sales
management
in canada

H.F. (HERB) MACKENZIE

Brock University

PEARSON

Prentice
Hall

Toronto

The first edition of this book is dedicated to the many salespeople and customers I have worked with during my sales and sales management career, and especially to James G. Stevens (retired) who has been a great influence and friend for many years.

—HFM

Library and Archives Canada Cataloguing in Publication

MacKenzie, H.F.
    Sales management in Canada/H.F. (Herb) MacKenzie.

Includes index.
ISBN 978-0-13-118989-8

1. Sales management—Textbooks. I. Title.

HF5438.4.M32 2008   658.8'1   C2007-902231-6

ISBN-13: 978-0-13-118989-8
ISBN-10: 0-13-118989-1

Vice-President, Editorial Director: Gary Bennett
Marketing Manager: Leigh-Anne Graham
Acquisitions Editor: Don Thompson
Developmental Editor: Toni Chahley
Production Editor: Marisa D'Andrea
Copy Editor: Laurel Sparrow
Proofreader: Ruth Bradley-St-Cyr
Production Coordinator: Patricia Ciardullo
Indexer: Belle Wong
Photo Researcher: Sandy Cooke
Compositor: Joan M. Wilson
Art Director: Julia Hall
Interior and Cover Design: Miguel Acevedo
Cover Image: Veer

3 4 5 6 7   14 13 12 11

Printed and bound in Canada.

Brief Contents

PART I   Sales Management and Strategy   3

    1   Introduction to Sales Management in Canada   4

    2   Planning Strategy for Marketing and Sales   24

PART II   Developing the Strategic Sales Program   69

    3   Organizing the Selling Function   70

    4   Estimating Potential and Forecasting Sales   92

    5   Developing and Growing Account Relationships   119

    6   Enhancing Customer Interactions   149

PART III   Implementing the Strategic Sales Program   193

    7   Recruiting and Selecting Salespeople   194

    8   Training Salespeople   225

    9   Motivating Salespeople   253

    10   Compensating Salespeople   280

    11   Leading Salespeople   307

    12   Ethical and Legal Responsibilities   337

PART IV   Evaluating the Strategic Sales Program   379

    13   Reviewing and Evaluating Sales Performance   380

Contents

Preface   xiii

PART I   Sales Management and Strategy   3

1   INTRODUCTION TO SALES MANAGEMENT IN CANADA   4

The Sales Management Process   6

The Changing Environment of Sales Management   8

Customer Environment   8

Competitive Environment   10

Changes in Selling and Sales Management   10

Competencies for Sales Managers Today   12

Strategic Planning and Implementation Competency   12

Leading and Coaching Competency   13

■ Sales Management Today

Making Better Management Decisions   14

Technology Competency   15

Managing Diversity Competency   16

Career Paths in Sales Management   16

Why Sales Management?   18

■ Sales Management in Action

Alternative Power   19

Summary   20

Key Terms   20

Review Questions   21

Application Exercises   21

CASE 1.1   Scotia Electric Sales and Service   22

CASE 1.2   Tortran Digital   23

2   PLANNING STRATEGY FOR MARKETING AND SALES   24

Market Orientation and the Sales Force   25

Business Strategy   25

The Importance of a Mission Statement   27

The Mission Statement and Corporate Goals and Objectives   27

Corporate Goals and Objectives and Business Strategies   28

Marketing Strategy   28

Segmentation, Targeting, and Positioning: A Three-Step Process   28

Marketing Program Development   29

■ Sales Management in Action

TalkSwitch: All Talk and Growing Action   32

Sales Force Investment   33

Right-Sizing the Sales Force   33

Additional Factors to Consider   35

■ Sales Management Today
Adding and Subtracting: Does It All Add Up?   37

Sales Force Budgeting   **39**

Planning the Sales Budget   39

Administering the Sales Budget   40

Summary   41

Key Terms   41

Review Questions   42

Application Exercises   42

CASE 2.1   Shoes for Moos   43

CASE 2.2   Electronics and More   44

■ COMPREHENSIVE CASES FOR PART I   46

CASE 1   Maritime Bank   46

CASE 2   Royal Corporation   56

PART II   Developing the Strategic Sales Program   **69**

3   ORGANIZING THE SELLING FUNCTION   70

Organizing the Selling Function   **71**

Geographic Specialization   72

Product Specialization   73

Market Specialization   74

Functional Specialization   76

■ Sales Management Today
IBM Software: Moving From Product Specialization to Market
Specialization   76

Telemarketing Programs   **77**

When To Use Telemarketing   78

Integrating Telemarketing With the Sales Force   78

Managing the Telemarketing Effort   78

The Future of Telemarketing   80

Independent Sales Agents   **80**

When to Use Independent Sales Agents   81

■ Sales Management in Action
The Stevens Company Has It All   81

How to Choose Independent Sales Agents   83

Managing Independent Sales Agents   83

Strategic Account Programs   **83**

Selecting Accounts for Strategic Account Programs   84

Managing Strategic Account Programs   84

The Increasing Complexity of Sales Force Organization   **86**

Summary   87

Key Terms   88

Review Questions   88

Application Exercises   89

CASE 3.1   Trecourt Valve and Fittings Reorganizes Its Sales Force   90

CASE 3.2   Tandy Safety Clothing   91

4   ESTIMATING POTENTIAL AND FORECASTING SALES   92

The Importance of Estimating Potential and Forecasting Sales   **93**

Preparing the Sales Forecast   **96**

■ Sales Management in Action
How Much Is Too Much Juice?   96

Looking at Past Sales Performance   97

Looking to the Future   102

Additional Topics in Forecasting Sales   **104**

Developing Territory Forecasts   105

Involvement in Forecasting   107

Familiarity With and Use of Various Methods   108

■ Sales Management Today
Collaborative Demand Planning: Working With Suppliers and Customers to Forecast Demand   108

Choosing Appropriate Forecasting Methods   111

Adjust Forecasts Early When Necessary   111

Looking Back: Review and Evaluation   113

Summary   114

Key Terms   115

Review Questions   115

Application Exercises   116

CASE 4.1   Trends   117

CASE 4.2   Centre for the Arts   117

5   DEVELOPING AND GROWING ACCOUNT RELATIONSHIPS   119

Managing Account Relationships   **120**

Types of Account Relationship Strategies   **120**

Transactional Relationships   121

Consultative Relationships   122

Partnering Relationships   122

Helping Customers Buy   **123**

Understanding the Customer's Buying Task   123

Understanding Who Is Involved in the Buying Decision   124

Understanding the Customer's Buying-Decision Process   125

■ Sales Management Today
Relationship Importance Increases for Technology Purchases   126

Guiding Relationship Evolution, Building Trust, and Creating Value   **129**

■ Sales Management in Action
Tenaquip Supply Program Provides Tools in Vending Machines   132

Prospecting For and Qualifying New Accounts   **133**

Finding Prospects   133
Qualifying Prospects   135

Managing a Portfolio of Accounts   **136**
When Is an Account Too Small?   136
Single-Factor Models   138
Using Portfolio Models   139
Decision Models   140
Sales Process Models   141

Summary   143

Key Terms   144

Review Questions   144

Application Exercises   145

CASE 5.1   Eastern Canada Pulp & Paper   146

CASE 5.2   Leisure Lady Lingerie   147

6 ENHANCING CUSTOMER INTERACTIONS   **149**

Three Selling Approaches   **150**
Transactional Selling   150
Consultative Selling   150
Relationship Selling   151

Prerequisites to Professional Selling Success   **152**
Your Personal Selling Philosophy   152
Relationship Strategy   152

◼   Sales Management Today
Selling Philosophy: Which Hat Today?   154
Product Strategy   155
Customer Strategy   155
Presentation Strategy   155

The Selling Process Model   **157**
Pre-Contact Phase   157
Face-to-Face Interaction Phase   159

◼   Sales Management in Action
2 Great Gals: Consultative Selling With Style   165
Post-Sale Phase   171

Summary   173

Key Terms   174

Review Questions   174

Application Exercises   175

CASE 6.1   Bridgehead Cutting Tools   176

CASE 6.2   Haines & Associates   176

COMPREHENSIVE CASES FOR PART II   178

CASE 1   TFI Food Equipment Solutions   178

CASE 2   Hi-T Mill Supply Inc.   183

PART III   Implementing the Strategic Sales Program   193

7   RECRUITING AND SELECTING SALESPEOPLE   194

The Importance of Recruitment and Selection   195

Planning for Recruitment and Selection   196
   The Role of the Sales Manager in Recruiting and Selecting Salespeople   196
   Sales Force Turnover and Personnel Needs   196
   Sales Force Culture   197
   Job Analysis   198

Recruiting Applicants   203
   Internal Sources   203
   External Sources   205

Selecting Applicants   208
   Résumés and Application Forms   208
   Personal Interviews   209
   Tests   211
   ■ Sales Management in Action
   Hire for "People Smarts"   214
   Background Checks   215
   ■ Sales Management Today
   Not Just Socially Unacceptable   217

Validating the Selection Process   218
   Summary   220
   Key Terms   221
   Review Questions   221
   Application Exercises   222
      CASE 7.1   Red Cow Enterprises, Inc.   222
      CASE 7.2   Custom Energy Reduction Systems   223

8   TRAINING SALESPEOPLE   225

The Importance of Sales Training   226
   Improved Sales Performance   227
   Improved Self-Management   227
   Improved Selling Skills   227
   Improved Customer Relationships   227
   Reduced Turnover   227
   Better Morale   228

The Sales Training Process   228
   Perform a Sales Training Needs Assessment   228
   Establish Sales Training Objectives   232
   Establish a Sales Training Budget   234
   Develop the Sales Training Program   234

■ Sales Management in Action
Come Join the Real Whirled   241

■ Sales Management Today
Engaging Trainees: Who Is Your Avatar?   242

Evaluate the Sales Training   245

Training for the Sales Manager   246

Summary   248

Key Terms   249

Review Questions   249

Application Exercises   250

> CASE 8.1   B.C. Business Equipment Sales (Part A)   251

> CASE 8.2   B.C. Business Equipment Sales (Part B)   251

9 **MOTIVATING SALESPEOPLE**   **253**

Motivation and Activity   **254**

General Model of Sales Motivation   **254**

Expectancy: The Relationship Between Effort and Performance   255

Instrumentality: The Relationship Between Performance and Reward   256

Valences for Rewards   257

■ Sales Management in Action
Motivating the 'B' Team   257

Specific Factors Related to Sales Motivation   **258**

Job-Related Factors   258

Job Value   258

Individual-Related Factors   260

Quotas   **265**

Why Use Quotas?   266

What Are Good Quotas?   266

Types of Quotas   267

Establishing and Managing Quota Plans   269

Sales Contests and Recognition Programs   **270**

Planning   270

Promoting   271

Rewarding   272

■ Sales Management Today
The Benefits of Tangible Incentives   274

Evaluating   275

Summary   275

Key Terms   276

Review Questions   276

Application Exercises   277

> CASE 9.1   Performance Auto Sales   278

> CASE 9.2   Robert Mendes   278

10 COMPENSATING SALESPEOPLE 280

Compensation Plans **281**
  Straight Salary 282
  Straight Commission 284
  Bonuses 286
  Combination Compensation Plans 287
  Compensation Plan Summary 288

Selling Expenses and Benefits **290**
  Unlimited Reimbursement Plans 290
  Limited Repayment Plans 290
  Per Diem Payment Plans 291
  Employee Benefits 291

Putting the Compensation Plan Together **293**
  Paying Low Compensation 293
  Paying High Compensation 294

■ Sales Management in Action
  Want a Raise? Vote One for Yourself 295
  Deciding the Appropriate Mix 296

Evaluating the Compensation Plan **297**

Special Issues in Sales Force Compensation **298**
  Customer Satisfaction and Sales Force Compensation 299

■ Sales Management Today
  Using Compensation to Focus Behaviour 299
  Pay Equity 300
  Team Incentive Compensation 301
  Global Considerations 302
  Summary 303
  Key Terms 304
  Review Questions 304
  Application Exercises 304

    CASE 10.1 Aries Corporate Coffee Services 305
    CASE 10.2 Prairie Ag Products 306

11 LEADING SALESPEOPLE 307

Leadership Is Not Management **308**

Leaders: Personal Traits, Personality, and Needs **309**

Power and Leadership **312**

Leading Change **313**

Leading Individual Salespeople **315**
  Situational Leadership Style 315
  Coaching 317

■ Sales Management in Action
  The Sales Leader as Coach 319

Leading the Sales Force **320**
  Building a High-Performance, Cohesive Sales Force 320
  Leading Sales Meetings 321

Personnel Issues   **323**

    Plateauing: Causes and Solutions   323

■ Sales Management Today
    Valuable Advice for Those Who Would Be Leader   324

    Conflicts of Interest   327

    Alcohol Abuse and Drug Dependency   328

    Harassment and Sexual Harassment   329

    The Uncooperative or Disruptive Salesperson   330

    Termination: Option of Last Resort   331

    Summary   332

    Key Terms   333

    Review Questions   333

    Application Exercises   334

    CASE 11.1   The First Challenge   334

    CASE 11.2   Bill Siddall's Sales Call Reports   335

12   ETHICAL AND LEGAL RESPONSIBILITIES   **337**

Ethics: The Foundation for Good Relationships   **338**

■ Sales Management Today
    Selling Ethics: The Good, the Bad, and the Ugly   339

    The Erosion of Character   340

Factors That Influence the Ethical Behaviour of Salespeople   **340**

    The CEO as Role Model   341

    The Sales Manager as Role Model   342

    The Values and Behaviours of Peers   342

    Company Policies and Practices   343

■ Sales Management in Action
    Making Ethical Decisions   343

    Toward a Personal Code of Ethics   349

Federal and Provincial Laws   **350**

    The *Competition Act*   350

    Provincial Consumer Protection Acts   354

    Canadian Law and Global Selling   355

    Summary   355

    Key Terms   356

    Review Questions   356

    Application Exercises   357

    CASE 12.1   Trouble at TPG Power Source   358

    CASE 12.2   Canadian Electrical Controller Corp.   359

■ COMPREHENSIVE CASES FOR PART III   361

CASE 1   General Electric Appliances   361

CASE 2   Hal Maybee's Ethical Dilemmas   372

PART IV   Evaluating the Strategic Sales Program   379

13 REVIEWING AND EVALUATING SALES PERFORMANCE   380

The Sales Performance Evaluation Process   381

The Sales Performance Evaluation Model   382

Sales Analysis at the Company, SBU, or Region Level   382

■ Sales Management in Action
   B.C. Court Rules a Warning Is Not a Dismissal   383
   Sales by Product   385

Expense Analysis at the Company, SBU, or Region Level   387
   Cost by Product   387

Evaluating Salespeople   388

Objective Measures   388
   Input Measures   389
   Output Measures   392

■ Sales Management Today
   Today's Push for Profitability   395
   Ratios   396
   Four Factor Model   399

Subjective Measures   400
   Problems With Subjective Performance Measures   400

360-Degree Feedback   402

Performance Matrices   403
   Summary   406
   Key Terms   407
   Review Questions   407
   Application Exercises   408
      CASE 13.1   Import Food Sales   408
      CASE 13.2   Upper Canada Clothing   409

   COMPREHENSIVE CASES FOR PART IV   410
      CASE 1   Stavanger Safety Equipment   410
      CASE 1   Power & Motion Industrial Supply   414

Glossary   418

Notes   424

Company/Name Index   435

Subject Index   437

Preface

For many people, there is nothing as personally satisfying as to be able to connect with people and improve their lives. The best salespeople regularly do this. They focus their attention on helping customers satisfy buying needs, and they are able to do this even when sometimes facing stressful challenges in their personal lives and selling jobs. The best sales managers do this by motivating and mentoring salespeople to become the best they can be— by having a genuine interest in developing and encouraging them as sales professionals.

This is a book about *sales management,* but the best sales managers must also have been at least credible salespeople. They must understand the selling process, and nearly every one of them, upon reflection, will be able to name two or three managers or colleagues who have had a tremendous impact on their development and career. Moving into management and then being able to influence the careers of others comes with great responsibility. For certain, what salespeople become is determined in no small measure to their own competence and initiative, but a good sales manager can be instrumental in developing a great salesperson while a poor sales manager can ruin promising sales careers. The intention of this book is to help people who aspire to become a sales manager to become *that* good sales manager, the one that salespeople will fondly remember throughout their lives.

Organization of This Book

This book begins with a discussion of the nature of sales management in Canada today, the changing sales environment, the competencies needed for sales management success, and the strategy planning process within organizations and the role that sales managers play in that process. Then, three interrelated processes that sales managers are responsible for are discussed: developing, implementing, and evaluating the strategic sales program. More specifically, the book is composed of four parts.

- **Part I—Sales Management and Strategy.** There are many important changes occurring in the sales environment today. Marketplace changes include rising customer expectations, decreasing supplier bases, increasing customer power, and a focus on value. Changes in the competitive environment include globalization of competition, shorter product and service life cycles, and competitor alliances. These changes are having an impact on all aspects of selling and sales management: the relationship between sales and marketing, sales force structure and design, the selling process, sales management activities, and performance evaluation. As a result, today's sales manager requires four important competencies to be effective: 1) strategic planning and implementation competency, 2) leading and coaching competency, 3) technology competency, and 4) managing diversity competency. A deficiency in even one of these areas limits the sales manager's ability to lead a team of superior sales professionals. Changes in marketplace and competitive environments and the competencies required by today's sales manager are discussed in Chapter 1. These changes in the sales environment are also creating changes in the internal environment of many organizations, including how strategy planning is conducted and coordinated across different levels of the organization. Many organizations are increasing the degree of coordination between sales and marketing. These topics are discussed in Chapter 2.

■ **Part II—Developing the Strategic Sales Program.** Sales managers are responsible for the development of the company's strategic sales program. First, they must decide how to organize the overall selling function within the company: whether to organize the sales force on the basis of geography, market or type of account, products or services sold, or functions or activities performed. They must decide whether to use telemarketers, independent sales agents, strategic account programs, or sales teams and, if so, how to integrate them within the selling function. Organizing the selling function is discussed in Chapter 3. Second, they must estimate market potential and forecast sales. This becomes the basis for setting individual sales quotas and establishing individual salesperson, as well as overall sales force, budgets. Estimating potential and forecasting sales is discussed in Chapter 4. Third, they must decide how to manage accounts, whether to use one or several account management strategies, how to balance resources across a portfolio of accounts, and how to prospect for and qualify prospects to maintain or grow the customer base. Developing and growing account relationships is discussed in Chapter 5. Finally, they must decide how to manage customer interactions; that is, how to manage the face-to-face communications with customers and prospects. This is the selling process that is implemented by the company's salespeople. Enhancing customer interactions is discussed in Chapter 6.

■ **Part III—Implementing the Strategic Sales Program.** Sales managers are responsible for the implementation of the company's strategic sales program. To do this, sales managers are actively involved in recruiting and selecting (Chapter 7), training (Chapter 8), motivating (Chapter 9), compensating (Chapter 10), and leading salespeople (Chapter 11). Sales managers must be aware of and fulfill their ethical and legal responsibilities while implementing all aspects of the strategic sales program (Chapter 12). As part of the implementation process, sales managers employ various policies and procedures that influence the aptitude, skills, and motivation of the sales force. In this way, they shape and direct the behaviour of individual salespeople to help them achieve their performance goals.

■ **Part IV—Evaluating the Strategic Sales Program.** Sales managers are responsible for reviewing and evaluating the company's strategic sales program. Because sales managers operate in a dynamic environment, there are changes constantly occurring that have implications for the company's strategic sales program. The needs of customers evolve and change, competitors change their marketing strategies, and economic conditions change from one period to the next. Internally, the sales manager's own company may change its marketing strategy and this may require adjustments to the strategic sales program. Effective sales managers must review and evaluate sales performance at two levels: the overall sales force level and the individual salesperson level. Reviewing and evaluating sales performance is discussed in Chapter 13.

This is an exciting time to be in sales management. Sales managers must look both ways—to the competitive environment and to the customer marketplace—to see the important changes that impact selling and sales management today, and they must constantly operate in an environment of change and development. It is certainly a job for those who love challenge. But it comes with many rewards.

Features of This Book

As the first Canadian textbook on the market, *Sales Management in Canada* contains a number of features designed to enhance learning and understanding for students, and make the course exciting and rewarding for instructors. The following features are found throughout this book.

FOCUS ON THEORY AND APPLICATION

Students of sales management benefit from current theory, but they are also very interested in practice. They want to know how theory is applied in the real world of the sales manager. In each chapter, this book tries to strike a balance between providing information on the latest sales management research and theory, and introducing students to real people and issues that are an exciting part of sales management. Each year, hundreds of trade books and magazines are published and are read by sales managers to help them enhance their sales management skills. Many of the most important of these are introduced throughout this book.

BALANCE OF ORGANIZATIONS FROM MANY INDUSTRIES

This book includes examples related to sales organizations of all sizes, from Canada's largest and best known to some of Canada's smaller, more entrepreneurial companies that have very limited sales resources. An attempt has been made to include examples from across Canada and from across a great variety of industries. There are industrial and consumer goods manufacturers, wholesalers and retailers, service companies, and companies from both high-growth, technology companies to companies that are managing sales in mature markets.

LEARNING TOOLS THAT ENHANCE INSTRUCTION

■ **Chapter Learning Objectives:** Each chapter opens with a number of important learning objectives that help focus student attention on what they are about to see throughout the chapter, and what they should be able to do after they read and understand the chapter.

■ **Opening Vignettes:** Following the learning objectives is a vignette that focuses on real sales professionals within Canadian sales organizations or Canadian operations of global sales organizations, and discusses timely issues that are important to them and that relate to the topic of the chapter. These vignettes are designed to attract student interest and attention, so they are often referred to in later chapter material as well.

■ **Boxed Features:** Each chapter contains two boxed features: *Sales Management Today* and *Sales Management in Action*. These boxes are tied directly to chapter content and provide interesting examples of what is current practice in sales management, and what today's sales managers can do to improve their chances of success.

■ **Chapter Summaries:** At the end of each chapter appears a summary of important information that is tied directly to the learning objectives introduced at the beginning of the chapter. These summaries provide an opportunity for students to reflect on what they have learned and what they should know after they have completed the chapter.

■ **Key Terms and Glossary:** Key terms are bolded throughout the text and listed with page references at the end of each chapter. A glossary is also included at the end of the book for quick reference to each term's meaning. Each of these terms is an important concept that students should understand once they have completed a chapter.

■ **Review Questions:** Each chapter provides ten review questions that allow students to test their knowledge of chapter content. They provide a focus of what the important topics are within the chapter.

■ **Application Exercises:** Each chapter provides four application exercises designed for in-class use and discussion. They focus on chapter-related issues and content, but often require students to bring their own experiences and perspectives to the classroom so that they can enhance the learning experience for everyone.

- **Short Cases:** Each chapter has two short cases. Although disguised, nearly all of these cases are based on real people and organizations. Some come from the author's experiences in sales management, and others come from interviews with practising salespeople and sales managers across Canada. While the cases can be assigned for out-of-class assignments, their length makes it possible to read and discuss these cases entirely within the classroom. While they might appear short, they have all been classroom tested, and personal experience indicates that many of them can generate considerable classroom discussion and provide useful vehicles for teaching and learning.

- **Long Cases:** Each of the four parts of the book concludes with two long cases chosen for their ability to generate interest and excitement and to provide more in-depth analysis and discussion on important sales management issues. All of these cases have been classroom tested and have proven to enhance student learning and enjoyment.

- **Indices:** Two indices appear at the end of the book: a subject index and a name index featuring people and companies so that readers can quickly find topics, companies, and people of interest.

Supplements

This textbook is supported by many materials designed to enhance learning and understanding for students, and to make the course exciting and rewarding for instructors. The following are the support materials available for instructors.

- **Instructor's Resource CD-ROM** contains the Instructor's Manual, PowerPoint Slides, Test Generator, and Image Library:

  - **Instructor's Manual:** The Instructor's Manual has been written by the author of this book, with very few exceptions—those being the teaching notes for three cases that were written by other case writers. That means there is a greater opportunity to include personal insights into how to use the features of this book as the author has tested most of them and certainly knows why these particular review questions, application exercises, and cases were chosen. In the suggestions for using these, the author has tried to add value so that instructors can get the most benefit possible from their classroom use. At the same time, an attempt has been made to add additional value for the classroom instructor by providing suggestions for classroom use of specific chapter material. The Instructor's Manual also provides a number of role-play exercises and student interview exercises for instructors who wish to incorporate these into their course design.

  - **PowerPoint® Slides:** PowerPoint slides are available for each chapter of the book. The slides contain links to websites and speaking notes with page references to relevant material in the textbook.

- **Pearson TestGen:** This computerized test item file enables instructors to view and edit the existing questions, add questions, generate tests, and print the tests in a variety of formats. Powerful search and sort functions make it easy to locate questions and arrange them in any order desired. TestGen also enables instructors to administer tests on a local area network, have the tests graded electronically, and have the results prepared in electronic or printed reports.
- **Image Library:** The tables and figures in the textbook are available in.jpeg or.gif format to instructors in the Image Library. Instructors can download these images to include in their own classroom presentations.
- **Companion Website (www.pearsoned.ca/mackenzie):** This student resource site offers additional case studies, practice quiz questions, internet exercises, company weblinks, and a variety of other resources. An online glossary with all key terms and definitions from the text is available for easy reference.

Acknowledgments

This text has been improved as a result of numerous helpful comments and recommendations. We extend special appreciation to the following reviewers: Kerry D. Couet, Grant MacEwan College; Tanya Drollinger, University of Lethbridge; David Hutchison, University of Windsor; Lea Prevel Katsanis, Concordia University; Frank Maloney, George Brown College; and Rae Verity, Southern Alberta Institute of Technology.

About the Author

Dr. H.F. (Herb) MacKenzie, Associate Professor, Brock University

Dr. MacKenzie is currently an Associate Professor of Marketing, as well as Chair, Marketing, International Business, and Strategy at Brock University, St. Catharines, Ontario. He has taught in the undergraduate, graduate, and executive education programs at universities in Canada, Europe, and the Middle East, and has been consulting to both private- and public-sector businesses since 1985. He has more than 15 years of industrial sales and sales management experience, and has published many cases, conference proceedings, and articles in the areas of sales management, buyer–seller relationships, and distribution channel management. He has authored and co-authored textbooks on personal selling, sales management, and marketing, and has edited three Canadian marketing casebooks. He has been recognized by his students in recent years: Professor of the Year, Marketing Professor of the Year, and twice with the Faculty of Business Faculty Award of Excellence.

A Great Way to Learn and Instruct Online

The Pearson Education Canada Companion Website is easy to navigate and is organized to correspond to the chapters in this textbook. Whether you are a student in the classroom or a distance learner you will discover helpful resources for in-depth study and research that empower you in your quest for greater knowledge and maximize your potential for success in the course.

Companion
Website

[www.pearsoned.ca/mackenzie] Enter

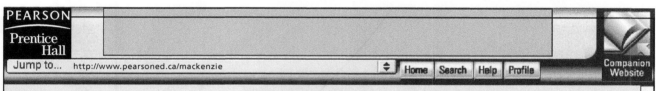

PEARSON
Prentice Hall

Jump to...   http://www.pearsoned.ca/mackenzie   ⇕   Home   Search   Help   Profile

Companion Website

Home >

Companion Website

Sales Management in Canada by MacKenzie

sales management in canada

Student Resources

The modules in this section provide students with tools for learning course material. Some of these modules include:

- Additional cases
- Practice quizzes, including multiple-choice, true and false, and short-answer
- Company websites
- Annotated weblinks
- Glossary

In the quiz modules students can send answers to the grader and receive instant feedback on their progress through the Results Reporter. Coaching comments and references to the textbook may be available to ensure that students take advantage of all available resources to enhance their learning experience.

Instructor Resources

The modules in this section provide instructors with additional teaching tools. Downloadable PowerPoint Presentations, Test Generator, and an Instructor's Manual are just some of the materials that may be available in this section. Where appropriate, this section will be password protected. To get a password, simply contact your Pearson Education Canada Representative or call Faculty Sales and Services at 1-800-850-5813.

Part I

Sales Management and Strategy

CHAPTER 1   Introduction to Sales Management in Canada

CHAPTER 2   Planning Strategy for Marketing and Sales

Comprehensive Cases for Part I

CASE 1   Maritime Bank

CASE 2   Royal Corporation

Today's sales managers are operating in increasingly complex and dynamic environments. Changes in these environments and the key sales management competencies required to succeed today are discussed in Chapter 1. These changes are also creating shifts in the internal environment of many organizations, including how strategy planning is conducted and coordinated across different levels and functions within the organization. Marketing and sales strategy planning are discussed in Chapter 2.

Introduction to Sales Management in Canada

LEARNING OBJECTIVES

After completing this chapter, you should be able to

1. Explain the sales management process.

2. Describe the changing environment of sales management in Canada and how these changes are affecting selling and sales management.

3. Describe four important competencies needed by sales managers today.

4. Describe the career paths for sales managers today.

Paula Shannon's colleagues have described her as a globetrotting, team-building energizer—among other things—and for good reason. She was hired by Boston-based Lionbridge Technologies in 1999 to manage its internet strategy and one-third of its global sales force. Following the collapse of the technology sector, Lionbridge's sales dropped, and the company restructured and downsized. Paula was placed in charge of the entire 70-person global sales force in more than 30 countries around the world.

Her first focus was to centralize sales management processes, but she did it by fostering communication with and getting buy-in from the various salespeople who would be affected. Everyone was encouraged to participate and become involved, and this ultimately gave everyone a sense of responsibility and ownership for the changes that were taking place. She changed the compensation plan and increased salesperson motivation through increased incentives to acquire new business. Both regional sales managers and salespeople who deal with multinational accounts received training to improve their skills and their performance. The entire sales force gets together every year to network and to share stories about and learn from innovative customer opportunities that they either won or lost. Through the company's global intranet, all salespeople access data concerning targets, quotas, goal attainment, and performance.

From her home office in Montreal, Paula Shannon regularly logs more than 130 000 air miles per year to build and motivate the Lionbridge sales force and to manage its global sales team. Shannon says, "A good sales team has balance; it has people who are rounding out the group personality. There's one who's a process master, one who's a real extrovert presenter, another who's a deep technical expert. They check their individual egos at the door and work collaboratively on the team solution."

As an indicator of Shannon's success at team-building, Lionbridge placed second in 2003 for Best Sales Team in the American Business Awards. As an indicator of her success as a sales executive, in 2004 Paula Shannon received the inaugural International Stevie Award for Best Sales Executive. The award recognizes leadership, innovation, perseverance, creativity, teamwork, and integrity. Rory Cowan, CEO of Lionbridge, said, "The nominees for this award consisted of sales leaders from some of the world's finest companies. Paula's selection as the winner does not surprise me. This prestigious award recognizes the high calibre of sales leadership, intelligence, ambition, and character that we see from Paula every day." [1]

This is a book about sales management and, to a lesser extent, about personal selling. We define **sales management** as simply the management of the company's personal selling function. **Personal selling** involves person-to-person communication with prospects or customers with the intention of discovering their needs, matching product solutions to their needs, and building satisfying relationships with them by satisfying their needs.

Sales managers and other sales executives can have a dramatic influence on the attitudes and behaviours of their salespeople. Paula Shannon, discussed at the beginning of this chapter, provides a perfect example. Her effectiveness as a sales executive is due to her ability to combine strong organizational and management skills with equally strong leadership and interpersonal skills. Sales managers are almost always promoted from professional sales positions in which they learn some, but not all, of the skills required to be effective sales managers. Usually, they have demonstrated above average sales ability. They must understand the selling process because they are responsible for training new salespeople, and for coaching them when they have difficulty implementing the selling process properly. It is not uncommon for sales managers to maintain responsibility for some customer accounts, particularly large or very important accounts. However, we do not suggest that the best salespeople necessarily make the best sales managers. In fact, the opposite is often the case. A vice-president we know for one of Canada's largest distributors once commented about a specific territory sales manager, "When we promoted him, we lost the company's best salesperson and we gained the company's worst sales manager." How could this happen?

The problem often arises because of a general belief that promotions go to those who have demonstrated superior ability, that performance should be rewarded. What would happen if the best salesperson were bypassed for a management position? Some salespeople would feel slighted; others would be concerned with what their colleagues thought. This creates social pressure for them to seek and accept a promotion, often without considering whether they have the aptitude or competencies necessary to do a good job. Companies often add to the problem as senior management often expects that the best salesperson should be able to accept the promotion and immediately function as an effective sales manager, with little or no support. Superior organizations recognize that sales managers and salespeople require different competencies. They have programs in place to ensure that everyone continually develops in accordance with their appropriate career path.

In the rest of this chapter, we discuss the sales management process (what sales managers do); the current environment for sales management (the context in which they must do their job); the competencies they need to perform effectively in this environment; and the career paths available to those who demonstrate effectiveness as sales managers.

The Sales Management Process

What do sales managers typically do? The list of activities that follows illustrates much of what a sales manager might do during a typical month. When you review this list, you will understand why sales management is one of the most rewarding and exciting jobs in business today. During any particular month, sales managers could:

1. Approve an advertisement to hire a new salesperson, interview one or several candidates for the position, and make a selection decision from among the applicants.
2. Attend a meeting with senior management to discuss changes in the marketplace, how these changes will affect sales strategy, and the resources the sales force will need to implement the sales strategy for the coming year.
3. Review sales performance for the previous period to identify where there are major variances from what was projected, and then decide what action to take with respect to the variances.
4. Make sales calls to specific accounts for which they are responsible or with salespeople to train or coach them, or they might attend a trade show to monitor competitors or meet important prospects.
5. Prepare a sales force budget for the next year, determine what the company needs to spend on its sales force to achieve its goals, and allocate the budget to individual salespeople.
6. Meet with the production manager to discuss production issues that might impact sales for the coming period and what actions the sales force might take as a result of changes in production levels.
7. Hold a meeting with the sales force to discuss what is happening with key accounts and important changes that may affect them in the coming weeks or months.
8. Attend a company meeting and present awards and recognition to members of the sales force who have met their performance goals.
9. Meet with the company's information officer to discuss information needs for the sales force.
10. Meet with the marketing manager to discuss how proposed changes in the company's marketing strategy will affect sales and changes that salespeople will need to make to communicate the new marketing strategy to the marketplace.

This is certainly not an all-inclusive list, but it will give you a feel for the scope of activities that sales managers might perform. It has been presented in no particular order so that you will get a sense of the action-orientation of much of what sales managers do. They are constantly involved with both strategic and tactical issues and are frequently required to switch from one to the other; they are always both planning and doing. They must communicate regularly with the company's sales force, and also with senior management, with functional mangers from almost every internal department in the firm, and with people from various other firms (including suppliers, channel members, customers, and even competitors). Lisa Gschwandtner, editor-in-chief of *Selling Power* magazine, describes today's sales manager as a leader, coach, mentor, facilitator, goal setter, motivator, number cruncher, and communicator.[2]

All of the activities that a sales manager might perform can be summarized as "managing the company's strategic sales program." To do this, sales managers are essentially involved in three interrelated sets of processes, as illustrated in Exhibit 1.1.

Exhibit 1.1

Model for Sales Force Management

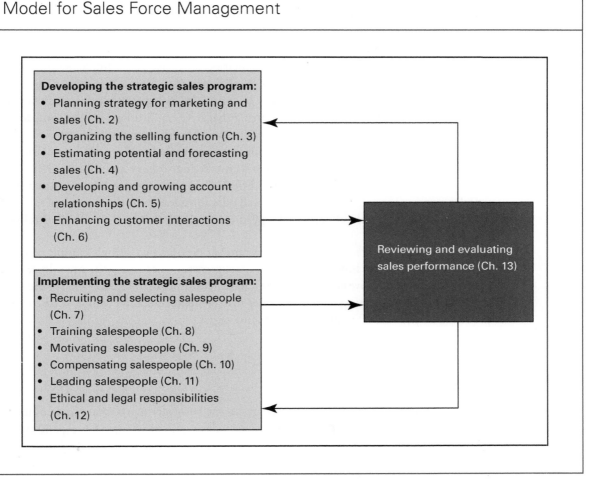

Developing the strategic sales program:
- Planning strategy for marketing and sales (Ch. 2)
- Organizing the selling function (Ch. 3)
- Estimating potential and forecasting sales (Ch. 4)
- Developing and growing account relationships (Ch. 5)
- Enhancing customer interactions (Ch. 6)

Implementing the strategic sales program:
- Recruiting and selecting salespeople (Ch. 7)
- Training salespeople (Ch. 8)
- Motivating salespeople (Ch. 9)
- Compensating salespeople (Ch. 10)
- Leading salespeople (Ch. 11)
- Ethical and legal responsibilities (Ch. 12)

Reviewing and evaluating sales performance (Ch. 13)

1. *Developing the strategic sales program.* First, they must decide how to organize the overall selling function within the company: whether to organize the sales force on the basis of geography, market or type of account, products or services sold, or functions or activities performed. They must decide whether to use telemarketers, independent sales agents, strategic account programs, or sales teams and, if so, how to integrate them within the selling function. Second, they must estimate market potential and forecast sales. This becomes the basis for setting individual sales quotas and for establishing individual salesperson and overall sales force budgets. Third, they must decide how to manage accounts and whether to use one or several account management strategies; how to balance resources across a portfolio of accounts; and how to seek and qualify prospects to maintain or grow the customer base. Finally, they must decide how to manage customer interactions; that is, how to manage the face-to-face communications with customers and prospects. This is the selling process implemented by the company's salespeople. Developing the strategic sales program is discussed in Part II of this book.

2. *Implementing the strategic sales program.* To do this, sales managers are actively involved in recruiting and selecting, training, motivating, compensating, and leading salespeople. Sales managers must be aware of and discharge their ethical and legal responsibilities while implementing all aspects of the strategic sales program. As part of the implementation process, sales managers effect various policies and procedures that influence the aptitude, skills, and motivation of the sales force. In this way, they shape and direct the behaviour of individual salespeople to help them achieve their performance goals. Implementing the strategic sales program is discussed in Part III of this book.

3. *Reviewing and evaluating sales performance.* Because sales managers operate in a dynamic environment, changes are constantly occurring that have implications for the company's strategic sales program. The needs of customers evolve, competitors modify their marketing strategies, and economic conditions shift from one period to the next. Internally, the sales manager's own company may redesign its marketing strategy and this may require adjustments to the strategic sales program. Effective sales managers must review and evaluate sales performance at two levels: the overall sales force level and the individual salesperson level. Reviewing and evaluating sales performance is discussed in Part IV of this book.

Managing the company's strategic sales program has become increasingly complex and challenging. This is an exciting time to be in sales management. Sales managers must look in two directions—to the competitive environment and to the customer marketplace—to see the important changes that are impacting selling and sales management today. We will now discuss these changes and how they are affecting today's sales managers.

The Changing Environment of Sales Management

Exhibit 1.2 shows some of the important changes in the customer marketplace and competitive environment that are creating unique challenges for today's sales manager. After expanding upon each of these shifts in customers' and competitors' ways of doing business, we will look at their effect on the sales–marketing relationship within the firm, sales force structures, the selling process, sales management activities, and sales force performance evaluation.

CUSTOMER ENVIRONMENT

Four major shifts in the customer marketplace have important implications for sales management.

1. *Rising customer expectations.* Sales managers need to recognize that today's consumer and organizational buyer expectations for quality, service, and overall value will continue to increase and are probably infinitely elastic.[3] An executive of J.D. Power & Associates, a consumer satisfaction research firm, provides a clear explanation of this: "What makes customer satisfaction so difficult to achieve is that you constantly raise the bar and extend the finish line. You never stop. As your customers get better treatment, they demand better treatment."[4]

2. *Decreasing supplier bases.* Customers today are buying from fewer and fewer suppliers. They see that reducing their supplier bases often contributes to savings that far outweigh any small price premium they pay as a result. Grand & Toy, a leading Canadian supplier of office products, has recognized this trend and has been expanding its product lines and service capabilities so that it can be a supplier of choice to those customers who see the benefit of buying all of their supplies from one source.

Exhibit 1.2

Changes in the Customer Marketplace and Competitive Environment that Affect Selling and Sales Management

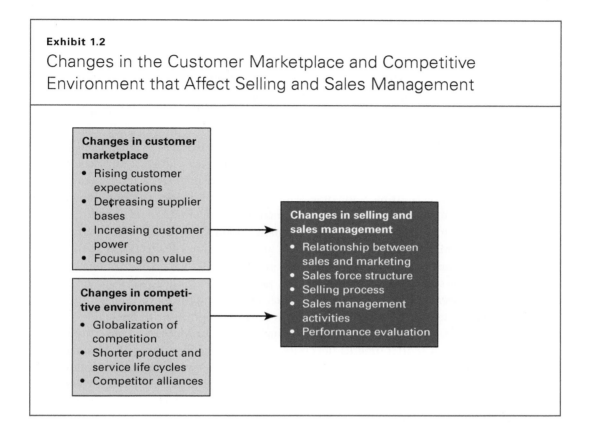

3. *Increasing customer power.* Many customers are increasing their power, or their ability to influence the actions of their suppliers. Many large retailers have grown larger than the manufacturers that supply to them and now demand that manufacturers sell to them directly, at lower prices and with other concessions. In organizational markets, where buying is done from wholesalers rather than retailers, large customers who are decreasing their supplier bases are putting pressure on wholesalers to consolidate so that they are capable of meeting the customers' needs for lower prices, greater product assortments, better service, etc. This increases wholesaler power as manufacturers who are not represented by the "right" wholesalers can effectively be blocked from the marketplace. Finally, both consumers and organizational buyers are increasing their power relative to their suppliers because of the knowledge that they are able to access through the internet. In many instances now, even when the purchase is not made over the internet, the customer has collected information, has evaluated products and suppliers, and has knowledge of a company's products and of competitive offerings that may be greater than the knowledge of the salesperson who is trying to sell to them.

4. *Focusing on value.* For most customers today, price is secondary to value. Sellers can increase value for customers either by reducing the cost to the customer, both in monetary and non-monetary terms, or by enhancing the value for customers by offering better product solutions, better service, or superior relationships. Xerox recognized the importance of value over price when it advertised to its customers, "There's a new way of looking at it." Xerox product solutions are not sold on price but on improving customer efficiency and reducing overall customer costs.

COMPETITIVE ENVIRONMENT

In the competitive environment, three major changes have important implications for sales management.

1. *Globalization of competition.* In 2004, Canada exported $352 billion in goods and $36.0 billion in services to the United States; in return, we imported $250 billion in goods and $41.8 billion in services from the United States.[5] We have a positive trade balance in goods but a negative trade balance in services with the United States. Unfortunately, Canada has a negative trade balance in both goods and services with most other countries with which it does business. Canadian firms are facing more international competition in their domestic markets. At the same time, while Canadian businesses are continuing to explore international markets, they are facing increased competition there as well. Canadian companies that want simply to maintain a domestic focus must recognize that competition from global markets will continue to increase and will affect their sales.

2. *Shorter product and service life cycles.* While product and service life cycles continue to exhibit the same stages—introduction, growth, maturity, and decline—they are increasingly shorter. Because technologies are rapidly changing—improving continually and becoming more reliable—customers are more willing to adopt newer technologies as they become available. Robert G. Cooper, a marketing professor at McMaster University in Hamilton, says that shorter product life cycles, driven by globalization of markets, technological advances, and continually changing customer needs, have made product innovation the strategic focus of many companies.[6] The sales force is particularly important when a product or service is early or late in its life cycle. Early in the life cycle, salespeople are needed to create awareness and to persuade customers to try products and services before they have achieved widespread acceptance, when the customer's risk is greatest. Late in the life cycle, product solutions, prices, and services among competitors might be so similar that the relationship bond between the customer and the salesperson may be the important differentiator that adds value for the customer.

3. *Competitor alliances.* Companies are increasingly forming alliances to increase their market power. One increasingly popular method is **co-branding**, the practice of using two established brands on the same product. For example, Ford and Eddie Bauer co-branded the Ford Explorer, Eddie Bauer edition. Many companies are using customers' testimonials in advertisements and press releases. This gives them instant credibility in the marketplace, and helps to cement relationships with important customers as well. Companies are also forming alliances to improve opportunities or to overcome weaknesses they may have in marketing their products and services. For example, Angiotech Pharmaceuticals, a Vancouver-based specialty pharmaceutical company, signed an agreement allowing Orthovita, a specialty orthopedics firm, to sell one of its products throughout North America.[7] Companies today must carefully monitor competitors to see what forms of alliances they may be making that will increase their presence in the marketplace.

CHANGES IN SELLING AND SALES MANAGEMENT

The shifts in the customer marketplace and competitive environment that we have described are having an impact on all aspects of selling and sales management. Sales departments are relating in new ways to other departments in the firm and, in particular, to marketing. Sales forces are evolving structurally, and this is changing the scope of responsibilities for sales managers. Salespeople are shifting their focus from "selling" to "serving," and this is affecting all aspects of the selling process. All of these changes are impacting the management activities of sales managers—how they recruit and select, train, motivate, compensate, and lead salespeople. Finally, sales managers are evaluating sales performance in new ways. We now turn our attention to the changes that are occurring in all of these areas.

1. *Changes in the relationship between sales and marketing.* In many large companies there has historically been poor communication between sales and marketing. Companies are recognizing that these two departments must cooperate to develop and implement effective strategic sales and marketing plans. In many small companies, it is even more important for marketing people to understand selling and for salespeople to understand marketing. If considerable customer contact is required, selling may be more important. Trevor Adey, president of Consilient Technologies, a St. John's-based wireless technologies solutions provider, says, " . . . I see many small- and medium-sized organizations that need good salespeople who understand marketing, more than they need good marketing people who might be able to sell."[8] The relationship between sales and marketing and how they work within the broader corporate structure is discussed in greater detail in Chapter 2.

2. *Changes in sales force structure.* Many sales forces today are evolving structurally; this is happening in two ways. First, sales forces are increasingly becoming organized on the basis of products sold, markets served, or functions performed instead of (or in addition to) geographical regions served. Second, sales forces are using new types of customer contact: telemarketing and telesales, selling teams, strategic or national account salespeople, direct mail, the internet, independent sales agents, new channel partners, etc. Sales managers are no longer managing just field salespeople but are increasingly concerned with managing an entire "sales mix," considering various ways to reach and manage communications with customers. These structural changes are discussed in greater detail throughout our book, and particularly in Chapter 3.

3. *Changes in the selling process.* The changes in the selling process have generally been made to build stronger relationships between buyers and sellers. The emphasis today is on relationships. In order to have close relationships, salespeople must begin with consultative selling, focusing on fully understanding customer needs and demonstrating a commitment to helping customers solve buying problems. Later, the focus shifts to demonstrating capability and commitment. The changes in the selling process when building and maintaining account relationships and enhancing customer interactions are discussed in Chapters 5 and 6, respectively.

4. *Changes in sales management activities.* Sales managers are still responsible for recruitment and selection, and for training, motivating, compensating, and leading salespeople. However, companies are changing the way they manage accounts. This means that the aptitudes and skills necessary to be an effective salesperson are changing, and the activities that sales managers perform are changing as a result. This is discussed in Chapters 7 through 12.

5. *Changes in sales performance evaluation.* Sales managers today are turning away from sales as the most important measure of sales performance and are increasingly focusing on profit. There is a growing recognition that a company's sales force is a limited resource, and careful allocation decisions must be made to maximize the benefits a company gets from that resource. This means more carefully targeting accounts that provide the greatest return for the resources invested, and this is why sales managers need greater involvement in developing marketing strategy. Sales managers must decide whom to call on, how to call on them, how often to call on them, and the service level that can be provided to various accounts. This is why there are so many changes in sales force structure and in the selling process.

Sales managers are increasingly becoming interested in the time and effort required to close a sale, price sensitivity of customers, promotional support needed to support a sale, the level of after-sale service required, gross margins on new sales, and the potential for future sales from the same account and from additional accounts as a result of making a particular sale. All of these decisions affect sales performance, and performance evaluation is discussed in greater detail in Chapter 13.

Competencies for Sales Managers Today

What sales managers do and the environment in which they operate have been discussed. We will now look at what competencies are required to be an effective sales manager today. **Competencies** are the knowledge, skills, aptitudes, and other personal characteristics needed to achieve superior performance. In the context of sales management, this refers to what sales managers have that enables them to manage and lead a sales force for superior performance. Exhibit 1.3 illustrates the four most important sales management competencies for sales managers today, which we will now discuss.

STRATEGIC PLANNING AND IMPLEMENTATION COMPETENCY

Strategic planning and implementation is the most important competency that a sales manager must possess. Strategic planning can take place at several levels within the organization: overall corporate strategy, strategic business unit (SBU) strategy, and functional sales force strategy.

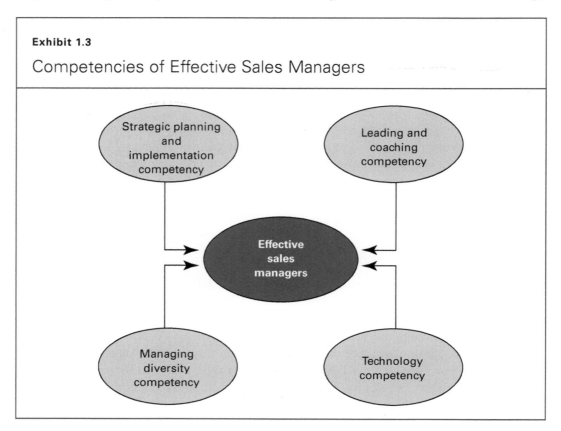

Exhibit 1.3

Competencies of Effective Sales Managers

There is tremendous interdependency between strategies at different levels and sales managers play a greater or lesser role depending on such factors as company size and structure, experience and ability, and competitive market conditions. Strategic planning and sales force strategy are discussed in greater depth in Chapter 2. However, regardless of the sales manager's level of involvement in strategic planning, she must completely understand the strategic plans at all levels of the organization, because she is expected to take action at the sales force level that will ultimately result in helping all levels of the organization achieve performance objectives. To effectively demonstrate competency at strategic planning and implementation, she must fully understand both the internal environment and the external environment of her firm.

Internally, the sales manager must understand the organization's overall mission, vision, strategy, and goals. She must know the firm's resources and capabilities, and how these can be effectively utilized to take advantage of market opportunities. Sometimes, she must negotiate with senior management to request additional resources or to change policies or procedures due to changing market conditions. Other times, in order to satisfy the needs of specific customers, the actions of many functional departments must be coordinated. The sales manager must know where to go and whom to go to in the organization when the need arises and she must have the ability to communicate and negotiate effectively with many internal people besides those within the sales force.

Externally, the sales manager must understand the industry within which her company competes: suppliers, competitors, channel members, and customers. The sales manager is ideally positioned in the organization to do this because she can manage contact with any or all of them. With respect to customers in particular, she can get a much broader view than any one salesperson as she is at liberty to make sales calls with salespeople on all key accounts. Good sales managers will encourage salespeople to share information with them and with other members of the sales force so that everyone learns. It is a visionary sales manager who can put in place the systems and processes to gather, aggregate, analyze, and disseminate information that can be of strategic importance to the sales force and to the organization as a whole.

Once the sales manager fully understands the firm's internal and external environments, she must be action-oriented. She must be able to decide on account selection, retention, and growth strategies. This often means identifying and targeting specific customer segments, a key strategic decision. She must determine account allocation within the sales force, set budgets and quotas, and manage salesperson and sales force performance. This requires a combination of strategic and tactical decisions and actions ultimately focused on achieving the firm's mission and strategic goals. The Sales Management Today box provides advice on how to make better decisions, because strategic planning and implementation competency is so important for today's sales manager.

LEADING AND COACHING COMPETENCY

A recent study involving 130 global firms indicated that leadership was the most important quality of sales executives.[9] A larger study involving 900 salespeople found that the most important qualities of sales managers included communication skills, motivational skills, and the ability to train and coach salespeople.[10] While it is a truism that customers buy from salespeople they like and trust, it is also true that salespeople follow sales managers they trust and respect.

How can sales managers build trust and gain respect? Dave Anderson, author of *No-Nonsense Leadership,* says, "You may think you are watching your reps. But, actually, they are watching you. Reps won't buy into what you say unless they buy into your character, your competence, and your consistency."[11] A sales manager who wishes to gain trust and respect must be visible, accessible,

SALES MANAGEMENT **TODAY**

Making Better Management Decisions

There has been a lot written recently on what sales managers do and how the role of sales manager has been changing. One thing is certain: sales managers make decisions—many decisions, every day. What separates good decision-makers from poor ones? The most important distinction is process. Good decision-makers follow a process. The following is a five-step process model that will reduce the probability of making poor decisions.

1. *What is the situation and what are the relevant facts?* At this stage, you need to be sure you clearly understand the situation. Are you facing a problem or an opportunity? Are things getting better, or worse?

2. *Who are the stakeholders that will be affected by any action?* Stakeholders should be identified early in the process. They can contribute important information concerning the situation, and their buy-in will often be critical to successful implementation of important decisions.

3. *What are the alternative courses of action that could be taken?* These may be readily apparent, but it is often a good idea to query all of the important stakeholders as well. Don't ignore the "do nothing" alternative. Sometimes it is the best alternative; at the very least, it provides a benchmark against which to evaluate all other alternatives.

4. *Carefully evaluate each of the alternatives.* Decide what criteria you will use to evaluate the alternatives. What are the pros and cons of each alternative? What are the constraints that might restrict particular choices? Who will be winners and who will be losers? You need to think about the short-term and long-term implications of each alternative.

5. *Make a decision and implement it.* Choose the alternative that fits best with the values of your organization, the sales force, other stakeholders, and yourself. Keep stakeholders involved so you will benefit from continued guidance and buy-in if further actions must be taken. Establish some benchmarks and periodically review the outcomes from your actions.

Linda Hanson, president of Toronto-based LLH Enterprises, describes why a good decision-making process is important for effective management today: "You can more easily defend your decision because of the process you followed and the stakeholders you involved. And if the outcome is not what you expected or you are not happy with it, you will have an easier time making changes if stakeholders are involved."

Source: Linda Hanson, "Better Decisions = Better Sales Performance," *Contact,* 7, 1, February 2004, pp. 10–11.

and able and willing to communicate. Salespeople need to know that they are important, not just collectively but as individuals. They must believe that their sales manager is working for them, representing their interests and willing to fight for them within their organization, and that the sales manager doesn't simply communicate and implement policies and strategies from senior management. The best sales managers listen and provide constructive feedback when salespeople have problems, and share in their glory and recognize their accomplishments when salespeople have reason to celebrate.

Research has demonstrated that both familiarity with the salesperson's job and perceived fairness enhance salespeople's trust of their sales managers.[12] Role modelling, or leadership by example, has also been demonstrated to increase salespeople's trust.[13] Sales managers today cannot simply manage from their offices: they must participate in field sales calls with their salespeople, and be capable and prepared to coach them when required. **Coaching** is an interpersonal process between the sales manager and the salesperson in which the sales manager provides constructive feedback and encouragement to the salesperson with the goal of improving sales performance. Truly effective sales managers are effective coaches who can teach and mentor their salespeople. Toronto-based consultant Elisa Leo, a self-described "sales guru" who works for a Toronto-based consulting firm, believes that there is not enough effective leadership in sales today. She says, "Good leaders truly teach and mentor their people . . . . They'll walk among their team, and know their desires, strengths, and weaknesses."[14]

TECHNOLOGY COMPETENCY

Today's sales manager needs to understand and know how to implement technology solutions to improve sales force efficiency and effectiveness. **Sales force automation** (SFA) includes a variety of information and communication technologies that address sales force efficiency: communicating with customers via email, managing account activity with customer contact management software, filing reports and entering orders electronically, developing and delivering sales presentations and demonstrations to prospects and customers. At one time, implementing SFA may have been a source of competitive advantage. However, it is so widespread among today's sales forces that it is now simply a necessity to remain competitive.

Increasingly, companies are moving beyond SFA to implement **customer relationship management** (CRM) solutions:

> Customer relationship management is a business strategy to acquire and retain the most valuable customer relationships. CRM requires a customer-centric business philosophy and culture to support effective marketing, sales, and service processes. CRM applications can enable effective customer relationship management, provided that an enterprise has the right leadership, strategy, and culture.[15]

The increased use of CRM technology is important because it is focused on the customer, and on the seller–buyer organizational relationship. CRM systems try to ensure that the customer's experience with the organization is seamless and consistent, regardless of what that experience might be. Whether the customer views a company's product literature, visits its website, calls for technical or service assistance, or is visited by a salesperson, a good CRM system will ensure that every customer contact point provides consistent information aimed at handling the customer as efficiently as possible while providing information that is both consistent and valued. CRM is about doing the right things right; therefore, it addresses both effectiveness and efficiency issues.[16]

Other technologies that are impacting how sales forces operate include the internet, electronic data interchange (EDI), and efficient consumer response (ECR). The internet, once thought to be a replacement for salespeople, is now recognized as an important sales tool. It can be used effectively to support the selling process through identifying prospects, making presentations and demonstrations, providing information, and servicing sales. EDI in manufacturing and ECR in retailing can both be used to tie customers' computers to the sales organization's computers. Inventories can be managed and orders can be placed electronically (for delivery or for manufacturing), improving inventory management and logistics throughout the entire distribution channel.

There are many opportunities to integrate technologies that impact the sales force. Successful implementation, however, depends on the implementation process. It requires that the purpose of the technology be clearly communicated, that the benefits of the technology be clearly demonstrated, and that management be clearly committed to the implementation and use of technology.

These initiatives are becoming increasingly important to the success of the sales force, and a sales manager needs technology competency to understand and implement them effectively.

MANAGING DIVERSITY COMPETENCY

One of the important challenges for sales managers today is managing increasing diversity in the sales force and in the companies with which they attempt to do business. **Diversity** increases as variance increases with respect to gender, ethnicity, culture, race, age, disability, sexual orientation, and religious affiliation. Sales managers need to consider diversity issues both at home in Canada and in international markets as these become more important.

In the domestic market, there are clear indications of increasing workforce diversity. A recent Conference Board of Canada survey of 53 large Canadian companies found that 81 percent of them had a workforce diversity policy and 79 percent had formal processes and practices in place to foster diversity.[17] Statistics Canada reported that the number of visible minorities in the labour force grew from 1.3 million to 2.0 million between 1991 and 2001. This figure could reach 3.3 million, or 18 percent of the total labour force, by 2016.[18] The Canadian workforce of tomorrow will clearly be different from today's.

Canada is also increasing its participation in international trade. Some of the best growth opportunities for Canadian businesses are in countries such as China and India, which are predicted to become the world's second and third largest economies, and many smaller countries such as Mexico and Brazil, where there is growing economic wealth and a rising middle class. Canadian companies will need to deal with increasingly diverse international partners, employees, and customers in these markets. Fortunately, relative to companies in many other countries, Canadian companies are in a good position to do so as Canada is one of the most multicultural countries in the world. Multiculturalism has been described as Canada's competitive advantage in the international marketplace.[19]

The sales manager of today must carefully consider his views on diversity in order to effectively manage in an increasingly diverse environment, and he must also foster appropriate attitudes and behaviours among the sales force as this will increasingly determine his company's sales success.

Career Paths in Sales Management

To fully understand career paths in sales management, we need to understand where sales managers come from and where they go. Sales managers almost always come from non-managerial sales positions in an organization, although many have some managerial or supervisory experience before getting their first promotion to sales management. Kevin Grantham, sales manager at Marmon/Keystone Canada Inc., is a typical example of someone who has worked his way through the ranks to sales management. He began his career as a warehouse person in 1979, then advanced to inside salesperson, inside sales supervisor, account manager, and finally, in 2004, to sales manager.[20] Many people finish their sales careers in sales management positions, although as you will see shortly there are many levels of sales management positions from front-line management, to middle management, to top management. It is also not uncommon for very senior people in organizations to have begun their careers in sales, often spending time in one or more sales management positions. Christina Gold, former president of Avon for North America, previously managed Avon sales in Montreal.[21] Anne M. Mulcahy, chair and CEO of Xerox Corporation, and Diane McGarry, former president and CEO of Xerox Canada, both began their Xerox careers in sales.[22]

Describing career paths in sales management is difficult without clearly understanding where sales managers fit within an organization. Unfortunately, this can vary considerably from one organization to another. Exhibit 1.4 illustrates a sales organizational hierarchy of some common sales positions, from non-managerial to top management. Four first-line and middle management positions are included: territory, district, regional, and national sales manager. It would be a very large organization that would have all four of these positions; most have no more than two of them.

Territory and district sales managers are usually described as **first-line managers**. They are responsible for non-managerial sales staff, including inside salespeople, field salespeople, and administrative assistants or sales secretaries. First-line managers report to more senior management. They have a short-term perspective and are generally focused on implementing company sales policies and procedures. They motivate their staff to achieve sales performance objectives: sales, profits, and customer service.

Regional and national sales managers are usually described as **middle managers**. By definition, this means that there are levels of management above and below them. A regional sales

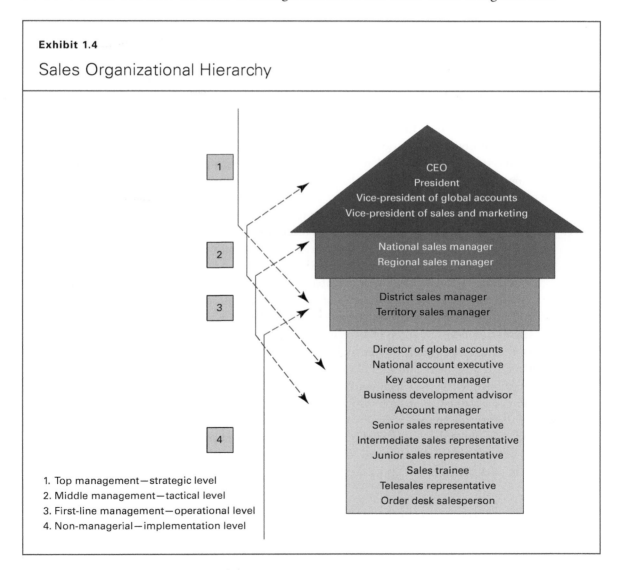

Exhibit 1.4

Sales Organizational Hierarchy

1
CEO
President
Vice-president of global accounts
Vice-president of sales and marketing

2
National sales manager
Regional sales manager

3
District sales manager
Territory sales manager

Director of global accounts
National account executive
Key account manager
Business development advisor
Account manager
Senior sales representative
Intermediate sales representative
Junior sales representative
Sales trainee
Telesales representative
Order desk salesperson

4

1. Top management—strategic level
2. Middle management—tactical level
3. First-line management—operational level
4. Non-managerial—implementation level

manager, for example, may report directly to a vice-president of sales and have a dozen or more territory managers who report to him. National and regional sales managers have a mid-term perspective and have increased responsibility because they manage larger groups of people; communicate policies and procedures from top management to lower management levels; and encourage teamwork and cooperation, resolve conflicts, and manage relationships among many people in the organization.

Some important factors affect sales organizational hierarchy and have been creating changes in sales management positions. Two important organizational factors are size and geographical market coverage. Smaller organizations and those that operate in smaller geographical markets may have a single level of sales management, and that person may simply be called the *sales manager*. Often, this sales manager will have direct account responsibility and may or may not manage field salespeople. This sales manager may even report directly to the president, or owner, of the company. In fact, in some of these organizations, the president or owner may fulfill the responsibilities of sales management and may directly manage the company's sales staff.

The nature of the product or service that a company sells may also affect positions within the sales organizational hierarchy. Many high-technology products and services are expensive and have strategic implications for the buying organizations. This means that salespeople must contact and sell to "C-level" people: chief executive officers, presidents, vice-presidents, chief financial officers, etc. To give them credibility with people in these positions, they are often given titles that reflect more who they prospect and sell to rather than their responsibilities. They may be called anything from global sales manager to vice-president of sales and marketing, yet may have no one within their own firm who reports directly to them.

Two important organizational trends are also affecting the sales organizational hierarchy. The first is the recent trend toward restructuring and downsizing. Organizational hierarchies are becoming flatter, and many middle management positions are being declared redundant. Besides increasing organizational efficiency, these changes have also improved sales effectiveness. Faster communication from the top to the bottom of the organization increases the speed with which decisions are made and allows companies to react more quickly in today's dynamic and competitive marketplace. At the same time, these changes have reduced the opportunities for promotion and have decreased job security in sales management.

The second trend involves inflating job titles in sales positions. A number of factors have contributed to title inflation. First, the role of salesperson has shifted from simply "selling" to "consulting." This enhances the value of the relationship between the salesperson and customer, and the salesperson becomes more of a "relationship manager." Second, new more prestigious titles reflect the increased education and skill levels needed by salespeople today.[23] Many salespeople are demonstrating their commitment to sales as a career by achieving sales accreditation through organizations such as the Canadian Professional Sales Association, where they can earn the designation of Certified Sales Professional (CSP). Third, with increased competition, more prestigious titles provide greater credibility for salespeople when they deal with prospects or customers. A good example of this is provided in the Sales Management in Action box on page 19.

What does all of this mean to you? That you might want to take a course and consider a career in sales management, as we'll explore next.

Why Sales Management?

Here is a statement that might shock you: *More business students will benefit from studying sales management (and personal selling) than any other aspect of business.*

SALES MANAGEMENT IN **ACTION**

Alternative Power

Ted Manning has more than 20 years' experience in marketing and sales and has been operating his own consulting firm, TT&T Marketing, in Thorold, Ontario, since 2004. Ted specializes in a number of services that help firms grow their sales: survey research, strategic marketing planning, competitive analysis, image building, sales forecasting, and tactical marketing (including product, price, and distribution strategy). But, that's not what has Ted excited these days.

In early 2007, Ted attended one of his Friday morning breakfast meetings with a group of local St. Catharines, Ontario, businesspeople, where he met an invited guest from Niagara Windpower Inc. She suggested Ted meet her business partner and, immediately following that meeting, Ted was hired as the company's director of marketing and sales.

Niagara Windpower is a small company with tremendous potential in an emerging and exciting industry: alternative energy solutions. It has two locations: Thorold and Grimsby, Ontario. In total, there are ten salespeople: six in Thorold and four in Grimsby; however, the company had as many as twenty salespeople at one time. There is a sales manager in Grimsby, but the sales manager in Thorold has recently resigned. Salespeople are paid entirely by commission. Each salesperson has an assigned

territory, but the territories are not entirely exclusive. A salesperson might, for example, live in one town but have a friend in another town. He would be allowed to sell to his friend even if that friend is located in another salesperson's territory. Territory problems are also created by the company's policy of having salespeople alternate to provide office duty in which they handle walk-in customers and telephone inquiries. Salespeople who get these leads then expect to be able to sell to them and earn commission if they are successful.

Why does this environment appeal so much to Ted Manning? Ted says, "I enjoy designing systems and processes, and creating order. This company is just beginning to grow, and it really needs someone with the ability to plan and organize." At this stage, Ted will be involved in planning strategy for marketing and sales, organizing the selling function, estimating potential and forecasting sales, and deciding account management strategies. At the same time, decisions will need to be made concerning recruiting, selecting, training, motivating, compensating, leading, and evaluating salespeople, and Ted expects to be involved in all of these. There is a real opportunity here to help a company grow and establish itself as an industry leader, and, for Ted Manning, that is a challenge.

Source: Personal interview, Ted Manning, February 23, 2007.

First, consider the importance of professional selling to the Canadian economy. Nearly 10 percent of the Canadian labour force is employed in sales occupations, and this does not include people in sales management positions. Selling drives the Canadian economy. This means there are tremendous opportunities in selling, and if you are interested in management, tremendous opportunities in sales management.

Within individual businesses, more money is spent on selling than on any other form of marketing communication. Selling costs often represent a company's single largest operating expense, as much as 8–15 percent of total sales revenue.[24] The sales force is the "revenue generator" for most businesses, and the best salespeople and sales managers are known throughout every organization. They are among the highest-paid people in most organizations. Of course, experience in sales also develops many of the competencies and provides much of the knowledge that is needed to be effective in more senior positions, and sales management provides training in the competencies needed to manage and lead people.

Even if you will eventually own your own business, selling skills will determine your success. Entrepreneurs need selling skills, or need to know how to manage people with selling skills. Most students in finance, accounting, and computer science eventually get careers in businesses where they have client contact responsibility and need to manage relationships.

You are invited to explore your options and to enhance your value.

SUMMARY

1. **Explain the sales management process.** Sales managers are responsible for all of the activities involved in managing the company's strategic sales program. These involve three interrelated sets of processes: developing the strategic sales program, implementing the strategic sales program, and reviewing and evaluating sales performance.

2. **Describe the changing environment of sales management in Canada and how these changes are affecting selling and sales management.** Many important changes are occurring in the sales environment today. Marketplace changes include rising customer expectations, decreasing supplier bases, increasing customer power, and a focus on value. Changes in the competitive environment include globalization of competition, shorter product and service life cycles, and competitor alliances. These changes are having an impact on all aspects of selling and sales management, including the relationship between sales and marketing, sales force structure, the selling process, sales management activities, and performance evaluation.

3. **Describe four important competencies needed by sales managers today.** The four important competencies that sales managers need to be effective today are: (1) strategic planning and implementation competency, (2) leading and coaching competency, (3) technology competency, and (4) managing diversity competency.

4. **Describe the career paths for sales managers today.** This is an exciting and challenging time to be in sales management. Sales managers usually bring with them the selling skills that they previously learned as salespeople and then develop management skills that position them for future promotions within their organizations. Sales management activities vary from one firm to another, depending on such things as firm size, markets served, or products sold. In large firms, the sales manager can fill a front-line management or a middle management position. In smaller firms, one person may have complete sales management responsibility. That person could be given the title of sales manager, or might even be the owner or president of the company. Two important trends affecting sales management careers today are restructuring and downsizing, and inflated sales management titles.

KEY TERMS

sales management   5

personal selling   5

co-branding   10

competencies   12

coaching   15

sales force automation   15

customer relationship management   15

diversity   16

first-line manager   17

middle manager   17

REVIEW QUESTIONS

1. A vice-president was heard to say, "When we promoted him, we lost the company's best salesperson and we gained the company's worst sales manager." Explain what he meant.

2. List and briefly describe three interrelated sets of processes that sales managers are involved with when managing the company's strategic sales program.

3. Briefly explain four major changes in the customer marketplace that are affecting selling and sales management today.

4. Briefly explain three major changes in the competitive environment that are affecting selling and sales management today.

5. Briefly explain the changes that are occurring in selling and sales management as a result of changes in the customer marketplace and competitive environment.

6. How can a company's sales department help its marketing department? How can a company's marketing department help its sales department?

7. List and describe four sales management competencies needed by effective sales managers today.

8. Define sales force automation (SFA) and customer relationship management (CRM). How are these concepts related?

9. Explain the difference between first-line sales managers and middle sales management positions.

10. One vice-president of sales was overheard to say, "It's always a catch-22. If we don't train people with the competencies necessary to become sales manager, we are forced to promote one of our best salespeople and see whether they sink or swim. If we do train people with the necessary competencies and a position does not open for them, they get frustrated and leave the organization." Do you agree with this person's views? Explain. What should this vice-president of sales do?

APPLICATION EXERCISES

1. Visit the website for the Canadian Professional Sales Association (**www.cpsa.com**). Explore this website and see what it offers both salespeople and sales managers. Does it seek to serve other stakeholders besides salespeople and sales managers? Explain.

2. Amy Anderson is about to complete her business program with a concentration in marketing. She has just interviewed for a sales position with a manufacturer of plastic components and parts that are sold to manufacturing firms across Canada. The interviewer has asked her to come for a second interview, but when she told her mother, Mrs. Anderson said, "Selling is no place for a woman, particularly a selling job where you have to travel. Why don't you see if you can get a marketing job where I'm sure you would be much happier?" Why do you think Mrs. Anderson feels this way? Do you agree with her position? Explain.

3. Consider two of the following sales positions:
    ■ selling website design services to large organizations (more than 1000 employees)
    ■ selling residential real estate
    ■ selling new and used automobiles
    ■ selling for a large consumer goods manufacturer

- selling home security systems door to door, or
- selling for a safety clothing manufacturer.

Describe how you think a sales manager's activities and responsibilities might differ when managing these sales forces.

4. Do men or women make better salespeople? Be prepared to defend your position. Do you think it is easier for a male sales manager to manage male or female salespeople, or does it matter? Do you think it is easier for a female sales manager to manage male or female salespeople, or does it matter?

CASE 1.1   Scotia Electric Sales and Service

Jim Walsh was excited when he was hired as the sales manager for Scotia Electric Sales and Service. He had been looking for a sales management job for several years and, although he had several interviews, none resulted in an actual job offer. Scotia Electric was a small company that sold electric motors and motor control equipment, along with some miscellaneous electrical supplies. The company had a total of only 23 employees who operated from two sales offices in Nova Scotia, although Scotia sold throughout the three Maritime Provinces. The sales department included nine field salespeople, three order desk salespeople (inside telephone salespeople), and three counter salespeople.

Jim's past sales experience had been with an electrical wire and cable manufacturer. Jim had begun with the company as an order desk salesperson and been promoted to field sales after three years. He had spent four years in field sales and managed his territory well. Throughout Jim's four years in sales, he had continued to grow the company's customer base throughout New Brunswick. Opportunities for career growth within the company were limited, so Jim had been forced to look externally for career advancement.

During his first few weeks at Scotia Electric, Jim noticed that the salespeople seemed to be unmotivated, which surprised him, as he understood that their compensation included a commission component that, on average, accounted for approximately 10 percent of their total compensation. When he investigated, he found that compensation for the best salespeople had remained relatively flat over the previous three or four years. Before he addressed his concerns with the salespeople, Jim decided that he would make joint sales calls with each of them so that he could assess their selling skills and get to know them better as individuals. He announced that he would be making calls with each of them over the next month, and that he wanted to begin with the company's highest-producing salesperson, Jeff Cormier. Unfortunately, one week before the first scheduled joint sales call, Jeff came into Jim's office and resigned. He said that he had a better job offer to sell for a general line industrial distributor and that he would be leaving in two weeks.

Over the next few weeks, Jim did make some joint sales calls with the other salespeople and his assessment was that none of them was really focused on increasing sales. They all seemed preoccupied. Jim noticed that they seemed to spend increasingly more time in the office, and much of it on their computers. For several nights, Jim stayed late and checked the search history on the office computers; he noticed considerable activity on employment sites, and this was apparent on several computers. Jim cleared the history from the office computers and tried to track who might be actively seeking to change companies. He quickly realized that his next best three salespeople were all looking for other jobs. Jim knew he could not afford to lose them all, and certainly not all at once.

CRITICAL-THINKING QUESTION

If you were Jim Walsh, what would you do?

CASE 1.2   Tortran Digital

Tortran Digital began operations as a small Canadian manufacturer of injection-moulded parts for the marine and electronics industries. Initially, the company had a single salesperson, but as contracts with major marine navigation manufacturers, telephone service providers, and an assortment of Canadian equipment manufacturers began to grow, the company expanded by adding two to three new salespeople each year. By 2007, the company had 15 salespeople, but Tony Gomes, the company president, was still managing all sales operations. As the company continued to grow its product design and manufacturing capabilities, Tony decided that it was time to appoint one of his senior salespeople to the position of sales manager.

When Tony reviewed his sales staff, three people immediately came to mind. However, when Tony quietly approached Ed Shilling, his first choice, Ed immediately indicated that he had no interest: Ed did not want to be a sales manager, and he enjoyed his current job too much to make a change. That left two alternatives: Heather Spadafora, the salesperson in Mississauga, and Patrick Li, the salesperson in Ottawa. Heather had been a top performer ever since she joined the company in 2001. Her sales growth had averaged 40 percent per year, and she let everyone know it whenever she could. She had ambition and had demonstrated a willingness to mentor junior salespeople. She had helped coach and train both of the other salespeople who operate in territories adjacent to her own. She had built solid customer relations with major accounts in her territory, and she was very much a "people" person. Typical of many salespeople, however, Spadafora seemed to dislike paperwork and had not always been the best at filing reports and sales documentation when needed.

Patrick, on the other hand, was one of the most organized and focused salespeople that Tony had ever met. He too had been growing his sales faster than almost everyone else in the company. He had an outstanding ability to manage and plan, and had helped Tony on many occasions in preparing budgets, planning territory allocations, and organizing sales training sessions at the company's headquarters in Brampton. If he had one weakness, it was his total focus on his work. He had always been very professional, but that sometimes resulted in his appearing cold and disinterested in interpersonal relations with company staff and sales colleagues.

CRITICAL-THINKING QUESTION

If you were Tony Gomes, what factors would you consider before making your choice? What action would you take?

Chapter 2

Planning Strategy for Marketing and Sales

LEARNING OBJECTIVES

After completing this chapter, you should be able to

1. Describe the business strategy planning process and the role of marketing strategy.

2. Explain how sales management interacts with elements of the marketing mix.

3. Describe how to right-size a sales force.

4. Explain the importance of the sales budget.

What is a google? Answer: 1 followed by 100 zeros. Think about it. A million has only six zeros; a billion has only nine zeros. A google, therefore, is a very large number, and Google Inc. is a very large company. It is one of the greatest marketing—or sales—successes of the last century, and was selected by *Fortune* in 2007 as number one among the 100 best companies to work for.

In 2002, Google had only 275 employees, including 90 salespeople, and sales revenue of US$440 million. By 2005, sales had topped US$6.1 billion, and by 2006, the company had 7942 employees (at June 30). Significantly more than half of all paid search-ad spending in North America goes to Google. The company now keeps the size of its sales force a secret, but it has grown to support 46 sales offices around the world—including one in Toronto that serves the Canadian market, where Google is the most widely used search engine. In major markets such as North America, Google now serves as many as 12 vertical markets (advertising segments), including retail, business services, travel, technology, consumer packaged goods, and others.

What has contributed to the company's phenomenal growth? It is easy to argue that it is its technology, and possibly that it has some marketing savvy. However, the sales force needs to be given its share of credit. The sales force plays an important role in both shaping and implementing the company's overall strategy. Salespeople meet regularly with product managers and customers. Google's vice-president of global online sales and operation, Sheryl Sandberg, says, "We are in a constant mode of change, so we are in a constant mode of collaboration." Information from customers is fed to the engineering group and the appropriate product teams in a constant effort to provide the best products to meet customer needs.

The strong customer orientation permeates the entire organization. Everyone is focused on giving customers exactly what they need—nothing more, nothing less. According to Marissa Mayer, vice-president of search products and user experience, Google spends most of its time and effort making its search engine bigger and better, rather than focusing on its competitors. Google's search index is three times larger than any other available today. At the same time, Google's simplicity is a main selling point. The company values the white space on its homepage: there are no bouncing balls, flashing lights, or annoying pop-up ads. Patrick Keane, director of field marketing and head of sales strategy, says, "What we really want to do is focus on a great user experience, and all else follows." "All else" means more people using Google.com or one of its 112 domains to search for information. More than 380 million unique users are on Google each month, and that means they see a large number of ads relevant to their search terms. Each time one of these ads is clicked, Google makes money. But, behind all of this, the sales force must convince advertisers that Google is the right place to spend their search-ad budget. Google salespeople must be able to build and manage strong relationships with top-spending customers, help them select the best keywords or search terms, and decide what sites to target with their advertising. To be successful, according to Sheryl Sandberg, Google salespeople must have passion, great communication skills, analytical ability, high intelligence, teamwork skills, and the ability to think strategically and execute sales plans effectively. Google's continued success depends on attracting the right salespeople to its sales force.[1]

Market Orientation and the Sales Force

Today, successful companies must continually adapt to a rapidly changing marketing environment. They need a strong **market orientation** or focus on aligning all business activities and processes toward maximizing performance in the competitive marketplace. This requires a lot of internal communication and collaboration, as illustrated by Google in the opening vignette. Firms with a strong market orientation differ from competitors in two important ways. First, they are better at market sensing. That is, they continually collect and analyze information concerning customers and competitors, and can use this information to identify market opportunities in advance of competitors. Second, they develop and maintain stronger relationships with their marketing channel intermediaries, if they exist, and with their customers.

For many of these firms, the sales force plays a central role. Salespeople have regular contact with customers, are first in an organization to become aware of customers' changing needs, and are often the first to understand competitor strengths and weaknesses and see competitor actions. Companies that use their sales force to collect and disseminate market information have an excellent source for market sensing, as these salespeople can bring valuable competitor and customer information inside their company. The sales force also plays an important role in managing relationships with customers and channel partners. Even if there are many contacts between people from these organizations and people from the sales organization, the quality of the overall organizational relationships is largely determined by the skill of the salespeople as relationship managers.

To position the sales force more clearly in the context of the organization, and with respect to marketing strategy, the next sections discuss business strategy and marketing strategy. Then, we will look at the factors that companies use to decide their level of sales force investment.

Business Strategy

Business strategy planning involves creating a **mission statement** (a statement that defines a firm's goals and objectives, which, if achieved, will enable the firm to become what it wishes to be) and developing business strategies to help the business achieve its goals or objectives. Business strategy planning may take place at the corporate level or at the strategic business unit (SBU) level, as illustrated in Exhibit 2.1. A **strategic business unit** is a business unit within a larger,

Exhibit 2.1

The Business Strategy Planning Process

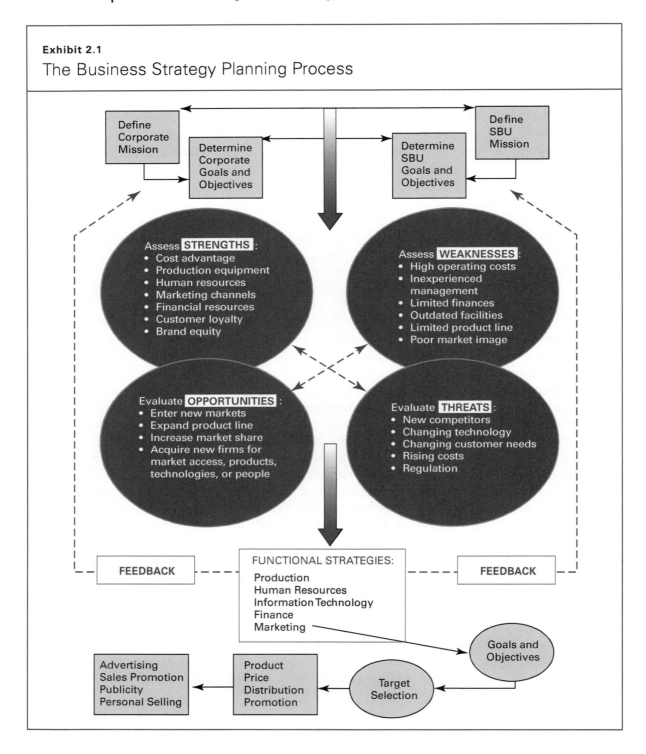

more diversified organization that has its own management, resources, objectives, and competitors, making it important that it manages its business strategy planning separately. At the same time, while the strategic business unit plans separately, it must support and be consistent with corporate-level business strategy planning. For many companies, however, the distinction between corporate-level and SBU-level business strategy planning is moot as there is only a single entity, which does not comprise separate strategic business units.

THE IMPORTANCE OF A MISSION STATEMENT

A firm's mission statement is what differentiates it from other firms. It is a firm's *raison d'être,* or reason for being. It defines what an organization is, and what it hopes to be. It also delimits an organization, as it (at least implicitly) defines what an organization is not, or should not be. Some firms call their mission statement a vision statement; other organizations have both a mission statement and a vision statement.

What is the value of having a mission statement? There is certainly debate. A group of managers from more than 20 companies identified the same mission statement as belonging to each of their companies.[2] Clearly, this mission statement, even if it does describe the firm's mission, does so in such general terms that it fails to differentiate among firms. A good mission statement needs to define what a company does, whom it serves, and how it accomplishes what it intends to do. The mission statement of Corporate Express Canada, Inc., shown in Exhibit 2.2, is an effective mission statement based on these criteria. It clearly communicates to management, employees, customers, and other stakeholders what the firm does, and it provides a guideline for opportunity analysis and strategic decision making.

THE MISSION STATEMENT AND CORPORATE GOALS AND OBJECTIVES

Once a firm has decided its mission, it must decide its **goals**—specific performance targets that a firm wishes to achieve—although these may not always be clearly measurable. For example, a firm's goals could focus on its product quality (to manufacture the highest quality electronic components in its industry), market position (to be the market leader in wave technology), customer satisfaction (to have the highest customer satisfaction ratings in the software development

---

Exhibit 2.2

Mission Statement: Corporate Express Canada, Inc.

We will be the Number One Office Supplies Business in Canada by putting the Customer at the Heart of Everything we do.

We will be the premier supplier of office, technology products, furniture, facility supplies, and integrated essentials to companies and organizations that value innovative procurement solutions.

We will leverage our other business lines, as well as our electronic commerce and systems technology, distribution infrastructure, and logistics capabilities to reduce our customers' total procurement costs, while making it easy for them to do business with us.

We provide our customers with what they need, when and where they need it, and always with the best service they can possibly imagine.

We will measure our processes and train our employees to continuously improve the way we prepare the world for business.

Source: Corporate Express Canada, Inc., http://www.corporateexpress.ca/en/company-info/office-supplies-company.asp, accessed November 1, 2006.

industry), or financial position (to improve profitability through continued new product introductions). **Objectives** are goals expressed in more specific terms (such as market share, sales revenue, unit sales, or gross margin), but they may also be expressed in terms of customer satisfaction levels, percentage of sales or margins from newer versus older products, or from direct sales versus sales through channel intermediaries, among other things. To clarify, as an example, a firm may have a goal to be market leader in providing logistics software solutions to the marine transportation industry. To achieve its goal, it may have one or more specific objectives: for instance, it could hope to increase sales revenue by 30 percent in the next year, or to increase the number of companies that use its software by 50 percent during the same period. Bob Urichuck (CSP), master trainer and author of *Up Your Bottom Line,* recommends that effective goals be S.M.A.R.T.: specific, measurable, attainable, relevant, and trackable.[3]

CORPORATE GOALS AND OBJECTIVES AND BUSINESS STRATEGIES

Once a firm has decided on its goals and objectives, it must develop **strategies**—means to achieve goals and objectives. Michael Porter, one of the world's best known business academics, argues that firms can gain a competitive advantage, and superior performance, through either cost leadership or differentiation. These two bases for competitive advantage, when combined with a choice of competitive scope—broad scope versus narrow scope—lead to three generic business strategies: cost leadership, differentiation, and focus (or niche). This third strategy, focus, gets its name from the fact that firms following this strategy narrow their focus to few or even a single market segment. These business strategies are termed *generic* because they may be employed by all firms, large or small, and regardless of industry.[4] Each of these generic business strategies has different implications for a firm's sales force, as described in Exhibit 2.3.

Marketing Strategy

Once a firm decides its corporate-level or SBU-level business strategy, it must develop functional area strategies, one of which is its marketing strategy. **Marketing strategy** is a set of integrated decisions that begin with market segmentation, target marketing, and positioning, and then include the **marketing program**, decisions that relate to the elements of the **marketing mix**: product, price, distribution, and promotion.

SEGMENTATION, TARGETING, AND POSITIONING: A THREE-STEP PROCESS

Segmentation, targeting, and positioning are a three-step process. **Market segmentation** refers to either aggregating customers into groups, or dividing the total market into smaller, relatively homogeneous groups. These groups are referred to as **market segments** and comprise people or businesses that share one or more common characteristics, or have similar needs and purchase behaviours. **Target marketing** occurs when the decision is made to allocate resources to gain a sales response from one or more of the identified market segments. At the extreme, a firm could decide that, after segmenting the market, its best option is to target the entire market with a single marketing program, a targeting strategy commonly referred to as **undifferentiated targeting**, or mass marketing. This market targeting strategy is growing less popular. Firms are more likely to target a single market segment, referred to as **concentrated targeting**; or to target two or more market segments with a specific marketing program for each segment, known as **differentiated targeting**. Today, it is increasingly popular to target at even a more micro level, selecting target customers by postal code, by occupation, or even as individuals—a market targeting strategy referred to as **micromarketing**.[5]

Exhibit 2.3

Porter's Generic Business Strategies and Their Sales Force Implications

Low Cost:	**Implications:**
Aggressive pursuit of cost reductions so the company can be the lowest cost provider in its industry. Often associated with high market share. Cost reductions can come from scale economies, experience or learning, technology, or tight cost and overhead controls.	• focus on large or volume accounts • focus on transactional customers (where price or convenience are the main purchase criteria) • order-taking an important task as current customers must be maintained while prospecting for additional large accounts
Differentiation:	**Implications:**
An attempt to become recognized for uniqueness and superiority. Successful companies often have high brand loyalty among customers, who are often less price-sensitive as well.	• focus on long-term buyer-seller relationships, with superior after-sales service • focus on consultative or relationship customers, where understanding needs and selling product benefits are more important than price or convenience • may require considerable prospecting and qualifying of customers • salespeople often better trained and compensated
Niche (or focus):	**Implications:**
A focus on meeting the specific needs of a particular target market, better than any competitor. Market share within its industry may be low, but a successful niche strategy lets a company dominate within the targeted segment.	• focus on understanding specific target market being served • must have superior knowledge of customers, competitors, products, and own company policies and capabilities

Once a decision has been made with respect to market targeting, the firm must then decide its positioning strategy. **Positioning** refers to creating and maintaining a firm's intended image with respect to its product, brand, or itself in the minds of target customers, relative to competition. Position in the customer's mind is achieved as a result of the firm's marketing program. Each element of the marketing mix can have a positive or negative effect on product, brand, or firm image.

MARKETING PROGRAM DEVELOPMENT

Any firm's success in the marketplace can be traced to the effectiveness of the marketing program that it has developed to achieve its objectives with respect to each of the target segments it decides to serve. In the following sections, each element of the marketing mix will be discussed, with respect to the implications for sales management.

SALES MANAGEMENT AND PRODUCT STRATEGY A generalization often made in marketing is that consumer products are more frequently promoted through advertising, and business products through face-to-face selling. This may be true, but consumer products manufacturers still need salespeople, and business products manufacturers must still advertise. Procter & Gamble, for example, is one of the best known consumer goods manufacturers in Canada, but it has a large and very professional sales force promoting its products to the many channel intermediaries who then sell the products to final consumers. Xerox Canada has a large and professional sales force who call on both channel intermediaries and business customers, but it advertises regularly in many magazines that are read by potential buyers or people who may influence the purchase decision for its products. What determines the extent to which salespeople are utilized is the characteristics of the product that is being sold. Business goods are often more complex, more expensive, and frequently more customized to meet the needs of specific customers. Under these conditions, salespeople are needed so that information can be shared and two-way communication and negotiation can take place. The selling firm needs to understand the customer's needs and the purchase process that will be followed, and then be able to negotiate product and price buying conditions that are satisfactory to both the buyer and the seller.

Salespeople play a central role in positioning their company and its product or brand within the marketplace. When the product is a commodity, or near commodity, salespeople can position the company based on service or price. When the product is one that can be clearly differentiated, salespeople can add value by promoting the uniqueness of the product and how it provides specific buyer benefits, or they can still position the company or product on the basis of value or superior before- and after-sale service. Strategic Technologies Inc. of Surrey, B.C., manufactures a product that is 40 percent more expensive than other products on the market. Doug Blakeway, the president and CEO, recognizes that to be successful, the product offering must add value for the customer. The company offers a 100 percent lifetime warranty and regular product upgrades. As a result, salespeople have regular contact with customers and take every opportunity to position the company as a provider of superior equipment and service.[6]

SALES MANAGEMENT AND PRICE STRATEGY As pointed out in the previous section, as product price increases, the likelihood of needing salespeople also increases. This is true regardless of whether the higher price is in absolute terms or simply relative to competition. As the absolute price of a purchase increases, the financial risk to the buyer also increases, and salespeople are needed to provide information and advice to buyers who are considering a purchase. At the same time, even if the value of the purchase is somewhat lower, if the price of the product being considered is higher than the prices of competitors' products, salespeople will be necessary to convince buyers why the product is better suited to the customer's needs, or will provide them better overall value.

Salespeople also fill an important role when prices must be negotiated with buyers. In many situations, the purchase decision involves product customization, and this may require "building" a price that reflects the product cost, the value of the product to the customer, or some combination of both. These situations often require extended negotiations, and the involvement of a professional salesperson. Even if the firm uses a one-price policy and charges the same price to all customers, a salesperson may be necessary to convince the buyer of the value of the product and why the price that is requested is reasonable.

SALES MANAGEMENT AND DISTRIBUTION STRATEGY The simplest and shortest way to get to market is to sell direct from the manufacturer to the end-customer. In many instances, this involves the use of salespeople. Most capital equipment—and even much raw material and most component parts—is sold directly in business-to-business markets. Recently, for example, Xerox Canada sold a digital production press valued at approximately $1 million to Swarm Enterprises, the company's first such sale in Edmonton. Swarm is now printing 500 000 pages per month on the new press.[7] Xerox salespeople sell much of the company's most complex and costly equipment direct in the business-to-business market. However, they also sell lower-priced products through channel intermediaries, such as retailers and office products resellers. Dell Inc., famous for its direct sales of computers to consumers, also employs a sizeable sales force that sells computers and related equipment directly to business accounts. Direct selling is growing too in popularity in the consumer market. Avon Canada, Pampered Chef, and Tupperware Canada are three of the many direct selling companies in Canada that employ salespeople, referred to as agents, dealers, or distributors.

Companies that utilize intermediaries, rather than sell direct, can use either a **push strategy**, where promotion is directed to channel intermediaries instead of end-users, or a **pull strategy**, where promotion is directed to end-users instead of channel intermediaries. In both instances, the sales force plays an important role. When a push strategy is used, the role of the sales force is to *sell to* the channel intermediary, often supported with sales promotion, and the channel intermediary sells (or pushes) the product to the next customer in the channel: another channel intermediary or the end-customer. When a pull strategy is used, the role of the sales force is to *sell through* the channel intermediary, meaning that they must fulfill a strong service role by ensuring that the intermediary has sufficient inventory, displays and promotes the product properly, and has trained salespeople who are capable of selling and supporting the product. In most instances, the decision is not whether to use a push or pull strategy, but how to combine the two to maximize sales through the channel. The Sales Management in Action box describes how Ottawa-based TalkSwitch sells through and supports its channel intermediaries, using a combined push and pull strategy.

SALES MANAGEMENT AND PROMOTION STRATEGY   There is growing recognition today that all forms of marketing communications—personal selling, advertising, sales promotion, publicity, and public relations—should provide a consistent, persuasive message to customers. This is referred to as **integrated marketing communications**, or IMC. Xerox Canada provides an excellent example of how to use IMC. Whether customers visit the company's website (**www.xerox.ca**), read an ad in *Canadian Business,* or receive a written proposal or presentation from a Xerox salesperson, they will be reinforced with the same theme: *There's a new way to look at it.* Integrated marketing communications increases the effectiveness of positioning because of the consistency of messages, but it also can increase the efficiency of promotion by reducing the communications budget when the same messages are being reinforced through various communications media.

Advertising can build awareness for a company and for its product, and can increase the likelihood that the sales force will gain access to prospects. Companies that have effective websites are finding that they gain a number of advantages, many of which support or assist the sales force. For example, many companies have product brochures, installation and maintenance manuals, and product catalogues on their website. Large amounts of information can be communicated to prospects and customers, and are available for review by buyers or other purchase influencers long after the salesperson has made a sales call. Tenaquip (**www.tenaquip.com**), one of Canada's largest industrial distributors, has its product catalogues online; these include its buyer's guide, which has more than 80 000 items and nearly 2000 pages. Interested customers may bypass salespeople and order directly online, but a salesperson is still key to creating awareness and beginning and building a relationship with buyers. In many instances, customers will phone for additional information or to make specific requests, and require the services of either inside or outside salespeople.

TalkSwitch: All Talk and Growing Action

Most technology companies use dual distribution as their go-to-market strategy. They commonly sell direct to end-customers, but also sell through some form of channel intermediary. Common intermediaries include original equipment manufacturers (OEMs), who add the product to whatever they manufacture or sell, or value-added resellers (VARs), who understand the product and its applications and can integrate it when necessary with products from several manufacturers to provide solutions to more complex end-customer needs.

Ottawa-based TalkSwitch manufactures telephone systems for small and multi-location businesses that have 32 or fewer telephone users per location. The company has more than 1300 resellers in North America, and has recently expanded to Ireland and the United Kingdom. There are many advantages of going to market through channel intermediaries, but the success of this strategy depends very much on the support that is provided to help these resellers succeed. Support is crucial, because simply selling a product to a reseller will not guarantee future sales. Only if the resellers are successful at moving product through the channel profitably will they be interested in continuing to purchase from a manufacturer. Recognizing this, TalkSwitch salespeople were instrumental in the company's strategy to train and support its resellers. TalkSwitch developed its *TalkSwitch-On-Tour* seminar series, which it rolled out late in 2005 and continued throughout 2006 at major cities across Canada and the United States. Speaking of the seminar series, Tim Welch, vice-president of sales for TalkSwitch, says, "It gives us the chance to meet existing and prospective resellers face to face, present them with new sales and marketing tools, and to share ideas and strategies about ways to increase their revenues by selling even more TalkSwitch product." At these seminars, resellers are provided with product demonstrations, informa-

tion on the small business market and tips on how to sell into it, and information on how TalkSwitch will manage its channel partner program. Working closely with its resellers allows a company such as TalkSwitch to leverage a small company-owned sales force into a very large sales force of reseller salespeople all focused on selling TalkSwitch product.

To further support its Canadian resellers, TalkSwitch added a national distributor to its channel structure. White Radio has warehouse facilities in Burnaby, British Columbia, and Burlington, Ontario. All Canadian resellers now place their orders through White Radio, which can provide them with better logistical capabilities from its two locations, resulting in faster order fulfillment. They also receive expanded technical support and access to a wider assortment of products that complement the TalkSwitch systems. Canadian resellers still get the same support from TalkSwitch, including access to its reseller website, dedicated account managers and technical support, webinars, and sales and marketing tools. TalkSwitch and White Radio will now tour across Canada together to introduce White Radio resellers to the TalkSwitch product line.

In 2007, TalkSwitch was again named to Pulvermedia's Pulver 100 list of the 100 privately held companies that represent the future of the IP communications industry. In 2006, TalkSwitch was named "Best of Show" at the Internet Telephony Conference and "Best New Exhibitor" at the Channel Partners Conference. Also in 2006, *VARBusiness,* a U.S. reseller-focused magazine dedicated to providing strategic insight to technology integrators and solution providers, named Tim Welch as one of the top 60 channel executives to watch. Tim Welch says, "We've put a lot of effort into developing a program that really works for our channel partners . . . . This recognition shows we're not only on the right path, but we're leading the way."

Sources: TalkSwitch website, http://www.talkswitch.com/, accessed December 27, 2006; CATA Alliance, "TalkSwitch Launches VAR Channel Sales Training Seminar Series Geared to Boost Revenue," http://www.cata.ca/Cata_Members/News/members_pr10260501.html, accessed December 28, 2006; TalkSwitch news release, "TalkSwitch Selects White Radio as Canadian Distributor," http://www.talkswitch.com/news/press/talkswitch_white_radio.asp, accessed December 28, 2006; Canada NewsWire, Ottawa, "TalkSwitch's Tim Welch Named to Prestigious VARBusiness Channel Executives List," April 11, 2006, p. 1.

Sales Force Investment

A key decision for many companies is how much to spend on their sales force. Companies spend more money on their sales force than on any other form of marketing communications.[8] In fact, companies regularly spend 4–8 percent of their sales revenue on personal selling, and that expenditure can be as high as 15 percent or more. North America's top 500 sales forces employ nearly 18 million salespeople. Among the manufacturing companies, salespeople comprise 5.9 percent of the total workforce, and the percentage rises to 7.9 percent for companies in the service sector.[9]

RIGHT-SIZING THE SALES FORCE

Right-sizing the sales force must begin with consideration of the company's business strategy. Companies that are focused on serving existing customers in a fairly stable environment with limited growth opportunities generally hold their sales force size stable; they may be able to reduce it if there are productivity gains as a result of employing new sales technologies; or they may restructure the sales force and shift some sales tasks to internal salespeople as discussed in Chapter 3. On the other hand, companies that are focused on growth through gaining market share or by introducing new products or serving new markets will constantly have to recruit, select, and train new salespeople. If financial resources are limited and the company cannot make an early investment in a sales force, other alternatives can be considered, including distributors, dealers, or manufacturer's agents. For larger sales forces, it is sometimes expedient to maintain a few extra salespeople in the pipeline—at the recruitment and selection stage, or at the training stage—recognizing that there will be sales force turnover. One company, which wishes to remain anonymous, keeps a salesperson in a territory knowing that there is insufficient potential to generate profit. It does this partly because the company wishes to have a national sales force, and also because the sales manager considers this particular territory a training ground for future salespeople. Salespeople who are hired to work in this territory understand that they will eventually be moved, when an opportunity arises.

How does a company determine the right-sized sales force? A number of methods can be used, including the breakdown sales approach, the percentage of sales approach, the workload approach, and the incremental approach. Each of these is now discussed.

BREAKDOWN SALES APPROACH The **breakdown sales approach** starts with the company's total sales forecast and divides it by the average expected sales per salesperson. The result is the number of salespeople who are needed to support the level of sales that is forecasted. This method is popular because of its simplicity. It is easy to understand and use, and it works reasonably well for a large sales force that is operating in a reasonably stable sales environment. For example, salespeople in the top 20 insurance companies average just under $1 million sales revenue each.[10] An insurance company that forecasted sales of $500 million could simply calculate that it needs 500 salespeople:

$$\text{Sales force size} = \frac{\text{Forecasted sales}}{\text{Average sales per salesperson}}$$

$$= \frac{\$500\ 000\ 000}{\$1\ 000\ 000}$$

$$= 500 \text{ salespeople}$$

While it is popular and intuitively easy, the breakdown sales approach has one major draw-back: it suggests that sales should determine the number of salespeople; however, it should be the number of salespeople that determines sales revenue.

PERCENTAGE OF SALES APPROACH   The **percentage of sales approach** is conceptually very similar to the breakdown approach. The sales manager starts with the company's total sales forecast, and then multiplies that by a predetermined percentage to estimate the sales force budget. This predetermined percentage may be the company's selling cost as a percentage of sales, determined from past data, or may be determined by reviewing costs as a percentage of sales within the same industry or for otherwise similar companies. Once the sales force budget is determined, it is divided by the direct cost per salesperson to determine the number of salespeople the company can afford. For example, the sales manager might note that sales force expenses as a percentage of sales revenue have historically been 20 percent. If forecasted sales are $20 million, then the sales force budget should be $4 million. From internal accounting data, the sales manager will be able to determine the total direct cost per salesperson, and she can then simply divide the sales force budget by the cost per salesperson to see how many salespeople should be employed. Assuming that the total direct selling cost per salesperson is $200 000, the sales force should employ 20 salespeople:

$$\text{Sales force size} = \frac{\text{Sales force budget}}{\text{Direct cost per salesperson}}$$

$$= \frac{\$4\,000\,000}{\$200\,000}$$

$$= 20 \text{ salespeople}$$

Of course, if other sales force-related expenses besides direct selling costs are included in the sales force budget, they will have to be deducted before the sales force size is determined. Such expenses could include, for example, costs related to the sales manager, sales supervisors, or administrative assistants.

Again, this method is popular because it is easy to understand and to use, but it also has a number of limitations. If a historical expenses as a percentage of sales figure is used, that percentage may no longer be valid. If the figure came from an industry average, or from similar companies, there is no guarantee that it is valid for individual companies. A more serious issue is that, as in the breakdown method, forecasted sales are used to determine the size of the sales force. If there is a downturn in sales, this method could result in prematurely downsizing the sales force, which could then contribute to a further sales decline. This might be particularly problematic if the company is also losing market share. In such a situation, the company might need to invest more heavily in its sales force, possibly increasing the number of salespeople well beyond what would be determined by the percentage of sales approach.

WORKLOAD APPROACH   The **workload approach** makes intuitive sense and is preferable to the previously discussed methods. With the workload approach, the sales manager starts with the total number of sales calls needed to cover the entire sales region, and then divides this amount by the average number of sales calls a salesperson can make. This approach determines the workload that is necessary, what can realistically be done by a single salesperson, and then how many salespeople will be needed to manage the entire workload. To determine the total workload, the sales manager needs to assess the total number of current and potential accounts and classify them on the basis of the resources (sales calls) that will be allocated to each one. For example, the sales manager might begin by allocating a specific number of sales calls to current customers based on sales to them the previous year: more than $100 000 is an 'A' account and should be seen 12 times per year on average; from $50 000 to $100 000 is a 'B' account and should be seen six times per year on average, etc. Based on his calculations, the sales manager might determine that a total of 14 700 sales calls are required across the entire sales force. On average, if salespeople work 200 days a year and make 3.5 sales calls per day, each salesperson will make 700 sales calls per year. The sales manager will need 21 salespeople:

$$\text{Sales force size} = \frac{\text{Total number of sales calls needed}}{\text{Average number of sales calls per salesperson}}$$

$$= \frac{14\ 700\ \text{sales calls needed}}{700\ \text{sales calls each}}$$

$$= 21\ \text{salespeople}$$

This approach has been described in its simplest form. The strength of the approach is that it can be tailored to meet the needs of individual sales forces. For example, this example classified accounts based on the sales to each account during the previous year. For companies that have a reasonably stable customer base, this may suffice. If there is opportunity to develop many new accounts, then some consideration would have to be given to these possible new accounts. If there are only a few prospective accounts, and the potential at each is known, the sales manager might simply allocate a certain number of sales calls to each of them. Of course, this process would benefit greatly from active salesperson involvement. If there are many such accounts and the maximum potential is relatively small, the sales manager might simply require each salesperson to make a certain percentage of sales calls to prospective accounts. In this way, sufficient resources are allocated to maintain existing accounts, and acceptable resources are allocated for growth or territory development. Of course, if there are many such prospective accounts, or a number of accounts with sufficient potential, taking all of them into consideration will most likely require an increase in the size of the sales force.

INCREMENTAL APPROACH   The **incremental approach** determines appropriate sales force size by adding additional salespeople until the cost of adding one more salesperson will not be covered by the estimated additional contribution dollars the salesperson will generate. This approach is not generally used to determine the size of a new sales force because this would require the sales manager to estimate relatively complex sales response functions to predict what sales would be at different sales force sizes [sales = f (sales force size)]. A typical sales function is illustrated in Exhibit 2.4. As the size of the sales force increases, sales also increase, but at a diminishing rate. Costs, however, tend to increase more directly as the size of the sales force increases. For sales forces that have been in existence for some time, the sales manager can think in terms of incremental sales and incremental costs. She can determine that the incremental cost of adding one more salesperson is, for example, $135 000. Now, all she needs to do is estimate whether this cost will be covered by incremental sales. If an additional salesperson could add $500 000 in sales revenue, and the contribution margin is 30 percent, the contribution increase would be $150 000. Since this is greater than the incremental cost, the sales manager should add another salesperson.

ADDITIONAL FACTORS TO CONSIDER

Determining the right size for a sales force is an important strategic decision because it has implications for company profitability, in both the short and the long term. A number of additional

Exhibit 2.4

Typical Sales Response and Cost Functions

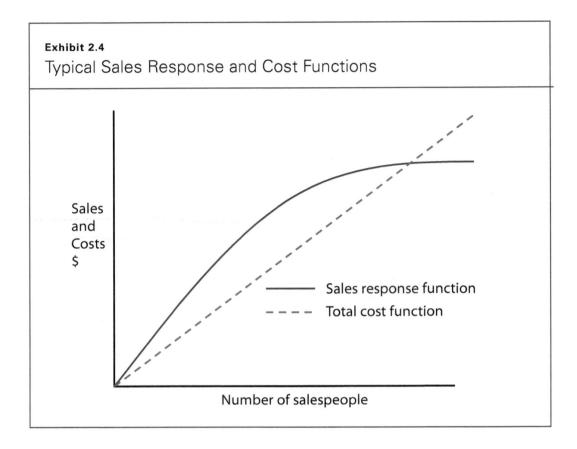

factors must be considered when sales force size decisions are made, including when and how to downsize the sales force, the impact that new product launches and new markets will have on sales force size, and the implications of sales productivity enhancements on sales force size. These are discussed in the following sections.

DOWNSIZING THE SALES FORCE Right-sizing the sales force usually means growing the sales force, and the previous sections described a number of approaches for determining how many salespeople are needed. However, right-sizing may also mean downsizing. The Sales Management Today box describes Pfizer's decision to downsize its sales force. The decision to downsize is no less important than the decision to add salespeople. In fact, downsizing can have a long lasting and very negative impact if not done carefully.

The main problems that result from downsizing are often due to severed relationships, between former salespeople and their customers, the sales company, and other people still within the sales organization.

When a salesperson leaves a sales company, her customers are forced to develop a relationship with a new salesperson. While this may be good for some customers, it may not be for others. Some customers may prefer the familiar salesperson; others may view this as an opportunity to change suppliers. They may have remained customers because of their longstanding relationship with a particular salesperson, and may see the change as the appropriate time to explore a relationship with another salesperson who has been trying to get their business. A situation even more damaging to the company occurs if its former salesperson begins to sell for a competitor,

SALES MANAGEMENT **TODAY**

Adding and Subtracting: Does It All Add Up?

One important aspect of sales force investment involves right-sizing the sales force so that customers and prospects get their desired level of service, and the sales force is able to properly represent the company's products and services in the marketplace. In profitable industries where there are frequent product introductions and where customer relationships are extremely important, there is a tendency to grow the sales force to remain ahead of the competition. Eventually, this inefficiency increases industrywide costs, and either reduces profits or results in higher than necessary prices for customers.

Sales forces in the pharmaceutical industry have been growing rapidly in recent years. There are so many pharmaceutical sales representatives now that the average sales call to a physician is down to approximately 1.5 minutes. Sales and marketing costs have risen to 25 percent of sales revenue, up from 20 percent just 15 years ago. The rate of sales growth has declined in major markets to 5 percent from 10–15 percent a year as competition from generic drug manufacturers continues to increase. Industrywide, companies spend 1.5 times as much on selling drugs as they do on research and development for new drugs. GlaxoSmithKline chief executive officer Jean-Pierre Garnier has argued that resources need to be re-allocated from promotion to new product development.

Pfizer, the world's largest drug manufacturer, made the first move. In late 2006, the company undertook a comprehensive review of its total operations and decided to reduce its North American sales force by roughly 20 percent; approximately 2200 salespeople will become unemployed. Citigroup analyst George Grofik estimates the move will save Pfizer US$440 million per year, assuming a cost per salesperson of approximately US$200 000. He sees this as a good move given the company's top-line revenue pressure. However, other industry analysts are not convinced. Roopesh Patel of UBS Investment Research recalls the 2005 sales force cuts that had a significantly negative effect on Pfizer's performance. Time, of course, will tell who is correct.

In the meantime, not all pharmaceutical companies will follow Pfizer's example. Daniel Vasella, chief executive officer of Novartis AG, plans to add approximately 1000 new salespeople to that company's North American operations. While its competitors are under pressure from generic drugs and may have limited near-term opportunities to introduce new drugs, Novartis has three new major drugs for the marketplace: Galvus, Tekturna, and Exforge. Vasella says, "There are other promotional activities you can do, but the rep is still the biggest lever."

Sources: Ben Hirschler, Reuters (November 29, 2006), "Pfizer to Cut 20 Percent of Sales Force, http://articles.news.aol.com/business/_a/pfizer-to-cut-20-percent-of-sales-force/20061129080509990024, accessed December 27, 2006. AP (November 29, 2006), "Analysts Mixed on Pfizer Job Cuts," http://money.aol.com/news/articles/_a/analysts-mixed-on-pfizer-job-cuts/n20061129080009990009, accessed December 27, 2006. Pfizer Canada, http://www.pfizer.ca/english/pfizer%20canada/corporate%20backgrounder/default.asp?s=1, accessed December 27, 2006. Pfizer Inc. news release, November 28, 2006, http://mediaroom.pfizer.com/index.php?s=press_releases&item=126, accessed December 27, 2006.

and some important customers value their relationship with the salesperson to the extent that their business follows her to the new company. If the salesperson remains in sales but does not stay within the same industry, if she harbours resentment against her former sales company she may still make things unnecessarily difficult for the replacement salesperson who takes over her accounts. Finally, the salespeople who remain with a sales company following downsizing may not have the same strong attachment to the company when other salespeople have left. The work environment has changed, and while this can be for the better, it often is not. This can be particularly problematic when the sales force consists of only three or four people. Having a friend or two leave an organization often leads to additional people leaving as well. Depending on why the sales force was downsized, the remaining salespeople may also have some level of concern and frustration. If this happens and the situation is not quickly resolved, salespeople other than those who were downsized may also leave, and it is usually the best ones—the ones with the most opportunity—who leave.

Aside from the problems that arise from changed relationships, there are also the administrative problems created by having to restructure sales territories, and the changes to the workload of the remaining salespeople. If the downsizing is incremental over an extended period, the environment of continual change can have a negative impact on morale. For this reason alone, once a decision has been made that downsizing is necessary, it is wise to do it quickly and as completely as possible. Those who are let go should be assisted with career placement, and those who remain should be told why downsizing was necessary and what the likelihood of continued downsizing is. If there is reason to believe that the conditions demanding downsizing will continue and possibly worsen, it might be wise to downsize slightly more than necessary when the initial change takes place. Salespeople will more likely accept an increased workload for a short period of time if they accept the reason for the downsizing and know that an attempt is being made to create stability for those who remain. When there is a heavier workload, it is sometimes possible to provide some temporary sales support until workloads return to a more acceptable level.

LAUNCHING NEW PRODUCTS—EXPLORING NEW MARKETS When a firm launches new products or decides to explore new markets, additional sales force investments are often required. Sometimes, the existing sales force is capable of handling the increased responsibility, and sometimes additional salespeople are required.

If the existing sales force is used to launch new products, or is required to call on new accounts, the amount of sales resources allocated to existing customers becomes reduced. This may or may not affect sales for some time if there are sufficient **carryover effects** (sales that continue in a territory after sales resources have been reduced in the territory). When salespeople reduce the number of calls made to or the time spent with some accounts, there may be no appreciable reduction in sales. This is more likely to happen when customers have a high level of loyalty to a supplier or a salesperson, or have high switching costs and must therefore continue to buy from a particular supplier. Sometimes, additional sales calls can be made by inside salespeople to keep the service level and number of contacts to important accounts stable and to offset the impact of fewer face-to-face sales calls by the field salesperson.

If launching the new products requires considerable selling effort, new salespeople are often required, and sales territory adjustments may also have to be made. Some companies outsource a new product sales force to manage the introduction of important new products, and then gradually transfer responsibility for sales of these products to the existing sales force as sales for the new products become established. Companies that do this often find that, even after a successful launch, some additional salespeople are required over the longer term, and the best of the salespeople who helped implement the initial launch of the new products make good candidates for permanent sales positions. Other companies hire and train new salespeople in advance of launching important new products. Ideally, the new salespeople are simply integrated within the existing sales force as sales for the new products increase. In the worst case, the company may be faced with downsizing or maintaining higher than necessary sales force expenditures until attrition reduces the size of the sales force.

PRODUCTIVITY AND THE SALES FORCE   Today, companies are increasingly interested in improving the productivity of their sales force. This sometimes includes better utilizing sales outsourcing, inside telesales, telemarketing, or other sales support people, or better targeting accounts so that sales resources are used more effectively. Companies—and even individual salespeople—are investing more in better account management activities with the help of personal digital assistants, sales force automation (SFA) tools, and customer relationship management (CRM) programs.

When productivity enhancements occur, a company's sales revenue may be increased as the sales resources are better used. However, some companies more than likely undertake sales force productivity enhancement initiatives with the intention of reducing selling costs, and frequently with the intention of reducing the size of the sales force as a means of doing that. However, wise companies understand that sales force productivity decisions and sales force size decisions need to be made independently.

Sales forces in most industries have experienced considerable productivity gains in recent years; that is, the sales volume per salesperson has been increasing. While this may partly be explained by price increases, the sizes of the sales volume increases certainly cannot be attributed only to that factor. Much of the increased average sales per salesperson most certainly resulted from improved account management practices. For example, the sales productivity among the largest manufacturing firms increased by 6 percent in 2006. Among the largest services sales forces, the number of salespeople was reduced by less than 3 percent, but sales increased by 19 percent. Productivity improved by 23 percent. Among the largest insurance companies, the number of salespeople remained relatively unchanged, but the average sales per salesperson increased by 14 percent.[11]

Sales Force Budgeting

An important sales management task is preparing and administering sales budgets. A **sales budget** is a document that itemizes planned expenses and provides a basis for the sales manager to monitor and control sales activities. Preparing a sales budget requires considerable thought concerning what sales are likely to be achieved, and the costs that will be necessary to achieve those sales results.

PLANNING THE SALES BUDGET

Sales budgets are usually prepared annually, but are often broken down by quarter (or even by month) to aid the sales manager in monitoring and controlling activities. Exhibit 2.5 illustrates a typical sales budget. Note that sales revenue is also estimated. In this example, sales are estimated by salesperson and by type of sale, whether direct or warehouse sale. Some companies will also estimate sales by product or product line, by particular account or market segment, and by particular regions within a salesperson's sales territory if the territory spans several regions. These sales estimates are the result of a company's sales forecasting process, described in greater detail in Chapter 4. However, sales are directly the result of particular marketing programs decided as part of the strategy planning process described in this chapter.

A good starting point for preparing a future sales budget is the current sales budget. A review of the current budget will identify whether changes must be made, considering inflation or any planned changes in marketing programs or selling activities.

Exhibit 2.5

Contribution (Loss) Projections

	Total	Wang	Kronlund	Maybee
Sales				
Whse	1 182 159	382 517	627 988	171 654
Direct	1 504 842	564 187	282 333	658 322
Total Sales	2 687 001	946 704	910 321	829 976
Cost of Goods Sold				
Whse	798 976	257 434	419 496	122 046
Direct	1 216 196	459 812	232 360	524 070
Total COGS	2 015 202	717 276	651 856	646 070
Gross Margin	671 799	229 428	258 465	183 906
Expenses				
Salary	160 650	57 000	48 150	55 500
Commissions	41 902	15 109	11 927	14 884
Travel & Entertainment	81 500	28 500	17 000	36 000
Sales Promotion	9000	2000	5000	2000
Total Expenses	293 070	102 609	82 077	108 384
Contribution (Loss)	378 729	126 819	176 388	75 522

ADMINISTERING THE SALES BUDGET

While planning the sales budget is important, administering it is equally important. The sales budget will help a sales manager identify where problems may exist. If sales are below forecast, the sales manager should investigate whether expenses are being made appropriately, and may decide to re-allocate expenses to other categories in an attempt to boost sales revenue. Money can be taken from the sales training budget, for example, to focus salespeople on a short-term sales promotion. Such decisions must not be made lightly, however. While short-term sales may improve, the cost could be the long-term sales that would result due to a better trained sales force.

There are instances in which sales expenses can be below budget, and this can negatively affect sales. Salespeople can, for example, spend too little on sales promotion, or for travel and entertainment. When sales expenses appear to be too high, again, the sales manager needs to carefully consider why. Sometimes sales revenue is higher than forecasted, but additional expenses are incurred to generate the additional sales. For this reason, companies that reward sales managers for controlling sales budgets should reward them based on selling expenses as a percentage of sales.

Sometimes, it becomes apparent well before the year-end that sales budgets need to be adjusted. When this happens, adjustments to the sales budgets should be made earlier rather than later so that they can remain effective tools for managing the sales force.

SUMMARY

1. **Describe the business strategy planning process and the role of marketing strategy.** Business strategy planning involves defining a mission, expressed as a mission statement; defining specific goals or objectives, which, if met, will help the business achieve its mission; and developing business strategies to help the business achieve its goals or objectives. Marketing strategy is one functional-level strategy. It is a set of integrated decisions that begin with market segmentation, target marketing, and positioning. Then, specific marketing programs must be decided, considering product, price, distribution, and promotion decisions for each target market.

2. **Explain how sales management interacts with elements of the marketing mix.** A common generalization is that personal selling is more frequently used in the promotion of business products, and advertising is more likely to be used in the promotion of consumer products. While the generalization is true, advertising is also important in business marketing, and personal selling is also important for promoting many consumer products. Personal selling is more often used as the price of the product or product complexity increases. While salespeople may sell directly to end-customers, many salespeople sell to and support channel intermediaries. Finally, personal selling is only one of several ways to promote products to customers. There is a growing attempt today to manage total marketing communications in an integrated fashion so that customers receive consistent messages from all sources. This is known as integrated marketing communications.

3. **Describe how to right-size a sales force.** Four methods are used to determine the appropriate size of a sales force: the breakdown sales approach, the percentage of sales approach, the workload approach, and the incremental approach. Right-sizing the sales force often means growing the sales force, but it can mean downsizing as well. When companies introduce new products or explore new markets, decisions must be made concerning whether additional sales resources are needed. Productivity is a growing concern today. Productivity increases may mean downsizing a sales force, but sales managers should recognize that sales force productivity decisions and sales force size decisions need to be made independently.

4. **Explain the importance of the sales budget.** A *sales budget* is a document that itemizes planned expenses and provides a basis for the sales manager to monitor and control sales activities. A good starting point for preparing a future sales budget is the current sales budget. A review of the current budget will identify whether changes must be made, considering inflation or any planned changes in marketing programs or selling activities. The sales budget will help a sales manager identify where problems may exist.

KEY TERMS

market orientation   **25**

mission statement   **25**

strategic business unit   **25**

goals   **27**

objectives   **28**

strategies   **28**

marketing strategy   **28**

marketing program   **28**

marketing mix   **28**

market segmentation   **28**

market segments   **28**

target marketing   **28**

undifferentiated targeting   28

concentrated targeting   28

differentiated targeting   28

micromarketing   28

positioning   29

push strategy   31

pull strategy   31

integrated marketing communications   31

breakdown sales approach   33

percentage of sales approach   34

workload approach   34

incremental approach   35

carryover effects   38

sales budget   39

REVIEW QUESTIONS

1. Discuss two important ways in which firms with a strong market orientation differ from competitors.

2. Define *mission* and explain why it is important to an organization.

3. Describe the relationship among the concepts of *segmentation, target marketing,* and *positioning.*

4. A sales manager leaving an annual business planning session was overheard to say, "This takes several weeks of my time every year. I could more effectively use my time managing the selling activities of the sales force." How would you respond to this comment? Be specific.

5. Describe how the four elements of the marketing mix—product, price, distribution, and promotion—relate to sales strategy.

6. Explain the difference between a *push strategy* and a *pull strategy,* and explain the role the sales force plays when each strategy is used.

7. Describe four methods that can be used to determine the right size for a sales force.

8. What factors must a sales manager consider when downsizing the sales force? Explain.

9. What is meant by *carryover effects?* Explain which of the following products would have the least sales carryover effects:
   a. door-to-door vacuum sales
   b. sales of standard industrial products
   c. sales of toothpaste, or
   d. sales of household furniture at a major retail outlet.

10. Describe a *sales budget* and explain why it is an important tool for sales managers.

APPLICATION EXERCISES

1. Mississauga-based 01 Communique (**www.01com.com**) is a leading provider of remote access and integrated communications software and services. Explore its website to see whether this company uses a push or a pull strategy. Be prepared to defend your choice.

2. In this chapter, the mission statement for Corporate Express Canada, Inc., was provided as an example of an effective mission statement. Explore the internet and find three additional mission statements of Canadian companies. Compare and contrast the four mission statements. Explain which mission statement is best, and which is the least effective.

3. Using the following information, decide how many salespeople the company should employ in its sales force.

Sales last year:	$32 million
Average sales per salesperson last year:	$1.6 million
Calls required to effectively cover the complete territory:	19 200
Sales force turnover	10 percent
Days worked per year on average:	200
Average calls made per day:	4.0
Cost for adding each new salesperson:	$120 000 per year
Marginal profit contribution for the next salesperson:	$150 000 per year
Amount by which marginal profit contribution decreases with each new salesperson added:	$7500

If you were the sales manager, what size sales force would you recommend? Be prepared to defend your answer.

4. In a recent conversation between the vice-president of sales and the vice-president of marketing, the topic turned to positioning. The vice-president of sales stated, "It is the role of the sales force to position the company and the product appropriately in the marketplace." The vice-president of marketing disagreed. She said, "No, I believe that positioning is the responsibility of the marketing department. The role of the sales force is simply to sell." Be prepared to discuss your views on positioning. Which vice-president do you support?

Shoes for Moos   CASE 2.1

Shoes for Moos was a rubber boot specifically designed to fit cows' "feet." The idea came to Jim Wells when he was the owner of Wells' Work and Casual Wear in Elmira, Ontario. A local farmer came to Jim's store to buy rubber boots for cows with infected hooves. With the help of his brother-in-law, Tom Byers, a classifier with the Holstein Association of Canada, Jim designed a special "shoe" that would fit over an infected cow's hoof and hold a poultice firmly in place to help with the healing process. The product was particularly attractive to dairy farmers because dairy cows with infected feet were frequently given antibiotics and their milk, during the entire period while on antibiotics and sometimes for many days afterward, became contaminated and unfit for sale. Using these special boots helped infected hooves heal faster and, in many instances, would completely eliminate the need for antibiotics. Hoof disease in cows was highly contagious and during bad weather, when the ground was wet and muddy, a farmer might have 2–20 percent of his herd with infected feet.

Jim eventually convinced Kaufman Footwear in Kitchener, Ontario, to manufacture the product for him. To help him develop his marketing plan, Jim asked his marketing class at Conestoga College, where he was teaching part-time, to collect market data for him. Students explored a number of sources for data and estimated that, in Canada, there were over 50 000 farms (approximately 35 percent in Quebec and 30 percent in Ontario) and nearly 1.5 million dairy cows (approximately 40 percent in Quebec and 35 percent in Ontario). At the same time, estimates placed the number of large farm animal veterinary clinics at about 600 and veterinarians at about 1000, across Canada.

Jim was also aware that there were several regional farm shows across Canada each year, including a large one in Toronto, where the Canadian Vet Show was also held. There were a number of trade magazines that could reach farmers, and others that specifically targeted veterinarians. Many farmers bought farm supplies from local farm dealers, and Jim estimated that there could be as many as 500 outlets in Ontario that might potentially sell such products to farmers. Veterinarians, on the other hand, bought mainly from veterinary supply wholesalers. However, most of these served mainly logistical functions and had limited sales force coverage.

While he was in the early stage of developing a marketing plan for his new product, Jim Wells wondered what role personal selling should play in his company's strategy.

CRITICAL-THINKING QUESTION

If you were Jim Wells, what else would you need to know, and what other decisions would you have to make, before you could decide what role personal selling should play in the company's marketing strategy?

CASE 2.2   Electronics and More

When Tim Reilly took over as vice-president of sales for Electronics and More, he was told by the president that his job was to focus the company on sales growth, and in particular on what was referred to internally as direct sales: sales for products that were not held in the company's inventory. Shipments were generally made direct from the manufacturer to the end-customer. Warehouse sales, by contrast, were sales for items that the company carried in its inventory.

Warehouse sales had higher gross margins, which were needed to offset inventory carrying costs. However, direct sales were seen as the future of the company and were therefore strategically more important. The company was in the process of expanding its product lines to include more complex products, and most of these would result in direct sales. In order for the company to be attractive to manufacturers of these types of products, Electronics and More's salespeople would need to be better trained technically, and the company would have to demonstrate to manufacturers that it could add value for them.

Across the entire company, direct sales currently accounted for approximately 60 percent of total sales, although that ranged from 52 percent in Quebec to 64 percent in Manitoba. One objective of the company was to achieve 70 percent of sales revenue nationally from direct sales within three years. Part of this change would come about through the addition of new product lines, but most would have to come from re-focusing the sales force on direct sales, hopefully without sacrificing any of the company's current warehouse sales.

There were three salespeople in the Atlantic Provinces sales office (see Exhibit 2.5 on p. 40). Overall, the branch was getting 56 percent of its sales revenue from direct sales. One salesperson, Hal Maybee, was currently getting 70 percent of his sales direct, but there was one important reason for that: his territory was a long distance from the company's warehouse, so his customers preferred to buy standard products from local suppliers rather than wait for delivery from Halifax, Nova Scotia. Hal was therefore forced to focus his effort on selling products that were not standard warehouse inventory items. Bob Leese, on the other hand, was getting most of his sales from warehouse inventory. Most of Bob's customers had been purchasing from Electronics and More for many years. He had not added many new accounts over the past five years. Given the types of accounts in his territory, it was surprising that his direct sales did not at least equal those of the other salespeople at the branch. Bob was getting the lowest sales commissions. The company paid commission of 1 percent of sales for warehouse sales and 2 percent of sales for direct sales. Tim discovered that the sales commission structure had been changed two years ago to focus salespeople on direct sales, and it did have considerable impact.

When Tim visited the Atlantic Provinces sales branch and discussed the situation with Gig Smith, the branch manager, Gig suggested that it might be time to adjust the commission structure again. After some discussion, Tim agreed. "Alright. Let's consider it. Of course, I will need to study what the impact will be on the national sales force before any changes are made. I don't think we can have different commission structures in different regions even though selling conditions may vary. There will always be some winners and some losers when these changes are made. In total, we cannot give more money away unless sales revenue increases. We either have to redistribute commissions, or come up with a plan that will give everyone a chance to benefit. For example, we could decrease the commission on warehouse sales to 0.5 percent, and increase it on direct sales to 3 percent. What do you think?"

After a few minutes, Gig replied, "Not in this branch. I think that if we really are serious about getting the salespeople to change their sales focus, we need to set a minimum level of sales for both warehouse and direct sales below which no commission will be paid. Then, we can make a commission payment for sales above the minimum. I need more time to think about it."

CRITICAL-THINKING QUESTIONS

1. Explain why Gig did not like Tim's suggestion.

2. If you were Gig, what recommendation would you make that would be effective for your sales branch?

3. Is it important that the same commission structure be used nationally to change the sales focus of the sales force? Explain why or why not.

Comprehensive Cases for Part I

Maritime Bank

Problems arise when a large bank, attempting to develop a stronger customer service orientation, enlarges the tellers' responsibilities to include selling activities.

CHRISTOPHER LOVELOCK

"I'm concerned about Karen," said Margaret Costanzo to David Reeves. The two bank officers were seated in Margaret's office at Maritime Bank. Costanzo was a vice-president of the bank and manager of the Scotia Square branch, the third largest in Maritime's large branch network. She and Reeves, the branch's customer service director, were having an employee appraisal meeting. Reeves was responsible for the customer service department, which coordinated the activities of the customer service representatives (CSRs, formerly known as tellers) and the customer assistance representatives (CARs, formerly known as new accounts assistants).

Costanzo and Reeves were discussing Karen Mitchell, a 24-year-old customer service rep, who had applied for the soon-to-be-vacant position of head CSR. Mitchell had been with the bank for three and a half years. She had applied for the position of what had then been called head teller a year earlier, but the job had gone to a candidate with more seniority. Now that individual was leaving—his wife had been transferred to a new job in another city—and the position was once again open. Two other candidates had also applied for the job.

Both Costanzo and Reeves were agreed that, against all criteria used in the past, Karen Mitchell would have been the obvious choice for head teller. She was both fast and accurate in her work, presented a smart and professional appearance, and was well liked by customers and her fellow CSRs. However, the nature of the teller's job had been significantly revised nine months earlier to add a stronger marketing component. CSRs were now expected to offer polite suggestions that customers use automated teller machines (ATMs) for simple transactions. They were also required to stimulate customer interest in the broadening array of financial services offered by the bank. "The problem with Karen," as Reeves put it, "is that she simply refuses to sell."

The New Focus on Customer Service at Maritime Bank

Although it was one of the largest banks in Canada, Maritime had historically focused on corporate business, and its share of the retail consumer banking business had declined in the face of aggressive competition from other financial institutions. Three years earlier, the board of directors had appointed a new chief executive officer (CEO) and given him the mandate of developing a stronger consumer orientation at the retail level. The goal was to seize the initiative in marketing the ever-increasing array of financial services now available to retail customers. The CEO's strategy, after putting in a new management team, was to begin by ordering an expansion and speed-up of Maritime's investment in electronic delivery systems, which had fallen behind the competition. To achieve this strategy, a new banking technology team had been created.

During the past 18 months, the bank had tripled the number of automated teller machines (ATMs) located inside its branches, replacing older ATMs by the latest models featuring colour touch screens and capable of a broader array of transactions in multiple languages. Maritime was already a member of several ATM networks, giving its customers access to freestanding 24-hour booths in shopping centres, airports, and other high-traffic locations. The installation of new ATMs was coupled with a branch renovation program, designed to improve the physical appearance of the branches. A pilot program to test the impact of these "new look" branches was already underway. Longer term, top management intended to redesign the interior of each branch. As more customers switched to electronic banking from remote locations, the bank planned to close a number of its smaller branches.

Another important move had been to introduce automated telephone banking, which allowed customers to check account balances and to move funds from one account to another by touching specific keys on their phone in response to the instructions of a computerized voice. This service was available 24/7 and utilization was rising steadily. Customers could also call a central customer service office to speak with a bank representative concerning service questions or problems with their accounts, as well as to request new account applications or new chequebooks, which would be sent by mail. This office currently operated on weekdays from 8:00 A.M. to 8:00 P.M. and on Saturdays from 8:00 A.M. to 2:00 P.M., but Maritime was evaluating the possibility of expanding the operation to include a broad array of retail bank services, offered on a 24-hour basis.

The technology team had completely redesigned the bank's website to make it possible to offer what were described as the region's most "user-friendly" internet banking services. Customers had online access to their accounts and could also obtain information about bank services, branch locations and service hours, location of ATMs, as well as answers to commonly asked questions. Maritime was also testing the use of web-enabled services for customers who had digital cell phones with internet access.

Finally, the bank had recently started issuing new credit cards containing chips with embedded radio-frequency identification (RFID), which speeded transactions by allowing customers to wave their cards close to a special reader rather than having to swipe them in the traditional way. All these actions seemed to be bearing fruit. In the most recent six months, Maritime had seen a significant increase in the number of new accounts opened, as compared to the same period of the previous year. And quarterly data released by the Bank of Canada showed that Maritime Bank was steadily increasing its share of new deposits in the region.

Customer Service Issues

New financial products had been introduced at a rapid rate. But the bank found that many existing "platform" staff—known as new accounts assistants—were ill equipped to sell these services because of lack of product knowledge and inadequate training in selling skills. As Costanzo recalled:

> The problem was that they were so used to sitting at their desks waiting for a customer to approach them with a specific request, such as a mortgage or car loan, that it was hard to get them to take a more positive approach that involved actively probing for customer needs. Their whole job seemed to revolve around filling out forms or responding to prompts on their computer screens. We were way behind most other banks in this respect.

As the automation program proceeded, the mix of activities performed by the tellers started to change. A growing number of customers were using the ATMs, the website, and automated telephone banking for a broad array of transactions, including cash withdrawals and deposits (from the ATMs), transfers of funds between accounts, and requesting account balances. The ATMs at the Scotia Square branch had the highest utilization of any of Maritime's branches, reflecting the large number of students and young professionals served at that location, Costanzo noted that customers who were older or less well-educated seemed to prefer being served by "a real person, rather than a machine." They were particularly reluctant to make deposits via an ATM.

A year earlier, the head office had selected three branches, including Scotia Square, as test sites for a new customer service program, which included a radical redesign of the branch interior. The Scotia Square branch was in a busy urban location, about one kilometre from the central business district and less than 10 minutes' walk from the campus of a large university. The branch was surrounded by retail stores and close to commercial and professional offices. The other test branches were among the bank's larger suburban offices in two different metropolitan areas and were located in a shopping mall and next to a big hospital, respectively.

As part of the branch renovation program, each of these three branches had previously been remodelled to include no fewer than four ATMs (Scotia Square had six), which could be closed off from the rest of the branch so that they would remain accessible to customers 24 hours a day. Further remodelling was then undertaken to locate a customer service desk near the entrance; close to each desk were two electronic information terminals, featuring colour touch screens that customers could activate to obtain information on a variety of bank services. The teller stations were redesigned to provide two levels of service: an express station for simple deposits and for cashing of approved cheques, and regular stations for the full array of services provided by tellers. The number of stations open at a given time was varied to reflect the volume of anticipated business, and staffing arrangements were changed to ensure that more tellers were on hand to serve customers during the busiest periods. Finally, the platform area in each branch was reconstructed to create what the architect described as "a friendly, yet professional appearance."

Human Resources

With the new environment came new training programs for the staff of these three branches and new job descriptions and job titles: customer assistance representatives (for the platform staff), customer service representatives (for the tellers), and customer service director (instead of assistant branch manager). The head teller position was renamed head CSR. Details of the new job descriptions are shown in the Appendix. The training programs for each group included sessions designed to develop improved knowledge of both new and existing retail products. (CARs received more extensive training in this area than did CSRs.) The CARs also attended a 15-hour course, offered in three separate sessions, on basic selling skills. This program covered key steps in the sales process, including building a relationship, exploring customer needs, determining a solution, and overcoming objections.

The sales training program for CSRs, by contrast, consisted of just two 2-hour sessions designed to develop skills in recognizing and probing customer needs, presenting product features and benefits, overcoming objections, and referring customers to CARs. All staff members in customer service positions participated in sessions designed to improve their communication skills and professional image: clothing and personal grooming and interactions with customers were all discussed. Said the trainer, "Remember, people's money is too important to entrust to someone who doesn't look and act the part!"

CARs were instructed to rise from their seats and shake hands with customers. Both CARs and CSRs were given exercises designed to improve their listening skills and their powers of observation. All employees working where they could be seen by customers were ordered to refrain from drinking soft drinks and chewing gum on the job. (Smoking by both employees and customers had been banned some years earlier under the bank's smoke-free office policy.)

Although Maritime Bank's management anticipated that most of the increased emphasis on selling would fall to the CARs, they also foresaw a limited selling role for the customer service reps, who would be expected to mention various products and facilities offered by the bank as they served customers at the teller windows. For instance, if a customer happened to say something about an upcoming vacation, the CSR was supposed to mention traveller's cheques; if the customer complained about bounced cheques, the CSR should suggest speaking to a CAR about opening a personal line of credit that would provide an automatic overdraft protection; if the customer mentioned investments, the CSR was expected to refer him or her to a CAR who could provide information on money market accounts, certificates of deposit, or Maritime's discount brokerage service. All CSRs were supplied with their own business cards. When making a referral, they were expected to write the customer's name and the product of interest on the back of a card, give it to the customer and send that individual to the customer assistance desks.

In an effort to motivate CSRs at the three branches to sell specific financial products, the bank experimented with various incentive programs. The first involved cash bonuses for referrals to CARs that resulted in sale of specific products. During a one-month period, CSRs were offered a $50 bonus for each referral leading to a customer's opening a personal line of credit account; the CARs received a $20 bonus for each account they opened, regardless of whether or not it came as a referral or simply a walk-in. Eight such bonuses were paid to CSRs at Scotia Square, with three each going to just two of the full-time CSRs, Jean Warshawski and Bruce Greenfield. Karen Mitchell was not among the recipients. However, this program was not renewed, since it was felt that there were other, more cost-effective means of marketing this product. In addition, Reeves, the customer service director, had reason to believe that Greenfield had colluded with one of the CARs, his girlfriend, to claim referrals that he had not, in fact, made. Another test branch reported similar suspicions of two of its CSRs.

A second promotion followed and was based on allocating credits to the CSRs for successful referrals. The value of the credit varied according to the nature of the product—for instance, a debit card was worth 500 credits—and accumulated credits could be exchanged for merchandise gifts. This program was deemed ineffective and discontinued after three months. The basic problem seemed to be that the value of the gifts was seen as too low in relation to the amount of effort required. Other problems with these promotional schemes included lack of product knowledge on the part of the CSRs and time pressures when many customers were waiting in line to be served.

The bank had next turned to an approach which, in David Reeves' words, "used the stick rather than the carrot." All CSRs had traditionally been evaluated half-yearly on a variety of criteria, including accuracy, speed, quality of interactions with customers, punctuality of arrival for work, job attitudes, cooperation with other employees, and professional image. The evaluation process assigned a number of points to each criterion, with accuracy and speed being the most heavily weighted. In addition to appraisals by the customer service director and the branch manager, with input from the head CSR, Maritime had recently instituted a program of anonymous visits by what was popularly known as the "mystery client." Each CSR was visited at least once a quarter by a professional evaluator posing as a customer. This individual's appraisal of the CSR's appearance, performance, and attitude was included in the overall evaluation. The number of points scored by each CSR had a direct impact on merit pay raises and on selection for promotion to the head CSR position or to platform jobs.

To encourage improved product knowledge and "consultative selling" by CSRs, the evaluation process was revised to include points assigned for each individual's success in sales referrals. Under the new evaluation scheme, the maximum number of points assignable for effectiveness in making sales—directly or through referrals to CARs—amounted to 30 percent of the potential total score. Although CSR-initiated sales had risen significantly in the most recent half-year, Reeves sensed that morale had dropped among this group, in contrast to the CARs, whose enthusiasm and commitment had risen significantly. He had also noticed an increase in CSR errors. One CSR had quit, complaining of too much pressure.

KAREN MITCHELL

Under the old scoring system, Karen Mitchell had been the highest-scoring teller/CSR for four consecutive half-years. But after two half-years under the new system, her ranking had dropped to fourth out of the seven full-time tellers. The top-ranking CSR, Mary Bell, had been with Maritime Bank for 16 years, but had declined repeated invitations to apply for a head teller position, saying that she was happy where she was, earning at the top of the CSR scale, and did not want "the extra worry and responsibility." Mitchell ranked first on all but one of the operationally related criteria (interactions with customers, where she ranked second), but sixth on selling effectiveness (see Exhibit 1).

Costanzo and Reeves had spoken to Mitchell about her performance and expressed disappointment. Mitchell had informed them, respectfully but firmly, that she saw the most important aspect of her job as giving customers fast, accurate, and courteous service, telling the two bank officers:

> I did try this selling thing but it just seemed to annoy people. Some said they were in a hurry and couldn't talk now; others looked at me as if I were slightly crazy to bring up the subject of a different bank service than the one they were currently transacting. And then, when you got the odd person who seemed interested, you could hear the other customers in the line grumbling about the slow service.
>
> Really, the last straw was when I noticed on the computer screen that this woman had several thousand in her savings account so I suggested to her, just as the trainer had told us, that she could earn more interest if she opened a money market account. Well, she told me it was none of my business what she did with her money, and stomped off. Don't get me wrong, I love being able to help customers, and if they ask for my advice, I'll gladly tell them about what the bank has to offer.

SELECTING A NEW HEAD CSR

Two weeks after this meeting, it was announced that the head CSR was leaving. The job entailed some supervision of the work of the other CSRs (including allocation of work assignments and scheduling part-time CSRs at busy periods or during employee vacations), consultation on—and, where possible, resolution of—any problems occurring at the teller stations, and handling of large cash deposits and withdrawals by local retailers (see position description in the Appendix). When not engaged in such tasks, the head CSR was expected to operate a regular teller window.

Exhibit 1   Maritime Bank: Summary of Performance Evaluation Scores for Customer Service Representatives at Scotia Square Branch During Latest Two Half-Year Periods

CSR Name[3]	Length of Full-Time Bank Service	Operational Criteria[1] (max.: 70 points)		Selling Effectiveness[2] (max.: 30 points)		Total Score	
		1st Half	2nd Half	1st Half	2nd Half	1st Half	2nd Half
Mary Bell	16 years, 10 months	65	64	16	20	81	84
Scott Dubois	2 years, 3 months	63	61	15	19	78	80
Bruce Greenfield	12 months	48	42	20	26	68	68
Karen Mitchell	3 years, 7 months	67	67	13	12	80	79
Sharon Rubin	1 year, 4 months	53	55	8	9	61	64
Swee Hoon Chen	7 months	—	50	—	22	—	72
Jean Warshawski	2 years, 1 month	57	55	21	28	79	83

[1]Totals based on sum of ratings points against various criteria, including accuracy, work production, attendance and punctuality, personal appearance, organization of work, initiative, cooperation with others, problem-solving ability, and quality of interaction with customers.

[2]Points awarded for both direct sales by CSR (e.g., traveller's cheques) and referral selling by CSR to CAR (e.g., debit card, certificates of deposit, personal line of credit).

[3]Full-time CSRs only (part-time CSRs were evaluated separately).

The pay scale for a head CSR ranged from $10.00 to $15.00 per hour, depending on qualifications, seniority, and branch size, as compared to a range of $8.40 to $12.00 per hour for CSRs. The pay scale for CARs ranged from $9.20 to $13.50. Full-time employees (who were not unionized) worked a 40-hour week, including some evenings until 6:00 P.M. and certain Saturday mornings. Costanzo indicated that the pay scales were typical for banks in the region, although the average CSR at Maritime was better qualified than those at smaller banks and therefore higher on the scale. Karen Mitchell was currently earning $10.80 per hour, reflecting her education, which included an associate's degree in business administration from the local community college, three-and-a-half years' experience, and significant past merit increases. If promoted to head CSR, she would qualify for an initial rate of $12.50 an hour. When applications for the positions closed, Mitchell was one of three candidates. The other two candidates were Jean Warshawski, 42, another CSR at the Scotia Square branch; and Curtis Richter, 24, the head CSR at one of Maritime Bank's small suburban branches, who was seeking more responsibility.

Warshawski was married with two sons in school. She had started working as a part-time teller at Scotia Square some three years previously, switching to full-time work a year later in order, as she said, to put away some money for her boys' college education. Warshawski was a cheerful woman with a jolly laugh. She had a wonderful memory for people's names and Reeves had often seen her greeting customers on the street or in a restaurant during her lunch hour. Reviewing her evaluations over the previous three years, Reeves noted that she had initially performed poorly on accuracy and at one point, when she was still a part-timer, had been put on probation because of frequent inaccuracies in the balance in her cash drawer at the end of the day. Although Reeves considered her much improved on this score, he still saw room for improvement. The customer service director had also had occasion to reprimand her for tardiness during the past year. Warshawski attributed this to health problems with her elder son who, she said, was now responding to treatment.

Both Reeves and Costanzo had observed Warshawski at work and agreed that her interactions with customers were exceptionally good, although she tended to be overly chatty and was not as fast as Karen Mitchell. She seemed to have a natural ability to size up customers and to decide which ones were good prospects for a quick sales pitch on a specific financial product. Although slightly untidy in her personal appearance, she was very well organized in her work and was quick to help her fellow CSRs, especially new hires. She was currently earning $10.20 per hour as a CSR and would qualify for a rate of $12.10 as head CSR. In the most recent six months, Warshawski had ranked ahead of Mitchell as a result of being very successful in consultative selling (Exhibit 1).

Richter, the third candidate, was not working in one of the three test branches, so had not been exposed to the consultative selling program and its corresponding evaluation scheme. However, he had received excellent evaluations for his work in Maritime's small Longmeadow branch, where he had been employed for three years. A move to Scotia Square would increase his earnings from $11.20 to $12.10 per hour. Reeves and Costanzo had interviewed Richter and considered him intelligent and personable. He had joined the bank after dropping out of college midway through his third year, but had recently started taking evening courses in order to complete his degree. The Longmeadow branch was located in an older part of town, where commercial and retail activity were rather stagnant. This branch (which was rumoured to be under consideration for closure) had not yet been renovated and had no ATMs, although there was an ATM accessible to Maritime customers one block away. Richter supervised three CSRs and reported directly to the branch manager, who spoke very highly of him. Since there were no CARs in this branch, Richter and another experienced CSR took turns handling new accounts and loan or mortgage applications.

Costanzo and Reeves were troubled by the decision that faced them. Prior to the bank's shift in focus, Mitchell would have been the natural choice for the head CSR job, which, in turn, could be a stepping stone to further promotions, including customer assistance representative, customer service director, and, eventually, manager of a small branch or a management position in the head office. Mitchell had told her superiors that she was interested in making a career in banking and that she was eager to take on further responsibilities.

Compounding the problem was the fact that the three branches testing the improved branch design and new customer service program had just completed a full year of the test. Costanzo knew that sales and profits were up significantly at all three branches, relative to the bank's performance as a whole. She anticipated that top management would want to extend the program systemwide after making any modifications that seemed desirable.

Appendix

Maritime Bank: Job Descriptions for Customer Service Staff in Branches

PREVIOUS JOB DESCRIPTION FOR TELLER

FUNCTION: Provides customer services by receiving, paying out, and keeping accurate records of all moneys involved in paying and receiving transactions. Promotes the bank's services.

RESPONSIBILITIES

1. Serves customers:
   - Accepts deposits, verifies cash and endorsements, and gives customers their receipts.
   - Cashes cheques within the limits assigned or refers customers to supervisor for authorization.
   - Accepts savings deposits and withdrawals, verifies signatures, and posts interest and balances as necessary.
   - Accepts loan, credit card, utility, and other payments.
   - Issues money orders, cashier's cheques, traveller's cheques, and foreign currency, and issues or redeems Canada savings bonds.
   - Reconciles customer statements and confers with bookkeeping personnel regarding discrepancies in balances or other problems.
   - Issues credit card advances.

2. Prepares individual daily settlement of teller cash and proof transactions.

3. Prepares branch daily journal and general ledger.

4. Promotes the bank's services:
   - Cross-sells other bank services appropriate to customer's needs.
   - Answers inquiries regarding bank matters.
   - Directs customers to other departments for specialized services.

5. Assists with other branch duties:
   - Receipts night and mail deposits.
   - Reconciles ATM transactions.
   - Provides safe deposit services.
   - Performs secretarial duties.

NEW JOB DESCRIPTION FOR CUSTOMER SERVICE REPRESENTATIVE

FUNCTION: Provides customers with the highest-quality services, with special emphasis on recognizing customer need and cross-selling appropriate bank services. Plays an active role in developing and maintaining good relations.

RESPONSIBILITIES

1. Presents and communicates the best possible customer service:
   - Greets all customers with a courteous, friendly attitude.
   - Provides fast, accurate, friendly service.
   - Uses customer's name whenever possible.

2. Sells bank services and maintains customer relations:
   - Cross-sells retail services by identifying and referring valid prospects to a customer assistance representative or customer service director. When time permits (no other customers waiting in line), should actively cross-sell retail services.
   - Develops new business by acquainting non-customers with bank services and existing customers with additional services that they are not currently using.

3. Provides a prompt and efficient operation on a professional level:
   - Receives cash and/or cheques for chequing accounts, savings accounts, taxes withheld, loan payments, MasterCard and Visa, mortgage payments, money orders, traveller's cheques, cashier's cheques.
   - Verifies amount of cash and/or cheques received, being alert to counterfeit or fraudulent items.
   - Cashes cheques in accordance with bank policy. Watches for stop payments and holds funds per bank policy.
   - Receives payment of collection items, safe deposit rentals, and other miscellaneous items.
   - Confers with head CSR or customer service director on non-routine situations.
   - Sells traveller's cheques, money orders, monthly transit passes, and cashier's cheques, Canada savings bonds, and may redeem coupons and sell or redeem foreign currency.
   - Prepares coin and currency orders as necessary.

- Services, maintains, and settles ATMs as required.
- Ensures only minimum cash exposure necessary for efficient operation is kept in cash drawer; removes excess cash immediately to secured location.
- Prepares accurate and timely daily settlement of work.
- Performs bookkeeping and operational functions as assigned by customer service director.

NEW JOB DESCRIPTION FOR HEAD CUSTOMER SERVICE REPRESENTATIVE

FUNCTION: Supervises all customer service representatives in the designated branch office, ensuring efficient operation and the highest-quality service to customers. Plays an active role in developing and maintaining good customer relations. Assists other branch personnel on request.

RESPONSIBILITIES

1. Supervises the CSRs in the branch:
   - Allocates work, coordinates work flow, reviews and revises work procedures.
   - Ensures teller area is adequately and efficiently staffed with well-trained, qualified personnel. Assists CSRs with more complex transactions.
   - Resolves routine personnel problems, referring more complex situations to customer service director.
   - Participates in decisions concerning performance appraisal, promotions, wage changes, transfers, and termination of subordinate CSR staff.
2. Assumes responsibility for CSRs' money:
   - Buys and sells money in the vault, ensuring adequacy of branch currency and coin supply.
   - Ensures that CSRs and cash sheets are in balance.

- Maintains necessary records, including daily branch journal and general ledger.
3. Accepts deposits and withdrawals by business customers at the commercial window.
4. Operates teller window to provide services to retail customers (see Responsibilities for CSRs).

NEW JOB DESCRIPTION FOR CUSTOMER ASSISTANCE REPRESENTATIVE

FUNCTION: Provides services and guidance to customers/prospects seeking banking relationships or related information. Promotes and sells needed products and responds to special requests by existing customers.

RESPONSIBILITIES

1. Provides prompt, efficient, and friendly service to all customers and prospective customers:
   - Describes and sells bank services to customers/prospects who approach them directly or via referral from customer service reps or other bank personnel.
   - Answers customers' questions regarding bank services, hours, etc.
2. Identifies and responds to customers' needs:
   - Promotes and sells retail services and identifies any existing cross-sell opportunities.
   - Opens new accounts for individuals, businesses, and private organizations.
   - Prepares temporary cheques and deposit slips for new chequing/NOW accounts.
   - Sells cheques and deposit slips.
   - Interviews and takes applications for and pays out on installment/charge card accounts and other credit-related products.
   - Certifies cheques.
   - Handles stop payment requests.
   - Responds to telephone mail inquiries from customers or bank personnel.

- Receives notification of name or address changes and takes necessary action.
- Takes action on notification of lost passbooks, credit cards, ATM cards, collateral, and other lost or stolen items.
- Demonstrates ATMs to customers and assists with problems.
- Coordinates closing of accounts and ascertains reasons.

3. Sells and services all retail products:
   - Advises customers and processes applications for all products covered in CAR training programs (and updates).
   - Initiates referrals to the appropriate department when a trust or corporate business need is identified.

NEW JOB DESCRIPTION FOR CUSTOMER SERVICE DIRECTOR

FUNCTION: Supervises customer service representatives, customer assistance representatives, and other staff as assigned to provide the most effective and profitable retail banking delivery system in the local marketplace. Supervises sales efforts and provides feedback to management concerning response to products and services by current and prospective banking customers. Communicates goals and results to those supervised and ensures operational standards are met in order to achieve outstanding customer service.

RESPONSIBILITIES

1. Supervises effective delivery of retail products:
   - Selects, trains, and manages CSRs and CARs.
   - Assigns duties and work schedules.
   - Completes performance reviews.

2. Personally, and through those supervised, renders the highest level of professional and efficient customer service available in the local marketplace:
   - Provides high level of service while implementing most efficient and customer-sensitive staffing schedules.

- Supervises all on-the-job programs within office.
- Ensures that outstanding customer service standards are achieved.
- Directs remedial programs for CSRs and CARs as necessary.

3. Develops retail sales effectiveness to the degree necessary to achieve market share objectives:
   - Ensures that all CSRs and CARs possess comprehensive product knowledge.
   - Directs coordinated cross-sell program within office at all times.
   - Reports staff training needs to branch manager and/or regional training director.

4. Ensures adherence to operational standards:
   - Oversees preparation of daily and monthly operational and sales reports.
   - Estimates, approves, and coordinates branch cash needs in advance.
   - Oversees ATM processing function.
   - Handles or consults with CSRs/CARs on more complex transactions.
   - Ensures clean and businesslike appearance of the branch facility.

5. Informs branch manager of customer response to products:
   - Reports customer complaints and types of sales resistance encountered
   - Describes and summarizes reasons for account closings

6. Communicates effectively the goals and results of the bank to those under supervision:
   - Reduces office goals into format which translates to goals for each CSR or CAR.
   - Reports sales and cross-sell results to all CSRs and CARs.
   - Conducts sales- and service-oriented staff meetings with CSRs/CARs on a regular basis.
   - Attends all scheduled customer service management meetings organized by regional office.

CASE 2	**Royal Corporation**

As Mary Jones, a third-year sales representative for Royal Corporation, reviewed her call plans for the following day, she thought about her sales strategy. It was only July, but Jones was already well on her way toward making 2005 her best year so far with the company financially. In 2004, she had sold the largest dollar volume of copiers of any sales representative in Eastern Canada and had been the third most successful rep in the country.

But Jones was not looking forward to her scheduled activities for the next day. In spite of her excellent sales ability, she had not been able to sell one of the products: the Royal Corporate Copy Centre (CCC). This innovative program was highly touted by Royal upper management, and Jones was one of the few sales reps in her office who had not sold a CCC in 2004. Although Jones had an excellent working relationship with her sales manager, Tom Stein, she had been experiencing a lot of pressure from him of late because he could not understand her inability to sell CCCs. Jones had therefore promised herself that she would concentrate her efforts on selling CCCs, even if it meant sacrificing sales of other products.

Jones had six appointments for the day: 9:00 A.M., Acme Computers; 9:45 A.M., Bickford Publishing; 11:45 A.M., ABC Electronics; 12:30 P.M., CG Advertising; 2:00 P.M., General Hospital; and 3:30 P.M. Pierson's. At Acme, Bickford, and ABC, Jones would develop CCC prospects. She was in various stages of information gathering and proposal preparation for each of the accounts. At CG, Jones planned to present examples of work performed by a model 750 colour copier. At General Hospital, she would present her final proposal for CCC adoption. Although the focus of her day would be on CCCs, she still needed to call and visit other accounts that she was developing.

Royal Products

In 2003, Royal had introduced its Corporate Copy Centre facilities management program (CCC). Under this concept, Royal offered to equip, staff, operate, and manage a reproduction operation for its clients on the clients' premises. After analyzing the needs of the client, Royal selected and installed the appropriate equipment and provided fully trained, Royal–employed operators. The CCC equipment also permits microfilming, sorting, collating, binding, covering, and colour copying, in addition to high-volume copying. The major benefits of the program include reproduction contracted for at a specified price, guaranteed output, tailor-made capabilities, and qualified operators.

The Royal Corporation established the Royal Reproduction Centre (RRC) division in 1979. With 17 offices located in nine Canadian provinces, the RRC specializes in high quality quick-turn-around copying, duplicating, and printing on a service basis. In addition to routine reproduction jobs, the RRC is capable of filling various specialized requests, including duplicating engineering documents and computer reports, microfilming, colour copying, and producing overhead transparencies. In addition, the RRC sales representatives sell the Royal 750 colour copier (the only piece of hardware sold through RRCs) and the Royal Corporate Copy Centre program (CCC). Although the RRC accepts orders from "walk-ins," the majority of the orders are generated by the field representatives who handle certain named accounts, which are broken down by geographic territory.

Royal 750 Colour Copier

The Royal 750 colour copier made its debut in 1996 and was originally sold by colour copier specialists in the equipment division of Royal. But sales representatives did not want to sell the colour copier exclusively and sales managers did not want to manage the colour copier specialists. Therefore, the 750 was not a particularly successful product. In 2002, the sales responsibility for the colour copier had been transferred to the RRC division. Since the RRC sales representatives were already taking orders from customers needing the services of a colour copier, it was felt that the reps would be in an advantageous position to determine when current customer requirements would justify the purchase of a 750 copier.

Acme Computers

As she pulled into the Acme Computers parking lot, she noticed that an unexpected traffic jam had made her 10 minutes late for the 9:00 A.M. appointment. This made her uncomfortable as she valued her time and assumed that her clients appreciated promptness. Jones had acquired the Acme Computers account the previous summer and had dealt personally with Betty White, the director of printing services, ever since. Jones had approached White six months earlier with the idea of purchasing a CCC but had not pursued the matter until now because Betty had seemed very unreceptive. For today's call, Jones had worked for several hours preparing a detailed study of Acme's present reproduction costs. She was determined to make her efforts pay off.

Jones gave her card to the new receptionist, who buzzed White's office and told her that Jones was waiting. A few minutes later, Betty appeared and led Jones to a corner of the lobby. They always met in the lobby, a situation that Jones found frustrating, but it was apparently company policy.

"Good morning, Betty, it's good to see you again. Since I saw you last, I've put together the complete analysis on the CCC that I promised. I know you'll be excited by what you see. As you are aware, the concept of a CCC is not that unusual anymore. You may recall, from the first presentation I prepared for you, that the CCC can be a tremendous time and money saver. Could you take a few moments to review the calculations that I have prepared exclusively for Acme Computers?" Betty flipped through the various pages of exhibits that Jones had prepared, but it was obvious that she had little interest in the proposal. "As you can see," Jones continued, "the savings are really significant after the first two years."

White countered, "Yes, but the program is more expensive the first two years. And what's worse is that there will be an outsider here doing our printing. I can't say that's an idea I could ever be comfortable with."

Jones realized that she had completely lost the possibility of White's support, but she continued. "Betty, let me highlight some of the other features and benefits that might interest Acme."

"I'm sorry, Mary, but I have a 10:00 meeting that I really must prepare for. I can't discuss this matter further today."

"Betty, will you be able to go over these figures in more depth a little later?"

"Why don't you leave them with me. I'll look at them when I get the chance," White replied.

Jones left the proposal with White, hoping that she would give it serious consideration. But as she pulled out of Acme Computers' driveway, she could not help but feel that the day had gotten off to a poor start.

Bickford Publishing

At 9:45 A.M., Jones stopped at Bickford Publishing for her second sales call of the day. She waited in the lobby while Joe Smith, the director of corporate services, was paged. Bickford Publishing was one of Jones's best accounts. Last year, her commission from sales to Bickford had totalled 10 percent of her pay. But her relationship with Joe Smith always seemed to be on unstable ground. She was not sure why, but she had always felt that Smith harboured resentment towards her. However, she decided not to dwell on the matter as long as a steady stream of large orders kept coming in. Jones had been calling on Bickford ever since Tim McCarthy, the sales rep before her, had been transferred. Competition among the RRC sales reps for the Bickford account had been keen. But Tom Stein had decided that Jones's performance warranted a crack at the account, and she had proven that she deserved it by increasing sales 40 percent within six months.

"Good morning, Miss Jones, how are you today?" Smith greeted her. He always referred to her formally as "Miss Jones."

"I'm fine, Mr. Smith," Jones replied. "Thank you for seeing me today. I needed to drop by and give you some additional information on the CCC idea that I reviewed with you earlier."

"Miss Jones, to be perfectly honest with you, I reviewed the information that you left with me, and although I think that your CCC is a very nice idea, I really don't believe it is something that Bickford would be interested in at this particular point in time."

"But Mr. Smith, I didn't even give you any of the particulars. I have a whole set of calculations here indicating that the CCC could save Bickford a considerable amount of time, effort, and money over the next few years."

"I don't mean to be rude, Miss Jones, but I am in a hurry. I really don't care to continue this conversation."

"Before you go, do you think that it might be possible to arrange to present this proposal to Mr. Perry (Tony Perry, the vice-president of corporate facilities, Joe Smith's immediate supervisor) in the near future? I'm sure that he would be interested in seeing it. We had discussed this idea in passing earlier, and he seemed to feel that it warranted serious consideration."

"Maybe we can talk about that the next time you are here. I'll call you if I need to have something printed. Now I really must go."

As Jones returned to her car, she decided that, in spite of what Smith had told her about waiting until next time, she should move ahead to contact Mr. Perry directly. He had seemed genuinely interested in hearing more about the CCC when she had spoken to him earlier, even though she had mentioned it only briefly. She decided that she would return to the office and send Perry a letter requesting an appointment to speak with him.

Although Jones was not yet aware of it, Joe Smith had returned to his desk and immediately begun drafting the following memo to be sent to Tony Perry:

To: Tony Perry, V.P., Corporate Facilities
From: Joe Smith, Corporate Services
Re: Royal CCC

Tony:

I spoke at length with Mary Jones of Royal this morning. She presented me with her proposal for the adoption of the CCC program at Bickford Publishing. After reviewing the proposal in detail, I have determined that the program: (a) is not cost effective, (b) has many problem areas that need ironing out, and (c) is inappropriate for our company at this time.

   Therefore, in light of the above, my opinion is that this matter does not warrant any serious consideration or further discussion at this point in time.

Jones arrived back at her office at 10:45. She checked her mailbox for messages, grabbed a cup of coffee, and returned to her desk to draft the letter to Tony Perry. After making several phone calls setting up appointments for the next week and checking on client satisfaction with some jobs that had been delivered that day, she gathered up the materials that she needed for the rest of her sales calls. Finishing her coffee, she noticed the poster announcing a trip for members of the "President's Club." To become a member, a sales representative had to meet 100 percent of his or her sales quota, sell a 750 colour copier, sell a CCC program, and sell a short-term rental. Jones believed that making quota would be difficult but attainable, even though her superior performance in 2004 had led to a quota increase of 20 percent for 2005. She had already sold a colour copier and a short-term rental. Therefore, the main thing standing between her and making the President's Club was the sale of a CCC. Not selling a CCC this year would have even more serious ramifications than she had thought.

Until recently, Jones had considered herself the prime candidate for the expected opening for a senior sales representative in her office. But Michael Gould, a sales rep who also had three years' experience, was enjoying an excellent year. He had sold two colour copiers and had just closed a deal on a CCC to a large semiconductor manufacturing firm. Normally everyone in the office celebrated the sale of a CCC. As a fellow sales rep was often heard saying, "It takes the heat off all of us for a while." Jones, however, found it difficult to celebrate Michael's sale. For not only was he the office "golden boy" but now, in her opinion, he was also the prime candidate for the senior sales rep position. Michael's sale had left Jones as one of the few reps in the office without the sale of a CCC to his or her credit. "It is pretty difficult to get a viable CCC lead," Jones thought, "but I've had one or two this year that should have been closed." Neither the long discussions with her sales manager nor the numerous in-service training sessions and discussions on how to sell the CCC had helped. "I've just got to sell one of these soon," Jones resolved.

ABC Electronics

On her way out, she glanced at the clock. It was 11:33 A.M.: she had just enough time to make her 11:45 appointment with Sam Lawless, operations manager at ABC Electronics. This was Jones's first appointment at ABC, and she was excited about getting a foot in the door there. A friend of hers was an assistant accountant at ABC. She had informed Jones that the company spent more than $15 000 a month on printing services and that they might consider a CCC proposal. Jones knew who the competition was, and, although their prices were lower on low-volume orders, Royal could meet or beat their prices for the kind of volume of work for which ABC was contracting. But Jones wasn't enthusiastic about garnering the ABC account for reproduction work: she believed she could sell them a CCC.

Jones's friend had mentioned management's dissatisfaction with the subcontracting of so much printing. Also, there had been complaints regarding the quality of the work. Investment in an in-house print shop had been discussed. Jones had assessed ABC's situation and had noticed a strong parallel with the situation at Star Electronics, a multi-division electronics manufacturing firm that had been sold CCCs for each of its four locations in the area. That sale, which had occurred over a year ago, had been vital in legitimizing the potential customers in the Northeast. Jones hoped to sell ABC on the same premise as Fred Myers had sold Star Electronics. Myers had been extremely helpful in reviewing his sales plan with Jones and had given her ideas on points he felt had been instrumental in closing the Star deal. She felt well prepared for this call.

Jones had waited four months to get an appointment with Lawless. He had a reputation for disliking to speak with salespeople, but Jones's friend had passed along some CCC literature to him, and he had seemed interested. Finally, after months of being unable to reach him by telephone or get a response by mail, she had phoned two weeks ago and he had consented to see her. Today she planned to concentrate on how adopting the CCC program might solve ABC's current reproduction problems. She also planned to ask Lawless to provide her with the necessary information to produce a convincing proposal in favour of CCC. Jones pulled into a visitor parking space and grabbed her briefcase. "This could end up being the one," she thought as she headed for the reception area.

Jones removed a business card from her wallet and handed it to the receptionist. "Mary Jones to see Sam Lawless. I have an appointment," Jones announced.

"I'm sorry," the receptionist replied. "Mr. Lawless is no longer with the company."

Jones tried not to lose her composure. "But I had an appointment to see him today. When did he leave?"

"Last Friday was Mr. Lawless's last day. Mr. Bates is now operations manager."

"May I see Mr. Bates, please?" Jones inquired, knowing in advance what the response would be.

"Mr. Bates does not see salespeople. He sees no one without an appointment."

"Could you tell him that I had an appointment to see Mr. Lawless? Perhaps he would consider seeing me."

"I can't call him. But I'll leave him a note with your card. Perhaps you can contact him later."

"Thank you, I will." Jones turned and left ABC, obviously shaken. "Back to square one," she thought as she headed back to her car. It was 12:05 P.M.

CG Advertising

Jones headed for her next stop, CG Advertising, still upset over the episode at ABC. But she had long since discovered that no successful salesperson can dwell on disappointments. "It interferes with your whole attitude," she reminded herself. Jones arrived at the office park where CG was located. She was on time for her 12:30 appointment.

CG was a large, full-service agency. Jones's colour copy orders from CG had been increasing at a rapid rate for the past six months, and she had no reason to believe that CG's needs would decrease in the near future. Therefore she believed the time was ripe to present a case for the purchase of a 750 colour copier. Jones had been dealing primarily with Jim Stevens, head of creative services, They had a good working relationship, even though on certain occasions Jones had found him to be unusually demanding about quality. She figured that characteristic seemed to be common in many creative people. She had decided to use his obsession with perfection to work to her advantage. Jones also knew that money was only a secondary consideration as far as Stevens was concerned. He had seemingly gotten his way on purchases in several other instances, so she planned her approach to him. Jones had outlined a proposal, which she was now ready to present to Jim.

"Good morning, Jim, how's the advertising business?"

"It's going pretty well for us here, how are things with you?"

"Great, Jim," Jones lied, "I have an interesting idea to discuss with you. I've been thinking that CG has been ordering large quantities of colour copies. I know that you utilize them in the presentation of advertising and marketing plans to clients. I also know that you like to experiment with several different concepts before actually deciding on a final idea. Even though we have exceptionally short turnaround time, it occurred to me that nothing would suit your needs more efficiently and effectively than the presence of one of our Royal 750 colour copiers right here in your production room. That way, each time that you consider a revision, one of your artists will be able to compose a rough and you can run a quick copy and decide virtually immediately if that is the direction in which you want to go, with no need to slow down the creative process at all."

"Well, I don't know; our current situation seems to be working out rather well. I really don't see any reason to change it."

"I'm not sure that you're fully aware of all the things that the 750 colour copier is capable of doing," Jones pressed on. "One of the technicians and I have been experimenting with the 750. Even I have discovered some new and interesting capabilities to be applied in your field, Jim. Let me show you some of them."

She reached into her art portfolio and produced a wide variety of samples to show Stevens. "You know that the colour copier is great for enlarging and reducing as well as straight duplicating. But look at the different effects we got by experimenting with various sizes and colours. Don't you think that this is an interesting effect?"

"Yes, it really is," Stevens said, loosening up slightly.

"But wait," Jones added, "I really have the ultimate to show you." Jones produced a sheet upon which she had constructed a collage from various slides that Stevens had given her for enlarging.

"Those are my slides! Hey, that's great!"

"Do you think that a potential client might be impressed by something like this? And the best part is you can whip something like this up in a matter of minutes if the copier is at your disposal."

"Hey, that's a great idea, Mary. I'd love to be able to fool around with one of those machines. I bet I'd be able to do some really inventive proposals with it."

"I'm sure you would, Jim."

"Do you have a few minutes right now? I'd like to bounce this idea off Bill Jackson, head of purchasing, and see how quickly we can get one in here."

Jones and Stevens went down to Jackson's office. Before they'd even spoken, Jones felt that this deal was closed. Jim Stevens always got his own way. Besides, she believed she knew what approach to use with Bill Jackson. She had dealt with him on several other occasions. Jackson had failed to approve a purchase for her the prior autumn on the basis that the purchase could not be justified. He was right on that account; their present 600 model was handling their reproduction needs sufficiently, but you can't blame a person for trying, she thought. Besides, she hadn't had Stevens in her corner for that one. This was going to be different.

"How's it going, Bill? You've met Mary Jones before, haven't you?"

"Yes, I remember Miss Jones. She's been to see me several times, always trying to sell me something we don't need," he said cynically.

"Well, this time I do have something you need and not only will this purchase save time, but it will save money, too. Let me show you some figures I've worked out regarding how much you can save by purchasing the 750 colour copier." Jones showed Jackson that, at CG's current rate of increased orders of colour copies, the 750 would pay for itself in three years. She also stressed the efficiency and ease of operation. But she knew that Jackson was really only interested in the bottom line.

"Well, I must admit, Miss Jones, it does appear to be a cost-effective purchase."

Jackson volunteered, "Not only that, but we can now get our art work immediately, too. This purchase will make everyone happy."

Jones believed she had the order. "I'll begin the paperwork as soon as I return to the office. May I come by next week to complete the deal?"

"Well, let me see what needs to be done on this end, but I don't foresee a problem," Jackson replied.

"There won't be any problem," Stevens assured Jones.

"Fine, then. I'll call Jim the first of next week to set up an appointment for delivery."

Jones returned to her car at 1:00. She felt much better having closed the sale on the 750 copier. She had planned enough time to stop for lunch.

During lunch, Jones thought about her time at Royal. She enjoyed her job as a whole. If it weren't for the pressure she was feeling to sell the Corporate Copy Centre program, everything would be just about perfect. Jones had been a straight 'A' student in college, where she had majored in marketing. As far back as she could remember, she had always wanted to work in sales. Her father had started out in sales and had enjoyed a very successful and profitable career. He had advanced to sales manager and sales director for a highly successful Fortune 500 company and was proud that his daughter had chosen to pursue a career in sales. They would often get together, and he would suggest strategies that had proven effective for him when he had worked in the field.

When Jones's college placement office had announced that a Royal collegiate recruiter was visiting the campus, Jones had immediately signed up for an interview. She knew several recent graduates who had obtained positions with Royal and were very happy there. They were also doing well financially. She had been excited at the idea of working for an industry giant. When she had been invited for a second interview, she'd been ecstatic. Several days later, she'd received a phone call offering her a position at the regional office. She'd accepted immediately. Jones had attended various pre-training workshops for six weeks at her regional office preparing her for her two-week intensive training period at the Royal Training Headquarters. The training had consisted of product training and sales training. She had excelled there and graduated from that course at the head of her class. From that point on everything had continued smoothly . . . until this problem with selling the CCC.

After a quick sandwich and coffee, Jones left the restaurant at 1:30. She allowed extra time before her 2:00 appointment at General Hospital (located just four blocks from the office) to stop into the office first, check for messages, and check in with her sales manager. She informed Tom Stein that she considered the sale of a 750 to CG almost certain.

"That's great, Mary. I never doubted your ability to sell the colour copiers, or repro for that matter. But what are we going to do about our other problem?"

"Tom, I've been following CCC leads all morning. To tell you the truth, I don't feel as though I've made any progress at all. As a matter of fact, I've lost some ground." Jones went on to explain the situation that had developed at ABC Electronics and how she'd felt when she'd learned that Sam Lawless was no longer with the company. "I was pretty excited about that prospect, Tom. The news was a little tough to take."

"That's okay. We'll just concentrate on his replacement now. It might be a setback. But the company's still there, and they still have the same printing needs and problems. Besides, you're going to make your final presentation to General Hospital this afternoon, and you really did your homework for that one." Stein had worked extensively with Jones on the proposal from start to finish. They both knew that it was her best opportunity of the year to sell a CCC.

"I'm leaving right now. Wish me luck."

He did. She filled her briefcase with the proposals and CCC demonstration kit that she planned to use for the actual presentation, and headed toward the parking lot.

General Hospital

Jones's appointment was with Harry Jameson of General Hospital. As she approached his office, his receptionist announced her. Jameson appeared and led her to the boardroom for their meeting. Jones was surprised to find three other individuals seated around the table. She was introduced to Bob Goldstein, vice-president of operations, Martha Chambers, director of accounting, and Dr. J.P. Dunwitty, chairman of the board. Jameson explained that whenever an expenditure of this magnitude was being considered, the hospital's executive committee had to make a joint recommendation.

Jones set up her demonstration at the head of the table so that it could easily be seen by everyone, and began her presentation. She presented slides verifying the merits of the CCC, and also explained the financial calculations that she had generated based upon the information supplied to her by Jameson.

Forty minutes later, Jones finished her presentation and began fielding questions. The usual concerns were voiced regarding hiring an "outsider" to work within the hospital. But the major concern seemed to revolve around the loss of employment on the part of two present printing press operators. One, John Brown, had been a faithful employee for more than five years. He was married and had a child. There had never been a complaint about John personally or with regard to the quality or quantity of his work. The second operator was Peter Dunwitty, a recent graduate of a nearby vocational school and nephew of Dr. Dunwitty. Although he had been employed by the hospital for only three months, there was no question about his ability and performance.

In response to this concern, Jones emphasized that the new equipment was more efficient, but different, and did not require the skills of experienced printers like Brown and Dunwitty. She knew, however, that this was always the one point about the adoption of a CCC program that even she had difficulty justifying. She suddenly felt rather ill.

"Well, Miss Jones, if you'll excuse us for a few minutes, we'd like to reach a decision on this matter," said Jameson.

"There's no need to decide right at this point. You all have copies of my proposal. If you'd like to take a few days to review the figures, I'd be happy to come by then," said Jones, in a last-ditch attempt to gain some additional time.

"I think that we'd like to meet in private for a few minutes right now, if you don't mind," interjected Dunwitty.

"No, that's fine," Jones said as she left the room for the lobby. She sat in a waiting room and drank a cup of coffee. Five minutes later, the board members called her back in.

"This CCC idea is really sound, Miss Jones," Jameson began. "However, here at General Hospital we have a very strong commitment to our employees. There really seems to be no good reason to put two fine young men out of work. Yes, I realize that from the figures that you've presented to us you have indicated a savings of approximately $30 000 over three years. But I would have to question some of the calculations. Under the circumstances, we feel that maintaining sound employee relations has more merit than switching to an unproven program right now. Therefore, we've decided against purchasing a CCC."

Jones was disappointed, But she had been in this situation often enough not to show it. "I'm sorry to hear that, Mr. Jameson, I thought that I had presented a very good argument for participation in the CCC program. Do you think that if your current operators decided to leave, before you filled their positions, you might consider CCC again?"

"I can't make a commitment to that right now. But feel free to stay in touch," Jameson countered.

"I'll still be coming in on a regular basis to meet all your needs for other work not capable of being performed in your print shop," Jones replied.

"Then you'll be the first to know if that situation arises," said Jameson.

"Thank you all for your time. I hope that I was of assistance even though you decided against the purchase. If I may be of help at any point in time, don't hesitate to call," Jones remarked as she headed for the door.

Now, totally disappointed, Jones regretted having scheduled another appointment for that afternoon. She would have liked to call it a day. But she knew she had an opportunity to pick up some repro work and develop a new account. So she knew she couldn't cancel.

Pierson's

Jones stopped by to see Paul Blake, head of staff training at Pierson's, a large department store with locations across Canada. Jones had made a cold call one afternoon during the previous week and had obtained a sizable printing order. Now she wanted to see whether Blake was satisfied with the job, which had been delivered earlier in the day. She also wanted to speak to him about some of the other services available at the RRC. Jones was about to reach into her briefcase for her card to offer to the receptionist when she was startled by a "Hello, Mary," coming from behind her.

"Hello Paul," Jones responded, surprised and pleased that he had remembered her name. "How are you today?"

"Great! I have to tell you that the report you printed for us is far superior to the work that we have been receiving from some of our other suppliers. I've got another piece that will be ready to go out in about an hour. Can you have someone come by and pick it up then?"

"I'll do better than that. I'll pick it up myself," Jones replied.

"See you then," he responded as he turned and headed back toward his office.

"I'm glad I decided to stop by after all," Jones thought as she pressed the elevator button. She wondered how she could best use the next hour to help salvage the day. When the elevator door opened, out stepped Kevin Fitzgerald, operations manager for Pierson's. Jones had met him several weeks earlier when she had spoken with Ann Leibman, a sales rep for Royal Equipment Division. Leibman had been very close to closing a deal that would involve selling Pierson's several "casual" copying machines that it was planning to locate in various offices to use for quick copying. Leibman had informed Jones that Tom Stein had presented a CCC proposal to Pierson's six months earlier but the plan had been flatly refused. Fitzgerald, she explained, had been sincerely interested in the idea. But the plan involved a larger initial expenditure than Pierson's was willing to make. Now, Leibman explained, there would be a much larger savings involved, since the "casual" machines would not be needed if a CCC were implemented. Jones had suggested to Fitzgerald that the CCC proposal be reworked to include the new machines so that a current assessment could be made. He had once again appeared genuinely interested and suggested that Jones retrieve the necessary figures from Jerry Query, head of purchasing. Jones had not yet done so. She had phoned Query several times, but he had never responded to her messages.

"Nice to see you again, Mr. Fitzgerald. Ann Leibman introduced us. I'm Mary Jones from Royal."

"Yes, I remember. Have you spoken with Mr. Query yet?"

"I'm on my way to see him right now," Jones said, as she thought that this would be the perfect way to use the hour.

"Fine, get in touch with me when you have the new calculations."

Jones entered the elevator that Fitzgerald had been holding for her as they spoke. She returned to the first floor and consulted the directory. Purchasing was on the third floor. As she walked off the elevator on the third floor, the first thing she saw was a sign that said, "Salespeople seen by appointment only. Tuesdays and Thursdays, 10 A.M. to 12 noon."

"I'm really out of luck," Jones thought, "not only do I not have an appointment, but today's Wednesday. But I'll give it my best shot as long as I'm here."

Jones walked over to the receptionist, who was talking to herself as she searched through a large pile of papers on her desk. Although Jones knew that the woman was aware of her presence, the receptionist continued to avoid her.

"This could be a hopeless case," Jones thought. But just then, the receptionist looked up and acknowledged her.

"Good afternoon. I'm Mary Jones from Royal. I was just speaking to Mr. Fitzgerald, who suggested that I see Mr. Query. I'm not selling anything. I just need to get some figures from him."

"Just a minute," the receptionist replied, as she walked toward an office with Query's name on the door.

"Maybe this is not going to be so bad after all," Jones thought.

"Mr. Query will see you for a minute," the receptionist announced as she returned to her desk.

Jones walked into Mr. Query's plushly furnished office. Query was an imposing figure: 6 foot 4 inches, nearly 300 pounds, and bald. Jones extended her hand, which Query grasped firmly. "What brings you here to see me?" Query inquired.

Jones explained her conversations with Ann Leibman and Kevin Fitzgerald. As she was about to ask her initial series of questions, Query interrupted. "Miss Jones, I frankly don't know what the hell you are doing here! We settled this issue over six months ago, and now you're bringing it up again. I really don't understand. You people came in with a proposal that was going to cost us more money than we were spending. We know what we're doing. No one is going to come in here and tell us our business."

"Mr. Query," Jones began, trying to remain composed, "the calculations that you were presented with were based upon the equipment that Pierson's was utilizing six months ago. Now that you are contemplating additional purchases, I mentioned to Mr. Fitzgerald that a new comparison should be made. He instructed me to speak with you in order to obtain the information needed to prepare a thorough proposal."

"Fitzgerald! What on earth does Fitzgerald have to do with this? This is none of his damn business. He sat at the same table as I six months ago when we arrived at a decision. Why doesn't he keep his nose out of affairs that don't concern him? We didn't want this program six months ago, and we don't want it now!" Query shouted.

"I'm only trying to do my job, Mr. Query. I was not part of the team that presented the proposal six months ago. But from all the information that is available now, I still feel that a CCC would save you money here at Pierson's."

"Don't you understand, Miss Jones? We don't want any outsiders here. You have no control over people that don't work for you. Nothing gets approved around here unless it has my signature on it. That's control. Now I really see no need to waste any more of my time or yours."

"I appreciate your frankness," Jones responded, struggling to find something positive to say.

"Well, that's the kind of man I am, direct and to the point."

"You can say that again," Jones thought. "One other thing before I go, Mr. Query. I was noticing the colour copies on your desk."

"Yes, I like to send colour copies of jobs when getting production estimates. For example, these are copies of the bags that we will be using during our fall promotion. I have received several compliments from suppliers who think that by viewing colour copies they get a real feel for what I need."

"Well, it just so happens that my division of Royal sells colour copiers. At some time it may be more efficient for you to consider purchase. Let me leave you some literature on the 750 copier, which you can review at your leisure." Jones removed a brochure from her briefcase. She attached one of her business cards to it and handed it to Query. As Jones shook his hand and left the office, she noted that she had half an hour before the project of Blake's would be ready for pick-up.

Jones entered the doughnut shop across the street and, as she waited for her coffee, reviewed her day's activities. She was enthusiastic about the impending colour copier sale at CG Advertising, and about the new repro business that she had acquired at Pierson's. But the rest of the day had been discouraging. Not only had she been "shot down" repeatedly, but she'd now have to work extra hard for several days to ensure that she would make 100 percent of quota for the month. "Trying to sell the CCC is even harder than I thought it was," Jones thought.

Part II

Developing the Strategic Sales Program

CHAPTER 3 Organizing the Selling Function

CHAPTER 4 Estimating Potential and Forecasting Sales

CHAPTER 5 Developing and Growing Account Relationships

CHAPTER 6 Enhancing Customer Interactions

Comprehensive Cases for Part II

CASE 1 TFI Food Equipment Solutions

CASE 2 Hi-T Mill Supply Inc.

Today's sales managers are responsible for developing strategic sales programs. Organizing the selling function is discussed in Chapter 3. Estimating sales potential and forecasting sales is discussed in Chapter 4. Developing and growing account relationships is discussed in Chapter 5. Enhancing face-to-face interactions with customers is discussed in Chapter 6.

Chapter 3

Organizing the Selling Function

Xerox has long been admired among sales professionals as a company that provides outstanding sales training for its sales force. *Selling Power* recently included Xerox in its top 10 list of companies for sales employment, ranking Xerox sixth among 379 companies employing a sales force of over 500, based on compensation, training, and career mobility. In Canada, *The Globe and Mail's Report on Business* magazine recognized Xerox Canada as one of the 50 best employers in Canada in 2007, for the third time since 2003.

The company went through some difficult times in recent years as competitors with less expensive products began to affect Xerox sales. The Xerox share price fell below US$5.00 per share on the NYSE in December 2000, but the company has started to fight back aggressively and its share price more than tripled by January 2004.

The start of the comeback was a recognition that the company needed to revamp its product line. In 2001, Xerox Canada added many new products with more competitive prices to its product line: a suite of 21 new and enhanced office products, including nine new digital copiers, basic multifunction products that print and copy, and advanced multifunction printers that print, copy, fax, scan, and email. Frank Albanese, research manager at IDC Canada, an information technology consulting provider, viewed former Xerox products as over-engineered and expensive when compared to competitor products that were increasingly more task-focused at lower and lower prices. However, Albanese says, "Their latest product line reflects that they are in touch with what customers are looking for. Now they are ready to compete and their pricing is proof of that."

As a result of changes to its product mix and the markets it now must serve to build its market share, Xerox has been changing its sales force organization, and has been exploring new ways to get to market. Xerox products were once sold exclusively through its own direct sales force. The company still employs approximately 27 000 direct sales, service, and support experts who serve larger companies and global accounts through its geographic and industry-focused business units in Canada and the United States. However, to supplement this direct sales force,

Xerox is expanding its worldwide distribution channels to include TeleWeb operations and a number of channel partners, including resellers, dealers, and independent agents.

Rob Stewart, vice-president of worldwide marketing for Xerox Office Group, says that about 60 percent of its products are still sold direct in Canada, but he feels the new products will provide a tremendous opportunity for the various Xerox channel partners to reach smaller-sized customers looking for more competitive solutions.[1]

Organizing the Selling Function

One of the most important decisions a firm makes is about how to organize the sales force. The opening vignette describes how the products a company sells and the markets it serves affect decisions on sales force organization. At the same time, how the sales force is organized affects many other decisions, as shown in Exhibit 3.1. First, it defines the roles and reporting relationships of

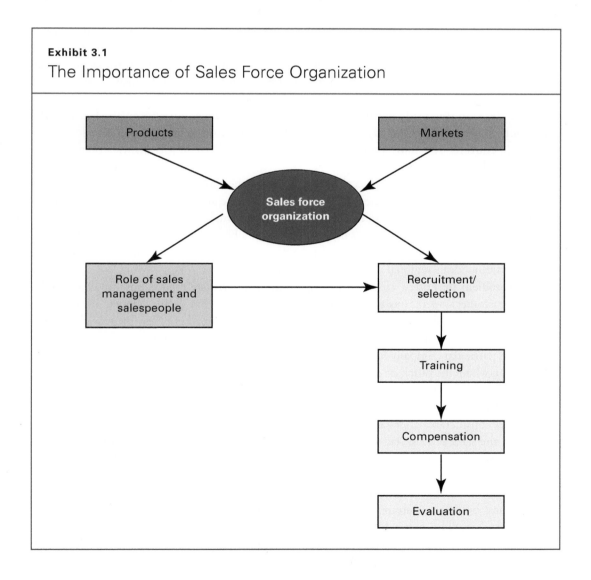

Exhibit 3.1
The Importance of Sales Force Organization

both sales management and salespeople. Second, it has implications for how salespeople are recruited and selected, trained, compensated, and evaluated.

The decision is one between geographic specialization (the most efficient way to organize the sales force) and one of several other methods that may be more effective, including product, market, or functional specialization. Even when these latter methods are used, many sales forces remain somewhat organized on a geographic basis. This chapter begins with a discussion on sales force organization. Then, telemarketing, independent sales agents, strategic account programs, and team selling are discussed.

GEOGRAPHIC SPECIALIZATION

Geographic specialization is the simplest way to organize the sales force. Salespeople are usually responsible for a specific geographic area and call on all accounts and potential accounts within that area, attempting to sell the company's complete product line. Exhibit 3.2 shows how one Canadian sales organization has divided the Atlantic district of Canada into six sales territories, each with one salesperson. The Atlantic District Sales Manager is one of three district sales managers who report to the Eastern Canada Sales Manager who—along with the Western Canada Sales Manager—reports to the National Sales Manager. Notice also that the division of sales territories is not strictly based on provincial boundaries. Territory potential and other factors may force some adjustments when territories are defined. In this instance, for example, the company determined that the salesperson who resided in northern New Brunswick also should cover the Gaspé Peninsula, a part of Quebec, rather than one of the salespeople from Quebec City. The decision was made partly based on geographic distance, but also on the fact that the salespeople in Quebec City already had sufficiently large territories, and the accounts located in the Gaspé Peninsula were more similar to the accounts in northern New Brunswick than to those managed by the Quebec City salespeople.

The efficiency of geographic specialization is due to the shorter distances between accounts within smaller geographic territories. This reduces travel time and expenses and allows salespeople to make a greater number of sales calls than they might make under alternative organization structures. This structure also allows salespeople to gain a better understanding of local culture, and competitive and economic conditions in their territories, all of which can be very important due to the tremendous regional diversity within Canada.

One problem that often arises when geographic structures are used is how to allocate sales when the customer's operations span more than one territory. What should happen, for example, when Jean Cormier calls on a Canada Cement LaFarge plant in northern New Brunswick, but the sale requires some coordination with the salesperson in Toronto who calls on the company's head office? This particular company has decided that sales will be allocated based on the following split: one-third on where the purchase order originates, one-third on where the shipment goes, and one-third on where the invoice goes. You can see why this would sometimes be contentious, particularly when large sales orders are involved, when commissions are due to salespeople, or when the sale requires considerable after-sale service by only one of the salespeople involved.

When the sales process, customers, and products are similar within a territory, this type of organization structure makes sense. It becomes increasingly more difficult to manage when these factors grow more diverse. Salespeople who sell many product lines tend to favour those products that are easier to sell or that they understand better, rather than those that are more profitable for the company or that are strategically more important because of their long-term potential. Salespeople who call on many different types of accounts begin to favour some more than others because they understand the needs of customers in some industries better than others. Whenever

Exhibit 3.2

Geographic Specialization

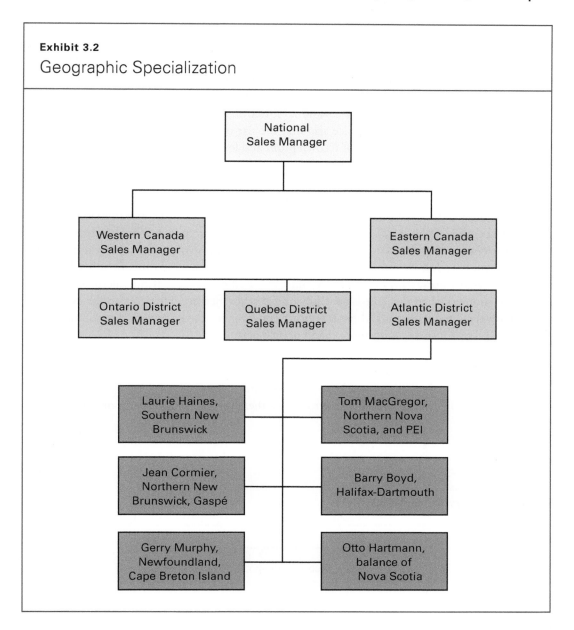

the sales process, product lines, or accounts become more heterogeneous (more varied), companies may benefit by organizing their sales force on some basis other than geographic specialization. Even so, many companies still maintain some geographic considerations. These other specialized forms of organization—products, customers, and activities—are now discussed.

PRODUCT SPECIALIZATION

In **product specialization**, salespeople are responsible to sell a limited number of products or product lines, thereby becoming experts on the products they do sell. This is one way to ensure that a product or product line receives the company's desired level of selling effort, and it is also advantageous when salespeople must become experts on specific and often unrelated products. When a sales force is organized on the basis of product specialization, the various product groups are often responsible for their own strategic planning as they often face different competitors. In addition, their product lines may or may not be sold to different customers, and these groups are frequently responsible for their own profit and loss. Exhibit 3.3 shows a sales force that has been organized on the basis of product specialization. Notice that coordination occurs only at the very senior levels of the organization. Notice also that the size of each sales force may be very different. Since each group is responsible for its own profit and loss, each must determine the resources it needs to compete in its own product market.

Product specialization does have some limitations. It is more costly than a simple geographic organization structure. If the company illustrated in Exhibit 3.3 had simply organized on the basis of geography, there would be 30 salespeople covering all of Canada, and individual territories would be quite small. Since 10 salespeople sell integral horsepower motors across Canada, their territories are considerably larger. Consequently, they will spend more time and money for travel and will have less time to perform selling activities. At the same time, the 20 salespeople who sell fractional horsepower motors also must cover all of Canada. If the salespeople call on different customers, then the issue is generally one of cost efficiency. However, to the extent that they call on the same customers, there is another concern: customers may find it confusing and inefficient if they must deal with more than one salesperson.

MARKET SPECIALIZATION

When organized on the basis of **market specialization**, salespeople are responsible to sell to a limited number of industries or vertical markets, thereby becoming experts on the needs of

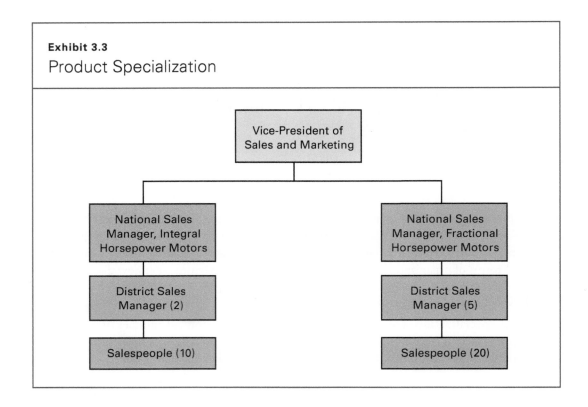

Exhibit 3.3
Product Specialization

specific types of customers. By focusing on a delimited market, the sales force can provide customers with greater value because the salespeople can better understand customer needs, and can better adapt their product solutions when customer needs and buying behaviours are changing. Exhibit 3.4 illustrates how a firm might be organized on the basis of market specialization. It is a very customer-oriented approach and is becoming increasingly popular in recent years. Notice that the specialized sales forces within the same sales organization are not necessarily structured in exactly the same manner. The manufacturing and construction sales force, because it is so much larger, has an additional level of line management.

Market specialization, like product specialization, is somewhat cost-inefficient as sales territories tend to be geographically larger, requiring additional travel time and costs. However, only one salesperson will call on any particular account and this is a potential benefit compared to a sales force organized on the basis of product specialization. An important disadvantage is that salespeople must again sell a complete range of products within their vertical markets. When several complex products are sold and product knowledge is a critical factor, this sales organization structure may not be the best choice because salespeople may not be able to gain sufficient knowledge across all products. In an effort to overcome this deficiency, however, some firms have added product specialists who work with salespeople from the various market-focused sales forces when required.

Other companies that have organized their sales organizations on the basis of market specialization include Hewlett-Packard, General Foods, and AstraZeneca. The Sales Management Today box describes how IBM Software is restructuring its sales force from five product divisions to serve 12 vertical markets.

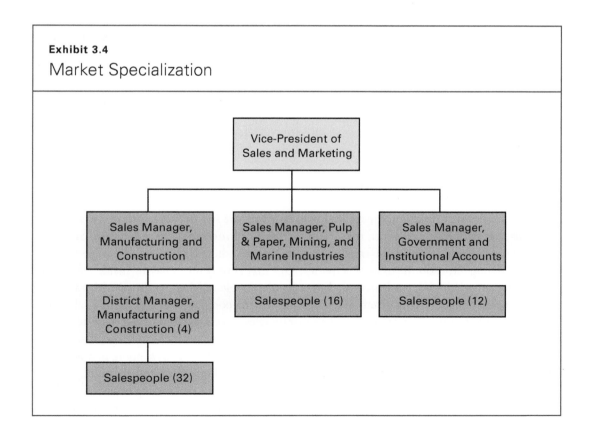

Exhibit 3.4

Market Specialization

SALES MANAGEMENT **TODAY**

IBM Software: Moving From Product Specialization to Market Specialization

IBM Software Group is in the process of restructuring its sales force from five product divisions to serve 12 vertical markets: insurance, banking, financial markets, automotive, retail/wholesale, consumer packaged goods, utilities, telecommunications, electronics, health care, government, and life sciences. The change will require additional support for companies that partner with IBM to provide industry-specific solutions. IBM will double the number of software account managers it employs to work with independent software vendors (ISVs) and partners. It will also introduce 60 new middleware products. Middleware is software that helps different networked computer systems communicate with each other. These industry-specific new products will, for example, help insurance companies handle claims, improve electronic payment processing for banks, or facilitate dealer collaboration in the automotive industry.

PureEdge Solutions of Victoria, British Columbia, is an award-winning ISV that has benefited from IBM's new focus. PureEdge develops electronic forms, principally for three vertical markets: banking, insurance, and government. As a result of IBM's initiative to build alliances to serve specific vertical markets, it introduced PureEdge to Kofax, a provider of document-capture software, and Document Sciences, a developer of content-processing software. Together, the three ISVs created a new joint solution for insurance and financial companies. Mark Upson, president and CEO of PureEdge, says, "Now IBM is educating its sales reps on the solution, and they engage us when they see a customer's requirement for it . . . . We are the model of how IBM wants this to work." IBM Software plans to have 75 percent of its sales force trained across product lines to sell industry-specific solutions within two years. The IBM technical sales force will, however, continue to sell based on product specialization.

Sources: Rochelle Garner, "IBM's Revamped Vertical Focus Could Benefit Solution Providers, ISVs," *CRN*, December 4, 2003, downloaded February 27, 2004, www.crn.com/sections/BreakingNews/dailyarchives.asp?ArticleID=46445; Rochelle Garner, "IBM Software Goes Vertical," *CRN*, December 8, 2003, downloaded ProQuest (ABI/INFORM Global) February 27, 2004; PureEdge Solutions website, www.pureedge.com/companyssss, downloaded February 27, 2004.

FUNCTIONAL SPECIALIZATION

Some companies are organizing their sales forces based on the specific selling-related activities or functions that salespeople perform, that is, on the basis of **functional specialization**. Since different selling situations require different skills and activities, there is often an advantage to structuring the selling effort on the basis of activities. This may simply mean having inside salespeople prospecting and qualifying customers, and outside salespeople making presentations and closing sales. However, functional organization also occurs when a company has a dedicated sales force for finding and closing new accounts, and a separate sales force for maintaining these accounts.

One reason this structure may improve effectiveness is that salespeople who are good at managing accounts may favour this activity and may not spend sufficient effort developing new accounts. Developing new accounts requires salespeople to prospect for and qualify customers, and to spend a lot of time collecting and evaluating information on customer needs and buying behaviours. This is usually a much more competitive selling environment as well, and this increases a salesperson's risk of rejection. If a firm has a lot of customer turnover, then generating new accounts is a critical activity for the firm's success and having a sales force dedicated to this activity will help. Sometimes too, salespeople may become comfortable selling a particular product mix, so having a separate sales force introduce new products makes sense. Then the accounts can be turned over to or continue to be serviced by the regular sales force. Exhibit 3.5 illustrates a functional sales organization.

Red Carpet (Canada) uses a functional sales force to sell its coffee services. One salesperson, who is responsible for business development, prospects, qualifies, and makes sales presentations to prospective accounts. If successful, a route salesperson takes over and maintains the account by servicing the customer's needs on a pre-determined schedule. The original salesperson continues to contact the customer, but with an increasing time interval between calls: for example, one week, three months, and then nine months after the close.[2]

Telemarketing Programs

Telemarketing is the practice of using telephone contact to prospect for, qualify, sell to, and service customers.[3] That is, telemarketing can be used at all stages of the selling process. While telemarketing is appealing for reasons we will soon discuss, important changes are currently taking place in the industry. In 2003, the United States passed the *Telephone Consumer Protection Act*, making it illegal to call consumers who register with a national do-not-call registry. Fines for companies who violate the rules can reach US$11 000. AT&T was fined US$780 000 after 78 complaints were received from 26 people.[4]

The Act is important for Canadian companies because many U.S. companies outsource their telemarketing operations to Canada, where they can save as much as 20 percent of the cost of telemarketing.[5] Canada has been a popular choice for outsourcing also because of the similarities in the cultures of the two countries, since Canadian telemarketers can easily relate to U.S.

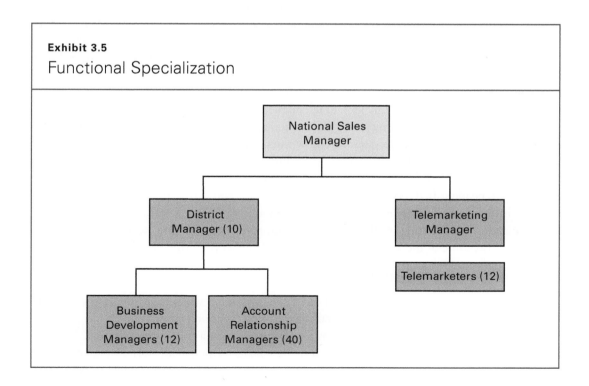

Exhibit 3.5
Functional Specialization

customers. Canadian companies that wish to service U.S. clients now need new technology that will allow Caller ID to display either their name or the name of the company they represent, where previously it was permissible to simply display "out of area." Companies are, however, normally allowed to contact consumers who made purchases within the previous 18 months. While the Act will seriously affect telemarketing to U.S. consumers, it will likely have little impact on business customers. Canada is currently considering new legislation related to telemarketing.

WHEN TO USE TELEMARKETING

There has been tremendous growth in the use of telemarketing in recent years, which promises to continue because telemarketing is both cost efficient and effective. Jim Domanski, of Ottawa-based Teleconcepts Consulting, says that a telemarketer can make as many customer calls in one day as a salesperson can make in one week. Due to decreased selling expenses compared to using field salespeople, Domanski estimates that contacting a customer by telephone costs one-tenth of the cost of making that same call in person.[6]

Integrating telephone and computer technology has allowed many companies to more effectively implement their telemarketing strategies. Telemarketers are able to view specific customer information—such as company address, credit rating, past purchase behaviour and service issues, pricing information, and much more—while they are actively serving the customer on the telephone. When the call is completed, customer information is automatically updated and is then available for the next service encounter, regardless of who in the company might then need to interact with the customer. In fact, for incoming calls, "smart systems" are now able to identify the specific telemarketer who handled the previous call and direct the new call to them.

INTEGRATING TELEMARKETING WITH THE SALES FORCE

One of the important decisions management must make is about how to integrate the telemarketing effort within the company. Historically, salespeople have viewed telemarketers as competitors, even when employed by the same company. Telemarketers were frequently distrusted, as they often became privy to sensitive information concerning how salespeople were servicing their accounts. When they solicited sales, salespeople feared that commissions would be split or reduced, or this would eventually happen. For these reasons, salespeople have in the past been reluctant to fully embrace telemarketers in the sales process.

Today, salespeople increasingly look to telemarketers to help them service their accounts and build sales. Companies that started using telemarketing to handle incoming calls for price information, order entry, or service requests are now using telemarketers to prospect for and qualify leads, and thereby improve the efficiency of the selling process for salespeople. Telemarketers also contact customers between face-to-face sales calls so that customer contact can be maintained, problems can be identified more quickly, and new products and special promotions can be introduced. This has meant an increased professionalism among telemarketers, requiring improved communication and selling skills, leading to improved salaries and working conditions. Exhibit 3.6 lists some of the activities that are currently being performed by telemarketers.

MANAGING THE TELEMARKETING EFFORT

There are several management issues that need to be considered when implementing a telemarketing program: reporting relationships, staffing, training, and motivating.

Determining the reporting relationships for telemarketers is a prime consideration. In larger firms, telemarketers usually report to a telemarketing manager. In smaller firms, telemarketers may report to an office manager, or directly to the sales manager. It is usually preferable to have them

Exhibit 3.6

Current Telemarketing Activities

Activity	Implementation
Prospecting and qualifying leads	Calling prospects and qualifying them (identifying product need, ability to pay, authority to buy, and willingness to buy) to improve the efficiency of face-to-face selling
Approaching customers and closing sales	Introducing new products that the sales force may not have time to sell; selling accessories and service contracts for products that the customer has already purchased; selling excess inventory or promotion items to both existing and new accounts
Account maintenance	Welcoming and thanking new accounts; providing information on product use, accessories, and complementary services; providing an internal point of contact for customers when the salesperson is not available; solving customer technical and service problems

report to someone in a management position and not directly to the salespeople with whom they may be teamed. This will ensure consistency in training, expectations, and performance evaluation.

Staffing is often a challenge because the types of people that are needed will vary greatly depending on the tasks they are expected to perform. Telemarketers who handle only inbound calls must have a strong customer service orientation. If they are taking orders, they must be able to accurately determine and record customer needs. They may also require some selling skills in order to suggest complementary items and services, and possibly up-sell the customer with better quality products or larger quantities. If telemarketers are to make outbound calls and basically be required to implement the complete selling process from prospecting to closing the sale, then to succeed they will need many of the personal attributes of good salespeople: enthusiasm, organization, emotional maturity, courteousness, and an obvious ambition. Telemarketing is often used to identify and train people who may later become field salespeople for their firm. While many companies staff their own telemarketing program, other companies outsource all or part of it. Companies such as Toronto-based Minacs Worldwide are capable of managing both inbound and outbound telemarketing activities for companies across all industries. Minacs, for example, has 4500 employees, over 20 years of experience, and 20 sites in Canada, the U.S., and Europe.[7]

Training and motivating telemarketers also provides challenges. Some companies train their own telemarketers, but teleconsultants are available across Canada with experience training telemarketers to perform many different tasks across many industries. It is often difficult to motivate inbound telemarketers whose main responsibility is to service customers' order entry or service needs; they are usually paid close to minimum wage, although salaries are higher when technical knowledge and skills are required. These jobs are not as boring, however, as some outbound telemarketing jobs, where low-cost, non-technical products are sold amid often considerable stress as telemarketers may be required to make 100 or more calls per day.

However, in many companies, telemarketers are improving their status where they are required to have all of the skills and knowledge needed by field salespeople, and where they have revenue-generating responsibility. Jim Domanski of Teleconcepts Consulting, mentioned previously, reports that compensation plans for telemarketers have been improving dramatically. Jim says that compensation is much higher in the U.S., where companies compensate more for performance—that is, lower salaries and higher commissions. However, Canadian companies now regularly pay salaries of $35 000 annually, with incentive plans that can increase total compensation by 40–50 percent. At the extreme, Jim Domanski reports knowing one Canadian telesalesperson who was compensated completely by commission and earned over $200 000 in one year.[8]

THE FUTURE OF TELEMARKETING

At the start of this section, we argued that current U.S. and pending Canadian legislation poses new challenges for telemarketing. However, there is reason to believe that telemarketing opportunities will continue to grow. Making Caller ID mandatory when selling to consumers, for example, may improve the image of telemarketing and may make it more difficult for the many disreputable telemarketers to continue to operate. Telemarketing will be further encouraged and enhanced as many companies now have "contact" buttons on their websites. Minacs Worldwide, for example, has a hot button that says "Live Contact—click here" so you can immediately be connected with a Minacs representative. For outbound telemarketers, having an internet site means that the interaction with customers who can also connect to the website can be enhanced. One of the major drawbacks to telephone selling has always been the ability to make product demonstrations over the telephone. However, a good telesalesperson with a supporting website can now overcome this weakness. Jim Domanski, for one, predicts that telesales will eventually overtake field sales as the dominant sales channel for many companies.[9]

Independent Sales Agents

An attractive alternative for many firms is, instead of having a company salesperson, to hire an **independent sales agent**—also called a *manufacturer's agent,* who sells for several non-competing manufacturers and receives a commission from each based on the sales made for each manufacturer. Some of these agents operate simply as individuals, while others operate as part of a sales agency where one or more additional salespeople along with several sales support people may be employed. Saint John–based J.F. Taylor is a sales agency that serves Atlantic Canada with a range of plumbing and heating products. It employs six people, including an outside salesperson in Halifax, and is typical of an independent sales agency.[10]

While some manufacturers use only their own sales force, some sell exclusively through independent sales agents, and some use a combination of both. It is common in Canada to see manufacturers with offices located in one or two regions using their own sales force where there is a

SALES MANAGEMENT **IN ACTION**

The Stevens Company Has It All

The Stevens Company Limited has been selling medical and health-related products for nearly 200 years and is one of Canada's largest, privately owned wholesalers. It sells more than 500 000 items from many hundreds of suppliers at its warehouse locations in Ontario, Manitoba, Alberta, British Columbia, and Nova Scotia. The Stevens Company sells to private practitioners and medical institutions, including hospitals, laboratories, and long-term care facilities.

The vice-president of sales and marketing is Bill Carson. The sales and marketing operations are organized on several bases. For example, at the Brampton, Ontario, branch, there are several acute care salespeople who are each responsible for assigned geographic territories. There are also alternative care salespeople, again assigned to specific territories, and some acute and alternative care (combined) salespeople who have territories in northern Ontario where travel times and distances

are longer. The Brampton branch also has a director of sales, a sales coordinator, a clinical specialist, a product specialist, and a salesperson responsible for industrial and commercial accounts. As well, a customer service manager oversees seven customer service representatives who handle incoming calls for service and sales, and who sell to smaller accounts and newer accounts that are not sufficiently large to justify the time and expense of a field salesperson. These inside salespeople manage accounts through the company's database of more than 8000 contacts. Jeff Stevens, the president of the company, says that with a single keystroke, Stevens Company people can bring up detailed customer profiles and account information so that they can provide outstanding customer service. The contact software program that the company uses also reminds salespeople when it's time to make follow-up sales calls.

Sources: The Stevens Company Limited website, www.stevens.ca, accessed February 23, 2007; correspondence from Jeff Stevens, May 3, 2007.

---

heavy concentration of customers or where they can service accounts without spending too much time or money for travel. They then supplement their sales force with independent sales agents so they can serve smaller markets. Elkay Canada manufactures stainless steel sinks in Coldwater, Ontario, and sells exclusively through a nationwide network of 35 independent sales agents. These agents perform the selling function within designated territories, and are compensated by an agreed-upon commission structure.[11]

WHEN TO USE INDEPENDENT SALES AGENTS

Independent sales agents provide several advantages to both small and large sales organizations. Small firms with limited resources sometimes favour this alternative to improve their cash flow. While a company must pay its own sales force on a regular basis, it usually pays agents a commission only after a sale has been made and the company has received payment from the customer. Also, companies that use independent sales agents can treat their selling expenses as a variable cost rather than having to commit to the largely fixed cost of their own sales force.

Exhibit 3.7 demonstrates why this would be important to a small firm. If the firm were to hire four salespeople at an annual total cost of $100 000 each, then it would have a $400 000 annual commitment regardless of its sales. Had the firm hired four independent agents instead, and paid them a 20 percent sales commission, it would have saved money unless sales exceeded $2 000 000. That is, for sales below this amount, independent sales agents are cost-efficient, but the firm would have saved money by hiring its own sales force if annual sales had exceeded this amount.

However, replacing an independent sales agent with a company salesperson when it appears the latter would be more cost-efficient assumes that the company would be able to generate the same amount of sales with its own salesperson. While a company salesperson would be able to devote 100 percent of his time and effort to selling the company's products, suggesting that he might actually increase sales, he would have to establish new selling relationships and might be hampered by the strong customer relationships the former independent sales agent has formed, particularly if the agent finds a competing manufacturer to represent.

In many instances, independent sales agents can provide better market coverage than a company's own sales force. They frequently have considerable knowledge of the markets and industries they serve, and can often develop a new territory for a manufacturer much faster than a manufacturer's salesperson because they have established relationships with key customers. Another important advantage is that they usually sell anywhere from five to 20 or more non-competing but complementary product lines. It is impossible for a manufacturer with a limited product line to match the service capability these agents can provide for many customers.

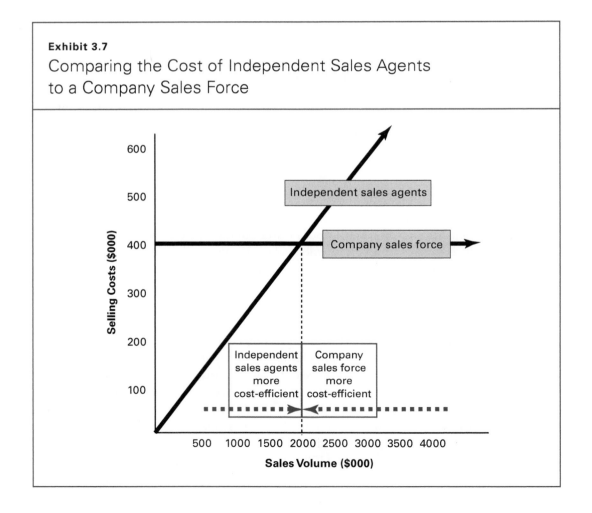

Exhibit 3.7

Comparing the Cost of Independent Sales Agents to a Company Sales Force

HOW TO CHOOSE INDEPENDENT SALES AGENTS

Choosing independent sales agents is no less important than choosing company salespeople. Wrong choices cost time, money, and lost sales. Discovering that a poor choice has been made may require severing the relationship with an agent, and this may impact future relationships that the manufacturer hopes to establish with other agents or customers in the territory.

A good independent sales agent carries a number of non-competing and complementary product lines. Some manufacturers prefer to use agents only where its products will be among the two or three most important product lines that the agent sells, as this will ensure the manufacturer gets the attention and effort it desires. Some smaller, lesser known manufacturers benefit when their products are sold by agents who also sell one or more brands that have strong market acceptance, as they are then assured of getting good market exposure.

Another important factor to consider is the territory that the agent covers. Ideally, a manufacturer would like to establish a network of agents that ensures maximum market coverage, but does not create a lot of conflict among agents who compete for the same customers where they sell in overlapping territories.

Manufacturers also evaluate agents' business practices and philosophies, which should be consistent with their own. They assess agents' financial stability, their past performance with the other lines they represent, and the services they can provide for the manufacturer: market information and feedback; product installation, repairs, and service; and trade show participation.

MANAGING INDEPENDENT SALES AGENTS

Managing independent sales agents is not without challenges. When many different agents are involved, their performance will vary due to their experience, their individual market conditions, and the particular mix of products that they sell. Some may need limited attention, while others may require considerable effort in order to train and motivate them. As they are independent business owners, they will establish their own priorities concerning what and where they will sell, and how much effort they will provide to any particular product line that they handle. They will naturally spend their greatest effort on those products they find easiest to sell and that provide them with the highest commissions. In some instances, they will also tend to focus more on selling activities to generate sales and commissions, compared to after-sales service activities that may be just as important to the manufacturers that they represent. Manufacturers must be willing to compensate them appropriately for their time and effort, and for the particular selling functions they perform. There is a trend today to pay higher commissions or even a fixed stipend for opening new territories, or some additional compensation when non-sales support activities are also required by the manufacturer.[12]

Strategic Account Programs

A significant change in sales force organization is the increasing emphasis on **strategic account programs** (also called key, major, national, or global account programs).[13] These programs are designed to provide increased attention and customized solutions for important accounts that require this level of support, and often require that both the seller and the buyer make considerable resource commitments to coordinate their strategies to increase profits for both organizations. On the seller side, this increased importance may mean using more senior people, or using cross-functional sales teams.[14] These teams may include sales and marketing people, production and finance people, or others. This change in sales force organization is made to provide better sales and service to select customers that often account for a large percentage of the firm's sales.

The classic example is, of course, the strategic account program that Procter & Gamble has developed for Wal-Mart. In Canada, Procter & Gamble has assigned several salespeople to handle this one account specifically.[15] Strategic account programs are currently used by many companies in Canada, including PepsiCo, Elizabeth Arden, McCain Foods, Cadbury Trebor Allan, and Bell Mobility, to name a few.

SELECTING ACCOUNTS FOR STRATEGIC ACCOUNT PROGRAMS

Two important and related decisions that must be made before implementing a strategic account program are how many and which accounts to treat as strategic accounts. Companies have tended to focus on account size, selecting accounts based simply on the sales volume generated from them. To some extent this makes sense, as companies are certainly at some risk when they lose one or two of their largest accounts. However, simply focusing on account size often results in wasted resources as many of these accounts may neither need nor wish to be treated as strategic accounts. Furthermore, many companies are now finding that their largest accounts are not necessarily their most profitable. A better approach is to consider only a large account that has some degree of complexity, exhibiting one or more of the following characteristics:

- It has operating locations in more than one territory, with centralized purchasing.
- People from several functional areas are involved in purchasing; particularly if senior management influences the purchase decisions.
- It requires special pricing considerations, special services, or customized product solutions that must be coordinated across sales territories.
- It has expressed a desire for and expects long-term cooperative working relationships with its major suppliers.

MANAGING STRATEGIC ACCOUNT PROGRAMS

While strategic account programs are growing in popularity, firms have found a number of ways to implement them. Some firms have even experimented with more than one approach, changing how they implement their strategic account programs as conditions change and as they gain experience. The most commonly used approaches for implementing strategic account programs are now discussed.

- *Using management.* This approach is one of the least costly approaches to strategic account program management, and is also popular among those who believe that strategic accounts are too important to be managed by regular salespeople. It works well for small organizations that have only a few such accounts, or that cannot afford other alternatives. This alternative is also appropriate when someone with management authority is required either because a lot of internal coordination is needed among functional areas of the selling firm or because management-level people are involved in the buying firm's purchasing decisions. On the other hand, this approach can cause problems when the manager's location is distant from the customers that she must manage or when these accounts require so much time to service appropriately that planning and other management activities suffer.

- *Using the existing sales force.* This is another cost-effective approach that is also favoured by smaller firms or those who are beginning to experiment with strategic account programs. It does have several advantages: it allows managers to focus on management activities; salespeople can be given one or two such accounts and can be trained for increasing responsibility; salespeople are often located closer to the accounts they service than are managers, so there may be some geographic efficiency; it requires few additional resources and so it limits the firm's risk.

On the other hand, it does have a few major disadvantages. Developing and maintaining long-term relationships with strategic accounts can be very different from the normal types of selling activities of the existing sales force. Additionally, if the salespeople are focused on short-term sales performance because of pressure to meet specific sales quotas, they may focus their activities on closing sales rather than on long-term relationship building.

■ *Creating a separate sales force.* Many firms that have achieved at least some success with one of the previous approaches eventually gravitate to establishing a separate strategic account sales force. These salespeople specialize in managing strategic accounts and have no other responsibilities to interfere with their efforts. If there are a number of such salespeople within the firm, they usually report to a strategic accounts manager who, in turn, reports to a national sales manager or someone in a more senior management position. Companies with a separate strategic account sales force have greater flexibility in providing career advancement options for their salespeople, because these positions are generally seen as being more senior sales positions. 3M Corporation, a global company with operations in more than 60 countries including Canada, assigns strategic account managers to work with local salespeople in many countries to coordinate activities for its many strategic global accounts. John McCarthy, global business manager for 3M Storage Systems Business, relates that prior to setting up IBM Storage as a strategic account, it was doing less than $1 million worth of business there. Afterwards, he says, business "went up by at least a factor of ten."[16]

■ *Developing cross-functional selling teams.* **Selling teams** are groups of people, often from different functional areas within a sales organization, who are responsible for managing strategic accounts when the buying process or product solutions are complex and customized. Selling teams are often required to manage strategic accounts in the following situations:

■ when people from several functional areas are involved in purchasing decisions,
■ when product solutions are very technical and customized, or
■ in service organizations where different people within the sales organization are responsible for selling the service and others are responsible for service delivery.

ZedIT Solutions is characteristic of the many information technology consulting and service providers whose salespeople regularly deal with complex solutions to meet the needs of a very diverse group of customers. While the salespeople can help identify customer needs, it often takes one or more technical service providers visiting the buying organization so that customer needs are clearly defined and understood. Then, the salesperson continues to manage the customer relationship, or more specifically, the many relationships between the selling firm and the customer firm as illustrated in Exhibit 3.8.

Cross-functional selling teams are increasingly common when technical products and services are being sold, in such industries as pharmaceutical, petrochemical, communications and information technology, industrial machinery, and business services selling. Selling teams are discussed at greater length in the next section where sales organization complexity is discussed.

Exhibit 3.8
Selling Team and Buying Team

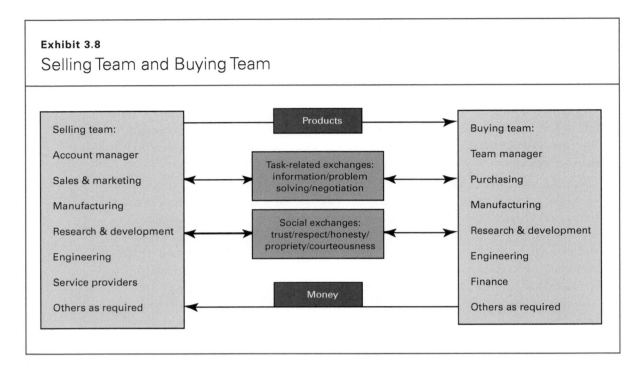

The Increasing Complexity of
Sales Force Organization

Today, many firms—even small ones—are increasingly using their creativity to organize their sales force. Smaller firms increase their sales force size as they see additional opportunities, or as they see specific customer needs that their current sales force cannot satisfy. This may require creating a hybrid sales organization structure.

There are, for example, several technology companies across Canada that started with two or three salespeople, generally organized by geography. As these companies began to grow, they simply added additional salespeople to handle sales in new geographic territories, to sell new products and services added to the company's product line, to meet the needs of specific large accounts, or to sell to a particular market, such as the government. Many times, these salespeople, whatever their focus, are supported by one or several telemarketers or product specialists within the sales organization. It is therefore very conceivable that a company sales force with only four or five salespeople could be specialized on the basis of geography, product, market, and function.

Maritz Canada has recently been recognized as one of the 50 best companies to work for in Canada. It provides a number of services to help companies improve their performance: loyalty marketing programs, travel and non-travel incentive programs, meetings and events programs, brand alignment strategies, learning systems, e-business solutions, communications, and research. Salespeople are generally employed to sell one or more of these product-based solutions to customers within specific territories. As the salespeople sell to specific accounts, they may gain some industry expertise and may become specialized on a specific industry. Maritz Canada currently has two vertical markets in which it has organized special selling teams: automotive and financial services. However, it has recently been developing expertise in the pharmaceutical industry and this may soon be added as an additional market focus.

Salespeople are regularly reviewed to see which have developed the skills or potential to serve as account managers working on selling teams focused on one of the company's eight strategic accounts. Ford Motor Company of Canada, for example, is Maritz's most important customer. It represents the highest percentage of the company's sales and uses the most diversified combination of services that Maritz provides. For this reason, four account managers serve this one client. Other important strategic accounts, all managed by strategic account managers, include Hewlett-Packard, IBM, Microsoft, Nortel, and Scotiabank.[17]

What does the future hold for salespeople? Changes in sales organization structure are increasingly being driven by customer needs. New ways of serving customers are being developed, and new people are constantly being given increased selling responsibility as they are required to communicate with customers before, during, and after a sale. The importance and status of telemarketers will continue to increase. At the same time, face-to-face salespeople will become increasingly more important, although their selling roles will certainly change. Phil Wallace, a senior vice-president with Aon Consulting in Toronto, says, "The salesperson of the future will increasingly become the client relationship manager, the business solution provider, or the leader of a sales team with the objective of launching new products, exploiting new markets, or uncovering the potential of new market segments."[18]

SUMMARY

1. **Describe four ways in which a sales force might be specialized.** There are four ways a sales force might be specialized: geographic, product, market, or functional specialization. Geographic specialization occurs when salespeople are organized simply on the basis of geographic territories. When separate sales forces are used to sell specific product lines, companies are using product specialization. Market specialization is used when salespeople are organized to specialize on specific industries, or vertical markets. Functional specialization is used when different people are responsible for different selling activities.

2. **Compare the advantages and disadvantages of each method of sales force specialization.** The simplest sales force organization structure is geographic specialization. It is the most cost-efficient way to organize a sales force. It requires relatively limited travel time and expense, and provides salespeople with the most time for face-to-face customer contact. It may not be effective when specific product or industry knowledge is important.

An advantage of product specialization is that salespeople possess specific product knowledge. It requires larger geographic territories, which means longer travel times, increased travel costs, less selling time, and, sometimes, account duplication.

Market specialization requires salespeople to have specific industry or market knowledge. Account duplication is not an issue, but this form of sales force organization otherwise has the same disadvantages as product specialization.

Functional specialization matches selling tasks to the salesperson's selling skills. It can improve selling efficiency when less important selling activities are performed by less expensive people, and more expensive people are employed strictly for revenue-generating activities. It ensures that all of the important selling activities are given the effort that the company desires. Functional specialization may result in geographic duplication, product duplication, and account duplication. It also requires additional coordination to ensure that it is effective.

3. **Explain when to use telemarketing programs and how to manage them.** Telemarketing can be used to prospect for, qualify, sell to, and service customers—in other words, for all stages of the selling process. Salespeople have historically distrusted telemarketers, but telemarketers have been gaining status and their working conditions have been steadily improving. Managing, staffing, training, and motivating telemarketers are important issues when implementing a telemarketing program.

4. **Explain when to use independent sales agents and how to manage them.** Independent sales agents are an important alternative to a company sales force, particularly when companies have resource constraints, need to manage cash flow, or want to cover newer or smaller territories. They often have the advantage of existing customer relationships and can leverage these to develop territories much faster than a company salesperson. They must be actively managed for performance: selected, trained, compensated, motivated, and evaluated. An important issue is control. Since they are independent sales agents, they often focus on products they find easiest to sell or that provide them with the best compensation. Also, they may tend to focus more on closing sales than on building long-term relationships by performing non-selling activities.

5. **Explain when to use strategic account programs and how to manage them.** Strategic account programs are designed to provide increased attention and customized solutions for specific accounts. Accounts selected for strategic account programs should be larger accounts, with some level of purchasing complexity and a desire to have long-term cooperative relationships with their suppliers. There are four ways to manage strategic account programs: use company management, use the existing sales force, establish a separate sales force, or develop cross-functional selling teams.

6. **Assess the role of team selling in the selling process.** Selling teams composed of an account manager and one or more other people from different functional areas are becoming increasingly popular. They are used when people from several functional areas are involved in the purchasing decision, when product solutions are technical and customized, or for service organizations where different people within the sales organization are responsible for selling the service and others are responsible for service delivery. Because selling teams require a selling firm to invest considerable resources, they are generally used when selling to strategic accounts or when very large sales are involved.

KEY TERMS

geographic specialization   **72**

product specialization   **73**

market specialization   **74**

functional specialization   **76**

telemarketing   **77**

independent sales agent   **80**

strategic account programs   **83**

selling team   **85**

REVIEW QUESTIONS

1. Explain how each of the following factors might affect the choice of a sales force organization structure:
   a. a company's size
   b. the company's products

   c. the company's customers
   d. the company's financial condition

2. Give reasons why a firm might decide to organize its sales force structure on each of the following bases:
   a. geographic specialization
   b. product specialization
   c. market specialization
   d. functional specialization

3. Discuss how a sales force could benefit from a telemarketing program. Identify some problems that might occur when telemarketing is first introduced within a sales organization.

4. Why would a firm consider using independent sales agents when it could have its own sales force? Explain.

5. Some sales managers believe that managing independent sales agents is no different than managing company salespeople. Do you agree or disagree? Explain.

6. One sales manager was heard to comment, "We have 10 customers that account for nearly 90 percent of our sales. I think we need to develop a strategic account program to manage these accounts." Discuss.

7. Discuss four ways to organize strategic account programs.

8. Explain the concept of a *selling team*. When is it appropriate to use selling teams in the selling process?

9. A company's sales force structure may change as it identifies new opportunities or specific customer needs that it cannot meet with its existing sales force. What are some of the problems and issues you would expect a sales manager to face as the sales force structure changes? Explain.

10. Increasing sales force complexity is an issue for larger rather than smaller Canadian companies. Defend or refute this statement.

APPLICATION EXERCISES

1. During a visit to a sales management class, a vice-president of sales and marketing for an industrial manufacturer stated, "It really does not matter much whether you are managing a company sales force or a group of independent sales agents. From a management perspective, there is really very little difference." Explain what you think he meant by this statement.

2. Procter & Gamble has one of the largest consumer goods field sales forces in Canada. Do you think its field sales force should be organized by geographic, product, or market specialization? What else should its sales management consider when deciding how to organize its selling effort?

3. Consider the increasing complexity of sales force organization today. Explain how you think the role of sales managers today differs from the more traditional one that may have existed four or five decades ago. What implications do you see for sales managers in the future?

4. Assume that you are the Canadian sales manager for a manufacturer of document handling equipment (photocopiers, fax machines, printers, etc.). Your company manufactures and

sells simple equipment designed for small businesses, as well as complex multi-function equipment that may cost $100 000 or more. The company has just come to Canada and is beginning to organize its sales force structure for the Canadian market. Prepare a report giving your recommendations for a sales force organization structure, and be prepared to defend your position.

CASE 3.1 Trecourt Valve and Fittings Reorganizes Its Sales Force

Joan Revello, the Alberta sales manager for Trecourt Valve and Fittings, had just returned from the annual sales meeting in Vancouver, her favourite city. At the meeting, she hadn't been surprised to learn that the other sales managers across Canada were experiencing the same problems that she had identified at her branch. Sales had decreased again for the fifth consecutive quarter, although the decline seemed to have slowed somewhat. Sales from active accounts—those that had made purchases within the past six months—were almost the same as in the previous period, after considering the price increase that had gone into effect in January. However, sales for the branch were down due to having lost approximately 4 percent of the accounts in the territory.

Joan had asked her salespeople to put additional effort into establishing new accounts to replace the ones they had lost. She had even implemented an incentive program to reward salespeople who were successful in doing this. Some new accounts had been opened, but not enough to reverse the declining sales trend. When Joan had mentioned this at the annual sales meeting, Tom Anders, the national sales manager, had commented, "We know. We have been tracking this for some time, and it seems to be an issue in almost every district. We are going to change the sales force organization so that we have two distinct sales forces. One will continue to service the customers we currently have, but the other will be responsible only for establishing new accounts." When he'd concluded his remarks, Tom had asked all of the district sales managers to return to their branches and decide how they could implement the new functional sales organization strategy at their particular branch.

When she heard this, Joan knew immediately that she was going to have a problem. After much thought, she decided that she would combine the four territories managed by the salespeople at her branch into two larger territories—one centred on Edmonton and one centred on Calgary. She could easily make a decision for new account development in the new Edmonton territory: it would go to Jayne Alexander, a recent hire who did not have many accounts where she had established very close relationships and who was also more aggressive than the other salespeople. Joan felt that she was an obvious choice. However, for new account development in the new Calgary territory, there was no easy solution. Both Brad Luchak and Tomas Causi had been with the company for over 10 years. They were both good at maintaining customer relationships and were both highly regarded by their customers. With respect to sales performance, both had been gradually losing sales due to a decline in the number of active accounts they serviced, and neither had shown any strength at opening new accounts.

Joan had a good working relationship with both Brad and Tomas; she respected them and they respected her. Both were very obliging, and dedicated to the company and their customers. But Joan knew she would have to allocate one of them to new account development, and she was quite sure that whoever it was, he would be unlikely to succeed. Joan was having a problem deciding how to make a choice, but she knew that the responsibility was hers and she would eventually have to choose.

CRITICAL-THINKING QUESTIONS

1. What other factors besides sales force organization should Joan consider?

2. Does Joan have any other alternatives for organizing her sales force? Explain.

3. If Joan decides to proceed with restructuring her sales force, what criteria should she use to decide whether Brad or Tomas gets reassigned to new account development? What would you do?

Tandy Safety Clothing

CASE **3.2**

Tandy Safety Clothing sold a complete range of safety clothing to businesses across Canada. The company manufactured mainly nylon and PVC rainwear, and supplemented its product mix with gloves, boots, hats, caps, glasses, respirators, and many other items that were all manufactured overseas under the Tandy brand name.

Originally, the company had been located in Ontario and sold only to that market. It had eventually expanded to Quebec and then decided it wanted to become a national supplier. To quickly gain representation across Canada, Bill Ferguson, Tandy's president, had decided to appoint a number of manufacturers' agents to serve new territories in both eastern and western Canada. From 1980 to 2007, sales had continued to grow, as had profits.

In 2007, Tandy Safety Clothing had been purchased by a U.S. company that wanted to quickly gain access to the Canadian market. The new company had added several new and more costly items to the product mix and it had served the entire U.S. market with its own sales force. The sales manager of the U.S. company had made it known that he would immediately replace all manufacturers' agents in Canada with company salespeople.

When Bill had called Tim Best of Canada West Safety Equipment in Saskatchewan, his most important Canadian agent, to let him know what was likely to happen in the near future, Tim had been devastated. "Bill. You can't let this happen to me. When you needed my help, I took on your line and helped you grow the business to where you are today. When you lost your agent in Alberta, you convinced me to open another sales location and to represent you across Alberta as well. I have made a considerable investment in both time and money and I need your product line if I am to continue with my business. I have turned down many competitors over the years who wanted me to sell their lines instead of yours; I always remained faithful to Tandy. There are many accounts here that think of Tandy when they think of Canada West, and vice versa. If I lose your line before I can find something to replace it with, I might as well close my business. Help me, Bill."

CRITICAL-THINKING QUESTION

If you were Bill Ferguson, what would you do? Be specific.

Chapter 4

Estimating Potential and Forecasting Sales

LEARNING OBJECTIVES

After completing this chapter, you should be able to

1. Understand the importance of four types of sales-related forecasts.

2. Use the most popular sales forecast methods.

3. Discuss involvement in, familiarity with, and current use of various sales forecast methods.

4. Assess the accuracy of sales forecast methods.

Do you want "really fast information detection"? No, that's not RFID. *RFID* stands for "radio frequency identification." It has certainly been in the news in recent years as businesses are beginning to explore new uses for the not-so-new technology. Wal-Mart has been pressuring its suppliers to use this technology if they want to do business with the world's largest retailer. Companies such as Procter & Gamble and Coca-Cola are beginning to use it, and some analysts predict that the technology could save Wal-Mart as much as US$8 billion over the next few years.[1] Small computer chips are placed on individual items, or on pallets, so they can be identified and tracked as they move from the manufacturer, to the shipping company, to the retailer, throughout the retailer's premises, and through the door after being purchased by a customer. The system reduces labour costs and helps reduce inventory stock-outs and theft. But, there are other applications. Cars can zip through tollbooths or along controlled access highways without stopping to pay. Employee ID cards can permit entry to restricted areas and track who enters and for how long, and who leaves and when. MasterCard and American Express are exploring its use in credit cards that no longer need to be swiped.

Of course, along with the growth in applications and use, there is tremendous growth in opportunities for manufacturers and resellers in this expanding market. OCR Ltd. (**www.ocr.ca**) is a Canadian company that has been providing automated data collection solutions for more than 30 years. It is now a key player in the RFID industry, selling automatic identification and data capture solutions that can include physical products such as readers, tags, and "smart" labels, to feasibility studies, custom software, installation, and service. Company sales have been growing rapidly but to predict its future in RFID solutions, the company must be able to predict where the industry is headed.

Recently, ABI Research reduced its 2007 revenue forecasts for RFID software and services by 15 percent to only US$3.1 billion.[2] How important is this revised forecast for a reseller and solutions provider such as OCR? The immediate question management needs to answer is why there is a change in the forecast. If the reason is because customers are having difficulty with the implementation of this technology within their operations, this could indicate future problems for the RFID industry. However, RFID practice director Michael Laird of ABI Research attributed the adjustment to four interrelated factors: "They are market consolidation, collaborative solutions, the growing availability of off-the-shelf commercial RFID software packages, and the improving skills of RFID project planning."[3] The decrease in projected market size is, therefore, a result of increased efficiencies and reduced costs, and after a short period of adjustment, there could be tremendous growth as the market expands. Customers who previously could not afford RFID solutions may begin to see them as affordable; companies that are already using RFID technology may look for additional applications as the costs continue to go down. Even if revenue for software and services is reduced, OCR might benefit from a faster rate of growth in related hardware sales. Its 2005 sales of wireless hardware, for example, were in excess of $7 million and that was a 30 percent increase over the previous year. Its 2006 sales began with another record high and the company expected to again set an annual sales record.[4]

To prepare a 2007 sales forecast, OCR may need to examine its current and target customers; current sales by product and product line; historical sales by product, by product line, and by customer; suppliers it has added or dropped, if there are any; and industry trends and forecasts such as those provided by ABI Research. The company's final sales forecast will most likely be determined by both quantitative and qualitative sales forecast methods. Once the quantitative analyses are done, management judgement will most likely be used to refine any forecast to account for changing industry trends that past data will not adequately capture. These are the topics of this chapter. First, quantitative methods of sales forecasting will be discussed. Then, qualitative methods and how to combine them with quantitative methods will be discussed.

The Importance of Estimating Potential and Forecasting Sales

Sales managers regularly consider and must understand four types of sales-related forecasts: (1) market potential, (2) market forecast, (3) sales potential, and (4) sales forecast. These types of forecasts vary on two dimensions: whether they are industry or company level, and whether they relate to the best possible or the most likely outcome. This is illustrated in Exhibit 4.1.

Exhibit 4.1
Four Types of Forecasts

	Best Possible Result	Most Likely Outcome
Industry Level	Market potential	Market forecast
Company Level	Sales potential	Sales forecast

Market potential is an industry-level forecast of the best possible sales that can be achieved across an entire industry, under ideal conditions. For example, if the total number of students entering post-secondary educational institutions in Canada in any year is considered a market, then the market potential for laptop computers in units would be equal to the number of students, assuming each student would buy one laptop computer. **Market forecast** is an industry-level forecast of the most likely sales that will be achieved, recognizing that ideal conditions do not exist. For example, some of these students may already own a laptop, some may share a laptop with siblings or friends, some may not be able to afford a laptop, and many may decide that while they might like to have one, owning a laptop is simply not necessary. Market forecast will therefore be lower than market potential.

Sales potential is a company-level forecast of the best possible sales that can be achieved by a particular company, under ideal conditions. For a company to achieve its full sales potential, it must have and implement a perfect marketing plan. Any factor that limits the implementation of the company's marketing plan will affect the company's ability to achieve its potential, and when this is considered at the forecasting stage, the sales manager will better be able to forecast the company's sales. **Sales forecast** is a company-level forecast of the most likely sales that will be achieved by a particular company, recognizing its limitations to develop and implement a perfect marketing plan. For example, to achieve its full sales potential, a company may need seven models of laptops (product strategy), larger reseller discounts (price strategy), stronger relationships with college and university bookstores (distribution strategy), and better national advertising and a larger, better trained sales force (promotion strategy). Recognizing any weakness in a company's ability to implement a perfect marketing plan will lower a company's sales forecast. By implication, a sales forecast is tied directly to a specific marketing plan, regardless of how close to perfect it may be. Any change to a company's marketing plan will result in a change to the company's sales forecast. Sales forecast will therefore be lower than sales potential. Exhibit 4.2 illustrates the relationships among the four types of forecasts.

While all of these types of forecasts are important for sales managers to understand, the most important one for sales managers is the sales forecast. This may explain why more than 50 percent of companies include sales forecasting in their sales management training programs.[5] Sales managers must be able to determine where their customers are, and how much and what they will buy. A sales manager who does not understand which customers are her company's best customers and where they are located will direct sales resources both to the wrong geographical territories, and to the wrong accounts within territories. A sales manager who cannot predict how much and what customers will buy may end up with too much or insufficient inventory to meet demand, or with the wrong inventory. Having too much inventory reduces inventory turnover, and hence reduces return on investment. This may also result in higher taxes, insurance, spoilage, and obsolescence costs. Having too little inventory, or being out of stock of important items, creates other problems. At the very least, there is an opportunity cost from lost sales. However, it could be more serious if customers begin to buy from competitors and ultimately evaluate their products or service as superior, and then continue to buy from them. The Sales Management in Action box describes the forecast process that Ocean Spray Cranberries uses to help ensure it has for sale just enough juice—not too much, and not too little.

The sales forecast is the basis for many of the most important decisions throughout the entire organization. At the corporate level, sales forecasts are used to allocate resources across functional areas, and to control operations throughout the company. For example, if senior management recognizes a large gap between sales potential and sales forecast, and the gap can be closed con-

Exhibit 4.2

Relationships Among Market Potential, Market Forecast, Sales Potential, and Sales Forecast

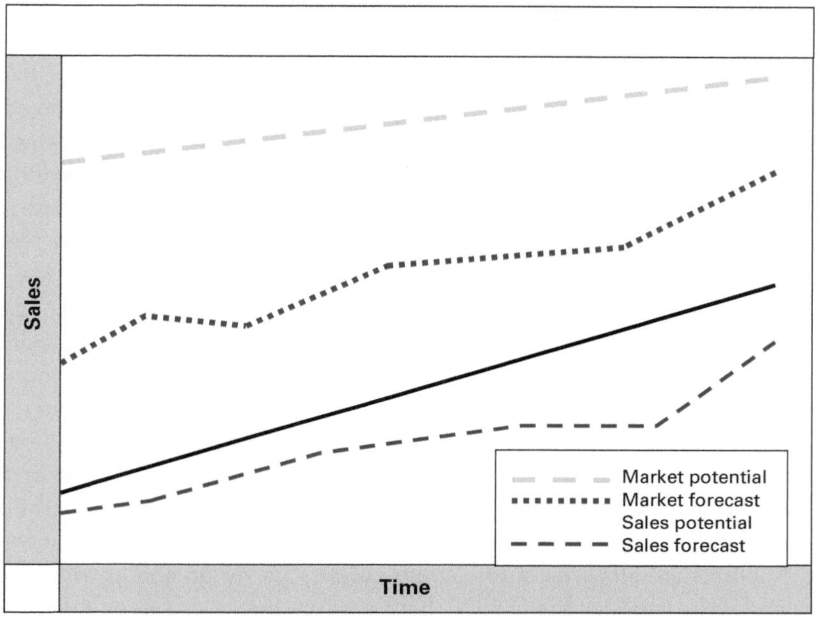

Legend:
- — — — Market potential
- ·········· Market forecast
- —— Sales potential
- – – – Sales forecast

(Y-axis: Sales; X-axis: Time)

siderably by increasing production capacity, more resources might be allocated to production: larger facilities, new equipment, more production employees, etc. Sales forecasts will also provide estimates of the resources the company will have in future periods for changes in corporate strategy: mergers, acquisitions, divestments, etc. Production will use sales forecasts to develop production schedules. Information from the production department will allow purchasing to plan purchase requirements, including what needs to be sourced and when it needs to arrive for production. Human resources will use the sales forecast as an early indicator of human resources needs and can begin planning the number and types of employees that may be required in the near future. The finance department will use the sales forecast to predict cash flows so it can better plan the need for or use of capital. The marketing department, in particular, needs to work closely with the sales force as pointed out in Chapter 2. While changes to marketing strategies affect sales forecasts, sales forecasts also provide information on the resources that are available to develop marketing strategies. Finally, the sales forecast is critical to the planning and management of the sales force itself. Sales managers use it to plan the selling effort across territories, to establish sales quotas for individual salespeople, and as the basis for sales force and salesperson evaluation. Accurate sales forecasting can improve both sales effectiveness and sales efficiency. Because sales forecasting is so important, and because sales managers play an important role in developing sales forecasts, they need to understand the most important sales forecasting methods that are used. These are discussed in the following sections.

How Much Is Too Much Juice?

Sean Reese is one of seven people in the forecasting group at Ocean Spray Cranberries. The company has been increasing the responsibility of the forecasting group as it continues to introduce new products—sometimes simply line extensions of existing products and sometimes entirely new product lines. Most of its products are time-sensitive. They must be sold within five to six months of production to maintain quality. As well, seasonality is a factor with many products. About 90 percent of cranberry sauce is shipped between August and November to prepare retailer shelves for Thanksgiving and Christmas. Grapefruit juices sell best in January and coincide with an increase in health club memberships as people realize what the Christmas season has done to their waistlines.

Sean Reese and the other members of the planning group must forecast demand by geographic area, and by product. Forecasts are prepared at the SKU level and at the category-size level, for one to six months, with emphasis on the first three months. Forecasting models use time-series data based on the previous three years. But, forecasts are adjusted based on event planning, such as promotions, advertising campaigns, and product reformulations. Sales and marketing people are heavily involved in this collaborative process. Of course, supply must also be considered. What happens when there is a shortage of cranberries? Marketing and sales must make adjustments to focus on juice blend drinks, such as cranberry apple and cranberry grape, which require a smaller percentage of cranberry juice.

Sales and marketing are also involved more heavily when new products are involved than when simple product line extensions are being introduced. Forecasting sales for product line extensions is easier as data from existing sales and lessons from the past can be used. Completely new products often involve consumer research, but the forecasting group still provides a "reality check" to what might be overly optimistic forecasts. At monthly "alignment" meetings, people from sales, marketing, operations, finance, and demand planning assemble to produce a single forecast. However, Tara Kowlaczyn, vice-president and managing director for logistics and planning, says, "It's a collaborative process, but at the end of the day, the demand planners have final veto power. And we do end up with one number—that's a policy that is driven by management down through the ranks—and that number goes right into the final systems, and we'll develop our financial plans off of it." Improvements to the demand planning process have increased forecast accuracy to 75 percent from only 55 percent in 1998. Accuracy is assessed by several measures depending on whom the information is prepared for, but generally, the planning group uses mean absolute percentage error (MAPE). (See page 113 for a discussion of MAPE.)

Sources: Jack Malehorn, "Forecasting at Ocean Spray Cranberries," *The Journal of Business Forecasting Methods & Systems*, Summer 2001, pp. 6–8; "Sponsor Profile: Manugistics/Ocean Spray," http://www.manugistics.com/documents/collateral/Ocean_Spray_ManuCS.pdf, accessed December 9, 2006; Kurt C. Hoffman, "Supply-Chain Reorganization is the New Flavor at Ocean Spray," *Global Logistics & Supply Chain Strategies*, September 2001, http://www.glscs.com/archives/9.01.ocean.htm?adcode=5, accessed December 9, 2006.

Preparing the Sales Forecast

There are many methods that can be used to forecast sales. Some methods are more quantitative; some are more qualitative. Some methods are top-down, and some are bottom-up. Each method has advantages and disadvantages, and experienced sales managers frequently rely on more than one method depending on the importance of forecast accuracy. The following sections describe many of the most used forecasting methods. The first methods discussed rely on past data to predict future sales. Then, we look at methods that are more useful when there are no historical data, or when those data will not adequately capture important other considerations. Following the exposition of the various sales forecasting methods, their familiarity and popularity in use and related issues are explored.

LOOKING AT PAST SALES PERFORMANCE

Many of the quantitative methods of sales forecasting rely on past sales data. This recognizes that the single best predictor of the next year's sales, when available, is last year's sales. The most popular methods of predicting future sales when looking at past sales performance include naïve forecasts, moving averages, exponential smoothing, decomposition, and regression analysis. Each of these is now described.

NAÏVE FORECAST METHOD   The simplest forecasting method is the **naïve forecast method**. This method simply assumes that sales in the next period will be equal to sales in the last period: March sales will be the same as February sales; third-quarter sales will be the same as second-quarter sales; etc. This method assumes stability and that sales conditions vary little from one period to the next. An example of naïve forecasts for the last five months of the year are provided here:

Month	Jul.	Aug.	Sep.	Oct.	Nov.	Dec.
Actual sales	137	153	162	181	172	180
Naïve forecast		137	153	162	181	172

For many situations, this forecast method may be perfectly satisfactory. In fact, 70 percent of Canadian companies reported that they use it.[6] For some companies, there may be limited information that can be used to improve this forecast, the assumption of reasonable sales stability going forward may be appropriate, or variance from forecast may not be particularly important. In any event, this method can still be used as a benchmark against which to compare other forecasting methods. Comparing forecast methods is discussed in greater detail in a later section of this chapter that explores forecast accuracy.

MOVING AVERAGES METHOD   The **moving averages method** is also a very simple forecasting method. It is similar to the naïve forecast method but calculates an average based on observations from two or more previous periods. It is called *moving* because each new data point that is available results in a change to the average that was calculated with the previous data. For example, if sales for January and February were $5240 and $6660, respectively, then the two-month average sales is $5950. If sales in March were $7280, then the new two-month moving average would be $6970, calculated by dropping the January sales amount, and adding the March sales amount. Examples of two-, three-, and four-month moving averages are provided in Exhibit 4.3.

The number of periods to be included in the moving average can only be determined by trial and error. Using a moving average to forecast sales can result in large error if there are considerable fluctuations in sales from one period to the next. Assuming that the fluctuations are simply

Exhibit 4.3
Moving Averages Forecast Method

Month	Sales	2-Month Moving Average	3-Month Moving Average	4-Month Moving Average
January	5240	—	—	—
February	6660	5950	—	—
March	7280	6970	6393	—
April	7680	7480	7207	6715
May	7160	7420	7373	7195
June	6840	7000	7227	7240
July	6450	6645	6817	7033
August	6630	6540	6640	6770
September	7860	7245	6980	6945
October	8270	8065	7587	7303
November	8890	8580	8340	7913
December	9620	9255	8927	8660

random, increasing the number of observations used when calculating the moving average should produce better forecast results. However, a smaller number of observations will capture important trends in the data better than a large number of observations. Exploring the accuracy of forecasts using the different numbers of observations will provide guidance as to which time period is better. One problem with moving averages, however, is that they equally weight all periods used in their calculations. That is, in a four-month moving average, the sales for January have as much influence as the sales for April when calculating a forecast of May sales. A forecasting method that overcomes this weakness is exponential smoothing.

EXPONENTIAL SMOOTHING METHOD   An easy way to conceptualize the **exponential smoothing method** is to view it simply as a moving average where the most recent sales data play a more important role and older data get systematically discounted. Logically, this method of forecasting should be superior to the moving averages method as it makes better use of more recent sales data, and this data should be a better predictor of sales in a subsequent period than older sales data. The key decision that the sales manager must make is to decide the smoothing constant (α), constrained between the values of 0 and 1, that will be used for calculating exponential smoothing. When sales fluctuations are greater, a higher value of α will give greater weight to more recent sales data. As the value of α decreases, more weight is given to older sales data. To determine the best value of α, the sales manager should test several values and then choose the value where forecasting accuracy is best. Examples of exponential smoothing using three values of α are provided in Exhibit 4.4.

Exhibit 4.4

Exponential Smoothing Forecast Method

Month	Sales	Smoothing $\alpha = 0.2$	Smoothing $\alpha = 0.5$	Smoothing $\alpha = 0.8$
January	5240	—	—	—
February	6660	5240	5240	5240
March	7280	5524	5950	6376
April	7680	5605	6615	7099
May	7160	6020	7148	7564
June	6840	6248	7154	7241
July	6450	6366	6997	6920
August	6630	6383	6724	6544
September	7860	6432	6677	6613
October	8270	6718	7269	7611
November	8890	7028	7770	8138
December	9620	7400	8330	8740

Equation for simple exponential smoothing:

Smoothed sales forecast for $t + 1 = \alpha\, Y_t + (1 - \alpha)\, F_t$, where:

α = smoothing constant, between values of 0 and 1
Y_t = actual value of time series in period t
F_t = forecast of the time series for period t

TREND PROJECTION AND REGRESSION ANALYSIS METHODS   The **trend projection method** includes a number of simple time-series forecasting methods that all assume that past sales and rates of change in past sales can be used to predict future sales. A sales manager using trend projection simply estimates the trend from the past two periods of sales data and adds it to current sales to predict future sales. The formula for calculating a trend projection is

$$\text{Sales forecast } (t) = \text{Sales from last period } (t-1) \times \frac{\text{Sales from last period } (t-1)}{\text{Sales from two periods ago } (t-2)}$$

Trends can be expressed as a unit change in sales, or as a percentage change in sales. Which to use is an important decision as they will result in very different predictions of future sales. For example, if a salesperson sold 15 vacuum cleaners this month but only 10 vacuum cleaners the previous month, his unit increase was 5, but his percentage sales increase was 50 percent. If he were to assume the trend would continue, basing his projection on unit sales, his forecast would be 20 vacuum cleaners (15 plus 5). However, if he were to base his projection on percentage sales increase, his forecast would be 22 or 23 (15 plus 50 percent). This latter estimate is 10–15 percent higher than the former estimate. In fact, when sales are increasing, the percentage change approach will project higher sales than the unit sales approach. Trend projection is often used with moving averages or exponential smoothing forecasts to improve sales forecast accuracy.

The example just described used only two time periods of data. If many time periods of data are available, a **time-series regression** can be calculated. This regression represents the relationship between sales (the dependent variable, Y) and time (the independent variable, X) and can be represented by a single straight line that best fits the data using the *ordinary least squares* method, which minimizes the squared errors between actual and predicted sales. This line is expressed by the equation $Y = a + bX$, where a is the intercept and b is the trend that shows the impact of time on sales. The equation $Y = 5697.60 + 259.10X$, illustrated in Exhibit 4.5 using the same data from the previous examples, indicates that sales are $5697.60 plus a trend of $259.10 for each additional month. Forecast sales, Y, for the next month would be $9065.90 ($5697.60 + $259.10 × 13 months). Time-series regressions can be calculated for varying time intervals: days, weeks, months, quarters, or years.

Of course, regression analysis does not have to use time as the independent variable. In fact, time, while it might be related to sales, does not cause sales. It is therefore more likely that other variables are better predictors of sales. When a single predictor or independent variable is used, we have a **single regression model**. Some possibilities include population, average household income, advertising expenditures, number of salespeople, birth or death rates, car registrations, or housing starts. A **multiple regression model** uses multiple predictors (or independent variables) to forecast sales. Regression models are now very easy to estimate, with statistical software packages such as SPSS or SAS, but also with more common software programs such as Microsoft Excel. These models should, however, be developed with care. They are subject to a number of problems, including spurious correlation, when a relationship exists just by chance; multicollinearity, when the independent variables

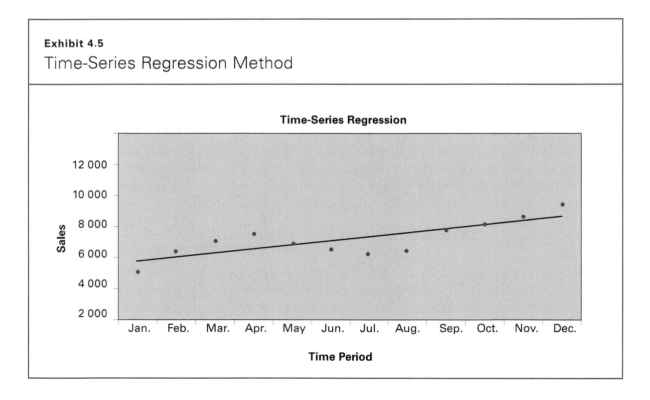

Exhibit 4.5
Time-Series Regression Method

are highly correlated among themselves; autocorrelation, when the observations on an independent variable are highly correlated; or simply using too many predictor variables.

DECOMPOSITION METHOD The **decomposition method** is used when the sales manager wants to predict sales for each period of a year (usually a week, month, or quarter), and a seasonal pattern is evident. Three steps are involved when performing a decomposition analysis: (1) calculate seasonal index values, (2) forecast sales for the next period, and (3) adjust the sales forecast to take seasonality into consideration.

Step 1: Calculate seasonal index values. The first decision is whether to calculate seasonal index values based on weeks, months, or quarters. At least three, and preferably more, years of sales data are required; however, it is possible to use too many years of data in the calculations so that changes in seasonality over time will fail to be captured effectively. Then, an average across specific time periods (weeks, months, or quarters) must be determined, and this average must be divided by the overall sales average for all time periods. This procedure is illustrated in Exhibit 4.6:

1. Determine the average sales for each quarter across years, shown in the column headed "Average Sales per Quarter."
2. Determine the average sales for all 16 quarters, which, in this example, is 125.19.
3. Divide the values determined in item 1 above by the value determined in item 2. This will determine the seasonal index value for the next year, which can then be used to determine the seasonal index values shown in the extreme right column.

Step 2: Forecast sales for the next period. In this step, the sales manager must decide which method to use to make the sales forecast for the next period. Using the data in Exhibit 4.6 and a trend projection, the forecast sales for 2008 are $512 017:

$$\text{Sales forecast} = \$523\ 000 \times \frac{\$523\ 000}{\$534\ 000} = \$512\ 017$$

With a sales forecast of $512 017 for 2008, if there is no seasonal component, then the sales for each quarter would be $128 004 ($512 017/4 quarters) as sales for each quarter would be equal.

Exhibit 4.6

Decomposition Method

Quarter	Sales ($000)				Avg. Sales per Quarter	Avg. Sales for All Quarters	Seasonal Index
	2004	2005	2006	2007			
1	95	105	107	120	106.75	125.19	0.853
2	109	112	123	116	115.00	125.19	0.919
3	105	120	132	124	120.25	125.19	0.961
4	140	160	172	163	158.75	125.19	1.268
Total	449	497	534	523			1.000 (avg.)

Step 3: Adjust the sales forecast to take seasonality into consideration. Next, the sales manager needs to adjust the quarterly sales forecasts to account for seasonality. In this example, the lowest seasonal index value is 0.853, for the first quarter, and the highest seasonal index value is 1.268, for the fourth quarter. Multiplying the unadjusted quarterly forecast by the seasonal index values adjusts the forecast for each quarter, predicting sales of $109 187 for the first quarter and $162 309 for the fourth quarter. Similar calculations can be made for the other two quarters. These data suggest a very strong seasonal component and a sales manager would certainly like to take this into consideration as it will impact many of the decisions that she must make, and many decisions that must be made throughout the entire company. Seasonality influences sales for retailers, automotive dealerships, beer and soft drink manufacturers, clothing and sporting goods manufacturers, and many other companies.

LOOKING TO THE FUTURE

While the previous forecasting methods all rely on past sales data, the following methods are more forward looking. Past sales data, when available, may enhance forecasting with some of these methods, but many of them are appropriate when little or no sales history is available. These methods include leading indicators, executive opinion, survey of buyer intentions, test markets, and sales force composite. Each method is now described.

LEADING INDICATORS   A **leading indicator** is a measurable indicator that is closely related to sales, but that changes before sales occur. When a sales manager sees this indicator change or has reason to believe that there will be a change in this indicator based on predictions from a valid source, the sales manager can predict a change in sales at some future point. The best way to explain leading indicators is to provide an example. A sales manager might read an economic prediction that housing starts will increase by 10 percent in Alberta next year. He can predict that sales of lumber, nails, and roofing materials will soon follow, and that sales of washing machines, dishwashers, bathroom fixtures, and many related items will follow a few months later. Leading indicators are particularly useful because they can predict when there are likely to be changes in sales trends; that is, sales are either going to go up or go down more rapidly than recent trends might predict, or sales might begin to level off following a period of rapid growth.

EXECUTIVE OPINIONS METHODS   Utilizing executive opinions to predict sales is particularly useful when there is no sales history upon which to base sales forecasts. There are two methods of forecasting that employ executive opinion. The first, the **jury of executive opinion method**, is so called because it employs the opinions of a group of people who might all add insight into likely future sales, and this is particularly important when qualitative factors must be considered. Among the many things that could be important are likely dealer or distributor reactions, end-customer reactions, competitor response, changes in economic climate, production resources, materials and components supply capabilities, human resources or labour issues, inventory management capability, and many others. This method of forecasting remains popular because it is fast and easy to use, and because so many factors can be considered; however, the accuracy of any forecast is most certainly related to the experience of the people who are providing estimates so that the assumptions under which each person is making predictions should be known to the group. Sometimes, the people involved in making forecasts are too far removed from the marketplace, and their estimates fail to consider customer behaviour. On the other hand, marketing and salespeople may be too close to the marketplace so that without mangers from other functional areas of the company involved in the process, they may miss important changes in financial resources, production, or human resources that could influence future sales.

A second method that employs executive opinion is the **Delphi method**. This is a more structured approach in which managers provide estimates of sales in writing rather than face to face. Its advantage is that all forecast estimates are independent and not subject to group influence. The "bandwagon effect" or "snowballing" is less likely to occur, but this is at the cost of time and, often, increased complexity. Following an initial round of forecast estimates, information is fed back to individual members of the group along with the assumptions that were used in making various sales forecasts. Group members are again asked for estimates, and the process continues until reasonable consensus is achieved. This technique is also commonly used to predict long-term technological breakthroughs or opportunities, and experts from outside the company may participate. In these instances, both time and cost are greatly increased. The Delphi method is somewhat easier to employ today now that computer communication is so common.

SURVEY OF BUYER INTENTIONS METHOD   The **survey of buyer intentions method** is very popular among sales managers for both consumer and business products. This method involves collecting information from individual customers or potential customers concerning their expected purchases for a future period. In the consumer goods market, Ipsos Canada, for example, has a large online panel who are regularly surveyed concerning their buying intentions or who are shown new product concepts and then estimate their likelihood of purchasing based on the products they are shown, their particular features or benefits, and their proposed price. In business markets, the number of important accounts that a company has is often very small, so information on their purchasing intentions is more easily collected. Sometimes surveys, telephone calls, or personal visits are employed. In fact, it is possible for salespeople to collect this information as part of a regular sales call. Sometimes there are problems with forecasts that are based on a survey of buyer intentions. Some customers may overestimate their likelihood of purchasing, or the amount they will use. Consumer goods companies such as Kraft Canada or Procter & Gamble, however, will have experience with this method and will be able to discount estimates based on their past experience with similar products. In business markets, some customers may be unwilling to estimate their future use as this could provide information on their planned production changes, and this might be considered proprietary information. However, there are instances where this method can provide very accurate forecasts and should be employed. Assume, for example, that you are the supplier of specific parts or components that Toyota uses in the Matrix or the Corolla models that it manufactures in Canada. If Toyota has a history of good sales forecasting, then knowing its planned production for the next period would allow a supplier to ensure that supply is available, and the supplier could adjust its manufacturing or inventory accordingly.

TEST MARKET METHOD   The **test market method** (sometimes called the market test method) is useful for predicting sales for new products as they are tested in the real marketplace under, hopefully, real market conditions. Products can be introduced to the marketplace with a complete marketing program. Test market locations are usually selected so that residents match as closely as possible the target customers in the larger Canadian marketplace on the basis of demographic characteristics. Test markets can provide valuable information on customer acceptance, trade support and acceptance, and customer satisfaction levels, repurchase rates, and price sensitivity. Sometimes, the same product can be tested in several locations with different marketing programs so that adjustments can be made before the final commercialization of the product. McDonald's test marketed its Boston Market restaurant concept in Sydney (Nova Scotia) and

Toronto even though it had been a successful concept in the United States where there were more than 600 locations. It wanted to ensure the likelihood of success across Canada before introducing the concept nationally.[7] Frequently, U.S. firms test market products in Canada before they are launched in their home market. If the product fails in the Canadian test market, the company will not damage its image at home, or waste the resources that would be needed to launch the product across the United States. McDonald's, for example, launched its Lighter Choices menu in Canada before it introduced the product in the United States.[8]

The test market method does have several disadvantages. It can be very expensive, easily costing $1 million or more. It is not a good method to use for all products, particularly for long-lived consumer durable products that require strong dealer support and servicing capabilities. Finally, test markets are often viewed by competitors who can then begin planning their reaction, or take action that can skew test market results. Kevin Burdett, group product manager for frozen foods at McCain Foods Canada in Florenceville, New Brunswick, for example, says, "You're tipping your hand. In years gone by, I could probably do something in Peterborough [Ontario], and it would take two years for the people in B.C. to know about it. You couldn't do anything in the world today that everybody wouldn't know about within two days."[9] While it may not be as popular as it once was, it will remain a valuable method for testing products before introduction, and for forecasting sales response based on one or more marketing programs.

SALES FORCE COMPOSITE METHOD   The **sales force composite method** is a popular method that uses estimates from individual salespeople to forecast the volume of their sales, what products, and to which customers they will sell. These estimates can then easily be aggregated into sales branch or region forecasts, and these can subsequently be aggregated into national sales forecasts. Estimates of its popularity for mid- to long-term forecasts range from 49 percent to 77 percent.[10] It is probably used more frequently among business-to-business customers because they have smaller customer bases, and salespeople will be more familiar with each of their important customers. In fact, this is a major strength of this forecasting method: sales forecast estimates are made by those closest to the customer and more likely to know what important changes will be occurring at key accounts or within their territory.

While salespeople may have the best knowledge of their customers, having them provide sales forecast estimates can also create problems. Salespeople are by nature optimistic and often overestimate their ability, and this can lead them to overestimate their sales forecast. However, if they are closely monitored in terms of achieving their sales quota, and if rewards are tied closely to quota achievement, salespeople could underestimate their sales forecast so that their subsequent sales quota will be set at a lower level. Sales managers need to monitor salespeople's estimates over time to see how well they are able to forecast their sales. Some sales managers use a "partial" sales force composite method. Most salespeople have from two or three to 10 or 20 key accounts. The sales manager can estimate the sales forecast for each salesperson, and then make adjustments to these estimates based on salesperson feedback on key accounts. If a small account bankrupts or doubles its purchases, it will have little impact on the salesperson's sales; however, even a 20–30 percent decrease or increase in sales for a major account needs to be forecast if possible.

Additional Topics in Forecasting Sales

Now that the most popular methods of estimating potential and forecasting sales have been introduced and explained, there are a number of important topics related to forecasting that must be considered.

DEVELOPING TERRITORY FORECASTS

For many companies, estimating overall demand is one issue, but allocating demand estimates to distinct territories is also important. Estimating territory demand recognizes that conditions may vary greatly from one territory to another, and demand estimates are important to the overall management process: planning, organizing, controlling, and evaluating. There are many ways to estimate territory demand.

As one example, let's assume that a consumer goods company that manufactures a product that it sells throughout the four Atlantic provinces estimates that its next year's sales will be $5 million. If the company has good distribution throughout the entire region, it might suspect that sales in each province will be related to population. It is easy to get population statistics by province and then calculate the percentage of the Atlantic provinces' population that resides in each province. Then, multiplying the total sales forecast by the percentage population in each territory provides a sales forecast for each province as shown in Exhibit 4.7.

If there is a single salesperson in Newfoundland and Labrador, then her sales quota becomes $1 095 000. Now the sales manager must decide what to do with the other territories: how to combine them, and how many salespeople are needed. One possibility is to have two salespeople in Nova Scotia and two in New Brunswick, making one of these latter salespeople also responsible for Prince Edward Island. Travel to Prince Edward Island is easier from New Brunswick than from any other province. Another alternative is to combine Nova Scotia and Prince Edward Island, as the combined sales forecast would be close to the combined sales forecast for the other two provinces, and have only two salespeople: one resident in New Brunswick, and one resident in Nova Scotia. This would assume that each salesperson could manage a territory with sales of approximately $2.5 million. Whatever is decided, the sales manager should attempt to correlate sales with population statistics to see whether there is a strong relationship. If there is, then this may be all that is needed for forecasting territory sales. If there is a weak correlation, then the sales manager needs to consider why and whether adjustments might be needed. For example, Sobeys has a large distribution centre in Nova Scotia. Sobeys could purchase product in Nova Scotia that it then ships to Newfoundland and Labrador, part of the other territory. This may require a

---

Exhibit 4.7

Using Population to Estimate Forecast Sales

Province	Population July 1, 2006	Percent of Total (%)	Sales Forecast ($)
Newfoundland and Labrador	509 677	21.9	$1 095 000
Prince Edward Island	138 519	5.9	295 000
Nova Scotia	934 405	40.1	2 005 000
New Brunswick	749 168	32.1	1 605 000
Total:	2 331 769	100.0	5 000 000

simple adjustment if the sales manager can get an estimate of the percentage of Sobeys purchases that was sold in each province.

Another possibility is to develop a **buying power index**—a method of forecasting sales for a particular sales territory as a percentage of total forecast sales. For consumer goods, a number of factors could be related to territory sales and should therefore be considered when making territory sales forecasts. Along with population, two other possibilities are disposable income and retail sales. These could be weighted and combined to form an index; for example, 2, 5, and 3, respectively. (Other weights could be chosen, but the reason for choosing these will become apparent shortly.) Assume that a national consumer goods company sells laundry detergent across Canada. If its national forecast for the next year is $100 million, forecasters need only calculate a provincial buying power index to determine the sales forecast for each province. Considering Newfoundland and Labrador, for example, a forecaster could find that it has 1.7 percent of Canada's population, 1.4 percent of Canada's personal disposable income, and 1.7 percent of total Canadian retail sales.[11] Calculating a buying power index would result in the following:

$$BPI = \frac{(2)P + (5)I + (3)R}{10} = \frac{(2)1.7 + (5)1.4 + (3)1.7}{10} = 1.55\%$$

Forecast sales for Newfoundland and Labrador for its laundry detergent would be $1.55 million. Again, how well this buying power index relates to sales across territories can be investigated empirically, and adjustments can be made if appropriate. Different weights could be applied, or different factors could be used. For example, a manufacturer of consumer automotive after-market products might find that new motor vehicle sales or housing starts is a better predictor than total retail sales.

This example was meant to be illustrative only; however, there is a buying power index that is published in the United States each year by *Sales & Marketing Management* magazine. It is based on population, income, and retail sales, weighted as in the previous example. These buying power indices are available for all areas of the United States, at various levels of aggregation: state, county, city, or metropolitan area. In Canada, this data is not readily available, but many companies have created a proprietary buying power index that they use for allocating forecast sales to specific territories.

A buying power index is less likely to be used to predict expensive, infrequently purchased consumer goods, or industrial products, although there is nothing that prevents a company selling any type of product from creating some form of buying power index. In industrial sales, companies more frequently choose a single factor such as total number of employees or number of production employees, value of purchases or value of shipments, or some other factor. Useful data is generally available both from Statistics Canada and from each province of Canada. Provincial labour, technology, or tourism departments, for example, publish lists of companies within their jurisdiction by NAICS code. NAICS stands for North American Industrial Classification System, and is a system that classifies companies on the basis of their economic activity. NAICS codes begin as two digits, and each additional digit refines the classification, increasing specificity. For example:

31	Manufacturing
312	Beverage and Tobacco Manufacturing
3121	Beverage Manufacturing
31213	Wineries
312130	Canadian Wineries

Notice that the last digit refers to a country, as the NAICS code is otherwise standardized across Canada, the United States, and Mexico. A company that sold corks to the wineries could easily get a listing of Canadian wineries, along with statistics on numbers of employees, possibly even production levels, or shipment or sales volumes. As well as federal and provincial government statistics, trade associations such as the Alliance of Manufacturers and Exporters Canada are a valuable source of information.

INVOLVEMENT IN FORECASTING

The sales forecast, as pointed out, has implications for almost every functional area of business. That explains why companies frequently involve people throughout the organization in the forecasting process, from the CEO to product line managers. The most popular sources for people involved in forecasting are marketing and sales.[12] However, 56 percent of companies use cross-functional forecasting teams. About half of the companies that employ cross-functional teams charge them with the responsibility to develop a single forecast, and about half of them use these teams to reconcile individual forecasts that come from different departments.[13]

Information that is used for forecasting purposes is also most likely to come from people in marketing and sales. In more than four out of five companies, marketing and sales contribute information, compared to approximately half of companies where forecasting, finance, or senior executives contribute information. In more than 70 percent of companies, information is contributed by four or more functional areas, and 15 percent of companies involve seven or more functional areas.[14] The academic background of people employed in forecasting also shows considerable variance: 50 percent have a bachelor's degree, 33 percent have a master's degree, and the remaining are equally represented by people with high school diplomas and Ph.D. degrees. Only about 13 percent of people have a background in statistics/mathematics, and another 13 percent have a background in finance/accounting. Many have a background in production, distribution, logistics, product/market knowledge, sales, marketing research, and information systems.[15]

A more recent trend is to invite both customers and suppliers to participate by providing information that will aid forecasting. More than one in four companies now employ a collaborative planning, forecasting, and replenishment (CPFR) program with their customers. Under these arrangements, customers provide information on their own forecasts, and on their inventories, planned promotions, and even point-of-sale (POS) data. Such arrangements create a win–win situation for both parties. Suppliers improve the accuracy of their forecasting, resulting in increased sales and turnover, and decreased inventories and obsolescence. Customers have fewer stock-outs and will also benefit from better customer service. These arrangements, however, do require considerable trust between collaborating parties.[16] Other collaborative, but less formalized, arrangements also exist. More than half of companies in a recent survey stated that they collaborate with customers when forecasting: nearly 70 percent of them with fewer than seven customers, but 10 percent of them with more than 20 customers. Approximately 30 percent of responding companies also indicated that they collaborated with their suppliers. The positive correlation between collaborating with customers and suppliers indicates that some companies are beginning to conduct demand planning across their entire supply chains.[17] The Sales Management Today box describes how Colgate-Palmolive Company collaborates with its suppliers and customers to forecast demand.

SALES MANAGEMENT **TODAY**

Collaborative Demand Planning: Working With Suppliers and Customers to Forecast Demand

Colgate-Palmolive Company is a US$9.4 billion consumer products company that manufactures and sells toothpaste and oral care supplies, soaps, pet foods, and other household products. It opened its first international subsidiary in Canada in 1914, and now does business in over 200 countries. Operating in so many countries has created problems. A lack of global standardization of systems and data increased IT and other costs. Serving global customers and sourcing from global suppliers created additional problems. Inventories became unnecessarily high, and order-related cycle times were long.

As a result, the company now uses SAP APO (Advanced Planner and Optimizer) for replenishment optimization and demand planning. Working collaboratively with its suppliers and customers, Colgate-Palmolive has given them access to business-critical data such as production plans and schedules, worldwide inventory status, forecasts, and current order status. Reuben Mark, chairman and CEO of the company, states, "Colgate people working around the world share a commitment to three core corporate values: sharing, global teamwork, and continuous improvement." The company has implemented three

initiatives, all consistent with these values: collaborative planning, cross-border sourcing, and vendor managed inventory (VMI). VMI is a pull process that helps match company supply with customer demand. Shipments are made to key customer distribution centres based on daily inventory and demand information that is transmitted from these customers to Colgate-Palmolive.

As a result of implementing these three initiatives, forecast errors have been reduced from 62 percent to 22 percent. Finished goods inventory has been reduced by 22 percent. On-time and complete order fill rates for intra-company replenishment have been improved, and overall customer order fulfillment has increased to 95 percent. VMI on-time and complete order fill rates have been improved from 70 percent to 98 percent, and replenishment cycle times have been reduced from five days to only one day. Colgate-Palmolive has improved its relationships with its suppliers and customers, and sales, market shares, and gross margins have all been steadily improving. Management is optimistic for future growth and improved performance as well.

Sources: Colgate-Palmolive, http://www.colgate.ca/english/aboutus/chairmansmessage.html, accessed December 9, 2006; Colgate-Palmolive 2005 Annual Report; SAP.com, http://www.sap.com/solutions/business-suite/scm/pdf/ SCM_Solution_Magazine_Colgate_new.pdf, accessed December 9, 2006.

FAMILIARITY WITH AND USE OF VARIOUS METHODS

Familiarity with various forecasting methods is a topic with important implications, and fortunately, we have longitudinal information concerning this. Exhibit 4.8 provides information on familiarity based on three U.S. surveys conducted at approximately 10-year intervals. One generalization readily apparent is that familiarity with forecasting methods is generally decreasing, although it's decreasing more quickly for some methods than others. While not as familiar as it once was,

Exhibit 4.8

Familiarity with Forecasting Techniques

	Percent Familiar			Percent Somewhat Familiar		
Naïve	**M&C (1984)**	**M&K (1995)**	**McC et al. (2006)**	**M&C (1984)**	**M&K (1995)**	**McC et al. (2006)**
Jury of executive opinion	81	66	57	6	16	17
Sales force composite	79	71	66	5	14	18
Customer expectations	73	64	62	7	19	21
Moving averages	85	92	84	7	6	16
Straight-line projection	82	85	71	11	11	20
Exponential smoothing	73	90	76	12	6	20
Regression	72	78	73	8	10	24
Trend-line analysis	67	73	69	16	16	23
Decomposition	42	43	38	9	20	16

Sources: Adapted from J.T. Mentzer and J.E. Cox, Jr., "Familiarity, Application, and Performance of Sales Forecasting Techniques," *Journal of Forecasting*, 1984 (1), pp. 27–36; J.T. Mentzer and K.B. Kahn, "Forecasting Technique Familiarity, Satisfaction, Usage, and Application," 1995 (5), pp. 465–476; T.M. McCarthy, D.F. Davis, S.L. Golicic, and J.T. Mentzer, "The Evolution of Sales Forecasting Management: A 20-Year Longitudinal Study of Forecasting Practices," *Journal of Forecasting*, 2006, pp. 303–324.

moving averages remains the most familiar quantitative forecasting method. Both sales force composite and customer expectations have declined in familiarity over the three studies, but slowly compared to jury of executive opinion. One method that seems to have increased in familiarity, particularly when those who rate themselves as somewhat familiar are considered, is regression.

When it comes to use of various forecasting methods, some generalizations can be made from the three U.S. studies; however, there are differences in use between Canadian and U.S. companies. Exhibit 4.9 shows use by rank of various methods longitudinally in the U.S. studies, across three time horizons: short horizons of three months or less, medium horizons of four months to two years, and long horizons beyond two years. It also shows cross-sectional percentage use of various methods employed by Canadian companies. A generalization from the longitudinal research is that there is a growing use of qualitative methods for all time horizons. In the U.S. studies, jury of executive opinion ranked highest or nearly highest across all three studies and all forecasting time horizons. Sales force composite and customer expectations were also commonly used, but decreased in use as the forecasting time horizon increased. Exponential smoothing was the most commonly used quantitative forecasting method in the United States, particularly for short and medium time horizons. Regression was popular for all time horizons and has increased in popularity, most likely due to increased familiarity and the current ease of performing regression analysis with personal computers and spreadsheet programs such as Microsoft Excel. The largest percentage of respondents—41 percent—stated that they used spreadsheet programs for forecasting, although spreadsheet programs are capable of providing forecasts using many methods.[18] Because of the nature of the data, it is not possible to make a direct comparison between Canadian and U.S. companies, but it would appear that exponential smoothing is more popular in the United States, and moving averages is more popular in Canada. It would also appear that sales force composite is more likely to be used in Canada, and jury of executive opinion is more popular in the United States. A possible reason could be related to different forecasting needs across the two countries if multinational companies are involved, where strategy planning is more likely conducted in the United States, and more tactical planning related to implementation issues is conducted by subsidiaries or sales branches in Canada.

Exhibit 4.9

Use of Forecasting Techniques

Technique	Short: 3 months or less			Medium: 4–24 months			Long: Over 24 months			Percent use
	M&C (1984)	M&K (1995)	McC et al. (2006)	M&C (1984)	M&K (1995)	McC et al. (2006)	M&C (1984)	M&K (1995)	McC et al. (2006)	K&F (2001)
Naïve										70
Jury of executive opinion	1	5	na	1	2	1	1	1	1	38
Sales force composite	1	3	2	2	2	3	8	4	3	60
Customer expectations	3	3	1	5	8	4	4	7	na	
Industrial survey										33
Intention to buy survey										38
Moving averages	4	1	6	6	6	7	10	9	na	37
Straight-line projection	8	3	6	8	9	8	6	10	6	
Percentage rate of change										36
Unit rate of change										28
Exponential smoothing	4	2	3	7	1	2	9	6	5	13
Regression	7	5	3	2	4	6	2	2	2	
Simple regression										21
Multiple regression										18
Trend-line analysis	6	8	3	4	5	5	3	3	4	
Decomposition	9	8	na	9	7	8	10	10	na	
Leading indicators										44

NOTES:

1. Three U.S. studies rank methods by use; Canadian study reports percentage use.

2. M&C, n = 160; M&K, n = 186; McC et al., n= 86; K&F, n = 118

3. na = no respondents indicated use for this time horizon

Sources: Adapted from J.T. Mentzer and J.E. Cox, Jr., "Familiarity, Application, and Performance of Sales Forecasting Techniques," *Journal of Forecasting*, 1984 (1), pp. 27–36; J.T. Mentzer and K.B. Kahn, "Forecasting Technique Familiarity, Satisfaction, Usage, and Application," 1995 (5), pp. 465–476; R.D. Klassen and B.E. Flores, "Forecasting Practices of Canadian Firms: Survey Results and Comparisons," *International Journal of Production Economics*, 2001, pp. 163–174; T.M. McCarthy, D.F. Davis, S.L. Golicic, and J.T. Mentzer, "The Evolution of Sales Forecasting Management: A 20-Year Longitudinal Study of Forecasting Practices," *Journal of Forecasting*, 2006, pp. 303–324.

CHOOSING APPROPRIATE FORECASTING METHODS

Forecasters have many forecasting methods from which to choose. Making the most appropriate choice is not easy. There are many factors that must be considered when making a choice: (1) amount, quality, and stability of data available, (2) the forecasting time horizon and the use to which the forecast will ultimately be put, (3) the hardware and software resources available for use, (4) the need for involvement of people from different functional areas and from different levels of the organization hierarchy, and (5) accuracy, cost, familiarity, and ease of use of particular methods. It is clear that different methods of forecasting will be superior under different conditions, so forecasters should clearly understand their specific needs and should attempt to choose the method or methods that best fit their needs. One concern is the greater apparent use of qualitative methods. If their use is increasing simply because of ease of use or increased familiarity, they are possibly being employed regardless of whether they are the best method for a particular application.[19] Exhibit 4.10 describes some of the strengths and weaknesses of many of the most popular forecast methods described in this chapter, and should help you choose appropriate forecast methods.

A solution to the choice issue is to employ multiple choices, and compare forecasts that result. In one Canadian study, forecasters used, on average, 3.5 forecasting methods.[20] A more recent study found that the average number of methods employed was 5.2 methods, with one respondent indicating that 15 methods were used.[21] Although most firms use multiple forecasting methods, approximately 60 percent of companies do not combine their forecasts. Among the companies that did combine forecasts, accuracy was improved, on average, by nearly 10 percent; however, the standard deviation of the improvement was quite high, meaning that there was considerable variance in the improvements so that decreases were also likely. This may explain the large percentage of companies that do not combine forecasts.[22]

Another forecasting trend that seems to be increasing is using judgmental input to overlay or adjust statistical forecasts. In one study, 83 percent of respondents stated that their company held consensus meetings where managers from different functional areas met after a forecast was prepared.[23] This provided the opportunity to improve forecasts by considering judgmental factors that could not be captured by statistical modelling. The inclusion of others after a forecast has been made should not be to share blame for a bad forecast, but to gain buy-in. If senior management is not involved, at some point they must still accept the forecast. It is easier to sell a forecast to senior management if they know that estimates and assumptions have been reviewed and accepted by the many stakeholders whose success depends on accurate forecasts.

ADJUST FORECASTS EARLY WHEN NECESSARY

A forecast is made at one point in time to predict results at a future point in time. Frequently, the accuracy of a forecast is called into question long before the forecast period ends. When this happens, it is wise to make an adjustment to the forecast as early as possible so that decisions that are made as a result of the forecast can be revised. If sales, for example, are well ahead of or well behind what is forecast after only one or two months or quarters, a review should attempt to identify whether this is a trend that is likely to continue. Employment or production changes, or changes to operating or capital budgets, may need to be made.

One change that should only be made after careful consideration is to sales quotas assigned to individual salespeople, particularly if compensation is tied to achieving sales quota. Adjusting a quota upward may later be seen to have been unfair if a salesperson achieves the original quota but fails to achieve the adjusted quota. At the same time, failing to adjust a quota downward

Exhibit 4.10

A Comparison of Some Sales Forecasting Methods

Method	Strengths	Weaknesses
Moving averages	Simple to use Works well when many products or territories involved Helps smooth random fluctuations	Assigns equal weight to each observation Requires several periods of historical sales data Adjusts slowly to trends
Exponential smoothing	Quite simple to use Gives greater weight to recent data Requires that little data be maintained Software makes calculations easy Generally good accuracy for short-term forecasts	May require effort to find best smoothing coefficient Less accurate as length of forecast period increases Large fluctuations in recent data may require changing the smoothing coefficient
Decomposition	Quite simple to use Can account for seasonality Intuitively simple but still managed easily with most software packages	Requires medium to large amounts of sales data Less accurate as length of forecast period increases
Jury of executive opinion	Collaborative and gains buy-in from many stakeholders Can be conducted quickly Often suitable when prior sales data not available Ensures that many factors other than past sales considered	Time and cost can be issues if many people are involved Snowballing or bandwagon effect may occur Senior people, or one or two strong individuals may dominate Some people far removed from marketplace
Delphi method	Communications can be managed by computer Eliminates snowballing or bandwagon effect Eliminates dominance or influence within the group People external to the company may participate	Time can be a real problem, especially if there are many iterations to reach consensus Difficult to gauge the importance of the outcome to all participants
Survey of buyer intentions	Involves actual customers in the forecasting May be inexpensive if only a few customers are involved Can build good relationships with important customers	Customers frequently over-estimate demand Some customers distrust intentions or will not provide information
Test market	Takes place in real world with real marketing program Can be used to help refine marketing program	Possible exposure to competition so that results may be skewed May invite early competitor reaction Very costly and often time consuming
Sales force composite	People closest to customers involved Salespeople have knowledge of territory, customers, and products May enhance morale as salespeople involved in the forecasting	Salespeople by nature often over-optimistic May forecast low if used to establish quota and compensation is affected Salespeople often lack larger macro perspective of the economy and things that could impact sales May take excessive time away from selling

could demotivate a salesperson who begins to see his quota as unachievable too early in a sales period. More will be said about this in Chapter 9, where sales quotas are discussed.

If one or more adjustments have been made to a forecast throughout the period covered by the forecast, care should be taken to compare forecast accuracy against the original forecast if accuracy tracking is important.

LOOKING BACK: REVIEW AND EVALUATION

Looking back—reviewing and evaluating forecasts and forecasting—is becoming increasingly important. There is evidence that forecast accuracy is decreasing.[24] One reason could be related to the selection of forecast methods. As forecasters become increasingly unfamiliar with forecasting methods, they may simply select those with which they have the most familiarity rather than the best choice given their forecasting needs. Ease of computer use and software packages, combined with decreased familiarity, may result in a reliance on computer outputs because "computers don't make mistakes." While the output may be accurate, the input or process may be faulty.

Another problem may be the decreasing involvement of senior management. Management attention may have become more focused on strategic linkages and long-term planning, and less focused on short-term market forecasting. This may be increasingly left to middle management or staff people who seldom are held accountable for poor forecasting or rewarded for forecast accuracy. More than two-thirds of survey respondents reported that there was no accountability for poor forecasting within their company, and three-quarters reported that there were no rewards for accuracy.[25] Among Canadian companies, it was reported that 38 percent did not monitor forecast results.[26] Another possibility could be related to the growing product proliferation. Forecasting becomes more complex and may become subject to greater error as the number of products involved increases. In one recent study, 40 percent of companies made more than 1000 forecasts at the SKU level, and 5 percent of companies made more than 100 000 forecasts.[27]

There are several ways to compare forecast methods for accuracy. One of the most commonly used is the *mean absolute percentage error,* or **MAPE**. This is the average of the absolute percentage forecast errors. Using the sales data for the month of August for the naïve forecast method discussed earlier in this chapter, the absolute percentage forecast error would be

$$\text{Absolute percentage forecast error} = \left| \frac{\text{Forecast sales} - \text{Actual sales}}{\text{Actual sales}} \right|$$

$$= \left| \frac{137 - 153}{153} \right|$$

$$= 10.5\%$$

The absolute percentage forecast error for each period is

Aug.	Sept.	Oct.	Nov.	Dec.
10.5%	5.6%	10.5%	5.2%	4.4%

Then, MAPE is calculated as the average of the absolute percentage forecast errors:

$$\text{MAPE} = \frac{10.5 + 5.6 + 10.5 + 5.2 + 4.4}{5} = 7.24\%$$

That is, using the naïve forecast method results in a mean absolute percentage error, or MAPE, of 7.24 percent. Using more information than just sales results from the last period should result in a lower MAPE, but the extent to which that is true will depend on the importance of other factors for making sales forecasts. Because the naïve forecast method is so popular among Canadian companies, and because MAPE is so easily calculated, it should be routine to do this as a benchmark against which to compare the accuracy of other forecast methods. Less than 10 percent of Canadian companies were found to use MAPE, but approximately 50 percent of U.S. companies did.[28] An equal percentage of U.S. companies also use percentage error, or PE, since MAPE does not consider the direction of the forecast error. This is a tremendous increase from the 3 percent who reported using percentage error in 1995. In Canada, the most popular method to check forecast accuracy was reported as visual monitoring.[29]

Clearly, there is a need for greater familiarity with forecast methods, and an opportunity for those who understand and can appropriately use forecast methods. A variety of forecast methods should be part of every sales manager's tool kit.

SUMMARY

1. **Understand the importance of four types of sales-related forecasts.** Sales managers regularly consider and must understand four types of sales-related forecasts: (1) market potential, (2) market forecast, (3) sales potential, and (4) sales forecast. These types of forecasts vary on two dimensions: whether they are industry- or company-level, and whether they relate to the best possible or the most likely outcome. The most important one for sales managers is the sales forecast. It is the basis for many of the important decisions throughout the entire organization.

2. **Use the most popular sales forecast methods.** Many of the quantitative methods of sales forecasting rely on past sales data: naïve forecasts, moving averages, exponential smoothing, decomposition, and regression analysis. Other methods of sales forecasting are more forward looking: leading indicators, executive opinion, survey of buyer intentions, test markets, and sales force composite. This chapter discussed how to use each of these methods. It also described how to construct a buying power index and how to use NAICS data to help allocate sales forecasts across sales territories.

3. **Discuss involvement in, familiarity with, and current use of various sales forecast methods.** People from product line managers to the CEO may be involved in the forecasting process. Nearly every functional area may be involved. Companies are increasingly involving suppliers and customers in the forecasting process. There appears to be growing use of qualitative methods for sales forecasting. Differences in forecasting methods between Canadian and U.S. companies may be the result of different forecasting needs. There are many factors that must be considered when making a choice of forecast methods: (1) amount, quality, and stability of data available, (2) the forecasting time horizon and the use to which the forecast will ultimately be put, (3) the hardware and software resources available for use, (4) the need for involvement of people from different functional areas and from different levels of the organization hierarchy, and (5) accuracy, cost, familiarity, and ease of use of particular methods. On average, companies use between 3.5 and 5.2 different methods when forecasting sales.

4. **Assess the accuracy of sales forecast methods.** There are several ways to compare forecast methods for accuracy. One of the most commonly used is the *mean absolute percentage error,* or MAPE. While it is used by less than 10 percent of Canadian companies, it is used by approximately 50 percent of U.S. companies.

KEY TERMS

market potential   **94**

market forecast   **94**

sales potential   **94**

sales forecast   **94**

naïve forecast method   **97**

moving averages method   **97**

exponential smoothing method   **98**

trend projection method   **99**

time-series regression   **100**

single regression method   **100**

multiple regression model   **100**

decomposition method   **101**

leading indicator   **102**

jury of executive opinion method   **102**

Delphi method   **103**

survey of buyer intentions method   **103**

test market method   **103**

sales force composite method   **104**

buying power index   **106**

MAPE   **113**

REVIEW QUESTIONS

1. What are the four types of sales-related forecasts? How do they differ?

2. Explain why sales forecasts are important for many departments besides the sales department.

3. Describe the differences between the moving averages method and the exponential smoothing method of forecasting sales. What advantage does each have over the naïve forecast method?

4. Describe the three-step process that is used with the decomposition method. What is the major reason why this method would be used?

5. How does the jury of executive opinion differ from the Delphi method? When would each method be appropriate to use?

6. Define buying power index and describe how to construct one.

7. What is a collaborative planning, forecasting, and replenishment (CPFR) program, and why are these programs becoming more popular?

8. List the factors that must be considered when selecting a sales forecast method, and explain why each is important.

9. Is it ever acceptable to combine quantitative and qualitative methods of forecasting sales? If no, why is it not acceptable? If yes, how can this be accomplished?

10. What is MAPE and why is it important? What is the main weakness of using MAPE?

APPLICATION EXERCISES

1. Dog Knit Sweaters has been selling sweaters made from dog hair yarn for almost one year. Its forecast sales and actual sales were as follows:

Month	Forecast	Actual
September	100	120
October	150	166
November	175	180
December	200	230
January	180	205
February	200	210
March	200	182
April		

   What are forecast sales for April using two-month, three-month, and four-month moving averages? Calculate MAPE for all three and compare your results. Which number of observations leads to the lowest MAPE? Would exponential smoothing be more appropriate here? Why or why not?

2. Ceilidh Electronics has been selling compact DVD players for several months. Historical data are as follows:

January	11		April	51
February	24		May	73
March	34		June	88

   What forecast method should be used to forecast future sales in units? (Assume that seasonality will not be an issue.) Use your recommendation to calculate a forecast for July and August.

3. Select any well known publicly traded Canadian company with sales of more than $50 million. Look at its latest annual report and find its sales for the past several years (by quarters if possible). Use at least three of the forecasting methods discussed in this chapter to assess its performance. This may require that you predict sales for periods for which results already appear. That is, you may find data for 2002 through 2007, for example. Looking at sales data for some of the first few years, forecast sales for several of the later years. Assess how well the company did when compared to forecast. Then, take the data you have and forecast sales for one or two future periods for which there are no reported sales figures. Which forecast method did you use? Be prepared to explain why.

4. Mark Moniz is the vice-president of sales for a large Canadian industrial distributor. During a recent trip to Europe, he discovered a new manufacturer of carbide cutting tools that is looking for distribution in Canada. Mark is thinking about taking on the line and he has asked you, a marketing consultant, to provide him with your thoughts. In particular, he wants to know two things: what factors he needs to consider when determining the Canadian market potential for this product line, and what factors he needs to consider when determining the sales potential for this product line. Write a report to Mark Moniz and provide him with your thoughts.

Trends

When Raechel Greve graduated from university, she was promoted to manager of a popular trendy restaurant called Trends, where she had been working on a part-time basis during the final three years of her business program. The restaurant was located in Southwestern Ontario and was noted for its wide selection of better quality Ontario-produced wines. Shortly after Raechel became manager, she completely changed the dinner menu, intending to bring the restaurant upscale to meet the needs of an increasingly affluent clientele. The menu was pricey, but most patrons rated the food quality and presentation as outstanding. As a result, sales continued to grow, but Raechel found she was occasionally having difficulty managing her inventory of beverages and food items. She realized that a better forecasting model would help her plan for future growth, and she was determined to improve her ability to forecast sales at least one year in advance. Sales records for the previous three years were used to compile the data in the table below.

PAST FOOD AND BEVERAGE SALES FOR TRENDS ($000)

	Three Years Ago	Two Years Ago	Last Year
January	212	228	246
February	207	214	237
March	202	216	242
April	158	171	193
May	163	164	196
June	147	151	168
July	145	157	172
August	152	160	176
September	130	136	141
October	125	138	149
November	159	166	177
December	197	204	236

CRITICAL-THINKING QUESTION

Given these data, what sales should Raechel expect for each month next year? Be prepared to explain to Raechel why you chose the forecasting method you did.

Centre for the Arts

The managing director for the Centre for the Arts (**www.arts.brocku.ca**) was considering how to forecast total person-seats that would be sold for the upcoming season. The Centre for the Arts is an integral part of Brock University. The Departments of Dramatic Arts and Music have scheduling priority as the Centre's facilities are needed for the practical components of their studies. Following this, priority is given to the Department of Education and other faculties within the university that might need the 538-seat Sean O'Sullivan Theatre to meet their needs. Time is also allocated to the Niagara Symphony Orchestra for its practice. Then, what time is left is at the discretion of the managing director to book professional entertainment events that are open to the Niagara Region community. Typical performers included John McDermott, Natalie MacMaster, Chantal Kreviazuk, Remy Shand, and Ron Sexsmith, and several Christmas specials and a number of theatrical performances were also held there. John McDermott was one of the most popular performers. He usually played for two nights and his shows were almost always sold out. Ticket sales for theatrical performances varied. While some sold very well, others failed to achieve sales of 50 percent capacity.

For the upcoming season, 42 performance nights have been booked. The following summarizes data for the previous seven seasons:

Season	Performance Nights	Total Attendance
2001	38	15 773
2002	40	16 620
2003	45	18 450
2004	42	17 682
2005	42	17 955
2006	40	17 316
2007	38	16 868
2008	42 (booked)	

CRITICAL-THINKING QUESTION

The president of Brock University has asked for a forecast of the total attendance for the 2008 season. If you were the managing director, what forecast would you make? Describe in detail the process you would use to make your forecast.

Chapter 5

Developing and Growing Account Relationships

LEARNING OBJECTIVES

After completing this chapter, you should be able to

1. Describe three types of buyer–seller relationships.

2. Describe three buying situations that customers face.

3. Explain the buying centre concept and who may be included in it.

4. Explain the customer buying-decision process.

5. Explain three stages in relationship evolution.

6. Explain prospecting and qualifying and why they are important.

7. Explain how to determine when an account is too small.

8. Describe how to allocate sales effort across a portfolio of accounts.

In less than 20 years, Burnaby, B.C.–based Creo Inc. has successfully transformed itself from a manufacturer of quality products to a complete solutions provider focused on creating value for its printer customers. It has won many awards for its products, corporate social responsibility, business development, and employee relations. Recently, it was ranked among the 50 best employers in Canada by *Report on Business* magazine. Creo has historically focused on the prepress segment of the printing industry. (Prepress begins after the graphic designer is finished with the graphic file, and ends when the job is ready for the printing press.) Today, Creo provides technologies that affect the entire print supply chain, from the creative function through the pressroom.

How does Creo create superior customer value? It starts when Creo salespeople, called business solutions advisors, make their first sales call on prospects. Patrick Morrissey, vice-president of sales for the Americas, says, "Our whole agenda is focused on the customer, not on Creo. We begin by fully understanding the customer's business. Companies with similar operating characteristics and that serve similar markets often face common problems. We have enabled our salespeople to become industry experts by focusing them on specific customer segments. We have salespeople who sell to small, entrepreneurial printers; to larger, commercial printers; to newspaper printers; and to packaging printers. We try to identify each customer's most important concerns and then we work closely with them to develop superior solutions that meet their individual needs. When necessary, we utilize selling teams that may include anyone from product experts, to financial people, to professional services people such as trainers, to technical sales support specialists."

Customers partner with Creo throughout the product development process. This has helped Creo become a learning organization and has enabled it to gain more than three times the market share of its nearest competitor. To ensure customers get maximum benefit from their systems, Creo offers flexible training options: classroom or on-site instructor-led sessions, learning guides, or web-based programs. Part of its customer relationship strategy is built around the Creo Users Association (CUA). Members can attend an annual conference where they can participate in numerous seminars, workshops, and roundtables. Attendees can book one-on-one meetings with Creo management, developers, and technical experts. Peer-to-peer networking is encouraged so customers can learn from each other. From the first prospect contact to long after a sale is consummated, Creo has a strategy for developing and growing strong account relationships.[1]

Managing Account Relationships

How an organization chooses to develop and grow its account relationships is an important strategic decision that must take into consideration products sold, markets served, and an organization's resources and capability. Therefore, this decision will have an impact on many sales management decisions, including sales force organization, and recruiting, selecting, training, compensating, and evaluating salespeople. As illustrated in Exhibit 5.1, the process includes deciding on an account relationship strategy; understanding customers and helping them buy; guiding relationship evolution, building trust, and creating value; prospecting for and qualifying additional customers; and managing a portfolio of customer accounts. We will now discuss each of these topics.

Types of Account Relationship Strategies

Sellers must decide how they will acquire, maintain, and grow customer accounts; that is, they must have an **account relationship strategy**. Some firms decide to use a single relationship

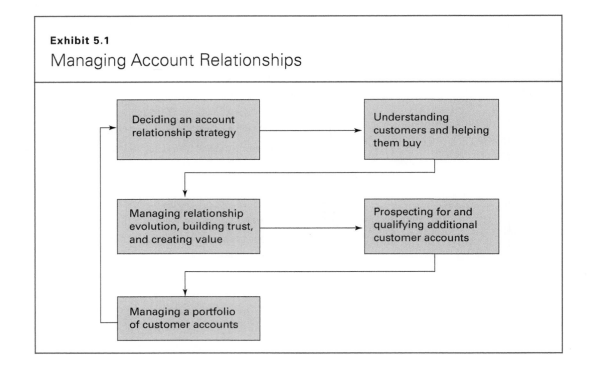

Exhibit 5.1
Managing Account Relationships

strategy; others decide to use different relationship strategies with different customers. The appropriate relationship strategy is one that meets the needs of both the seller and the buyer. The three main types of relationships are illustrated in Exhibit 5.2. As relationships move from merely transactional to partnering relationships, they become increasingly closer and longer-term. Closer relationships are indicated when there is a willingness to communicate and share information, to adapt technologies and processes to those of the other party, etc. Long-term relationships are often indicated by formalized contracts, but even in the absence of such contracts, there is often an implicit willingness to maintain and grow a relationship as long as each party continues to make the necessary resource commitments to meet the needs of the other party.

Selecting an appropriate account relationship strategy for each account is very important. Different account relationship strategies require salespeople to develop different selling philosophies and buyers to adopt different buying philosophies. A chosen account relationship strategy may affect the organization of the sales force, the activities that the salespeople are required to perform, and hiring, training, motivating, and compensating decisions made by sales management. Choosing an inappropriate account relationship strategy will result at best in wasted resources as too much time and effort are spent on accounts that do not require or value them. At worst, it will result in lost sales if insufficient resources are allocated to meet the needs of an account and a competitor is willing to make the necessary investment.

TRANSACTIONAL RELATIONSHIPS

Transactional relationships are appropriate when value-conscious customers are interested primarily in price or convenience. Sellers who try to develop closer, longer-term relationships with customers who only wish transactional relationships will waste time and effort that could better be utilized elsewhere. In many transactional relationships, however, there may be a strong

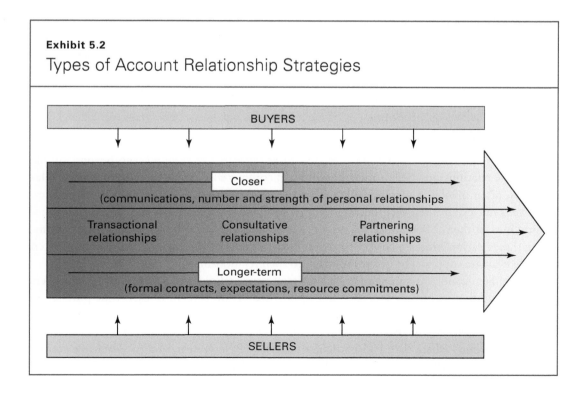

Exhibit 5.2
Types of Account Relationship Strategies

personal relationship between individual buyers and salespeople. A first sale might be made because the product being offered is superior to what the customer is currently using, or the price might be lower than what the customer is currently paying. However, it is unlikely that the sale will be made unless the customer has some level of trust in the salesperson, her product, and the company. The buyer may continue to buy from the salesperson indefinitely and, over time, the personal relationship between the buyer and seller may become very close. If, however, the buyer's firm is only interested in a transactional relationship, then continuing sales are always at risk either if a particular buyer or salesperson changes jobs, retires, or dies, or if another salesperson approaches the buyer with a superior product or lower price. Because some customers value only transactional relationships, some marketers are developing lower-cost selling channels: direct mail, telemarketing, and the internet. One recent study concluded that 68 percent of firms attempt to develop transactional relationships with at least some of their customers.[2]

CONSULTATIVE RELATIONSHIPS

Consultative relationships are appropriate when the customer's problem is not clearly understood by the seller, or even possibly by the customer; when the solution is complex and must be customized to meet specific customer needs; when after-sale service is important and may include delivery, installation, or ongoing product repairs or upgrades; or when the price or profit margin is sufficiently high to justify the seller's costs and the buyer is willing to pay that price. Consultative relationships are more common in business markets than in consumer markets.[3] The role of the salesperson differs greatly from the role he must perform when only a transactional relationship is involved. Consultative salespeople act as business consultants for their customers and they must therefore fully understand the customer's needs before offering a product solution. This will involve considerable two-way communication between the buyer and seller, bilateral problem solving, and considerable negotiation between the two parties so that at the end of the process both parties will gain from the relationship. If the seller desires a truly consultative relationship, then the customer must be viewed as someone to be served, and the salesperson must be willing to be the customer's advocate within the sales organization. This often requires that the salesperson actively negotiate and marshal resources inside his firm to ensure that the customer is served. While it might at first appear that consultative selling practices are easily mastered, the truth is that consultative selling is a complex process that puts great demands on salespeople.[4]

PARTNERING RELATIONSHIPS

Partnering relationships, sometimes referred to as *enterprise relationships,* go beyond simple consultative relationships. Sellers must be willing to commit considerable resources to these relationships, often involving many people within their organization to support and manage sales. Customers must want these relationships in order for them to succeed and, in fact, customers frequently initiate them.[5] Because of the resource commitments by both buyers and sellers, terminating these relationships can be very costly for both parties. For this reason, customers will often carefully evaluate suppliers before committing to such relationships.

Nortel Semiconductors implemented a series of commodity partnerships with key suppliers when it found that its buyers were spending approximately 80 percent of their time purchasing items that accounted for only about 20 percent of their purchases. These partnering relationships were developed with suppliers who would become a one-stop shopping source for one or a few commodity groups where they had particular expertise. By concentrating its purchases among fewer suppliers, Nortel would increase its bargaining power for lower overall costs. There would be fewer transactions and this would reduce activity in the stockroom and in the company's accounts payable department. Inventory levels at Nortel could be reduced as responsibility for inventory would be passed to suppliers, and reduced inventory would mean reduced obsolescence and insurance costs as well. Having fewer suppliers would mean that there would be fewer salespeople to deal with, and this would allow Nortel to do a more careful analysis of remaining suppliers. An analysis of these programs was conducted after two years and the results were very positive. Nortel had been adding new suppliers over that period because the company was expanding into new technologies, but even so, it was able to reduce its total supplier base for commodity products by approximately 20 percent and also achieve substantial cost savings.[6]

Sellers must be careful not to attempt to manage so many of these relationships that their servicing capability is exceeded and customers become dissatisfied. Many of these relationships begin with a formal contract but, because of the time and cost to develop them, there is often an expectation by both parties that the relationship will continue well beyond any formal contract. From the seller's perspective, these accounts may be considered as strategic, key, major, national, or global accounts, and they may develop specific programs to manage them.

Helping Customers Buy

Regardless of which account relationship strategy is appropriate for a particular account, it is the salesperson's responsibility to help customers buy. To do this, the salesperson must understand the customer's buying task or situation, who in the customer firm will be involved in the buying decision, and the process that the customer will use to solve a particular buying problem. Each of these issues is now discussed.

UNDERSTANDING THE CUSTOMER'S BUYING TASK

Before a salesperson can help a customer solve a buying problem, she must understand which of three buying situations the customer faces: a new task buy, a modified rebuy, or a straight rebuy. Each buying situation presents the buying firm with unique issues and therefore has different implications for the salesperson.

NEW TASK BUY   The most complicated buying situation a customer faces is a **new task buy**. It is a relatively rare situation for established companies since they make most purchases from regular, known vendors and from within known product categories. However, when a customer does need a good or service not previously purchased, the customer may initiate an extended problem-solving process to carefully collect and evaluate information before making a purchase decision. If the purchase is technical or costly, many people may be involved to help determine product and vendor specifications, and to decide on a purchasing process both for the immediate purchase and for subsequent purchases. New task purchases are important to salespeople because there are many people involved in the purchase decision and this provides greater potential to influence the customer's evaluation process and help establish new patterns of future buying behaviour.

MODIFIED REBUY   Customers who face a **modified rebuy** situation generally initiate a limited problem-solving process where they consider product modifications or one or more alternative vendors. In some instances, the customer may wish new or additional product features, a lower price, faster service, a different level of quality, or a lesser or greater purchase quantity. In other situations, the customer may decide it is time to consider alternative vendors to evaluate whether improved purchase conditions are possible. Since the customer has some product and vendor knowledge, the search for additional information and the alternative evaluation process will be shorter, and fewer people may be involved in the purchase decision.

STRAIGHT REBUY A **straight rebuy** is the simplest buying situation. Customers tend to simply repurchase the same products from vendors that have provided satisfactory past performance. There is limited involvement by people from the customer firm and these purchases are frequently delegated to the buyer or purchasing agent. In many instances, these purchases have become so routinized that orders may be generated electronically and placed over the internet. In some instances, a salesperson may even monitor the customer's inventory and suggest what and when additional purchases should be made.

UNDERSTANDING WHO IS INVOLVED IN THE BUYING DECISION

In organizational buying, the term **buying centre** is commonly used to designate all of the people who will be involved in a particular purchase decision. (The concept also applies to some consumer purchases as well but is more commonly referred to as the family decision-making unit, or DMU.) The size of the buying centre varies depending on the purchase situation (new task, modified rebuy, or straight rebuy) and membership in the buying centre changes over time with people entering and leaving depending on the stage of the customer's buying decision process.[7] Salespeople must understand the buying centre concept because when several people are involved in the buying decision, they will have different priorities and personalities, will have different levels of influence, and will use different evaluative criteria when assessing alternatives. The common roles that buying centre members fill are now discussed.

- *User buyer.* **User buyers** are concerned primarily with operating characteristics and costs when the purchase will affect their job performance or operating budget, or those of the department for which they are responsible. User buyers tend to focus more on tactical versus strategic issues. Salespeople need to identify who will actually use a product and how choosing various alternatives will affect them. This is more complicated than it may at first appear in organizational selling. For example, a salesperson must consider the manufacturer who might use his product in the manufacturing process and the impact this might have on the manufacturer's customer. Sometimes the sale may depend simply on the ease of use by the manufacturer. Other times, the salesperson may have an advantage if he can convince the manufacturer that customers will see increased value in the manufacturer's product as a result of using the salesperson's alternative.

- *Technical buyer.* **Technical buyers** influence and sometimes determine product specifications. The technical buyer may be also the user buyer. A production manager may have influence in a purchase decision because it directly affects his operations and as a result, he may also be given responsibility for determining exactly what is acceptable as an alternative. Engineers, information technology managers, or even purchasing agents may also fill the role of technical buyer. Although the technical buyer may have a lot of influence in the buying decision, he seldom has the authority to make the final decision. That is, he frequently is able to say "no," but seldom can say "yes." Salespeople should attempt to contact and influence these people as early as possible in the buying process as it is sometimes possible to influence product specifications to their advantage. However, naïve salespeople often rely too much on the influence of these people and are then disappointed when they find that a competitor has cultivated someone else in the buying centre with greater decision-making authority.

- *Economic buyer.* The **economic buyer** has ultimate authority in a buying decision. She may say "yes" when everyone else says "no"; she may say "no," when everyone else says "yes." In some instances, the economic buyer may be a committee charged with the responsibility to make important financial decisions. Salespeople sometimes have difficulty identifying or contacting economic buyers because they may be at higher levels within the organization and are often "buffered" by people at lower administrative or operational levels. Economic buyers are likely to be higher in an organization when there is greater impact on the organization as the result of the decision; that is, when the outcome of the decision is more strategic. For less strategic decisions, the purchasing manager may be the economic buyer, charged with the responsibility of balancing purchase cost against other considerations. Salespeople can identify the economic buyer by finding out who initiated a purchase decision, who has the most to gain from it, and who is most at risk if a wrong decision is made.

Two other important buying influence roles that salespeople need to consider are those of the advocate and the gatekeeper. When the buying decision is a complex one, salespeople benefit from having an **advocate**, or champion, to help them in the process. Advocates are strong supporters who provide information concerning who will be influential in the buying decision, what criteria are important to them, what are competitors' strengths, and anything else that might affect final choice. Advocates may want to see a particular salesperson win because they truly believe he offers the best alternative, or simply because they like him or dislike his competitor. Sometimes, when it is difficult to contact the economic buyer, an advocate can promote the salesperson's position within the buying centre. It is therefore wise to cultivate an advocate who is both competent and trustworthy.

The person who fills a **gatekeeper** role controls the flow of information to members of the buying centre. Purchasing people are frequently gatekeepers as they are the ones who directly interact with salespeople and can then decide what information is passed on to others who may be influential in the decision process. The technical buyer frequently performs the role of gatekeeper by deciding which alternatives can be considered and which cannot. Departmental secretaries may be gatekeepers as they can influence information flows between salespeople and buying centre members. A common problem many salespeople face is getting past a gatekeeper to contact other buying centre members. An important objective of many companies participating in trade shows is to prospect for buying influencers whom they can then directly contact by mail or telephone without having to depend on selling only through the purchasing department. Getting past gatekeepers can be difficult and salespeople can create clashes when bypassing them. For this reason, it is important to find out who will be involved in purchasing decisions as early as possible in the process and to make initial contacts as high as possible within the buying organization. The Sales Management Today box describes changes that have been made to the composition of some buying centres for technology purchases in recent years. Salespeople need to be aware of these changes.

UNDERSTANDING THE CUSTOMER'S BUYING-DECISION PROCESS

Both consumers and organizational customers follow a **buying-decision process**. Exhibit 5.3 illustrates a simplified process that can explain the behaviour of both types of buyers. The process begins with need recognition and then proceeds to information search, alternative evaluation, purchase decision and implementation, and, finally, post-purchase evaluation. Each of these stages is now discussed.

Relationship Importance Increases for Technology Purchases

Salespeople who sell technology products have noticed a tremendous change in the composition of buying centres. Twenty years ago, companies frequently gave complete responsibility for making purchasing decisions for technology products to information technology departments. These departments were provided with a budget for purchases, and were then allowed to make decisions concerning what was needed and where it should be purchased. Frequently, companies ended up with technologies they did not need and could not implement.

Today, technology purchase decisions are likely to involve everyone from users to senior executives as these strategic decisions affect the buyer's ability to effectively manage its operations. The alternatives for both technology products and suppliers have increased so that each buying decision must focus on return on investment. That is, for any given investment, senior executives want to know how much each investment will cost, and how greatly it will benefit the firm. When companies make purchase decisions for many of these products, they have to live with their decisions for years or even decades. Errors can be very costly in terms of both purchase costs and lost revenues if the technology reduces a company's ability to serve its customers relative to its competitors.

Computing Canada editor Patricia McInnis relates a story of a chief information officer who decided to upgrade notebook computers within his organization. Instead of just asking several suppliers

for competitive proposals, he thought it was time to establish a relationship with one key supplier who would be committed to a relationship with his firm. He asked each of the potential suppliers to spend some time understanding his company and its needs: What were his firm's goals and how would technology help it meet its particular objectives? Who would be affected by technology decisions and how would they be affected? When the various proposals arrived on his desk, some clearly attempted to address his concerns. Others submitted regular proposals as if his conversation with them had never happened. To these he gave no consideration.

When Acadia University decided that every student in its business program would have a portable computer, considerable time and effort was put into the purchase decision. Twelve suppliers were carefully evaluated to determine which would become the university's technology partner. According to president David Ogilvie, the university needed "to have absolute confidence that the technology being provided would meet the objectives and standards required for the program, and that the company would be in business in the long term to provide us with critical long-term support. Then once you get beyond that absolute requirement, you get into your confidence in your ability to work with the corporation in a partnership arrangement." Buyers today are seeking closer relationships with suppliers because they recognize the importance of these long-term committed relationships.

Sources: Patricia McInnis, "Partnership in Need of a Rescue," *Computing Canada,* March 12, 2004, p. 12; Allan Lynch, "Secrets of a Super Salesman," *Atlantic Progress,* April 1999, pp. 50, 52.

■   *Need recognition.* **Need recognition** is the first stage of the buying-decision process. Nothing will happen until customers recognize a need: there is a difference between their current situation and their desired state. Need recognition may occur for any of a number

Exhibit 5.3

A General Model of the Customer's Buying Decision Process

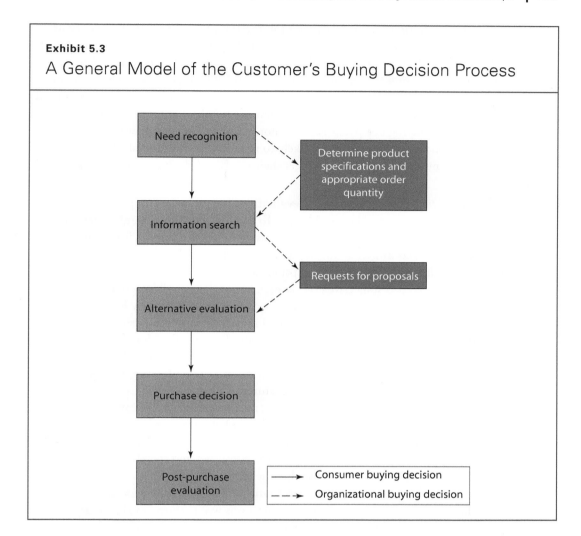

of reasons: products malfunction or become obsolete as technology changes; organization, family, or personal conditions change; new products or processes offer advantages over current ones; expendable items simply get used and must be replaced.

Often customers have needs of which they are unaware. It is the role of marketing and sales to trigger need recognition. One major distinction between consumer and business buying behaviour is what happens immediately following need recognition. Consumers generally proceed immediately to the information search stage, but businesses often more clearly define their specific need and may involve many people in determining product specifications before proceeding further with the buying process.

■ *Information search.* Following need recognition, consumers or businesses will engage in product or vendor **information search**. This search usually begins with an *internal search* of memory for what is known about potential products or vendors and then proceeds to an *external search* if sufficient information is not already available. External search may involve talking to current users of the product or vendor; viewing catalogues, advertisements, and trade directories; searching the internet; visiting trade shows and fairs; and contacting companies and requesting product and price information, including sales presentations and demonstrations. A buyer's search effort is affected by the level of involvement a buyer has in the purchase decision. Buyer involvement increases as a buyer perceives more risk with the purchase decision. There are several types of risk: financial risk if a wrong choice will result in financial loss, functional risk if a wrong choice will not solve the buyer's need, or social risk if other consumers or businesses view the purchase choice as inappropriate. At this stage, business buying behaviour is often more formal than consumer buying behaviour. Organizational customers are more likely to request formal proposals that clearly outline how potential vendors may best meet their needs and the buying conditions they require.

■ *Alternative evaluation.* During **alternative evaluation**, buyers make comparisons among whatever alternatives they may be considering. To do this, they use **evaluative criteria**: objective and subjective characteristics of the product or vendor that are important to the buyer. For example, a consumer about to purchase a new car will likely consider several objective criteria such as price, gas consumption, seating capacity, and safety features. She might also consider several subjective criteria such as styling, overall image of the dealership, and professionalism of the salesperson. Few consumers will actually formalize the evaluation process, but most will consider several important evaluative criteria and will then rank their alternatives based on their assessment of how well each rates against specific criteria. Salespeople can have an impact on a buyer's evaluation by carefully **framing** their offering for them; that is, by describing their offering in a particular way. A salesperson might, for example, describe all of the safety features of a car for the consumer as well as discuss how well the car has performed on independent safety tests. He can also provide some anecdotes of how these features have benefited other customers and what the consequences are of not having these features. In this way, the salesperson tries to increase the importance of safety as a selection criterion for the consumer and thereby increase the probability that the consumer will choose this alternative.

Organizational buyers are more likely to formalize the evaluation process and, at least outwardly, favour objective criteria. Some organizations will perform a **value analysis**—a systematic, formal process to evaluate alternatives—particularly as the differences among alternatives increase. As part of the value analysis, they will consider materials, design, quality, purchase and operating cost, and anything else that might affect the overall cost of acquiring and using the product. Firms sometimes use **vendor analysis**—a systematic, formal process to evaluate potential vendors—to ensure they choose the vendor that performs best on a number of important criteria: price, quality, service, responsiveness, reliability, and financial stability.

■ *Purchase decision.* During the **purchase decision** stage, the terms of sale are negotiated, including final price, delivery method and timing, payment method and credit arrangements, installation and maintenance agreements, warranties and guarantees, etc. Organizational buyers must also decide whether they will place a single order or issue a contract for an extended period of time guaranteeing all such purchases will be made from the winning supplier. Some customers prefer to use **multiple-sourcing** and buy from several suppliers to ensure guaranteed supply in the event of supplier strikes, product shortages, or bankruptcies. Increasingly, however, organizations are employing **sole-sourcing** where they buy all similar products from a single supplier. The increased volume from a single supplier will reduce the buyer's cost while increasing the supplier's total profit, so both companies win. Customers also benefit from having to deal with fewer suppliers, and this often provides the greatest cost improvements: fewer salespeople to see, consolidated shipments of products, better communications, and reduced accounting and financial activity.

■ *Post-purchase evaluation.* Following purchase, buyers are involved in **post-purchase evaluation**. They use many of the same criteria that they used for alternative evaluation to evaluate a purchase decision. The outcomes from this process range from satisfaction at one extreme to dissatisfaction at the other. Results of the evaluation process influence future purchase decisions. Repeat purchase probability increases as satisfaction increases and decreases as satisfaction decreases.

Consumers may experience **cognitive dissonance** following an important purchase. Cognitive dissonance is simply doubt in the buyer's mind whether the correct purchase decision was made. As involvement and risk increase in the purchase decision, so too will cognitive dissonance. Therefore, it will increase as the price of the purchase increases. It will also increase as the number of alternatives increases and as the similarity between the chosen alternative and the next best alternative increases. Salespeople should recognize that this is a common feeling among buyers and should take actions to reduce cognitive dissonance when possible. Actions could include providing written materials about and testimonials for purchased products, phoning the customer following the purchase to reinforce the purchase decision, sending a letter congratulating the customer on the purchase decision, and encouraging the customer to call the salesperson if any concerns arise. Salespeople should recognize that cognitive dissonance also occurs among organizational buyers.

Organizational buyers are increasingly formalizing the post-purchase evaluation process. This has become easy to do as a result of readily available computer capabilities. Buyers increasingly use these formalized evaluations as a basis to open discussions with suppliers and shape their future behaviours. That is, they create the suppliers they want by shaping supplier product offerings, service capabilities, and internal operations to better meet the buyer's needs. This process is referred to as **reverse marketing** and is increasingly used when customers wish to establish long-term partnerships with their suppliers, often reducing the number of suppliers they use.

Guiding Relationship Evolution, Building Trust, and Creating Value

There is greater awareness today of the value of long-term customer relationships. Companies that successfully build closer customer relationships with key customers are rewarded with lower customer defection rates and higher profitability.[8] Salespeople have a key role in establishing and maintaining customer relationships and need to understand how relationships evolve over time—from awareness, to exploration, expansion, and commitment. Descriptions and selling implications for these stages are provided in Exhibit 5.4. The following sections focus on the latter three stages as these distinguish long-term, strategic relationships from mere transactional market exchanges.

Exhibit 5.4

Stages in Buyer–Seller Relationship Evolution

Relationship Stage	Description	Selling Objectives
Exploration	Limited investment by both parties. Transactions tend to be smaller. Stage may extend for a considerable period of time.	1. Close a trial order. 2. Demonstrate capability. 3. Foster trust.
Expansion	Both buyer and seller increase investment in the relationship. Order size and frequency may increase.	1. Sell larger quantities. 2. Sell additional items. 3. Sell higher quality. 4. Continue to foster trust.
Commitment	Both buyers and sellers willing to make increased investments with an expectation of closer, longer-term, and sometimes exclusive relationship.	1. Build closer, longer-term relationships: increased communication, cooperation, and involvement throughout both organizations.

- *Exploration stage.* The **exploration stage** begins with the first transaction between the buyer and seller. Over time and following a number of transactions, the relationship may proceed to a later stage, but it is also possible that a relationship may never get any closer than exploration. During this stage, the buyer and seller gradually develop performance expectations, trust, and personal relationships. The first transactions are critical to the development of long-term relationships. The seller's performance will be carefully monitored during the early transactions to evaluate quality, service, price, and reliability. Following several successful transactions, if the seller fails on some important criterion, the customer may excuse the failure as abnormal behaviour for that supplier. However, failing on one of the earliest transactions may lead the customer to conclude that the supplier is not capable of performing satisfactorily. For this reason, it is important that salespeople establish realistic customer expectations early in a relationship and then meet or, preferably, exceed them. Salespeople should particularly follow up with customers following initial orders to ensure that the customer is satisfied with all aspects of the purchase and that the customer understands how to use and maintain the product or service to receive full benefit from it. If there are problems, the salesperson needs to accept full responsibility and demonstrate commitment to solving problems for the customer. When people other than the buyer are involved with product or service use, salespeople need to ensure that everyone involved is contacted and is entirely satisfied. Research indicates that users may be dissatisfied for a considerable time before decision makers become aware of it.[9]

- *Expansion stage.* Trust continues to develop during the **expansion stage**. Salespeople may increase sales through repeat purchases, often convincing customers to buy increasingly larger volumes from them. Salespeople should recognize that many customers will be unprepared to place substantial business with them until after they have performed satisfactorily during an exploration stage. The exploration stage may continue over several transactions before a customer will expand business for important products or services to a relatively unproven supplier. For this reason, salespeople should strategically plan to grow an account by selling those things that they know customers will value most and that best demonstrate their service capability before attempting to become a preferred supplier.

■ *Commitment stage.* The **commitment stage** is the pinnacle of buyer–seller relationships, when both parties are committed to a long-term working relationship. Sellers benefit from decreased selling costs and increased and assured sales volumes, and customers benefit from supply guarantees and reduced purchasing and administrative costs. Committed customers are reluctant to switch suppliers because of the high level of trust in and satisfaction with them. Research has found that suppliers who can reduce customer turnover by as little as 5 percent can almost double profits.[10]

Salespeople succeed when they achieve increased sales, assuming they are profitable sales. Increased sales must come from new or established accounts. The cost of attracting a new customer is frequently greater than the cost of keeping a current customer, meaning that account profitability is often lower, and possibly negative, early in a relationship. This is further supported by an important study demonstrating that the amount of time spent prospecting for new accounts did not improve sales performance—the amount of time spent with established accounts did.[11] The stages in relationship evolution indicate that customers are unlikely to commit to a new supplier at the beginning of a relationship. Therefore, salespeople should be focused on convincing customers to first explore a relationship with their firm. They should give customers a chance to try their product and service. Following successful early transactions, the salesperson might then focus on guiding the customer through subsequent stages, increasing sales and profitability. The salesperson's ability to do this is dependent on her ability to build customer trust and create value for her customers. The Sales Management in Action box describes how Tenaquip Industrial Equipment and Supplies has been growing its relationship with one important customer.

Trust is important for both establishing relationships and growing accounts. Customers must have trust in both a supplier organization and its salespeople. Trust at the organization level means that a company will meet its commitments; that is, it has the capability to meet or exceed the customer's expectations and it consistently does so. These promises are, however, made most frequently by a salesperson. It is important for the salesperson to be seen as trustworthy in order to get initial sales from a customer. If the organization fails to deliver on the salesperson's promises, this will most likely affect the customer's trust of the salesperson, which is why salespeople must carefully monitor initial orders from an account to ensure that promises are kept and customers are satisfied. The following are some trust-creating attributes of salespeople:

1. *Dependability.* Salespeople must deliver on all promises: appointments, promised deliveries, quality, after-sale service.
2. *Competence.* Salespeople must have product, company, competitor, and industry knowledge. They must understand the selling process and be professional.
3. *Customer orientation.* Salespeople must be able to demonstrate that they are focused on a win–win relationship and that they have the customer's best interests at heart.
4. *Character.* Salespeople must be honest and act with integrity in all their business dealings.

SALES MANAGEMENT IN **ACTION**

Tenaquip Supply Program Provides Tools in Vending Machines

When it first started to become popular in the late 1980s, *partnering* was described as "one of the most profound changes to hit the American industrial marketplace in five decades." Partnering refers to the building of closer, longer-term buyer–seller relationships. Buyers initiated partnering relationships as a way to reduce purchasing costs. Maintenance, repair, and operating (MRO) supplies—such as office and warehouse supplies, safety equipment, cutting tools, electrical and welding supplies, etc.—were logical products to focus on as they were found to account for only 17.5 percent of purchases, but 26.2 percent of purchasing costs. As partnering became more common, progressive sellers recognized the value of selling their capability to partner with customers to help reduce buying costs.

Tenaquip Industrial Equipment and Supplies is one of these progressive companies. Sales manager Mod Baldassarre began his career at Tenaquip as an inside salesperson approximately 20 years ago, shortly after completing a part-time degree in English at McGill University. His first position was inside salesperson. At that time, Tenaquip sold across Canada exclusively through its catalogue of MRO supplies. When the company eventually decided to employ a field sales force, Mod moved to outside sales, and now has 25 inside and six outside salespeople who report to

him at the Montreal office. Tenaquip now sells more than 110 000 products through its catalogue and its eight locations in Quebec and Ontario.

With its ability to sell so many MRO items, Tenaquip is capable of managing integrated supply programs for major customers. These programs require a considerable investment of resources as each program must be tailored to meet specific customer needs. The supply program that Tenaquip has developed with one important customer in Quebec is unique. This customer initially invested in nine vending machines located to dispense fairly expensive cutting tools at strategic locations throughout its manufacturing facilities. Each vending machine holds between 55 and 70 products, and production workers can access tools where and when they are needed. A system records who has taken tools from each machine. Mod Baldassarre says, "These are expensive production tools and our customer cannot afford to be out of stock of any of these items without risking production downtime. We have reduced the customer's costs by taking the entire purchase process from them. We procure, stock, package, and replenish these items for the customer and ensure they always have inventory when and where they need it." The customer now has 13 vending machines and is considering more.

Sources: Mod Baldassarre, interview May 19, 2004; *Industrial Distribution*, "A New Age of Opportunity in the Industrial Marketplace," 78 (April 1988), p. 3; James P. Morgan, "JIT Casts Its Shadow Across MRO," *Purchasing*, May 22, 1986, pp. 52–55.

5. *Likeability.* Salespeople need to be respectful and well mannered, and be able to build rapport with prospects and customers.

These attributes are interindependent. A salesperson highly rated on two or three of these attributes is likely to be highly rated on the other attributes as well. In the final analysis, the deciding factor might simply be whether the customer likes the salesperson. One purchasing agent candidly remarked, "If I don't like you, I won't buy from you. If I do like you, I'll help make sure you have the offer that best meets my needs."

Salespeople who develop trusting relationships create value for customers. Salespeople regularly find that they can compete on product quality, price, and service but still fail to get a customer's business because of the relationship bond between that customer and a competitor. The relationship with the customer may be the only value-added feature that the competitor has, but it may also be the most difficult one to overcome.[12] How salespeople can create value for customers as they manage customer interactions is the focus of Chapter 6. The following section discusses prospecting for and qualifying new accounts.

Prospecting For and Qualifying New Accounts

Prospecting is a systematic process of identifying potential customers. The success that many salespeople achieve today comes from the prospecting they did last week, or even several months ago. Yet, prospecting for customers is one task that most salespeople do not enjoy, and that many ignore or do poorly. Some companies that recognize prospecting's importance to sales success formalize the prospecting requirements so that salespeople must find a specific number of prospects on a regular basis because they know that it takes a certain number of prospects to create a customer.

Good prospecting requires good planning and should be a systematic process. Salespeople such as Joe Girard—arguably "the world's greatest salesperson," and a popular sales trainer— know the value of good prospecting. Joe uses the "Ferris wheel" concept to explain why prospecting is so important. Customers continually get off the Ferris wheel because they die or go bankrupt, acquire or merge with other customers, move to new locations, change technologies or find other suppliers, no longer have a need for a product or service, or simply decide to develop new supplier relationships for any of a number of reasons beyond the salesperson's control. Salespeople need to continually recruit new riders (prospects) for the Ferris wheel to replace those lost to attrition. From shoeshine boy, newsboy, delivery boy, and dishwasher, Joe went on to become the Number 1 car salesperson for each of the 12 consecutive years he sold cars: a record of 174 cars in one month, 1425 cars in one year, and 13 001 cars during his career—and all of them one car at a time (no wholesale, lease, or fleet sales).[13] Great salespeople like Joe know that prospecting is important to their success and use more than one method for prospecting.

FINDING PROSPECTS

Each salesperson should develop a system of prospecting suited to his particular selling situation. For example, a new salesperson may be given a geographic territory and told to "cold call" on every potential prospect in that territory. Established salespeople are more likely to use referrals or networking to find prospects. These and other popular methods of prospecting are now discussed.

- *Cold calling.* **Cold calling** requires salespeople to contact, by phone or in person, each prospective customer among a group of identified prospects. Many new salespeople rely on this method because they do not have an established customer list that they can use for referrals.[14] One large international business solutions company, for example, regularly assigns new sales trainees to large business parks and requires them to "knock on every door." While many salespeople fear making cold calls, it has proven to be a very effective way to prospect for certain products and services. Steven J. Schwartz, president of SJS Productions, Inc., and author of *How to Make Hot Cold Calls,* suggests that all cold calls can be turned into "hot" calls through a telephone contact system that uses careful call planning, strategic message scripting, and effective script delivery.

■ *Referrals.* A **referral** is a prospect who has been recommended by a current customer or by someone familiar with the product or salesperson. Existing customers are the primary source of referrals.[15] A salesperson who successfully sells to a customer may ask for one or more referrals by saying, "Mr. Cormier, now that you fully understand our service, who else do you know who might benefit from it as well?" When the salesperson calls on the referral, he may say, "Miss Zhang, Mr. Cormier at St. Joseph's Hospital has suggested you might benefit from seeing what we have to offer." Salespeople who are adept at managing the referral process may even employ a technique called *endless chain referrals.* These salespeople use each prospect contact to identify new prospects. Note that it is not necessary to successfully sell to a prospect in order to ask them for a referral. Once a customer understands what you offer, they may recognize that, although you cannot meet their needs, you may meet the needs of other prospects they know. Referral cards and letters can also be effective. You may use these with explicit (testimonial) or implied permission. If you can document how your solution has benefited a customer, you can send prospects a letter or card that might say, for example, "Want to know how our company improved operating efficiency at Acme Manufacturing by over 20 percent? Our salesperson, Tony Rykse, will phone you Tuesday morning at 10:15 A.M. to discuss it with you."

■ *Directories, websites, and trade publications.* There are numerous directories available to help salespeople prospect for customers: *The Blue Book of Canadian Business* (top 2 percent of Canada's businesses); *The Canadian Key Business Directory* (top 20 000 businesses); *Canadian Directory of Industrial Distributors* (distributors by product specialty and geographic territory); *Canadian Trade Index* (26 000 manufacturers, service firms, and distributors); *Fraser's Canadian Trade Directory* (350 000 manufacturers, distributors, and agents); *Scott's Directories* (businesses by region; also available on CD-ROM); *Polk City Directory* (1100 individual directories covering 6500 communities in Canada and the United States); *Yellow Pages* (available for all regions of Canada, and also available on the internet at **www.yellowpages.ca**). Other websites that are valuable for prospecting include **www.canada411.ca** and **www.dnb.ca**, as well as any of a number of search engines such as **www.google.ca**. Some salespeople, particularly consultants, use e-newsletters to prospect for clients. These newsletters are sent on a regular basis to interested people and provide valuable tips and information that they hope these prospects will value. Salespeople who serve specific industries may benefit from trade publications that provide information on those industries' problems, innovations, new product solutions, and emerging trends. Some examples of trade publications include *Canada IT, Canadian Plastics Magazine, Women's Wear Daily, Canadian Underwriter, Pulp & Paper Canada, Canadian Grocer,* and *Canada Computers.*

■ *Trade shows and educational seminars.* One of the primary objectives of trade show participation is to make face-to-face contact with purchasing decision makers and key influencers. Barry Siskind, Canada's foremost trade show authority, says that when trade shows are carefully selected, they provide an opportunity to contact more targeted people more quickly than can be done by any other marketing method. Trade show managers recognize the value trade shows offer to participants as a venue for generating sales leads and are increasingly incorporating lead retrieval systems in their shows. When visitors to the shows register, contact information is collected and card readers available at participating booths read this information, which can then be supplemented with additional manually collected information on decision-making authority, budgets, needs and priorities, and likely timing of purchases. Research from the Center for Exhibition Industry Research found the cost of closing sales leads generated at a trade show to be 56 percent less than leads generated in the field.[16] Unfortunately, according to Siskind, nearly 80 percent of leads generated at trade shows are not followed up properly.[17]

Selling seminars provide an opportunity to attract specific target customers and showcase products or services. Charon Systems, Inc., a Toronto-based systems integrator, regularly organizes seminars for up to 100 technology people from target firms. President David Fung estimates that 25 percent of participants become clients.[18] Polaroid Canada, IBM, Microsoft, and Xerox have also used selling seminars at many Canadian locations.[19] Banks, investment firms, accounting firms, consultants, and wine merchants all use seminar selling to find prospects.

■ *Networking.* Simply put, **networking** is people meeting people and benefiting from the personal connections. Barry Siskind, author of *Making Contact,* describes networking as a three-act process: in act one, you approach a person and engage them; in act two, you "netchat," quickly collecting as much information from the other person as you can, but providing information about yourself to them as well when appropriate; in act three, you disengage from the other person so you can continue to network with others. Networking skills are important especially for new salespeople who do not have a large base of satisfied customers for referrals.

QUALIFYING PROSPECTS

Good salespeople recognize that all prospects do not provide the same opportunities and they become adept at assessing the likelihood of turning a particular prospect into a satisfied customer. The process of assessing prospect opportunities is called **qualifying the prospect**. Salespeople need to determine the answers to four questions:

1. Does the prospect have a *need* for my product or service?
2. Does the prospect have the *authority* to buy my product or service?
3. Does the prospect have the *financial resources* to buy my product or service?
4. Does the prospect have the *willingness* to buy my product or service?

If a salesperson determines that a prospect does not need her product or service, she should discontinue the qualifying process and allocate her time where there may be greater opportunity. If a need is established, then she should determine that she is talking to someone with the authority to make the purchase decision. Salespeople who do not do this often find they waste considerable time and increase the difficulty of getting to the real decision maker at some later point in the sales cycle without offending their initial prospect. Once authority is established, the salesperson needs to determine that the prospect can pay for the product or service. To encourage responsibility for establishing ability to pay, some companies pay commissions after customers pay their invoices, and may require that salespeople support the accounts receivable department with credit collection if problems arise. Even when prospects meet these first three conditions, some prospects may be unwilling to make a purchase decision. Sometimes customers will withhold purchase decisions because of expected future economic or market conditions. If this is the case, the salesperson should find out when would be a more appropriate time for the purchase, and follow up as that time approaches. In other instances, the prospect may simply be buying from a salesperson's competitor and may be unwilling to change suppliers.

Managing a Portfolio of Accounts

Sales managers today are becoming more focused on profitability than sales, and this means that the size and number of accounts is more carefully considered. Too many customers drain a company's resources so that too little effort can be focused on accounts with the best opportunities. This is a particular problem when salespeople spend too much effort on accounts that have limited potential. Sierra Wireless of Richmond, B.C., had a problem with too many small, demanding, and price-sensitive customers. CEO David Sutcliffe gave them information on his competitors. He said, "I know they're thinking I'm out of my mind. But if your competitors are so busy choking on those small orders, you can focus on and win the more profitable opportunities."[20]

WHEN IS AN ACCOUNT TOO SMALL?

Salespeople must decide which accounts deserve their personal attention, how often they should visit each account, and which accounts they should ignore or sell by some method other than personal selling. A good place to start is to calculate a **break-even sales volume per sales call**. This will require two pieces of information: an estimate of the cost to make a sales call, and an estimate of the salesperson's target direct selling expenses as a percentage of sales. **Direct selling expenses** include compensation, travel and entertainment, samples and promotional materials, and communications. These are referred to as direct selling expenses because they are attributable to a specific salesperson and the company would not have incurred these expenses if the salesperson were not employed. Exhibit 5.5 illustrates how to estimate a cost per sales call.

Determining the direct selling expenses as a percentage of sales is more complicated than it might at first seem. It would be very easy to simply take the total direct selling expenses we calculated in Exhibit 5.5 and express this as a percentage of that salesperson's total sales. Unfortunately, this would make the break-even sales volume sensitive to costs related to the performance of that particular salesperson. It may be better to have management provide a target for selling expenses as a percentage of sales, leaving the management of actual selling expenses and sales performance to the salesperson and the sales manager. Sales costs as a percentage of sales can vary greatly depending on industry; however, looking at the industry average is a good place to start.

Once the information is available, it is a simple exercise to use the following formula:

$$\text{Break-even sales volume per sales call} = \frac{\text{Cost per sales call}}{\text{Target direct selling expenses as a percentage of sales}}$$

$$= \frac{\$196.49}{0.08}$$

$$= \$2456.13$$

What does this mean? The salesperson must generate $2456.13 per sales call in order to cover her direct selling expenses. She could call on an account once per month and cover her direct selling expenses if the account purchases this sales volume per month. If this salesperson were to call

---

Exhibit 5.5

Calculating a Salesperson's Cost Per Sales Call

Compensation		
Salary, commissions, and bonus	$77 500	
Fringe benefits (EI, CPP, medical, pension, etc.)	12 400	
		$ 89 900
Direct selling expenses		
Automobile	$ 10 420	
Travel and entertainment	32 400	
Communications	2 300	
Samples, promotional materials	1 475	
Other	1 050	
		47 645
Total direct selling expenses		$137 545
Days worked 2004 =		
(days available – vacation, paid holidays,		
training days, sick days) =	200 days	
Average number of calls per day =	3.5 calls	
Total number of sales calls 2004 (200 × 3.5)	700 calls	
Average cost per sales call ($137 545 / 700)		$ 196.49

---

on this same account 10 times per year, she would have to generate sales of $24 561.30 to cover her direct selling expenses.

Should the salesperson stop calling on an account because the sales from that account do not cover her direct selling expenses? This requires judgment of the account's long-term potential. It is often necessary to invest time and effort to develop an account. An account may not be profitable early in a relationship. Some accounts may also pay higher prices as a result of the specific products they purchase or because they buy in smaller quantities, and they therefore provide a higher gross margin, which means they can be profitable at lower sales levels. Sometimes, an account may simply be conveniently located or can be a source of valuable information for the salesperson. An unidentified salesperson for an industrial distributor related the following example:

> One of my best customers is a pulp mill and one of my favourite customers is a small machine shop located near it. I call on them both every four weeks although the sales at the machine shop would suggest I should call there three or four times a year at most. However, all of the costs of making the call other than my time are necessary to visit the pulp mill. The owner of the machine shop likes to see me at 8:00 A.M., just after his workers have been allocated their daily work and he needs a coffee. No one at the mill wants to see me that early so it would be wasted time for me otherwise. During coffee, I often get information on what the machine shop is doing for the pulp mill and what is being quoted for the future, so I know more about the mill and can discuss this with appropriate people at the mill when I get there. Finally, I always get an order from the machine shop. Even if it is a small order, it's a positive start to my day.

It is also possible to allocate junior salespeople to smaller, unprofitable accounts when they are first hired as it provides them with some field experience and training before they are given responsibility for more important accounts. In such a situation, any losses a company incurs could be considered a training expense.

Determining the break-even sales volume per call is helpful information, but salespeople often must allocate a scarce resource (their time) across many accounts that vary in both size and growth opportunity. **Account analysis** refers to estimating sales potential for each prospect and customer in a sales territory. It is a necessary step before deciding how to allocate sales calls across accounts. There are several ways to do this and the most popular ones are now discussed.

SINGLE-FACTOR MODELS

The most commonly used method of allocating sales calls across accounts is referred to as the A–B–C account classification method. This is a **single-factor model** of account classification because accounts are classified based on a single factor, most commonly sales. Exhibit 5.6 illustrates how this account classification works.

Many companies identify their top accounts and determine the percentage of sales from these accounts. In this example, the top 10 percent of accounts generate $961 000, or 50 percent of total sales in the territory. This would be fairly typical of many companies as most find the top 10 percent of their accounts generate 30–60 percent of sales revenue. Also typical, most companies find that a large percentage of their smallest accounts generate a disproportionately smaller percentage of total sales. In this example, the smallest 60 percent of accounts generate only 20 percent of total sales.

After estimating her break-even per sales call, the salesperson can think about allocating her 700 available annual sales calls across her 120 accounts, recognizing that (1) she needs $2456.13 in sales per sales call to cover her direct selling expenses, and (2) she will need to keep some percentage of available sales calls to call on prospects who are not currently included in her base of 120 customers. Further, there is an upper limit to the number of calls that should be made to any one account, either because increasing sales calls will not contribute a marginal increase in sales to cover the cost of the additional calls or because customers will not see the value of increased calls and will be unwilling to commit the time to the salesperson.

Now the salesperson can begin to think about allocating calls across account classifications. She might decide, for example, to call on 'A' accounts once each month, 'B' accounts bimonthly, and 'C' accounts two times per year. She will have allocated 504 sales calls (12 × 12 calls + 36 × 6 calls + 72 × 2 calls), and this leaves 196 calls that she could use to make calls on prospective customers.

Exhibit 5.6

A–B–C Account Classification

Account Classification	Accounts (n)	Accounts (%)	Sales ($000)	Sales (%)	Sales per Account ($000)
A	12	10	961	50	80.1
B	36	30	577	30	16.0
C	72	60	384	20	5.3

Using the A–B–C account classification method has several advantages. It is easy to understand and communicate. It provides some consistency with respect to how accounts of different sizes are managed both within a territory and across territories. To some degree it allocates effort to where there is greater opportunity while ensuring that sufficient resources are allocated to the largest and most demanding accounts, and the ones that would likely be the most targeted by competitors. Finally, it can help new or inexperienced sales managers control activities within a sales force because the resource allocations are based on objective data.

One disadvantage of this method is that it treats all accounts within a category the same, when there sometimes are only minor differences between the larger accounts in one category and the smaller accounts in another category. For example, the largest 'C' account may be virtually the same size as the smallest 'B' account, yet this method would suggest that one be seen three times as often as the other. A second disadvantage is that the classifications are based on past sales data and therefore ignore account opportunity. Some accounts could generate increased sales volume with increased effort. Both of these disadvantages can be somewhat overcome by allowing salespeople leeway in deciding how to allocate their sales calls within categories. For example, this salesperson has 36 'B' accounts and can make a total of 216 calls on these accounts. The smaller of these accounts may not require six calls per year, and the larger ones may require more than six calls per year. Other factors such as geographic location, customer wishes, and competitive activity may need to be considered at each account as well. Allowing the salesperson to allocate her 216 calls among these 36 accounts will ensure a better allocation of effort than simply treating all accounts the same.

USING PORTFOLIO MODELS

A **portfolio model** is somewhat more complicated as multiple factors are considered when classifying accounts and a critical assessment of many accounts may be needed before they can be allocated to one of the account classifications. Portfolio models usually include four cells, although it is possible to develop six-cell or nine-cell models as well. Exhibit 5.7 illustrates a typical four-cell model based on overall account opportunity for the seller and the selling firm's ability to capitalize on these opportunities; that is, its competitive strength.

Portfolio models are more subjective than single-factor models. They become even more difficult if there is disagreement concerning how to define account opportunity or competitive position. For example, account opportunity might simply be an assessment of the potential sales volume that the account could generate. However, it could also be a weighted composite of current sales, growth potential, and gross margin. Competitive position could be an estimate of the share of the account's purchases that are made from the selling firm, or could be determined by an assessment of the number and types of relationships the account has with competing firms, the account's attitude toward the selling firm, how well the selling firm's products meet the specific needs of the account, etc. While implementing this type of model is often difficult, one of its real strengths is that it does provide a framework to facilitate communication between sales managers and salespeople so that they can develop improved strategies for allocating sales calls across accounts within each territory.

Portfolio models are most effective where a sales force must understand individual customer needs and where relationship strength is important to sales success.

Exhibit 5.7

Portfolio Model of Accounts

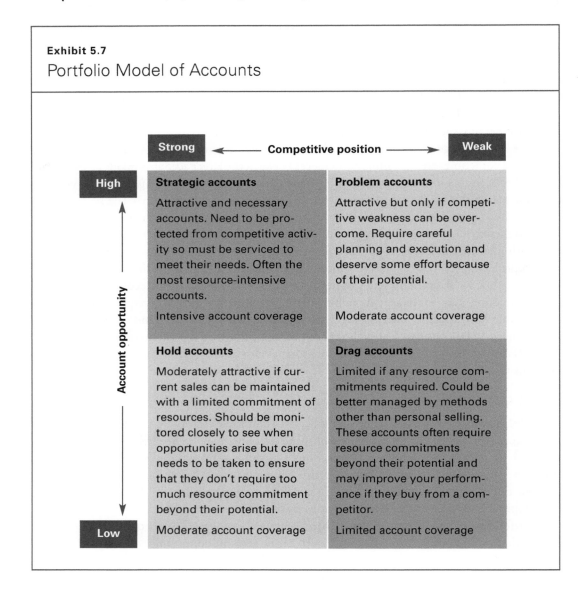

DECISION MODELS

Decision models attempt to determine the optimum allocation of sales calls across accounts. These models comprise two stages. First, a **sales call response function** must be estimated for each account in a sales territory: this is the relationship between the number of sales calls and actual sales. This may be done through regression analysis if there is sufficient data available, but is more commonly done judgmentally. Salespeople are given information concerning the number of calls and sales at each account in a previous period. They are then asked, for each account, what the impact on sales would be if sales calls were increased or decreased. Exhibit 5.8 shows a typical sales call response function. Making one or two calls on this account will produce only a

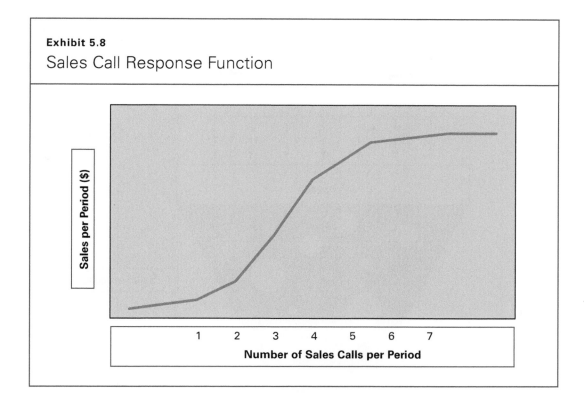

Exhibit 5.8
Sales Call Response Function

(Y-axis: Sales per Period ($); X-axis: Number of Sales Calls per Period, labeled 1 through 7)

small sales volume. Calls three, four, and five result in a reasonable sales increase; however, smaller increases in sales result with additional sales effort.

The second stage considers all of the individual sales response functions and then allocates sales calls where they will result in the largest increase in sales. Because this is a complex mathematical task, it is usually done with computer-based models that are generally simple to learn and use. In Exhibit 5.8, for example, rather than continuing to allocate additional sales calls to this account, a decision model might allocate this sixth or seventh sales call to another account where it would generate a greater volume of sales.

SALES PROCESS MODELS

A **sales process model** classifies accounts based on where they are in the sales process. For example, an account might be simply a prospect, ready for a formal sales presentation, in serious negotiations with the salesperson, or nearly ready to place an order. Where an account is in the sales process has implications for if and when the salesperson will be able to close the sale. One popular sales process model is the sales funnel, illustrated in Exhibit 5.9.

The sales cycle for complex technical sales might be several months in duration. Insurance salespeople know they need to contact a large number of people to gain permission to make a smaller number of presentations, to make an even smaller number of sales. In these selling situations, it is important that salespeople balance a portfolio of accounts that are at various stages of the selling process. This means that salespeople must ensure that sufficient prospects are regularly

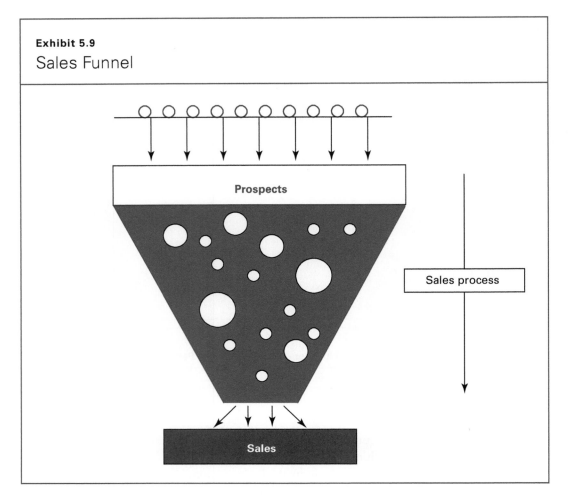

Exhibit 5.9

Sales Funnel

added to the funnel so that it does not become empty. The quality of the prospects added to the funnel and the ability of the salesperson to manage the sales process will affect the number of sales opportunities that are successfully closed. Salespeople need to ensure that they "work" the whole funnel so that it is always in balance. They should work on sales opportunities near the bottom of the funnel first; that is, close those that are near the end of the sales process. Then, they should work on the top of the funnel; that is, add new prospects. Prospecting is an activity that many salespeople dislike, but if it is not given sufficient attention there is a real danger that the funnel will empty. Finally, salespeople should work on those opportunities that are in the sales process, moving them along through the funnel and ensuring there are regular, predictable sales over time.[21] We have indicated the size of each sales opportunity by the size of the circle that represents it in Exhibit 5.9. Salespeople should consider not only where sales opportunities are in the sales process, but also the size of the sale that will result if the opportunity is successfully closed.

Sales process models are valuable tools for opening the lines of communication between sales managers and salespeople. They also improve a sales manager's ability to diagnose where a salesperson might need to increase activity to improve sales performance.

SUMMARY

1. **Describe three types of buyer–seller relationships.** Transactional relationships are based on meeting the needs of price-sensitive customers who seek price or convenience, with little expectation of relationship continuity. Consultative relationships involve two-way communication, bilateral problem solving, and considerable negotiation between the two parties so that each gains from the relationship. Partnering—or enterprise—relationships are focused on the long term and frequently involve considerable resource commitment by both parties.

2. **Describe three buying situations that customers face.** Customers face three buying situations: new task buy, modified rebuy, and straight rebuy. These are distinguished by the customer's experience level and the amount of risk the customer perceives in the purchase decision. Therefore, the buying situation will have an effect on the customer's buying-decision process.

3. **Explain the buying centre concept and who may be included in it.** The buying centre comprises all of the people who are involved in the buying decision. At various stages of the buying-decision process, members may enter or exit the buying centre. Common buying centre roles include the user buyer, the technical buyer, the economic buyer, the advocate, and the gatekeeper. One person may fill several roles, and several people may fill one role.

4. **Explain the customer buying-decision process.** The customer buying-decision process begins with the need recognition stage when the customer recognizes there is a difference between their current situation and their desired state. It progresses through several other stages: information search, alternative evaluation, purchase decision, and post-purchase evaluation. The time and effort that a customer will devote to any particular stage depends on the buying situation that the customer faces and the importance of a particular decision for the customer.

5. **Explain three stages in relationship evolution.** Three stages in relationship evolution are the exploration, expansion, and commitment stages. While relationships will not necessarily progress through all stages, and some relationships may cycle backwards, it is normal for buyers and sellers to increase commitment gradually as they become accustomed to each other's capabilities and processes. Customers may place a trial order and, if satisfied, expand their business with a supplier. The pinnacle relationship stage is commitment, where both buyers and sellers invest in long-term relationships as they recognize mutual advantage.

6. **Explain prospecting and qualifying and why they are important.** Prospecting is a systematic process of identifying potential customers. Prospects become qualified prospects when a salesperson has determined that they meet four conditions: they have an identified need, they have the authority to purchase, they have the ability to pay, and they have a willingness to buy. It is important that salespeople continually prospect and qualify prospects to continue to grow business, or to replace customers who have for any of a number of reasons stopped buying from the salesperson.

7. **Explain how to determine when an account is too small.** An account is too small when the sales it generates are not enough to cover the costs required to sell to that account. Alternatives are to ignore the account; to explore other, less costly ways to sell to the account; or to reduce the number of sales calls made to the account, thereby reducing the cost of handling the account.

8. **Describe how to allocate sales effort across a portfolio of accounts.** The single-factor model allocates sales calls on the basis of past sales. This model is popular and works well in stable territories, but it ignores future account potential. For this reason, some companies have begun using portfolio models that consider more than one factor when classifying accounts to categories. These are more subjective but provide an excellent basis to open communications between sales managers and salespeople. There are also various decision models and sales process models that can be used to allocate sales effort across a portfolio of accounts.

KEY TERMS

account relationship strategy **120**

transactional relationships **121**

consultative relationships **122**

partnering relationships **122**

new task buy **123**

modified rebuy **123**

straight rebuy **124**

buying centre **124**

user buyers **124**

technical buyers **124**

economic buyers **125**

advocate **125**

gatekeeper **125**

buying-decision process **125**

need recognition **126**

information search **127**

alternative evaluation **128**

evaluative criteria **128**

framing **128**

value analysis **128**

vendor analysis **128**

purchase decision **128**

multiple-sourcing **128**

sole-sourcing **128**

post-purchase evaluation **129**

cognitive dissonance **129**

reverse marketing **129**

exploration stage **130**

expansion stage **130**

commitment stage **131**

prospecting **133**

cold calling **133**

referral **134**

networking **135**

qualifying the prospect **135**

break-even sales volume per sales call **136**

direct selling expenses **136**

account analysis **138**

single-factor model **138**

portfolio model **139**

sales call response function **140**

sales process model **141**

REVIEW QUESTIONS

1. Consider the three types of relationships discussed in this chapter: transactional, consultative, and partnering relationships. Describe the conditions under which each of these relationship strategies would be appropriate for a sales organization.

2. Explain how the buying situation that an organization faces (new task buy, modified rebuy, or straight rebuy) might affect the composition of the buying centre and the customer's buying-decision process.

3. Explain how the composition of the buying centre might differ when each of the following purchases is being considered.
   a. a new textbook for a sales management course
   b. 50 new computers for a student computer lab
   c. chicken feed for a very large, professionally managed chicken farm
   d. a new chair for the office secretary
   e. services of a sales training consultant
   f. a new family automobile

4. Describe appropriate selling objectives for each stage of relationship evolution.

5. List and explain five trust-creating attributes of salespeople.

6. What is meant by "qualifying the prospect"? What four questions must you answer to qualify a prospect?

7. You made an average of 5 sales calls per day and sold for 200 days per year. Your direct selling expenses for the year were $150 000. You visited Ankar's Machine Shop 24 times last year and Ankar placed a total of $3750 business with you. Your direct selling expenses as a percentage of sales were 10 percent. Should you make 24 sales calls on this account next year? What other alternatives do you have?

8. Compare and contrast single-factor models and portfolio models of account classification. What are the strengths and weaknesses of each and when is each appropriate?

9. Sales managers frequently find that as few as 20 percent of their customers can account for as much as 80 percent of their sales. However, one sales manager was recently overheard to say, "I'm sure that 20 percent of my customers create 120 percent of my profit." What did he mean? If you were this sales manager, what would you do?

10. What is meant by a sales process model? For what types of selling situations are they most appropriate? Explain how a salesperson would use one.

APPLICATION EXERCISES

1. Interview a buyer for a local manufacturer. Ask the buyer about a recent straight rebuy and either a modified rebuy or a new task buy that was made. Write a report explaining how the buying-decision process differed for the two purchases. Explain how a salesperson could benefit from knowing this information.

2. Visit a car dealership of your choice. Interview a salesperson and determine what the dealership does to reduce a customer's cognitive dissonance after a purchase has been made. Does the salesperson himself specifically do anything to reduce it? What suggestions can you offer that might improve either the dealership's or the salesperson's performance in this respect?

3. Write a report describing how your relationship with your college or university has evolved, beginning with the exploration stage. Have you reached the commitment stage yet? Explain. What behaviours would indicate that you have reached the commitment stage?

4. You have just been hired to replace a veteran salesperson and have been given his territory, a large industrial park and the area surrounding it, which, in total, comprises approximately 500 businesses. Your sales manager has told you to spend the first week planning how you will manage your territory. She has asked you to present your plan to her on Friday afternoon before making your first call on Monday morning. This is your first sales job and you want to impress her. Explain what you will do during your first week.

CASE 5.1   Eastern Canada Pulp & Paper

Tony Hartmann was making one of his regular weekly calls to Eastern Canada Pulp & Paper. It was his largest single account. However, Tony was continually frustrated trying to get the mill to order valve and pump packing from him. Tony recalled the conversation that had taken place in Joe Yu's office during his last visit. Joe was the senior buyer for the mill operations.

TH: "Morning, Joe. Glad to see you again," Tony extended his hand.

JY: "Tuesday. I can always count on you. What's on your agenda today?" They shook hands.

TH: "I would like to explore the possibility of getting your valve and pump packing. You know we just signed an agreement to represent a major Canadian packing manufacturer."

JY: "Yes. But you know that Scott Wiebe, our maintenance foreman, has been using the same packing for decades and he's very happy with the quality and service we get from your competitor."

TH: "But they are several hundred kilometres from here and they bring their packing in from the U.S. What happens if you need something in a hurry?"

JY: "Not a problem. We have lots of inventory they consign to us and their salesperson checks it every month and then simply invoices us for what we have used."

TH: "How about price?"

JY: "We do pay a premium, I know. But we justify it based on quality and the service we get."

TH: "I am confident we have an exact equivalent for every item you are currently buying and we can certainly guarantee excellent service. We'll carry everything you use in inventory."

JY: "I don't know. If I make a change to save a few thousand dollars and your packing fails and Scott has to come in to solve a problem at 3:00 A.M. or we have to shut down production, I'll certainly not be popular. You will need to get Scott to agree to a change first before I'll change."

TH: "So, if I can get Scott to agree to using our packing, you will change?"

JY: "No. But I will consider it."

TH: "What else is there to consider?"

JY: "Well, we do give you nearly $400 000 in business each year. We spend only $20 000 annually for packing. If we stop buying from your competitor, he will have no reason to visit us. There is little else we can buy from him. We really enjoy seeing him when he visits. He's always cheerful and puts everyone here in a good mood for the rest of the day. I'd hate to take the business away from him."

TH: "I know that packing is a relatively unimportant purchase for you, but it is very important to us so that we get established with our supplier, and you use more packing than any other customer in my territory."

JY: "Talk to Scott. No commitment, but I will at least talk to you if you get Scott to agree."

With that, Tony had left. He had tried many times over the next few months to talk to Scott. The few times he'd succeeded, Scott had always listened and said he would consider it. But, Tony had never been able to get any commitment beyond that.

Today, Tony decided, he would focus on safety footwear because he'd heard that the mill was going to standardize on their safety boots and simply offer all employees a selection of five or six styles. Tony's company represented a Canadian manufacturer and was one of two distributors that sold safety footwear to the mill.

Joe entered the waiting area and greeted Tony. "Come into my office," Joe motioned and Tony followed. "I have some good news for you today."

Tony smiled. "I'm always glad to hear that. What's up?"

"We are going to standardize our safety footwear program and you will be our exclusive supplier. Your sales of safety boots will double next year," Joe continued.

Tony grinned. "Wow! That's great. What brought this on?"

Joe said, "Mostly a need to rationalize our supplier base. Head office wants me to reduce the number of suppliers we buy from by 50 percent within the next year. Also, your competitor's boots come from the U.S. and the recent devaluation of the Canadian dollar has made them considerably more expensive. I also want to talk to you about your valve and pump packing."

"I've been trying to get Scott to consider us and he says he will but nothing has happened yet," Tony responded.

Joe ignored Tony's remark. "Well, let's start with pricing and then we'll discuss what you are prepared to do to ensure we always have inventory when we need it." Can you get me a list of equivalents and prices by next week and be prepared to discuss inventory issues with us?"

CRITICAL-THINKING QUESTIONS

1. What buying centre roles were being filled by Joe Yu and Scott Wiebe? How might these roles be changing in the future? Explain.

2. How might Tony Hartmann use this information to help him sell valve and pump packing to this customer?

Leisure Lady Lingerie   CASE 5.2

Cindy Leitch was somewhat apprehensive as she left work Thursday evening. She had been hired as a territory account manager for Leisure Lady Lingerie and had started work on Monday of that week. The first days were spent at head office—meeting with human resources people and senior management; touring the manufacturing and warehouse operations; making sales calls with a local salesperson; and learning about company culture and policies, and procedures that salespeople were to follow when placing orders, preparing call reports, and otherwise operating within their designated sales territories. As she had been about to exit the building, Tim Betts, the national sales manager, had been just entering. "I hope you enjoyed today, Cindy. Tomorrow is your last day before you fly home and begin to make sales calls on your own customers. I'll give you a few months and then I'll come out to your territory to make some calls with you." Tim had smiled, then added, "I've got a special task for you tomorrow, so try to get a good rest tonight."

Unsure how to answer, Cindy had simply smiled and said, "Certainly. I'm looking forward to it." Now she was wondering what *it* was.

When she met with Tim the following morning, he surprised her with a computer printout summarizing account activity in her territory the previous year. (See Table 1.) "You have 150 active accounts in your territory. There are also 30 to 40 inactive accounts that bought from us previously but not last year. Why they are inactive, I can't say. Some may have just stopped buying from us and some may be bankrupt. According to research we have done on your territory, there are approximately 380 retailers that sell the types of products we manufacture and that are potential accounts. I would like you to review this territory information and prepare a general sales call plan for me."

"Are there any assumptions I should make or guidelines I should consider?" asked Cindy.

"I would say you should call on every account at least once each year and your best accounts twice a month. Assume you will be selling 200 days next year and you know the company average is 4.5 sales calls per day. Can you prepare a sales call plan for me by noon? I'll buy lunch if you can."

Cindy laughed, "You'll buy lunch anyway. If you don't pay for it, you'll see it on my expense account. I'll see you at noon."

TABLE 1

Summary Account Information	
Accounts	**Total Sales**
Top 10	$300 200
Next 10	180 500
Next 10	164 200
Next 20	135 600
Next 20	128 800
Next 20	99 300
Next 30	135 210
Last 30	53 460

CRITICAL-THINKING QUESTIONS

1. Prepare a sales call plan for Cindy's territory and be prepared to defend it.

2. What other recommendations would you advise Cindy to make to Tim Betts?

Chapter 6

Enhancing Customer Interactions

LEARNING OBJECTIVES

After completing this chapter, you should be able to

1. Describe three selling approaches that are used by salespeople today.

2. Describe five prerequisites to successful selling.

3. Explain the skills involved in the pre-contact phase.

4. Explain the skills involved in the face-to-face interaction phase.

5. Explain the skills involved in the post-sale phase.

Who wants to be a salesperson? If your instructor asked your class this question, you should not be surprised if only a few hands went up. However, if you were to check where most of your classmates got jobs after they graduated, or where they ended up 10 years after graduation, you would mostly likely be surprised at the number who had developed successful selling careers. That's because sales careers provide advantages over many other careers that college and university graduates initially consider.

When Brenda Fisher graduated with a B.Ed., she intended to have a teaching career. Unable to get a teaching job, she eventually got a pharmaceutical sales position with Janssen-Ortho Inc. She now enjoys an income considerably higher than she would have, had she successfully gotten a teaching position. At the same time, she enjoys the job flexibility she has as she works at her professional sales career while managing her young family.[1] Susan Green, now a real estate broker in New Glasgow, Nova Scotia, actually spent 10 years as a teacher. She does not regret her decision either. Susan says, "I have more freedom to be creative and I'm financially much better off. I love this business. Many people think that real estate is about selling houses, but it's really about providing service to clients, both buyers and sellers."[2]

Many people start their sales careers very early. Jim Pattison, who describes himself as "having no other skills except as a salesman," now owns the third-largest privately owned company in Canada, with more than 25 000 employees and $5 billion in revenue. He started selling garden seeds, then pots and pans, door to door.[3] Joe Murphy, now retired from Xerox Canada, began selling knives and cutlery door to door before he was hired by Xerox, where he became one of the company's most respected salespeople. Joe eventually got responsibility for a single account that was very important to his company—Memorial University of Newfoundland. "Joe Xerox," as he became known there, managed the account so well for over 20 years that when he retired, the university threw him a retirement party and gave him a "retirement certificate" recognizing the outstanding service he had provided to them over his career. The certificate was even signed by the university's president.[4]

Three Selling Approaches

There are really three approaches that are used by salespeople today. The door-to-door sales made by Jim Pattison and Joe Murphy, described in the opening vignette, are examples of transactional selling. Successful real estate salespeople, such as Susan Green and the agents who work for her, must be skilled at consultative selling. Joe Murphy would be skilled at consultative selling as well, as this approach is mastered by Xerox salespeople. The ability that Joe Murphy demonstrated at managing his one major account also demonstrates his skill at relationship selling. Relationship selling does not replace consultative selling, but enhances it when conditions are right for developing close, collaborative relations with customers. These three selling approaches are now described in greater detail.

TRANSACTIONAL SELLING

The **transactional selling approach**, the most traditional selling approach, is still applicable today when either of two conditions exists. First, the salesperson has a limited product offering and uses a relatively scripted sales presentation to "push" products on customers. In this instance, the salesperson has no interest in maintaining a relationship with the customer. He wants to complete a sales transaction and then simply proceed to another prospect, common in door-to-door selling. Second, the salesperson is attempting to sell to customers who see the product or service as having little differentiation among suppliers, and who are not interested in long-term supplier relationships. In this instance, the customer makes individual purchase decisions based on price and convenience each time a need arises. The salesperson who tries to create value for these customers, or to build long-term relationships with them, will often waste his time.

CONSULTATIVE SELLING

The **consultative selling approach**, the foundation for selling in many of today's sales organizations, dates back to the late 1960s. The consultative salesperson views the customer as central to the sales process, and the customer's satisfaction is the salesperson's ultimate goal. The consultative salesperson sees herself as a consultant to the customer. She must assess customer needs early in the process, and to do this, the salesperson must be skilled at asking appropriate questions. Note that this will require considerable two-way communication between the salesperson and the buyer. The salesperson must be a good listener in order to understand the buyer's problem completely, from the buyer's perspective. Then, she must select and offer a solution that meets the buyer's needs. This approach requires that the salesperson invest more time and effort in managing the sales process and is therefore appropriate only when customers are willing to invest in the process as well.

The previous discussion suggests two conditions that are necessary for consultative selling to be used successfully. First, due to the increased allocation of resources by both the salesperson and the customer, the product or service being sold must have a significant dollar value, either from the initial sale or from the opportunity to sell or service additional future needs. Second, the fact that the salesperson must completely understand the customer's needs suggests that different customers will have different needs. Hence, the salesperson must be able to tailor customized solutions to meet each customer's needs.

RELATIONSHIP SELLING

The **relationship selling approach** has become more prominent as both salespeople and customers now recognize the value of closer, longer-term buyer–seller relationships. Customers are often the impetus for this type of selling. Some customers need highly customized product solutions that may require many people from the seller's firm to interact with many people within their firm to design the correct product or service solution to meet their specific needs. Even then, the customer may require long-term maintenance or servicing, or upgrades, from the seller. Some customers need guaranteed inventory and quick supply of less complex supplies, such as MRO (maintenance, repair, and operating) supplies. In these instances, sellers agree to maintain inventories of specific items for customers, and to deliver them when and as needed by these customers. Salespeople may also attempt to focus on relationship selling when the products or services they sell have become commoditized—that is, viewed as being very similar by customers so that there is little opportunity to sell based on specific features. In these instances, for many customers, relationships become more important than products. As the ability to differentiate based on product solutions diminishes, salespeople may find increased opportunities to differentiate themselves based on their ability to establish and build long-term relationships.

There is no selling approach that is best under all conditions, for all companies. Some companies may use a single selling approach. Other companies may require that salespeople be proficient using all three approaches, selecting the approach to use based upon what specifically is being sold, the dollar value of the transaction or the potential long-term dollar value of the account, and the needs of the particular customer. For example, a salesperson for a transportation services company may call on one account where the buyer wishes to send a shipment from Montreal to Regina. For this customer, this is a reasonably infrequent transaction, delivery time may not be critical, and all road transportation companies are viewed as being the same. In this instance, success for the salesperson will likely be determined by how low he can price the delivery service. A second customer may be wishing to import products from Central Europe and have them delivered to several distribution centres in Canada. The salesperson will have to determine what exactly is being shipped, what it will weigh and what is its value, how it will be packaged and if there is some flexibility in the packaging of the shipment, and what part of the shipment will go to each location. Then, the salesperson will be in a position to design what will most likely be an intermodal delivery system that will incorporate the use of road, rail, and ocean transportation. The salesperson who can best assess the buyer's needs and then best meet those needs will likely get the account. This customer now has a base solution and can negotiate future shipments with other transportation companies based on whether they can improve on the intermodal transportation system, or offer either a better price or faster service. Other companies, however, may have many shipments originating from many places but requiring deliveries in various sizes to various locations within Canada. The selection of a single transportation company may prove beneficial for these companies if they want a close working relationship with a supplier that will help them solve both current and future transportation requirements.

A salesperson's success will depend on his ability to match the appropriate selling approach to the customer and situation. There are other things as well that will help determine success. Important personality traits and behaviours are discussed in later chapters on recruiting and selecting, training, and motivating and compensating salespeople. The next section of this chapter will focus on five prerequisites to successful selling.

Prerequisites to Professional Selling Success

Success in selling does not just happen. Being successful requires considerable strategy planning before a sales call is made, effective use of face-to-face interaction practices during a sales call, and, often, long-term relationship management through appropriate follow-up and servicing activities. The strategic/consultative selling model, shown in Exhibit 6.1, features five strategic steps, each based on three prescriptions. The next sections will discuss each of the five strategic steps.

YOUR PERSONAL SELLING PHILOSOPHY

Successful salespeople must develop their own **personal selling philosophy**. First, they must value personal selling. Companies are making increasing investments in personal selling in response to several important changes in the marketing environment: competition, including from global sources, is increasing; products and services are becoming increasingly complex; and customers are demanding greater value from the companies with which they do business. The best salespeople take pride in helping customers solve buying problems, and recognize the value they provide to their companies as they are often the most important element responsible for generating revenue.

Second, successful salespeople must adopt the marketing concept. The value of the marketing concept, formulated in the 1950s, is that it made the customer the focus of marketing attention. Companies that adopt the marketing concept coordinate their activities to create customer satisfaction and build profitable relationships. For salespeople, an important part of adopting the marketing concept philosophy involves helping customers solve buying problems.

Third, salespeople must see themselves as consultants or partners to their customers and must have their customers' best interests in mind at all times.

RELATIONSHIP STRATEGY

A **relationship strategy** is a well thought out plan for establishing, building, and maintaining quality relationships.[5] Successful salespeople understand the psychology of human behaviour and use it to develop and project a positive professional image. In *The Professional Image,* author Susan Bixler says, "All of us make entrances throughout our business day as we enter offices, conference rooms, or meeting halls. And every time we do, someone is watching us, appraising us, sizing us up, and gauging our appearance, even our intelligence, often within the space of a few seconds."[6] That means salespeople must be concerned with their relationship strategy from their first appearance before a customer. Such things as clothing, facial expressions, tone of voice, self-confidence, handshake, and general manners will influence how the customer views a salesperson and will affect how he or she reacts to the salesperson from the first interaction.

Second, as part of a relationship strategy, salespeople must be able to communicate appropriately with customers. Nearly every major sales training program classifies customers into four communication styles based on high or low dominance and high or low sociability. Salespeople must be able to identify a customer's preferred communication style and then adjust their own style accordingly. For example, people who fit into the low dominance, low sociability category have been labelled Reflective, Analytical, Conserving–Holding, Thinker, or Cautiousness/Compliance, by various training programs.[7] These people, as the labels suggest, value information. Salespeople need to use a very well-organized sales approach when dealing with them, providing charts, graphs, and other documentation to support everything that is said. These people

Exhibit 6.1

The Strategic/Consultative Selling Model

Strategic/Consultative Selling Model*	
Strategic step	Prescription
Develop a personal selling philosophy	• Value personal selling • Adopt marketing concept • Become a problem solver/partner
Develop a relationship strategy	• Project positive, professional image • Practise communication-style flexing • Behave ethically
Develop a product strategy	• Become a product expert • Sell specific benefits • Configure value-added solutions
Develop a customer strategy	• Understand customer behaviour • Discover customer needs • Develop prospect base
Develop a presentation strategy	• Understand buying process • Prepare objectives • Provide outstanding service
* Strategic/consultative selling evolved in response to increased competition, more complex products, increased emphasis on customer needs, and growing importance of long-term relationships.	

Marketing Concept:
• co-ordinate all activities
• to create satisfied customers
• and achieve company goals.

Source: Gerald L. Manning, Barry L. Reece, and H.F. (Herb) MacKenzie, *Selling Today: Creating Customer Value,* 4th Canadian edition. (Toronto, ON: Pearson Prentice Hall, 2006), p. 20.

Selling Philosophy: Which Hat Today?

What does it take to become a successful salesperson? Well, it all starts with your hat. You cannot have a successful selling career today unless you wear the right hat. Or—if you listen to Dave Kahle, author of *Take Your Sales Performance Up a Notch*—the right six hats.

The selling environment today is characterized by rapid discontinuous change as new technologies bring new products and new competitors, and create constantly changing customer needs. Salespeople need better knowledge and training to keep up with product, competitor, and customer changes. Newer forms of competitors emerge today, and growing global competition adds to the competitive landscape. All of these changes in the selling environment mean that salespeople are increasingly faced with more time pressure and must work increasingly harder, or smarter, to keep up. As a result, salespeople are compelled to wear six hats—that is, build competencies in six areas—if they want to have a successful selling career.

■ *An astute planner.* Salespeople must be able to organize and manage information, and to plan whom to see, when to see them, and what to say to them, long before they make an initial customer approach. Time is an increasingly scarce resource, and effective salespeople must allocate their time effectively across their accounts.

■ *A trusted friend.* People do business with people they trust and like. Salespeople must be able to establish, build, and then maintain trusting relationships with their customers. In an increasingly complex world, customers value relationships with competent, ethical salespeople.

■ *An effective consultant.* Salespeople who can help customers solve buying problems and make good purchase decisions are more adept at identifying opportunities, and are better able to match customized product solutions to specific customer needs.

■ *A skillful influencer.* Today's effective salesperson must understand the strategies and tactics that are important throughout the entire sales process: approach, presentation, demonstration, negotiating buyer resistance, closing, and servicing the sale.

■ *An adept human resources manager.* In particular, salespeople must take responsibility to manage themselves. They often work without direct supervision, so they need to be self-motivated and take responsibility for their accounts and their own actions. They must be able to handle both rejection and stress.

■ *A master learner.* With constant change in products, programs, and services, as well as in competitors and customer needs, salespeople must be dedicated to lifelong learning. Superior salespeople must constantly seek to upgrade their skills and knowledge.

Source: Dave Kahle, *Take Your Sales Performance Up a Notch* (Grand Rapids, MI: The DaCo Corporation, 2002).

need to reflect on everything that has been provided before making a decision, and a salesperson who tries to close a sale too quickly will be seen as "pushy" and will be resisted.

Third, salespeople must behave ethically. Salespeople constantly face situations where they may be pressured to compromise their ethical standards: the sales manager wants the salesperson to focus on closing a new account, but the salesperson knows she needs to service an existing account based on a previous promise; the salesperson is opposed to bribery but a customer has just promised a sizeable order if the salesperson will provide a personal incentive; a competitor has lied to a customer concerning their product capability and now the salesperson must decide whether to tell the same lie in order to close a sale. Salespeople are increasingly finding that unethical selling practices undermine their reputation and hinder their ability to build long-term relationships with customers, ultimately reducing sales for their company as well. Chapter 12 describes the importance of ethical leadership, and its significance for establishing and maintaining an ethical sales force.

PRODUCT STRATEGY

A **product strategy** is a plan that helps salespeople make correct decisions concerning the selection and positioning of products to meet identified customer needs.[8] First, salespeople must recognize the importance of becoming product experts. This requires that they be able to answer any customer questions concerning their product: what benefits it offers, along with information on such things as product development, quality improvement processes, specifications, performance characteristics, maintenance and service requirements, lifetime costs of operation, delivery availability, and price. To answer these questions, salespeople must also be knowledgeable concerning their own company and their competitors.

Second, salespeople must know the features of their products, and must understand and be able to communicate the benefits these features provide to customers. This is where salespeople must be careful. They often have a tendency, when they know too much about product features and specifications, to communicate this knowledge while forgetting that customers value the benefits they receive, not the product features. Successful salespeople always match features to benefits, and then communicate the benefits to customers.

Third, as part of their product strategy, salespeople must understand how to create value-added product solutions for their customers. They understand that customers often seek a "cluster of satisfactions" that arise from the product itself, from the company that manufactures or sells the product, and from the salesperson who sells and services the product. Salespeople who understand this will determine where they can best differentiate their product offering in the customer's mind.

CUSTOMER STRATEGY

A **customer strategy** is a carefully conceived plan that will result in maximum customer responsiveness. As part of a good customer strategy, a salesperson must first develop an understanding of general customer behaviour: how customers make buying decisions, and what factors affect their buying decisions. Second, the salesperson must learn as much as possible about individual customers. A salesperson who wishes to sell to a specific customer and then obtain repeat business from that customer must learn to collect and systematize information about that customer. Hammer and Champy, authors of *Reengineering the Corporation,* say, "Customers—consumers and corporations alike—demand products and services designed for their unique and particular needs. There is no longer any such notion as *the* customer; there is only *this* customer, the *one* with whom a seller is dealing at the moment and who now has the capacity to indulge his or her own personal tastes."[9] Therefore, salespeople must understand the specific needs of individual customers, and what will motivate them to make specific buying decisions. Third, salespeople must systematize how they prospect for customers to ensure they always have a list of quality prospects they can turn to when they need to generate sales. More will be said about prospecting later in this chapter when the selling process model is discussed.

PRESENTATION STRATEGY

A **presentation strategy** is a well-developed plan that includes preparing the sales presentation objectives, preparing a presentation plan to meet these objectives, and renewing commitment to provide outstanding customer service.[10] As the first prescription, salespeople must develop one or more objectives for each sales call. Second, they must consider the face-to-face activities that will occur during the sales call and decide how they will proceed and how they will handle issues that may arise. Third, they must be prepared to provide outstanding customer service both during and after the sales presentation.

Exhibit 6.2 illustrates how the five strategic steps involved in the strategic/consultative selling model are interrelated. The personal selling philosophy is critical to the development of the other four strategic steps. A salesperson who does not value personal selling, who does not adopt the marketing concept, and who does not see himself as a customer's consultant/partner, will be unlikely to develop a strong relationship, product, customer, or presentation strategy. Once a salesperson has developed his relationship, product, and customer strategies, these will influence the development of his presentation strategy. A salesperson might, for example, decide on one relationship-building activity to use when the customer is first approached, another to use during the presentation stage, and another to use after the presentation as part of a sales follow-up process.

Exhibit 6.2

The Five Strategic Steps in the Strategic/Consultative Selling Model

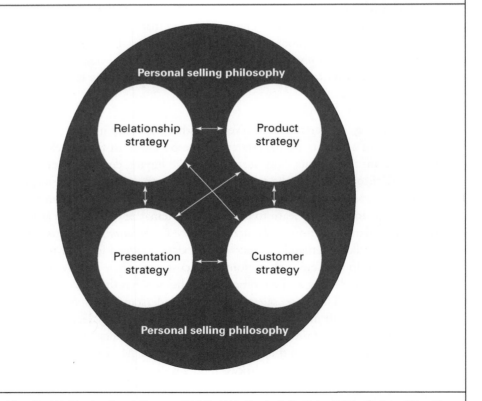

Source: Adapted from Gerald L. Manning, Barry L. Reece, and H.F. (Herb) MacKenzie, *Selling Today: Creating Customer Value*, 4th Canadian edition. (Toronto, ON: Pearson Prentice Hall, 2006), p. 22.

The ultimate purpose of considering these five strategic steps is to prepare the salesperson for the selling process. The next section of this chapter presents the selling process model—"where the rubber hits the road." Salespeople who understand the selling process and who implement it effectively have positioned themselves to have successful and rewarding sales careers.

The Selling Process Model

This section describes the selling process model. The selling process has three major phases: a pre-contact phase, a face-to-face interaction phase, and a post-sale phase. Exhibit 6.3 illustrates how these three phases are related.

PRE-CONTACT PHASE

While many salespeople understand that success is determined by how well they manage the face-to-face interaction with the customer, the most successful salespeople know that how well they do during this phase is largely determined by their pre-contact planning skills. Salespeople who bypass planning because they are interested in action are more likely to call on the wrong customers, talk too much or ask the wrong questions, appear awkward and unsure of how to handle customer questions, and waste valuable time for both customers and themselves. Astute customers will recognize this and will be less willing in the future to see these salespeople. Superior salespeople consider the pre-contact phase critical to their success and are well prepared before making contact with prospects or customers. There are two important activities for salespeople

Exhibit 6.3
The Selling Process Model

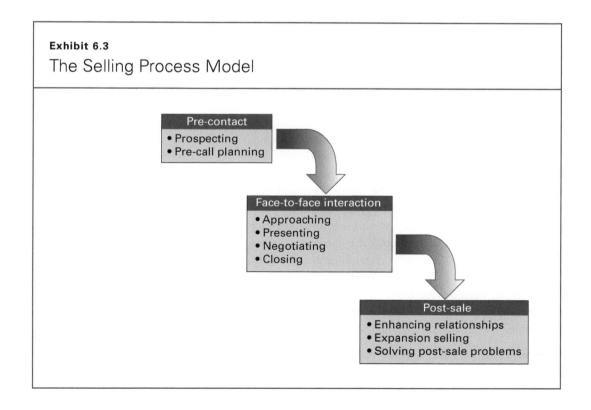

Pre-contact
- Prospecting
- Pre-call planning

Face-to-face interaction
- Approaching
- Presenting
- Negotiating
- Closing

Post-sale
- Enhancing relationships
- Expansion selling
- Solving post-sale problems

during the pre-contact phase: prospecting and pre-call planning. Prospecting was discussed at length in Chapter 5 because this important activity is required for developing new accounts. Prospecting and qualifying activities may be done by salespeople or by others within the sales organization. Pre-call planning, however, includes activities that are done exclusively by salespeople during the pre-contact selling phase. Effective pre-call planning involves several activities: gaining as much information concerning prospects or customers as possible, setting objectives for sales calls, and planning for the presentation and interaction. Pre-call planning was ranked as the most important among 14 selling skills for long-term success in a survey of 1500 sales managers and sales representatives.[11]

GAINING PROSPECT OR CUSTOMER KNOWLEDGE   As part of the prospecting and qualifying processes, it is sometimes possible to gain considerable prospect information. For existing customers, some companies maintain databases that keep all relevant information and account histories available to everyone who has customer contact responsibility. Whether a salesperson is collecting initial information concerning a prospect, or updating customer information in a company database, there are two types of information that are important: information about the prospect as an individual, and information about the prospect as a business representative.[12]

Each prospect and customer is unique. Being able to relate to each of them on an individual basis is important to building long-term relationships. A starting point is to know how to pronounce and correctly spell the person's name. Then, it is important to acquire information on educational background, work history, and any personal information that is available. Interviewing other industry people, including salespeople, and people within the prospect's company can provide valuable information. A lasting business relationship is often based on a strong personal relationship, so the better a salesperson knows, understands, and can relate to a prospect on a personal level, the more likely it is that she can develop a strong, supportive business relationship. More than 70 years after Dale Carnegie wrote *How to Win Friends and Influence People*, it remains arguably the greatest self-help book ever written. Dale Carnegie recognized the value of knowing and taking a personal interest in other people. He said, "You can make more friends in two months by becoming interested in other people than you can in two years trying to get other people interested in you."

As well as personal information concerning a prospect or customer, a salesperson also needs information on them as a representative for their business. As part of the qualifying process, a salesperson must determine what role the person will play in his company's buying decisions. For which decisions will the person be the decider, and under what conditions will he be an influencer in the buying centre? The salesperson should also know the prospect's business: what it makes or sells, who are its current suppliers and customers, whether it is an industry leader or follower, whether the individual and the company are risk-takers and innovators or conservative risk-avoiders, if the company is expanding or contracting, and any business conditions that are likely to change for the company in the future. It is also good to know how long a prospect or customer has been buying from current suppliers, whether he is satisfied with the products, the service, and the salesperson he is currently buying from, whether he previously bought from the salesperson's company and, if yes, then why he stopped.

SETTING SALES CALL OBJECTIVES AND PLANNING THE INTERACTION   Many sales managers recognize that a sales call without a sales objective is a wasted sales call. The worst sales call is the "because I was in the neighbourhood, I thought I would drop in" sales call. This salesperson has just indicated that the customer is unimportant, and that he has no reason for calling other than his own convenience. If he gets a warm reception, he will be fortunate.

Seldom does a salesperson close a sale on the first sales call. Multi-call sales presentations are becoming increasingly popular in many industries. A good objective for a first sales call might be to gather information concerning a prospect's needs. A second sales call might be needed to present a formal proposal that has been developed to satisfy the prospect's needs. One or more additional calls may be necessary to provide further information, clarify and negotiate customer concerns, and close the sale. Finally, ongoing sales calls might be necessary to help with product installation, train the customer's staff in proper use and care of the product, solve product performance problems, or provide maintenance and upgrading. Taken together, it is apparent that for any particular sales call, a salesperson may have one or several sales call objectives:

1. Introduce the salesperson or the company to the prospect and qualify the prospect to ensure she does have a need for the product.
2. Identify who all of the members of the buying centre will be, and establish the buying process that will actually be used to make the purchase.
3. Collect information on the prospect's usage history, including what he bought, how much he uses, where he bought it, what his purchase criteria were, how satisfied he is with current suppliers, etc.
4. Make a formal presentation of a sales proposal and involve the customer in a product demonstration.
5. Provide post-sale service and secure one or more referrals for additional prospects.

A salesperson with more than one objective for a sales call is more likely to achieve some success, and this will increase his confidence and provide a sense of accomplishment. At the same time, if the salesperson clearly understands what needs to be accomplished during a particular sales call, he is also more likely to bring to the sales call the resources necessary to achieving his objectives. For example, if the sales call is being made to several individuals who comprise the buying centre, then the salesperson should identify who within his own company will be needed to address any areas where he is not expert. The salesperson will be viewed as more professional and better prepared, and will be more likely to close the sale or at least shorten the sales cycle.

Depending on the sales call objectives, the salesperson should consider the interaction with the prospect. Of course, one of the biggest surprises for salespeople is that once they are face-to-face with the prospect, they often have little control over what is discussed and what happens during the face-to-face interactions. Suggestions will be provided later to help maintain some control, at least early in the process. However, even if there is little control, a well-prepared salesperson will still anticipate many of the things that might occur during the sales presentation and will be prepared for them. Superior salespeople see the sales call as a game of chess, not checkers. That is, they do not say something, wait for the customer to respond, and then make their next move. They often plan several moves into the future by having a number of "what if" alternatives.

FACE-TO-FACE INTERACTION PHASE

The face-to-face interaction phase is where the salesperson's planning and selling skills are put to the test. Being well prepared before meeting directly with the prospect will greatly increase the chance of success. If qualifying has been done immediately after prospecting, or at least before the salesperson makes the sales call, then the salesperson does not have to qualify the prospect at the initial meeting. If, however, the prospect has not been qualified prior to the face-to-face sales call, then failure to properly qualify the prospect during the initial stage of the sales call will often result in a waste of the salesperson's time. In any event, the critical first step is the *approach*—making the initial face-to-face contact with the prospect or customer.

APPROACHING THE CUSTOMER   The salesperson should keep three objectives in mind during the approach. He must: build rapport, gain the prospect's full attention, and make the transition to the need discovery stage of the sales presentation.[13] If the salesperson has already contacted the prospect to make an appointment, the prospect most likely has a positive or negative impression of the salesperson even before the face-to-face sales call. It is useful for salespeople to make an initial contact to arrange an appointment because this demonstrates professionalism and a concern for the customer, and allows the salesperson to begin the process of building the prospect's interest. It also helps ensure that the customer is prepared for the sales call so that he will have arranged his time accordingly and will be more prepared to devote his full attention to the salesperson.

When the salesperson makes that first physical contact with the prospect, he has a very short period of time—minutes—to create a positive first impression. This period of time is what Dr. Leonard Zunin, co-author of *Contact: The First Four Minutes,* describes as the "four-minute barrier." In this first four minutes, a relationship can be developed or denied. Susan Bixler, author of *The New Professional Image* says this about the importance of the first impression:

> Books are judged by their covers, houses are appraised by their curb appeal, and people are initially evaluated on how they choose to dress and behave. In a perfect world this is not fair, moral, or just. What's inside should count a great deal more. And eventually it usually does, but not right away. In the meantime, a lot of opportunities can be lost.[14]

The first few minutes of the approach should be used to attempt a social contact. The salesperson needs to dispel any anxiety that either he or the prospect might feel at a first meeting, and try to establish a friendly atmosphere. Good ways to start a conversation include commenting on here and now observations, offering sincere compliments, and attempting to discover mutual acquaintances or interests.[15] Commenting on the here and now could include comments concerning the morning news, the previous night's hockey game or another recent event, something that is unique about the prospect's company or office, or even the weather. Some prospects take pride in personalizing their work area or office, and if this is apparent, a sincere compliment might be welcome. If, however, the salesperson notices a work area that is designed specifically for business, this could be an indication that the prospect has little interest in social contact and that the salesperson should be prepared to move more quickly to the purpose of the sales call. If the salesperson is fortunate enough to notice something in the meeting environment that suggests a possible mutual interest or acquaintance, a question or comment about it is certainly appropriate. From the time of the initial contact, the salesperson should always be alert to demonstrating propriety—respect for the prospect's office and time. Nothing works better than "do you mind" questions: "Do you mind if I come in?" "Do you mind if I sit down?" "Do you mind if I place my briefcase here?" And, a good way to move from the opening social contact to the more formal business contact is to ask, "Do you mind if I ask you a few questions?"

A similar approach to gaining the prospect's attention and helping build interest is to suggest the questions to the customer. Newer salespeople often find that this gives them some control early in the sales call, and helps them get past initial nervousness. At the same time, this helps the salesperson manage the agenda by ensuring that he gets the opportunity to state important things that he may wish to state. Used deftly, the salesperson can easily involve the prospect at this stage too, and help establish an environment of friendly interaction. Consider making a statement similar to the following: "Mr. Davis, when I was preparing for our initial meeting today, I considered a number of things that, if I were you, I would like to know about the product I am selling, the company I represent, and the way I do business as a sales professional." Of course, the order of topics and questions can be changed to suit the individual situation. If the salesperson decides to focus on his company first, he may continue, "For example, you might want to know a little about Dinkus & Doofus Manufacturing and what are our capabilities for serving large accounts such as yours." Now the salesperson will most likely get the prospect's permission to proceed, and he can deliver a reasonably rehearsed answer to this question and then follow it with additional questions, or involve the customer by adding, "Can I ask a few questions about your company?"

Another popular way of moving from the social contact to the business contact is the **product approach**, where the salesperson focuses immediately on the product that he sells, and may include a product display, a demonstration, or even simply a picture or brochure. Some salespeople prefer the **referral approach**, where the salesperson uses a third-party referral to gain the prospect's attention and interest. For example, the salesperson might say, "Ms. Murphy, my name is Hannah Simpson, and I represent Saskatchewan Farm Outlet. We specialize in smaller shipments of specialized farm products that are often difficult to locate. Mr. Boast, the manager at the local farm market, suggested that you might be interested in what we sell. Mr. Boast has been one of our faithful customers for several years now." If Ms. Murphy knows and respects Mr. Boast, she will likely give Hannah her attention at this point. Another popular approach is the **customer benefit approach**, where the salesperson immediately focuses on the superior benefit his company can offer to its customers: "Mr. Chahley, my company has been able to cut operating costs for our major customers by anywhere from 30 to 75 percent. I am confident we can achieve these same savings for you." There are other approaches that can be used, and ultimately, a salesperson should experiment to find the one or two that work best for his product, his company, or himself.

CRAFTING EFFECTIVE SALES PRESENTATIONS Highly effective consultative salespeople think of the sales presentation as a three-step process: need discovery, selection of the product, and delivery of a need-satisfaction presentation. Each of these steps is now described.

Need Discovery There are sales positions in which the salesperson has a very limited product line and the product being sold is relatively unsophisticated. In these situations, the salesperson has a fairly simple task in identifying whether the customer has a need for her product, and she can proceed to making a need-satisfaction presentation. More often, the salesperson must implement the process of **need discovery**—asking questions and carefully noting the responses to clearly establish the prospect's needs. The process of need discovery is important for two reasons. First, without clearly establishing the buyer's needs and buying motives, the salesperson risks attempting to sell the wrong product, or appealing to the wrong buying motives. Second, and often more important, the need discovery process establishes the need in the prospect's mind. Many prospects do not recognize that they have a need, and unless they do, a purchase is unlikely.

Need discovery begins with questions. Asking questions signals intent to understand, and this is important because it says to customers that the salesperson will not try to sell something until she can establish that there is a need, and understand what is needed. Noting responses, especially if they are written down, signals to the buyer that his responses are important and that the salesperson wants to ensure she fully understands them. Writing the answers serves another important purpose for the salesperson because she can use this information when it comes time to ask confirmation questions, a specific type of question that will be introduced shortly. Simply asking questions promotes two-way communication, ensures buyer involvement in the process, reduces tension, and helps build trust. A sales presentation without questions is usually one where the salesperson does too much talking, and not nearly enough listening. Four types of questions are commonly used as part of an effective consultative sales presentation:

1. *Survey questions.* A **survey question**, or *information-gathering question,* is designed to gain knowledge concerning the buyer's current situation. There are two types of survey questions: the **general survey question**, which helps the salesperson discover facts, and the **specific survey question**, which is designed to give buyers a chance to describe in greater detail their current buying problem, issue, or dissatisfaction that they are experiencing. Either of these questions, as well as other types of questions, can also be a **closed question**, which requires a simple "yes" or "no" response, or an **open question**, which requires the buyer to provide more thoughtful and insightful answers.

2. *Probing questions.* A **probing question** is designed to help the salesperson uncover and clarify the buyer's problem, or what has sometimes been referred to as "pain." These questions expose the buyer's concerns, fears, frustrations, or anxiety, so they are more likely to be used in situations where there is some risk to the buyer: financial risk due to the value of the purchase, functional risk due to the complexity of the product, or social risk due to the visibility of the purchase decision to relevant others. A series of effective probing questions encourages the buyer to share ideas and feelings, and may actually help the buyer to discover things that even he has not considered previously.

3. *Confirmation questions.* A **confirmation question** is designed to verify the accuracy and assure a mutual understanding of information shared between the buyer and the salesperson. As the sales interaction progresses, the buyer will suggest one or several **buying conditions**—that is, qualifications that must be fulfilled or available before the buyer will agree to make a purchase. The salesperson should confirm with the customer when there is an indication of a buying condition. After several buying conditions are identified, the salesperson should use a **summary confirmation question** to bring these buying conditions temporally close for the customer and ensure that the customer understands and remembers what his buying conditions were. For example, the salesperson could say, "To summarize where we are currently, you have stated that you want our first truck at your loading dock by 7:00 A.M. each morning, you want an additional truck each hour until noon, and you want a refrigerated unit on the last truck each day?" If the buyer agrees, the salesperson can continue. "And, you want our billing to be monthly, a guarantee on overnight delivery, and our drivers are not permitted to smoke on your property?" Once a salesperson has uncovered all of the buying conditions, he is in a position to prepare a proposal. In a multi-call situation, a salesperson is wise to begin subsequent sales calls with a summary confirmation question that re-establishes what was agreed during a previous sales call.

4. *Need-satisfaction questions.* A **need-satisfaction question** is designed to move the buyer to commitment and action. This is a fundamentally different type of question. Where the

previous types of questions focused on understanding and clarifying the buyer's problem, this type of question helps the buyer recognize how the product will solve his buying problem. These are powerful questions because they build desire on the part of the buyer and give him ownership of the solution.

A good suggestion when preparing for a sales call is to prepare a need discovery worksheet. Exhibit 6.4 illustrates one example. Preparing a worksheet ensures that all relevant information

---

Exhibit 6.4
Need Discovery Worksheet

Customer: Mr. Sanjay Khosla   Date: September 17, 2008

Questions:

1. Do you currently have both registered and non-registered investments?
    (*Survey/General/Closed*)

2. Please describe your current portfolio of investments for me. (*Survey/General/Open*)

3. At this point in your life, what are the major financial concerns that you have?
    (*Survey/Specific/Open*)

4. Are you concerned with the probable cost of education for your three children when they
    begin university or college? (*Probing/Closed*)

5. If I am correct, you are telling me that you are concerned with providing for your children's
    education. Am I correct? (*Confirmation/Closed*)

6. To summarize what we have covered this morning, you are prepared to make a monthly
    contribution to save for your children's education. You would prefer a registered plan that
    will allow growth accumulation tax-free. You like the R.E.S.P. plan where the government
    makes an additional contribution to your savings. And, you prefer a family plan where, if any
    one of your children decides not to attend college or university, you can designate that the
    savings go to your other children without penalty. Do we agree?
    (*Summary Confirmation/Closed*)

7. Can you see how slowly moving money from the non-registered investment that you have
    started for your children's education to a registered plan will help you accumulate wealth much
    faster due to the government contribution of $400 per year, and the tax free growth that the
    plan will achieve? (*Need-Satisfaction/Closed*)

8. Are there any other benefits you see from making these changes to your investment portfolio?
    (*Need-Satisfaction/Open*)

gets collected during a sales call, that there is a logical sequence to the questions that are asked, and that the salesperson avoids asking unnecessary questions that might suggest poor preparation on his part. A further advantage is that a prepared need discovery worksheet saves time. The salesperson does not need to write the questions—only the responses to them—during the sales call. The Sales Management in Action box describes how two innovative businesswomen discover their clients' needs, craft a customized product, and make a need-satisfaction presentation during a single sales call.

Selection of the Product   Step two involves the selection of the product that satisfies the needs and matches the buying motives of the buyer. This might be a simple task, or it could be very complex. If the salesperson has many options, then configuring a product solution might require considerable time—maybe days or even weeks. In such instances, the salesperson will need to arrange another sales call to make a formal presentation that may include a written proposal. Salespeople should consider here that buyers frequently have many motives, or seek many **satisfactions**—positive benefits from a purchase. These satisfactions can relate to the product itself, the company that supplies the product, or the particular salesperson who sells the product. Taken together, these satisfactions have been referred to as a *cluster of satisfactions* as illustrated in Exhibit 6.5. The complexity of configuring a product solution is also increased if there are many people involved in the buying centre. In such instances, the salesperson must identify the buying motives of each person and attempt to address the needs of each of them. Each of these people

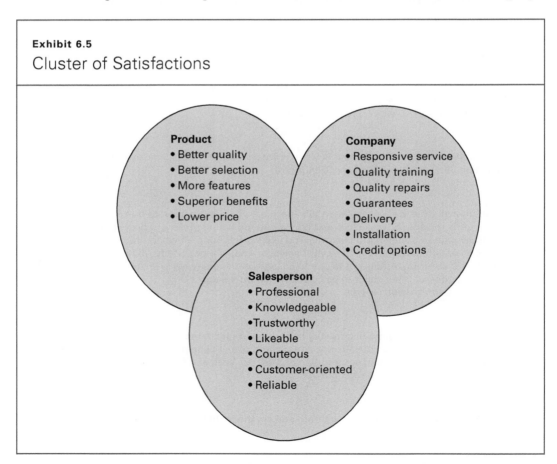

Exhibit 6.5
Cluster of Satisfactions

Product
- Better quality
- Better selection
- More features
- Superior benefits
- Lower price

Company
- Responsive service
- Quality training
- Quality repairs
- Guarantees
- Delivery
- Installation
- Credit options

Salesperson
- Professional
- Knowledgeable
- Trustworthy
- Likeable
- Courteous
- Customer-oriented
- Reliable

2 Great Gals: Consultative Selling With Style

Susan Abramson and Rachel McGarry are two great gals (**www.2greatgals.com**) who first met while improving their interior decorating skills at Seneca College. They became friends and soon recognized that they had complementary skills that they could use to offer decorating and organizing advice for homeowners. They have since been guest designers on the W Network, HGTV, Food Network, and Rogers Cable 10. They have also appeared in magazines and newspapers, including *Canadian House & Home, Home To Go,* and *Kitchen Equipped.*

Customers who contract with 2 Great Gals can expect a visit from both gals. In a single session, the two gals discover the customers' needs, create a personalized decorating plan that the customers can implement as their time and budget allow, and make a need-satisfaction presentation to the customers. Susan, the gal with the business skills, says, "We like our clients to do some homework before we visit—finding photos of rooms, styles and ideas they like—so we can begin to see what they are after. Then we spend about half an hour or so visiting rooms and asking lots of questions. We need to know who lives there, what they value, and how they use their home. Do they have children? Pets? Do they entertain a lot? How is the home situated for natural sunlight? It's a very consultative process. Our goal is to ensure the customer gets exactly what they want and that they are satisfied with our service."

Rachel, the gal with the artistic skills, says, "Once we have enough information, we can begin to explore ideas with the homeowners. Before we leave, I prepare a customized attractive binder with drawings and visuals to help them implement the decorating and organizing ideas we discussed."

As part of their relationship-building strategy, the two great gals provide superior after-sale service. Clients are entitled to free email Q&A following the initial consultation.

Source: Personal interview with Susan Abramson and Rachel McGarry, April 6, 2004.

---

may be seeking a different cluster of satisfactions. It is not unusual that the buying influencer seeks satisfactions related to the salesperson or company, but the user or technical influencer seeks satisfactions related to the product, for example.

Once a salesperson has configured a product solution, he must make appropriate recommendations to the customer. There are three options. The salesperson can make a recommendation and the customer can decide to make an immediate purchase. More commonly, the salesperson must make a need-satisfaction presentation—presenting the benefits to the customer, negotiating buyer concerns or points of resistance, and finally closing the sale. There is even the possibility that the salesperson, after fully understanding the customer's needs, will recognize that the best solution for the customer is from another source. While this might seem counterintuitive, responsible salespeople who have the customer's best interests in mind should recommend the other source. This is in the salesperson's best long-term interests as well.

Making a Need-Satisfaction Presentation   Once a salesperson has decided on the product solution, and depending on where the customer is in the buying cycle, the salesperson must choose which type of presentation to make: an informative, persuasive, or reminder presentation.

■   *Informative presentations.* An **informative presentation** is one where the primary purpose is to inform the buyer concerning factual information about the product, its superior benefits, and its technical or operating specifications. This type of presentation is frequently made to introduce new or fairly complex products. Technical influencers often prefer informative presentations; they respond better to rational argument than to emotional appeal. If the product is sufficiently superior, clearly offers a solution to the customer's purchasing problem, and the customer is educated concerning the product that is being presented, then a factual presentation that emphasizes clarity, simplicity, and conciseness is often what is needed.

■ *Persuasive presentations.* A **persuasive presentation** is one where the primary purpose is to influence the buyer's beliefs and attitudes, and ultimately to move the buyer to take action and make a buying decision. Persuasive presentations combine both rational and emotional appeals, although the amount of weight given to each may vary depending on the particular person to whom the salesperson is presenting. True sales "hunters" are often masters of the persuasive presentation. Such presentations are certainly appropriate when it is clear that the buyer will benefit from the product solution that is being presented. Persuasive presentations require planning, practice, and skill, but when they are made effectively, they build buyer trust of the salesperson and the product solution.

■ *Reminder presentations.* A **reminder presentation** is one where the primary purpose is to remind or reinforce to the buyer what is already known. This type of presentation is often used by sales "gatherers," salespeople who must manage or maintain existing accounts. For example, a salesperson for an office supply company might make a regular Monday morning visit to one of her accounts. This ensures that the customer remembers the salesperson and knows the schedule by which she will regularly make a sales call and ask for orders or check on service. Another type of reminder presentation may be made by salespeople who have already made informative and persuasive presentations to the buyer. The buyer may not see sufficient reason to change from an existing supplier, particularly if it is one that he is satisfied with and has been buying from for some period of time. The salesperson who is trying to gain business from this prospect may need to make regular reminder presentations to ensure that she is "top of mind" for the buyer if something goes wrong with the current supplier and the buyer decides to make a change. This is one of the reasons why, particularly in business markets, salespeople need to make regular calls on prospective accounts. It may take months, or years, before they get an opportunity to sell to a particular customer, but reminder presentations reinforce to buyers that the salesperson is interested in their business.

Some Guidelines for Persuasive Sales Presentations   The guidelines that follow relate more to persuasive presentations because these are the presentations that require the most planning, practice, and skills; however, some of these suggestions might be useful to keep in mind for all presentations.

1. *Place emphasis on the relationship.* Customers like to buy from those they trust and those they believe will be around after the sale to ensure their satisfaction. Salespeople build good relationships when they are honest, sincere, and helpful, and when they do what they say they will do.

2. *Always connect features to customer benefits, and gain customer reactions.* Customers do not buy features; they buy benefits. Gaining reactions increases customer involvement, and allows the salesperson to ensure that the customer understands or values the benefit being

discussed. For example, the salesperson using the feature–benefit–reaction (FBR) approach might say, "Our service technicians are all trained at the factory, which means that the generators we supply to you will be maintained to operate at peak efficiency. Is efficiency an important concern for you?"

3. *Place the strongest appeals at the front and end of the presentation.* Prospects remember the first part of a presentation (primacy effect) or the last part of a presentation (recency effect) better than they remember the middle of a presentation. Opening a presentation with a strong appeal gains attention; closing a presentation with a strong appeal prepares the prospect and the salesperson for the close.

4. *Target emotional links.* An **emotional link** is a connector between what the salesperson says and the prospect's emotions.[16] Persuasive words help establish emotional links: *improved, new, efficient, enhanced, convenient, superior, proven, guaranteed,* and *unsurpassed.* Salespeople should think how these words can be used to describe benefits the prospect seeks, such as proven operating efficiency, unsurpassed product quality, superior customer service, improved market share, enhanced reputation, or guaranteed on-time service and delivery.

5. *Tell stories, use metaphors, and supply testimonials.* Stories not only help salespeople sell, they help salespeople relate to customers. A good story focuses the customer's attention, improves communication, and is memorable. Metaphors, sometimes referred to as *figurative language,* help create visual images in the customer's mind. A salesperson who wants to impress a customer with the performance of his laser printer compared to the one the customer now owns might say, "Comparing the speed of this printer to your current printer would be like comparing a gazelle to a water buffalo." The customer now has a clearer image of the comparative speeds of the two products. Finally, providing third-party testimonials helps assure customers that others have tried and have been very satisfied with the product.

6. *Use an appropriate demonstration when possible.* Demonstrations enhance communication, improve retention of information, and can involve the customer more actively in the presentation. Most important, demonstrations help prove claims a salesperson makes; that is, they are proof devices that add credibility to the product, the company, and the salesperson. The best demonstrations, of course, involve the actual product, or plant tours. These are, however, not always possible. Salespeople can also rely on many other proof devices: models, photos, illustrations, brochures, portfolios, reprints of articles, catalogues, graphs, charts, spreadsheets, test results, audio-visual support, websites, and bound formal presentations. Of course, some of these provide greater "proof" than others.

NEGOTIATING BUYER CONCERNS   **Negotiating**, in a selling context, is the process of working to reach a win–win agreement between the buyer and seller; that is, finding a solution that both parties can agree on and that will create satisfaction for each of them. Negotiations may begin long before an actual sales presentation, and may be about the date and time of a meeting, the duration and place of a meeting, and even its agenda and who will attend the sales presentation. During a sales presentation, buyers will frequently raise issues or concerns. Older selling texts and sales training programs refer to these concerns as *objections*. However, objections have a negative connotation, and also imply that a salesperson must "overcome" objections to win a sale, suggesting that the process results in a win–lose condition. *Concerns* is a more appropriate term because, in many instances, the buyer is simply asking for more information about one or more of the buying conditions that she may have. Buyers who raise concerns must have some level of interest in the product, so a salesperson who receives lots of questions from a buyer is in a better position to receive an order than a salesperson who meets buyer indifference.

What concerns do buyers usually have? To the inattentive salesperson, it might appear that buyers have dozens or even hundreds of concerns. However, a careful analysis of buyer concerns will soon demonstrate that there are really only five topics that raise concerns for buyers: need, the product, the price, the source, and time. Most salespeople can simplify things even further as, when customers raise concerns with a particular salesperson, they tend to raise the same concerns as other customers. This means that a salesperson should learn to anticipate specific concerns from customers, and practise his response to them. Each of these five concerns will now be briefly discussed.

1. *Concerns related to need.* The buyer is really asking, "Why do I need this product?" What could be more natural than to ask a salesperson to describe the benefits that will be received as a result of making a purchase? A salesperson who knows the benefits his product delivers and is in a position to offer proof of those benefits to the buyer is in a good position to ask for business.

2. *Concerns related to the product.* The salesperson must understand what specific concerns the buyer has with the product. (1) "The product is new or untried": The salesperson should have testimonials or other proof devices. The salesperson could encourage the buyer to place a trial order, or he could provide the customer with samples. Providing guarantees or warranty information might also help. (2) "Another customer has tried the product and didn't like it": This is more difficult to handle, and the salesperson needs to ask lots of questions to determine information about the dissatisfied customer and specific problems they had. At this point, the objection is a very general one, and it is quite possible that the other customer involved a completely different application for the product. (3) "This product will not be a good seller": This concern will be raised sometimes by a prospect who would buy the product for resale. Salespeople can discuss the success of other resellers, describe research that was done before the product was developed, offer guarantees or trial orders, or describe the advertising and promotion strategy the salesperson's company has undertaken to support the product in the marketplace and help create demand.

3. *Concerns related to the source.* These concerns are particularly difficult to handle when they are raised by a "relationship" buyer. For example, "I have been buying from your competition for many years": The salesperson needs to find out about the relationship between the buyer and his current supplier. Sometimes it can simply be an indication of buyer inertia, or unwillingness to expend effort to investigate or consider a new supplier. At other times, it could indicate genuine loyalty, personal relationships, or even long-term contracts with a competitor. Salespeople who encounter this should consider rewording the concern as a question: "If I understand, what you are saying is that you really want me to explain how our company can add value over our competition?" Often, the customer will indicate that the salesperson should proceed, and a well-prepared salesperson can then discuss the cluster of satisfactions that a buyer could receive from changing suppliers. At the same time, the salesperson should look for other people within the buyer's organization who could become champions or supporters of the salesperson, his company, or his product. For example, concerns by the economic buyer may be overcome when there is strong support from the user buyer or the technical buyer.

4. *Concerns related to price.* These concerns can always be expected from the "transactional" buyer who will remain almost totally focused on price. However, almost all buyers will raise price concerns. Professional buyers who are trained in negotiating have a number of

tactics they use: "I'm sorry, but it's beyond my current budget." Or, "This is what I am prepared to pay. Take it or leave it." Or, "Okay, let's split the difference and we will both be happy."[17] Salespeople need to be trained in how to deal with each of these and other tactics, or risk sacrificing margin on sales and reducing their profitability. Some of the tactics salespeople can use to manage price concerns include focusing on a clearly superior benefit, or a cluster of satisfactions; pointing out the relationship between price and quality, or between price and cost (which includes the long-term cost of owning and operating the product); only giving a price concession when the customer also gives a concession, such as offering a lower price if the buyer will forgo a feature; or clarifying the price concern by asking questions. It is possible that although price is raised as a concern, it may not be a real concern, or it may be hiding another concern. Depending on the specific price concern raised, the salesperson could ask: "What price would you expect to pay for this product?" Or, "If you had sufficient budget, would you buy this product?" Or, "If we can agree on price, is there any other concern that might prevent you from making a purchase?" Once the salesperson clearly understands the buyer's price concern, he can begin to look for satisfactory solutions.

5. *Concerns related to time.* This is another commonly raised concern. Sometimes it is legitimate, but frequently it is a *stall* technique. Buyers may say, "I need time to think about this." Or, "I must speak to Bob before I make a decision." In the former instance, the buyer may be a Reflective (low dominance, low sociability preferred communication style), and may be a person who thinks about almost everything before making a decision. In the latter instance, the buyer may be indicating that he is simply not the decider in this buying decision. In both instances, these stalls may simply be what are sometimes referred to as *quasi-concerns*—not really legitimate concerns, but an effort to postpone making a decision. Many people feel increasingly uncomfortable as a buying situation approaches because they are about to effect a change. There is some risk and always some change when a buying decision is made, and buyers remove themselves from an uncomfortable situation through the stall. Salespeople may suggest that the product offer is limited and will not be available shortly, or a price increase is expected. But, they should do this only when they are being honest. Good customer relationships cannot be built on deception.

Salespeople have many ways to handle buyer concerns, but one of the most effective demonstrates empathy for the buyer by suggesting that what he is feeling is a common and legitimate concern. This is called the "feel–felt–found" technique. It is regularly used by George Hutchison, chairman and CEO of North Bay, Ontario-based Equisure Financial Network Inc. When a prospect raises a concern, George will often say, "I know how you *feel*. Others have *felt* the same way. However, they've *found* that . . . ." Using this strategy also shows prospects that other customers have successfully overcome the same concerns.[18]

There are occasions when a concern cannot be adequately addressed and the salesperson should look for opportunities elsewhere. For example, if a prospect really does not have the budget or authority to make a purchase decision, then this prospect is an unqualified prospect and will likely waste the salesperson's time. Productive salespeople know when to stay and when to walk away.

CLOSING   This stage of the face-to-face selling process has been one of the most feared by salespeople and, historically, many have handled it poorly. One commonly heard comment in the past was, "Think A–B–C: Always Be Closing." Another was, "The difference between a good salesperson and an excellent salesperson is the ability to close." While both statements have some value, there is a whole new philosophy of closing in selling today—to the point where some companies have dropped closing as a topic from their sales training programs. Bill Goodwin, manager of training, sales, and marketing at 3M, believes that more diagnostic efforts to understand the customer throughout the sales process will result in fewer concerns as the salesperson moves toward a closing situation.[19] The result is that closing becomes a natural part of the sales process and not a point in the process where salespeople should feel fear. Problems at the close often indicate that there were problems at one or more earlier stages of the selling process: the prospect was poorly qualified, the presentation was poorly planned and delivered, or buyer concerns were not adequately addressed.

There are many ways to attempt to close a sale, but a professional salesperson will quickly discover that many of them are questionable and not conducive to building long-term customer satisfaction. Salespeople should consider using a **trial close** at any point in the sales presentation. A trial close—sometimes called *minor point close*—is a comment or question designed to help the salesperson discover how close the prospect actually is to making a purchase decision. Using probing or confirmation questions can be effective here: "We can ship the product to you next Wednesday. Would this be acceptable?" Or, "Would you like me to be present when the system is being installed?" Remember feature–benefit–reaction (FBR)? After a salesperson presents a product feature, converts it to a buyer benefit, and gains a positive reaction from the prospect, this is an appropriate time to try a trial close. Effective salespeople may use several trial closes throughout a sales presentation. If, following a trial close, the prospect agrees, the salesperson can simply assume the sale, summarize the superior benefits of the product, or ask directly for the sale. This last close is the simplest and, for many salespeople, the best close. If the salesperson has qualified the customer, has gotten agreement that there is an acceptable solution, and truly believes he is adding value for the prospect who buys the product, it should be a natural thing to simply look the customer directly in the eyes and ask for the order: "Mr. Jiang, we seem to agree that our product is acceptable for your application and that our price is competitive. I would be honoured to supply your needs and can promise that I will provide you with excellent service. May I have your order?" This will get either a "yes" or a "no" response, or will uncover any concerns that are remaining and need to be further addressed.

If the buyer says "yes," the salesperson should reassure the customer that he has made the right decision. This is referred to as the **confirmation step**. It is important to do this as, in almost any purchase decision requiring face-to-face negotiations prior to close, the customer will experience **buyer remorse** (sometimes called *cognitive dissonance*). This is a feeling that occurs fairly soon after a decision has been made, where the customer begins to question whether he has made the right decision. That is, he may not feel he has made a wrong decision, but there is some doubt as to whether the best decision was made. Buyer remorse is more likely to occur as the importance of the purchase increases (economically, functionally, or socially), and as similarity increases between the chosen and the next best—but rejected—alternative. A new home buyer may be forced to make a decision between two attractive homes. Once the decision is made, and the sale is completed, it is natural to then think about the rejected alternative and the things that were liked about it. Compliments and reassurances by the successful salesperson help, as does a sincere "Thank you."

If the buyer says "no," the salesperson needs to ensure that the prospect remains open to the possibility of future business. Initially, the salesperson can try to summarize the benefits of the product to the customer and attempt another close. The salesperson should also ask for clarification and feedback from the prospect to better understand why a sale was not made. Finally, the salesperson should do a "curb-side review" and carefully analyze the entire process and consider where the sale was lost and what can be done better in future selling situations. Of course, sometimes, the sale is lost simply because there really is not a good fit between the product and the prospect's needs. When it is clear that the sale is lost, the salesperson should thank the prospect for the opportunity, and express an interest in being considered for future business.

POST-SALE PHASE

The third phase is the post-sale stage—what the salesperson does after the sale is made. This phase involves servicing the sale, expansion selling, and managing dissatisfied customers.

SERVICING THE SALE   **Servicing the sale**, or providing post-sale service, includes all of the activities that are performed to facilitate or enhance the purchase and use of the product. These activities are very important as studies have found that 50–70 percent of customer attrition is due to poor customer service.[20] The cost to regain a lost customer can be four to five times more than the cost of keeping the current customer satisfied.[21] That is why companies today are focused on getting—then keeping—customers. There is a growing recognition of the lifetime value of customers, or what they can contribute to a company over an extended relationship. Larry Rosen, chairman and CEO of Harry Rosen Inc., a fashionable men's clothing retailer with many Canadian locations, embraces this customer-for-life philosophy. He says, "We don't look at a person that walks into our store as an immediate sale. We look at him with a potential lifetime value."[22] Salespeople at Harry Rosen Inc. focus on providing outstanding customer service.

EXPANSION SELLING   More companies today recognize the value of **expansion selling**, which includes any of three techniques to expand business from an existing customer: full-line selling, cross-selling, and up-selling. Once a customer has a relationship with a salesperson, it is easier for the salesperson to gain additional business from that customer. When those products are related to the product that the customer is already buying, this is called **full-line selling**. Salespeople need to recognize that adding additional related items to a sale helps customers gain greater satisfaction from their purchase. For example, a customer might order a lower-end Dell computer, either by talking directly to a salesperson or through the Dell website. The computer may come with a minimal amount of software, but for a very small additional price, the customer may be able to include the latest version of Microsoft Word. This would increase the value of the product considerably for many customers, but many of them might not think to make the small additional investment unless prompted to do so. There are jokes about "Do you want fries with that, sir?" However, it is used because it works, and while a few customers may be upset by being asked, many understand that it is an attempt to increase the satisfaction they get from their food experience. The cashier who politely asks this question will invariably have a higher average revenue per customer served than the cashier who does not. To be successful at full-line selling, the salesperson should consider what primary items he is selling, and what additional complementary items can be sold if he is successful. Suggestions for additional items should be made only after the customer's primary needs have been met.

Cross-selling involves selling items that are unrelated to the items that a customer is currently buying from the salesperson. It relies on good relationships between the buyer and seller, and when there are good relationships, customers welcome the attempt by the salesperson to sell them additional items. It allows customers to rationalize their supplier bases and add convenience by buying from fewer and better suppliers. Increasingly, Canadian banks are training people with customer contact responsibility in how to cross-sell to existing customers. These people have customer information available that allows them to target products to those people who might need them or who will benefit most from them. One financial services company, Quick & Reilly, increased its sales by 35 percent after it trained its people to cross-sell products.[23]

Up-selling refers to the attempt to sell better quality products. Most customers are concerned with making the right product choice rather than simply purchasing the least expensive alternative.[24] Considering this, the responsible salesperson owes it to her prospects to show them when and how, for a few extra dollars, they can receive more value and greater satisfaction. Mike Weber, sales manager at Young Electric Sign Company, says that a salesperson who is successful at up-selling must first have a good relationship with the customer—one that is built on trust. Second, he says, the salesperson must continually qualify the prospect throughout the selling process and pay particular attention to their needs so that opportunities to up-sell are not missed. According to Weber, salespeople at Young Electric begin up-selling at the design stage when the prospect and the salesperson are establishing exactly what is needed. Salespeople produce a sketch of the desired sign, and another "possible" sign that shows something better the prospect could buy. The prospect usually sees the value of the better alternative.[25]

Whatever technique a salesperson uses to expand sales to an existing customer, the salesperson should ensure that she only attempts expansion selling when she is sure it is in the customer's best interest. She should make any attempt at expansion selling in an honest manner, not with the intent just to increase revenue, but with the intent to better satisfy the customer's needs.

MANAGING DISSATISFIED CUSTOMERS   One of the greatest risks for sales organizations is that dissatisfied customers will exit rather than voice. That is, they simply leave the relationship rather than complain. Salespeople should consider themselves fortunate when customers do complain. The salesperson then has an opportunity to salvage the relationship, and even strengthen it. There are a number of things that the salesperson should do when dealing with complaining customers. The following are some suggestions:

1. *Encourage the customer to complain.* They are going to do so anyway, so the best thing a salesperson can do is to get customers to completely divulge their complaint. There is sometimes a catharsis once the customer gets everything out in the open. On the other hand, any attempt to interrupt a customer who wants to express his total frustration will most likely heighten the customer's anger and escalate the situation to a point where the relationship cannot be salvaged.
2. *Accept responsibility.* The salesperson should not take the complaint personally, but should recognize that he is hearing the complaint because he is the representative of the company to the customer. Rather than pass blame elsewhere in the company, the salesperson would be wise to empathize with the customer, and then express intent to try to remedy the situation. Nothing works better than, "I'm sorry this happened. I hope I can help solve this issue for you to your satisfaction."
3. *Clarify anything that is not clear.* The salesperson needs to be sure that he clearly understands the problem, from the customer's perspective. At this point, it is only the customer's perspective that counts.
4. *Express your perspective on the problem.* This is particularly important if there is information that the customer may not know, or if there are some constraints that will place some limits on the possible actions that might be taken.

5. *Problem solve with the customer.* Explore with the customer some possible solutions. This may evolve into a negotiating process, of course, but that is what good salespeople often do. At the end of the process, remember that both parties must feel satisfied. It must be a win–win solution.

6. *Gain the customer's commitment.* It is very important at this stage to ensure that the customer will be pleased with whatever action is decided. It may simply require asking the customer, "If we follow through on this action, will you be satisfied with what we have done?"

Salespeople who receive complaints have a valuable source of information that may not otherwise be available. It allows salespeople to re-evaluate their company's selling strategy and make or recommend changes, when either is appropriate. When customers complain, salespeople also have a unique opportunity to demonstrate their company's commitment to servicing customers. Customers who complain and who are subsequently satisfied often become more loyal customers.[26]

SUMMARY

1. **Describe three selling approaches that are used by salespeople today.** Salespeople today use three selling approaches: transactional selling, consultative selling, and relationship selling. Transactional selling is appropriate when the salesperson has a scripted sales presentation and is selling a limited product offering, or when customers know exactly what they want and are focused on price, or convenience, or both. Consultative selling is appropriate when the salesperson fills the role of consultant and is focused on understanding the customer's needs before making a product selection and a sales presentation. Relationship selling is not a replacement for consultative selling, but complements it when customers want long-term relationships with their suppliers.

2. **Describe five prerequisites to successful selling.** The five prerequisites to selling success are (1) developing a personal selling philosophy, (2) developing a relationship strategy, (3) developing a product strategy, (4) developing a customer strategy, and (5) developing a presentation strategy. The personal selling philosophy is critical to the development of the other four strategic steps; however, the five steps are all interrelated.

3. **Explain the skills involved in the pre-contact phase.** Two important skills are required in the pre-contact phase. First, salespeople must be able to identify and qualify prospects. They have many sources from which they can choose when prospecting. Salespeople must quickly qualify prospects, which requires that they establish that the prospect has a need for the product or service, the authority to make the purchase decision, the ability to pay for it, and the willingness to actually make the purchase decision. Second, salespeople must be good at pre-call planning. This will involve gaining as much information as possible about prospects or customers, setting objectives for sales calls, and planning for the sales presentation and interaction.

4. **Explain the skills involved in the face-to-face interaction phase.** During this phase, salespeople must know how to approach prospects or customers, make presentations, provide demonstrations, negotiate buyer concerns, and close sales. This is where the salesperson's planning and selling skills get their "road test."

5. **Explain the skills involved in the post-sale phase.** The post-sale phase involves servicing the sale, expansion selling, and managing dissatisfied customers. Servicing the sale includes all of the activities that are performed to facilitate or enhance the purchase and use of the product. Expansion selling includes any of three techniques used to expand business with an existing customer: full-line selling, cross-selling, and up-selling. Managing dissatisfied customers is important because only a small percentage of dissatisfied customers actually complain. Complaints provide valuable information for salespeople, an opportunity to demonstrate their company's commitment to service, and the potential to increase customer loyalty once a customer becomes satisfied.

KEY TERMS

transactional selling approach   **150**

consultative selling approach   **150**

relationship selling approach   **151**

personal selling philosophy   **152**

relationship strategy   **152**

product strategy   **155**

customer strategy   **155**

presentation strategy   **156**

product approach   **161**

referral approach   **161**

customer benefit approach   **161**

need discovery   **161**

survey question   **162**

general survey question   **162**

specific survey question   **162**

closed question   **162**

open question   **162**

probing question   **162**

confirmation question   **162**

buying conditions   **162**

summary confirmation question   **162**

need-satisfaction question   **162**

satisfactions   **164**

informative presentation   **165**

persuasive presentation   **166**

reminder presentation   **166**

emotional link   **167**

negotiating   **167**

trial close   **170**

confirmation step   **170**

buyer remorse   **170**

servicing the sale   **171**

expansion selling   **171**

full-line selling   **171**

cross-selling   **171**

up-selling   **172**

REVIEW QUESTIONS

1. Distinguish between a transactional selling approach and a consultative selling approach.

2. One sales manager was overheard to say, "It is impossible to implement a relationship selling approach unless you also understand and use a consultative selling approach." Do you agree or disagree? Explain your answer.

3. Briefly describe the importance of the five prerequisites to selling success as illustrated in the strategic/consultative selling model (Exhibit 6.1).

4. Distinguish between a *prospect* and a *qualified prospect*.

5. Describe six sources available for prospecting. Would the best source for prospecting be the same for established salespeople and people new to sales? Explain your answer.

6. What is *need discovery* and why is it important? Should a salesperson always attempt need discovery? Explain.

7. Explain what is meant by *cluster of satisfactions*. Explain why this would be an important concept for salespeople to understand.

8. Describe three types of sales presentations and explain when each would be most appropriate.

9. One sales trainer told his trainees, "You may think there are hundreds of concerns that buyers will raise, but they really only fall into five categories. Once you understand this, you will be better prepared to handle concerns effectively." Describe these five categories of buyer concerns.

10. What is *expansion selling?* Explain why this is a useful concept for salespeople to understand.

APPLICATION EXERCISES

1. Steven J. Schwartz is a Canadian author and sales trainer who is internationally known for his expertise in helping salespeople book appointments. Visit his website at **www.hotcoldcalls.com** and hit "Toolbox." One of the items here is a 24-question self-assessment tool that can help you identify initial mistakes you might make when first contacting prospects by telephone. Complete the survey and assess how well you did. Continue until you get all answers correct.

2. You have just graduated and have a job interview with a small computer retailer that is known for its outstanding customer service. During the interview, the sales manager says, "We want salespeople who will only sell products that meet customer needs. We are in business to build and maintain our position for honesty and outstanding service. I want you to take 15 minutes and write at least six questions that you would ask a customer who approaches you in our store and who appears not to know exactly what they want to buy. I will also want to know why you have chosen the questions you have chosen." What questions will you ask? Defend your choice.

3. You have just been through a fairly lengthy interview process with one of Canada's largest consumer packaged goods companies. At the end of your third interview, the sales manager says, "It has been our practice to hire new sales recruits at $28 000 per year. Most also earn another $4000 on bonus programs. I notice you state that you want a minimum starting salary of $40 000. I think you place too much value on yourself. Why would we consider paying you that much premium?" How would you respond? Be specific.

4. Canadian Tire has just hired you as a "paint consultant" to service customers who come to the store's paint department. You have just completed a sale to a customer who has purchased 40 litres of exterior house paint. List the items that you think would be appropriate for you to attempt to sell to the customer now (expansion selling). After you have attempted to sell a few additional items, the customer says, "Look, if I wanted anything else, I would have asked." What would you say to this customer? Be specific.

Bridgehead Cutting Tools

Tom Bannister was the sales manager at Bridgehead Cutting Tools, a North American manufacturer of cutting tools, including drills, taps, dies, reamers, and hacksaw blades. The company sold through a network of industrial distributors. However, it maintained a strong sales force that serviced its distributors and made sales calls on end-customers but directed them to place orders through a recognized distributor. As a result of sales growth, Tom had to hire a new sales representative, and that precipitated adjustment to several sales territories. Stan Klassen was the new salesperson, and he was assigned to the province of Alberta, including Edmonton and everywhere north of the city.

Stan seemed to be doing quite well. In fact, during his first four months, Stan added nearly 30 new accounts and sales seemed to be growing. That is why Tom was surprised when he received a telephone call from Tony Caputo, the owner of Wellhead Distributors, the largest distributor that Bridgehead Cutting Tools had in Western Canada and one of only four that were in Stan's territory. Tony was noticeably upset, and he wasted no time getting to the reason for his call. "Tom, we have been a distributor for your tools for nearly 20 years and we do a good job for you. Our companies have always had a good relationship, but that will quickly change if you don't assign another salesperson to call on us. I don't want that new guy of yours looking after us. We deserve better."

Tom replied, "I'm sorry there seems to be a problem, Tony. I certainly value your business and our friendship. Would you mind telling me specifically why you don't want to have Stan service your account? He has seemed to be doing an excellent job for us in the short time he has been here, so you have taken me completely by surprise."

"Well," Tony responded, "old Ed always treated us much better. Ed always had a reason for visiting, and we appreciated that. He was a 'no-nonsense' guy. He valued our time, and he treated us with respect. This new guy has only been to see us twice and he wants to spend half his day with us when he comes. He never seems to have a real reason to visit. He only wants to take us to lunch or out golfing. He spends most of his time talking about the Edmonton Oilers and telling jokes. I don't know where you got him, but we don't want him. Whatever happened to Ed? Ed was your senior salesperson, I know. He certainly wasn't ready to retire. If we can't get Ed back, can we get someone similar?"

CRITICAL-THINKING QUESTION

If you were Tom Bannister, what would you do? Be prepared to defend your answer.

Haines & Associates

Haines & Associates is a sales agency that represents seven U.S. manufacturers of industrial products. The company carries no inventory as most of the products it sells are customized solutions to meet specific customer needs. An exception, however, is a line of fairly inexpensive solenoid valves that are sold to mines, pulp mills, marine accounts, and manufacturing companies.

This U.S. manufacturer advertises in a number of U.S. trade magazines, many of which are also distributed in Canada. As a service to advertisers, these magazines include a "bingo card" insert. Each advertisement in a magazine has a number. Interested readers can go to the bingo card that is inserted near the back of the magazine and can circle the number of any advertisement that they are interested in. Once they return the bingo card to the magazine publisher, their name and address is passed along to the company whose advertisement generated the interest, and this becomes a sales lead, or prospect, for the advertiser.

The U.S. manufacturer sent additional information to all interested prospects, informing them that Haines & Associates was its Canadian sales agency. It then sent copies of all of the prospect names and addresses to Haines & Associates, requesting that it have a salesperson follow up on all leads. Initially, Bob Haines, president of the company, distributed the sales leads from the manufacturer to the five salespeople who worked for his agency. When the U.S. manufacturer asked for a report concerning how many leads were followed up, and the results of the follow-ups, Bob decided to ask his salespeople what they had done. He first approached Trevor Zavitz, his most senior salesperson. Trevor responded, "Well, to be honest, I threw them away. So did the rest of the salespeople. We don't have time to call on all of those leads to find the one or two who are legitimately interested in the valves. I know the customers in my territory, and the customers know me. The manufacturer has already informed these leads that we are the Canadian sales agency so if they are really interested, they'll call us. I spend my time selling products, not chasing magazine collectors."

CRITICAL-THINKING QUESTION

If you were Bob Haines, what would you do? Be prepared to defend your answer.

Comprehensive Cases for Part II

TFI Food Equipment Solutions

It was early 2007, and Alex Pettes had just recently been appointed as president of TFI Food Equipment Solutions (TFI) (**www.tficanada.com**) of Brampton, Ontario. Sales for 2006 were approximately $20 million, just slightly below 2005 sales. In fact, sales had been reasonably stable for several years, but Alex was now considering how he could take TFI to the next stage in its growth. TFI was a well-established, privately owned industrial distributor that had begun in 1954. Its two major product lines were Henny Penny and Taylor. TFI held exclusive rights to sell both lines of products in Ontario and in the four Atlantic provinces (New Brunswick, Nova Scotia, Prince Edward Island, and Newfoundland and Labrador). Alex recently secured for TFI the Canadian rights for One-Shot Corporation's "Revolver" and for R-O International's automatic french fry machine. Both products were manufactured outside Canada and had to be imported. The issue that Alex Pettes was considering was how and to what extent TFI should develop the national market for these two new product lines. In the back of Alex's mind was also a recent change that one of his current key suppliers was making in the U.S. market, and Alex could not help wondering whether this might eventually have implications for his Canadian operations.

> *I was able to convince Henny Penny to keep him [John Frishman] out of our territory, and all of Canada. We have built this territory without his involvement, and we will continue to have exclusive rights here, I understand. Still, I worry about the long-term implications of what is happening in the United States.*

—ALEX PETTES

Company Background

TFI is a well-established industrial distributor headquartered in Brampton, Ontario, that in 2006 earned approximately 90 percent of its sales revenue (divided equally) from sales of its two major product lines: Taylor (a division of Carrier Commercial Refrigeration Inc. of Rockton, Illinois, **www.taylor-company.com**), and Henny Penny Corporation (headquartered in Eaton, Ohio, **www.hennypenny.com**). Both Taylor and Henny Penny produce equipment for use in restaurants, stores, and institutional food service operations. Taylor focuses on ice cream and beverage equipment (batch ice cream machines, shake and slush machines, etc.). Henny Penny manufactures equipment for food service applications (fryers, rotisseries, blast chillers/freezers, heated food display units, holding cabinets for storing cooked food while maintaining its quality, etc.). Essentially, there is no overlap or risk of cannibalization between the two product lines, and they do complement each other very well.

Source: This case was written by H.F. (Herb) MacKenzie and James Doyle, both at Brock University, Faculty of Business, St. Catharines, ON, L2S 3A1. It was prepared as a basis for class discussion and is not intended to illustrate effective or ineffective handling of a management situation. © 2007 by H.F. (Herb) MacKenzie. Reprinted with permission.

TFI has been recognized by both manufacturers for its sales performance. In 2003, TFI was named Henny Penny's "Distributor of the Year," and in 2004 and 2005, the company was named Taylor's "Distributor of the Year." Alex believes that the market potential for both product lines will continue to be strong, but he is concerned that growth might be difficult to achieve as long as he is restricted to his current sales territory. Sales for 2006 look like they will be down approximately 4 percent from 2005, but final sales figures will not be available for a few months yet. This small decline is certainly within normal sales variance, but Alex's greater concern is his desire to see TFI grow.

Alex Pettes is highly regarded by TFI employees, suppliers, and fellow distributors who sell the same and similar products in other regions of Canada and the United States. Deeply knowledgeable in sales and marketing, Alex came to the position of president of TFI after several years as vice-president of sales and marketing. During his period in the previous position, the company achieved considerable success. Alex developed many of the important relationships TFI has with its suppliers and customers, and he was instrumental in the establishment and growth of the firm's sales force. Now, as president, Alex reports directly to the two owners, Tom and Jerry Kappus, who are currently the majority shareholders of the company. The owners have removed themselves from the daily operations of the company and are gradually selling their shares to Alex and two other minority shareholders. Due to his experience and expertise in sales and marketing, Alex is still closely involved in many of the important sales and marketing decisions that are made by the organization.

TFI has good relations with the other two industrial distributors who represent Henny Penny and Taylor in other regions of Canada. D.S.L. Inc. (**www.dslinc.com**) distributes Henny Penny and Taylor products throughout Western Canada and much of Northern Canada (as well as Alaska, Washington, and Oregon). It has been in business since 1916 and has Canadian sales branches in Winnipeg, Manitoba; Calgary, Alberta; and Port Coquitlam, British Columbia. Bazinet Taylor Ltee (**www.bazinet-taylor.ca**), established in 1954, is the exclusive Quebec industrial distributor. Though there are no contractual arrangements, the three "sister" distributors often help each other by trading or transferring inventory when one has a need and another has inventory. Taylor products, for example, may take as long as eight weeks to get after a distributor places an order on the factory. Being able to transfer, lend, or trade inventory, therefore, helps all of the distributors provide better customer service, and sometimes reduce inventory if there is an over-stock situation, or when older models of equipment must be sold. Arrangements are also made among distributors for installation, parts, or service when a product is sold by one distributor, but is being delivered and installed in the territory of another distributor.

The TFI Sales Force

TFI currently employs two types of salespeople who sell to two distinct markets. There are four salespeople who serve national accounts. Judi Saliba, Joanne Shearer, and Vico Singh sell to such companies as 7-Eleven, Wendy's, Burger King, McDonald's, Harvey's, KFC, Milestone's Grill & Bar, Mac's Convenience Stores, Esso, and other large, multi-outlet businesses. Dean Robinson serves the supermarket chains, such as Loblaws, Sobeys, A&P, and Wal-Mart. Because of their size, these accounts generally receive discounts on the products they buy, and these discounts can be as high as 25 percent from TFI list prices depending on the particular products, the number of product-units purchased, and the overall size of the sale. (Exhibit 1 illustrates pricing and product information for three models of Taylor single flavour soft serve machines.) These accounts

Exhibit 1   An Example of Product and Pricing Information

Taylor Single Flavour Soft Serve Machines

	Model 142	Model C707	Model C706
Capacity	93 cones/h	284 cones/h	426 cones/h
Impact	3 cones	25+ cones	40+ cones
Production	3.3 gal/h	10 gal/h	15 gal/h
	12.4 L/h	37.9 L/h	56.8 L/h
Weight	180 lb	335 lb	385 lb
	81.8 kg	152 kg	174.6 kg
Width	16.0"	18.25"	18.25"
	406 mm	464 mm	464 mm
Depth	24.5"	32.5"	34.0"
	622 mm	864 mm	864 mm
Counter clearance	4"	33.88"	33.88"
	101 mm	860 mm	860 mm
Price—Single Unit	$7899 each	$13 890 each	$17 943 each
Price—Multiple Unit	$7346 each	$12 918 each	$16 687 each

Source: Information taken from TFI 2006 price list.

contribute approximately 43 percent of total company sales revenue (national accounts—15 percent, supermarket chains—24 percent, and McDonald's—4 percent). Each of these salespeople receive annual base salaries ranging between $50 000 and $70 000, and commissions on sales of 1–4 percent. Commissions earned by these salespeople typically add 40 percent or more to their base salary. The national accounts market is relatively stable and predictable, although Alex can recall a circumstance where one grocery chain required a large amount of equipment with very short notice as it was preparing for a store "grand opening" and had forgotten to order its equipment with sufficient lead time. With considerable effort, TFI delivered all of the equipment to the customer's satisfaction. Most equipment, however, was planned and ordered long in advance of need, so that salespeople generally filled a high-service, customer relationship role.

Ten salespeople service the "independent" market. It is very different from the multi-outlet market, and contributes approximately 31 percent of the company's total sales revenue. Comprising primarily small, locally owned operations, including convenience stores and independent restaurants, this market is divided into numerous exclusive territories. In each territory, a TFI salesperson has been granted permission to sell the complete TFI product line, including Henny Penny and Taylor. The busiest sales period for this market is the few months leading to the summer season when consumer demand is high for ice cream and cool beverages. On average, salespeople are expected to sell $400 000 of equipment annually (which usually works out to about 35 to 50 sales), and, apart from the provision of company vehicles and reimbursement of out-of-pocket expenses, are compensated by commission, which generally ranges between 12 percent and 18 percent of sales. These salespeople have considerable flexibility in negotiating selling prices with customers; however, when discounts are given, the salesperson's commission is reduced accordingly. Alex was recently forced to terminate agreements with two of TFI's salespeople for consistent underperformance in their sales territory. Fortunately, this is uncommon, as losing salespeople creates a disruption to operations while new salespeople must be hired and trained.

Parts and service revenue contributed approximately 26 percent of total sales revenue.

A Recent Channel Change in the United States

Recent changes to Henny Penny's distribution strategy in the United States concerned Alex, at least for the longer term. He needed to consider what he should do in case similar changes were implemented in the Canadian market. Henny Penny was beginning to upset some of its U.S. distributors by forming a strategic alliance with J. Frishman Associates of Pompano Beach, Florida, to sell one of its products, the combi-oven, to the institutional market. Henny Penny's U.S. distributors claimed that this move was tantamount to the creation of a dual distribution system that was sure to harm sales in their respective territories. Though sales for the manufacturer would likely increase, distributors were starting to argue that what was good for Henny Penny might not be so good for them; Alex Pettes expected this issue would cause considerable tension at an upcoming meeting of North American distributors, which Henny Penny had scheduled to be held in Las Vegas, Nevada. Although Henny Penny had indicated to Alex that it did not have similar plans for Canada, he was somewhat concerned with the possibility of changes in its distribution strategy in his territory if this new channel structure proved successful in the United States. Alex was aware, however, that, sometimes, legitimate reasons existed for dual distribution systems, and he wondered what the impact would be for TFI if this happened.

New Opportunities for TFI

Alex Pettes was characteristically enthusiastic about the market potential for the two new products that TFI recently added to its product mix. The Revolver system (**www.one-shot.com**) is a single portion blending machine that is described as "the 'blend in cup' beverage system." It can blend a host of favourite drinks, including iced cappuccino, malts, milkshakes, etc. The machine can sit on a countertop as it is only 9" by 9.25" in size, stands only 30.5" tall, and weighs only 35 lb. The countertop unit provides users with unparalleled convenience; as an "all-in-one" system, the Revolver requires no clean-up. The machine uses a patented and unique design, and the cup lids come equipped with a built-in blade that mixes milkshakes and smoothies within the cup. A Revolver system would list for approximately $2200, approximately double the cost to TFI. Alex is confident that the user-friendliness and low cost of the Revolver will make it very attractive to every business from national accounts to independent convenience stores and small restaurants and cafés.

The second product is an automatic french fry vending machine manufactured by R-O International (**www.rointernational.com**). The machine produces hot french fries, "coin-to-cup" in just 45 seconds. It is 40" by 40" by 72" high, and weighs 970 lb. The machine is a revolutionary and innovative product that cooks french fries without oil, and it accepts multiple payment types: coins, tokens, cards, etc. The unit is also self-cleaning and claims to generate a gross margin for businesses of 70 percent. Alex is also convinced that this product has tremendous market potential. In particular, Alex feels that the automatic french fry unit should perform well in convenience store chains (which was a key motivating factor in taking on the product), and in institutional settings such as university and college campuses. A typical french fry vending machine would list for approximately $20 000, again, approximately double the cost to TFI.

Alex does recognize, however, that this product is relatively new to the market and consumers are generally unfamiliar with it. Many consumers would most likely question the quality of french fries distributed through a vending machine.

The Decision

Having secured distribution rights for the Revolver system and the automatic french fry vending machine, Alex Pettes was now unsure how and to what extent he should penetrate the Canadian market. He really had two related decisions to make: (1) how should the new products be sold in territories where TFI did not currently operate, and (2) how should they be sold in existing TFI territories? Since TFI had exclusive rights to sell these products throughout Canada, both decisions were important as the two new suppliers expected national distribution in Canada. Alex was also concerned that the two new products would appeal to different types of customers, and a different sales strategy might be appropriate for each of them. Alex considered several alternatives:

- First, Alex wondered whether he should hire TFI company salespeople for the new territories, even though they would not be allowed to sell the other products that TFI salespeople currently sold. TFI had a strong market presence and was quite profitable in Ontario and the four Atlantic provinces selling mainly two product lines. Alex understood how to manage this type of sales force structure, and using company salespeople ensured that all important market information stayed inside TFI where competitors or potential competitors could not make use of it.

- Second, Alex wondered whether TFI's relations with Bazinet-Taylor Ltee and D.S.L. Inc., the other Taylor and Henny Penny distributors in Canada, could be leveraged. Alex believed that these two distributors would be willing to add the two new product lines to their product mix, assuming that they could earn a good margin by doing so. The question immediately became what Alex would be prepared to offer them as a discount from the list price if they would become sub-distributors for these products.

- Third, Alex considered the possibility of using manufacturers' agents to sell the new products in the new territories. There was considerable risk and uncertainty associated with the new products, and using manufacturers' agents would be a more conservative sales strategy. These salespeople would be paid strictly by commission, and would otherwise pay their own selling expenses. Of course, they would also represent other product lines as well as the two that they would sell for TFI.

- Finally, Alex wondered, if he decided to hire TFI company salespeople for the new territories (the first alternative above), should he also consider an entirely new sales force for these products in Ontario and the Atlantic provinces as well? Alex was not so much concerned that the two new products would cannibalize sales from the existing product lines, but he was concerned that if current salespeople allocated too much of their time and effort to the new products, sales for Henny Penny and Taylor could be negatively affected. These two suppliers were too important to TFI to jeopardize losing either of them. Of course, if Alex did decide to hire new salespeople for these existing territories, having salespeople organized on the basis of product lines was only one alternative. Alex might also consider simply making each of the current sales territories smaller so that all salespeople could sell the complete product mix in their respective territories.

Alex was keen to ensure that any decisions he made would enable TFI to generate sufficient sales to satisfy the company's two new suppliers. At the same time, he wanted to ensure that the company's ability to maintain sales for his current products, particularly Henny Penny and Taylor, was not compromised.

Hi-T Mill Supply Inc.   CASE 2

Derek Anders was excited as he walked into Hi-T Mill Supply's head office in early 2008. It was Monday morning and he was about to begin his first two days with the company before flying to Calgary on Tuesday night. On Wednesday morning, Derek would begin work at the Calgary branch as sales manager for Western Canada. For his first day, he was scheduled to meet with Bob Smith and Tauri Colli, the company's two owners, and with Bill Stockley, the sales manager for Eastern Canada. Derek would meet Danny Ogg and Hal Maybee on Tuesday. Danny Ogg was a senior salesperson who lived in Winnipeg and who was responsible for Hi-T Mill Supply sales in Western Ontario and Manitoba. Danny was in Toronto to make a sales visit to the head office of a national account that was headquartered there, but that had several operating locations in his territory. Danny was scheduled to fly to Calgary with Derek and would introduce him to the rest of the staff there on Wednesday morning. Hal Maybee was a consultant who had just been hired to provide sales training to Hi-T Mill Supply, but who had also been asked to provide advice or assistance to Derek while he established himself in his new position. While Derek was recognized as a very competent salesperson, he had no sales management experience prior to joining Hi-T Mill Supply.

Derek Anders

Derek Anders received his early education in Newfoundland, and moved to Cambridge, Ontario, with his family in the late 1980s when his father took a job in the automotive industry. Derek completed a sales program at a nearby community college in 1996 and was hired by a manufacturer of valves as an inside order desk salesperson. Within three years, Derek demonstrated his ability to provide application assistance to customers and he was promoted to outside field salesperson, responsible for handling distributor accounts in Ontario and the Atlantic Provinces. Derek worked closely with his distributors and was largely responsible for their sales growth over the next several years. In 2006, when the sales manager retired, the position was given to Jay Trerice, the salesperson who managed distributor accounts in Western Canada. Derek was not surprised, although he was a little disappointed. Jay worked out of his home in Calgary, but he had a very good relationship with the company's senior management. Although Derek felt he was a better salesperson, he recognized that Jay was also very competent. Derek felt, unfortunately, that there were unlikely to be any opportunities for advancement in the near future as Jay was only a few years older than himself.

Derek began to think about looking elsewhere for a sales management job, but he did not actively pursue it until one of his distributors, Hi-T Mill Supply, indicated that it was looking for a sales manager for Western Canada. At first, Derek was unsure he wanted to apply as he was

Source: This case was prepared by H.F. (Herb) MacKenzie, Brock University, Faculty of Business, St. Catharines, ON, L2S 3A1. It is intended as the basis for classroom discussion and is not meant to demonstrate either effective or ineffective management. Names and places in this case are disguised. © 2007 by H.F. (Herb) MacKenzie. Reprinted with permission.

comfortable in his present position. He knew the products that he sold very well and one issue he had with working for a distributor was that he would have to learn about many different product lines. Hi-T Mill Supply represented more than 300 manufacturers, and carried inventory for about one-third of them. The more he thought about it, however, the more he thought this might be just the challenge he needed. During the interview and hiring process, Derek was able to convince the owners of Hi-T Mill Supply that he would be able to do the job. He knew a lot about valves and associated products, and he had enough technical aptitude that he could learn enough about the other products quickly. He had good planning skills, he seemed to understand time and territory management issues, and he had a good understanding of the value of qualitative and quantitative sales performance analysis. He also recognized his weakness was likely to be his inexperience at handling "people issues," and knew that this would ultimately determine his success as a sales manager.

Hi-T Mill Supply

Hi-T Mill Supply was a Canadian-owned industrial distributor with a head office and warehouse in Toronto, and offices and warehouses in Montreal and Calgary. The company had originally sold maintenance, repair, and operating (MRO) supply items such as hand tools, safety equipment, fasteners and fittings, and many items that were commonly bought by almost all types of businesses. It began operations in Toronto as Industrial Fasteners and Supplies Ltd. The company name was changed to Hi-T Mill Supply in 1985 when more technical product lines—such as pneumatic and hydraulic valves and cylinders, electric motor control equipment, vibration dampening equipment, power cable reels, and solid and liquid level control equipment—were added. It bought the Montreal and Calgary locations of another industrial distributor that went bankrupt in 1988. Gradually, salespeople were hired who worked from these branches but who resided in the territories where they sold. In 2007, there were three of these salespeople: Danny Ogg in Winnipeg, Bruce Stratton in Ottawa, and Rebecca MacIsaac in Halifax.

Bob Smith explained to Derek how the company's growth changed the way it managed sales. "At one time, things were very simple. We sold only MRO supplies. Everything came from our inventory and customers only bought from us when they needed supplies quickly for their operations. Now, however, things are more complicated. We assign all sales to one of three categories: warehouse (W), direct (D), or in-and-out (I&O). When we sell something that is normally an inventory item for us, the sale is coded as a warehouse sale. Those are usually the less technical, MRO supplies items, or sometimes things that we inventory because we have promised to do so for specific customers. A direct sale is one where we place an order with a manufacturer, and the manufacturer then ships the order direct to our customer so that we don't have to physically handle it. We simply get an invoice from the manufacturer, and we in turn invoice our customer. These are usually more complex items or items that we could not afford to carry in inventory because the turnover rate or gross margin for them would be too low. In-and-out sales are orders that we have the manufacturer ship to one of our warehouses and that we then immediately reship to our customer. We may do that for any of several reasons. Maybe we don't want the manufacturer to know who our customer is. Sometimes we may wish to consolidate items to save freight or brokerage fees. Sometimes we may need to make some product modifications before items are shipped to our customer. Or, in some instances, we need to consolidate shipments in our warehouse because customers request it to save them freight expenses or order processing costs. As we have added more and more technical products, the percentages of direct and in-and-out sales have increased."

"It's created other problems for us too," added Tauri Colli. We have some salespeople who have adapted very well as the company has changed. One or two have resisted selling our newer product lines, maybe because they don't have the technical skills to be comfortable with them, or maybe because some people simply don't like change. We have one or two, like Danny Ogg, who have focused almost exclusively on the newer product lines."

"Yes, that's true," Bill Stockley interjected. "But that's largely because salespeople such as Danny Ogg who have territories more distant from our warehouses have to focus more on these types of products. Many customers buy MRO supplies from local sources where they are assured of faster deliveries. A customer in Winnipeg doesn't want to wait one or two days to get nuts and bolts or safety clothing from Calgary. On the other hand, vibration dampening shock mounts will take anywhere from four to twelve weeks regardless where they are ordered from, and there may not even be a distributor located in Winnipeg that sells them."

Derek was following the conversation until there was a brief pause. He felt they were expecting him to ask a question or make a comment, so he said, "I guess you are telling me that when I look at the sales figures, I need to consider many factors when evaluating performance."

"Yes," said Bill, "and it gets even more complicated." He looked at Tauri. "Should I tell him now?" Tauri shrugged and Bill took that as a sign to continue. "I have a very unhappy salesperson here in Toronto," said Bill. "Annie Cormier worked for several years to sign a contract to become the sole supplier for all MRO supplies for National Cement, headquartered here in Toronto. She finally got the contract effective January 2000. The account means nearly $3 million for our company. National Cement has manufacturing plants from New Brunswick to Alberta. With our accounting system we split the credit for many of these sales based equally on three factors: where the order originates, where the shipment is delivered, and where the invoice is mailed."

"I can see how that could create problems," Derek interrupted, sorry he did as soon as he spoke. The conversation stopped, waiting for him to continue. "I mean, in some instances, the salesperson who is responsible for the sale might get credit for only one-third of the sale and in other instances they might get credit for two-thirds of the sale. When a salesperson in my territory has to service a sale and only gets credit for one-third of the sale because it was ordered from a centralized purchasing department in Toronto and invoiced to that office, he might feel he deserves more credit."

"But in this case," Bill continued, "National Cement places local orders that are then shipped to their local operating locations with the invoice following to its head office in Toronto. Annie was a bit upset that she only got one-third credit, but she was prepared to live with it. About a month ago, however, she came into my office in a rage. Tom Johns, your most senior salesperson, has two of National Cement's operating plants in his territory. In January 2001, he convinced them to request that all invoices go to the local plants to be matched with receiving reports before being sent to head office, and the head office agreed even though that policy has not been implemented anywhere else. In effect, that gave Tom 100 percent credit, and Annie got none. She just found out that she lost credit for $125 000 in sales last year that she feels should have been credited to her. If we can't come to some agreement on this, she's going to make my life miserable, and I agree with her."

Derek thought about it for a moment. "I can certainly sympathize with Annie and I'm sure we can solve the situation. But I must request that you give me a few months so I can get to discuss it with Tom. Can we talk about this later, once I get settled?"

"I'll stall Annie. She's easy to manage as long as she knows I'm working for her, and she trusts me to do that."

"Well, I haven't even met any of my sales staff yet, and already I've got some people issues." At that point, Derek made a few notes in his folder and then the group decided it was time for lunch. They spent the rest of the day talking about where the company planned to go over the next few years and Derek quickly decided he was pleased to have taken his new position. He respected the two owners as he realized they knew their business well, and they were not simply putting in time until they decided to retire. They were committed to actively growing the company, but they seemed willing to delegate authority, at least where they felt it was warranted. Bill Stockley was an interesting person. In many ways, he seemed to be very much like Derek himself, and Derek thought they would get along very well.

When Derek arrived at the office on Tuesday morning, he was introduced to Danny Ogg and Hal Maybee. Hal was preparing to make a sales call with one of the Toronto salespeople but had been scheduled to meet with Derek again later in the day. Danny was asked to spend the morning with Derek so they could talk about the Calgary operations. Derek had many questions he wanted very much to ask. He decided that he would ask Danny some of them now, but there were a few sensitive ones he thought best to save until he better understood his situation.

"Where do you want to start?" asked Danny.

"Well, I thought I'd like to know something about the man I'm replacing. What can you tell me about Eric Crouse? What was his management style? What would you consider to be his strengths and weaknesses?"

Danny looked directly at Derek. "Okay." There was a lengthy pause. "Eric was not a strong manager, but he did a reasonable job and I respected him a lot. Everyone liked him because Eric found it very easy to say 'yes,' and very difficult to say 'no.' He was smart enough to identify problems, but then never really wanted to solve them. He was a good man with numbers and he used them a lot for planning. He shared all his analysis with everyone on a regular basis, but he was never willing to push people when they needed it. He knew most of the older products very well, but as I'm sure you know, the company has changed considerably in the past few years. Eric never kept up with the newer products, so he was always uncomfortable visiting customers with me because that's where I focus most of my attention. Consequently, I think he made one trip to Winnipeg in the last three or four years. I didn't really need him, but sometimes I felt very isolated from everything. If you ask some of the others in Calgary, you might get a different perspective."

"One thing I do promise you, Danny, is that you will see me more regularly. You may not see me as often as the other salespeople do, but you will see me regularly and for longer periods of time than the others do. Once I get organized, you'll get my plans and you'll see that once I make them I treat them seriously." Danny nodded, and Derek continued, "Can you tell me if I'm going to run into problems coming to the organization from outside?"

"What you really mean is whether someone else is going to be upset because they didn't get a promotion. Right? Another good question, Derek. But you're lucky in that regard. Tom Johns is the oldest member of the sales force. I'm glad he didn't get the promotion although, again, I like Tom a lot. I don't think he would like the responsibility. He's been around a long time and he's very comfortable in his territory. Besides, he'll be retiring in four or five years so it might not make sense to promote him now. I'm the second most senior salesperson but I'm certainly not interested. I don't plan to leave Winnipeg. I don't know about Peter Luchak. He certainly is an excellent salesperson, but he's a very independent guy. He gets along well with his customers, but he sometimes causes friction internally. He's not disliked, mind you. But I don't think he would get any support as sales manager either."

They continued to talk over lunch, when Derek asked directly what Danny expected of him. Derek decided they were going to get along well and he was glad to have someone with Danny's maturity on his sales force. As the lunch proceeded, Danny seemed to grow more hesitant until Derek finally noticed. "I think there is something else you want to tell me, but you're not sure how to say it. I know we have only just met but I hope you feel comfortable enough to trust me with any problems you have. I am committed to working with you and for you wherever I can, and I hope we can be open with each other."

"Yes . . . no . . . I mean, I don't have any problems right now. I'm very happy and I'm sure we'll get along well. But, yes, I do have something I want to mention because I think it's important and you should know. I am hesitant though because I don't want anyone to know I was the source of the information, and I don't want to tell you where I got the information."

"You have my word. I won't ask where you got your information, and I won't tell anyone that I heard it from you. If it concerns the company, I would appreciate knowing, but if you're very uncomfortable and prefer not to tell me, I can respect that too."

"Well, it concerns another salesperson. Brian Smith covers Northern Alberta and Saskatchewan. He basically goes to Saskatchewan every four weeks. I heard that he submitted an expense report for a trip to Saskatchewan last month but that he never left home. I won't tell you my source and you said you wouldn't ask, but I'm sure that everyone in the Calgary office knows about this."

"Thanks for your trust," said Derek. "That is information I should have, and I'll be sure to watch the situation." With that, they returned to the office, where they parted ways so that Derek could spend some time with Hal Maybee. Hal had been scheduled to do some work at the Calgary branch, but that was now postponed until Derek had an opportunity to evaluate the branch situation. Hal would spend his immediate time in Toronto, but was "on call" to help Derek if needed. Derek thought it would be a good idea to make his own sales calls with his sales staff so that he could make his own assessments before having any outside involvement. Hal had agreed, as that would give Derek an opportunity to get to know his staff better and to do some of his own sales coaching.

"I really only have one question," Derek looked at Hal. "What exactly should I do tomorrow morning?"

"Let me ask a few questions first," replied Hal. "I heard you were a pretty strong 'numbers' guy so I expect you'll do a careful analysis of the numbers before you decide anything. I've given them a scan, but I have been asked not to discuss them with you for a few weeks unless you have some specific questions. Bob and Tauri want you to make your own assessment first. I must ask though whether you plan to make sales calls with your salespeople?"

"Regularly. I have seen many sales managers who let this responsibility slip and I am committed to not do that. I plan to spend at least one day every month with each salesperson except Danny, the guy in Winnipeg. Because he is farther away, I plan to visit him quarterly, but I'll spend several days with him during each visit."

"Eric Crouse didn't do that, so I'm sure you'll get some resistance as soon as you announce your intentions."

"All the more reason to announce them immediately and to follow through quickly. They need to see my commitment to that and that my main purpose is to help them. I also want them to see that I do it regularly and I do it with everyone. Otherwise, it might be taken as a sign there are problems with specific people. I also think that once they see my intentions are good, it can be motivating for them."

"Alright. That's certainly a reasoned approach," Hal responded, impressed with the answer. "Then, if that's your approach, I would recommend you call a group meeting tomorrow morning to introduce yourself. Give them some of your philosophy as a sales manager and as a manager in general. Let them know that you will be making sales calls with them every month and that you are looking forward to helping them grow personally and professionally. Promise to meet with them all individually in the next few days, but ask for some time to properly evaluate the region before you do that. Then, spend a few days doing your analysis. You won't have to ask all of your salespeople to meet individually with you. My hunch is that you will get a visit or two before you even finish your sales analysis. Anyway, that's my advice."

Derek looked puzzled. "Are you saying I should do things differently, Hal?"

"No. Not at all. You asked for my advice. I took what you gave me and added a few points to it for you to consider. I think your approach is the right one but unless I miss my guess, you will get some resistance early. The sooner you get a feel for the sales figures, the sooner you'll be able to predict from where."

"Any other advice?" Derek asked.

"Yes. Once you have looked at the sales figures by salesperson, you should look at how they are allocating their time across accounts."

"The old 20/80 rule," Derek commented.

"Yes, but in this company, you might want to group customers into the old A–B–C classification scheme. Maybe include each salesperson's 10 largest customers as 'A' accounts, their 20 smallest customers as 'C' accounts, and classify all the rest as 'B' accounts."

"Have you already done this?" Derek asked.

"No. Just experience. I do have a sense of account distribution in this industry, by size of account. I may be wrong, but if there is anything of interest, this data should let you find it."

With that, the two men parted company, promising to be in contact within the next two weeks.

The First Few Days at the Calgary Branch

On Wednesday morning, Derek and Danny arrived early and went immediately to Derek's office. When the sales secretary arrived, Danny motioned her into the office and closed the door so they could all talk. Derek was also hoping to wait until everyone else arrived before meeting them as a group. Derek mentioned that as the branch sales secretary, she would be working for him as well as the sales staff, and he trusted she would handle any sensitive material she might see as confidential within the office. They continued to make casual conversation and Derek realized he liked her a lot. Gillian Strong was the type of person who would make an excellent administrative assistant. She was quite serious but friendly, and she had a lot of confidence and poise.

Shortly after 9:00, Gillian invited everyone to the boardroom. Once they were inside and seated, Derek and Danny entered, and Danny made the introductions. He pointed out each person in the room and told Derek who they were before Derek made his own introduction. "Let me tell you first how pleased I am to be here. I have been an employee of Hi-T Mill Supply for only two days but I am excited about this company. I know Eric Crouse managed this branch for nearly 20 years, and I am sorry he didn't live to see his scheduled retirement next year. I do hope to gain the same support that you gave him as we continue to grow this branch in the years ahead. I promise all of you my full support. I am dedicated to helping each and every one of you to develop personally and professionally, whether you are in sales or in sales support positions. I plan to spend the next few days assessing sales data for this branch and then I will meet with you individually to see how I can help you. You won't see much of me for the next few days. After my tour of the office and warehouse, I want to analyze our performance for the last few years. I will, however, have my door open and you will always find it open to you if you wish to discuss anything with me. Once I get a better understanding of our operations, I will begin making regular sales calls with each of the salespeople on a monthly basis." Before he could continue, Tom Johns interrupted.

"Not with me, you won't. I've been with this company for 20 years. I have the highest sales in this branch. I know my customers and my territory." Tom challenged.

"We can discuss this when me meet in the next week or so, Tom." Derek tried to change the subject.

"You can make calls with the others if you wish, but you won't be making any with me. I don't need any help or interference." Tom had become more aggressive.

"I'm sorry, Tom. This is not open for discussion. Once I understand more about your accounts, I'll be in a better position to select which customers we will visit together." This time, Derek was successful at changing the topic as he asked Rick Mansour, the office manager, to give him a tour of the office and warehouse. But, he noticed that Tom had left the boardroom and didn't seem to be in the office while Rick showed him around.

For the rest of the week, Derek stayed mostly in his office reviewing sales figures. When he looked at recent expense reports from the sales force, he knew he had justification to speak to Brian Smith without having to acknowledge that he was suspicious because of a conversation with another employee. Derek asked Brian to come to his office for a minute and when he did, Derek closed the door behind him. After a few social comments, Derek looked directly at Brian and confronted him with the reason for wanting the meeting. "Brian, I don't know quite how to put this to you, so I'll be somewhat direct. I have reason to suspect that you submitted an expense report last month for a trip you did not take." Derek expected Brian to either show some embarrassment or become defensive and ask where the information originated, but he did not. "Yes. I did. In fact, I did it twice in the last year. Eric suggested that I do it because I get the lowest base salary on the sales force, and he had no way to get me up to what we both agreed would be appropriate. An alternative, he suggested, would be for me to submit a few expense reports and claim some expenses. It would be tax-free and would raise me to the same income level as some of my peers."

"Does anyone other than you or I know about this?" Derek asked.

"It was supposed to be a secret between Eric and me. But, if no one else knows, you now have me curious as to how you became suspicious."

"It was simple, really. All your expense reports for travel show hotel receipts, and credit card receipts for gas and meal expenses. This expense report shows hand written receipts from a bed and breakfast, and cash receipts for meals and gasoline." Derek nodded toward an expense report on his desk.

"Yes, I know. But Eric knew too and he approved my expenses."

"Okay. I can accept that. Mind you, I'm not happy with it and I certainly won't be party to it in the future. I am pleased it was done with Eric's blessing. If there is a problem with your salary, I'll find some way to compensate you appropriately, but it won't be on your expense account. We can talk about this at a more appropriate time. I'd like to have breakfast with you on Monday morning if you can manage it. This is just a way to meet people outside the office so we can get to know each other better. I'm hoping to eventually have a breakfast meeting with everyone a few times each year." They agreed to meet first thing the next week, and Derek got back to analyzing his sales figures.

By the weekend, Derek had put together the information he thought he needed (see Exhibits 1, 2, and 3). His major problem was immediately apparent, but he wasn't sure what to do about it. He wished he had some advice, and he looked forward to discussing it with Hal Maybee. But, he knew Hal's first response would be to ask what he had found in the sales data, and what his own recommendations would be. Derek thought back to his job interview and his first few days at head office. He was certainly right that his biggest problems were likely to be people problems.

Exhibit 1 Salespeople

	Active Accounts	Sales Calls	Direct Selling Expenses	Gross
Barry Cullen	87	843	118 645	
Danny Ogg	77	868	124 688	
Brian Smith	103	930	108 227	
Peter Luchak	122	1240	94 566	
Tom Johns	130	1146	104 258	
Total	*519*	*5027*	*550 384*	

Exhibit 2 Sales by Salesperson, 2003–2007

		Sales ($000)				
		2007	2006	2005	2004	2003
Barry Cullen	W	464 661	454 214	433 824	424 071	388 699
	D	209 400	190 302	182 901	160 422	140 238
	I&O	191 230	186 745	173 209	151 265	145 256
	Total	*865 291*	*831 261*	*789 934*	*735 758*	*674 193*
Danny Ogg	W	368 908	347 371	336 600	323 540	317 655
	D	187 607	173 206	151 390	140 243	125 751
	I&O	231 750	201 202	189 879	160 444	153 243
	Total	*788 265*	*721 779*	*677 869*	*624 227*	*596 649*
Brian Smith	W	608 377	567 463	525 429	527 539	466 848
	D	152 346	142 302	130 917	115 231	118 918
	I&O	222 153	208 962	190 902	170 345	163 183
	Total	*982 876*	*918 727*	*847 248*	*813 115*	*748 949*

continued

Exhibit 2 *continued*

		Sales ($000)				
		2007	**2006**	**2005**	**2004**	**2003**
Peter Luchak	W	833 214	771 494	694 414	638 836	587 165
	D	185 901	184 129	170 774	145 148	157 236
	I&O	266 222	254 562	232 938	191 452	204 376
	Total	*1 285 337*	*1 210 185*	*1 098 126*	*975 436*	*948 777*
Tom Johns	W	995 341	888 342	654 449	634 529	645 287
	D	129 567	108 241	106 789	94 536	109 258
	I&O	283 766	263 998	238 756	242 873	232 388
	Total	*1 420 198*	*1 260 581*	*999 994*	*971 938*	*986 933*

Exhibit 3 Sales Force Sales Calls and Sales Revenue ($000) by Account Importance

	Top 10 Accounts	**Middle 70 Accounts**	**Smallest 20 Accounts**
Barry Cullen	108–302 599	552–512 816	41–49 876
Danny Ogg	112–397 256	578–342 253	32–48 756
Brian Smith	128–414 215	545–488 907	47–79 754
Peter Luchak	188–523 336	807–670 801	104–91 200
Tom Johns	133–878 662	822–502 548	166–38 988
Total	*669–2 516 068*	*3304–2 517 325*	*390–308 574*

Part III

Implementing the Strategic Sales Program

CHAPTER 7	Recruiting and Selecting Salespeople
CHAPTER 8	Training Salespeople
CHAPTER 9	Motivating Salespeople
CHAPTER 10	Compensating Salespeople
CHAPTER 11	Leading Salespeople
CHAPTER 12	Ethical and Legal Responsibilities

Comprehensive Cases for Part III

| CASE 1 | General Electric Appliances |
| CASE 2 | Hal Maybee's Ethical Dilemmas |

Today's sales managers are responsible for implementing strategic sales programs. To do this, sales managers are actively involved in recruiting and selecting salespeople (Chapter 7), training salespeople (Chapter 8), motivating salespeople (Chapter 9), compensating salespeople (Chapter 10), and leading salespeople (Chapter 11). Ethical and legal responsibilities of sales managers are discussed in Chapter 12.

Chapter 7

Recruiting and Selecting Salespeople

After completing this chapter, you should be able to

1. Discuss planning for recruitment and selection.

2. Explain how to conduct a job analysis.

3. Describe the different sources used for recruiting applicants.

4. Describe the selection and validation process.

When Jim MacDonald walked into the office of a large, Canadian industrial distributor, he greatly impressed the manager and inside salesperson who interviewed him. The sales branch urgently needed someone for a warehouse and counter-sales position. There were only a few job qualifications: a secondary school education, physical strength to help with receiving and shipping, and good appearance and communication skills for interacting with customers. There was potential also for future promotion to inside sales, and possibly later to field sales.

Jim was recommended by a manager at a local government employment office who said that he knew Jim's family and they were all respected in the local community. When Jim first appeared for his interview, he was well dressed and polite. He stated on his application that he had attended Acadia University but that he had left after only a few months. He stated that he had no job experience, but he was motivated and wanted to work toward a sales career because he loved interacting with people. In fact, he so impressed the people who interviewed him that Jim was immediately offered the job.

Within a few days, a customer queried why Jim had been hired. He said Jim had told him that he was about to go back to St. Francis Xavier University. Before the manager could speak to Jim, a second customer had the same query. However, Jim had told this customer that he was about to return to Acadia University. When the manager approached Jim, the confusion seemed resolved. Jim said that he had told both customers that he had studied at Acadia University but was now considering taking some night courses from St. Francis Xavier University. He wanted to do some business courses to further his career aspirations. The manager told Jim that taking courses would be a good idea, and that the company had an education program for employees and would pay his tuition and for his textbooks.

Unfortunately, a third customer came in and wanted to know why Jim had been hired. The customer said that he had been at a local grocery chain location when Jim had gotten fired, and that the manager might want to investigate further. However, a call to the personnel manager for the grocery chain did not provide much information—just that there was a note on Jim's file that under no circumstances would he ever be considered for re-hire. Then, the personnel manager added that Jim had worked for a local media outlet as well. Since Jim's new manager was a friend of the media outlet owner, he called for more information.

The owner said that when he had hired Jim, he had thought that Jim had studied for one year at Acadia University. Within weeks, Jim had stolen several employee paycheques and tried to cash them. He had then tried to obtain money in the company's name from a local bank. After he had fired Jim, the owner had discovered that Jim had never attended university. In fact, Jim's parents thought Jim was still in high school, and the school's principal thought that Jim was taking a year's leave to recover from major surgery.

Jim was immediately terminated. Two days later, the manager got a visit from a local bank manager, who had been trying to locate Jim for months. Jim had cashed many cheques in Montreal as James A. MacDonald from St. Francis Xavier University, and many more in Toronto as J. Andrew MacDonald from Acadia University. Jim did not even have an account at the bank. The day Jim was terminated, he cashed approximately 30 fraudulent cheques within several blocks of the office, giving the manager's name as a personal reference.

The following week, Jim's father visited the sales office and asked why Jim had been fired. In subsequent conversation between him and the manager, both men discovered that the only two true things on Jim's application were his name and his social insurance number. He had lied about his age, his father's first name, his father's occupation, his address, his phone number, his prior employment (by omission), and his education. There was considerable evidence for termination with cause.

Lesson learned.[1]

The Importance of Recruitment and Selection

If you read many companies' annual reports, you will often see the statement, "Our most important asset is our people." Many companies, if they wanted, could more specifically say, "Our most important people are the members of our sales force." The only purpose of a sales force is to generate revenue, directly through getting orders, or indirectly through establishing and building relationships with customers. The quality of a company's sales force affects its revenue-generating ability, and that is why superior companies need to manage the recruitment and selection process so carefully. That process, shown in Exhibit 7.1, involves planning for recruitment and selection,

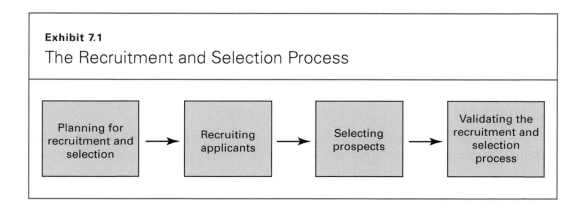

Exhibit 7.1
The Recruitment and Selection Process

Planning for recruitment and selection → Recruiting applicants → Selecting prospects → Validating the recruitment and selection process

recruiting applicants, selecting prospects, and validating the recruitment and selection process. When the process is managed carefully, the chance of hiring a good salesperson is much higher. When it is not, as the manager in the opening vignette discovered, the consequences can be serious.

Planning for Recruitment and Selection

The first stage of the recruitment and selection process—planning for recruitment and selection—is the most important stage of the entire process. Without proper planning, everything that follows is simply hit or miss. One businessperson, who wishes not to be identified, stated, "The problem with small businesses such as mine is that we are too quick to hire and too slow to fire. We don't realize we need someone until we really need someone, and then the first person who looks good gets hired. Then we constantly make excuses for them because we don't want to fire them. We think that with just a bit more experience and training they will become good salespeople." She went on to add, "I have two [salespeople] now that I should fire, but I know them personally and firing them is hard to do so I will live with my mistakes as long as I can, or until they decide to leave."

While this person was the owner of a small business in Atlantic Canada, many hiring mistakes are made in large organizations as well. DDI International, a global human resources consulting firm, surveyed nearly 1600 hiring managers and concluded that one in five new hires is a mistake, and over one-third of respondents admitted to making a poor hiring decision due to time pressure to fill open sales positions.[2]

THE ROLE OF THE SALES MANAGER IN RECRUITING AND SELECTING SALESPEOPLE

The first decision that a company must make when planning for recruitment and selection is to decide who will participate in the process, and who will have responsibility for making the final selection decision. In very small companies—or companies where sales force turnover is very high, qualifications for salespeople are few, and the selling job is relatively standardized—the sales manager frequently is the only person involved in the process and therefore makes the hiring decision. When companies are large enough to have a personnel department, or when a company needs to be very selective when choosing its salespeople, recruitment specialists often assist the sales manager with the process. In these instances, the recruitment specialists help attract and evaluate applicants, but the final decision frequently still rests with the sales manager. There is one situation, however, where the sales manager has less responsibility in the final hiring decision but will still certainly have influence: when the company is hiring salespeople with the longer-term goal of promoting them to management or even executive positions, a greater number of people will be involved in the recruitment and selection process, and recruitment specialists may have influence equal to or greater than the sales manager's. Even senior executives in the company may be involved, and may make the final selection based on the management potential of the applicant.

SALES FORCE TURNOVER AND PERSONNEL NEEDS

An analysis of sales force personnel needs is an important aspect of planning for recruitment and selection. Company sales may be growing or declining, and this sometimes requires sales managers to make territory re-alignments or to increase or decrease the number of salespeople. Even when the economic environment is stable and sales forecasts are more predictable, companies frequently make recruitment and selection decisions to replace salespeople lost due to sales force turnover. To conduct an assessment of sales force turnover, the first step is to calculate the sales force **turnover rate**: the percentage of salespeople who leave the sales force each year. The calculation requires dividing the number of salespeople who leave the company each year by the average size of the sales force. For example, if there were 51 salespeople on January 1 and 57 salespeople on December 31, then the average size of the sales force was 54 salespeople. If 7 people left the sales force during the year, then the sales force turnover rate is calculated as follows:

$$\text{Sales force turnover rate} = \frac{7}{54} = 13.0\%$$

Is this an acceptable turnover rate? To assess this, a sales manager should know how the rate compares to the sales force turnover rate for other firms in the same industry, and whether this rate has been increasing or decreasing over time. In some industries, sales force turnover rates can exceed 50 percent, while other industries have rates well below 10 percent. Companies in the pharmaceutical industry consider a 10 percent turnover rate normal, but management was surprised to find a 40 percent increase in the turnover rate in one recent year, when the turnover rate jumped from 10 percent to 14 percent across the industry. The two most important reasons were compensation and dissatisfaction with an immediate supervisor.[3]

Salespeople have one of the highest turnover rates of all employees. A recent Canadian Professional Sales Association survey found that 57 percent of salespeople who responded might consider actively pursuing employment with other firms within the following year.[4] Why do so many salespeople consider changing jobs? Perhaps Herbert Greenberg—CEO and president of Princeton, New Jersey-based Caliper Corp, a human resources consulting firm with offices in Toronto and Vancouver—has the answer. In his book, *How to Hire & Develop Your Next Top Performer*, he estimates that 55 percent of salespeople should not be in sales, and another 20–25 percent are selling the wrong product.[5] If he is correct, then only about one in five salespeople are employed in jobs where they have the skills required for success. Many will eventually leave the sales profession, but others will continue to sell while they search for the right product or company.

While the greatest concern is often with having turnover rates that are too high, management should be concerned about turnover rates that are too low as well. When turnover is very low, the sales force may become too entrenched in the ways they do things and they may be unable to adapt to a changing sales environment. As a worst-case scenario, the best salespeople may have already left the sales force as they will be the ones with the greatest opportunities to do so, and the company may have remaining only those whom no other company would hire. These salespeople will never voluntarily leave. A good sales manager will ensure sufficient sales force turnover to maintain enthusiasm and adaptability, but not so much that management time and other resources are wasted continually recruiting and selecting new salespeople, or that customers become apprehensive or dissatisfied with the company, or that remaining salespeople become nervous or demotivated.

SALES FORCE CULTURE

A careful assessment of the company's sales culture is important as part of the planning for recruitment and selection. Understanding a company's internal sales culture and then aligning the recruitment and selection process to that culture will result in better hiring decisions, and should result in better satisfied employees, lower sales force turnover, and better overall sales performance. Sales managers who are not careful risk hiring salespeople to fit a desired sales culture rather than the existing sales culture. In these instances, new salespeople may quickly become dissatisfied and leave the company. To understand the company's sales culture, sales managers need to assess a number of factors: how much direction and support a new salesperson will be given; how sales territories are established and maintained; what expectations exist concerning salesperson performance; what happens if quotas are exceeded or not reached; and how a new salesperson will be compensated or otherwise rewarded. Then, they can begin to recruit and select salespeople who will fit the existing sales culture.

Further complicating the issue is that sales cultures may not only vary across companies, but may vary across sales offices within the same company. Some companies carefully establish and maintain a corporate sales culture; other companies are more decentralized and sales cultures vary depending on individual sales managers, unique territory selling conditions, or the sales force that exists in particular sales offices. Sales managers need to be cognizant of this to ensure that new salespeople are hired to fit the particular sales environment where they will work.

JOB ANALYSIS

One thing that should be apparent after reading previous chapters is that there are many different types of sales jobs: inside and outside sales jobs; face-to-face and telesales jobs; transactional and relational sales jobs; technical and more general sales jobs; business development and account maintenance sales jobs. Before applicants can be recruited for a sales job, the recruiter must conduct a **job analysis**—a systematic approach to define specific tasks and responsibilities that must be performed in a particular job (job description), and to determine the knowledge, skills, abilities, and personal characteristics that an applicant should possess (job qualifications) in order to perform successfully in the job. Some organizations spend time and other resources to prepare job descriptions but fail to realize that environmental or other conditions have changed since the last time someone was hired for a particular job, so that the job description being used has little resemblance to the job that a new recruit will actually be required to fill. This problem is more likely to occur in smaller sales forces where tasks sometimes get changed by informal agreement because someone is particularly good (or poor) at doing a certain task that is essential to the operation. Once tasks have changed for a particular position, when an employee leaves that position the sales manager is faced with: (1) hiring someone based on an old job description, and making other changes to remaining employees' jobs to accommodate the extra tasks that will not be part of this position for the new recruit; (2) changing the job description and trying to find someone who can do all of the things that the former employee did; or (3) hiring someone based on the old job description and having that person quickly become dissatisfied if she does not like the extra tasks she is required to do. An astute sales manager will recognize, at least, that there are three options, and he will most likely adopt the first or second of these. The sales manager who selects the third option is, in effect, hiring someone for a job other than the one that exists. Research suggests that, in several sales contexts, when actual jobs do not meet recruits' job expectations, turnover increases.[6]

JOB DESCRIPTION The **job description** is a formal written document that describes the tasks and responsibilities for a particular job. Job descriptions are frequently prepared by the sales manager in smaller firms. In larger firms, job analysis staff from the human resources department may be used. An option for firms of all sizes is to use an external consultant who specializes in this aspect of recruiting. Regardless of who prepares the job description, a minimum of two sources should be used to collect information on the job: the sales manager who will supervise the new recruit and who will be able to describe the job as he expects it to be; and current employees who are doing the job and who will be able to describe the job as it actually exists. In the event that the job is being filled due to retirement or termination, an exit interview with the employee who is leaving should be conducted, and this would be particularly important if the position is unique. In some instances, input from other companies in the distribution channel, including customers, can provide useful information.

Once this information is collected, it is possible to prepare a good job description, one that includes all of the information that is necessary to attract the best applicants for the job, while dissuading poorly qualified people from applying. Among the most likely information to be found in a good job description is the following:

1. *The relationship between this position and other positions in the company.* To whom does the person in this position report, and who, if anyone, reports to her? What will her relationship be with other members of the sales department?
2. *The nature of the goods or services to be sold.* In some situations, salespeople may be required to sell both goods and services, but the salesperson may have to focus mainly on one or the other.
3. *The types of customers to be called on.* Many salespeople service both end-users and dealers or distributors. Salespeople will need to know the frequency of calls to various types of customers; for example, a packaged goods company may expect a salesperson to make eight calls per day to grocery chain locations. Finally, salespeople need to know who within customer organizations will be called on; that is, whether they will be seeing purchasing personnel, or whether they will also have to see other people within customer accounts.
4. *The specific tasks and duties to be performed.* Some companies require outside salespeople to prospect for new customers, while other companies delegate this responsibility to inside salespeople. Some salespeople manage customer accounts from the prospecting stage to long-term retention. Others may be the new business development person who then transfers the account over to another salesperson who has account management responsibility. Salespeople also need to know their role in collecting information, preparing presentation material, collecting delinquent accounts receivable, preparing sales call reports, taking customer inventories and refilling bins or shelves, and any other tasks that may be required.
5. *The mental and physical demands of the job.* Salespeople will want to know what technical knowledge they must have or will be required to acquire, and how frequently they will need to upgrade their knowledge. How frequently will they have to travel and how often will they be away overnight? Will they have to carry heavy demonstration material or equipment?

Many companies have a variety of sales positions from inside or counter sales, to field sales, to sales management. Exhibit 7.2 provides job descriptions for three positions at Dell Computer Corporation. Note that each job description specifies different duties and responsibilities. The job qualifications also vary from one job to another. In the following section, job qualifications are described in greater detail.

JOB QUALIFICATIONS   **Job qualifications**—unlike the job description, which specifies tasks and responsibilities—specify required knowledge, skills, and abilities, or KSAs. Exhibit 7.2 shows the job qualifications for several jobs at Dell Computer Corporation and, again, you should note that job qualifications vary considerably depending on the job. For one job, inside sales manager, both required and preferred KSAs are indicated.

Exhibit 7.2

Job Descriptions at Dell Computer Corporation

A. **Bilingual Inside Sales Manager — Relationship Sales — Ottawa — 060007NW**

The successful candidate will be responsible for managing the internal sales force selling to REL accounts. He/she will motivate the sales force to sell products and services through effective management of sales incentive, career development, reporting mechanisms and one-on-one relationship building. The Inside Sales Manager will help drive growth in the REL market.

PRINCIPAL DUTIES AND RESPONSIBILITIES:

- Attain targeted sales goals and performance through the effective management of the daily operations of the sales force
- Analyze various sales reports to determine buyer/buying influences and project sales to establish quotas
- Resolve complex customer concerns regarding the sale/delivery of products with customer and internal departments such as manufacturing, customer service, and financial services
- Participate and close large sales opportunities with sales representatives
- Provide management to a unit by establishing goals and objectives, assigning tasks and reviewing work at frequent levels

REQUIRED KNOWLEDGE, SKILLS, AND ABILITIES:

- Post-secondary education
- Fluently bilingual in English and French
- Minimum of 3 years of sales management experience
- Must have proven success in consistently achieving sales goals
- Must have experience mentoring and coaching other employees
- Strong organizational and presentation skills
- Strong verbal and written communication skills in English and French

PREFERRED KNOWLEDGES, SKILLS AND ABILITIES:

- Strong knowledge of computer hardware, software and peripherals

B. **Bilingual Technical Sales Representative — Corporate Accounts — 060004AV**

The Technical Sales Representative (TSR) is responsible for supporting Dell Canada's sales team in their efforts to configure and sell Dell Enterprise products and related services within. The TSR must have the ability to identify customer requirements through a consultative selling approach and must be able to consider the customer requirements from an enterprise rather than a single system perspective. The successful candidate will have proven time management and project management skills. He/she has strong verbal and written communications skills. Candidates with previous working knowledge of multi-platform network hardware and software, LAN software and hardware, SAN infrastructure and with multiple network operating system certifications such as UNIX, NT, NTAS, LAN Server will be highly valued.

REQUIRED SKILLS:

- 2 years end user technical sales experience
- Proven sales experience required
- Working knowledge of multi-platform network hardware and software
- Working knowledge of SAN infrastructure
- Minimum 2–3 years working in a sales support environment
- Strong presentation skills
- Proven experience using coaching skills in training

PREFERRED SKILLS:

- Thorough knowledge of LAN architecture Dell/EMC product knowledge
- Knowledge of the English and French languages (written and verbal)

C. **Calgary Sales Representative—Dell Direct Store—060009HF**

RESPONSIBILITIES:

- Sell Dell products and services through face to face direct customer interaction
- Qualify opportunities by understanding customer needs, budgets, decision-makers, timelines
- Answer customer questions regarding Dell products and recommend solutions
- Provide technical and administrative information and price quotes to customers
- Close sales and process customer orders
- Meet and exceed stipulated goals
- Maintain awareness of market conditions and competitors' products and pricing.
- Establish and execute plan to meet or exceed all sales/business objectives
- Sell the targeted set of Dell products/services
- Understand the Dell business model
- Overcome competitive sales objections/position product against competition and customer needs

QUALIFICATIONS:

- At least one year experience in retail sales or related field
- Results driven
- Self-motivated
- Quick learner
- Thrives in a fast-paced environment
- Excellent verbal and written communication skills
- Strong organizational and presentation skills
- Team player with initiative
- Good interpersonal skills
- Flexible and able to prioritize
- Proven multi-tasking ability

All candidates must be currently legally eligible to work in Canada.

Note: All three job descriptions included the following statement:

We recognize the value of diversity in our workforce, and encourage all qualified candidates to apply. We thank all candidates who choose to apply; however, only those selected for an interview will be contacted.

Source: © 2007 Dell Inc. All Rights Reserved.

Whether a company uses specific KSAs or a more general approach, effective employee selection involves using valid selection criteria and predictors of job performance.[7] This, of course, requires that there is a clear understanding of what is meant by performance, the topic of Chapter 13. Whatever definition of performance a company chooses, it must determine the KSAs that will lead to success. **Selection criteria** are characteristics that are necessary for a person to be successful at a specific job; common ones for sales jobs might include extroversion, conscientiousness, self-motivation, enthusiasm, persuasiveness, cognitive intelligence, and creativity, among others. In particular, extroversion and conscientiousness, two of "The Big Five" personality dimensions discussed later in Chapter 11, have been found to be related to sales success, particularly in sales jobs having a higher percentage of incentive-based compensation (e.g., commission and bonuses).[8] To determine whether an applicant is conscientious, for example, a company will need to identify one or more **predictors**—that is, measurable or visible indicators of that selection criterion. Depending on the selection criterion the company is trying to predict, predictors can take many forms: university or college degrees or diplomas, specific university or college programs, or courses; professional development or certification certificates; tests or quizzes; years of general sales or specific industry experience; interviewer assessments; or others. The key is to ensure that only *valid* predictors are used; that is, ones that predict what they purport to predict. Valid predictors will help a recruiter select the right candidate; invalid predictors may lead to selecting the wrong candidate.

SELECTING VALID PREDICTORS There are many ways to choose valid predictors. For a very small company, management may have to settle for face validity of predictors; that is, "on the face of it," a predictor looks good. Sometimes, these predictors can be supported by books, magazine articles, or newspaper stories that describe others in similar situations who have found these predictors to be useful. This will increase the predictor's face validity, but not its statistical validity because, while the predictor may be supported by many sources, they are dissimilar enough and usually sufficiently few that any statistical analysis would be meaningless. A sales manager might, for example, believe that new sales recruits need a degree in information technology and two years of inside sales experience. His face validity will be increased if he finds that his competitors require the same job qualifications. If he successfully hires someone who meets these qualifications and that person is successful, again, his face validity is increased. Of course, if he will not hire someone with lower qualifications, he does not know that these are truly necessary for job performance.

Larger companies may evaluate members of the current sales force to build a profile of their most successful salespeople. Edward Jones, a highly decentralized financial services firm with over 4000 investment representatives, with the help of The Gallup Organization's management consulting unit, developed a profile of its best sales producers. Through interviews with high-level sales managers and the company's best sales producers, a composite profile was identified with three key personality traits: a strong work ethic, a high degree of motivation, and an ability to build rapport. How does the selection process work at Edward Jones? The company gets about 1000 applicants per month. Those who look the most promising get turned over to Gallup, which then conducts a phone interview composed of 60 questions that are designed to identify whether the applicant has the three key personality traits. Those who do are then referred back to Edward Jones and are invited for an interview to further see whether the applicant has the necessary competencies identified in the composite profile. In the end, approximately 20 percent, or 200, are hired. In the first four years that Edward Jones implemented this selection strategy, the attrition rate among salespeople fell from 21 percent to 9 percent.[9]

In some larger organizations where there are a number of salespeople performing the same job, it is possible to look at the predictive validity of particular predictors through statistical analysis. Predictors can be correlated with performance, or used in a regression analysis. Some companies may even use discriminant analysis. For example, a company may divide its sales force into three or four groups based on performance, and then compare the best performers to the worst performers. The middle third, or middle half, is often dropped from the analysis so that predictors that really discriminate—or contribute most to the difference—between the two groups are more apparent.

Recruiting Applicants

The goal of *recruiting* is to attract a pool of applicants who may qualify for sales positions. Recruiting has become more important in recent years for several reasons. For less complex and less attractive selling jobs, companies need large numbers of applicants due to regular turnover. For more complex selling jobs, companies may have to recruit a large number of applicants to find only a few who might meet the qualifications they are looking for. The insurance industry, for example, reports that it is getting increasingly more difficult to attract new applicants to the industry, and it must now interview between 60 and 120 applicants to make a single hiring decision.[10] There is a growing awareness that good recruitment programs result in a better pool of applicants from which to choose. The success of the recruiting process depends very much on where the company searches for talent. Companies use a number of sources—internal and external—when recruiting applicants.

INTERNAL SOURCES

Many companies use internal sources when recruiting for sales positions. Among the internal sources commonly used are current employees (that is, promoting from within), employee referral programs, and co-op students or interns.

PROMOTING FROM WITHIN   There are several advantages to hiring internally for sales positions. First, current employees have a history with the company; their attitude and aptitude are better known, and their future performance can be better predicted. Internal candidates who transfer to the sales force can be expected to have better long-term performance than candidates from other sources.[11] Second, internal recruits require less orientation. They frequently know the company history, culture, markets served, and products. This will also reduce the amount of training that is necessary to get them established in their sales position. Third, recruiting internally boosts morale for all employees. It demonstrates for everyone that the company provides opportunities for career advancement. Most employees would view a move to the sales department as a promotion as there is greater independence and salaries are frequently higher. In some companies, there are also opportunities for advancement within the sales force. Approximately 90 percent of companies that have national account salespeople recruit them from their existing sales force.[12]

Promoting from within is not without its problems though. When too many people are promoted from within, the company loses the opportunity to bring some new sales approaches inside the company. People from other departments also bring previously established attitudes and behaviours with them to the sales department. Engineers, for example, may be more inclined to focus on product features than on customer benefits. Inside salespeople and customer service people, because of their strong customer service orientation, may find it difficult to handle tough negotiations with customers. At the same time, management from other departments may resent their best employees moving to the sales department. Lastly, if the only source of sales recruits is internal, an attitude of entitlement may develop where employees feel that they should always be the source of new sales recruits. A strong personnel department can help solve many of these issues. When employees from the personnel department know qualifications and needs across the organization, they are better able to recruit for all departments, and to ensure that there are appropriate programs in place to assist employees with career advancement aspirations to succeed.

A good recruitment program will search for both internal and external candidates to ensure that the company makes the best selection decision to meet its particular needs. Some companies may ultimately have a bias for internal recruits, while others may favour external sources for recruits. Michael Stern, head of Toronto-based executive search firm Michael Stern Associates, suggests that a good rule of thumb is to favour internal candidates unless an external candidate is at least 25 percent better for the position. Stern says, "Outside people can often bring a lot to the party, but they can also bring surprises, too."[13]

EMPLOYEE REFERRAL PROGRAMS   A second important internal source of recruits is referrals from current employees. Many larger organizations now have formalized *employee referral programs,* rewarding employees who refer successful new hires to the company. Marlene West, an employee at Vancouver-based Business Objects, received $1000 for her role in attracting Jeff Propp, a family friend, to the company. Business Objects hired nearly one-third of its 300 new hires in 2005 through employee referrals.[14] There are a number of reasons that companies use these programs:

- It takes less time and is less expensive to find new recruits.
- Applicants are usually better qualified for positions in the company.
- Turnover is lower among referred new hires.
- Referred new hires adapt to the company culture more quickly.
- Referred recruits accept an offer more readily because they already trust the employment experience the company will deliver.[15]

General Mills Canada, with manufacturing, sales, and distribution offices from Nova Scotia to British Columbia, rewards employees who refer new hires with bonuses. The company recognizes that current employees know what it takes to be a success at General Mills Canada, and referred employees are more likely to have the experience, skills, and loyalty important to the company. These employees are more likely to achieve superior performance standards.[16] Employee referral programs can also be motivational for current employees because these programs give employees influence in deciding who will be their future co-workers.

CO-OP STUDENTS OR INTERNS   Many Canadian colleges and universities now have co-op programs where students can spend from one to three terms in intern or co-op positions with companies. Procter & Gamble Canada is just one such company, but one where many students aspire to gain experience. Students are an important part of its business strategy and when employed as interns, they get important responsibilities and challenges within the company, they get to interact with senior management, and they get regular coaching and performance feedback throughout their work terms.[17] Programs such as these greatly benefit students who gain experience and earn money while still in school, but these programs are also an important recruitment tool for companies that use them. They provide an opportunity to get important work done, while assessing potential future employees with limited risk as there is no long-term commitment.

EXTERNAL SOURCES

While an internal company search may be a good place to start the recruiting process for new salespeople, it is also a good idea to perform an external search for candidates. Even if the final decision is to choose an internal candidate, an external search will ensure that an informed decision is made and will also help establish a pool of potential candidates for future hiring decisions. Among the common external sources for sales recruits are print advertisements, private employment agencies, colleges and universities, professional and trade associations, company websites and other online sources, and competitors, suppliers, and customers.

PRINT ADVERTISEMENTS   Print advertisements remain popular, although their popularity is declining. Their strength is in attracting job applicants, although this may also be their greatest weakness. A well-crafted ad can attract many applicants, but when they are poorly qualified or only marginally interested, the large number can quickly overburden the selection process. Only about 15–20 percent of new job openings in Canada get advertised in newspapers.[18] When companies are hiring for less demanding, general sales positions, local newspapers are an inexpensive source of applicants. As the complexity of the sales position increases, companies often use a newspaper that reaches a provincial, or even national, audience. For sales positions where special qualifications are required, advertisements in industry trade magazines or association bulletins or newsletters may be a better source of applicants. However, the lead time to place an advertisement in these sources may be weeks or even months, compared to only a few days for newspapers.

One issue that needs to be addressed is whether to place an *informative ad*—one that discloses the company, the product that is sold, the specific job responsibilities, and the compensation—or a *blind ad*—one that provides little more than contact information. Many sales managers argue that informative ads generate better-quality applicants, reduce selection costs, lower turnover rates, and help avoid ethical questions related to deception. However, for some less attractive sales positions with high turnover—such as telemarketing positions or door-to-door sales jobs that pay exclusively based on sales performance—blind ads work well. Companies that advertise for these types of sales jobs frequently provide minimal information concerning both the job itself and the company that is hiring. In fact, the only identity on the ad might be a telephone number, encouraging people to call. This gives the company the opportunity to discuss the best features of the job and encourage interested applicants to come for a personal meeting. Occasionally, however, companies will place blind ads when they are considering replacing a current employee but only if they can find a suitable applicant. A favourite story among sales managers is about a job applicant who responded to a blind ad for his own position.

PRIVATE EMPLOYMENT AGENCIES   A *Sales & Marketing Management* survey found that nearly one in three companies that responded used private employment agencies to help fill vacancies.[19] There are approximately 3000 such agencies in Canada, and they fill 20–40 percent of positions.[20] The percentage is higher for higher-level and higher-skilled positions. These agencies normally charge 15–20 percent of a successfully placed applicant's first-year salary. The fee may be paid by the job seeker or by the employer, but is more likely to be paid by the employer as the difficulty in finding appropriate hires increases due to higher applicant qualifications.

Many agencies, such as Sellutions Inc. (**http://www.sellutionscanada.com**) and Brock Placement Group Inc. (**http://www.brockplacement.com**), specialize in filling sales and marketing positions. Another agency, jobWings, operates a number of more highly targeted sites: for sales management and sales representative positions (**http://www.salesrep.ca**); for retail sales and management positions (**http://www.retailjob.ca**); and for call centre positions (**http://www. callcenterjob.ca**).

To make the best use of private employment agencies, a company should provide a clear job description and a list of job qualifications. The agency can then recruit and screen applicants so that only the most qualified ones actually contact the employer. Companies that pay for the services of a private employment agency often find that they save on their total recruiting and selection costs as they eliminate the cost of advertising and much of the cost associated with screening applicants. In addition, the employer often saves time for sales managers and others who might be involved in the process that they can use more effectively performing other duties. Companies should, however, gauge the quality of any private employment agencies they use and carefully track from which ones they gain their best salespeople. Some less professional companies simply want to place recruits and earn a fee. There are enough agencies in Canada that companies do not have to deal with those who send poorly qualified candidates.

COLLEGES AND UNIVERSITIES   Many companies find that colleges and universities are an important source of new sales recruits. Career development offices assist graduating students in finding jobs. They advertise positions for companies that are recruiting salespeople, and frequently arrange on-campus interviews between recruiters and applicants. Colleges and universities often hold career fairs where recruiters from many companies attend to promote sales opportunities to students.

Post-secondary students are attractive to many employers because they are educated and more socially poised than inexperienced applicants who do not have a diploma or degree. They frequently can be hired at lower salaries than more experienced salespeople, and they do not have the poor selling habits that some experienced salespeople have developed. They are enthusiastic and have already demonstrated that they can learn, so they are often capable of quickly absorbing product and sales process knowledge. Courses and grades can provide an indication of their aptitudes, abilities, and interests: analytical thinking, interpersonal communications, quantitative, writing, time-management, and many other skills that are important for particular sales positions.

When recruiting from colleges and universities, it is important to be selective. Colleges often provide specific sales programs and are a good source of recruits for general sales positions. University business programs are more likely to prepare graduates for marketing or general management positions. Some of the best sales candidates, however, come from science and general arts programs. A common complaint many companies have with recruiting recent graduates is that there is considerable turnover as these hires will "job-hop" when other opportunities arise, particularly if they find increased salaries or more challenging positions, or simply become bored in their current position. Of course, the best solution is to describe the job responsibilities and career advancement possibilities honestly when hiring, and then to recruit and select employees who are neither under- nor overqualified for the position.

PROFESSIONAL AND TRADE ASSOCIATIONS   Professional and trade associations are sometimes a good source of sales recruits. Members join professional associations to network with others who have similar backgrounds and interests, so these organizations provide a good source of recruits with specific experience or industry knowledge. Some associations publish newsletters where recruiters can advertise. The Canadian Professional Sales Association (**http://www.cpsa. com**) has approximately 30 000 members and offers an online career mall for its members. It also has a website (**http://www.salesjobsCanada.com**) where members can post résumés and where employers can automatically pre-screen candidates and receive automatic notification when there are profile matches between job seekers and their company's recruitment needs.

COMPANY WEBSITES AND OTHER ONLINE SOURCES   Canadian companies—large and small—are increasingly using their websites to attract job applicants and requesting that applicants submit their résumés over the internet. Xerox, IBM, Microsoft, Procter & Gamble, General Mills, Pfizer, Dell, and many other companies receive thousands of résumés each day. It might seem that companies could be overcome with the volume of applications received through the internet. However, this is actually an effective way to recruit for sales positions as applications can be efficiently pre-screened by modern software programs so that only the most qualified applicants proceed through the recruitment and selection process.

COMPETITORS, SUPPLIERS, AND CUSTOMERS   Competitors, suppliers, and customers are often a good source from which to recruit salespeople. These people will be familiar with the business and are likely to understand the tasks and responsibilities required to be successful in the sales job.

Competitors' salespeople can be an attractive source of recruits because they already have established relationships with customers or potential customers. In fact, some companies target salespeople who have strong relationships at specific accounts. Hiring from a competitor also makes sense if training resources are limited. These salespeople already know the industry, the customers, the products, and how to sell, at least to some extent. They can become productive quickly after being hired. In some industries, companies have a policy of not hiring salespeople from competitors until they have left the industry for a specified period of time. In these instances, salespeople are often required to sign a non-compete clause as part of the initial employment contract. Hiring from competitors is not always a good idea, however. Since satisfied employees are unlikely to leave a position simply for financial gain, there is the possibility of hiring someone who may continue to be an unhappy, problem employee for their new employer as well. A study of pharmaceutical salespeople concluded that while new hires from competitors were initially higher sales producers, the cost of acquiring them quickly offset their sales productivity, making competitors' sales forces the least profitable source of new salespeople.[21] Some companies also have a policy of not hiring salespeople from competitors so they do not have to "unlearn" bad habits or adjust to a new sales culture. These and other reasons may be why only 10 percent of respondents to a *Sales & Marketing Management* study indicated that competitors were the best source of sales recruits.[22]

Hiring from suppliers makes sense for wholesalers and retailers, particularly if the supplier for whom the salesperson works is an important one in the reseller's product line. A distributor for electrical equipment, for example, might find a salesperson who works for a manufacturer of motors or motor control equipment that it sells. Such a salesperson would not only know the products and the industry well, but would often be familiar with the sales culture within the distributor firm. Customers may also be a good source of salespeople. If the customer is a wholesaler or retailer, a salesperson from that customer will have some experience with the product and the manufacturer. Even if the customer is an end-user account, the customer will have some experience with the company and its product line. Hiring from customers and suppliers does have some risks. Care should be taken to ensure that relationships with other people within the customer or supplier firm remain positive.

Selecting Applicants

The third stage of the recruitment and selection process is *selection*—choosing from among a pool of applicants only those who meet the job qualifications. This actually involves two steps: (1) evaluating the pool of recruits, and (2) selecting one or more recruits and negotiating employment. It is helpful when evaluating a large pool of recruits to be able to reduce the number of potential hires to only a few, and then to make a more careful selection from among those that seem best suited for the job. As the selection process proceeds, the cost of processing each applicant increases so companies want to reduce the pool of applicants as early as possible in the process. There are a number of selection tools, including résumés and application forms; personal interviews, tests (intelligence, aptitude, and personality tests), background checks, physical examinations, and drug testing. The HR Chally Group, specialists in salesperson selection, suggest that recruiters use the "30–30–30–10 rule" when making a final selection decision:[23]

- 30 percent should be based on assessment results
- 30 percent should be based on background information and reference checks
- 30 percent should be based on interview results, and
- 10 percent should be based on perceived fit with the company's culture

The following section will describe many of the tools that recruiters use as part of the selection process.

RÉSUMÉS AND APPLICATION FORMS

Résumés and application forms both provide recruiters with information concerning job applicants, including contact information, education and employment history, and other relevant personal information such as skills, activities, and interests that might be job-related.

Résumés are often the first contact between job seekers and recruiters. Some organizations receive thousands of résumés daily. When résumés are submitted electronically, most submissions are immediately discarded. Résumés that receive additional attention are those that include key words or phrases that are part of the automatic search list. If résumés are visually scanned, creativity and uniqueness, either in the résumé itself or in the cover letter, can be a deciding factor when selecting candidates for an interview. One creative business student printed her résumé to resemble a folded business card. The cover looked like a regular business card, and included a personal logo and contact information. Inside was the information she wanted to present. Another student demonstrated his creativity in his cover letter. He concluded his letter with a section, "Five Reasons Why You Want Me to Work for You." This provided him with a way to present benefits (why) along with features (what). For example, he explained that he had excellent time management skills: "I have achieved solid grades while working part-time to support my education and exercising regularly to maintain my personal health and well-being." His number one reason: "You wouldn't want your competitor to hire me." Both applicants were hired very soon after they began their job search, unlike the applicant who closed his cover letter with the salutation, "I hope to hear from you shorty."

Application forms are still popular and provide a number of advantages. They provide identical information on all applicants, in a form that makes it easy to find and compare information across applicants. They can be completed as part of the interview process, meaning that they can be a source to check for neatness, accuracy, attention to detail, and writing skills. Another reason for using application forms, whether written or electronic, is that they restrict the information that applicants can include when applying for a job. Discrimination when selecting job applicants is a growing concern for many companies. It is not possible to restrict information on a résumé that the applicant may later use to charge discrimination in the hiring process. By having a standardized form, companies can ask for appropriate information, and some companies protect themselves by including a statement that applications with unsolicited information will be automatically discarded.

PERSONAL INTERVIEWS

Most companies include one or more personal interviews as part of the selection process. Historically, interviews have been poor predictors of job performance in many occupations, but they are used extensively in the recruitment and selection of salespeople. Through the interview process, managers can better assess a candidate's sociability and interpersonal communication skills; ambition and aggressiveness; and, when necessary, competitor, industry, and product knowledge. Furthermore, the interview process helps ensure that successful candidates will fit with the culture of the organization and, in particular, with the sales manager or supervisor to whom they will directly report. The usefulness of interviews can be further increased by training sales managers or other interviewers on how to interview, and providing them with feedback on who were their best and poorest previous hires. Formal structured interviews ensure that everyone is asked the same questions, and this makes it easier to make comparisons across applicants. These interviews are particularly helpful when more than one person is conducting interviews, or when the interviewer is inexperienced. Semi-structured interviews are more appropriate when interviewing more experienced applicants as they will often control much of the interview process. These allow the interviewer to explore in-depth anything that is raised during the interview process that may be important in the selection process, while ensuring that all relevant information is collected. To provide some consistency in interviewing or evaluation across applicants, or when multiple interviewers or evaluators are used, some companies provide formal applicant interview forms. Exhibit 7.3 illustrates one such form.

SCREENING INTERVIEWS   Companies frequently use screening interviews as a tool to reduce the applicant pool early in the selection process. Screening interviews serve two purposes. First, candidates can get information on the job and its requirements to ensure that they are still interested in pursuing the position. Glynne Jenkins, a Toronto-based business consultant, suggests that when you have a superior applicant, you may wonder during the interview process who is interviewing whom. He says, "It is likely a good sales person thinks he or she is interviewing you."[24] Second, they provide the recruiter with a forum to select potentially outstanding candidates—those who appear to have the job qualifications the recruiter is looking for—and to deselect applicants who are clearly unacceptable. That is, recruiters can use a number of criteria to eliminate applicants from the pool of recruits. Applicants who have poor appearance, poor communication skills, or a lack of maturity may be quickly eliminated from further consideration. One sales manager recently eliminated a job applicant from her pool of recruits because he came to the interview with scuffed shoes. The anonymous sales manager said, "It indicates poor attention to detail. He would likely present himself to customers this way too. We expect better of our salespeople." Eliminating weaker applicants early allows the best candidates to proceed through the selection process to one or more subsequent interviews.

Exhibit 7.3

Applicant Interview Form

Business Services Division
Sales Applicant Interview Form

Name of applicant: _____

Interviewers in attendance:

1. _____
2. _____
3. _____

Date: _____   Time: _____

Rating:
5 = Excellent
4 = Satisfactory
3 = Marginal
2 = Poor
1 = Unacceptable

First impressions:	1	2	3	4	5	Comments:
Carriage and posture						
Composure and confidence						
Professional image						
Demonstrates propriety						
Maturity						
Sales potential:						
Speech and expression						
Verbal ability						
Persuasive						
Enthusiastic						
Self-confident						
Ambitious						
Adaptable						
Experience (prompt):						
Managing a sales territory						
Managing major accounts						
Cooperative teamwork						
Leadership						
Ethical standards						

Overall evaluation (rate 0 to 85, where 70 = average) _____

Would you recommend we hire this applicant? _____

Why or why not? _____

_____

SUBSEQUENT INTERVIEWS Screening interviews are often conducted by one or a very few people. As companies get closer to making a hiring choice, the number of people involved in the interview process may increase, and the level of the interviews within the company hierarchy may also increase, particularly for more senior positions or for candidates for whom there is an expectation of promotion to management or to more senior sales positions.

Recruiters will usually invite any candidate they are seriously considering to come to a company location where the applicant may meet with several people who will all have an influence in the hiring decision. Care should be taken to ensure that these interviews are coordinated so that all important topics are covered, and to avoid redundancy. Otherwise, everyone may simply gain the same information and the same impression, and "groupthink" can result in a poor hiring decision.

An alternative to a series of interviews is a single group interview. A number of interviewers may participate, each with specific responsibility for part of the process. The advantage is that everyone gets to see the applicant's reaction to the entire process. In some instances, one or more of the interviewers will be critical of the applicant or otherwise try to put him under some stress so that they can gauge how well he can think and respond under such conditions. A favourite of some sales managers is to simply ask the applicant, "Sell me this pen." For applicants who are new to sales, the goal may simply be to judge how well they respond in a stressful situation. For more experienced salespeople, the goal may be to judge how well they really do understand the selling process. Of course, some salespeople are well prepared for this request as it has been used now for many years. Ken Blanchard, chairman of Blanchard Training and Development, has another approach. He asks each applicant to take an hour and write an essay on what he will be doing over the next several months. This allows the interviewer to evaluate both written and oral communication skills, and to see how well the applicant can think under pressure. Alex Pettes, president of TFI Food Equipment Sales in Markham, Ontario, uses a similar approach, but earlier in the process. He asks candidates during a telephone interview to develop a territory business plan for the first month and be prepared to present it to him during the first face-to-face interview. He has even had applicants at this stage decide that maybe the job is not for them, saving him from wasting time on applicants who would most likely be poor hires anyway.[25] Another group interview process involves interviewing several applicants simultaneously. This works best when there are multiple interviewers present. It is a good way to assess how well applicants relate to other people, and to see who is most comfortable and most likely to take initiative in a group setting.

In addition to the more formal interview process, many companies include several informal elements in their interview process. Some companies invite applicants for dinner, often inviting the applicant's spouse or significant other as well. This helps ensure that recruits have a supportive home life and someone who understands the sales process and what might be involved in a sales position. Other sales managers invite candidates to play golf, go to a sporting event, or join them or another salesperson for a day in the field. Applicants are more likely to exhibit their true personalities and sales aptitude in these situations.

TESTS

Larger companies tend to use a larger number of selection tools, and, to their advantage, are most likely to include one or more types of formal tests as part of the selection process. Valid tests have been found to be valuable predictors of job performance, and help remove much of the subjectivity from the selection process. When companies rely mainly on interviews as the primary selection tool, candidates have been rejected for such things as hair style or length, wearing short-sleeved shirts or light-coloured suits, or having a beard or moustache. Three types of tests are frequently used to help make hiring decisions for salespeople: (1) intelligence or cognitive ability tests, (2) aptitude tests, and (3) personality tests.

INTELLIGENCE OR COGNITIVE ABILITY TESTS Intelligence, or cognitive ability, is the best predictor of overall job performance for many jobs. It may be more or less important depending on the qualifications for particular sales jobs. Many companies require a minimum score on intelligence tests but tend not to favour candidates simply because they have the highest scores. That is, there is usually a "hump" score beyond which applicants remain in the selection pool and below which they are rejected. The most popular intelligence test is the Wonderlic Personnel Test, a 50-item test that can be administered in 12 minutes and is available in more than 15 foreign languages. The questions include making word comparisons, rearranging disarranged sentences, identifying sentence parallelism, following directions, making number comparisons, extending a number series, and analyzing geometric figures or story problems requiring either mathematical or logical solutions. The following are three sample questions:

1. One of the numbered figures in the following drawing is most different from the others. What is the number of that figure?

2. A train travels 20 feet in 1/5 second. At this same speed, how many feet will it travel in three seconds?

3. Which number in the following group of numbers represents the smallest amount?

7	.8	31	.33	2

The test is designed to measure an applicant's ability to learn a specific job, solve problems, understand instructions, apply knowledge to new situations, benefit from specific job training, and be satisfied with a particular job. Applicants must complete the test without the use of a calculator or other problem-solving device. Over 120 million people have taken this test since 1937.[26]

APTITUDE TESTS Aptitude tests are designed to measure a person's interest in, or ability to perform, certain tasks or activities. One of the most widely used is the Strong Interest Inventory® (**www.cpp-db.com**). Aptitude tests determine whether an applicant's interests are similar to or different from those of successful people in a variety of occupations. The HR Chally Group (**www.chally.com**) has been helping clients select sales and marketing people for more than 30 years. According to the company, data analysis may validate from four to nine critical success factors for particular sales positions, but it also is common that top salespeople within a company may have different mixes of these important characteristics.[27] Mitch Anthony, author of *Selling With Emotional Intelligence,* tells of a job applicant who was almost rejected for an insurance sales position. The company wanted an energetic go-getter, and this person was a methodical analyzer. He eventually convinced the company that, while he was not a "rah-rah" person, he was good at servicing clients and building relationships. Within three or four years, he was the top producer for the company.[28]

Aptitude tests can also be useful to assess specific aptitudes and skills that may be good predictors for specific selling jobs, such as mechanical or mathematical aptitude, or technology skills. A potential problem with aptitude tests is that, used inappropriately, they may simply indicate extant skill levels and may ignore the fact that many of the important skills required for a successful selling career can be taught with an effective training program.

PERSONALITY TESTS   There are many types of personality tests. Among the more popular ones are the Myers-Briggs Type Indicator (MBTI), the 16 Personality Factors, the Occupational Personality Questionnaire, the California Psychological Inventory, and the Edwards Personal Preference Schedule (EPPS). The MBTI is more useful for employee development than employee selection, but many companies do misuse it for employee selection even though it has been criticized due to lack of empirical support for its validity.[29] The EPPS measures 24 separate traits, including aggressiveness, independence, and sociability. Tests such as this one include many questions, take considerable time to complete, and gather information concerning many traits of questionable importance when it comes to evaluating a candidate's suitability for a sales position. The fact that there are so many traits means that, by chance alone, one or two traits will likely correlate significantly with performance (i.e., a Type I statistical error). Psychologists have begun to focus on a smaller number of underlying traits for which there is now a growing body of research support. The most popular personality traits are included in "The Big Five," the importance of which was discussed previously in this chapter and will be discussed again in Chapter 11 on sales leadership. A measurement instrument that has become quite popular in recent years is the test of emotional intelligence, defined by an EQ (emotional quotient) score. It is described in the Sales Management in Action box. Although there are five dimensions of EQ, comprising 15 sub-dimensions, a small number appear to have high validity when used to predict performance in a number of sales jobs.

CONCERNS ABOUT THE USE OF TESTS   Using tests as part of the selection process has its adherents and its opponents. People who have taken many tests may be "test-wise," while even intelligent people with less test experience can "fake" answers to test questions and provide answers that recruiters seek. Some test developers realize this and include questions that provide a "desirability" or "lie" scale. When these are included, the argument to use only professional scoring of personality tests in strengthened. This may make the cost prohibitive for many smaller employers.

Employers have more legal requirements today to ensure that any tests used as part of the selection process are reliable, valid, and job-related, and do not discriminate against any applicant based on gender, age, race, religion, or another factor covered by human rights legislation. For a test to be reliable, a test-taker must get the same result if she takes the test more than once. If someone can write a cognitive ability test and score 450 the first time and 270 on a second version of the test, then the test is not reliable. Of course, if it is not reliable, it cannot be valid because a valid test must measure what it is purported to measure. If it does not measure what it is supposed to measure, or is not job-related, then there can be no justification for using it. Many tests available through commercial test developers have questionable reliability and validity, and

SALES MANAGEMENT **IN ACTION**

Hire for "People Smarts"

Steven J. Stein and Howard E. Book, two Ontario researchers, are strong supporters of *emotional intelligence* (EQ), and they are not alone. What is emotional intelligence? Well, it is difficult to define in a few words, but you will get a sense of what it means if you think of "common sense," "street smarts," and "people smarts." It is different from IQ, which measures your cognitive intelligence, and many supporters will tell you it is far more important. If you look around your classroom, you will see people you recognize as having an IQ that may be near the class average, but you know that when they graduate, they will be "the most likely to succeed." Some people see the difference between IQ and EQ this way: IQ will get you an interview and *may* get you a job. EQ *will* get you a job and is frequently necessary if you want to get a promotion.

Stein and Book say that there are five dimensions to EQ, comprising a total of 15 sub-dimensions:

1. *The Intrapersonal Realm:* Emotional Self-Awareness, Assertiveness, Independence, Self-Regard, and Self-Actualization

2. *The Interpersonal Realm:* Empathy, Social Responsibility, Interpersonal Relationships

3. *The Adaptability Realm:* Reality Testing, Flexibility, Problem-Solving

4. *The Stress Management Realm:* Stress Tolerance, Impulse Control

5. *The General Mood Realm:* Optimism, Happiness

Stein and Book estimate that IQ can predict on average only 6 percent success in a given job, but EQ can predict between 27 and 45 percent success, depending on the job. There are, of course, different dimensions of EQ that are important for different jobs.

What do you do if you have a low EQ? Well, the good news is that it is probably easier for you to raise your EQ than it is to raise your IQ. EQ tends to improve throughout your life, but IQ remains relatively stable. Men and women have approximately the same overall EQ scores, although they do show some differences on sub-scale scores. Men tend to score higher on stress tolerance; women tend to score higher on empathy and social responsibility. There are a few other differences that were noted only in North America: women scored higher on interpersonal relationships and men scored higher on self-regard. Racial differences in EQ scores were non-existent, a criticism often made concerning IQ bias.

Stein and Book do not report the particular sub-dimensions that distinguish high performers from low performers in sales management, but they do for senior managers, for general salespeople, and for customer service representatives. The following is a list for these selected positions:

Senior Managers (*n* = 260)	General Sales (*n* = 1254)	Customer Service Representatives (*n* = 334)
Self-Regard	Self-Actualization	Self-Actualization
Happiness	Independence	Reality Testing
Interpersonal Relationships	Self-Regard	Optimism
Reality Testing	Optimism	Happiness
Self-Actualization	Assertiveness	Interpersonal Relationships

Source: Adapted and reprinted from the publication *The EQ Edge: Emotional Intelligence and Your Success*, Revised & Updated Edition by Steven J. Stein and Howard E. Book with permission of John Wiley & Sons Canada, Limited, a subsidiary of John Wiley & Sons, Inc.

could create legal problems for companies that use them for selection purposes. Also, some tests have been shown to discriminate against applicants on the basis of race or gender, and their use for making a selection decision is illegal. It was argued earlier in this chapter that there are a variety of sales jobs, and the selection criteria and job qualifications vary considerably from one job to another. If this is true, then the use of a particular test may prove valid for one sales job, or one company, but not for others. Without carefully validating specific tests for specific jobs, a company runs a risk of using invalid tests as part of its selection process. The time, cost, sample size, and expertise required to properly validate a particular test make the process infeasible for most companies.

In the final analysis, tests must be carefully used and should be only one of many factors considered in the final selection decision. Applicants should not be eliminated strictly on the basis of test scores. Tests should measure a small number of skills or abilities of interest, and should include some checks for "fake" responding. Finally, the validity of tests should always be questioned so that there is some analysis after a hiring decision has been made to see how good the test was at predicting performance.

BACKGROUND CHECKS

There are four important reasons to do a thorough background check as part of the employee selection process: to show that due diligence was exercised in hiring; to provide factual information about a candidate; to discourage applicants with something to hide; and to encourage applicants to be honest on applications and during interviews.[30] The cost of conducting a comprehensive background check is approximately $200.[31] Abiding by the relevant privacy acts when conducting background checks is important, and employers should protect themselves by obtaining written consent from individuals before collecting, using, or disclosing personal information on an applicant.[32]

Many people provide inaccurate information on their job applications and résumés, including information about previous jobs and length of employment; past job responsibilities, job titles, and performance; and even educational background and accomplishments. Gerlinde Herrmann, president of the Human Resources Professionals Association of Ontario, acknowledges that unscrupulous job applicants are getting more sophisticated due to internet technology. She claims that educational background is where the most embellishment takes place.[33] People who are willing to tell lies or half-truths to get a job are also the ones most likely to do the same when dealing with prospects and customers.

In some instances, background checks are more important, and these should be more comprehensive: driving record, criminal record, credit history, work history, and education. When applicants provide references, it is almost certain that they will be biased in favour of the applicant. Everyone should be able to find three referees who will say something good about them. Some recruiters ask for additional referees during the interview process, and some ask for referees who can comment on specific aspects relating to the job applicant. The most important references usually relate to past work experience. When checking these references, it is a good idea to ask specific questions of the referee. The following are good examples:

■ What dates was she actually employed by your company?

■ What were her actual job responsibilities?

■ How well did she perform compared to other people with the same responsibilities?

- What were her greatest strengths?
- What would be the most important thing for her to improve?
- How well did she relate to customers, to management, and to co-workers?
- Why did she leave her job with your company?
- Would you rehire her if she were to reapply to your company?

Many companies will not provide information on past employees. In these instances, it is a good idea to ask them at least to confirm employment dates. Many applicants lie by omission rather than commission. That is, an applicant may leave important information off their application. If the applicant had a poor work experience, it is easy to gloss over it by simply adding a few months to the period of employment with another employer. The value of asking for a number of referees and carefully checking them is illustrated by the vignette at the beginning of this chapter. A good last question to ask, even if the interviewee has indicated that he will not provide information, is whether he or his company would ever consider re-hiring this person at any future time. It requires a simple "yes" or "no" response, and a recruiter should be wary if the response is "no." A follow-up "Why not?" is worth a try, but may not get an answer. Another good suggestion is to keep an interview form. Even if a referee provides very little information, the form will provide some proof later that you attempted due diligence if the candidate is hired and there are serious future problems. Recruiters should document all efforts to check background information on applicants—who was contacted, when, what was asked, what information was or was not provided—in case there is a later lawsuit for negligent hiring. **Negligent hiring** occurs when an employer hires an employee and fails to do an adequate background check, and that employee later harms another employee. Another situation, **negligent retention**, occurs when an employer retains an employee when the employer is aware that the employee is unfit for employment, and the employee later causes harm to another employee.[34]

Some firms use printed interview forms that are sent to referees and ask for written responses. These forms may contain a statement signed by the applicant so that those who give information are released from responsibility by the applicant. This allows the respondent completing the form to provide more candid information.

CREDIT CHECKS   Many companies request credit checks on job applicants. The assumption is that financial responsibility and job responsibility are positively related, but this may be a dubious assumption. To ensure that they comply with federal, provincial, and territorial legislation, companies that request credit checks should ensure that the request is work-related, and that they have written consent from the job applicant to conduct the credit check. They also must be prepared to release any information they receive related to the credit check to the applicant.

Equifax, Inc., a global company with 5800 employees in 13 countries (600 in Canada), claims 50 million commercial files and 310 million consumer files, and to sell hundreds of thousands of credit reports each year to thousands of employers.[35] Canadian consumers can visit Equifax Canada and order a free copy of their own credit report by mail, or for a very small fee get an electronic copy immediately (visit **http://www.equifax.com/EFX_Canada/**).

PHYSICAL EXAMINATIONS AND DRUG TESTING   Historically, companies required physical examinations prior to making a job offer to an applicant. However, this is no longer an acceptable practice. Companies cannot ask questions concerning a disability during an interview, nor can they reject an applicant because of a disability. It is acceptable to ask an applicant whether he can perform the functions of the job, and whether he is able to otherwise meet requirements necessary

SALES MANAGEMENT **TODAY**

Not Just Socially Unacceptable

What do you think your smoking dependency is costing you? Okay, ignore your health. Forget that a friend your age (assuming you are approximately 20 years old) who invested the same amount you spend daily on cigarettes would retire with over a million dollars in the bank. The real cost, you will never know.

Research in the United States indicates that smokers make considerably less money than non-smokers, after accounting for education, birth order, gender, race, and other factors. The reason is most likely prejudice that keeps smokers from being hired, and when hired, keeps them from promotions that their non-smoking peers enjoy. Smoking seems to stunt careers.

Is this happening only in small companies? Not according to Barbara Hackman Franklin, a director on the boards of Aetna Life & Casualty, Black & Decker, Dow Chemical, Westinghouse Electric, and several other large corporations. She says many companies have adopted an unwritten rule: "If you want to advance, don't smoke." The chairman at Ralston Purina verbally attacked smokers among the company's senior executives for their lack of respect for others. Word immediately got around the company and many young executives quickly sought medical advice from the company's medical director on how to quit smoking. One manager at Johnson & Johnson says, "In a culture like ours, where everyone is looking good and smelling good, the last thing you do is stick a cigarette in your mouth." The president of Provident Indemnity Life Insurance recently interviewed a personal friend for a position, but did not hire him because of "nicotine fingers" and "reeking" clothes. These are but a few of dozens of examples, and unfortunately, the people who are not hired and not promoted are frequently not told why, or they are given another reason.

Is this legal? Who knows? Approximately one-third of the states in the United States have legislation that prevents discrimination against smokers, but most do not. In the European Union, a 2006 advertisement for telemarketers in Ireland sparked debate when it stated, "Smokers need not apply." The European Commission ruled that companies in the 25 member countries of the EU could discriminate against smokers in hiring practices. In Canada, the issue remains unclear. In one test case in British Columbia, the arbitrator ruled that nicotine addiction is similar to alcohol or drug dependency, which suggests that discrimination against smokers in the selection process would be illegal. Will that prevent it? One sales executive, who wishes to remain anonymous, said, "We have lots of smokers in our company, but you can count the ones who have direct customer contact for us on less than one finger. Is this discrimination? I don't think so. I've never heard of someone that would buy from you because you smoke, but I have certainly known some people who would not buy from you if you did smoke." He may not be totally correct . . . signs at the R.J. Reynolds head office say, "Thank you for smoking."

Sources: "Okay to Spurn Smokers, EU Tells Companies," http://www.theglobeandmail.com/servlet/story/RTGAM.20060807. weusmoke0807/EmailBNStory/International/; Susan Sachs, "Smokers Needn't Apply, EU Decides," *Globe and Mail,* August 10, 2006, p. A3; Alix M. Freedman, "Harmful Habit: Cigarette Smoking is Growing Hazardous to Careers in Business," *Wall Street Journal,* April 23, 1987, p. 1.

to effectively do a job. It is acceptable, for example, to ask whether the applicant holds a valid driver's license, or can handle the stress of frequent flying. Once a conditional offer is made, the employer can then ask for a physical examination, at the company's expense. The recruiter should ensure that the applicant understands that the job offer is conditional on successfully completing the physical examination. Employers are obligated by law in Canada to make reasonable accommodation for people with a disability, if it will not cause undue hardship for the employer.[36]

Drug testing as part of the employee selection process is controversial in Canada, but the practice is increasing. Drug dependency is considered a disability under federal legislation, and will likely be interpreted in the same manner provincially. While there are no Canadian laws that prohibit drug testing, a number of Supreme Court decisions do provide some guidelines. Drug testing appears to be acceptable "as part of an investigation in an unfit for duty (reasonable cause) or post accident/incident situation, as part of a monitoring program after treatment, as a condition of return to duty after a policy violation, and on an on-going follow-up basis."[37] In all circumstances, however, drug and alcohol dependency testing must be part of a comprehensive policy that includes accommodation for those with a dependency. If used as part of the selection process, just as with a physical test, a drug or alcohol dependency test cannot be administered until after a conditional job offer has been made. The conditional offer should stipulate that random drug tests will continue during employment because, if this is not necessary for work-related reasons, then testing should never have been done to begin with.

Current indications are that a more common dependency—tobacco dependency—will be considered similar to drug and alcohol dependency when it comes to human rights in the workplace in Canada. But, as described in the Sales Management Today box, other countries do not all agree with Canada, and, even if it is illegal to discriminate against tobacco users in the selection process, they will most likely face increasing discrimination in both selection and promotion decisions.

Validating the Selection Process

The last stage of the recruitment and selection process involves validating the process. This, of course, involves validating all stages of the process to ensure that both recruitment and selection decisions are made correctly. Simply tracking where successful applicants came from, and which sources provided the highest percentages of poorly qualified applicants, can help a recruiter improve future recruitment. Spending money for expensive print advertising, for example, is wasteful if this medium provides only a few, or very poor, applicants.

Validating selection criteria is more complicated. What needs to be known is which selection criteria are the ones that best predict a salesperson's future performance. How important is education? Is sales experience really necessary and, if it is, what length of sales experience should be the minimum requirement? Which tests are valid, and what is an acceptable score for a candidate to achieve? Is the overall test score important, or should the recruiter look at specific dimensions of the test? How important is the interview, and is an appropriate process being used? Some of these questions are easier to answer than others. The usefulness of validation increases as the size of the sales force increases. An ongoing investigation of the validity of selection criteria allows a company to track the success of newer candidates, and provide feedback to the validation system so adjustments can be made for future selections. Even when only a very few salespeople are involved, the sales manager should constantly be reassessing who proved to be the best sales force recruits and who were the worst, and recognize how they differed on selection criteria. Of course, using these differences for future selections must be done with greater care when the analysis involves only a small sample.

Most companies use a number of selection criteria when making a selection decision. To simplify the process, they frequently use an incremental approach to selecting candidates. That is, applicants must pass a number of "hurdles" to proceed to a subsequent stage in the selection process. For example, to be hired, an applicant for a sales job must achieve a minimum education level and have a minimum level of required sales experience, pass a screening interview, obtain a certain score on the MBTI and the EPPS tests, receive a minimum evaluation score on a final structured interview, and then pass a series of background checks. As an applicant proceeds through this lengthy process, the cost to the company increases, so it is in the company's best interest to eliminate applicants who are unlikely to be successful as early as possible in the process. Exhibit 7.4 shows how an incremental approach to the selection decision would work.

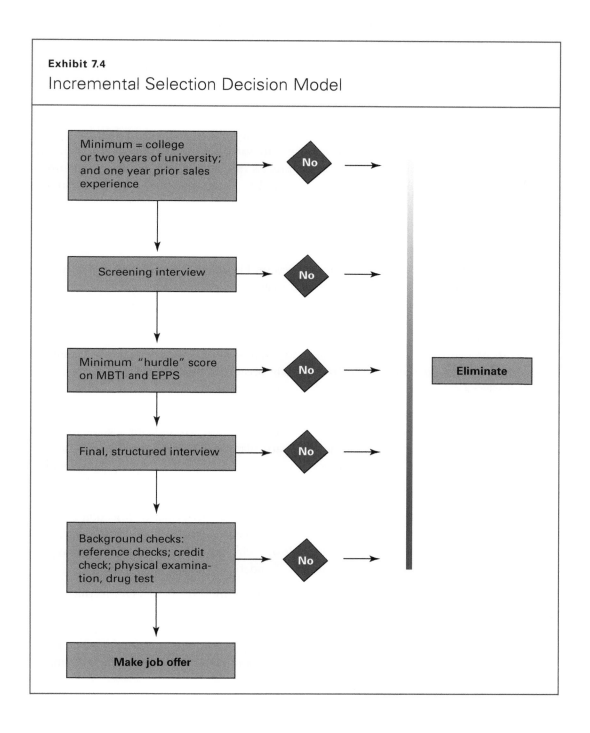

Exhibit 7.4
Incremental Selection Decision Model

To validate the first stage of the process, for example, the sales manager might check to see whether the best-performing salespeople meet or exceed this criterion level, and whether poorly performing salespeople do not. In such an instance, the selection criterion should be maintained in the future. If the sales manager notices that the best recruits have completed university, but the worst recruits have not, the hurdle should be increased so that new applicants must have, at minimum, a university degree. Of course, she might also find that those with a college education stay with the company and remain successful in their jobs while those with a university degree tend to leave within six months to one year of being hired. In this instance, she should consider not hiring university graduates, or only a small number that can be given increasing job responsibilities or otherwise kept satisfied. All other selection criteria should be validated following a similar procedure. Validation helps ensure that the most qualified candidates are selected for sales positions. Of course, no system can be 100 percent correct. Some recruits who meet all criteria will be poor performers and, as the example provided by Mitch Anthony earlier in this chapter illustrates, strictly following selection criteria means that some recruits who might be top performers could be eliminated. Good recruiters need to watch for the exceptional candidate who will most likely demonstrate somewhere in the process that they should remain in contention. With a good validation process, better decisions will be made, and that is what validation is intended to do.

SUMMARY

1. **Discuss planning for recruitment and selection.** Planning for recruitment and selection—the first stage—is the most important stage of the process. Who will be involved in the process and who will make the final selection decision must be decided, but the sales manager will most certainly play an important role. An important aspect of planning for recruitment and selection is to analyze the sales force turnover rate: what it is currently, how it compares to other firms in the industry, and how it has been changing over time. Understanding a sales force culture is important because, ultimately, the sales manager must select a candidate who will fit with the current culture.

2. **Explain how to conduct a job analysis.** An important part of the recruitment and selection process is to conduct a job analysis—a systematic approach to define specific tasks and responsibilities that must be performed in a particular job (job description), and to determine the knowledge, skills, and abilities (KSAs) and personal characteristics that an applicant should possess (job qualifications) in order to perform successfully in the job. Whether a company uses specific KSAs or a more general approach, effective selection involves using valid selection criteria and predictors of job performance. Selection criteria are characteristics that are necessary for a person to be successful at a specific job (e.g., cognitive intelligence). Predictors are measurable or visible indicators that a candidate has a particular selection criterion (e.g., score on a Wonderlic Personnel Test).

3. **Describe the different sources used for recruiting applicants.** Sources for recruiting applicants can be internal or external. Three popular internal sources are promotion from within, employee referral programs, and co-op students and interns. External sources include print advertisements; private employment agencies; colleges and universities; professional and trade associations; company websites and other online sources; and competitors, suppliers, and customers.

4. **Describe the selection and validation process.** The third stage of the process is selection. Résumés or application forms are often where the selection process starts. Candidates who pass this preliminary assessment then usually proceed to one or more of the following types of interviews: screening interviews, a series of individual interviews, team interviews, or even group interviews. Candidates may then continue on to testing, including intelligence, or cognitive ability testing, aptitude testing, or personality testing. While there are some concerns with tests, including falsifying answers or the validity of tests, most companies use tests as only one of a number of selection criteria. Once a candidate passes all of these hurdles, companies should conduct background checks: checking references, credit checks, physical examinations, driving records, drug testing, or other checks depending on the particular company and job involved. Finally, whatever is used for selection purposes should be validated. That is, there should be care taken to ensure that selection criteria and predictors are valid ones that do predict performance. This will help ensure better selection decisions are made.

KEY TERMS

turnover rate   **197**

job analysis   **198**

job description   **198**

job qualifications   **199**

selection criteria   **202**

predictors   **202**

negligent hiring   **216**

negligent retention   **216**

REVIEW QUESTIONS

1. Define *turnover rate*. Explain why it is important for a sales manager to know his company's sales force turnover rate.

2. What is a job analysis? Why is it important?

3. What is the information most likely to be found in a good job description?

4. What is the relationship between selection criteria and predictors? Explain.

5. Distinguish between validity and reliability (of either predictors or tests).

6. Describe three important sources of internal sales candidates.

7. What are the advantages of using print advertising and private employment agencies as external sources of sales applicants?

8. A sales manager says, "Even if someone sends in a résumé, when I ask them to come for an interview, I have them complete a company application form in my office." Explain why the sales manager would require that applicants do this.

9. Describe three types of tests that can be used as part of a salesperson selection process.

10. What are the primary reasons to conduct a background check on sales applicants? Explain.

APPLICATION EXERCISES

1. The Myers-Briggs Type Indicator was described as a popular, if questionable, test instrument for measuring personality. Visit **www.google.ca** (or another search engine if you prefer) and hit "advanced search." Type "Myers-Briggs + personality profiles" under "Find with exact phrase." Limit your search by typing ".ca" under "domain." Does the number of hits indicate anything about the validity of this test instrument for the selection of salespeople? Explain. Also, visit some of the websites that discuss this test instrument, and be prepared to discuss what you have found in class.

2. Ten predictors of sales aptitude follow:

Persuasiveness	Enthusiasm
Reliability	Verbal ability
Honesty	Well organized
Sociability	Sales experience (general)
Ambition	Sales experience (specific)

    Rank the three predictors that you believe would be the most important (1 = most important), and the three predictors that you believe would be the least important (10 = least important). Be prepared to defend your choices.

3. GlaxoSmithKline is one of many companies that use the team interview process, which is growing in popularity. Candidates meet with several managers concurrently, and each manager gets to ask several rounds of questions and provide input in the selection decision. What are the advantages and the potential pitfalls of using a team interview approach? Search the internet and see what suggestions you can find to help you if you suddenly discover that you are about to participate as an interviewee in a team interview environment.

4. As part of the selection process, one sales manager gives recruits a pad of paper on which is written a single "focus" word: INCOMPREHENSIBILITY. He then instructs the recruit to write as many words as he can within 10 minutes, with the constraint that only letters that are found in the focus word may be used, and no more frequently than they appear in the focus word; that is, no more than one C, two N's, or three I's, etc. What do you think the sales manager is trying to measure? What do you think of this exercise as part of the selection process? Explain.

CASE 7.1   # Red Cow Enterprises, Inc.

Carla Carruth was starting to feel the pressure. Her salesperson for Southern Ontario had just given two weeks' notice of leaving, and Carla wanted to replace her quickly before she left. The primary reason for such time pressure was that Carla wanted her departing salesperson to provide at least one week of on-the-job training for the new recruit.

Carla had called several sources of job applicants, and had been able to find 22 people who were looking for a junior sales job. However, after reviewing the applications, Carla had quickly reduced the pool of possible candidates to only five applicants. Carla had been dissatisfied with all five following subsequent interviews. The first woman who had appeared for an interview "was too old." Carla knew that there were laws against age discrimination, but with such a small sales force, she insisted that the salespeople who worked for her display the proper image for the company. Target customers were in their mid-to-late teens, and salespeople often had to interact directly with them as well as with retail accounts that sold her products. The second candidate had had three jobs in the past year, and none of them showed any progression. The third candidate was a man. Again, Carla knew it might be discrimination, but her customers were women, her other employees were all women, and she had decided that this one was going to be a woman also. The fourth candidate had looked good initially, but as soon as she talked, Carla could smell stale tobacco on her breath. It had been all Carla could do to continue the interview, but she had decided very early that this candidate would not do. The fifth candidate had had visible tattoos on her arm, and jewellery attached to several parts of her face. Carla realized that some of her customers would certainly find this acceptable, but she wasn't going to have this person represent her company.

It looked quite certain that a new salesperson would not be in place in time to learn the territory and company policies before the existing salesperson left. Carla was wondering what alternatives she should consider, and how she might ensure that this situation did not occur again.

CRITICAL-THINKING QUESTION

If you were Carla Carruth, what would you consider? What could you do to reduce the possibility of this situation occurring again should another salesperson decide to leave?

Custom Energy Reduction Systems   CASE 7.2

Custom Energy Reduction Systems was in the process of hiring a new technical salesperson to sell its customized equipment to mining and construction accounts across Canada. After assessing nearly 40 applicants, five were short-listed for interviews with management and with existing salespeople. As a result, two final contenders remained. There were some people who favoured Bill Tandy and some who favoured Ed Jiang. Both candidates were evaluated on a number of criteria by each of the interviewers, and the ratings for each candidate were averaged for each criterion. Hank Murray, the sales manager, prepared a summary of the information.

	Bill Tandy	Ed Jiang
Current salary	$66 000	$60 000
Education	B. Comm.	B. Eng.
Persuasiveness during presentation	8.1	7.3
Sociability and likeableness	8.6	8.5
Ambition and enthusiasm	7.7	8.4
Planning and organization	7.7	8.1
Relevant sales experience	8.5	7.4

Barry Burrows, the company president, told Hank, "I do have a preference, but I'm not going to tell you. This person will report directly to you, and you should make the decision. I want you to decide carefully. We have very few salespeople who will earn a salary of $70 000, so making the right choice is important. Let me know what you decide, and we can talk about it afterward."

CRITICAL-THINKING QUESTION

If you were Hank Murray, which candidate would you choose? Be prepared to defend your answer. What would you do if you subsequently discovered that the president was really hoping for the other candidate?

Chapter 8

Training Salespeople

Maxim Transportation Services has been operating from its head office in Winnipeg for more than 25 years. The company has five divisions: Maxim International Trucks, Maxim Trailers, Maxim Rentals and Leasing, Maxim Truck Collision, and Maxim Truck Recycling. Maxim Truck Collision operates in Winnipeg; Maxim Rentals and Leasing operates from Quebec through British Columbia; the other divisions operate in Manitoba, Saskatchewan, and Alberta.

The company has benefited for many years from having common management services for its more than 300 employees, but one area where it needed to standardize was in sales. When the company recently consolidated all of its head office operations in a new modern location, it wanted to make sure customers were getting a consistent message from all of the Maxim customer contact people that might service them. Maxim put all of its 60 salespeople through the Canadian Professional Sales Association's Certified Sales Professional program and made maintaining a certified designation a condition of employment. The program was delivered on-site in Winnipeg for the majority of salespeople. The Toronto salespeople were trained there; the Quebec salespeople received their training in French.

Ed Holloway, CSP, vice-president, rentals and leasing, says, "Now the terminology 'sales funnel' will mean the same thing to everyone, whether they're selling a part, a truck, a collision service, or a rental leasing service, which allows us to tie together our processes." This is an important first step that will help Maxim Transportation Services to integrate terms and processes from the various divisions into a company-wide CRM program so it can continue to improve its customer service.[1]

The Importance of Sales Training

The importance of the recruiting and selecting process in building a superior sales force was discussed in Chapter 7. Recruiting and selecting the best salespeople for the organization is an important first step. However, what is done to them or for them after they are hired is just as critical for their development and the company's success, as the example of Maxim Transportation Services illustrates in the opening vignette. Salespeople are among the most frequently trained people in business, and those who work for the best companies often receive sales training throughout their entire careers. A report published by *Training* magazine estimates that salespeople annually receive nearly 40 hours of training, approximately four times as many hours of training as senior executives.[2] Training can reinforce existing skills and knowledge, or help develop new skills and knowledge. It is not just for large sales forces. Training can be important to companies with only one salesperson.

The first step to develop a training program is to perform a training needs assessment and decide what is appropriate for the company and the situation that its sales force faces. As a second step, the sales manager must establish sales training objectives—ones that are both realistic and measurable. Third, the sales manager must decide the budget that is available for sales training, as this will determine many of the factors related to the design of the sales training program: who will be trained, what will be trained, and when, where, and how training will be done. Finally, the training must be evaluated, as the justification for training is always to improve skills, knowledge, and attitudes that will ultimately improve sales performance.

Before the sales training process is presented, a number of outcomes from sales training are discussed, as these are what justify investing money in sales training programs: improved sales performance, improved self-management, improved selling skills, improved customer relationships, better morale, and reduced sales force turnover. Exhibit 8.1 shows how these outcomes are interrelated.

Exhibit 8.1
Outcomes From Sales Training

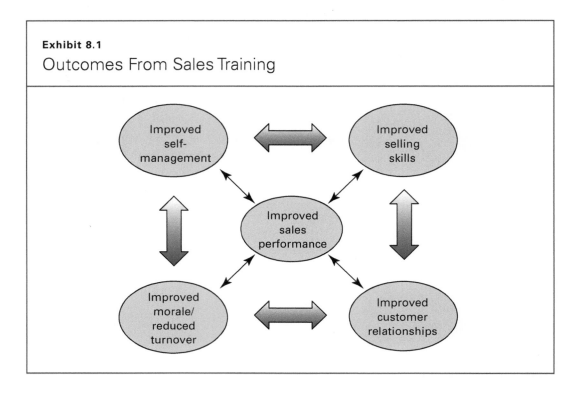

IMPROVED SALES PERFORMANCE

The ultimate justification for investing in training for the sales force is to improve sales force performance. Training provides several other advantages to the company and the salesperson, but ultimately, the justification for the investment is long-term improvement in sales that will generate financial contribution that exceeds the cost of the training. Companies that wisely spend money, make money. Nabisco, for example, implemented its two-day Professional Selling Program, which included role plays, videos, quizzes, team exercises, and feedback. In a follow-up assessment of 104 salespeople who were trained compared to 386 similar salespeople who were not, the company reported an average quarterly sales increase of more than $30 000. This equated to $120 000 in annual sales, and a projected increased operating contribution of more than $20 000—a high return on the estimated $1008 that the company invested to train each salesperson.[3]

IMPROVED SELF-MANAGEMENT

Salespeople with appropriate training take more responsibility for managing actions and enjoy their job more. They are more organized and are better able to manage their time. They have better territory planning skills and take more responsibility for deciding which customers to contact, and when, and how often. They better understand the value of keeping sales and expense records, and customer and competitor information. They know the warning signs for stress, and they have good strategies for managing stress in their work and their personal lives. Better time, territory, records, and stress management can all have a positive impact on sales performance.

IMPROVED SELLING SKILLS

Almost 80 percent of companies provide selling skills training for their salespeople.[4] How to manage customer interactions was discussed in Chapter 6; this is the face-to-face selling process that has a tremendous effect on a salesperson's ability to sell. Salespeople must understand how to prospect for and qualify customers, how to approach customers appropriately, how to make value-added sales presentations and demonstrations, how to handle customer resistance (once referred to as objections), how to negotiate sales conditions, and how to close sales. After they understand all of this, they must also understand how to service customers after the sale and manage long-term customer relationships. Younger salespeople may understand the process reasonably well if they were trained in selling in their college or university program, but only practice, and training, and more practice will make them better salespeople. Older salespeople often benefit from selling skills training as it reinforces for them what they do well, and helps them see where they may have developed poor selling habits.

IMPROVED CUSTOMER RELATIONSHIPS

Salespeople who have good time, territory, records, and stress management skills—and who understand and implement the selling process well—develop better customer relationships. Customers respect salespeople who are professional and organized. These salespeople have a better understanding of their customers and the industries they work in, and are less likely to waste time.

REDUCED TURNOVER

Salespeople who receive appropriate training will have a better understanding of what it is they do or should do to be successful. This could involve product training, or training to improve how they implement the entire selling process. This increases their confidence and helps them better handle customer questions and manage customer relationships, reducing conflict and improving sales performance. Increased knowledge, better relationships, and less conflict will all increase satisfaction, and increased satisfaction will decrease sales force turnover. A survey of salespeople employed by a *Fortune* 1000 company demonstrated that training increased satisfaction among salespeople because it reduced uncertainty concerning what they were required to do in their role as a salesperson, and it increased their perception of their ability to meet conflicting expectations of customers and their own management that might arise as part of their job.[5] Lower satisfaction was demonstrated to be related to an increase in sales force turnover. However, this relationship is moderated by economic conditions, and when salespeople do not have other job opportunities.[6] Of course, improved retention means that seller–buyer relationships are more stable; that is, there are better relationships.

BETTER MORALE

Attitude is arguably the most important personal characteristic of successful salespeople. Training indirectly improves attitude by improving salespeople's knowledge and selling skills. Most sales training involves one or both of these. When salespeople know their products and understand better how to sell, their confidence and sales performance both improve. That is the whole purpose of sales training—to get new salespeople up to speed faster and to improve the performance of all salespeople beyond what it would be without training. Increased performance improves morale and, in some cases, considerably improves the salesperson's income. A large study of salespeople in the insurance industry found that only 16 percent of low-performing salespeople remained with the company after 24 months, compared to four times as many high-performing salespeople.[7]

The Sales Training Process

The sales training process involves five steps: (1) performing a sales training needs assessment; (2) establishing sales training objectives; (3) establishing a sales training budget; (4) developing the sales training program, which includes deciding who, what, when, where, and how to train; and (5) evaluating the effectiveness of the sales training. This process is illustrated in Exhibit 8.2.

PERFORM A SALES TRAINING NEEDS ASSESSMENT

A sales **training needs assessment** involves a comparison. It requires that management carefully decide what salespeople should know, what should be their attitude, and how they should sell. These benchmarks must then be compared to the existing knowledge, attitudes, beliefs, and behaviours of the sales force. Where there are differences between what exists and what is desired, there is a need for training to close the gap. Deciding what should be is part of the planning process and requires vision. It begins with reviewing management objectives. Determining what exists requires management to collect and analyze information from several sources, including company records, customers, and salespeople.

MANAGEMENT OBJECTIVES The most important place to start is with organizational needs; that is, the organizational objectives for sales training. Without having one or more objectives for a sales training program, it is impossible to tell whether the program was a success or a waste of organizational resources. For many organizations, the realization that training is needed follows a slump in sales. The "fix" is to quickly train the sales force so that sales will improve. Implementing a sales training program under this type of pressure often results in a program that trains the wrong people, and the wrong things, and there is often little thought concerning how

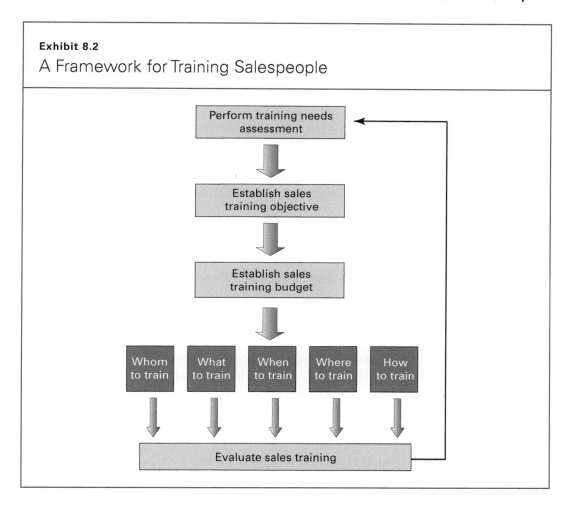

Exhibit 8.2
A Framework for Training Salespeople

Perform training needs assessment

Establish sales training objective

Establish sales training budget

Whom to train | What to train | When to train | Where to train | How to train

Evaluate sales training

to evaluate the training program. Good training programs are proactive. They are developed with specific, measurable objectives. Some companies have a training program for new employees, which specifies what will be trained and when so that there is continued development throughout their career.

Companies often make changes to their marketing strategy as a result of changes in their marketing environment. They may change their target market. They may introduce new products to their product line. They may become more aggressive due to increased competition, or simply change their selling style to a more consultative or relationship approach. In all of these instances, carefully deciding why training is needed and what objectives need to be accomplished with the training helps ensure success.

COMPANY RECORDS When used wisely, company records can be invaluable when performing a sales training needs assessment. Sales managers today have much more sales data available than ever before, and it can often be provided to them in almost any format they wish to have it—either on a daily, weekly, monthly, quarterly, or annual basis, or to meet their needs when they wish to investigate a specific question.

Exhibit 8.3

Type of Sales by Region

	Sales ($)	
	Dealer	**Direct**
Western Canada	4 546 827	10 255 354
Central Canada	2 655 198	14 435 988
Eastern Canada	3 336 928	8 521 276

A useful technique is to cross-tabulate data, a method used to look at two or more variables together. For example, the data in Exhibit 8.3 allow a sales manager to see if there are differences in sales in dealer versus direct sales in different regions of the country.

Even without making further calculations, it is easy to see that sales are highest in Central Canada, but dealer sales there as a percentage of total sales are lowest. There may be good reasons for this. It is possible that good dealers are not available in Central Canada. It may be that the company has a much greater sales presence in Central Canada and it may be more actively soliciting direct business there. The sales manager may decide after reviewing these data that the situation is acceptable, or she may decide to investigate further. Exhibit 8.4 compares average number of items per invoice and average dealer order size by region.

Again, a difference is readily apparent, but the possibility still arises that the situation is acceptable. The lowest average order size and the lowest average items per invoice are in the Central Canada region. If the sales distribution centre is in this region, it could be that customers carry less inventory and order more frequently. It could be that the company's marketing strategy is to rely less on dealers and to increase direct sales effort. If this is the situation, then the Central Canada region is the best region. However, if dealers are an important part of the marketing channel, then allowing the dealer network to weaken has strategic implications for the future of the company. A weak dealer network may allow competition to increase access to the market. If this is the situation, then the sales manager needs to take quick action to focus more effort on selling to dealers. One possibility, of course, is training. It is possible that the sales force needs additional training on how to sell to and support dealers. This, though, may not be the only solution. Another possible solution is to focus attention on dealer sales by changing the compensation plan

Exhibit 8.4

Average Dealer Order Size and Items per Invoice by Region

	Average Order Size ($)	Average Items per Invoice
Western Canada	2622	7.1
Central Canada	1788	5.3
Eastern Canada	2772	7.8

to motivate the sales force to sell through dealers. The best solution might involve both training and adjusting compensation to change behaviour.

So far, the focus has been on the sales force, but sales managers must often be concerned with individual salespeople. Cross-tabulating data can also suggest where training for individuals is needed. Exhibit 8.5 compares calls per day, sales per order, and gross margin by salesperson.

One question that is quickly raised is why Bob Constantine has the highest sales calls per day, but the lowest average sales per order and below average gross margin. Could he need training on how to close sales? Is he rushing through his sales calls? Horton Dewtie suggests other needs. His gross margin is the lowest, but his average sales are just above the sales force average. Is he cutting price to get business? Would he benefit by getting training in negotiation? Or, is he selling a mix of products with lower gross margins, possibly because he is uncomfortable selling more profitable items? If this is the situation, he could benefit by increasing his product knowledge—another training possibility.

Notice that the data suggest possibilities. The real value of data is that they raise questions. They often do not provide answers. A good sales manager will use the data to provide her with direction for further investigation. She should now look for alternative reasons to suggest why she sees particular patterns in the data. This may involve talking to salespeople, making sales calls with salespeople, or talking to customers.

SALES FORCE OBSERVATION AND PERFORMANCE TESTING   Many sales managers spend time in the field with their salespeople, and this provides an opportunity to identify whether individual salespeople have poor product knowledge or difficulty with specific parts of the selling process. If these are minor weaknesses, the sales manager may decide to address them with a "curb-side review" immediately after the sales call. In other instances, the observation may indicate a problem that may affect the entire sales force, and this will require more formal and extensive training at a future time. Sales managers should also be aware that observing the best salespeople in a sales force can suggest training that will benefit the entire sales force as well.

There are companies that require salespeople to undergo regular performance testing. Sometimes this may simply involve product knowledge tests to ensure that salespeople are keeping up with product changes. In other instances, salespeople may be assessed on their ability to probe for information and make consultative sales presentations, to effectively use product demonstrations, to handle buyer resistance, or to close sales, all in a simulated sales environment. Sometimes these performance tests may provide the opportunity for immediate sales training.

Exhibit 8.5

Calls per Day, Sales per Order, and Gross Margin by Salesperson

	Average Calls/Day	Average Sales/Order ($)	Gross Margin as a Percent of Sales (%)
Karen Smythe	3.6	3212	26.0
Bram Samila	4.0	3987	23.0
Judy VanderWillik	3.9	3822	24.3
Bob Constantine	5.1	2956	23.8
Terry Trite	3.4	3962	25.2
Horton Dewtie	3.3	4146	22.5

When these performance tests are performed in a group setting, there is an opportunity to compare and discuss everyone's performance and to explore ways to improve poor performance.

Sales managers who wish to may also use any of a number of training needs assessment instruments that are commercially available or that have been developed by sales training consultants. One commonly used training needs assessment instrument is the Sales Strategy Index available from Target Training International. Salespeople view 54 sales scenarios and choose what they believe to be the best strategy for each selling situation. The scenarios are related to six areas of the sales process: prospecting, first impressions, qualifying, demonstration, influence, and closing. They then receive a comprehensive report that compares them to top sales performers so they can identify their own strengths and weaknesses. (A copy of a sample report can be viewed at **www.ttidisc.com**.) This assessment instrument is also offered through many human resources and sales consultants around the world. Ontario-based SalesForce Training & Consulting offers this as part of its assessment possibilities (**www.salesforcetraining.com**). Past-president Brian Jeffrey has also developed a "Quick Assessment" tool that can be used for assessing tactical and strategic selling skills, and time management and organizational skills. Exhibit 8.6 provides an example of some of the tactical selling skills items that are assessed along with an indication of how the assessment is scored. This instrument can be used by a sales manager to assess the training needs of the entire sales force, or of each salesperson. Brian suggests that, when the sales manager assesses each salesperson, having each salesperson complete the instrument as well can be an interesting exercise. The sales manager's and salesperson's perceptions of the salesperson's training needs can be compared.

ESTABLISH SALES TRAINING OBJECTIVES

After performing a sales training needs assessment, the next step is to establish one or more sales training objectives. Sales training objectives need to be specific and measurable, and should be put in writing. There are many advantages to establishing and communicating clear training objectives.

1. *Helps define the sales manager's expectations.* When a sales manager is forced to think of and communicate objectives, he is forced to think through why training will be beneficial, and what the expected outcomes of training will be.
2. *Helps gain support from upper management.* Clearly defined objectives will help get support from senior management. Support may come in the form of an adequate financial budget, but interest and participation by senior management in the process will also help ensure sales training success.
3. *Helps gain support from the sales force.* Brian Jeffrey, introduced earlier in this chapter, says there are three types of salespeople who attend training sessions: Participants, who actively participate and try to get as much as they can from a training session; Vacationers, who see a training workshop as time away from work; and Prisoners, who would rather not be there and who are therefore negative and ruin the session for everyone.[8] If the sales manager can get support from the sales force before the training session begins, there will likely be more Participants and fewer Vacationers and Prisoners.
4. *Helps a sales manager determine if the training was a success.* A clearly defined and measurable training objective provides a standard against which the training outcome can be compared.
5. *Helps the sales manager prioritize training and plan a program for the longer term.* It is seldom that a sales manager will have the resources—money or time—to implement all needed training initiatives. Once the objectives are clearly established, the sales manager is in a better position to decide what is most important, and to decide on a plan for additional training needs.

Exhibit 8.6

Quick Assessment Tool for Sales Training

Tactical Selling Skills	Do well	Could be better	Need to be better	Need help
Prospecting for new business				
Cold calling				
Making appointments				
Establishing rapport with the prospect				
Gaining the prospect's interest				
Differentiating your company from the competition				
Understanding the buying/selling process				
Understanding the impact of personality on the sale				
Ability to adjust to the prospect's personality				
Understanding the prospect's needs before selling				
Listening skills				
Qualifying the prospect before selling				
Recognize non-verbal buying signals				
Using trial closes				
Closing the sale (asking for the business)				
Partnering with the prospect/client				
Using the telephone as an effective selling tool				
Providing strong after-sales follow-up and support				
Getting enough referral business				
Getting more business from existing accounts				
TOTALS				

SCORING:
Do well _____ × 3 = _____
Could be better _____ × 2 = _____
Need to be better _____ × 1 = _____
Need help _____ × 0 = _____

Total _____ × 100 = _____%
60

Source: Permission granted by Tim Flater, vice-president, sales and client development, SalesForce Training & Consulting Inc., 120 Eglinton Ave. E., Suite 500, Toronto, ON, M4P 1E2, (416) 779-0011 or (800) 461-7355.

Sales managers have many training objectives from which they may choose. The following is only a partial list:

1. Increase sales, gross margin, or market share.
2. Introduce new products or promotional programs.
3. Improve performance on specific aspects of the selling process.
4. Reinforce the importance of ethical selling practices.
5. Improve morale and motivate salespeople.
6. Prepare salespeople for management positions.
7. Prepare salespeople to sell to new market segments.
8. Improve cooperation and teamwork.
9. Train salespeople for team selling or national account management.
10. Introduce new technology to the sales force.

While a sales manager may choose a single objective against which to evaluate training outcomes, these objectives are often interrelated. For example, salespeople could be trained in how to prepare a spreadsheet analysis. As a result, they may make better sales presentations, which may then lead to increased sales or improved gross margin.

ESTABLISH A SALES TRAINING BUDGET

The sales training budget may be one of the most important items in a sales manager's overall annual budget. The sales manager needs to be able to estimate the number of new sales employees she will have each year, and the cost to train each new employee during the first year. She also needs to have a plan for annual sales force training needs, and for training of individual salespeople. When these figures are combined, the sales manager has a budget for which she can request senior management approval. As already noted, it is important to have a budget to force a sales manager to think about what is needed, prioritize training initiatives, to get senior management support for training, and to have a guide against which to make expenditures.

DEVELOP THE SALES TRAINING PROGRAM

After performing a training needs assessment, establishing appropriate objectives and a sales training budget, the sales training program itself must be designed. This requires the sales manager to make decisions relating to who, what, when, where, and how. Each of these questions is discussed in the following sections.

WHOM TO TRAIN   Companies commonly have training programs for new sales recruits. These may range from a few days to several months. New sales employees at Red Carpet Vending & Refreshment Services, Canada's largest office coffee service operator, all spend six days at parent company A.L. Van Houtte in Montreal where they learn selling skills based on the Canadian Professional Sales Association's Skills for Success program.[9]

Some companies have annual sales training programs where the venue and content regularly change. They recognize the importance of making regular and continued investment in salespeople. The Western Markets Group of Toronto-based Marsulex organizes quarterly meetings for its 40 employees, including its five salespeople, who all operate from different locations. The focus can range from sales training to customer service training and communications. Whether at a hotel in Fort Saskatchewan or at a resort in Jasper, Alberta, these sessions provide an opportunity to interact, have fun, and learn new skills.[10]

One major issue for sales managers is whether to train the entire sales force, or to provide specific training to individual members of the sales force based on their individual needs. For example, if a salesperson is destined for a sales management position, a careful assessment of his present skills and abilities and his needed skills and abilities might indicate specific training that will make the transition to management easier and reduce the number of problems he will face. Another salesperson whose career path will involve promotion to major or strategic account selling may need special training on how to manage multiple relationships within customer organizations. A separate, important issue, presented at the end of this chapter, is training for employees once they have been promoted to sales management.

WHAT TO TRAIN   There are many topics that can be covered in sales training programs, and the need for specific topics will vary depending on the industry the company operates in, the background and experience of its salespeople, the technology level and rate of introduction of new products, changing customer buying habits, and the actions of competitors. However, there are a number of topics that are common across many sales forces, as shown in Exhibit 8.7.

Product Knowledge   More companies train salespeople on product knowledge than on any other topic. However, high performers among the sales force may not have significantly better product knowledge than moderate performers.[11] Art Sobczak, author of *How to Sell More in Less Time, With No Rejection, Using Common Sense Telephone Techniques,* once asked a buyer what was important to his company. The buyer replied, "I want someone who knows my business, my competition, and their own product inside and out and can apply that knowledge to what I want. Get my attention quickly by telling me what you might be able to do and be prepared to ask questions to learn what I want. Then you are ready to make a presentation."[12] This suggests that product knowledge is a necessary, but not a sufficient, criterion for success. Salespeople must be able to apply their product knowledge to meet specific customer needs.

Salespeople should know several dimensions of product knowledge:

1. *Product development and quality improvement processes.* Wabi Iron and Steel Corp. of New Liskeard, Ontario, has been able to keep ahead of its competition by systematically developing and testing new alloys for the machinery that it manufactures. Company salespeople must continually be made aware of changes and improvements to be effective at finding solutions to customer buying problems.[13]

Exhibit 8.7
Common Sales Training Topics

Knowledge	Skills	Other
Product	Managing time	Company
Market	Managing territory	—history
Customers	Prospecting	—values
Competitors	Approaching	—expectations
	Presenting/demonstrating	Budgeting
	Negotiating/closing	Goal-setting
	Communicating	Pricing
	Decision-making	
	Servicing customers	

2. *Performance data and specifications.* Prospects commonly want to know product specifications, and how these compare to competitors' specifications. A salesperson selling household appliances should know the energy consumption of these products, as that is an important feature for many customers who want energy savings. Natural Resources Canada publishes an annual directory of the energy consumption of products based on manufacturer and model number.

3. *Maintenance and service contracts.* Salespeople who educate customers on the proper use and maintenance of products ensure that the products are used properly and that customers get the benefits they wish. Salespeople need to know what maintenance and service contracts are available for customers, and increasingly are asked to customize them to meet specific customer needs. Customized service contracts can help protect business from competition.[14]

4. *Price and delivery.* Some complex products require that a salesperson be able to price various features that may be configured to meet the specific needs of the customer. Prices will also vary due to quantity, delivery method, payment plan, and other factors. A salesperson who cannot quickly price a product and provide a prospect with accurate delivery information may be at a serious disadvantage.

Sales Process Knowledge   Anne Babej, director of professional development at the Canadian Professional Sales Association, says, "If you don't have sales-process training, you don't even really know who you're selling to."[15] This is the most important part of selling. It distinguishes the best salespeople from the rest of the sales force. Most companies train salespeople on the selling process applicable to their particular situation: company philosophy, target customers, and products. The purpose may be to provide, reinforce, or enhance their selling skills, and ultimately to increase sales.

Inexperienced salespeople need to have basic training on selling skills. Many salespeople are promoted to sales from other positions in the company. They may have product and customer knowledge, but only a general knowledge of what is required in their role as salesperson. Others have sales experience with another company or another product, but it is a mistake to assume they don't need additional training when they change selling jobs. Even experienced salespeople within a company can benefit from sales training that reinforces selling skills, as many will have developed poor habits if they have not benefited from regular training and reinforcement. The breadth and depth of topic coverage will vary depending on particular company objectives. The topics covered most frequently include prospecting, approaching customers, making effective presentations and demonstrations, negotiating buyer resistance, closing sales, and servicing the sale. All of these topics have been previously covered in detail in Chapter 6.

Competitive Knowledge   Salespeople who know their competitors' strengths and weaknesses can use this to their advantage when presenting their own products. Prospects often have knowledge of competitive offerings, and they may want to make comparisons during sales presentations. A salesperson who knows how his products differ from competitors' products can best focus on his own products' advantages and is better able to handle buyer resistance when it arises during a sales presentation.

Regardless of what a salesperson knows or thinks about a competitor's products, it is important to display the correct attitude toward competitors while face-to-face with customers. Knowledge will allow a salesperson to respond to questions concerning competitors, but the salesperson should never raise the issue of competition first. If the customer raises issues related to the competition, it is often wise to acknowledge the competition but then to focus on the positive aspects of your own product rather than the competition. A salesperson should never criticize the competition, and should certainly be sure that any claims made concerning the competition are accurate. Salespeople who make inaccurate statements about competitors quickly lose credibility with knowledgeable customers, and may also open themselves to libel or slander suits.

Salespeople who do not know the competition well may be at a disadvantage when negotiating with informed prospects. Salespeople who do not know competitors' prices may give lower prices than necessary, and thereby sacrifice margin. Salespeople who do not know the weaknesses of a competitor's product may provide lower prices than necessary or add features that are important to the customer at lower prices than they otherwise would charge. Knowing your competition is as important as knowing your own company and product.

Industry and Customer Knowledge   Sales success often depends on understanding how customers buy. Kenji Tomikawa, president and CEO of Toyota Canada, understands this. He says, "In the past, we didn't have many salespeople who knew the truck market well enough to understand what a typical truck buyer wants to use their vehicle for." Now, he has salespeople for Toyota trucks participate in a comprehensive sales training program that teaches them how truck buyers differ from car buyers.[16]

As we discussed in Chapter 5, when a buying centre is involved, salespeople must understand who is in the buying centre and the particular role of each person. Some sales forces are organized with sales specialists who focus on different vertical market segments, as discussed in Chapter 3. The reason for this is that customers within an industry often face similar problems and have similar needs when it comes to sales solutions. At the same time, they may have very different issues than customers in other industries. When this is the situation, industry and customer knowledge is critical to a salesperson's success, and salespeople need to have a thorough understanding of these customers' needs.

Training is often focused on discovering and understanding customer needs, and the buying motives they will use to make a buying decision. Two customers may purchase exactly the same product, but for different reasons.

Company Knowledge   Salespeople have a boundary-spanning role between the organization they work for and the customer organizations they serve. Often, the image the customer has of the salesperson's organization is formed entirely through interaction with the salesperson. For this reason, salespeople need to fully understand their own company.

First, they should know their company culture and organization. Many salespeople take pride in their company. Pfizer Canada salespeople are proud that their company has regularly been chosen among the best Canadian companies to work for.[17] Smaller companies, such as Vancouver-based Intrinsyc Software Inc., can instill pride in their employees through their company culture. Intrinsyc's president, Derek Spratt, says, "We're a young, high-tech firm with an environment that challenges employees to learn more. You don't stagnate at Intrinsyc. People roll out of bed and get excited about going to work every day."[18] Every company has its unique organizational culture that has evolved over time to include distinct norms and practices. When a company has developed a supportive culture for its salespeople and encourages them to seek unique solutions to buyer problems, it has set the stage for long-term seller–buyer relationships.[19]

Second, salespeople must understand the company support for the product they sell. Knowing this and communicating it to customers can be the difference between getting or losing an order. Mike Urquhart, vice-president of sales for Husky Injection Molding Systems Ltd., of Bolton, Ontario, says, "Our spare parts manager is one of the key people we often include in our sales presentations. It's his role to say, 'Here's how we back you up. Here's how we can help you when you have problems.' This is one way we convince customers that we are committed to helping them, before, during, and after the sale."[20]

Self-Management   Self-management is becoming increasingly important as companies recognize that individuals make decisions that affect both their efficiency and their effectiveness as salespeople. Research has demonstrated that salespeople who have been trained in self-management can increase both their short-term and long-term performance.[21] While there are many dimensions of self-management, four of the key ones are time management, territory management, records management, and stress management. We briefly discuss each of these.

1. *Time management.* Time for salespeople is a very limited resource. When 1300 salespeople were asked to rank 16 work-related challenges they faced, not having enough time was ranked first.[22] Salespeople spend less than one-third of their time face-to-face with customers. Increasing this time is one way to improve sales performance. Cy Charney, a Toronto-based performance improvement consultant and president of Charney & Associates, says, "Plan each day the afternoon or evening before. Doing this will give you assurance that your day will be productive and enable you to have a good night's sleep."[23] A small amount of time spent planning can pay huge dividends for many salespeople. Mark Elwood, another Toronto-based productivity consultant, says that the average person spends only 1.3 hours per week planning, 13.2 hours on administrative tasks, and 3.7 hours on non-essential activities. However, people who spend 3.4 hours per week planning and prioritizing spend only 9.5 hours per week on administrative tasks and 1.5 hours on non-essential activities. That is, 2 additional hours of planning provide a net gain of more than 4 hours.[24]

2. *Territory management.* Territory management is closely related to time management as the goal is to allocate time and effort across a group of customers and prospective customers assigned to a single salesperson, called a **sales territory**, so that each customer gets seen as often as necessary to maximize sales performance, but no more often than that. The Royal Bank of Canada had its account managers segment customers into 'A,' 'B,' and 'C' categories based on their dollar activity and profitability. By focusing more effort on the best accounts, the profit on the 'A' accounts, for example, was increased 268 percent, and the number of these accounts increased 292 percent over a two-year period.[25]

3. *Records management.* Sales managers need to be careful that they do not burden salespeople with too much paperwork. Time spent keeping records is often time away from selling, or it requires too much effort outside normal working hours and is quickly resented. Therefore, the only records that should be required are ones that provide benefits to the customer, the salesperson, the sales manager, or others in the sales company who support the salespeople. The most common records that meet these requirements are customer or prospect files and call reports. Some salespeople still use recipe cards or notebooks to maintain contact information, but most now use personal digital assistants. In larger companies, more sophisticated CRM systems are maintained, but salespeople often must be trained on their use and on the value of helping to keep them current. Call reports provide a review of what was done over time, and can also be used to provide information to others in the company, either for planning purposes, or to follow up on things the salesperson has

identified that need to be done to service an account. In many instances, good information management improves planning and saves time.

4. *Stress management.* Selling can be stressful, certainly at times. One reason, of course, is the type of people who are attracted to a sales career. Many salespeople put undue pressure on themselves to perform. They are driven to succeed. Other things that cause stress are deadlines, the non-routine nature of the job, travel, time away from family and leisure activities, and long hours. Lucille Peszat, executive director of the Canadian Centre for Stress and Well-Being, says, "Changes in your behaviour—you're more sarcastic, preoccupied, and inclined to procrastinate—could indicate you're overstressed."[26] Training to manage stress can help salespeople cope with it and become more productive. Effectively managing stress often requires a better lifestyle: healthier eating, more sleep, less alcohol, increased exercise.

Other Topics   There are many other topics that can be the basis for sales training. With the increase in technology that is being used to improve sales efficiency, many sales forces are finding it challenging to train salespeople how to use the technology, assuming they can motivate salespeople to want to learn new skills and selling techniques. Many veteran salespeople have still not mastered basic keyboarding skills, to the point where even to use word processing packages or send email is time consuming and challenging.

Making ethical decisions is part of personal selling, and with the growing awareness of unethical selling practices and the willingness of customers to pursue legal redress, companies are beginning to provide increased training to salespeople regarding corporate expectations of ethical conduct. Sales managers and top management serve as role models for salespeople. If a company wants its salespeople to behave ethically, providing training reinforces the importance of ethics to the company and increases the probability of this happening. Companies should also have a written code of ethics. Al Rosen, a retired accounting professor from York University, says that once you are hired by a company, "People are telling you to forget this and that—it becomes a birds-of-a-feather atmosphere."[27] When companies have written policies, it means someone has formalized a stand on business ethics.

Some companies have also supported various specialized training programs. Salespeople have been trained to read body language, interpret eye movements, overcome fear of making sales calls, or even identify whether they are dealing with "left-brained" or "right-brained" customers so they can determine their decision-making style. Companies will undoubtedly find that some of these sales training programs are more beneficial than others.

WHEN TO TRAIN   The issue of when to train deserves some consideration. The decision often depends on the objective of the training and on business conditions. Some companies use sales training as a reward. The top members of the sales force get recognized, and get to attend an annual sales training session at an attractive destination. When this is the situation, the training is generally scheduled for the same time each year, and it is promoted to the sales force as an annual sales contest or recognition event.

Sales managers should plan as far in advance as possible when implementing sales training. This provides the opportunity to communicate the objectives of the training, and to build both awareness and interest. If there are new product introductions, then sales training should occur before or coincide with the introduction. If the objective of the training is to prepare someone for a management position, then the training should be planned, prioritized, and held on a regular basis to help ensure interest and continued personal growth. Sometimes, sales training becomes an annual event simply because there are periods during each year when sales are slow.

For example, a sales force might regularly kick off each year with a sales meeting and training session. This gets everyone motivated for the new year, and the first week of each year is often a slow season when customers are getting back to work and may themselves be planning for the upcoming year, or catching up on things that may have built up over the holiday season.

Some training, such as the indoctrination of new salespeople, may need to be ongoing throughout the year.

WHERE TO TRAIN   Where to train is an important consideration for sales managers. There are really three interrelated dimensions to this question. Companies must consider whether to use (1) centralized or decentralized training, (2) internal or external people as trainers, and (3) whether to use company or external facilities.

Centralized Versus Decentralized Training   The first consideration is whether to use centralized or decentralized training. Centralized training occurs in a central location. That is, everyone comes together for the training session. When centralized training is used, it is more likely that external trainers or internal staff training specialists will be used.

There are a number of advantages to using centralized training: consistency, timing, and quality. When everyone is brought to a single location, everyone gets the same training, at the same time, and trainers can often utilize superior resources. The Sales Management in Action box illustrates how Whirlpool was able to use superior resources by bringing groups of its trainees to a centralized location. Planning for these sessions can include a number of team-building activities, either throughout the day, or through special entertainment events during the evenings. Senior executives from the company can attend and reinforce the importance of the training and help boost employee morale. The major disadvantage is cost. Centralized training requires that everyone come to a single location, and this often involves travel time and expenses, as well as the cost of accommodations, meals, and entertainment. Because of the high cost of centralized training, Sam Mazzotta, former director of product management at WorldCom Canada, now MCI Canada, estimates that webcasting, for example, can cut the cost of centralized training by more than 80 percent.[28]

Decentralized training usually takes place in regional sales offices and directly involves sales managers, or even the salespeople themselves as sales trainers. The advantages include travel time and cost savings, and a better focus on specific regional issues. When branch management is involved in the planning and delivery of training programs, the programs can focus on specific products, services, and customers relevant to the branch. Managers often become a more integral part of the process. In some branches, managers may require salespeople to take responsibility for certain training aspects and deliver short training sessions at regularly scheduled sales meetings.

Some companies, such as Xerox Canada, use a combination of centralized and decentralized training, gaining the benefits of both. New recruits may get their initial training at field sales offices where they are exposed to the company culture and its products. They then may get an intensive training session in Toronto designed specifically for recently hired salespeople. Salespeople who realize that this is not what they were hoping to do as a career, or that this is the wrong company for them, may leave at these early stages before the company has invested considerable resources in their development. Those who decide to continue return to their branch office. There, they are given territory responsibility and continue to develop as they are managed and coached by their sales manager. As they develop through their career, they may be required to attend a number of more advanced or specialized training sessions in Toronto, or other centralized locations. This process ensures continued growth for Xerox salespeople.

Come Join the Real Whirled

How boring can it be for a new salesperson to sit in a classroom and learn how to sell? Well, for many, it can be quite boring. That's why Whirlpool Corporation is taking new salespeople to "The Real Whirled." No, it's not a reality television program. It's an eight-bedroom red-brick farmhouse that has been renovated and completely equipped with Whirlpool products: dishwashers, refrigerators, washers, dryers, and microwave ovens. Groups of eight new salespeople from across Canada and the United States, many fresh from college or university, come to the Real Whirled for training. They live together for eight weeks, constantly trying and testing Whirlpool products. Sometimes competitors' products are added so that salespeople understand where to make important comparisons for customers as well. To see how well the products work, the new salespeople may prepare 900 plates of food, wash 120 bags of laundry or more, and spend hours loading, unloading, and reloading dishwashers, refrigerators, and dryers. They smear white bags with mustard, relish, and other condiments to see how well they can clean them. They cook pasta—three times as much as they need—to see how convection and microwave ovens compare to traditional ovens. They take tests and quizzes almost daily, and make oral presentations. Sometimes, they even take products apart alongside a company engineer, so they can understand the reason for their design. Then, when they graduate from the Real Whirled, they go out into the real world and train sales staff at many of the retailers that sell Whirlpool products: The Brick, Sears, The Bay, Future Shop, Leon's, and many others. For salespeople who are going to train customers, their own training is very important.

Sources: David Barboza, "New Recruits Get a Taste of 'Real Whirl,'" *Globe and Mail*, September 15, 2000, p. M2; Betsey Cummings, "Welcome to the Real Whirled," *Sales & Marketing Management*, February 2001, pp. 87–88; personal interview, Don Powell, divisional sales manager, Whirlpool Canada, August 10, 2006.

Internal Versus External Trainers Another important consideration is whether to use internal trainers or external trainers. The common trainers include company training specialists, field sales managers, and external sales training consultants. Companies may use a combination of trainers depending on specific training objectives, costs, and availability. Some companies are even being more creative and using a completely new type of sales trainer, as described in the Sales Management Today box.

1. *Company training specialists.* Larger companies that require lots of training, and that can afford to, often have internal sales training specialists. These people often have experience designing and delivering programs that meet the specific needs of the company's sales force. If there is good feedback concerning the results of the training sessions, then they can incorporate this feedback into the design and delivery of subsequent programs. In some situations, internal training specialists may train sales managers and provide training materials for them to use when training field salespeople. A frequent criticism of company training specialists is that much of what they teach is not immediately applicable to field selling situations since many of these trainers lack field selling experience.

SALES MANAGEMENT **TODAY**

Engaging Trainees: Who Is Your Avatar?

David Anderson, author of *Selling Above the Crowd: 365 Strategies for Sales Excellence,* says, "Effective training engages the trainee, it uses multimedia, it's interactive, and it's customized to fit specific individual and organizational needs." Engaging today's younger, computer-literate sales trainees is becoming increasingly challenging. Many like the classroom setting because they are familiar with it if they have recently graduated from college or university, but it is very easy to sit in a lecture and not be engaged.

Enter the avatar, a computer representation for a real person. In the electronic world, avatars date back more than 20 years to the Ultima IV computer game. Now, they are being used in sales training programs. They offer the advantage of being easily changed to suit a particular audience. They can be any race, old or young, male or female. When they are used in electronic sales training programs, they have the advantage of not tiring as the day goes on. They never look at their watch, or yawn (unless you want them to). The things they say and the situations they are in can be changed or modified easily from one presentation to another. They can be started, stopped, rewound, and required to perform at 3:00 A.M.

Other advantages compared to using live, in-person trainers are speed and cost. BT Group PLC, a British telecommunications company, was able to train 4500 salespeople in just over four weeks with an avatar-based course. Training manager Mick Taylor estimated that both cost and time were about half of what would have been required had the company used face-to-face training. Toronto-based Franklin Templeton Investments is just one of many Canadian firms that is increasing its use of web technology for sales training. The company wanted to connect its salespeople with investment advisors across Canada who sell Franklin Templeton funds, particularly advisors in remote locations. It settled on web conferencing technology, and now uses it for sales training and product announcements to its 700 employees across Canada as well. Many of these new web-based training programs are likely to incorporate avatars in future as they become increasingly popular.

Sources: Jeanette Borzo, "Computer-Generated 'Teachers' Improve Coaching, Role-Playing," *The Ottawa Citizen,* June 2, 2004, p. F2; Suzanne Wintrob, "The Right Connections Can Pay Off," *National Post,* April 4, 2003, p. BE7.

2. *Field sales managers.* Having field sales managers actively involved in the design, delivery, and follow-up of sales training programs reduces the criticism about using company training specialists. This is because sales managers usually have considerable field sales experience, either for their present company or with a previous company. They are more likely to recognize implementation problems that field salespeople will have once they take the training into the field. Having field sales managers involved in the training also provides an opportunity for the sales managers to interact with the sales force and to improve their own coaching and management skills. Sometimes, sales managers, rather than salespeople, may be taken to a centralized location for training. They then may take the training back to their own regional offices and provide it to their sales force. Federal Express now brings its sales managers to head office, trains them, and relies on their getting the training to their salespeople. Regional sales director Michael Bourke says that this has been a real benefit to the company. Salespeople get training from the same person they deal with daily—the sales manager—and sales managers are delighted because they enjoy working more closely as coaches to their salespeople.[29]

There are also some negative aspects to using field sales managers as trainers. They may understand selling techniques and may be very good at coaching individual salespeople, but they may not be particularly good at communicating information to groups of people. If they have lots of administrative and planning responsibilities, they may not have the time to be actively involved with training as well.

3. *External sales trainers.* Most companies that have sales training programs use external sales trainers for at least part of their training. Estimates range from 54 percent to 84 percent of companies.[30]

The most effective external sales trainers tailor their programs to meet the needs of individual clients. In fact, some external trainers manage the complete training programs for some of their clients. These trainers have an established history with their client and often fully understand their business and selling process. A criticism of some external sales trainers, however, is that they really do not understand the selling situation faced by the company. If they do not understand the company's products and its marketing strategy, the company's customers and how they buy, and the competitive environment of the company, they can easily make mistakes that will make them lose credibility with the sales force.

HOW TO TRAIN   Depending on the source, the estimates of usage for various sales training methods vary considerably. However, sources do generally agree that classroom instruction, role-playing, CD-ROM and audiotapes, the internet and other electronic media, and on-the-job training are all important. Companies today are more likely to use a combination of methods as opposed to a single method, as they recognize that different methods are better depending on the training content and objectives. These popular methods of sales training are now described.

Classroom Instruction   Classroom instruction is a popular method to train salespeople on product knowledge, how to use new technologies, ethics and ethical behaviour, or company policies and procedures. It is perhaps the most popular training method among new salespeople who are recent graduates from college and university. They are familiar with this method, and they do not have the pressure of actively demonstrating their level of selling skill in a group setting. There are many advantages of classroom training:

1. Experts can be used to teach specific topics.
2. All participants receive standardized training and have common knowledge at the end of the training.
3. Audiovisual materials can be effectively incorporated as part of the training.
4. Senior executives can make appearances and build morale without having to participate throughout the entire training session.
5. It can involve more than just lectures: case studies, role-plays, and presentations can all be used to increase active participation.

Classroom training has been a very popular traditional training method. Many companies that are turning to new training methods for the advantages they have still retain classroom training as part of their overall training program.[31]

Role-Playing   Role-playing is a popular training method and is used by nearly 44 percent of companies that have a sales force training program.[32] Role-playing can be very effective because it provides the opportunity through realistic situations and active interaction to practise and reinforce things that have been covered in lectures and audiovisual presentations. Typically, one person role-plays the salesperson, while another person, either the trainer or another salesperson, role-plays the prospect or customer. Sometimes role-playing takes place with only the participants present, but it more commonly takes place in a group setting where everyone gets to contribute to an analysis of the salesperson's performance. In these situations, there can be a lot of stress for the salesperson, therefore feedback should be given immediately following the role-play, and it should focus on both areas for improvement and what the salesperson did well. Videotaping role-plays is also common. Building a library of video role-plays allows trainers to use particular ones in later training sessions where specific examples may be needed.

CDs and Audiotapes   CDs and audiotapes are very popular training tools and are used by approximately 40 percent of companies.[33] They both offer the benefit of portability. Salespeople can use them while travelling in the field, and sales managers can ensure that all members of the sales force can easily access them. At one time, CDs were simply used as sales training presentation media. However, there is growing interest today in interactive CDs. Several Canadian companies have developed technology that can be delivered on CD (or over the internet) that allows salespeople to interact with people who are role-playing situations. Salespeople view simulated sales calls, answer questions or make choices, and then get feedback immediately concerning their performance.

These tools are quite inexpensive. Many companies create an internal library of CDs and audiotapes that can be borrowed by sales managers or salespeople as required. The Canadian Professional Sales Association maintains a large selection that can be borrowed by its members, and it will ship the materials to members anywhere across Canada. These tools can be used for training, for reinforcing previous training, or for motivational purposes. Many salespeople listen to audiotapes between sales calls and find that the tapes motivate them, help them reduce sales call reluctance, and relieve stress.

Online Training   Online training is growing as companies find it necessary to deliver more training to more people, more quickly. Nearly 50 percent of companies now use online training, although only about 60 percent of users do so more than once per year.[34] Century 21 has developed its CREATE21 modular 120-hour training course and has now used it to train more than 126 000 brokers, sales agents, and other staff. The program uses a number of tools and methods, but online training is an important component that allows trainees to access on-demand instruction, something that is very important to busy salespeople who cannot take time from their daily schedules to attend classroom training sessions. The program increased sales revenue per salesperson by 16 percent in less than one year, and reduced salesperson turnover from 40 percent to 11 percent in just two years.[35] Automotive manufacturer Saab uses a company website to provide its "Saab Way" training program. It provides product training, checklists and guides for salespeople, and customized sales process training online. Salespeople who have completed the program average 2.4 more car sales per month than those who have not.[36]

Webcasting is a newer online training method that is also growing in popularity. Instead of putting a training program on the internet and allowing salespeople on-demand access, webcasting presents sales training to salespeople in remote locations but requires that they all participate at the same time. It has some of the advantages of classroom training: everyone gets consistent and timely training. But, unlike classroom training, it can be delivered in shorter sessions that help salespeople comprehend and absorb material. Avanade Inc., a joint venture between Microsoft and consulting firm Accenture, uses webcasting for 80 percent of its technical classes for consultants. The company estimates that webcasting has saved about $1 million per year in travel expenses that would otherwise have been spent on trainees.[37]

On-the-Job Training   Nearly 85 percent of companies use some form of on-the-job training.[38] It can begin almost as soon as a new salesperson assumes her sales position, and it can continue throughout her entire career. The most common form of on-the-job training occurs when the sales manager makes sales calls with the salesperson. The actual training can begin before the sales call and can continue throughout the feedback, which should occur immediately after the sales call. A sales manager may, for example, ask the salesperson what the current status of the account is, what the salesperson's objectives for the pending sales call are, what resistance the salesperson will likely get from the buyer, how the salesperson plans to handle this resistance, and what the salesperson expects will be the outcome of the sales call. The sales manager may or may not attend the face-to-face meeting with the buyer. If he does, he should allow the salesperson to manage the interaction. Following the sales call, the sales manager should then conduct a "curbside" review with the salesperson, asking such questions as "How well do you think you did?" "What did you do well?" "What would you do differently next time if you could do it again?" and "What will you do next?" These training sessions can help build a good relationship between the sales manager and the salesperson. Once the salesperson sees a pattern to the process, she can begin to prepare and review each sales call on her own.

Sales managers who use individual coaching should consider making sales calls on a regular basis with each salesperson. They might make one sales call per month with veteran salespeople and make sales calls more frequently with junior salespeople. Senior salespeople can often benefit from coaching as well as junior salespeople, and the sales manager can sometimes learn new approaches that he can use to help train junior salespeople. If a sales manager makes irregular calls with salespeople, or starts making sales calls selectively with salespeople, this can signal to everyone which salespeople are having problems. It is also easier to establish a policy and always follow it than to be selective because, if calls are not made with veteran salespeople, they will soon resist any attempt to interfere with their behaviour or their customers.

Another common method of on-the-job training is to mentor new sales trainees with senior salespeople. This can be very effective and can certainly help establish new people into their selling role. One concern, however, is that selling is often very individualistic and what works for one salesperson may not work quite so well for another. Also, if senior salespeople and junior salespeople have entirely different selling roles, using a mentor system may not work very well. Senior salespeople often have established territories and are more concerned with relationship management. Junior salespeople are new to a territory and have to establish and build relationships. The skills required are not the same. There is also a danger that a veteran salesperson will teach the junior salesperson all his bad habits.

EVALUATE THE SALES TRAINING

Companies spend considerable resources for sales training, but generally spend limited resources to evaluate its effectiveness. A recent *Sales & Marketing Management* survey found that only 28 percent of respondents had a definitive method to measure the value or impact of their sales training.[39] There are many reasons why evaluation may not occur. Evaluation is difficult. It takes time and money, and there is often difficulty getting data or information that is needed to perform the evaluation. When companies have a reasonable history of sales growth and have been training salespeople for some time, management may simply accept that training is partly responsible for growing sales. In this instance, they may not see the value of investment in evaluation.

The most popular model for evaluating sales training is Kirkpatricks' four-stage model:[40]

1. *Participant reactions.* Measuring sales training participant reactions is conceptually similar to measuring customer satisfaction. You want to know whether salespeople were satisfied with the training they received. Their reactions should be measured on a number of aspects of the training: satisfaction with the trainer—was she engaging, entertaining, well-informed, easy to approach and relate to, and professional; satisfaction with the content—was it current, organized, and relevant; and, of course, there should be an overall satisfaction measure. Research suggests there is a positive relationship between participant reactions and retention of knowledge; that is, the more participants are satisfied with the training, the more they retain and learn from it.[41]

2. *Participant learning.* Measuring participant learning can be done through written quizzes and tests when the objective of the training was to provide company, product, or competitor knowledge. However, when the objective was to train salespeople on sales process, role-plays provide better measures. Research suggests there is a positive relationship between knowledge acquisition and the likelihood of transferring the learning to actual selling situations.[42]

3. *Behavioural changes.* The third level for evaluating sales training involves behavioural measures. This is sometimes referred to as "transfer of learning" and is critical to the success of a training program. Learning is valueless if it cannot be transferred to application. Sales managers often accompany salespeople on sales calls following sales training so they can assess the level of transfer of training. Research suggests that the more transfer of training that takes place, the better salespeople are able to meet company objectives: increased sales volume, enhanced customer relationships, and increased loyalty and commitment to the company.[43]

4. *Organizational objectives.* This is the most difficult level of training to assess. For example, it is possible to see a 10 percent increase in sales within six months of sales training. But, how do you conclude that sales training was responsible—either directly through establishing better selling skills, or indirectly through increasing salesperson motivation? It could be that a change in marketing strategy (any of product, price, distribution, or promotion), a change in the competitive environment, or a change in the economic environment was responsible. One solution would be to implement an experimental design, but this is not always possible. For example, supposing there is a sufficiently large sales force, a random selection of salespeople could be provided with sales training (the experimental group), and following the training, their percentage sales increase could be compared to a similar group of salespeople who did not receive training (the control group). Assuming the groups were similar, a greater change in sales performance could be attributed to the sales training. Measurement should be taken shortly after the training (one to three months) and again at a later period (six months to a year) to see whether the improvement is only for the short term or the longer term. If improvement is only noted in the short term, additional or reinforcement training should be considered.

The difficulty in assessing sales training at this level means that few companies do it effectively. Fortunately, as pointed out above, research suggests that when there is measurable transfer of training, there is improved performance meeting company objectives.

TRAINING FOR THE SALES MANAGER

Sales managers not only have to plan, implement, and evaluate sales training programs, but in many instances they are an important part of the program and its success often depends on the sales manager's ability to evaluate selling skills and coach salespeople who may need improvement. Dave Kahle, who sells himself as "The Growth Coach," is the author of over 500 articles and five books, and has worked with hundreds of companies as a consultant and sales trainer. Dave says, "Sales managers are, for the most part, the least trained for their jobs of any classification within the larger sales arena."[44] A survey of randomly selected sales managers supports his contention, as only 57 percent of respondents indicated that their companies provided training for sales managers.[45]

Given the importance of the sales manager to sales force performance and the amount of time and money spent to train salespeople, it is surprising that more training is not provided to sales managers. It could be that everyone expects that the sales manager does not need training because he was an excellent salesperson before he became sales manager. Even assuming this were true, this only ensures that the sales manager was at one time able to sell. If the selling environment has changed and the sales manager has not kept up, he may need sales training as well. It is also possible that the sales manager is an excellent salesperson, but he may be unable to effectively motivate or coach others. Salespeople achieve their success largely on their own effort and ability, but sales managers achieve their success through the efforts and ability of other people.

Among sales managers who received training, what topics were covered? An empirical study of sales management investigated 42 topics included in sales management training programs. Exhibit 8.8 lists the 12 topics where more than 50 percent of respondents said they received training.

Exhibit 8.8
Most Popular Topics Covered in Training Programs for Sales Managers

Planning and Organizing Activities (total = 13 topics)

Topic	%
Goal setting for salespeople	76%
Developing sales strategies	58%
Strategic sales planning	56%
Recruiting new salespeople	52%
Organizing salespeople	52%
Sales forecasting	50%

Management and Development Activities (total = 19 topics)

Topic	%
Motivating salespeople	82%
Leading salespeople	66%
Training salespeople	64%
Territory management	62%
Time management	60%

Evaluation and Control Activities (total = 10 topics)

Topic	%
Evaluating salespeople	64%

Source: Adapted from Rolph Anderson, Rajiv Mehta, and James Strong, "An Empirical Investigation of Sales Management Training Programs for Sales Managers," *Journal of Personal Selling & Sales Management*, Summer 1997, Table 6, p. 61. Copyright © PSE National Education Foundation. Used by permission of M. E. Sharpe, Inc.

While Exhibit 8.8 illustrates the most common topics on which sales managers received training, perhaps the most important issue is what is missing from the list. On only one of 10 evaluation and control topics did more than one-third of sales managers receive training. Among the evaluation and control topics that were missing, only a small percentage of sales managers in the study received training on profitability analysis: profitability by market segment, customer type, territory, salesperson, or product category. This suggests that sales managers are expected to focus on revenue generation, and do not have accountability or responsibility for profitability.

A second study that used the same data set investigated sales manager satisfaction with sales management training. Lower-level sales managers had higher satisfaction levels when general management activities were included in the training program: business ethics, conducting sales meetings, social responsibility, integration of sales and marketing, company knowledge, customer relations, and competitor knowledge. Higher-level sales managers, on the other hand, had higher satisfaction levels when control activities and channel relationship activities were included in the training program: profit analysis by market segment, by customer type, by territory, by salesperson, and by product category; analysis of company sales; market share analysis; analysis of selling costs; and selecting, managing, training, motivating, and evaluating wholesalers and dealers. The results of this study suggest that training programs for lower-level sales managers should focus more on general management activities, the things that they need to practise on a daily basis. Training programs for higher-level sales managers should focus on control issues and channel management issues, two areas where sales managers are unlikely to have developed skills through their previous sales-related positions. These are also areas where higher-level sales managers will need greater knowledge and skills as they become (1) more profit-oriented and (2) more involved in marketing versus strictly sales-related issues.

SUMMARY

1. **Discuss the importance of sales training.** Salespeople annually receive approximately four times more training hours than senior executives. There are a number of reasons why: improved sales performance, improved self-management, improved selling skills, improved customer relationships, better morale, and reduced turnover.

2. **Describe the five stages of the sales training process.** The sales training process consists of five steps: (1) performing a sales training needs assessment; (2) establishing sales training objectives; (3) establishing a sales training budget; (4) developing the sales training program, which includes deciding who, what, when, where, and how to train; and (5) evaluating the effectiveness of the sales training. Sales training needs assessment is a systematic assessment of existing knowledge, attitudes, beliefs, and behaviours, compared to desired ones. This leads to one or more sales training objectives which should be specific and measurable, and against which the training outcomes can be assessed. A sales training budget is important because it forces a sales manager to decide what is needed and prioritize those needs, and it provides a guide for making expenditures. It also helps get senior management support for training initiatives. The sales training program includes decisions related to who (new or experienced salespeople, individuals or the entire sales force), what (product, sales process, competitor, industry and customer, company, self-management skills, or specialized topics), when (regularly scheduled, or as-needed), where (centralized versus

decentralized; also including whether to use staff trainers, consultants, sales managers, or the salespeople themselves), and how (classroom instruction, role-playing, CDs and audio-tapes, online training, or on-the-job training).

3. **Describe different methods for evaluating sales training.** Among the popular methods of sales training are classroom instruction, role-playing, CD-ROM and audiotapes, the internet and other electronic media, and on-the-job training. Companies today are more likely to use a combination of methods. Classroom instruction is best used to train salespeople on product knowledge, how to use new technologies, ethics and ethical behaviour, or company policies and procedures. Role-playing provides the opportunity through realistic situations and active interaction to practise and reinforce things that have been covered in lectures and audiovisual presentations. CDs and audiotapes are portable and inexpensive, and are easily distributed among salespeople. Online training is growing in popularity as companies find they need to deliver more training, to more people, and faster. It also provides considerable flexibility. Most companies use some form of on-the-job training. Coaching and mentoring are popular forms of on-the-job training.

4. **Discuss sales manager training.** While salespeople are among the most trained people in a firm, sales managers are among the least trained people in selling-related positions. In particular, they get limited training on topics related to salesperson evaluation and control. Lower-level sales managers seem more interested in and satisfied with training on general management topics. Higher-level sales managers seem more interested in and satisfied with training on control activities and channel relationship activities.

KEY TERMS

training needs assessment   **228**
sales territory   **238**

REVIEW QUESTIONS

1. Explain six reasons why sales training is important.
2. What is a sales training needs assessment and why is it important?
3. Explain how to complete a sales training needs assessment.
4. Explain why it is important for a sales manager to establish and communicate clear training objectives.
5. What are the important aspects of product knowledge that a salesperson must know?
6. Describe four key dimensions of self-management that may be included in a sales training program.
7. Distinguish between centralized and decentralized training and explain the advantages and disadvantages of each.
8. What are the advantages of using staff trainers, consultants or outside trainers, sales managers, and salespeople themselves to conduct sales training sessions?

9. What are the advantages and disadvantages of using role-playing as a training technique? Provide some guidelines for a sales trainer that would use this technique.

10. What sales management training topics are most valued by lower-level and by higher-level sales managers for their own training? Explain why there is a difference.

APPLICATION EXERCISES

1. SalesForce Training & Consulting has been providing sales training and consulting for more than 20 years. What types of services does this company provide that would benefit salespeople and sales managers? Visit **www.salesforcetraining.com** and hit "Free Stuff" and "Articles." Be prepared to discuss in class one article relevant to salespeople, and one article relevant to sales managers.

2. Several of the best known consumer goods companies have established sales training programs that begin when a new recruit first joins the company, and continue through the recruit's sales career. A typical training program begins with classroom training, where the recruit learns about the company, its products, its marketing program, and particular selling techniques that its sales force uses. From there, the sales recruit may begin to make sales calls with an established salesperson before being assigned a specific sales territory, or may be assigned a sales territory and begin to make sales calls with a district sales manager. After three to six months in the field, the salesperson is given a refresher sales course that involves more advanced selling skills and time and territory management skills.

   Assess this type of sales training program. What are its strengths and weaknesses? Which of the two approaches do you feel is better for initial sales training in the field? Defend your answer.

3. When Jon Zhang graduated from college, he was excited to be hired to sell real estate in Vancouver. His manager told him, "Jon, we are going to pay you a full 3 percent commission for every property you sell. Most new salespeople get less and only get to 3 percent after they have been selling for a year or two." Jon was pleased because he thought that this would assure him a fair income. However, after six months, Jon was not pleased with his commissions. He realized that the problem was his sales ability; it certainly was not his motivation or willingness to work. When he approached his sales manager to see whether there was any training he could take that would help him sell, his manager told him, "Jon, there are lots of evening seminars on sales that could help you. You have to take these on your own because you are a commission salesperson. However, before you do that, I suggest you simply study a few of our top performers. Find out how they do it. You'd be surprised at how easy it is once you know what you are doing." Why do you think the manager made these comments? What would you do if you were Jon? Defend your answer.

4. You are a call centre manager and you have 200 telesales representatives working for you. Recently, you met a salesperson at a friend's wedding who promised that if you hired her to train your representatives, she would guarantee you an additional 5 percent sales growth next year, or you would not have to pay her training cost. A 5 percent increase in sales would be well worth the cost of the training, but you are not sure how you would ever tell whether the sales increase was due to the training. At a cost of $75 per salesperson, you know that your president will ask how you can ensure that you got the benefits you paid for. How can you show that the training does, in fact, increase sales 5 percent more than otherwise would occur by chance?

B.C. Business Equipment Sales (Part A)

Terri Henderson had been thinking for some time about training for her sales force of 11 sales rep-resentatives. The company had never had any formal training for its salespeople, and she thought the main reason for this was likely because only experienced salespeople were hired until the last few years. She was beginning to have some concerns, since only one of the last five salespeople that she hired had remained with the company for more than 12 months. Terri had two concerns: establishing a complete training program for new hires, and deciding what type of training she should provide for the current sales force. The implementation of training was her immediate con-cern, as she was about to hire two new salespeople within the next few days.

One possibility she was considering was to have each of the salespeople spend a week with Andy Lutes, the most senior salesperson on the sales force. Andy was 52 years old and had been with the company for almost 30 years. He had an established territory and was liked by his cus-tomers. Terri thought that giving this added responsibility to Andy would also be good for him. Andy seemed to have slowed down considerably over the past few years. While his sales were reasonably stable, sales among most of the other established salespeople were continuing to increase. This could be just the thing to motivate Andy and also get the new salespeople off to a good start.

A second possibility she was considering was to make joint sales calls with the new salespeo-ple one day a week for the first month, and gradually reduce her involvement to one-half day per month. Terri thought that she should gradually begin to make joint sales calls with the rest of the sales force as well. Even though this would be some time in the future, when she mentioned it to Andy, he angrily said, "I don't care what you do with the rest, but you're not making any sales calls with me." Although she was surprised by his reaction and was tempted to respond, Terri thought the best thing to do was simply to let it go for now. That would be an issue for another time.

CRITICAL-THINKING QUESTION

If you were Terri Henderson, what would you do?

B.C. Business Equipment Sales (Part B)

Terri Henderson had finally decided it was time to invest in training for her sales force. She had noticed over the past two years that unit sales of business machines were going up, but total sales revenue was going down. The sales decline was only approximately 2 percent both years, but Terri knew the company could not afford for this trend to continue.

One option she was considering was to make Bob Roberts responsible for training the other salespeople. Bob was the one salesperson whose sales had grown by more than 5 percent during each of the past two years. He was a real sales professional, and Terri knew he had experience as a sales trainer for an insurance company before he'd decided to sell office machines. Bob's compensa-tion was approximately $120 000, although one-quarter of that came from the 4 percent commis-sion that all salespeople received on sales. Terri was thinking of making Bob responsible for training two days per week, and letting him continue to sell the remaining three days. She knew that she would need to make a territory adjustment as Bob would not be able to give the territory as much attention as he had in the past. Terri knew that if she made Bob responsible for all sales training, she would have to adjust his salary to make up for the commissions he would most likely lose.

Another alternative was to hire an outside training specialist. She had heard of one who had been a salesperson for a global manufacturer of office equipment and who now operated his own consulting business as a sales trainer. Jason Chui charged a flat fee of $3000 to $5000 per day depending on the type of training involved. He charged more for group training and less for training that involved field sales calls with individual salespeople.

CRITICAL-THINKING QUESTION

If you were Terri Henderson, what would you do?

Chapter 9

Motivating Salespeople

LEARNING OBJECTIVES

After completing this chapter, you should be able to

1. Define motivation and explain the sales manager's role in motivating salespeople.

2. Describe and explain a general model of sales motivation.

3. Discuss specific factors related to salesperson motivation.

4. Describe different types of quotas and how to manage quota plans.

5. Describe how to manage sales contests and recognition programs.

Motivation is big business—big, big business. That's because everyone wants to motivate someone to do something, and people who are motivated will do more, do it better, and do it longer. Just how big is it? Take a look at the world's largest performance improvement company, Maritz Inc.

Maritz Inc. has been in business for more than 100 years, and describes itself as "practising the science and art of people and potential." Worldwide, it has more than 4000 employees and revenues of more than $1.4 billion, making it the 166th largest privately held company in a recent listing of the *Forbes* "500 Biggest Privately Held Companies." It has offices in Canada, the United States, the United Kingdom, Germany, France, and Spain, and alliances in other European countries, Africa, the Middle East, Asia Pacific, and the Americas.

In Canada, Maritz has 350 employees based in Mississauga, and revenues of $100 million. It has been operating in Canada since 1992, and has recently been recognized as one of the "50 Best Companies to Work For in Canada" and third in *Marketing Magazine*'s "Top Marketing Communications Companies." Although it manages many types of incentive programs for its clients, which happen to include 28 of the world's 50 largest companies, it has been particularly active recently with its incentive travel services. In a recent three-year period, Maritz Canada executed 350 group travel programs that involved more than 95 000 people. Travel programs bring lasting memories to winners and they are remembered for years after a person wins. They also provide a chance for companies to bring winners together to collectively celebrate their success, and build productive, long-lasting relationships.[1]

In this chapter, the importance of motivation is explored, along with suggestions that a sales manager can use to help ensure she manages a highly motivated and highly productive sales force.

Motivation and Activity

In the context of sales management, **motivation** can be defined as an internal drive to initiate and expend sufficient effort over time to perform appropriate selling activities to accomplish specific sales objectives. There are several important dimensions to this definition. First, it describes motivation as an internal drive. That is, motivation resides within the individual and is therefore unique to each person. Second, it describes the focus of the drive—"to initiate and expend sufficient effort over time," which means that two dimensions of motivation are intensity and persistence. *Intensity* is the magnitude of the physical and mental effort that the individual will make. Someone who is highly motivated has an intense inner drive and will work hard to do the things he believes to be important. *Persistence* is the willingness to expend effort over time. Someone who is highly motivated will perform his actions for long periods of time. Third, it describes these actions as effort "to accomplish specific sales objectives." That is, motivation results in goal-directed behaviour. Thus, the third dimension of motivation is direction. *Direction* recognizes that the individual will decide where he wishes to direct his behaviour.

If motivation is an internal drive and the individual decides his level of effort, what activities he will perform and for how long, and which goals he will try to achieve, then what is the role for the sales manager? Quite simply, the sales manager's responsibility is to manage the motivation of the sales force, which is often determined by her ability to manage the motivation of individual salespeople. Ultimately, sales managers are concerned with performance. Performance is determined by a combination of opportunity, ability, and motivation, and requires at least a minimal level of each. The following formula expresses this relationship:

$$\text{Performance} = \text{Opportunity} \times \text{Ability} \times \text{Motivation}$$

Because the relationship among these three factors is multiplicative, deficiencies in any one of these factors can be offset by a higher level on another, assuming that none of them has a value of zero. The sales manager is instrumental in helping salespeople identify opportunities, and ensuring they have selling ability by providing appropriate resources such as training, technology, and sales support. The sales manager can also increase a salesperson's motivation by carefully managing past performance and by recognizing and reinforcing it. Successfully achieving sales objectives will enhance a salesperson's self-concept, and this will increase the salesperson's motivation. More will be presented later concerning the role of the sales manager as a factor affecting a salesperson's motivation. First, however, a general model of sales motivation will be described.

General Model of Sales Motivation

Research has consistently shown that the effort salespeople will make to achieve sales objectives is related to three factors: (1) **expectancy**, the belief that making an effort to perform specific activities will, in fact, help the salesperson achieve the desired level of performance; (2) **instrumentality**, the belief that achieving the desired level of performance will be instrumental in helping the salesperson achieve specific rewards; and (3) **valence**, the personal value that the salesperson places on receiving these specific rewards. This model of motivation, shown in Exhibit 9.1, is based on Vroom's expectancy theory. It is a useful model for sales managers as it provides a good framework for making sales management decisions.

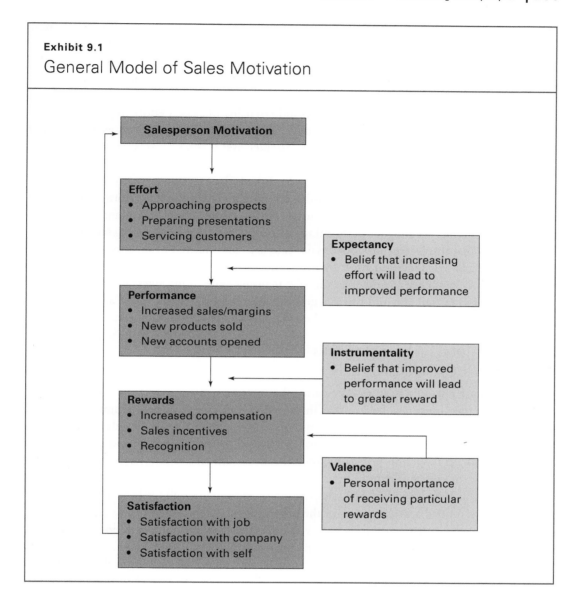

Exhibit 9.1

General Model of Sales Motivation

EXPECTANCY: THE RELATIONSHIP BETWEEN EFFORT AND PERFORMANCE

Generally, people expect a positive relationship between effort and performance. *Expectancy* refers to a salesperson's belief that such a relationship exists. A salesperson may hold a belief, for example, that increasing the average number of sales calls from 5.5 to 6.5 per day (increased effort) will lead to a 15 percent sales increase (increased performance) over a one-year period. The salesperson may believe this relationship to be highly probable, somewhat probable, or just possible (their expectancy strength). The salesperson's expectancy strength will therefore determine whether he will initiate effort and the amount and duration of effort that he will make.

Sales managers must be concerned also with the salesperson's expectancy accuracy. *Accuracy* refers to how accurate the salesperson's perception is that increased effort on a specific activity will lead to improved performance. There are dozens of activities that the salesperson could perform that might have an effect on sales performance. He could increase prospecting activity, do more pre-call planning, prepare better presentations, practise negotiating skills, or perform any number of other sales-related activities. Using the previous example, the salesperson may increase his average sales call activity because he has a strong expectancy that making one more call per day will increase his sales performance. If his increased activity does lead to his expected performance, then he will confirm his expectancy and conclude that his increased effort improved his performance. He will likely continue to maintain his sales call effort in future. But, what happens if he increases his sales call activity and his sales do not increase? Was his expectancy inaccurate simply because it was not confirmed? This is where the role of the sales manager is important. The sales manager should note the increase in effort and the lack of change in performance. A good sales manager will help the salesperson see which activities lead to increased performance and help the salesperson "work smarter" rather than simply "work harder." If the sales manager has evaluated the difference between higher-performing salespeople and lower-performing salespeople and has concluded that the average number of sales calls is a factor related to superior sales performance, then the fact that increased effort by this salesperson has not led to increased performance suggests another possibility and deserves the sales manager's attention. The salesperson may simply need better sales training, and this is where the sales manager should make some joint sales calls to experience firsthand the quality of the sales calls that the salesperson is making.

INSTRUMENTALITY: THE RELATIONSHIP BETWEEN PERFORMANCE AND REWARD

Salespeople must not only have an expectancy that increased effort will lead to improved performance, but they must also believe that improved performance will be instrumental in their receiving a reward. This is one reason why straight commission plans are popular among salespeople. They clearly understand the relationship between their performance and their compensation or reward. A salesperson who earns straight commission on sales knows that increasing her sales by 35 percent will also increase her compensation by 35 percent. On the other hand, consider a three-month sales contest. The salesperson's *instrumentality* will likely be affected by how winners are determined and the nature of the reward. If the sales contest awards all participants with points that can be redeemed for a variety of prizes based on the number of points each salesperson has accumulated, then the salesperson's instrumentality still will be high. If the reward is based upon achieving an individual sales target, again instrumentality will be high as each salesperson understands that if she achieves her target, she will receive a reward. However, if the reward is given to only a percentage of the sales force based on best performance, then a salesperson's instrumentality will be lower because the salesperson will not know what level of performance is required. She may believe that she can increase her performance by 10 percent, but she may also believe that this is unlikely to make her a winner. Her motivation to increase her effort is low because she does not see a relationship between performance and reward.

Instrumentality for salespeople who are on a straight salary compensation plan may be very low. One problem is that rewards often follow performance by a considerable period of time, so that the connection between performance and reward is not apparent. A salesperson may receive a very large order early in the year, but an increase in salary may come at the end of the year. It also may require several years of increasing performance to receive a promotion. Complicating things is the fact that others may receive the same reward for the same level of performance, or even for lower performance. At the end of the year, the entire sales force may receive a 5 percent salary increase. The salesperson who has expended extra effort to achieve superior performance

SALES MANAGEMENT **IN ACTION**

Motivating the 'B' Team

Everyone does not agree that incentive compensation is a good thing. Perhaps its best known critic has been Archie Kohn, author of the book *Why Incentive Plans Cannot Work*. He attacks incentives for several reasons. First, he says, pay is not a good motivator, and for many people gets ranked only fifth or sixth. Second, incentive plans are instruments of control; they are manipulative and they can have a punishing effect. Third, incentives increase competition, and decrease cooperation, which is important in a team environment. Fourth, incentive programs allow managers to abrogate their responsibility to manage and let the reward programs manage for them. Fifth, incentive programs undermine creativity and risk-taking. Finally, extrinsic rewards undermine employees' intrinsic motivation. Kohn argues that intrinsic motivation leads to innovation and excellence.

Certainly, it would appear, few people agree. At least if the number of sales organizations that use incentive programs is an indication. However, one important change that has been occurring recently is a greater concern with motivating the 'B' team, that is, the middle group of employees who are sometimes ignored. Martin Cozyn, vice-president of human resources for Nortel Networks, says, "You need to know who your top people are, but you also have to watch out for the message you're sending, because a disenfranchised middle can be just as damaging to your business as the loss of all of your top talent." Rodger Stotz, vice-president of Maritz Inc., introduced at the beginning of this chapter, provides an excellent suggestion. Instead of just having a "President's Club" where only the top 2–10 percent of the sales force win, leaving many to feel they might never succeed, another possibility is to set individual quotas and reward everyone who reaches their own targets. People then compete against themselves, and the overall performance of the sales force will improve even more.

When Nortel broadened its employee categories from simply critical or non-critical to include top, high, core, and low contributors, and eliminated the forced distribution that would allow only a certain percentage to be rated in the top category, there were noticeable improvements. The attrition rate among the top contributors was approximately one-half of what it was for core contributors, and about one-eighth of what it was for low contributors. This, according to Cozyn, was exactly what he wanted.

Sources: Alfie Kohn, "Why Incentive Plans Cannot Work," *Harvard Business Review,* September 1993, pp. 54–58; Alfie Kohn, "Alfie Kohn Responds," *Harvard Business Review,* November–December 1993, pp. 48–49; Alfie Kohn, "How Incentives Undermine Performance," *The Journal for Quality and Participation,* March–April 1998, pp. 6–13; Alix Nyberg Stuart, "Motivating the Middle," *CFO,* October 2005, pp. 63–70.

may then feel some level of inequity. She may feel herself treated unfairly, and her motivation will be decreased. The Sales Management in Action box describes a number of additional issues concerning sales incentive programs and motivating sales performance, and how companies are showing a greater interest in motivating the 'B' team. These people are the backbone of many sales organizations and they must also see that their performance is valued and will lead to recognition and reward.

VALENCES FOR REWARDS

The *valence*, or value, that a salesperson places on a particular reward will also influence her motivation to achieve the reward. Each salesperson has unique needs and will therefore have a different valence for any particular reward. One salesperson may want status or recognition; another simply may want a higher income. Sales managers need to understand individual valences when deciding how to reward performance.

Some sales managers fail to recognize that many salespeople are internally—as opposed to externally—motivated. Internally motivated salespeople will perform an activity simply because they get inner satisfaction from performing the activity. Some salespeople simply enjoy calling on customers, building relationships, and helping people solve problems. These salespeople are likely to be self-motivated. Some sales managers argue that internal motivators—personal growth, achievement, challenge, responsibility, advancement, involvement, work itself—have a longer-term effect on a salesperson's motivation to expend effort.[2] Other sales managers argue that financial rewards are valued most by salespeople, and often focus their attention on providing money as a reward. The extent to which a particular salesperson values more money will likely be influenced by several factors: her current career stage, her current financial situation, her income compared to other salespeople, or other factors. A salesperson who earns higher income than other salespeople in the same company, or in the same industry, may place more value on non-monetary rewards. She might prefer an extra week of vacation with her family, for example.

Sales managers need to establish rewards that meet the needs of individual salespeople in order to motivate them. Now that a general model of sales motivation has been described, several specific sets of factors related to sales motivation are examined.

Specific Factors Related to Sales Motivation

Many factors are related to salesperson motivation. Two sets of factors that are particularly important include job-related factors and individual-related factors. We will look at each of these sets of factors now.

JOB-RELATED FACTORS

One of the most important determinants of a salesperson's motivation is the sales job itself. Five job-related factors are important: job value, skill variety, autonomy, opportunity, and feedback.

JOB VALUE

Salespeople who value the sales job will be more motivated to do it. Salespeople are increasingly recognizing that their individual success helps create their firm's overall success. They know that if they do not achieve success outside the firm, nothing will happen inside the firm. This is simply another way of saying that nothing happens until somebody sells something. When management also recognizes this truism, they place more emphasis on selling and openly recognize the value the sales force contributes to the company's success. This reinforces the value of the sales job for salespeople. There was a very short period during the ascendancy of technology companies when some people were arguing that the role of the sales force in organizations would diminish. Many of the companies that took resources from their sales force and placed them elsewhere are no longer operating. Firms may find more efficient ways of communicating with customers, but personal selling has always been and will always be the most effective method of communicating with customers under most circumstances. Some salespeople are motivated simply because they value the close working relationships they develop with their customers, and the value they provide to their customers by helping solve their problems.

SKILL VARIETY   The wide variety of sales jobs requires a wide variety of skills for sales success. Salespeople who are simply order-takers (gatherers) require some skills, but fewer and at a lower level than salespeople who are order-getters (hunters). This latter group of salespeople often need a combination of skills: interpersonal and relationship-building skills, oral and written communication skills, analytical and problem-solving skills, and planning and strategy skills. Salespeople whose job requires them to use a wide variety of skills must manage more complex selling situations, will feel a greater sense of accomplishment and satisfaction when they succeed, and will likely be more motivated to achieve success.

AUTONOMY   There are few jobs that provide people with the same level of autonomy as sales jobs. Salespeople, assuming they are performing at a satisfactory level, have considerable autonomy to decide what to do, and when and how to do it. Most salespeople work well beyond the 35–40 hours that most people work in a week, but they do have flexibility. Some salespeople decide to work mostly from their office, while others decide to work mostly from home. Although they usually must work within a sales expense budget, they can often decide which customers to see, how often, and when, where, and if to entertain customers. The level of autonomy and the flexibility that is inherent in many sales jobs is one of the reasons why so many women are attracted to selling today. Women in sales often find it easier to balance their career and family.

OPPORTUNITY   Many salespeople begin careers in sales because of the opportunity that sales careers provide. Gavin Semple, now a member of the Canadian Professional Sales Association's Sales Hall of Fame, began his sales career selling vacuum cleaners, duck decoys, and insurance. He describes his motivation "to make a lot of money" so he could buy a television, a car, central heating, and other things he did not have when growing up on a farm in rural Saskatchewan. In 1972, he started selling agricultural, trenching, and golf course equipment. In his first year, he increased sales revenue fivefold, and, in 1976, he became company president. He is still president of Brandt Group of Companies in Regina.[3]

The first opportunity that a sales career provides is financial opportunity. Regardless of whether a salesperson earns straight salary, straight commission, or a combination of salary and commission, salespeople are among the highest paid people in organizations. It is not unusual to see a salesperson who earns a higher income than his sales manager or other executives in his company. The second opportunity that a sales career provides is the opportunity for advancement. Of course, not everyone can progress to management, but when companies are searching for candidates to move into supervisory or management positions, good salespeople are often among the first people to be considered. Some of the skills they have learned in sales will benefit them in management positions. As well, good salespeople are very visible within an organization, and this makes them good candidates for promotion as their previous performance is well known. Most other employees will see them as deserving candidates for promotion and are less likely to question if successful salespeople get fast-tracked into management roles. This opportunity for advancement makes sales careers particularly attractive to women and minorities who have career aspirations. Companies are beginning to increase diversity in their sales force to gain better access to the more diverse market segments in Canada today. Many companies now have top-producing salespeople who are members of various minority groups.

FEEDBACK   Feedback is valued by most people because it provides them with a sense of how well they are doing and when changes need to be made to improve their performance. Salespeople probably receive more feedback than people in any other job. Salespeople regularly receive feedback from management, but also from their peers. They also get feedback, directly or indirectly, from customers. Some salespeople are more attuned to this feedback than others. That is because some have taught themselves to more critically evaluate their performance after each sales call. They ask themselves what they did well, what they did poorly, and what changes they will make for future sales calls.

INDIVIDUAL-RELATED FACTORS

A second important set of factors that affect a salesperson's motivation are individual-related factors. Many individual-related factors have an influence on a salesperson's motivation, but two in particular will be described in the following sections: individual motives and career stages.

INDIVIDUAL MOTIVES Motivation is one of the oldest and most researched topics in psychology. Many theories have been developed over the years, and most still maintain some degree of relevance today. Some of the more important theories of motivation for sales managers are summarized in Exhibit 9.2. Most of these theories propose that human behaviour is motivated by one

Exhibit 9.2
Motivation Theories and Their Application

Theory	Brief Description
Maslow's Hierarchy of Needs Theory	There is a hierarchy of needs: physiological, safety, social, esteem, and self-actualization. As each lower-level need is satisfied, people strive to achieve the next higher need on the hierarchy.
Herzberg's Motivation–hygiene Theory	There are hygiene factors (pay, working conditions, interpersonal relationships, etc.) that can prevent dissatisfaction, but will not lead to motivation. Motivation is created by intrinsic job factors such as challenge, responsibility, and achievement.
McClelland's Theory of Learned Needs	People have three basic needs: achievement, affiliation, and power. People with higher need for the first two perform well in sales; people with higher power need perform better in sales management.
Alderfer's ERG Theory	People have three basic needs: existence, relatedness, and growth.
Adams' Equity Theory	People compare their effort, performance, and rewards to those of significant others to decide if they are treated fairly. A feeling of inequity (unfair treatment) will result in dissatisfaction. Equity theory suggests that reducing inequity may be more important than increasing incentives.
Vroom's Expectancy Theory	This theory says that motivation is determined by a person's expectancy that effort will lead to improved performance, which will be instrumental in their achieving a reward. Motivation will also be affected by the personal value of the reward as well.

Exhibit 9.3

Satisfying Common Needs of Salespeople

Needs	Company Policies, Programs, or Actions
Safety/security	Provide health, dental, insurance, and pension plans. Provide a safe work environment.
Social/affiliation/ relatedness	Schedule meetings and encourage participation. Encourage some non-work group activities.
Esteem/status/respect/ recognition	Publicly recognize and praise good performance. Seek advice and input on important decisions that affect the sales force.
Self-actualization/ growth	Provide training programs to improve selling or management skills. Share responsibility with the sales force.
Achievement/ accomplishment	Set short-term goals and acknowledge success. Publicly communicate achievements.
Power/control/ independence	Allow salespeople to determine their account call schedule. Encourage active involvement setting sales quotas.
Stimulation/variety/ excitement	Provide surprise short-term sales contests.
Routine/consistency	Perform regular sales management tasks such as making joint calls or providing performance feedback on a regular basis for all members of the sales force.
Equity	Ensure everyone knows how rewards are earned, and then reward fairly. Share workload and responsibilities evenly across the sales force.
Leadership/feedback/ communication	Demonstrate competence, empathy, integrity, and respect. Share information regularly with the sales force.

or more individual needs. While the various theories focus on different needs, Exhibit 9.3 suggests that some of these theories propose needs that are closely related to needs put forward by alternative theories. Examples of company policies, programs, and actions that can help salespeople satisfy individual needs are also provided in this exhibit.

CAREER STAGE   Another important individual-related factor that will affect a salesperson's motivation is **career stage**. Typically, salespeople who have had a long sales career will have progressed through a series of career stages, as diagrammed in Exhibit 9.4. These career stages include exploration, establishment, maintenance, and disengagement. As salespeople progress through

Exhibit 9.4
Career Stages

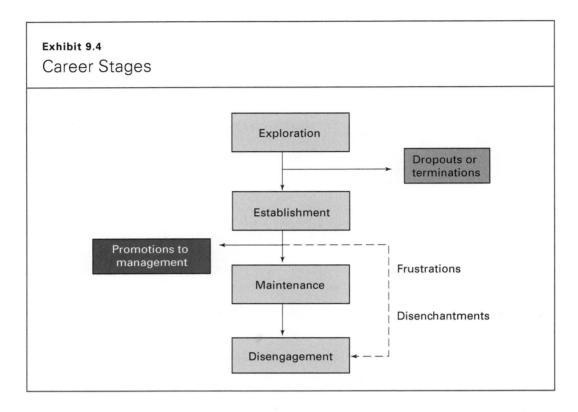

these stages, their experience and skill levels increase, their financial concerns and conditions change, and the rewards that they seek and that will motivate them change. Personal career concerns, developmental tasks, challenges, and psychosocial needs at each career stage are summarized in Exhibit 9.5. This exhibit also summarizes career stage impact on motivation, and implications for sales managers who must manage salespeople at each stage.

Exploration   The first career stage, exploration, can be considered a trial or test stage. This begins when a salesperson gets her first sales job and usually occurs very shortly after graduation from school, college, or university. However, some salespeople begin their first sales job after an exploration stage in one or more other occupations. In any event, the first few months in a sales job can be very stressful for inexperienced salespeople. There is usually a lot to learn, and this is all happening at the same time that the salesperson is trying to decide if this will be what she wants to do for the rest of her life, or if it will provide future opportunities for advancement. However, the exploration stage can extend well beyond a first job, possibly to several jobs as salespeople begin to explore other selling situations that may better fit their personal interest and aptitude.

Sales managers play a very important role when new salespeople are beginning a sales career and evaluating whether it could be suitable for them. Feedback, direction, and encouragement reduce stress and demonstrate concern and interest. Recognition of small successes and reinforcing accomplishments provide some level of security at a time when new salespeople are feeling insecure. Taking time to socialize with new salespeople and communicating the value of long-term sales careers also helps foster a feeling a belonging and greater security. Some companies help new salespeople through the exploration stage by designating a mentor for them from among more senior salespeople.

Exhibit 9.5

Career Stages: Characteristics and Implications for Sales Managers

	Exploration	Establishment	Maintenance	Disengagement
Personal career concerns	• To find a rewarding occupational field	• To establish a successful career in a selected occupational field	• To maintain career standing; may reassess and possibly redirect career	• To emotionally prepare for career end
Personal developmental tasks	• Learn job-related skills • Become a contributing member of the organization	• Use skills to produce results • Increase autonomy • Improve decision making and innovativeness	• To develop a broader view of work and organization	• Establish a self-identity outside of work • Maintain respectable performance level
Personal challenges	• To develop a good initial professional self-concept	• To produce superior performance with goal of promotion • Balance work–family demands	• To maintain motivation and performance • To adjust to aging and changed career expectations	• To accept career accomplishments • To adjust to new self-concept
Psychosocial needs	• Sense of acceptance and security • Challenge and growth	• Achievement • Esteem • Autonomy • Competition	• Reduced competitiveness • Security • Helping younger colleagues	• Self-respect • Detachment from organization and career
Impact on motivation	• Low expectancy and instrumentality perceptions • High valences for personal growth and recognition	• Highest expectancy and instrumentality perceptions • High valences for compensation but even higher for recognition and promotion	• Lowering expectancy perceptions and valence for promotion • Valences for recognition and status still high • Highest valence for compensation	• Lowest instrumentality perceptions and valences for all types of rewards
Implications for sales managers	• Need to provide encouragement and sense of early success • Need to help explore possible career paths	• Must keep expectations realistic • Need to focus on career paths and appropriate skill development	• Focus effort with pay for performance as highest level of skills combined with established client relationships	• Recognize that detachment is a normal process at this career stage • May need to begin territory succession plan

Source: Adapted from William L. Cron, "Industrial Salesperson Development: A Career Stages Perspective," *Journal of Marketing*, Fall 1984, pp. 41–52.

Establishment Some salespeople will enter the establishment stage very soon after beginning their first sales job. For example, a person who has decided very early that she wants a sales career in the pharmaceutical industry may be fortunate and get her first sales job with her first choice of employers. Her initial enthusiasm and preparation quickly indicate her aptitude, and positive reinforcement from management along a known career path leads her to quickly decide that sales is a good career. Other people may spend many years trying several companies, industries, or professions before deciding that sales is the career for them. Some people will therefore enter the establishment stage in their mid-twenties; others may enter this stage in their mid-thirties or even later. Many salespeople at this stage have increased financial obligations and are beginning to have family demands as well as career demands.

Salespeople in the establishment stage have moved from exploring career options to committing to a sales career. They are more competitive and willing to work longer hours and invest more time and effort improving their selling skills or increasing their product knowledge. They are now concerned with increasing their autonomy and demonstrating their performance capabilities. It is during this stage that salespeople have their highest expectancy and instrumentality perceptions. While they have high valence for increased compensation, their highest valences are for recognition and promotion. Unfortunately, advancement often slows as competition increases among people who are in the establishment career stage.

A major concern for sales managers when salespeople are in this stage is to manage expectations while also providing adequate rewards for performance. If sales managers fail in either of these areas, salespeople will seek alternative opportunities, and turnover will increase. Companies that are concerned about this usually have career paths for salespeople, and these are often communicated to salespeople regularly during this period. A typical sales career path may begin with inside salesperson or sales trainee, and progress to intermediate salesperson, senior salesperson, and then to national, key, strategic, or major account representative. The sales manager needs to be able to manage salespeople's progression so they remain committed not only to a sales career, but to staying on as high-performing salespeople within the firm.

Maintenance Many salespeople eventually are faced with a career re-evaluation. They begin to question where they are career-wise, and what options are still available to them. This frequently happens shortly before or after the age of 40, and is often precipitated by a particular event in their lives—possibly a personal life event, or perhaps a work-related event such as being passed over for promotion. Regardless, the re-evaluation will lead to a number of choices for most people.

Some will decide to leave the firm and look for opportunities elsewhere. Some may change companies; others may change careers. Some may decide to start their own business; others may decide to return to college or university. While many M.B.A. students, for example, are studying to advance their careers, many others are enrolled because they are hoping to change careers. Fortunately, many who re-evaluate their career during the maintenance stage decide to remain in sales. A sales manager needs to be sensitive to the salesperson just entering the maintenance stage, because this is where the decision to stay or leave is made. Maintenance-stage salespeople are the backbone of many sales forces. Maintenance-stage salespeople were rated highest in many aspects, including ability to meet sales goals, product knowledge, commitment to serving customers, and creativity in solving problems.[4] At age 58, Al Clark became the top-performing salesperson among the 16 000 State Farm agents across Canada and the United States.[5]

Sales managers need to recognize the importance of these salespeople to the firm and to carefully manage their motivation. These salespeople have decided that further promotion is unlikely, and they lower their expectancy perceptions and valence for promotion. They now will be motivated by other things. Many salespeople in this stage have the highest valence for financial rewards because they have increased financial commitments as their children enter post-secondary educational programs. Some are also beginning to plan ahead for financial needs during retirement. Other salespeople still will be motivated by recognition and status within the sales force. Giving these salespeople increased responsibility often helps. Many welcome increased involvement in training and mentorship programs, or inclusion on special-project teams. Many of these salespeople will remain strong contributors throughout this stage, but management is sometimes challenged to find ways to keep others motivated.

Disengagement   Disengagement is the final career stage. This is the stage where salespeople finally recognize that their sales career is coming to an end, and they begin to establish other priorities in their life. They may participate more in non-work activities such as golf or other hobbies. Their sales may continue at acceptable levels throughout this period as they have established accounts that they now manage as "gatherers." They still attempt to meet their sales quotas, but they curtail their "hunter" activities and they open fewer new accounts. This can provide opportunities for competitors and can sometimes have serious negative consequences for their firm, so sales managers need to closely watch what is happening in their territory during this period.

Managing these salespeople can sometimes be challenging. They generally have the lowest instrumentality perceptions and lower valences for all types of rewards. Some simply no longer respond to recognition programs, and others may now have reduced financial needs so that financial rewards no longer have much motivational impact. Sales managers should recognize disengagement as an important stage in a salesperson's career, and should help them through the process. Working closely with salespeople at this stage will provide better territory succession planning so customers remain satisfied and loyal.

A more serious problem for sales managers is the salesperson who enters the disengagement stage too early in his career. He may have recognized very early that his sales career has reached a plateau and he is unlikely to advance further in the company. He may simply bypass the maintenance stage and proceed directly to the disengagement stage as illustrated in Exhibit 9.4. If he is many years from retirement and has decided to do only as much as necessary to maintain job security, closer supervision becomes necessary. He is more likely to miss opportunities in his sales territory, providing opportunities to competitors who will quickly take advantage of the situation. Attempts to motivate him may fail, and may even lead to resentment. In the worst scenario, this salesperson may become openly negative concerning his job and company, and he can poison the atmosphere for the entire sales force. A sales manager who can find no other solution may eventually have to terminate this salesperson. How to manage salespeople who have reached an early career plateau and how to terminate salespeople will be discussed in greater detail in Chapter 11.

Quotas

A **quota** is a quantitative goal assigned to an individual salesperson. A good quota should be considered by the salesperson as both an objective and a challenge. Quotas, managed properly, can be one of the most important tools in a sales manager's tool kit. That is why almost all sales organizations have some form of quota system.

WHY USE QUOTAS?

There are many reasons why quotas are used in sales organizations. This section describes how sales quotas help sales managers motivate salespeople. As motivators, quotas serve two main purposes:

1. *To motivate salespeople to achieve superior performance.* Salespeople, by nature, like to have objectives. They enjoy the sense of accomplishment and like to know what is expected of them by management. A quota that is realistic but achievable will motivate salespeople to perform better than they otherwise might. As well, it can be used as the basis to communicate with and provide feedback to salespeople throughout the year.
2. *To provide direction for salespeople so they understand what is important.* Without direction, salespeople are free to sell whatever they wish and, not surprisingly, they will spend their time selling whatever is easiest to sell or whatever will provide the most sales volume. If this is acceptable to management, then simply stating the sales quota in terms of sales dollars will be sufficient. However, many companies need to ensure that time is also allocated to targeting new accounts, selling new or strategic products in a product line, focusing on specific customer segments, or moving high profit items. Under these conditions, salespeople should be focused on more than just dollar volume sales. At the same time, however, management must not have so many quotas that salespeople lose sight of what is really important to the organization.

WHAT ARE GOOD QUOTAS?

Good quotas have a number of characteristics. In particular, they are simple, complete, accepted, and managed. Simple quotas or quota plans are easier to explain to salespeople, and much easier for salespeople to understand. When quotas are complex or not understood, salespeople are unlikely to focus on the behaviours necessary to achieve them. Salespeople are also more likely to be suspicious of quotas that are difficult to understand.

A good quota plan is complete. It focuses salespeople on all of the activities that are important, or all of the criteria on which their performance will be evaluated. When the sales cycle is fairly long and often requires several face-to-face meetings to close a new account, for example, the salesperson must perform a number of activities to ensure there are always prospects at various stages of the buying process. Simply asking salespeople to close three new accounts per week could result in their achieving the quota for several weeks, but failing to meet the quota in the longer term. A solution is to break down the important activities that will lead to closing a sale, and establish a quota for each of them. A salesperson could be required to add 30 new prospects to her prospect list, make eight initial customer presentations, make four follow-up sales calls, and close two new accounts each week. As another example, a salesperson could be required to have annual sales revenue of $750 000 with 65 percent of it through dealers or distributors. In this example, salespeople have an annual sales quota, but the company is saying that dealers and distributors are important in the company's overall marketing strategy so that salespeople must remain focused on working with them.

Good quotas are accepted. In fact, if they are not accepted by the salespeople who must achieve them, they will act as demotivators rather than motivators. The importance of salesperson buy-in is suggested by the fact that more than 60 percent of sales managers receive input on sales quotas from the sales force.[6] The key to establishing good quotas is to balance the input and knowledge of both management and individual salespeople. A good place to start is with management. Sales managers, for example, will have information on past sales in each territory, and may be privy to key information that will be important in setting future sales quotas, such as changes in general economic conditions, proposed price changes, or likely new product introductions. Once the initial quota is determined, the sales manager should be able to explain to the salesperson all of the assumptions that went into deciding the initial value. The salesperson can then provide input based on information she has concerning her particular sales territory that may affect her likelihood of meeting the sales quota. A major customer may be making important changes to its level of production that will affect its purchase volume, competitor activity may be increasing or decreasing in the territory, or other factors may be involved. In any event, at the end of the process, the resulting sales quota should be acceptable to both parties, and that will get the salesperson's commitment. Some sales managers are concerned that salespeople will try to have their sales quota set too low, particularly if their compensation or reward system is based on their achieving sales quota. However, research suggests that salespeople are as likely to overestimate as to underestimate their quota, and errors were most frequently within plus or minus 10 percent. Only one in 20 sales managers thought that their salespeople tried to have their quotas set low so that they could benefit from it.[7]

Finally, good quotas are actively managed. Too frequently, quotas are established and then forgotten until it becomes necessary to see whether the salesperson has achieved his quota. Good quotas are regularly checked and performance against quota is discussed between the sales manager and the salesperson. Doing this early enough to identify potential problems allows interventions to be made so that there are no surprises at the end of the period. When it is apparent that a salesperson is tracking close to quota, recognition and encouragement from the sales manager can be motivating. It also sends the message that quotas are important and that performance is being monitored. When there are problems with performance, finding out early allows the sales manager and the salesperson to investigate the reasons and take corrective action. In some instances, the corrective action might require an adjustment to the sales quota. If it becomes apparent in June that a salesperson is unlikely to meet quota, then simply keeping the same quota for the balance of the year will result in a demotivated salesperson. If the reason for failure is beyond the salesperson's control, then adjusting the quota can improve motivation for the rest of the year. Care must be taken, however, when adjusting the quota upwards. If salespeople see this as a tactic to avoid rewarding them for their performance, this can create problems. Care should be taken before making adjustments, but there should be enough flexibility to make adjustments when they are truly necessary. Nearly one-half of the 1925 respondents to a recent survey reported that they did not make any changes to sales quotas within the previous year; just over one-quarter reported that they made one change, and almost as many indicated that they made two or more changes.[8]

TYPES OF QUOTAS

There are three widely used types of sales quotas: sales volume quotas, profit-based quotas, and activity-based quotas. The most popular among the three is sales volume quotas, which are used by the majority of companies, regardless of size. Profit-based and activity-based quotas are more likely to be used by larger firms.

SALES VOLUME QUOTAS   **Sales volume quotas** are the most commonly used quotas and are the most readily accepted by salespeople as they are generally easy to explain, and they are consistent with what salespeople believe they should do: sell. Sales volume quotas can be based on dollar sales, unit sales, or a point system. Sales volume quotas establish target sales for a specific period of time—usually monthly, quarterly, or annually. However, they can be specified daily or weekly.

Setting a dollar sales quota is common when the salesperson sells a broad product line and when management has little preference for what is actually sold. An industrial distributor salesperson, for example, may simply be given a sales quota of $400 000 based on the previous year's sales of $380 000, with an adjustment for price increases and an otherwise stable sales territory. Unit sales quotas are frequently used when high-priced or bulk items are sold. It may take a dealership salesperson as much time and effort to sell a $20 000 or a $60 000 vehicle, and both may be important to the dealership that must sell a complete line of vehicles for the manufacturer. The salesperson's sales quota is most likely to be stated as a specific number of units per month or per year. Salespeople may also be given unit sales quotas when goods are sold in cartons, on pallets, or by truckloads. With both dollar volume and unit sales quotas, sales targets may also be set for specific products, or for particular segments of customers. For example, a salesperson selling office equipment could be required to sell 60 office machines per month: 20 photocopiers, 20 computers, 15 printers, and 5 fax machines or scanners. This quota system ensures that the salesperson sells the complete product line and also means they will place more emphasis on higher dollar value sales as well.

Point-based quotas are a bit more complex but they do have an advantage of being more flexible. Salespeople earn points based on sales dollars or units sold. For example, a salesperson could earn for each $1000 of sales: three points for valve sales, two points for pipe fittings sales, and one point for pipe sales. A sales quota could be established as 10 000 points annually. The salesperson has some flexibility around how he wishes to achieve his point quota. At the same time, the sales manager has some flexibility as she can add some short-term sales contests over the year to redirect sales efforts to specific products. She might, for example, award double points during March for each new account opened, or, to encourage full-line selling, give an extra two points when all three items are sold on the same order. This flexibility also allows the sales manager to intercede throughout the year without seeming to change the sales quota. If the sales manager sees that economic conditions have deteriorated and it is likely that only 20 percent of the sales force will achieve their sales quota, then these short-term sales contests can boost sales performance until it looks like the target percentage of salespeople will be successful.

PROFIT-BASED QUOTAS   Profit-based quotas focus on profits rather than just sales revenue. When quotas are simply based on dollar sales volume, salespeople will focus on what they can sell with the least effort, and in the largest quantities. Sometimes this means selling volume at low margin, simply to get revenue. One solution is to focus salespeople on more profitable products or accounts by rewarding them for reaching profit quotas. Many profit-based quota plans focus on gross margin (net sales minus cost of goods sold) or contribution margin (gross margin minus direct selling expenses). Gross margin is frequently the fairest measure to use as salespeople are not always able to control even direct selling expenses. If a salesperson is paid a high salary because of his experience and product knowledge, or if he has higher travel expenses because his geographic territory is large, then he would be penalized because his direct selling expenses would be higher and he could not control these. On the other hand, when direct selling expenses are largely under the control of the salesperson, then profit-based quotas that use contribution margin make more sense. Salespeople would then be encouraged to control their direct selling expenses to maintain higher contribution margin. Some companies use net profit as the basis for setting sales quotas. However, it is questionable whether salespeople should be held accountable for things that are beyond their control. The accounting method the company uses to allocate overhead costs, for example, will affect the net profit on sales.

ACTIVITY-BASED QUOTAS   A short-term focus on dollar sales volume or profit-based quotas may lead salespeople to neglect account management activities that are critical to maintaining long-term customer relationships, or activities that will maintain an adequate number of prospects in the sales pipeline to ensure that sales are achieved with some degree of regularity in future periods. **Activity-based quotas** help ensure salespeople do the right things so that sales and profits are generated in the long term as well as in the short term. Companies that use activity-based quotas view activities as investments. Among the activities that can be used are the following:

- Number of sales calls per day
- Number of sales calls on prospective new accounts
- Number of prospects added to prospect list
- Number of prospects qualified
- Letters or telephone calls to prospects
- Number of sales proposals prepared
- Number of sales presentations made
- Number of product demonstrations made
- Number of dealer training sessions held
- Number of displays arranged
- Number of service calls made

There are, of course, many others depending on what is important in a particular selling situation. Because the behaviours on which activity-based quotas are based are largely under the salesperson's control, he can be held more accountable for achieving satisfactory performance. A good sales manager will look beyond simply meeting activity quotas, however. If all salespeople make a required 25 product demonstrations per week, but two of the salespeople have sales dollar volume considerably below average, the sales manager should investigate the reason why. It could be the quality of the demonstration or problems with some other part of the selling process, such as handling buyer resistance or closing sales. A major issue with activity-based quotas is that the data used to measure performance is frequently collected from the sales call reports of the salespeople who are being evaluated.

ESTABLISHING AND MANAGING QUOTA PLANS

Now that you have an appreciation for why quotas are important for managing salespeople, what makes a good quota, and the various types of quotas that can be used, some considerations for establishing and managing quotas will be discussed. Ideally, a number of factors should be considered when establishing a sales quota: territory potential, the previous year's sales, forecast sales for the next period, and adjustments that may need to be made because of changing conditions in the sales territory. (Methods to estimate sales potential and forecast sales were described in Chapter 4.) When possible, it is good to use sales potential as a starting point, but relying on sales potential alone as the basis to establish quotas will seldom provide a good solution. Here is why.

First, sales potential, you may remember, is what the firm could sell under ideal conditions. Sales forecast is smaller than sales potential because it is estimated sales based on a particular marketing program and other factors such as production capacity or financial resources within the firm. Second, the previous year's sales must be considered. This figure is an indication of how well the territory has been developed, and therefore provides some indication of what is possible for the next period. Third, within specific territories important changes may be taking place that require consideration and adjustment. The firm may have just added or lost an important distributor in the territory, and will have to consider the impact this will have on sales. If sales in the territory are largely from long-standing customers, the impact on sales of having a new salesperson in the territory will not be as negative as it might be if an inexperienced salesperson is added to a territory where salespeople must constantly search for new business. Considering all four factors together therefore requires considerable management judgment.

As well as judgment, the final selection of quotas will be influenced by the beliefs or philosophy of the sales manager. Should he set quotas low so that all salespeople succeed, or should he set quotas high so that only the very best salespeople meet their sales target? There is no correct answer, and what works best will change as conditions in the sales force change. A common rule of thumb is to set quotas so that 60–80 percent of salespeople achieve quota. A sales manager could set the percentage higher if achieving quota results in salespeople getting financial compensation that is seen as an important part of their total compensation package. If achieving the sales quota results in only a minor financial reward for the salesperson, and the company has numerous other shorter-term sales contests throughout the year, then setting the percentage lower may be better. The best advice is to be conservative when changes will have an impact on the reward system and, hence, motivation of the sales force. Gradual change is likely to meet with less resistance.

Another issue that often arises when managing quota plans is what to do when a salesperson meets one quota but fails to meet a second one. For example, a salesperson might achieve dollar sales quota but fail to achieve unit sales quota. Or, a salesperson may achieve total dollar sales quota, but fail to achieve quota in a particular target segment.

Sales Contests and Recognition Programs

Sales contests are very popular among salespeople and are generally implemented to serve very specific short-term objectives. Although sales contests do provide financial as well as non-financial rewards to salespeople, they should not be considered as part of a company's overall compensation package. **Recognition programs** are programs designed to recognize salespeople for superior sales performance. They are important and popular among salespeople as well. Recognition programs require as much management attention, but they are more likely to be formalized within an organization so that they are more stable from one period to the next. Exhibit 9.6 provides a ranking of the six most important ways that respondents to a recent survey indicated that incentives impacted their quality of work or performance.

Management should follow a four-step process to design and implement sales contests and recognition programs: (1) planning, (2) promoting, (3) rewarding, and (4) evaluating.

PLANNING

Sales contests are designed to motivate sales effort toward specific objectives. Therefore, it is important to clearly define the objective for each sales contest early in the planning stage. Popular objectives might include maintaining or building overall sales, or sales for specific products, or sales to specific accounts. It is important that the sales objective for a sales contest be consistent with other sales objectives for the organization. For example, a sales organization may have an annual sales objective to increase sales 15 percent over the previous year. Establishing a sales contest to intro-

Exhibit 9.6

Incentive Impact on Quality of Work or Sales Performance

Improved individual motivation	1
Made you feel good or created a sense of personal well-being	2
Increased sales activity	3
Improved team motivation	4
Motivated sales team to reach increased targets	5
Encouraged to sell new products/premium product lines	6

Source: *2006/2007 CPSA's Guide to Incentive and Recognition Programs*, ed. Anna Fredericks (Toronto, ON: Sales Resource Centre, Canadian Professional Sales Association, 2006).

duce a new product that requires considerable time and effort to sell could refocus the efforts of the sales force on the new product and result in lower overall sales, causing the company to miss its more important annual sales objective.

A second important decision at the planning stage is to decide the budget for sales contests. Without a budget, a tendency to simply add sales contests as a response to short-term conditions could develop so that sales contests proliferate with little effort to coordinate them or consider how they fit with long-term sales objectives. A general rule of thumb is to spend approximately 75 percent of the budget on prizes and the remainder on promotion.[9] Unfortunately, only 40 percent of respondents to a survey of Canadian sales organizations indicated that they have a budget for sales programs.[10] Other decisions that need to be considered during the planning stage include how to promote the sales contest, contest duration, the probability of winning, and the type of reward. These are discussed in later sections.

Recognition programs also require some planning, although these are frequently long-standing programs that change little from one period to the next. More formalized programs would include such things as President's Club membership; Salesperson of the Month or Year; or Bronze, Silver, Gold, or Platinum Sales Club membership. Some sales managers may be more effective than others at simply recognizing salespeople for individual effort or performance on a regular basis, but this may occur outside of formal recognition programs.

PROMOTING

The effectiveness of sales contests and recognition programs will be greatly affected by their promotion. Smart planners will decide how to promote before, during, and after these contests and programs are implemented. The promotion of sales contests will be enhanced if there is an exciting theme that can be used to build motivation and encourage positive word-of-mouth prior to the launch of the sales contest. A "Heart of Darkness" contest could lead winners to an "African Safari," or a "Top Gun" contest could provide winners with an experience flying fighter jets.

Depending on the duration of the sales contest, promotion may be needed to maintain or continue to build enthusiasm. Popular methods of communicating performance progress include email updates, monthly newsletters or reports, and public postings on company notice boards. Each of these methods has been used by approximately 60 percent of sales companies.[11]

The duration of sales contests can range from one week to one year. For shorter contests, prizes are usually lower value, and the number of winners is usually higher. The duration of

Exhibit 9.7
Duration of Recognition Programs

Duration	Percentage of Responding Companies with These Programs
Annual programs	70
Semi-annual programs	10
Quarterly programs	20
Monthly programs	40

Source: "CPSA's Guide to Non-Financial Rewards and Recognition," ed. Anna Fredericks
(Toronto: ON, Sales Resource Centre, Canadian Professional Sales Association, 2003).

recognition programs tends to be longer. Many companies have several types of recognition programs during the year. Exhibit 9.7 shows the popularity of recognition programs by duration. Promoting recognition programs should be an ongoing effort as the most effective promotion often comes during and after the presentation of the awards.

REWARDING

There are many decisions that must be made with respect to particular sales contests or recognition programs: Who will be eligible to win a prize or receive an award? What will the prize or award be? How many people will win a prize or receive an award? Where and when will prizes and awards be presented?

1. *Who will be eligible to win a prize or receive an award?* Some sales contests and recognition programs are focused only on sales performance, and therefore are designed mainly to reward field salespeople. Increasingly, sales organizations are beginning to reward sales support people as well. They are beginning to realize that sales support people can have both a direct and an indirect impact on sales performance. A direct impact would result when a customer service representative, for example, up-sells a customer to a larger quantity, a more expensive alternative, or complementary products. Indirectly, the same customer service representative can have an impact on sales performance by simply providing outstanding service that will foster customer loyalty and additional sales.

2. *What will the prize or award be?* The success of a sales contest will depend on the valences that the participants have for the prizes. Cash was preferred more than non-cash rewards by 85 percent of respondents to a recent survey by the Canadian Professional Sales Association.[12] However, many companies offer non-cash prizes and awards because they remain as reminders of accomplishment longer after they have been won. As the Sales Management Today box describes, tangible incentives are remembered longer than cash. Also, the value of some non-cash prizes can be higher than their cash equivalents. A $500 cash prize is worth $500 to the recipient, and costs the company $500. At the same time, it is a $500 taxable benefit for the winner. On the other hand, the company might be able

to provide a $500 non-cash prize that it pays considerably less for, meaning the company could distribute more prizes, or it could increase the value of the rewards it provides. These would still be a taxable benefit for the recipients, but valued at the company's cost. The valences that participants have for particular prizes are not necessarily related to the monetary value of the prizes. An established salesperson in mid-career who owns two widescreen HD televisions may have low valence for a third television. On the other hand, if he is a golf enthusiast, a quality golf bag has "trophy" value as it can be shown to friends and colleagues. Recognizing that different people value different things, there is a trend today to allow winners to choose prizes that they individually value. Paul Gallant, a vice-president at Carlson Marketing Group in Toronto, says, "Overall, people want to pick what they want to pick . . . . Gift cards and certificates have been on top for quite some time."[13]

3. *How many people will win a prize or receive an award?* There are several methods used to select winners in sales contests. Historically, salespeople competed as individuals, with only top performers winning sales contests. This is still popular and is appropriate where all salespeople have a reasonable chance of winning, and particularly if the prize is substantial. Even when there is a single top prize, companies can increase the number of winners by selecting a winner in each region, or at each sales branch. To overcome unequal opportunities among salespeople, some companies establish individual quotas, and salespeople who achieve their quota get rewarded or recognized. There is always a trade-off between rewarding so few that many become demotivated as they do not believe they can win, and rewarding so many that the accomplishment of winning becomes devalued. For sales contests with smaller value prizes, a good rule of thumb might be to aim for 70 percent of the sales force to win. Another possibility that allows more participants to win is to design the program so that the sales performance is based on improvement over a previous period. Salespeople who had poor performance one period would be better positioned to win the next period. The Sales Management in Action box on page 257 described the growing interest in motivating the 'B' team as well as the top performers, and rewarding each person based on improved performance is one of the valued suggestions.

   Another method of deciding winners that is growing in popularity is to group salespeople into teams, and then reward them with group and individual prizes. With a little creativity, inside salespeople and sales support people can also participate. When it is not possible to add these people to the teams, it is a good idea to have separate contests for them. Otherwise, having only field salespeople receive rewards and recognition can be demotivating. Of Canadian companies that responded to a survey concerning incentive programs, 70 percent indicated that salespeople were eligible for participation, but only 40 percent reported that outbound salespeople and customer support personnel were eligible. Only 30 percent of inbound salespeople were eligible.[14]

4. *Where and when will rewards and awards be presented?* This will be determined partly by the nature and value of the reward. National awards should be given at national meetings, and promoted through national media if possible. Many companies advertise winners in *The National Post* and *The Globe and Mail.* Monthly awards can be given at monthly sales meetings. Sales managers that wish to get the most from sales contests and recognition programs should ensure that the recipients get maximum exposure. It fosters pride among winners and increases motivation among others to become future winners.

The Benefits of Tangible Incentives

Respondents to a recent survey by World Incentives, Inc., overwhelmingly agreed (84 percent) that merchandise incentives are remembered longer than cash. Yet, the majority of salespeople (88 percent) responding to a recent CPSA survey indicated that they prefer cash to non-cash rewards. Both cash and non-cash rewards are popular in incentive programs, but Dr. Scott Jeffrey at the University of Waterloo has been researching tangible, non-cash incentives and makes some convincing arguments that they deserve more consideration.

Dr. Jeffrey suggests four psychological processes that may make tangible incentives better motivators than cash incentives of equal value: justifiability and social reinforcement (which may increase the value of earning the reward), and evaluability and separability (which may actually increase the perceived value of the reward). Here is how each of these four psychological processes may operate:

1. *Justifiability.* Employees may see some rewards as highly desirable, but may be unable to justify buying them. For example, a salesperson might like to own a set of new Calloway golf clubs, but could not justify buying them knowing that his children are about to start school and will need new clothes and school supplies. The opportunity to win the reward provides a way for the salesperson to achieve what he desires, without having to violate his family responsibilities.

2. *Social reinforcement.* Winning a tangible reward such as the Calloway golf clubs has a high level of visibility. Other members of the sales force can offer acceptable social reinforcement to the winner: "Job well done, Bob. Great set of golf clubs you won there." Each time Bob hears this, or simply uses his clubs, he will be reminded of the performance that allowed him to earn his tangible reward. While initially winning cash might be highly visible, it is less socially acceptable to acknowledge it, especially with the passage of time. Other members of the sales force would

likely be uncomfortable acknowledging the reward months after it is received: "Well, Bob, what did you do with the $1000 you won last year?"

3. *Evaluability.* Hedonic goods, such as a vacation trip to Hawaii, are difficult to attach an actual value to. Winners, when recalling the trip, are likely to recall a warm beach, a cool drink, a refreshing breeze, and other affective attributes that are difficult to value. Winners may increase the perceived value of the reward beyond its actual monetary value because they may cognitively alter the predicted utility of the reward. Particularly if the winner worked hard to get the reward, cognitive dissonance research suggests they will convince themselves that it is highly valued by them, bringing their self-perceptions in line with their behaviour. Dr. Jeffrey suggests this can even produce a vicious circle: The harder a salesperson works to get the reward, the higher it is valued. The higher it is valued, the harder the salesperson will work for the reward.

4. *Separability.* Since a monetary reward is earned as part of the salesperson's job, the reward will likely become mentally aggregated as part of total income, and will have little meaning beyond any recognition that is provided at the time the reward is won. The cash bonus simply becomes "more salary." Salespeople are also much better with numbers than most employees, so they are likely to compare the cash reward to their salary without the reward, and this may actually diminish the value of the reward. For example, top salespeople regularly earn $100 000 or more. Giving these people a $1000 cash reward will mean that they see their "income" go up by 1 percent, or less. A $1000 set of golf clubs has the same monetary value, but the win will not be aggregated as part of salary. It will remain separate from income.

While much of Dr. Jeffrey's work is conceptual, he has begun a research stream to empirically investigate his hypotheses. In his first study, he has found considerable support for justifiability. In an experimental design, respondents who found the purchase of the non-cash incentive most difficult to justify expressed a clear preference for a cash incentive of equal value. However, they performed better as well.

Sources: World Incentives, Inc., http://www.worldincentives.com/2005%20Incentive%20Federation%20Study.pdf, accessed August 19, 2006; also see Incentivecentral.org, http://www.incentivecentral.org/Federation_Study_2005__Incentive_Federation_Survey_of.571.0.html#6; Scott A. Jeffrey and Victoria Shaffer, "The Motivational Properties of Tangible Incentives," working paper, Department of Management Sciences, University of Waterloo, Waterloo, Ontario; Scott A. Jeffrey, "Justifiability and the Motivational Power of Tangible Non-Cash Incentives," working paper, Department of Management Sciences, University of Waterloo; Waterloo, Ontario; "2006/2007 CPSA's Guide to Incentive and Recognition Programs," ed. Anna Fredericks (Toronto, ON: Sales Resource Centre, Canadian Professional Sales Association, 2006).

EVALUATING

Once a contest is over, or after award presentations at a formal recognition event, the results need to be evaluated. The sales manager needs to review the results at the individual salesperson and at the sales force level. He should evaluate the level of participation among the sales force, whether salespeople were satisfied with the process and the results, and what changes need to be made to future events. While evaluation is an important part of the overall process, only 40 percent of companies have a measurement to evaluate their incentive programs. Of those that do, 70 percent use subjective measures, 60 percent use sales volume increases, and 50 percent use monetary objectives.[15]

SUMMARY

1. **Define motivation and explain the sales manager's role in motivating salespeople.** Motivation is an internal drive to initiate and expend sufficient effort over time to perform appropriate selling activities to accomplish specific sales objectives. The sales manager is instrumental in helping salespeople identify opportunities, and for ensuring they have selling ability by providing appropriate resources such as training, technology, and sales support. By helping salespeople manage their performance, and by recognizing and reinforcing successes, the sales manager has an impact on the salesperson's self-concept, and this will increase the salesperson's motivation.

2. **Describe and explain a general model of sales motivation.** Expectancy theory provides a general model of sales motivation. It describes the relationship between effort, performance, and reward. The effort salespeople will make to achieve sales objectives is related to three factors: (1) expectancy, the belief that making an effort to perform specific activities will, in fact, help the salesperson achieve the desired level of performance; (2) instrumentality, the belief that achieving the desired level of performance will be instrumental in helping the salesperson achieve specific rewards; and (3) valence, the personal value that the salesperson places on receiving these specific rewards.

3. **Discuss specific factors related to salesperson motivation.** Two sets of factors that are important to a salesperson's motivation include job-related factors and individual-related factors. There are five important job-related factors: job value, skill variety, autonomy, opportunity, and feedback. Two important individual-related factors are individual motives and career stages. There are four career stages: exploration, establishment, maintenance, and disengagement. A salesperson's motivation changes as he progresses through these career stages.

4. **Describe different types of quotas and how to manage quota plans.** Quotas are used to motivate salespeople to achieve superior performance and to provide direction for salespeople so they understand what is important. Good quotas are simple, complete, accepted, and managed. Quotas may be sales volume quotas, based on dollar sales, unit sales, or a point system; profit-based quotas, based on profit rather than sales; or activity-based quotas, based on sales-related activities to ensure salespeople do the right things. Sales managers must consider a number of factors when establishing sales quotas, including territory potential, the previous year's sales, forecast sales for the next period, and adjustments that may need to be made because of changing conditions in the sales territory. They must also decide what percentage of the sales force should achieve quota, and what to do when a salesperson does not meet quota.

5. **Describe how to manage sales contests and recognition programs.** Sales contests provide rewards to salespeople for achieving specific sales objectives, and usually shorter-term ones. Recognition programs are designed to recognize sales performance. Sales managers should follow a four-step process to design and implement sales contests and recognition programs: (1) planning, (2) promoting, (3) rewarding, and (4) evaluating.

KEY TERMS

motivation **254**

expectancy **254**

instrumentality **254**

valence **254**

career stage **261**

quota **265**

sales volume quota **267**

profit-based quota **268**

activity-based quota **269**

sales contests **270**

recognition programs **270**

REVIEW QUESTIONS

1. Define *motivation* and explain the sales manager's role in motivating the sales force.

2. Using expectancy theory, explain the relationship between effort and performance, and between performance and reward.

3. Explain what factors might increase or decrease a particular salesperson's valence for financial rewards.

4. List five job-related factors that affect a salesperson's motivation and explain how they do so.

5. What must a sales manager do to manage salespeople at each of the four career stages?

6. What are the two main purposes for using sales quotas? Explain what makes a good sales quota.

7. Describe three types of sales quotas and when each is most appropriately used.

8. Identify one major concern with activity-based sales quotas and explain why sales managers must often look beyond simply achieving this type of quota.

9. Explain the difference between a sales contest and a recognition program.

10. Describe the importance of the four-step process that sales managers should use to design and implement sales contests and recognition programs.

APPLICATION EXERCISES

1. Max Power, the company CEO, has just called you in to discuss sales force motivation. Max says, "I want you to design an incentive plan that will increase the motivation of our salespeople to sell more. They are currently on straight salary, but I think a good bonus plan is what we need. I don't know whether we should pay a small percentage of sales or profits once salespeople reach their quota, and then increase the percentage as their sales above quota increase, or whether we should pay a sizable bonus when they reach quota, and then gradually decrease the percentage the further above quota they go. One of our competitors even begins to pay bonuses long before its salespeople reach quota. I don't understand why they would even consider doing that. What are your thoughts?" As the company sales manager, what specifically would you tell Max Power?

2. Elaine Cheong has been selling for the Canadian sales branch of a global consumer goods company. She originally applied for a marketing position with the company but was offered a job in sales. Now, she is beginning to understand that a transfer to marketing is highly unlikely. She does not dislike selling, and she really does enjoy travel, meeting and working closely with people, and the flexibility that her selling job provides. However, she still has a desire to move to a marketing position within the company. As her sales manager, what would you do to increase Elaine's motivation to remain in sales?

3. Consider two of the following sales positions:
   - selling website design services to large organizations (more than 1000 employees)
   - selling residential real estate
   - selling new and used automobiles
   - selling for a large consumer goods manufacturer
   - selling home security systems door to door
   - selling for a safety clothing manufacturer

   Describe how a sales manager's role would differ when trying to motivate salespeople in the two sales positions you have chosen. What are the more effective things that a sales manager might do for each of the two positions? Explain.

4. Humaid Khan recently completed a sales program at a community college and has just taken a sales job with a large Canadian insurance firm. He initially had some concerns about selling insurance but, although he is still apprehensive, he does want to prove that he can be successful and that he can establish a career in insurance sales. When Humaid talked to other salespeople with the company, they all assured him that they too had been somewhat apprehensive early in their careers. As his sales manager, what would you do to increase Humaid's motivation and relieve his apprehension? Explain.

CASE 9.1 Performance Auto Sales

Andy Jones, sales manager for Performance Auto Sales, arrived early at his office as usual on Saturday morning. He was in a good mood following the contest celebrations the previous night. Andy had initiated a sales contest almost ten years ago as a "fun" event and had continued it on a monthly basis once he saw how it improved morale among the members of the sales force. The contest was known as "Steak and Beans Night." Each month, the sales staff would hold a sales meeting to discuss sales performance and plan the following month's activities. Following each meeting, Andy would announce the names of the top three salespeople among the 10-member sales force, and then everyone would gather at the restaurant across the street for dinner and drinks. The winners of the monthly contest originally got steak but were now allowed to order anything they wanted from the restaurant menu. The rest of the sales force got a plate of beans. Andy based his own reward on the total monthly sales objective for the dealership. If unit sales of new vehicles met the monthly quota, Andy sat at the "steak" table; otherwise, he sat at the "beans" table. When he sat with the winners, Andy would, in a joking manner, let the others know how good it felt to be with the winners and that they should aspire to join the group "sometime." When he sat with the non-winners, Andy jokingly pointed out that the reason he was eating beans was because of their poor performance.

On this particular Saturday morning, Jane Thompson was also scheduled to work early. Jane was the first and so far the only woman on the sales force. Andy was impressed with her professionalism and he was pleased to see that she really seemed to enjoy selling cars. Her monthly sales certainly met his expectations for someone new to sales. She had good relationships with her customers and he knew that several had recommended her to other people who eventually came to purchase a vehicle from her. When he mentioned the sales contest to her and told her that she should be at the steak table, he was surprised by her response. She seemed genuinely disappointed as she responded, "There really isn't much point in my trying to win. The same people seem to win every month and as a new salesperson it will be a long time before I have an established customer base that I can count on. I'll just continue as best I can."

CRITICAL-THINKING QUESTION

Why do you think Jane Thompson responded this way? Should Andy Jones be concerned? If you were Andy Jones, what changes would you consider making to your sales contest and recognition program?

CASE 9.2 Robert Mendes

Robert Mendes had been the top salesperson in the Atlantic region for more than five years. He asked one day to have lunch with Hal Maybee, the regional sales manager for Power & Motion Industrial Supply, Inc. During the table conversation, Robert turned quite serious. "Rumour has it that you are likely to be the next vice-president when Jim retires later this year. I just want you to know that I expect to replace you if that happens. I've been here for almost 10 years now, and I know my sales performance is among the best in the entire country. I have been dedicated to this company and I know I have a lot to offer, but I can't stay around forever as simply a salesperson. I want your job and if I don't get it, I'll have to leave."

Hal had to acknowledge that Robert was correct about his being one of the top salespeople nationally. He was, however, surprised by Robert's approach. Furthermore, Robert had never previously given any indication that he was interested in sales management, and Hal did not believe that he was ready for a sales management position. Hal was considering what his response would be. He had heard the rumour about his possible promotion as well, but so far it was nothing but rumour.

CRITICAL-THINKING QUESTION

If you were Hal Maybee, how would you respond to this situation?

Chapter 10

Compensating Salespeople

LEARNING OBJECTIVES

After completing this chapter, you should be able to

1. Discuss the strengths and weaknesses of various compensation methods.

2. Explain the role of selling expenses and employee benefits in compensation plans.

3. Design an effective sales force compensation mix.

4. Discuss several special topics related to sales force compensation.

In 2006, FedEx was recognized for the ninth consecutive year as one of *Fortune*'s "100 Best Companies to Work For." Even companies that are among the best can have difficulty designing and implementing an effective compensation plan for their salespeople. The latest changes to FedEx's compensation plan were made to respond to two problems. First, salespeople were complaining because their existing compensation plan was too confusing and unpredictable. Mark Jennings, director of sales planning and sales variable compensation programs, says, "We had tweaked our plan so many times that it became almost impossible for the salespeople to understand. We were constantly hearing complaints that the plan wasn't paying out in a timely manner, and the unpredictability on commissions and bonuses was frustrating for the sales force." Second, the company had recently expanded its product mix and needed to gets its 5000-member sales force focused on selling three product lines instead of just one.

The solution: FedEx initiated a "linked sales compensation design." Salespeople were each given targets to meet for all three product lines. Salespeople who concentrated on a single product line and sold it well could earn a reasonable income, but to earn a higher income through incentive compensation, they would have to meet targets for all three product lines. The new program was introduced to the sales force by their front-line sales managers as salespeople indicated that this was how they wanted to receive information. FedEx trained the managers, and had the managers present the plan to the salespeople. Each salesperson was given a chart that explained what income would be earned at every possible achievement level. Weekly updates on sales performance were also provided, as opposed to the monthly or quarterly reports previously provided.

The result: There was a dramatic improvement. Salespeople provided greater focus on selling the entire product mix. Sales force motivation was greatly increased, and frustration with the compensation plan was reduced considerably.[1]

In this chapter, we discuss the role that compensation plays in managing salespeople. Chapter 9 explained a general theory of motivation, and looked at many of the factors that motivate salespeople. It also discussed how job-related and individual-related factors influence a salesperson's motivation, and how a salesperson's motivation changes depending on career stage. In this chapter, the discussion is focused specifically on sales force compensation, including expenses and benefits. This topic gets special coverage because of the special role that compensation plays in motivating salespeople for superior performance. After all, many people are initially attracted to a sales career because of the above average compensation that salespeople earn. The opening vignette provides an excellent example of how an ineffective compensation plan can frustrate salespeople, and how an effective plan can motivate them to meet personal and company objectives.

Compensation Plans

An effective **compensation plan** combines both direct monetary payments—salary, commissions, bonuses, and, in some instances, stock options—and indirect monetary payments—expense accounts, health and dental benefits, pension and insurance plans, and paid vacations. Compensation plans are beginning to focus on **total target compensation** (TTC); that is, the total monetary compensation that a salesperson can earn assuming that she meets target sales results.[2] Companies can, of course, mix salary and various incentive components to establish TTC. Aflak, Inc., for example, is increasing the bonus payments and launching new short-term incentive programs for its salespeople. Cisco, on the other hand, is increasing base salaries and taking money from its short-term incentive programs. Yet, both companies share the same aggressive growth goals.[3]

Compensation plans are very important to a company's success as they determine the quality of sales recruits who will want to work for the company, and they have a considerable impact on the satisfaction and behaviour of the existing sales force. Sales managers must begin their compensation planning by considering the role that various members of the sales force perform, and the behaviours that are desired for salespeople in each role. The sales strategy model shown in Exhibit 10.1 provides a tool to help sales managers think about salesperson roles and what might be the appropriate compensation plan. *Diversification selling* is the most demanding selling role for salespeople. They must sell new products to new customers. Since this type of selling requires the most initiative by salespeople, those who do well should be compensated considerably more highly than those who do not. These salespeople should have a higher incentive opportunity (higher commission and bonus to salary). *Leverage selling* involves selling new products to existing customers, and *penetration selling* involves selling existing products to new customers. Both types of selling require moderate initiative by salespeople, and the incentive opportunity for them should, therefore, be moderate. *Account maintenance selling* involves servicing existing accounts. This role requires the least initiative by salespeople and should have the lowest incentive compensation to salary ratio. These salespeople are frequently paid by straight salary.

Designing an effective compensation plan requires research, intuition, and experimentation. Before deciding on a specific mix of compensation components, a sales manager should research such things as the range of salaries and incentives paid by competing firms in the same industry, and what mix of compensation components the company's sales force most desires. Of course, any compensation plan that is adopted must also take into consideration what the company can afford. The final compensation plan design will still be somewhat intuitive, which will ultimately mean that tweaking and adjustment will be required following implementation.

Exhibit 10.1
Sales Strategy Model

	New customers	Existing customers	
	Penetration selling	Account maintenance	**Existing products**
	Diversification selling	Leverage selling	**New products**

The various methods for compensating salespeople are now discussed, including straight salary, straight commission, bonuses, and combination plans.

STRAIGHT SALARY

When salespeople are paid on a **straight salary plan**, they receive a fixed monetary income that is paid at regular intervals for the performance of specific duties or responsibilities. Salary is not related directly to any particular performance measure and is given to the salesperson regardless of what they do or what they achieve. Although high-performing salespeople may be rewarded with salary increases following performance reviews, research indicates that salespeople who receive salary plus incentive programs earn, on average, approximately 40 percent more than those on straight salary.[4] Care must be exercised when interpreting this statistic, however. Straight salary compensation plans are most frequently used because of the nature of the sales activities involved. These plans most frequently compensate salespeople who are simply gatherers rather than hunters. Only a small percentage of salespeople are compensated by straight salary.[5]

ADVANTAGES   Straight salary plans offer a number of advantages for the company, the sales manager, and the sales force. For the company, salary expense becomes a fixed cost: five salespeople with an average annual salary of $80 000 means the company's total annual salary expense will be $400 000. Budgeting and administration are easy to manage. Total wage levels can therefore easily be managed as well. When the annual budget is prepared, an average salary increase can be determined based on economic and competitive conditions, and sales projections. Some companies simply adjust all salaries by this percentage, while others provide the total increase to the sales salary expense budget to the sales manager and allow him to allocate increases among various members of the sales force. With a straight salary compensation plan, selling expense as a percentage of sales tends to decrease as sales increase. Straight salary plans also foster company loyalty. Salaried salespeople are more loyal to their company and turnover is therefore lower among them.

When salespeople earn straight salary, sales managers have considerable more control of their activities and get greater cooperation when non-selling activities are required. Salespeople are more likely to spend time on non-selling activities, such as inventory replenishment and shelf-management programs; equipment installation, maintenance, and customer training; and accounts receivable and other account management problems. When compensation is straight salary, sales managers also find it easier to manage salespeople who have a large geographic territory to cover, or who must sell a broad range of products. Sales managers can require salespeople to cover all accounts based on long-term account opportunity, and not have them "cherry-pick" accounts based on short-term sales potential. Salespeople can also be required to allocate their sales efforts across product lines, and not simply focus on those items that are easiest to sell or that pay the highest commissions. Sales managers also find straight salary attractive when sales potential varies considerably among sales territories. There is less competition among salespeople for the best sales territories, and it is easier for sales managers to divide sales territories or reassign salespeople among territories when required.

For salespeople, a straight salary plan provides predictable income and the greatest level of security. Such plans are simple to understand. People new to sales often prefer straight salary compensation plans because none of their compensation is at risk for poor performance. Customers sometimes also prefer salespeople to be paid on straight salary as salespeople are then less likely to unnecessarily up-sell them, or try to sell them products that they do not need.

LIMITATIONS   A common criticism of straight salary compensation plans is that they underpay top performers and overpay the least productive members of the sales force. Many sales managers argue that, due to this, performance deteriorates as top performers become demoralized and reduce their selling effort. The best salespeople will often leave for better opportunities, and the salespeople who are left are the ones that other companies would not want. While this certainly overstates the impact of straight salary plans on sales force turnover, it is likely that there is some effect.

WHERE USED   Straight salary plans are more likely to be used when the company philosophy is to actively manage the sales force, when the sales manager has the time and skills required to closely supervise and adequately motivate salespeople. Under these conditions, the sales manager is aware of who are the best salespeople and who can be coached to become top performers, and can reward them accordingly.

Straight salary plans are also used to compensate sales trainees or new sales recruits who may not have the skills or the prospect base to achieve sufficient sales to earn an adequate income. Many companies begin new salespeople on a straight salary plan and increase the commission component of their salary as sales grow. New recruits might otherwise be financially unable to begin a career in sales.

Straight salary plans are commonly used to pay internal or inside salespeople, or salespeople who perform sales support or account management activities. Salespeople who are paid straight salary are more service-oriented and more willing to help customers solve problems and make decisions than salespeople who are paid a commission based on what customers buy. This is a reason why missionary salespeople—manufacturer's sales representatives who call on end-customers to increase demand for the manufacturer's products even though purchases are made through other channel intermediaries—and technical salespeople also are frequently paid by salary. In the former instance, it is often difficult to determine which or how much sales are directly attributable to the efforts of the salesperson; in the latter instance, the salesperson's focus is on advising rather than selling to the customer. When salespeople spend considerable time on service and when it is difficult to assess their performance, they are more likely to be paid a salary.[6]

STRAIGHT COMMISSION

Salespeople who are compensated with a **straight commission plan** are rewarded for performance. They must sell to earn money as their remuneration is tied directly to their sales performance. Traditionally, salespeople were paid commission based on dollar sales volume or unit sales, but companies are increasingly paying commission based on profitability. Some commission payment plans have become more complex, partly due to a growing awareness that simply paying a single commission rate across all products, territories, and accounts is often not the best policy, and partly due to the increased ability to manage and communicate commission earnings accurately and quickly with improved computer technology. AccountPro, for example, includes a Sales Commission application that allows users to design, process, and communicate relatively complex commission programs. Approximately 15 percent of salespeople are compensated completely based on sales performance, either with a straight commission compensation plan or with such a plan combined with other types of incentive payments.[7]

ADVANTAGES   Straight commission plans offer several advantages. Straight commission plans provide salespeople with the greatest possible monetary incentive and foster independence so that they require less direct management by the company. In fact, many commission-paid salespeople resent management intrusion when it affects their ability to make sales that will maximize their own income.

Straight commission plans are easy to administer and explain to salespeople. But this is not the only thing that helps improve sales force morale. Straight commission plans are inherently fair, assuming that sales territories are designed equitably. If all salespeople have equal opportunity, then those who perform well will be rewarded accordingly, and poor performers will be motivated to improve their performance or even leave the industry.

Since commissions are directly related to sales performance, companies do not have high selling expenses unless sales are good. When the economy is poor or sales decline, selling costs are reduced to match the decreased level of sales. This is particularly important for companies that have limited resources, frequently those that are smaller or newer companies. When working capital is scarce, they often can put it to better use than paying a sales force that is not performing.

For the company, a straight commission plan results in compensation being a variable cost, the same as the cost that the company has when it employs independent sales agents, previously discussed in Chapter 3. A straight salary plan, by comparison, results in compensation being a fixed cost for the company. Exhibit 10.2 demonstrates the relationship between the two compensation plans. A company that has five salespeople earning an average of $80 000 straight salary has a fixed selling expense of $400 000. If the company decided to pay a 10 percent straight commission instead of a straight salary, then selling expenses as a percent of sales would be lower as long as total sales were below $4 000 000 (i.e., $400 000/0.10 = $4 000 000). However, if sales exceed $4 000 000, then the company would save selling expenses if it moved to a straight salary compensation plan. This explains why companies sometimes begin with straight commission plans when they are new, and move toward salary plans as they mature. Wise companies do so gradually, as major changes to a compensation plan that negatively impact the income of the sales force can be demotivating and can result in large numbers of salespeople leaving the sales force. Unfortunately, when this happens, it is frequently the best salespeople who are the first to leave as they are the ones most likely to have good opportunities elsewhere.

LIMITATIONS   Straight commission compensation plans have a number of limitations. The most serious limitation is that sales management loses considerable control over the sales force.

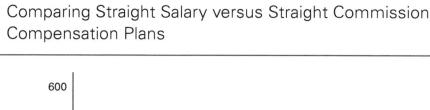

Exhibit 10.2

Comparing Straight Salary versus Straight Commission Compensation Plans

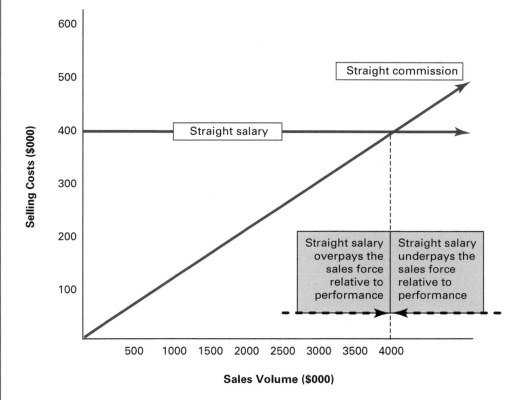

When salespeople are paid by straight commission, they view anything that interferes with their ability to earn commission as an infringement. They generally want to focus on closing sales, and often will "cherry-pick" opportunities to do so for their own short-term advantage. They may resist account management activities, and may sell products that customers really do not need. Salespeople will resist changing sales territories unless it is apparent to them that the change is to their advantage. That means that redesigning territories to increase account coverage will often be resisted because salespeople may have to focus on some less attractive accounts to increase their sales once territories have been split. A final limitation of straight commission plans is that there is often very wide variation in pay and this may decrease morale and increase turnover. This problem becomes particularly acute when economic conditions worsen and poor performers earn even less than usual. For example, many salespeople are attracted to real estate sales when home sales are good. When real estate sales decline, many poorer performing salespeople leave the industry. An equally important issue is that high performing salespeople often resist any attempt to attract them to management positions unless they see it as a step to additional promotion within the company. Many enjoy selling too much, while they also recognize that income potential is reduced if they move from sales to management.

WHERE USED   Straight commission plans are generally used where (1) companies want salespeople to focus on short-term transactional sales, often found in door-to-door selling or telesales, (2) where product complexity is low so that salespeople are not required to do a lot of customer training or service, or (3) where there are limited account management or missionary selling activities. Straight commission plans have traditionally been popular in real estate, automotive, insurance, and financial services selling. Some retail salespeople are also currently compensated by straight commission. There is a trend away from straight commission, at least among retail and car salespeople. Salespeople who are paid by commission may earn as little as 2–3 percent of sales for high value items to as much as 30–40 percent of sales for low value items or high margin items that require considerable effort to sell a small number of units.

BONUSES

Another way to increase a salesperson's income is to provide a **bonus** for sales performance. Bonuses may be paid to individual salespeople or to sales teams, and may include cash or some form of cash equivalent such as trips, merchandise, or reward cards. Bonuses may be used to focus salespeople to achieve both long- and short-term objectives.

Bonuses that are paid to direct sales effort toward long-term objectives are often viewed by salespeople as a major component of their compensation package. Many companies pay a bonus, for example, if salespeople achieve annual sales revenue or gross margin targets. Many companies are beginning to experiment with these bonus plans, as an "all-or-none" approach to paying a bonus can be demotivating for salespeople who fail to meet their target by only a small amount. As a result, some companies pay bonuses throughout the year. Instead of paying a 10 percent bonus for achieving an annual sales target, they might pay, for example, a 2 percent bonus when salespeople achieve each of four quarterly targets, and an additional 2 percent bonus if salespeople meet their annual target. Other companies begin to pay bonuses when a percentage of the annual sales target is achieved, and they may continue to increase the bonus payment as sales increase beyond the annual sales target. The following are three example plans that pay a bonus as a percent of the salesperson's salary, based on achieving a specified percent of target:

Percent of Target	Plan 1 Bonus (%)	Plan 2 Bonus (%)	Plan 3 Bonus (%)
70	40	–	40
80	60	30	50
90	80	70	70
100	100	100	100
110	120	120	140
120	140	130	200

These represent only three of hundreds of possibilities, but notice that they are all designed to achieve different things. Plan 1 is similar to many plans; however, notice that the reward to the salesperson for increasing from 70 percent to 80 percent of target is exactly the same as the reward she gets for increasing from 100 percent to 110 percent of target. Plan 2 pays the greatest increase in bonus payments at lower levels of target achievement, and increases in bonus decrease as performance increases. Plan 3 recognizes that as target achievement increases, it becomes more difficult for the salesperson to continue to improve performance, and this plan is designed to get the most effort from the salesperson. Important issues, of course, are at what level to begin paying a bonus, and whether bonuses should be capped beyond a certain level of performance.

Bonuses are very effective at directing sales effort toward short-term objectives. In this regard, they are the same as sales contests. Examples would include achieving a 25 percent gross margin in April, adding the largest number of new accounts during the first quarter, being among the first 10 salespeople to sell a new product, or having the highest sales increase for a particular period (either as total dollar sales volume or as a percentage increase over the previous period's sales). When bonuses are used to achieve short-term objectives, companies generally decrease the value of the bonuses, but may increase the percentage of winners or offer many bonuses during the year so that multiple objectives are achieved.

ADVANTAGES   There are many advantages to using bonus plans. They are generally simple to administer and for salespeople to understand. They can be designed to meet numerous objectives and can be changed easily, making it possible for almost everyone to achieve some bonus as a result of their performance. In fact, bonuses are particularly advantageous to reward sales teams, including support staff, when it is not always possible to decide the degree to which each person contributed to achieving the team objectives.

LIMITATIONS   One limitation of bonus plans is that it is difficult to find objectives that everyone will support. Another is that it is often difficult to find a bonus, other than cash, that will motivate everyone equally. Winning a free trip to Paris is not a bonus to a salesperson who is afraid of flying. These limitations reinforce the importance of rewarding achievement of multiple objectives, and designing flexibility into the non-cash bonuses so that those who achieve their targets get positively rewarded.

WHERE USED   Bonus plans are used extensively in Canada. Companies that focus on long-term objectives often carefully plan their bonus programs each year. Companies that focus on short-term objectives may do so within the context of their annual sales expense budget, or may simply implement short-term bonus programs as the need arises. Bonuses are usually paid when salespeople accomplish measurable performance objectives such as total dollar sales volume, gross margin, new accounts opened, new product sales, etc. However, they are sometimes tied to customer satisfaction. This is discussed more in a later section concerning special issues in sales force compensation.

COMBINATION COMPENSATION PLANS

The advantages and limitations of straight salary and straight commission plans have led many companies to adopt a **combination compensation plan**. These plans include some combination of salary, commission, and bonus, and are used by the majority of sales organizations in Canada. Salary usually accounts for the largest percentage of compensation within these plans; however, there are straight commission and bonus combination plans as well as plans that include all three components. Salespeople currently earn approximately 40 percent of their total compensation through performance-based incentives.[8] A recent Canadian study found, however, that this varies depending on the experience of the salespeople. Senior salespeople receive approximately 49 percent of their total compensation from commissions and bonuses, intermediate salespeople receive 28 percent, and junior salespeople receive 16 percent.[9] While it is often difficult to determine the appropriate mix of salary, commission, and bonus that should be included in a total sales compensation package, when combination plans are designed well, they provide a balance of control over sales force activities with incentive for sales force performance.

ADVANTAGES Combination compensation plans provide a maximum of flexibility to the sales organization. These plans allow companies to recognize all appropriate behaviours of the sales force, including non-selling activities, while also motivating them to achieve both long-term and short-term objectives through various incentive programs. Specific behaviours can be stimulated with short notice, such as selling older or overstocked inventory items, selling new products, opening new accounts, etc. Salespeople can be rewarded often throughout the year, providing many opportunities to recognize performance and build motivation and loyalty.

LIMITATIONS While flexibility is the major advantage of combination compensation plans, it is also their greatest weakness. Combination compensation plans tend to be more complex and difficult to administer than either straight salary or straight commission plans. There is sometimes a tendency for management to continually make adjustments to these plans, particularly if bonus programs play an important role. Managers who do not carefully plan and coordinate their short- and long-term objectives may find that when they design bonus programs to achieve short-term objectives, it reduces effort by the salespeople toward achieving more important long-term objectives. The tendency to make adjustments to combination compensation plans can also be demotivating unless changes are carefully communicated to the sales force and they are in agreement. Changes to compensation plans risk creating winners and losers, so they must be made with care.

WHERE USED The great majority of sales forces are compensated with a combination compensation plan. Some plans, though, are weighted more heavily toward salary than other plans. There are a number of reasons for this. One is most likely historical as, at one time, straight salary plans were more common than they are today. As an increasing number of companies began experimenting with performance-based pay components, others have had to follow suit to remain competitive and attract or retain good salespeople.

In business-to-business selling, or in selling where a consultative or relationship selling approach is used, the compensation plan is often heavily weighted toward salary to ensure that servicing customers remains important to salespeople; however, some incentive component is usually included to also ensure motivation to perform. In a team-selling environment where it is difficult to assess the contribution of individual members, salary will also be more important. If the company (or brand) has a strong position in the marketplace so that marketing becomes a critical part of the overall communication strategy and is important for generating sales, then, again, salary will be more important. Finally, some companies use combination plans for recent sales recruits or for salespeople in territories where opportunities may be more limited. College and university students who are new to sales often shun companies that pay straight commission. For this reason, some companies pay salary with a small commission component for a limited term, and gradually move the salesperson to a commission plan as they become more established. There are also instances where a salesperson is needed in a territory where there is limited opportunity for sales. In such instances, the sales manager may increase the salary component for this salesperson to offset the limited opportunity to earn commission.

COMPENSATION PLAN SUMMARY

This chapter began with a discussion of straight salary and straight commission compensation plans. While both of these compensation plans are used by many firms, we also pointed out that the great majority of firms do not use either but do, in fact, use combination compensation plans

Exhibit 10.3

Comparison of Characteristics of Various Compensation Methods

Compensation Method	Advantages	Limitations	Where Used
Straight salary	Fixed cost makes budgeting and administration easy; provides maximum security for salespeople; promotes loyalty and reduces turnover; provides sales manager with more control over non-selling activities.	Fixed cost means selling expenses remain high during economic downturns; provides no incentive for salespeople to improve performance; sales managers may need to more closely supervise salespeople.	Often used for new recruits while they become established; used to compensate salespeople whose primary role is to provide customer service.
Straight commission	For the company, variable cost ties compensation directly to sales; provides maximum incentive so aggressive and experienced salespeople can earn high incomes.	Selling costs are less predictable; sales managers lose considerable control over the sales force; salespeople have less company loyalty; wide variations in income may exist and during economic downturn some salespeople likely to leave; high earners may resist becoming a manager.	Often used where aggressive selling is needed, such as door-to-door sales or insurance sales; used when product complexity is low and salespeople do not need to provide much service or training; used where there is little account management or missionary selling; used when it is difficult to closely supervise sales force.
Combination plan	Provides some security and incentive for salespeople, and some control over sales force activities for the sales manager.	Tends to be more complex and difficult to administer; requires considerable management thought and control to ensure both short- and long-term company objectives are met; can be de-motivational if too many adjustments or changes made.	Most popular type of compensation plan and now used in almost all selling environments; however, mix of salary versus incentive depends on desire for management control or compensation plan control, and desired level of motivation.

that have both a salary component and an incentive component which could include commission or bonus. Exhibit 10.3 summarizes the advantages and limitations of the three types of compensation plans, and illustrates where each is most appropriately used.

Selling Expenses and Benefits

Other important dimensions of sales force compensation are selling expenses and benefits. **Selling expenses** include all of the expenses that salespeople incur as a result of selling-related activities that they perform for their company. How companies choose to reimburse salespeople for selling-related expenses and which expenses they reimburse directly impact the total compensation available to salespeople. Selling expenses as a percentage of sales can be very large, so it is understandable that companies will manage this carefully to ensure expenses are judiciously spent and recorded. There are three types of selling expense reimbursement plans: unlimited reimbursement, limited reimbursement, and per diem plans.

UNLIMITED REIMBURSEMENT PLANS

The most liberal reimbursement plan simply asks salespeople to submit itemized expense reports and then the company reimburses them for whatever was spent. This plan gives salespeople the maximum discretion when it comes to both travel and entertainment. That is one reason why these expense plans are usually used by companies that sell to executive-level clients, sell very expensive items, or sell in highly competitive markets. Some smaller companies also use unlimited reimbursement plans, although there is probably some understanding as to when the level of expenses gets to be too high. While management in a smaller company may not monitor expenses every week, it will still most likely make periodic comparisons from one sales period to another so that if expenses increase much faster than sales, future selling expenses will be more carefully managed.

One issue with unlimited reimbursement plans is that they more frequently lead to padding than do limited reimbursement plans. **Expense account padding** occurs when salespeople claim either inappropriate expenses, or expenses that were not actually made. A *Sales & Marketing Management* survey of 327 executives found that 49 percent of them believe that one or more of their salespeople falsify expense reports by at least $50 per month.[10] Salespeople can be very creative when it comes to padding expense accounts. One of the most popular items used by salespeople to pad their expenses is taxi expenses, as few taxis will actually complete receipts for salespeople, and some will even give salespeople several blank receipts if they are asked. Another common way to pad expenses is to claim mileage beyond what has actually been driven for business purposes. Some salespeople have a percentage they add to each expense report.

LIMITED REPAYMENT PLANS

The most commonly used expense reimbursement plan sets a dollar limit up to which salespeople will be reimbursed. In some instances, the limit may be expressed as a total dollar value, giving salespeople some freedom to decide where they wish to allocate their expenses. In other instances, the limit may be expressed as a percentage of sales or gross margin, giving salespeople some flexibility with respect to selling expenses as long as increases in selling expenses are related to increases in sales volume or gross margin.

Companies frequently provide limits for individual expense items. For example, a company may reimburse up to $10 for breakfast, $15 for lunch, and $30 for dinner. Another company may simply reimburse up to $50 per day for meals. For some companies, alcohol with meals is an acceptable expense; for others it is not. Some companies pay a car allowance and include all car expenses; others provide a mileage allowance, which may range from below $0.35 per kilometre to more than $0.50 per kilometre. Some companies restrict air travel to economy class, and set nightly limits for travel accommodations. Most companies recognize that there must be some flexibility in reimbursement policies across Canada because selling expenses may vary considerably from one region to another.

PER DIEM PAYMENT PLANS

A per diem, or per day, expense plan is less commonly used than other plans, but there are companies that use this method of sales expense reimbursement. It is, however, more commonly used by government departments, or for employees other than sales employees who must travel on company business. In some instances, the per diem amount covers total daily expenses, and in other instances, it covers only certain expense items. For example, a salesperson might be given $200 per day and be expected to cover total accommodation, travel, and meal expenses with this amount. In another company, a salesperson might be given $60 per day for meals and incidentals, for example, and be reimbursed for accommodations and travel separately.

Administratively, these plans are easy to administer. Some people do profit from such plans by underspending the per diem allowance. This is a potential problem if salespeople are expected to have face-to-face meetings with customers on a regular basis, or entertain prospective or regular customers. If travel costs are included in the per diem allowance, salespeople may try to manage customer relationships by telephone, most particularly those who are distant and costly to contact in person. Failing to entertain important customers could reduce sales revenue, and while this might benefit the salesperson, it would certainly not be good for the company.

EMPLOYEE BENEFITS

"**Employee benefits** constitute an indirect form of compensation intended to improve the quality of the work lives and personal lives of employees."[11] Benefit programs are important to salespeople and can be used to both attract and reward good salespeople. To some degree, salary, commission, and bonuses, and expenses and benefits, are interchangeable as, to the salesperson, they create a comprehensive compensation package. Companies are increasingly providing flexible benefit packages to salespeople, recognizing that the same things are not equally important to all members of the sales force. Sales managers need to carefully explain the company benefits to salespeople because while some understand the true value of particular benefits, some may simply not recognize that benefits are part of the total reward package they receive. At issue, sometimes, is whether the company or the employee pays for the benefits. When companies pay, the employees receive the benefits tax-free. When the employees pay, sometimes the company will increase the employees' incomes to cover the cost of the benefit, but the increased income they receive is taxable for the employee.

The first group of benefits that sales employees receive are usually common benefits offered to all of a company's employees. Exhibit 10.4 provides a list of selected benefits and the percentage of respondents who indicated that they received these benefits from their employer. The second group of benefits that sales employees receive are ones that are generally provided only to sales employees. Many of these benefits include equipment used to improve salesperson efficiency and effectiveness. Exhibit 10.5 provides a list of selected benefits and the percentage of respondents who indicated that they received these benefits from their employer. Finally, Exhibit 10.6 provides a list of some of the other perquisites that are frequently provided to sales employees, and that are, in many instances, provided to other employees as well.

Exhibit 10.4

General Employment Benefits Offered to Sales Employees

Benefit	Percentage of Respondents Who Receive These Benefits
Accidental death insurance	84%
Day care subsidy	6%
Dental coverage	78%
Drug card benefits	80%
Individual life insurance	78%
Long-term disability	76%
Maternity benefits top-up	14%
Orthodontics	46%
Stress management program	26%
Travel/accident insurance	73%
Tuition reimbursement	44%
Vision coverage	63%

Source: "CPSA's Guide to Benefits and Perquisites for Salespeople," ed. Anna Fredericks (Toronto: ON, Sales Resource Centre, Canadian Professional Sales Association, 2005).

Exhibit 10.5

Communications Equipment and Services Benefits for Salespeople

Equipment	Percentage of Respondents Who Receive These Benefits
Cell phone	78%
BlackBerry	14%
Fax machine	60%
Laptop computer	68%
Personal computer	28%
Internet access	68%
Personal digital assistant	17%
Peripheral devices	34%

Source: "CPSA's Guide to Benefits and Perquisites for Salespeople," ed. Anna Fredericks (Toronto: ON, Sales Resource Centre, Canadian Professional Sales Association, 2005).

Exhibit 10.6

Other Perquisites Provided to Salespeople

Type of Perquisite	Percentage of Respondents Who Receive These Benefits
Company parking	60%
Parking allowance	29%
Education subsidies	58%
Fitness program	11%
Group legal services	3%
Group auto insurance	16%
Group home insurance	6%
Health, social, golf club memberships	10%
RRSP matching	41%
Stock purchase plan	17%

Source: "CPSA's Guide to Benefits and Perquisites for Salespeople," ed. Anna Fredericks (Toronto: ON, Sales Resource Centre, Canadian Professional Sales Association, 2005).

Putting the Compensation Plan Together

When putting the entire compensation package together, management should have in mind the total income it would like its average salesperson to make. This is a critical decision. Salespeople will look at their compensation and compare it with a number of significant others: (1) other salespeople in the same company, (2) competing salespeople in the same industry, (3) other salespeople in other industries, and (4) non-sales employees in the same company. Salespeople who feel they are being treated inequitably will be dissatisfied that they are being paid too little. Some salespeople may also decide that they are being paid too much. Both of these conditions create problems for a sales organization.

Exhibit 10.7 illustrates a compensation–performance matrix that is particularly useful when looking at the compensation of individual salespeople relative to their performance. This matrix has implications for sales managers, who should have a good idea where various members of the sales force fit. It is also good if the sales manager can determine where the various members of the sales force see themselves. At Windsor Factory Supply, illustrated in the Sales Management in Action box, everyone has input into the compensation plan on an annual basis, so it is not simply a management decision.

PAYING LOW COMPENSATION

Some companies are forced to pay too little because they do not have the financial resources to meet compensation standards in their industry. When this happens, they generally get below-

Exhibit 10.7
Compensation/Performance Model

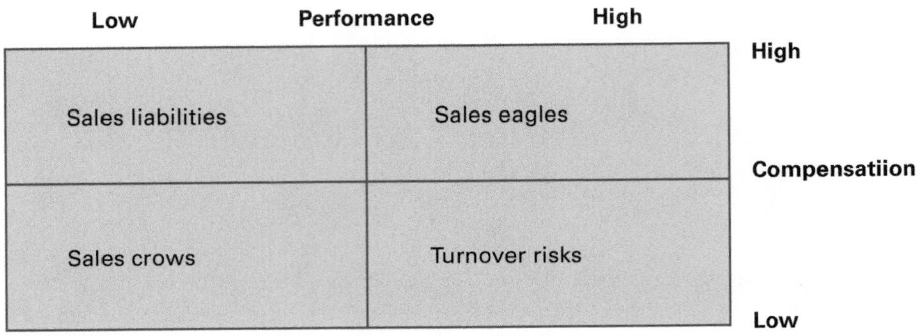

	Low	Performance	High	
	Sales liabilities		Sales eagles	High
				Compensatiion
	Sales crows		Turnover risks	Low

average salespeople. The company risks having a sales force comprising mainly *sales crows:* low-compensation, low-performance salespeople who pick up the crumbs left by competing sales forces. This can be a sales force issue or an individual salesperson issue because these salespeople frequently generate below-average sales volume, and the cost to the company is reduced revenue, reduced profit, and decreased market share where this issue exists. If a sales force has only a few sales crows, it might seem at first glance that this is not a very serious problem; however, these salespeople can quickly demotivate other members of the sales force.

A company that is fortunate to hire good salespeople, but that pays them poorly, will most likely have higher than industry-average sales force turnover, resulting in increased recruiting, selection, and training costs, and possibly damaged seller–buyer relationships. This situation creates a relatively unstable sales force and, over time, there is a risk that many of the remaining salespeople will be sales crows. Low-compensation, high performance salespeople are referred to as *turnover risks,* recognizing that they are somewhat unstable and more likely to leave the company. If there are only a few of these salespeople in the sales force, then the sales manager needs to assess whether they might be motivated to stay with the company for some reason other than compensation. Hiring too many salespeople who are good performers but failing to pay them for their performance can also result in a demotivated sales force. As the sales crows see too many turnover risks come and go, they quickly come to believe that good salespeople do not stay with their company.

PAYING HIGH COMPENSATION

Some sales forces are known to have high-quality salespeople who are generally paid above the industry average. A respected company with a superior product line and training and growth opportunities for its sales force often is a target company for many younger, but promising salespeople who will eventually build a career with the company. A company that has a high-compensation, high-performance sales force is fortunate to have *sales eagles.* This would be the dream of most sales managers. Sales eagles can create problems, however, when there are only a few of them in the sales force. They can create morale problems among other salespeople if their compensation is perceived to be too high for what they do. That is why a sales manager who has

Want a Raise? Vote One for Yourself

Windsor Factory Supply (WFS) began as a two-man industrial distributorship in 1955 and has since grown to be one of the largest and most important industrial distributorships in Canada. It now employs more than 170 people, including more than 30 salespeople who work from the company's seven branches. The company values customer service highly and employees are all empowered to make decisions whenever customer service is an issue. According to president Wes Delnea, "Happy employees help make happy customers." To keep employees happy, they share many group experiences, including attending major sporting events, parties, and picnics, and twice, all employees went to Las Vegas.

All decisions that affect company employees, including compensation and benefits, are decided by popular vote. Each year, the company holds a meeting of the entire staff. Everyone has information on company performance, and they discuss and vote on the next year's compensation plan. They decide, for example, how much of the profit will go to shareholders (who are employees or former employees),

how much will be paid to employees as bonuses, and how much will remain as retained earnings. Various evaluation committees, which had been voted to their positions earlier in the year, provide input on individual employee performance, and this helps determine each person's bonus. Employees also decide the benefits package each year, but it is generally superior to any offered by its competitors. Among the many things it normally covers are medical and dental expenses, education and recreation allowances, and even a generous clothing allowance if employees have the company name on any clothing they buy.

Sound unusual? Yes, it does. But, Windsor Factory Supply is an unusual company. At one point, the company had gone four years without a single employee absentee day. Employee involvement in all facets of the company has created involved and motivated employees who have helped make Windsor Factory Supply one of the most profitable companies in its industry—and one that pays higher salaries as well.

Sources: Interview with Wes Delnea, president, Windsor Factory Supply Ltd., March 20, 1997; correspondence from Wes Delnea, March 19, 1999; Richard J. Long, *Strategic Compensation in Canada* (Toronto, ON: Nelson Thomson Learning, 2006) p. 176.

a small number of sales eagles must ensure that they are paid for current performance and not simply because of past performance or windfall sales. A sales force should be proud to have some sales eagles among its members, but they should deserve to be sales eagles, and they should have a compensation level that others can achieve with ability and effort. It then becomes the sales manager's job to help other salespeople become sales eagles.

A sales force comprising *sales liabilities*—low-performance, high-compensation salespeople—puts the entire company at serious risk. This implies that selling costs as a percentage of sales will be higher than industry standards, and the company will be less profitable and have fewer financial resources to invest in sales force training, research and development, marketing communications, and many of the other things it must do to grow. While a sales force made up of sales liabilities puts the company at risk, having only a few sales liabilities on the sales force can put the sales force at risk. At best, they become ostracized by the other members of the sales force, but their poor performance keeps their territory at risk. At worst, they become resented by the other members of the sales force, who then become demotivated.

Much of this discussion suggests that performance-based compensation certainly has an important role in most sales forces. As the percentage of performance-based compensation increases relative to total compensation, the numbers of sales liabilities and turnover risks in the sales force are likely to decrease. The number of sales eagles is likely to increase, and the number of sales crows is likely to decrease. However, this is far too simplistic. There are important reasons why some sales forces have higher and some have lower percentages of performance-based compensation, and these will be discussed shortly. There are still a few issues that need to be considered by sales managers as the level of compensation among the sales force increases.

First, when salespeople are paid too much, they become less interested in promotion to management positions as this may mean that they must take a reduced income along with the promotion. Second, if market conditions change or if management realizes sales force salaries are too high, they may implement changes to the sales compensation plan in an effort to get better control over selling expenses. When this happens, the best salespeople are likely to be the ones most affected and, therefore, the ones most likely to become dissatisfied and leave. The worst salespeople, lacking other opportunities, will stay. The sales force quality decreases.

It is not always necessary to pay high compensation levels. Salespeople, once they achieve a certain standard of living or a satisfactory level of income, are more likely to reduce their motivation to achieve higher income. That is, their valence for money is reduced and their valence for other things may increase. As stated, sometimes salespeople will trade higher income to work with companies that have superior products, that are more favourably positioned in the marketplace, or that provide better growth opportunities. There are differences in the valence for income from one country to another. In one survey of approximately 41 000 salespeople across nine countries, salespeople in the United States chose money as their top motivator. Canadian salespeople, on the other hand, were motivated more by the opportunity to use their talent.[12] Deciding the appropriate mix of compensation components is now discussed.

DECIDING THE APPROPRIATE MIX

Deciding the appropriate mix of salary, commission, and bonus requires some creativity on the part of management. There are many ways this can be done, but we will demonstrate one practical approach. Let us assume that the company has sales projections of $80 million and wants to keep sales force compensation expenses equal to approximately 10 percent of sales, assuming that sales projections are achieved. That means the company would budget $8 million for sales force compensation, and if it has 800 salespeople, then the average compensation per salesperson would be $100 000.

Part of this $100 000 will be salary and part will be performance-based income. The first, and most important decision, is the percentage of total compensation each will contribute. (The reason this is the most important decision will be discussed shortly.) Suppose management decides that salary will account for approximately 90 percent of total compensation. The sales manager might calculate the average commission payment currently being made to the sales force. Assume, for example, that salespeople are paid 2 percent commission on sales to established accounts and 5 percent commission on sales to new accounts. Further, assume that 80 percent of sales are to existing accounts and the remaining sales are to new accounts. This means that total commission paid at targeted sales projection would be $2 080 000 (80 percent × $80 million × 0.02 plus 20 percent × $80 million X 0.05). This is an average commission of $2600 ($2 080 000/800). Average compensation without commission is, therefore, $97 400. The sales manager has approximately $7400 on average that he can allocate as bonus income ($100 000 minus $90 000 salary, minus $2600 commission). At this point, the sales manager might decide that bonuses for salespeople who achieve quota will be 10 percent of salary, and he may have set quotas at a level he estimates will result in 70 percent of salespeople achieving their quota. This means that, on average, bonuses will equal 7 percent of salary (10 percent of salary × 70 percent of sales force). Now, he has an average bonus estimate of $6300 ($90 000 × 0.07). Notice that this is $1100 below what should be available ($7400 minus $6300). The sales manager may use this as a "buffer" in the event that more than 70 percent of the sales force achieves quota. Alternatively, this may provide the sales manager with a budget for sales contests throughout the year (800 salespeople × $1100 = $880 000).

An important point must be made. First, this example shows how to make a very rough estimate of the various components of the compensation mix. However, the calculations are simple and can be done very quickly. It is possible to add some degree of sophistication to these calculations and create what might appear to be greater accuracy. However, in the real world, reasonable estimates are just as valuable and are more likely to be used. This is because, at the end of the year, the actual amount paid to the sales force for compensation will probably differ as total sales are unlikely to be exactly $80 million, and the mix of sales between established and new accounts is unlikely to be exactly 80 percent/20 percent.

The critical decision, as stated, is the percentage of total compensation that will be provided by incentive or performance-based income. It can range from 0 percent (straight salary) to 100 percent (straight commission or commission plus bonus). Most companies include a performance-based component somewhere between these two extremes, as already discussed. The size of the performance-based component should be decided based on the sales manager's preferred balance among (1) directing sales force effort on important customers, products, or activities, (2) motivating sales force effort, (3) controlling sales force cost, and (4) using mechanisms other than incentives to control the sales force. Exhibit 10.8 illustrates how various levels of performance-based compensation impact each of these factors. It is commonly accepted that 30 percent is the tipping point above which the compensation plan becomes the primary means of controlling sales force behaviour. "The 30 percent rule states that sales leadership's ability to influence sales force activity through means other than incentives diminishes as incentives grow beyond 30 percent of total compensation."[13]

Evaluating the Compensation Plan

Once a new compensation plan has been decided, management must carefully evaluate the plan prior to implementation to see the impact on individual salespeople. A good place to start is by looking at the compensation previously earned by each salesperson, and then estimating what compensation each will earn under the new plan.

There are two types of changes that can be made to compensation plans. The first is to increase the incentive component of the plan. The goal of the company is to foster increased sales performance, and to pay the sales force an incentive for achieving this. When successful, both the company and the salespeople win. If salespeople see the change as designed for the company's benefit rather than for their own, there will be resistance, and sales force turnover will likely result. The best salespeople will be the first to leave. This is one reason why, unless management is confident that the new compensation plan will immediately benefit the sales force, a change to increased incentive is usually gradual and often has a guarantee to salespeople for some period of time to ensure that they do not lose. Sometimes, however, a company may wish to increase

Exhibit 10.8

The Impact of Increasing Performance-Based Compensation

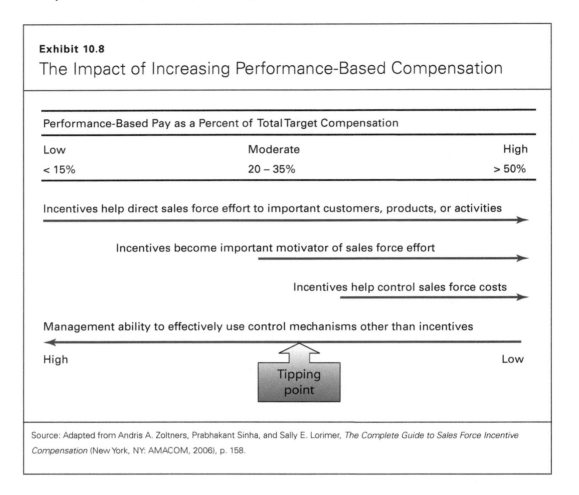

Source: Adapted from Andris A. Zoltners, Prabhakant Sinha, and Sally E. Lorimer, *The Complete Guide to Sales Force Incentive Compensation* (New York, NY: AMACOM, 2006), p. 158.

turnover. Without offering a compensation guarantee, increased incentive may help convince the poorest performing members of the sales force to leave as they may be unable to earn a good salary under a strong performance-based incentive plan.

The second type of change would involve reducing the incentive component and increasing salary. This is probably done less often, but it certainly does happen. There are times when performance-based programs can create an aggressive sales force, or one that loses interest in servicing accounts. They may even develop some questionable, or unethical, practices. In these instances, increasing the salary component may refocus their behaviour. However, care must be taken to ensure that the best salespeople do not lose when such changes are implemented, nor that sales force performance decreases with lower incentive. The Sales Management Today box describes what three companies decided to do to adjust their sales compensation program.

Special Issues in Sales Force Compensation

There are several important compensation issues that require attention. A few have been briefly mentioned in previous sections, but we now discuss these and other issues in some detail. The following sections focus on customer satisfaction and sales force compensation, equal pay, team compensation, and global considerations.

SALES MANAGEMENT **TODAY**

Using Compensation to Focus Behaviour

Companies are increasingly recognizing that adjustments to compensation plans can be used to help redirect the behaviour of salespeople. Some examples follow:

- *Refocus on more profitable products.* When ConAgra Foods wanted to refocus its salespeople to sell more profitable items in its product mix, it changed its commission structure so that salespeople got rewarded for gross margin (50 percent) and for growth (50 percent). This allowed the salespeople to sell the things that were easy to sell (go for growth) and sell the things that increased profitability for the company (go for gross margin).

- *Refocus on more profitable customers.* When a residential carpet manufacturer noticed that its profitability was declining, it needed to refocus its salespeople to sell higher margin products. But, to succeed, the key was to refocus on customers who would buy the higher margin products: upscale retailers and medium-sized dealers.

Compensation was 60 percent salary and 40 percent performance-based, including 3 percent commission on specific "emphasis" products. After one year, sales had grown by 1 percent, but sales of emphasis products had grown by 3 percent, and gross margin was up 12 percent.

- *Refocus on team selling.* Eaton Cutler-Hammer was finding that its salespeople were unable to become experts on all of the products in its broad and complex product line of motor control and electric distribution equipment. As a solution, the company organized its salespeople into three- and four-member groups, where each person was an expert on a subset of the total product line. About 30–40 percent of their sales calls were made as a team. To refocus the salespeople to work as a team, commissions were based on total team performance, but were then split among the various members of the team based on each person's salary grade. This way, senior salespeople, who earned higher salaries, also received higher payout.

Source: Personal interview with Tom Gunter, vice-president sales, ConAgra Foods, August 9, 2006; Andris A. Zoltners, Prabhakant Sinha, and Sally E. Lorimer, *The Complete Guide to Sales Force Incentive Compensation* (New York, NY: AMACOM, 2006), pp. 15–16, 74–76.

CUSTOMER SATISFACTION AND SALES FORCE COMPENSATION

Some companies use customer results measurements in their sales incentive plans. The more common measurements include customer satisfaction, customer loyalty or retention and repeat sales, and customer complaints or returns. These measurements help reinforce to the sales force that the company culture values strong customer relationships. Approximately 10 percent of companies in one research study were found to allocate some portion of their incentive compensation to customer satisfaction.[14] Customer results measurements can isolate the true impact of the salesperson on the customer. They can be particularly valid when they provide a better measure of the salesperson's performance than sales or profitability measures that can be affected by competition, market conditions, the economy, or other factors beyond the salesperson's control. There are several situations where customer performance measurements are more likely to be used:

1. *Company success depends on strong, long-term seller–buyer relationships.* Bill Gates predicts that customer service will become the primary value-added function that a business can offer.[15] Assuming this is true, salespeople will need to be more responsible for servicing customers and for managing customer satisfaction, and management should consider rewarding salespeople who can do this.

2.   *The company sells a commodity product.* As products become more commodity-like, a company's product strategy becomes less important, and its relationship strategy becomes more important. Marketing professor Jim Barnes, author of *Secrets of Customer Relationship Management,* says, "It is my view that a company's ability to set itself apart from its competitors increases as we move away from focusing on the core product (which in many industries today is virtually nondifferentiable) and pay greater attention to the effect on the customer of the interaction with employees."[16] The single employee having the most interaction with the customer is the salesperson.

3.   *The salesperson must invest considerable time learning about the customer.* This is often the situation in information technology and other high-technology markets. Salespeople must spend considerable time understanding the customer's current situation and assessing their needs before they can even begin to think about providing a solution. When successful, they have usually established a sufficiently good seller–buyer relationship and understand the customer's business so well that it becomes easier to sell additional products to the customer than to find new customers. Siebel Systems, for example, pays approximately 40 percent of a salesperson's incentive compensation based on customer satisfaction surveys.[17]

Using customer results measurements in sales incentive plans is not without some drawbacks. One issue is the small sample size that is sometimes available to survey regarding a particular salesperson. At the extreme, a salesperson may have a single account. A related issue is whom to survey within a customer firm. Often, the salesperson must manage multiple relationships within each customer firm. When there is a buying centre involved, should all or only certain members be surveyed? When more than one is surveyed, do the evaluations of all respondents carry equal weight? For some surveys, selection bias may also create problems. That is, some customers are more likely to respond than others. Customers who feel very strongly in favour of the salesperson are more likely to respond than other customers. At the same time, customers who are very dissatisfied with the salesperson or her company are most likely not going to be surveyed as they are no longer customers. Additional selection bias can be introduced if the salesperson selects who can respond to the survey, or if the salesperson can influence the results in other ways.

The use of customer results measurements as a contributor to incentive compensation appears to be declining, at least at the individual salesperson level.[18] However, these types of measurements can be very useful when looking at an entire sales district or region, or across an entire company. A general measure of customer satisfaction at a more aggregate level provides an indicator of whether the particular sales force is doing better or worse.

PAY EQUITY

Pay equity is an important issue for sales managers. All Canadian provinces have pay equity legislation supporting the principle of equal pay for equal work. However, women, in general, still earn far less than men although the gap is closing.[19] Much of the difference can be attributed to conflicting needs of both society and employers that leave women in lower-paying jobs; however, approximately 10 percentage points of the pay difference appears to be due to discrimination.[20] In sales, some sales managers may discriminate against women due to personal beliefs that women are less dedicated to building careers, or have family responsibilities that will interfere with their ability to manage more responsible positions. While gender salary differences may exist across sales positions, the differences are likely to be less in sales than elsewhere in an organization. One reason is because of the incentive component of the total compensation package which pays strictly for performance. There is no reason to suggest that women fail to perform as well as men in sales positions and, in fact, there is a good possibility that women are better at selling, on average. Women are finding career opportunities in real estate, advertising, insurance, financial planning, and many other areas of sales. Ron Burke, professor of organizational behaviour at York University, says, "Obviously, all men aren't the same, nor are all women, but men are more task-oriented and women are more people-oriented."[21] Being people-oriented is important today with the current sales focus on relationship maintenance and building. At the same time, the number of women graduating from Canadian universities is greater than the number of men, and as education and skill become more important, the pay equity issue should diminish. Responsible sales managers will be vigilant to ensure that pay equity is achieved within the sales force. Research supports that both motivation and performance increase when salespeople are paid fairly.[22]

TEAM INCENTIVE COMPENSATION

As mentioned frequently throughout this book, the use of sales teams is growing in popularity. Providing incentive compensation for sales teams creates challenges for many sales managers. An important first consideration is the composition of the sales team. Sometimes sales teams include senior and junior salespeople. Sometimes they include field and inside sales support people. Sometimes they include people from different functional areas within the organization. Regardless of the team composition, there is usually one individual with responsibility for account management. When salespeople manage the interface with the customer, they often view their own contribution to the selling effort as most important, and they often expect the greater incentive contribution. Salespeople who are used to being rewarded for individual effort often view any attempt to move toward team-based compensation unfavourably. This is particularly true the more equal the reward becomes for all members. Most, but not all, team-based incentive plans do reward members differently.

Given the difficulty managing team-based incentive compensation, sales managers are probably wise to move slowly in this direction, experimenting and obtaining feedback as they proceed. One approach might be to provide independent incentive compensation for both individual and team performance targets. If they are independent, then one or more team members can receive individual incentive compensation regardless of whether the team achieves its performance target. At the same time, it would be possible for a team member to get team incentive, even if that person missed his individual performance target. A second approach is to make individual incentive compensation contingent upon team performance. In this instance, sales managers still have a number of options to consider. First, a decision must be made whether all team members receive the same incentive compensation, or on what bases the total incentive will be distributed. Second, a decision must be made whether the allocation of incentive compensation will be made before performance is measured or after performance is measured. In the latter instance, it is possible to adjust incentive compensation allocation on the basis of who has contributed the most to achieving the team performance target. However, the issue now arises as to who will make the allocation decision. The responsibility may rest with the sales manager, or may be given to one or more team members.

By now, you should see how this issue can quickly become complicated. Potential problems are more likely as the relative size of the incentive compensation increases. They are also more likely to arise if the incentive compensation is financial. Some companies consider making individual incentive compensation financial, and team-based incentives non-financial. It is possible to provide everyone on the team with individual performance targets, and individual financial compensation, but provide all members with a non-financial incentive. If the goal of rewarding the team is really to foster team morale, then a team-building performance reward should be considered. Rewards could include a white-water rafting or fishing trip, a round of golf, tickets to a professional sporting event, or a weekend at a resort or spa.

GLOBAL CONSIDERATIONS

As growth in domestic markets declines, companies are increasingly looking to global markets for growth. Many companies simply appoint local distributors or hire manufacturer's agents for global markets, as these approaches limit risk since compensation is simply paid based on sales performance. That is, they earn distributor discounts or commissions based on the level of their sales. Other companies must open global sales offices, particularly if their product and service knowledge are complex, or if they are serving global customers who require consistency across their global locations. In these instances, the global sales organization must carefully decide the appropriate mix of national and expatriate salespeople for each global market. Each type of salesperson creates compensation issues.

Particularly when companies hire national salespeople, there are often legal and cultural compensation issues which differ from one country to another. Because Canadians view individual performance highly, we are likely to pay higher incentive compensation in Canada than would be paid to salespeople in many parts of the world. Some countries require employers to pay higher taxes and more fringe benefits than Canada does. Productivity issues are also a concern as work ethic also varies from one country to another, meaning that in some countries, you may have to pay more for less.

Expatriate salespeople provide a host of different problems. Historically, expatriate salespeople received a group of supplementary benefits, which could include moving expenses to and from their assigned country, housing and cost-of-living allowances, education reimbursement for children who might have to attend private institutions, annual paid return home for the salesperson and her family, and, sometimes, an overseas premium to offset any inconvenience of living abroad.[23] However, as one human resources manager says, "The definition of expatriates used to be people who lived off their expenses and banked their salaries."[24] At many companies now, including hers, the attitude toward compensating expatriates has changed and the goal is now to provide compensation packages that allow salespeople to maintain the same standard of living that they would have at home. Many companies are also beginning to find an increased interest in global traffic, and newer employees often welcome the experience of working abroad. As well as the cultural experience, global experience also helps position salespeople for promotion in companies that value this.

There are, of course, global assignments where salary premiums are appropriate. Some assignments involve personal risk or hardship. There are also instances where, if the assignment is for an extended period, the wealth accumulation that is possible in an offshore location might be considerably lower than would be possible at home, and simply allowing a salesperson to maintain the same standard of living as she would at home would mean that she actually would be at a disadvantage upon her return to Canada. Many of the factors that must be considered when designing compensation plans for expatriates are complex ones that most sales managers seldom have experience with, so human resources professionals should be involved in the compensation planning process.

SUMMARY

1. **Discuss the strengths and weaknesses of various compensation methods.** Straight salary and straight commission compensation plans represent two extremes when it comes to compensating salespeople. Straight salary plans provide maximum control over salespeople's activities, but provide little incentive for salespeople to strive for superior performance. They provide the company with a fixed cost, making budgeting and administration easy, and they also foster higher levels of employee loyalty. For salespeople, they provide maximum security. Straight commission plans provide minimum control over salespeople's activities, but provide maximum incentive for salespeople to strive for superior performance. They provide the company with a variable cost, but this can be an advantage for companies with limited financial resources. They do not foster high levels of employee loyalty, as salespeople are more likely to perceive that they work for themselves. Salespeople often have less security, but with the right company or product, superior salespeople can earn outstanding incomes. The great majority of companies use combination compensation plans to take advantage of the best of both straight salary and straight commission plans.

2. **Explain the role of selling expenses and employee benefits in compensation plans.** Selling expenses include all of the expenses that salespeople incur as a result of selling-related activities that they perform for their company. Companies reimburse selling expenses through unlimited, limited, or per diem repayment plans. Employee benefits constitute an indirect form of compensation intended to improve the quality of the work lives and personal lives of employees. Selling expenses and employee benefits are both an important part of a salesperson's compensation package.

3. **Design an effective sales force compensation mix.** When putting the entire compensation package together, management should have in mind the total income it would like its average salesperson to make. There is a danger of paying too little or too much. Deciding the appropriate mix of compensation requires some creativity. The size of the performance-based component should be decided based on the sales manager's preferred balance among (1) directing sales force effort on important customers, products, or activities, (2) motivating sales force effort, (3) controlling sales force cost, and (4) using mechanisms other than incentives to control the sales force. The compensation plan becomes the primary means of controlling sales force behaviour when the performance-based component exceeds 30 percent.

4. **Discuss several special topics related to sales force compensation.** Several special topics related to sales force compensation were introduced. First, customer satisfaction is beginning to play a more important role in the compensation of salespeople. Second, pay equity legislation is becoming increasingly important and all provinces now have pay equity legislation. Third, in a team-selling environment, there are issues of deciding the impact each member has on achieving sales, and the percentage of incentive compensation that should be given to each member of the team. Finally, many sales forces now operate globally. There are issues related to using expatriate salespeople and national salespeople when operating in global markets.

KEY TERMS

compensation plan **281**

total target compensation **281**

straight salary plan **282**

straight commission plan **284**

bonus **286**

combination compensation plan **287**

selling expenses **290**

expense account padding **290**

employee benefits **291**

REVIEW QUESTIONS

1. Define *total target compensation* and explain why it is important.

2. What are the advantages and disadvantages of a straight salary compensation plan?

3. Under what conditions might a company consider using a straight commission compensation plan?

4. What is a *per diem expense repayment plan?* Why would a company choose to use this type of plan?

5. Compare and contrast *sales eagles* and *sales crows*. What percentage of a sales force would be an acceptable level of sales crows? Be prepared to defend your answer.

6. Explain the "30 percent rule" and what happens when it is violated.

7. Should salespeople always be responsible for customer satisfaction? Why or why not?

8. Is *pay equity* always a good principle to follow? Be prepared to defend your position.

9. What are some issues that must be considered when compensating selling teams with incentive compensation?

10. Explain when it would be appropriate for a sales manager to pay a salary premium for a global sales assignment.

APPLICATION EXERCISES

1. Visit **www.google.ca** or another search engine of your choice. Under "advanced search," type "commission only sales" in the "with the exact phrase" space, and "Canada" in the "with at least one of the words" space. How many hits do you get? Are any of them potentially of interest to you? Why or why not? Why do you suppose these types of sales positions are so frequently offered? Before you would accept such a position, what would you like to know about the company or the product?

2. Superior Car Sales is a dealership that sells cars for several manufacturers. It sells a relatively inexpensive but very popular line of cars (approximately 1500 units per year) and a very high-end line of cars for another manufacturer (approximately 180 units per year). The company has two distinct sales forces that report to separate sales managers. All salespeople are paid a base salary, which gets increased each January, and a commission for each vehicle sold. For the less expensive line of vehicles, the salesperson gets a commission of $100 per unit, paid at the end of the month that the vehicle is sold. For the more expensive line of vehicles, the salesperson gets a commission of $600, but gets $50 per month for each month during

the year following the sale, assuming that the salesperson remains with the company. Which of these two commission payment methods would you prefer (ignoring the value of the commission)? Explain why the company might not want to use the same method of paying commissions for both sales forces.

3. When Urvi Dosanjh was hired as sales manager for a well known consumer packaged-goods company, her vice-president of sales instructed her to increase the gross margin percentage on sales for her branch. Selling prices were not under her control, nor were costs. Urvi realized that the only thing she could do would be to focus salespeople on more profitable items in the company's product line. At the same time, she knew that her boss would not be happy if the total sales revenue from the branch were to decline. She therefore needed both sales growth and an increased gross margin percentage. Currently salespeople received 80 percent of their compensation as base salary, and 20 percent for reaching target sales revenue quotas. Recommend a new compensation strategy that Urvi could use and explain why you have chosen it.

4. You are the sales director of a company that employs selling teams to sell expensive communications equipment for remote locations. Each team includes a lead generator and qualifier whose responsibility is to find sales leads and qualify them, a customer relationship management person whose main responsibility is to coordinate all face-to-face interactions with the customer, a technical support person whose responsibility is to assess customer needs and ensure that the proper system is selected and installed, and a customer service representative who is basically an inside sales contact person who ensures the customer gets good service after the sale is made. Commissions on sales are 20 percent. What alternatives could be considered for dividing the commission equitably among the four-member teams? What are the strengths and weaknesses of the alternatives you have identified? What would you recommend?

Aries Corporate Coffee Services   CASE **10.1**

Aries Corporate Coffee Services rents quality coffee machines to business customers and sells a variety of coffee making supplies to be used with its equipment. For larger customers, coffee machines are sometimes supplied free, as long as coffee beans and supplies are purchased from Aries. Unlike its competitors, Aries supplies whole beans that are then ground by the customer immediately before the coffee is brewed.

The company originally paid straight commission to salespeople but had grown to the point where it could afford to utilize a combination compensation plan, providing greater security for its salespeople. It hoped to reduce sales force turnover and also attract some younger sales recruits who had been dissuaded by the straight commission plan. The redesigned sales compensation plan was implemented in 2005. Salespeople received a base salary: $24 000 per year for new sales recruits, and it increased by $1500 per year for each additional year of service. Commissions started at 6 percent of sales for inexperienced salespeople and were reduced in increments of 0.5 percent as sales revenues grew. Salespeople who generated revenue in excess of $400 000 received the lowest commission rate, 4 percent. The following schedule illustrates the relationship between salary and commission:

Sales Level ($)	Commission Rate (%)
200 000	6.0
250 000	5.5
300 000	5.0
350 000	4.5
400 000	4.0

Some of the younger, less experienced salespeople seemed to like the plan, but two years after it was implemented, you overheard Laura Dunne, your highest performing salesperson, talking to several other salespeople in the staff lounge. "I hate this new compensation plan. If I was new to the company, it might be okay. But, I've been here almost 10 years and I feel like I'm working harder and harder for less and less. It isn't really worth the extra effort to sell more because the company keeps reducing your commission rate."

CRITICAL-THINKING QUESTION

As Laura's sales manager, what would you do? Be prepared to defend your recommendations.

CASE 10.2 Prairie Ag Products

Prairie Ag Products, formerly known as Prairie Fertilizer, sold a complete range of fertilizers, chemicals, seeds, and feed to farmers in Alberta, Saskatchewan, and Manitoba. The company changed its name because of its expanding product line, and soon afterward, it changed its compensation plan. The goal of the company was to pay just slightly more than similar firms so that it could attract and retain better employees. The company was planning on an average total target compensation of $50 000 for its salespeople, with 60 percent coming from salary, and 40 percent coming from performance-based bonuses.

The new compensation plan was implemented on January 1, 2007, but by the end of June, it was apparent that salespeople were unlikely to meet their sales quotas. In fact, it looked like they would be unlikely to get much more than 25 percent of their total compensation from performance-based bonuses. One of your salespeople in Saskatchewan has just tendered his resignation because "he has an opportunity to make considerably more money elsewhere." You are concerned that you may lose more salespeople if changes are not made quickly.

CRITICAL-THINKING QUESTION

As the sales manager for Prairie Ag Products, what would you do? Be prepared to defend your recommendations.

Chapter 11

Leading Salespeople

After completing this chapter, you should be able to

1. Understand the personal traits, personality, and needs of effective sales leaders.

2. Explain how effective sales leaders use power.

3. Understand how to effectively lead change.

4. Explain how to effectively lead individual salespeople.

5. Explain how to effectively lead the sales force.

6. Understand the range of personnel issues that a sales leader must face.

In all high-performing companies, there is strong leadership. Nowhere is leadership more important than in turn-around strategies. Everyone admires the strong leader who takes over an ailing company and makes it an industry star.

Bill McDermott is one such star. He became CEO of SAP America in 2002, a time when the Canadian and U.S. subsidiary of the German software giant was experiencing growth that was less than half that of its European division. By 2006, SAP America was the leader in its field. How did he do it? Bill McDermott says, "Change is only possible when it is tied to a very specific vision." His vision was to transform the company's message: no longer would they try to sell customers on how good SAP was, but instead would show customers how good they could become if they used SAP software solutions. It was a very customer-centric solution that clearly put the customer first. Bill estimates that he spends 70 percent of his own time dealing directly with customers. Other leadership traits Bill McDermott believes you need include enthusiasm, integrity, time-management, a future-orientation, and an ability to deal with and learn from disappointment.[1]

When Mark Hurd became CEO of Hewlett-Packard in 2005, the company was clearly in trouble. Sales and profits were down considerably. What impact his early sales experience had on his view of selling is not clear, but Mark Hurd tells a story about his third day in sales at NCR in 1980. He got a $250 order from a customer but was told by a person in his billing department that he had not completed the order correctly. When Mark told his manager what had happened, his manager phoned the billing department and reportedly said, "Hey, did my man just come down there with an order? The next time he does, I want you to get your ass out from behind your desk, and I want you to shake his hand. And I want you to thank him for keeping your ass employed. If there's anything wrong with the order, I want you to fix it so he can get about the job of continuing to keep you employed." Hurd swears the story is true, and he now has a customer-centric vision at Hewlett-Packard. One of his first actions was to decentralize the company's 17 000-strong sales force into the business units whose products they were selling. One sales executive who reports to Mark refers to him as "our chief sales officer." He says that when there are sales problems, if Mark is not already dealing with a customer, he'll stop whatever he is doing to see how he can help.[2]

Teresa Cascioli is another star. When she became CEO of Hamilton-based Lakeport Beverage Corporation in 1999, it was a small struggling brewery. Speaking of her leadership, she says, "Have the courage to do what's right and not necessarily what's popular. What other people think you should do might not be what's right for the entire company. You always have to think what's right for the entire business all the time." What was right? Lakeport sales now exceed $50 million and it owns the first beer from a small brewery to make The Beer Store's top-10 list in Ontario. A niche marketing strategy focused on both product and price and an aggressive sales team led to the company's success. Teresa Cascioli says, "Sales is not just about selling; it's about collecting information and passing it along so that an organization can be more successful."[3]

In all of these examples, you can sense strength, vision, enthusiasm, and focus. These are all "C-level" executives in their organizations, but they all have a customer-centric focus. They all know and support the value of a strong sales force. They are the types of senior executives who instill confidence throughout their organization and who support and empower sales managers and salespeople to do what needs to be done to keep happy customers. This chapter is focused on the importance of leadership skills for sales managers. The next section begins by discussing the difference between management and leadership.

Leadership Is Not Management

Searching the word *leadership* on Google gets 163 000 000 results. A search for books on leadership at Amazon.com gets 223 729 results; at Chapters.indigo.ca, it gets 17 747 results.[4] Leadership is a popular topic. Even a small search will reveal many definitions and many theories. In the context of sales management, **leadership** can be defined as the manager's ability to influence the actions of salespeople to achieve the goals of the organization.

Leadership is different from management. Management is concerned with steady-state process: problem-solving, planning, budgeting, and controlling. Leadership is concerned with influencing salespeople's actions by appealing to their emotions so that they are inspired to help achieve superior results. A true leader is held in high esteem and is admired by those who follow him. He inspires trust and loyalty. Management has formal authority, given to its members through titles, such as "sales manager." Leadership does not come with a title. People have leadership skills to varying degrees. Therefore, a sales manager may be a good leader, or he may have limited leadership skills. When a sales manager has weak leadership skills, sometimes an informal leader will arise among the sales force and provide the leadership that is needed. Managers are not necessarily leaders, and leaders are sometimes not managers. In an ideal situation, however, the sales manager should have strong leadership ability as well as management ability if he wants to achieve superior results, and if he wishes for promotion beyond sales management.

What is it that sets leaders apart from others? In the following section, the traits, personality, and needs of leaders are discussed.

Leaders: Personal Traits, Personality, and Needs

Personal traits are distinguishing characteristics that people have; they are, for example, submissive or authoritarian, decisive or hesitant, shy or bold, aloof or friendly, controlled or expressive. There are many personal traits that effective leaders may have, but there are nine in particular that have strong research support.[5] Of course, not all researchers support the same list of traits, nor is it suggested that you must have every trait to be an effective leader. It is also possible that you can develop some of these traits, although it will likely be easier for you to develop some than others. The nine traits are shown in Exhibit 11.1 and include the following:

1. *Dominance.* Effective leaders are dominant. They are take-charge people who want to be involved and who want to make decisions. They are assertive. Dominance is perhaps the most important trait because it affects all of the other traits. Without dominance, a sales manager will likely lack self-confidence. He may feel stressed and become insensitive to others. He may lose energy and be less stable in his job.
2. *High energy.* With high energy comes enthusiasm, drive, desire, and stamina. People with high energy tolerate stress and frustration. They are doers. They get things done because they take initiative to do so.
3. *Self-confidence.* Self-confident people believe they can. They trust their judgment and their ability to make decisions. They are more likely to challenge themselves through higher but realistic objectives, and to foster confidence in others.

Exhibit 11.1
Personality Dimensions, Leadership Traits, and Motivational Needs

"Big Five" Personality Dimensions	Traits of Effective Leaders	Motivational Needs
Extraversion	Dominance ⟶	Power
Conscientiousness	High energy	
	Self-confidence ⟶	Achievement
	Integrity	
Agreeableness	Sensitivity to others ⟶	Affiliation
Emotional stability		Affiliation
	Stability ⟶	Power
Openness to experience	Intelligence ⟶	Achievement
	Flexibility ⟶	Affiliation
	Locus of control ⟶	Power

Source: Adapted from Robert N. Lussier and Christopher F. Achua, *Leadership: Theory, Application, Skill Development,* Second Edition. (Toronto, ON: Thomson Southwestern, 2004), pp. 30–43.

4. *Locus of control.* People with an internal locus of control are referred to as *internalizers.* Effective leaders are internalizers. They take responsibility and believe that they control their own fate; their behaviour affects their performance.[6] Externalizers, by contrast, believe they have no control over their fate and are quick to place blame elsewhere for their failure.

5. *Stability.* Leaders who are stable are in control of their emotions, are positive, and feel secure. Effective leaders know their strengths and weaknesses, and are concerned more with self-improvement than being defensive.[7]

6. *Integrity.* Integrity is demonstrated when you achieve congruence between what you know, what you say, and what you do.[8] People with integrity are honest, ethical, and trustworthy.

7. *Intelligence.* Cognitive intelligence refers to the ability to analyze situations, think critically, and solve problems. It is measured by IQ. An alternative type of intelligence, emotional intelligence, has been demonstrated to be important to leadership success. It is measured by EQ and is a strong indicator of ability to work well with others. There are five components of EQ, as described in the Sales Management in Action box, "Hire for 'People Smarts,'" in Chapter 7 on page 214.

8. *Flexibility.* Effective leaders must be flexible so they can embrace change. They have to be able to adjust to changing situations if they hope to lead others to accept change.

9. *Sensitivity to others.* Being sensitive to others means being able to both feel and express empathy. Effective leaders can relate to other people as individuals and understand their needs and how they feel.

Personality is a combination of personal traits that classifies a person's behaviour. A person's personality affects his perceptions, attitudes, and behaviour. Knowing a person's personality helps predict his behaviour and, therefore, his job performance. There are many methods to classify personality, but one method that is currently popular because of its strong research support is referred to as the Big Five Model of Personality.[9] The purpose of this model is to categorize all of the personal traits used to describe someone into one of five dimensions.[10] These five dimensions are shown in Exhibit 11.1 and include the following:

1. *Extroversion.* Extroverts are dominant people who are willing to take charge and, if necessary, confront others. They are comfortable in social settings and often have a network of close associates that they have been able to develop because of their outgoing nature.

2. *Conscientiousness.* People who are conscientious are hard-working and achievement-oriented. They are dependable, organized, and responsible.

3. *Agreeableness.* Agreeable people are compassionate, easygoing, friendly, sociable, and warm, and get along well with other people. They are liked by others and have many friends.

4. *Socially adjusted.* Leaders who have emotional stability display self-control. They are comfortable recognizing the accomplishments of others. They are positive, relaxed, secure, and calm under stress—all the things that you will not find in neurotics. (*Neuroticism* is the term used for one of the original factors, but it is changed here to a positive descriptor.)

5. *Openness to experience.* People who are open to new experiences are willing to try new things. They are innovative, are willing to accept or even initiate change, and will take risks when necessary.

Employment experts estimate that personality profiles are used by as many as 40 percent of employers to predict job success.[11] While it is easy to see the importance of having some degree of all five of these dimensions of personality to be an effective leader, it is also informative to see why

---

Exhibit 11.2

Why and How Successful Executives Get Derailed

1. They had specific performance problems.
2. They were insensitive to others (bullying, intimidating, abrasive).
3. They were cold, aloof, and arrogant.
4. They betrayed their trust.
5. They over-managed and failed to delegate or build a solid team.
6. They were overly ambitious and focused on promotion.
7. They failed to staff effectively.
8. They were not strategic thinkers; often hid inability by becoming mired in detail.
9. They were unable to adapt to a new boss with a different style.
10. They were over-dependent on a mentor or advocate.

Source: Morgan W. McCall, Jr., and Michael M. Lombardo, "Off the Track: Why and How Successful Executives Get Derailed," © Center for Creative Leadership, Technical Report Number 1, January 1983, p. 6.

---

and how successful executives have their careers derailed. Exhibit 11.2 provides of list of 10 reasons cited by 21 managers whose careers were derailed. On average, they had two of these characteristics.

McClelland's Theory of Learned Needs, introduced in Chapter 9 (see Exhibit 9.2), tries to explain behaviour based on three specific needs: power, achievement, and affiliation. McClelland argues that all people possess these three basic needs, although one need tends to be dominant in each of us and motivates our behaviour. McClelland found one particular leader motive profile that was a reliable predictor of leader effectiveness: higher need for power, which was greater than the need for affiliation. Need for achievement was usually somewhere between the need for power and the need for affiliation.[12] Why this profile?

Effective leaders have a strong need for power. Power is necessary to influence others. As you will soon discover, there are many kinds of power. McClelland argued that power is neither good nor bad. *Personalized power* is power that is used for personal gain at the expense of others. *Socialized power* can be used to help oneself and others.[13] This is the preferred type of power of effective leaders and includes the personal traits of sensitivity to others (from the agreeableness personality dimension) and sensitivity (from the emotional stability personality dimension).

Effective leaders have a moderate need for achievement. People who have a very high need for achievement, in contrast, tend to use personalized power as they are overly ambitious and focused more on promotion—one of the reasons for career derailment in Exhibit 11.2. Leaders score high on the conscientiousness personality dimension and also possess personal traits of the openness-to-experience personality dimension.

Effective leaders have a lower need for affiliation than for power or achievement. Leaders with a high need for affiliation have been found to show favouritism to friends.[14] They are more likely to let their relationships with subordinates get in the way of their doing some of the things that are often necessary, such as implementing unpopular changes, or dismissing underachieving or disruptive employees. Recall Teresa Cascioli's comment in the opening vignette about always making the right decision for the whole organization.

Now that you have a clearer view of an effective leader's personality profile, the next section will discuss the various types of power that may be used to influence others.

Power and Leadership

Effective leaders must have power; otherwise, they could not influence others. **Power** is the ability to influence others in order to get things done. Power does not have to be exercised, as long as it is perceived to exist. There are seven bases of power that organizational leaders may use. The original five bases of power included legitimate, reward, coercive, expert, and referent power.[15] More recently, information and connection power have been added.[16] Each of these is now described.

- *Legitimate power.* Legitimate power is power that a sales manager has because of the formal position she has in the organization's hierarchy. It comes with the title that she is given. For example, she might say, "As your new sales manager, I have decided that I will make two sales calls per month with each of you." This sales manager is indicating that, because of her position, she has the authority to make this decision.

- *Reward power.* Reward power exists when the sales manager can provide rewards to salespeople for meeting specific sales objectives. For example, she might say, "I will arrange a three-month gym membership for any salesperson who meets this quarter's sales target." This sales manager is indicating that she can reward salespeople for their performance. Note, however, that if anyone has a very low valence for this reward, the sales manager's reward power is reduced. Another issue with the use of reward power is that, unless managed carefully, it tends to diminish over time.

- *Coercive power.* Coercive power exists when a sales manager can use punishment or can withhold a reward to gain compliance. For example, she might say, "Salespeople who do not complete their sales call reports in a timely fashion will have a warning letter placed in their employee file." This is clearly a threat. Note, however, that coercive power exists only if the salesperson cares about the punishment. A salesperson who has already decided to leave the company will care little, and this will reduce the sales manager's coercive power over him. Salespeople may come to resent the use of coercive power. If used often, or used against a large percentage of the sales force at one time, hostile opposition to the sales manager could result. Coercive power is best used to enforce rules and policies and to maintain discipline, but it should still be used with caution.

- *Expert power.* Expert power exists when the sales manager has skills or knowledge that is valued by the sales force. A sales manager should have experience as a successful salesperson in order to have some credibility with the sales force. She can increase her expert power by attending training programs, keeping current with technology, joining relevant associations, and reading job-related material. She must then make all of this visible to the sales force so they perceive her as having relevant expertise. Salespeople, particularly less experienced ones, will also ascribe expert power to a sales manager who has had a long and distinguished management career with one or several companies.

- *Referent power.* Referent power exists when a sales manager's personality leads others to identify with, respect, or admire her, and want to emulate or follow her. Referent power is not related to a person's position within the organization. Referent power may be gained by understanding and appealing to people's emotions. Research has demonstrated that referent power, and expert power, are related positively to salespeople's satisfaction with their sales manager.[17]

- *Information power.* Information power exists when the sales manager has data (information) desired by salespeople. This differs from expert power and recognizes that a sales manager may have access to specific information and decide whether she wishes to share it with others, and in what form she will disseminate it. She plays a role similar to the role played by a gatekeeper in a buying centre (refer to Chapter 5). A sales manager can increase information power by managing information flow, making sure that information flows through the manager where possible.

- *Connection power.* Connection power exists when a sales manager has or is believed to have relationships with influential people. The sales manager who is believed to have personal connections with an influential senior executive will have stronger connection power. Connection power can be increased through developing a network of influential associates.

In order for the sales manager to have power over a salesperson or the sales force, the salesperson or sales force must be dependent on the sales manager. That is, power and dependence always coexist. Without dependence, there is no power. Some examples have already been provided that suggest the difficulty of using reward power or coercive power when a salesperson is not dependent (does not value the reward, or does not care about the punishment). Problems sometimes occur when the sales manager and members of the sales force have and exercise different bases of power. For example, a new sales manager may have to resort to using legitimate, reward, and coercive power to influence members of the sales force. Expert power may reside with several senior members of the sales force. Referent power may belong to an informal leader of the sales force that other salespeople admire. Another member of the sales force may have connection power due to a personal relationship with executives senior to the sales manager. It is easy to see the difficulty that could arise for an inexperienced sales manager who might attempt to use legitimate power, and who then must deal with members of the sales force who attempt to countervail her power by using their own bases of power.

It is wise, therefore, for sales managers to limit the use of legitimate, reward, and coercive power and to attempt to develop both expert and referent power as early as possible.

Leading Change

Organizations today are constantly changing. There are increasingly intense domestic and global competition, innovative new technologies, and constantly evolving market demands brought about as a result. Organizations respond by re-engineering business processes, adding more advanced products and broadening product lines, focusing on new markets, and acquiring or merging with other companies or forming strategic partnerships with customers, suppliers, or even competitors. Perhaps nowhere in an organization is change more apparent than in the sales force. Sometimes the change required is a major one; frequently the change is simply an adjustment to market conditions or the result of an improvement initiative. Effective leaders need to be comfortable with change and must be able to lead and manage the change process. Regardless of whether the change is major or minor, there will always be some resistance. The "20–50–30 rule" suggests that 20 percent of people will embrace change, 50 percent will be neutral, and 30 percent will resist change. Effective change leaders work with those who embrace change, try to gain the support of those who are neutral, and do not waste effort on those who resist change.[18] Exhibit 11.3 illustrates one model for managing the change process that can be used to discuss both major and minor changes affecting the sales force. Each of the five stages is now described.

Exhibit 11.3

A Model for Managing the Change Process

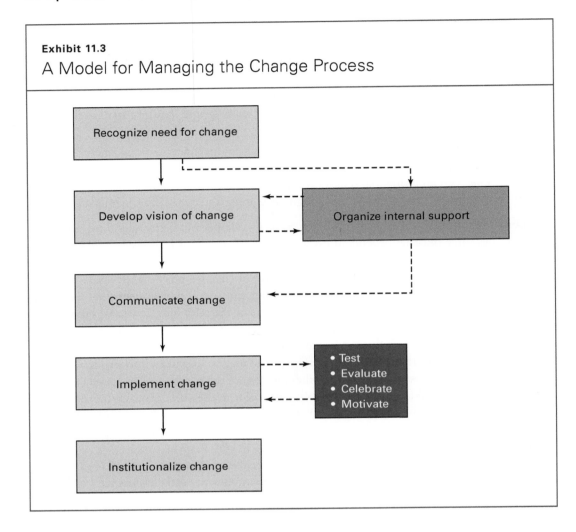

1. *Recognize need for change.* Nothing will change until someone recognizes the need for change. Change can be reactionary or proactive. It can be crisis-driven or evolutionary improvement. It can be directed from a higher corporate level, or it can be initiated by the sales manager or within the sales force. However, the need must still be recognized.

2. *Develop change vision.* Once a needed change is recognized, it is important to have a change vision, including a guideline for achieving change and an idea of what will be different as a result of the change. At this stage, the sales manager must decide the role that other members of the sales force will play in the change process. If the change is a crisis change that has been directed from higher up in the organization, the sales manager may simply have to move to the next stage. She may or may not have been involved with developing the change vision. If it is a minor change, the sales manager may again decide to communicate the change without seeking input, or may decide to involve a select number of important salespeople before a formal announcement is made. This will help motivate these salespeople and gain their commitment as they become involved in the process. For any change

that is sufficiently important that it is likely to engender resistance, the sales manager should most likely organize internal support for the change early in the process. This does two things. First, it gets input from the more important people who will be affected by the change and allows them to provide valuable input that will help establish the change vision. Second, these people can informally communicate ideas and solicit responses from other salespeople who will be affected. Again, this might help improve the change vision, and will be an important factor in gaining general support for the change.

3. *Communicate change.* It is important that the sales manager communicate the change once the change vision is decided. Even if the change has been communicated by the informal communications network, a formal announcement should follow from the sales manager. This is the signal that things are about to happen. The communication should include information on what change will occur, rationale for the change, and expected benefits from the change. For crisis change, the sales manager needs to be decisive and direct when announcing change. While support will not necessarily be higher, resistance will likely be less if people understand that there is total commitment for the change. In the event that people will be negatively affected by the change, the sales manager may need to have one-on-one communication with individuals following a group communication. Of course, once communication begins, it should be an important part of the process from that point forward.

4. *Implement change.* This is a critical stage in the process. For some changes, the sales manager may have to commit to a course of action early, and there may be no opportunity to reverse the change once an action is started if the change timeframe is very short. In these instances, the opening moves should be bold and dramatic, and should signal that the change is proceeding. For some changes, the process should proceed incrementally. In these instances, small changes can be tested and the outcomes evaluated to see whether the appropriate step is the next previously planned step or whether adjustments now need to be made. Small successes should be celebrated, and recognized and rewarded to help motivate continued internal momentum for change. Small and early successes can foster pride, and build confidence and enthusiasm.[19]

5. *Institutionalize change.* This is the final stage in the change process. It involves institutionalizing new values and behaviours into the culture. This will help prevent a reversal to old attitudes and behaviours following change.

Leading Individual Salespeople

Sales managers must lead both individual salespeople and a collection of salespeople, the sales force. The success of the entire sales force depends on the sales manager's ability to lead and get the best performance from each salesperson. Two topics will be discussed with respect to leading the salesperson as an individual: situational leadership style and coaching.

SITUATIONAL LEADERSHIP STYLE

Situational leadership is an approach to leadership based on the theory that the most effective leadership style is one that matches the particular situation that the leader faces. In the case of sales managers, it means that a single leadership style will not be effective when dealing with individual salespeople. Salespeople vary in terms of personality and personal maturity, skills and ability, motivation, and experience. A leadership style that works with a new sales recruit fresh from college or university will not work well with a 20-year veteran who knows her territory and products well. Exhibit 11.4 illustrates one situational leadership model with four leadership styles: telling, persuading, partnering, and delegating. The leader's behaviour depends on whether he is more or less *task-focused*, and more or less *relationship-focused*. As he becomes more task-focused, his behaviour will become more directive. His primary goal is to accomplish the task. As he becomes more relationship-focused, his behaviour will become more supportive. His goal to create and maintain a positive working relationship is increased. Exhibit 11.4 suggests that the normal pattern of leadership style changes from telling, to persuading, to partnering, to delegating as a salesperson's career develops. This is more likely to be true if the salesperson who is being led has started as a very inexperienced salesperson and has grown continually in the sales position. However, there will be some variability in this pattern depending on other factors related to particular situations. Sometimes, a sales manager may move forward in this normal sequence only to find that he must backtrack for a period. Each of the four situational leadership styles in this model is now discussed.

When the leader is *high task-oriented and low relationship-oriented*, he will be very direct and will not provide much support. This is the *telling style*. The sales manager simply tells the salesperson what to do: "I want you to make one call per month on your 'A' accounts and one call every three months on your 'B' accounts." This style works well when the salesperson is inexperienced. She may have limited ability but high commitment to do as directed because she trusts that the experienced sales manager knows best and she wants to succeed. It could also be necessary

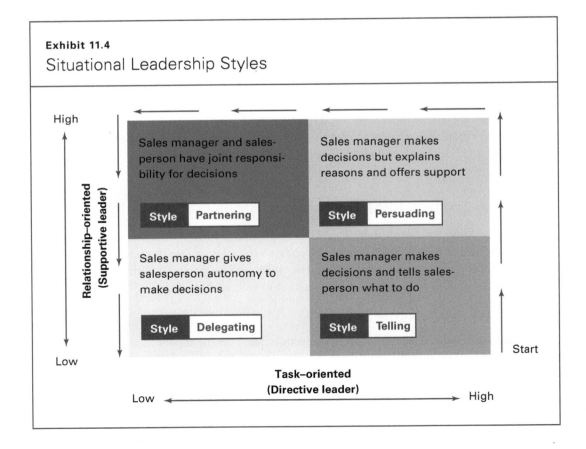

Exhibit 11.4
Situational Leadership Styles

Sales manager and salesperson have joint responsibility for decisions **Style Partnering**	Sales manager makes decisions but explains reasons and offers support **Style Persuading**
Sales manager gives salesperson autonomy to make decisions **Style Delegating**	Sales manager makes decisions and tells salesperson what to do **Style Telling**

Relationship-oriented (Supportive leader): Low → High

Task-oriented (Directive leader): Low → High

Start

to use this approach on a more experienced salesperson who refuses to follow guidelines but whose performance is low. With this leadership style, communication is one-way. Allowing two-way communication might lead to a situation where the salesperson perceives there to be some flexibility allowed with respect to what is required. This style seldom works for a long period of time. It does not take a new recruit very long to establish some experience and want to experiment and have more control over what they do. Experienced salespeople may accept this leadership style for a short period of time or with respect to one or more aspects of their job, but will likely resent continued intrusion and direction from the sales manager.

When the leader is *high task-oriented and high relationship-oriented*, he will be very direct, but he will also be supportive of the salesperson. This is the *persuading style*. The sales manager tries to persuade the salesperson to perform required behaviours: "It is important that you call on your 'A' accounts once each month. These are important accounts we must cultivate for new business. Calling regularly lets them know you are interested and willing to provide outstanding service. Is there anything I can do to make it easier for you to do this?" This style works well when the salesperson is still somewhat inexperienced, but her motivation and commitment may be declining as she wants to gain greater control over her own activities. It could also be necessary to use this approach on a more experienced salesperson who needs some direction, but who will do as she is directed as long as she understands the reasons for any requested behaviour. Communication in this situation is still largely one-way, but there is some two-way communication as the sales manager tries to be more supportive. There are some sales forces that will need this style of leadership indefinitely: sales forces comprising salespeople who are experienced but have limited ability or commitment, in particular.

When the leader is *low task-oriented and high relationship-oriented*, he will be supportive of the salesperson, and will provide limited direction. This is the *partnering style*. The sales manager encourages active participation in the decision-making by the salesperson and supports their suggestions or helps them recognize better solutions: "Geeta, you have done an excellent job getting that account to buy our expendable items. Now, how can we get them to purchase more capital items?" This style works well when the salesperson is experienced, but her commitment is variable. This salesperson needs little direction from the sales manager as she will more than likely know what to do. She will, however, need encouragement, challenge, and recognition for success. Two-way communication is important here. The salesperson and sales manager share the decision-making.

When the leader is *low task-oriented and low relationship-oriented*, he will provide limited, if any, support or direction for the salesperson. This is the *delegating style*. In effect, even if the actual words are not used, the sales manager is saying, "Geeta, this is your territory. These are your customers. You know what is expected of you and you know how to do it. If you need help, let me know." This leadership style works best with experienced salespeople who know what to do and have the commitment to do it. They don't need much encouragement. However, a wise sales manager will ensure that they still get lots of recognition for any success they do achieve. While they are motivated by things other than recognition, everyone likes to be appreciated and to have their accomplishments known.

COACHING

Coaching can be used for several purposes. It was first introduced in Chapter 7 because it is frequently used as part of the company's sales training program. However, in this chapter, **coaching** is defined as an interpersonal process between the sales manager and the salesperson in which the sales manager provides constructive feedback and encouragement to the salesperson with the goal of improving sales performance. This is certainly training as well, but it is specific intervention training rather than general sales training. When coaching is used to correct performance deficiencies and is done by the sales manager, its success depends on the leadership ability of the sales manager. The appropriate leadership style, with respect to the four leadership styles recently discussed, should be a *persuading style*. The sales manager needs to be highly directive because a specific problem is the focus of the coaching, and he needs to be highly supportive because this intervention will only work if the sales manager and the salesperson share a good working relationship. The salesperson must see that the sales manager's goal is to help her develop attitudes and behaviours that will improve sales performance. Donald Cooper—Canadian consultant, international speaker, and award-winning retailer—jokes, "When you die there is an express line at the Pearly Gates for coaches." He recognizes the value of a good coach. Someone who has the ability to motivate others to succeed while also giving them the ability to succeed is both important and rare.[20]

Among the specific sales process problems that can be addressed through coaching are poor prospecting habits, inadequate pre-call planning, weak sales presentations, inability to handle buyer resistance appropriately, poor negotiating skills, weak closing skills, and failure to service customers after the sale. The coaching process, therefore, needs to be focused on two things: getting the salesperson to recognize that a problem exists, and then getting the salesperson's commitment to improve. The following discussion describes one four-step process for coaching salespeople who need to improve their performance:[21]

1. *Document the performance problem.* In some instances, the salesperson may request help, but more often it will be necessary to uncover problem areas that she might have. Any of a number of quantitative measures could signal a problem: sales per sales call, average dollar sales per order, average number of line items per order, number of prospects in a salesperson's sales funnel, number of customer complaints, number of inactive or lost accounts, plus many more. Note that none of these identify a problem, but any one of them could indicate a need for further investigation.

2. *Get the salesperson's agreement that there is a problem.* If the sales manager identifies a problem, it is critical to get the salesperson to agree that the problem does exist. The salesperson could have a completely logical reason for her behaviour or performance. If the salesperson fails to see a problem, she will not commit to fixing it.

3. *Explore solutions.* A sales manager who is truly committed to the coaching process will let the salesperson suggest solutions at this point. This also has the advantage of increasing motivation to take appropriate action as people will commit more to their own solutions.

4. *Get a commitment to take action from the salesperson.* The final step is to get commitment to take action by the salesperson. A written formal contract is sometimes helpful as putting things in writing helps clarify expected action and outcomes. If a written contract seems too formal, then the sales manager should at least prepare a statement of what was agreed and provide a copy to the salesperson. Having a paper trail is important if there is a possibility of further review or action.

A word of caution is appropriate here. The goal and intent of coaching under these circumstances should always be to help salespeople overcome problems or improve performance. There must be both trust and respect in the relationship for this to succeed. The Sales Management in

SALES MANAGEMENT **IN ACTION**

The Sales Leader as Coach

Christian Sauvageau is a sales director for Merck Frosst Canada, the pharmaceutical company that many people see as the gold standard when it comes to sales force training. He attributes this, at least in part, to the fact that the company sales managers who oversee the field salespeople are also the sales coaches. The most effective sales managers see the need to work with salespeople during all three stages: pre-call planning, face-to-face interaction, and post-call feedback.

■ *Pre-call planning.* Mark Fulton, national sales manager, Skin Health, 3M Medical, recalls working with one underachieving salesperson. During the pre-call coaching period, he recalls asking her what her objectives were for the sales call. She responded with a long list of the things she hoped to accomplish. Fulton says, "She hadn't really thought 'I only have 30 minutes with the customer. If I could accomplish one thing, how am I going to go about doing it?'" Coaching her to narrow her goals and become more focused helped her improve her performance.

■ *Face-to-face interaction.* One of the greatest challenges for many salespeople is to learn how to talk less and listen more. This is a challenge for sales managers as well when they are making a coaching call with a salesperson. Court Carruthers—vice-president, national accounts and sales, Ontario, for industrial distributor Acklands-Grainger—says this is even a larger problem for sales managers with extensive sales experience. He says, "The big challenge for many sales managers, myself included, is we often know the answer to the question the customer's asking. The real focus is having the discipline to be quiet." He has a solution for them: sales managers who have a checklist to complete following the sales call must pay attention to the salesperson and the customer, and they cannot do that if they are talking.

■ *Post-call feedback.* Linda Richardson, founder and CEO of the global sales training and consulting firm, Richardson, suggests that the sales manager should let the salesperson talk first. She says, "If you just start telling people what they've done wrong they're going to get very defensive or passive–aggressive." She suggests asking questions to lead them through a self-analysis. Done effectively, the entire process is nonconfrontational, helps build rapport between the sales manager and the salesperson, and becomes internalized by the salesperson into their daily behaviour.

Source: Geoffrey James, "Establish a Coaching Chain," *Selling Power,* April 2006; Laura Pratt, "Training the Team? Start at the Top," *National Post,* April 12, 2004, p. FP7; Brett Ruffell, "Coaching in Action," *Contact,* April 2006, pp. 28–32.

Action box describes how to effectively manage the coaching process during the pre-call planning, face-to-face interaction, and post-call feedback stages.

If the sales manager starts to take coaching action only when there is an apparent problem with a particular salesperson, and his purpose is to document the problem so that the salesperson can be terminated, then the entire sales force will quickly recognize this. Effective coaching with other salespeople could be sabotaged in the future. Salespeople quickly begin to think, "He's making sales calls this month with Tom. I wonder if Tom will be with us next month?" A regular routine of sales calls with all salespeople will prevent this. Some joint sales calls can be made to foster better relationships with key accounts; some can be made to bond with salespeople and motivate them to greater performance; some can be made with the goal of coaching individuals for superior performance.

Leading the Sales Force

Leading individual salespeople is important to a sales manager's success. This is the foundation for building a strong and cohesive sales force. But, leading the sales force is at least as important. Two topics will be discussed with respect to leading the sales force: building a high-performance, cohesive sales force, and leading sales meetings.

BUILDING A HIGH-PERFORMANCE, COHESIVE SALES FORCE

Building a high-performance, cohesive sales force requires building and maintaining a strong sales force culture that is results-oriented, and where each member values his association with and involvement in the group. **Sales force culture** is the total of values, attitudes, and behaviours that are shared by members of the sales force and that are expected of and reinforced to new members. As the sales leader, you can help build and reinforce this culture through the principles of internal marketing, practising the four "E" behaviours: energizing, enabling, and empowering your team members, and ensuring that they achieve objectives and are recognized and rewarded for their accomplishments."[22] This will help build "E" employees, distinguished by the following characteristics:

- They are risk takers and make suggestions.
- They support others and motivate their co-workers.
- They smile frequently and they like their work.
- They are trustworthy and they like their customers.
- They define service as whatever the customer needs (either an external customer buying a product or service, or an internal customer who depends on their performance).[23]

Perhaps nowhere is a sales leader's role more important than in building a strong sales force culture. It starts by displaying interest in and respect for others. People like people who like them. That is simply another way of saying that if you like someone and you let it show, the chances are very good that that person will like you in return, and this is particularly true in a working environment where people interact with the same people on a regular basis. Responsibility for establishing good relationships within a sales force rests with the sales leader. Richard Branson, CEO of Virgin, expresses his philosophy concerning people who work for him: "We give top priorities to the interests of our staff; second priority to those of our customers; third to shareholders. This is not only a reflection of the importance of our people, it is also the most positive way of fitting together these three priorities. Working backwards, the interests of our shareholders depend upon high levels of customer satisfaction . . . which depends on high standards of service from our people, which depends on happy staff who are proud of the company they work for."[24]

Creating happy employees does not mean that you must always give them what they want. Your role as sales leader for your sales force must be balanced against your role as sales manager for your company. However, as sales leader, you energize your sales team through your optimism and enthusiasm. You enable your sales team by ensuring they have the resources necessary to serve the customer. You empower your sales team by giving them the authority to make decisions, recognizing that sometimes there may be mistakes. When Kevin Johnson was head of U.S. sales and marketing at Microsoft, he created a "Make It Right Fund," giving his sales team unlimited resources to solve customer problems. During his very short period in this position, customer satisfaction went from an all-time low to an all-time high. (He is now co-president of the Windows platform and services division and a contender to become a future president of Microsoft.)[25] Finally, you ensure your sales team succeeds and that they get recognized and rewarded for doing so. You succeed through the success of the sales team, and you fail when your sales team fails.

LEADING SALES MEETINGS

Sales meetings are a key venue to demonstrate leadership skills and provide a way to foster communication to and among members of the sales force. Properly managed, meetings can also be a source of invaluable information for management. However, holding meetings is a two-edged sword: they can boost or ruin morale; they can motivate salespeople to perform, or can simply take salespeople from the field so that their sales decline; they can promote the leadership skills of the sales manager, or can simply demonstrate his inability to communicate to a group of people. There are many types of sales meetings, but one thing they all have in common is that there must be one or more important objectives for the meeting or it will be a waste of time at best, and a complete failure at worst. Sales meetings can be used for many things:

- *Strategy planning meetings.* This is one of the more important reasons to hold a meeting. Strategy planning meetings are often held annually and may extend beyond a single day. Having more salespeople involved in strategy planning meetings increases participation and commitment, and reduces the need to inform everybody of strategy changes. For longer meetings, Friday and Saturday is a popular period. The evenings can be used for entertainment and to increase "psychic bonding" among attendees.

- *Recognition and reward meetings.* These provide a public venue to recognize sales achievement. These meetings demonstrate the importance of performance to the organization, and reinforce the value of superior performance if one or more senior executives from the company also participate.

- *Training meetings.* Training meetings can be organized to introduce new products and make the information available to the entire sales force congruently. They can also be organized to improve selling skills, and may include an internal sales trainer or an external sales consultant. Some companies take advantage of visits from vendor salespeople and get them involved in training their own salespeople. Other companies make their own salespeople responsible for aspects of sales training—particularly those who are product or industry experts, or those who have recently been successful selling a new product or type of account.

- *Motivational meetings.* These meetings are designed to simply boost morale and increase interpersonal bonding among salespeople. They can be longer meetings or very short meetings, held frequently or infrequently. One sales manager for a global office equipment company had his sales force meet every morning for coffee at a local coffee shop. The sales manager had a number of reasons for holding these meetings: it got his sales force out early, but did not get them to the office where they could get involved in unnecessary activities; it got them all to reflect on recent activities and performance; and it got them to plan and commit to action for the coming day. Successes were also recognized each day. This was not done as a result of company policy but became ingrained in the culture of that particular office, and it became one of the best producing sales offices in Canada.

■   *Gathering feedback meetings.* These meetings, rather than being used to communicate to salespeople, provide opportunities for salespeople to communicate to management. Holding special meetings reinforces the importance of sales force input to management, with respect to either current polices and conditions, or future possible ones. The success of these meetings depends on the ability of the meeting leader to facilitate discussion rather than simply communicate. If the sales manager is not the best person to do this, a trained facilitator should be used. Whether management should be present depends on the nature of the content for discussion.

Meetings can be very costly. Just bringing four or five salespeople to a national location for a two-day meeting can cost thousands of dollars. Even holding too many meetings at a local sales office can be costly in terms of lost sales. When salespeople do not see the benefit, meetings can do more harm than good. Salespeople will be particularly critical if they are compensated mainly by commission and they see meetings as reducing their ability to earn income. The following are some suggestions for increasing the value and importance of sales meetings for salespeople and for the company:

1. *Communicate the reason for a meeting in advance.* There should be an agenda to keep the meeting on schedule and so everyone knows what the objectives are for the meeting. Their involvement should be encouraged if they feel there are items that should be on the agenda.

2. *Plan for the meeting process.* Make sure all necessary audiovisual equipment is present and that there is back-up for technology problems, which still frequently occur. Make sure the room is organized appropriately and is comfortable for attendees, and that snacks or drinks are available if required.

3. *Encourage participation.* Ask open-ended questions, reinforce good comments or contributions, and ignore comments that are off-topic. Sometimes having a few "seeded" participators in the audience is a good idea. For example, you might mention to a salesperson that you will be asking her to comment on a new account that she just sold. This will encourage others to participate and does not embarrass the salesperson, who has time to prepare what she wants to say.

4. *Manage time.* If you have asked for a one-hour meeting, then be sure the meeting lasts for only one hour. Stick to the agenda so everyone knows that agendas are important. If new topics are introduced, try to move them to the next meeting. This will encourage people to take meetings more seriously and think ahead to what they may want to discuss. For longer meetings, think about "chunks" of time. Most adults have difficulty keeping focused for long periods of time. Don't give long lectures or training sessions. Make sure there are frequent breaks, active participation, and changes of topics. Break-out groups work well, and particularly if someone from each group must report on the outcome from the break-out session.

5. *Be prepared, but have some fun.* The meeting leader needs to be able to start discussions and keep them on topic. Coming unprepared sends a message that this is acceptable behaviour and the meeting is not really important. That is why process and focus are both important. However, there needs to be a bit of humour occasionally. The trick is to add humour without allowing everyone to contribute to the point where the objectives of the meeting are lost.

6. *Summarize and distribute minutes.* This is a reminder of what happened. It is also a permanent record, and provides an opportunity to reinforce positive contributions to the meeting and to recognize individuals and the team's overall sales performance.

The timing and frequency of meetings is important. Short meetings can be held more frequently, assuming the logistics of getting everyone to the meeting are manageable. If salespeople regularly spend some time each week in the office, then having a weekly or monthly meeting is possible. Having them every Friday afternoon, or the second Monday of every month, for example, allows salespeople to plan, and for everyone to know when a meeting is coming and to have some responsibility for the agenda. If enthusiasm for meetings is dropping, that is an indication that more objectives for the meetings are necessary, the meetings should be shorter, or the meetings should be held less frequently. Technology can sometimes help reduce the need for face-to-face meetings. Some items can effectively be handled by email. Some meetings might be held by teleconferencing or webconferencing. For sales forces that are geographically dispersed, using technology can reduce costs considerably, in terms of both money and time. You can get a sense of the cost saving by reviewing the section on using technology for sales training in Chapter 7.

Personnel Issues

One of the most challenging aspects of sales management for many sales managers is dealing with personnel problems. Many of these problems result because of weaknesses with recruiting, selection, training, compensation plans, or motivational programs. Having clearly stated policies and procedures will help reduce the incidence of personnel problems. Among the challenging problems that sales managers face are plateauing, conflicts of interest, alcohol abuse and drug dependency, harassment and sexual harassment, the uncooperative or disruptive salesperson, and salesperson termination. Tom Gunter, vice-president of sales, ConAgra Foods, provides some of his thoughts on many of these important personnel issues and other sales leadership issues in the Sales Management Today box. These important personnel issues are now each discussed further.

PLATEAUING: CAUSES AND SOLUTIONS

Plateauing occurs when salespeople reach the disengagement career stage too early in their career (discussed previously in Chapter 9). They stop growing professionally and are satisfied with maintaining performance standards, often well below their capability. A survey of 340 sales managers estimated that 17.5 percent of salespeople have plateaued.[26] While the greatest percentage were in their 40s, some plateaued as early as their 20s. In a second study, nearly 20 percent of respondents estimated that the percentage of plateaued salespeople in their sales force was only 1–5 percent; however, some respondents thought it could be as high as 40–50 percent in their sales force. This study also found that plateauing was a greater problem for smaller sales forces with fewer than 10 salespeople, and for larger sales forces with more than 100 salespeople.[27]

CAUSES OF PLATEAUING There are many causes of plateauing, as listed in Exhibit 11.5. The most frequently cited reason was having no clear career path. This reinforces the importance of developing a career path for salespeople at the time they are first employed, and regularly revisiting it as they continue in their sales position. This is especially important if they are unlikely to be promoted to a management position for any reason: their lack of interest or ability, or the lack

Valuable Advice for Those Who Would Be Leader

Tom Gunter has spent most of his life in sales: Scott Paper, Frito-Lay Canada, Molson Canada, and now as vice-president of sales for ConAgra Foods in Toronto. Tom has eight directors of sales who report to him, and each of them is responsible for four to six account managers. Tom has lots of good advice for aspiring sales leaders. The following are some of Tom's comments:

- *Managing change.* When you must change a culture, you have to create stability and put the appropriate structures and processes in place to succeed. The biggest challenge is getting some people to understand the importance of change, and then training them so they can make the change. The ones who can't get to where you want them may have to go elsewhere.

- *Plateaued salespeople.* Every company has a number of people who don't want to move up in the organization, and you need those steady performers as long as they are open to new concepts and ideas. But, if they have lost their motivation, you must have an open and honest talk with them about where they fit and let them decide if they want to stay or not. Some may become remotivated and get excited about helping someone else develop into the company's next senior executive.

- *Sales meetings.* Attendees must be aware of the preparation required and the decisions to be made at the meeting. In addition, the facilitator, timekeeper, and note-taker should be briefed on their roles and responsibilities. If a meeting room is unfamiliar or there are materials to set up, the manager should arrive early to prepare. This ensures that the meeting starts on time, as starting late shows disrespect to the participants.

- *Coaching.* You should involve the salesperson when delivering feedback. You must offer praise where due, but rather than spout criticism, you are better to ask questions that create a dialogue about possible ways to improve the result of what was seen or experienced.

- *Alcohol and drug abuse.* If a salesperson has identified the problem and is seeking help to deal with it, you are required to provide employee assistance to help them to overcome the problem. If they fail to acknowledge the problem and continue with the abuse, in spite of your efforts to offer assistance, you should move to termination. It's always advisable to seek legal counsel and involve human resource professionals in these situations as they are delicate, and can put your organization in jeopardy if handled poorly.

- *Harassment.* Personalities and outcomes of harassment are very diverse and each situation requires a different course of action. If a salesperson reports harassment, a sales manager must reserve judgment, listen actively, take many notes, and begin an investigative process. The outcome could include third party counselling, a meeting with the two individuals, a written apology, suspension of duties, or termination.

- *Termination.* Termination should be the last step after all other options are exhausted, but sometimes it is inevitable. If the employee leaves and feels as though he was treated fairly and respectfully, even if he does not agree with the assessment, it reflects well on the company and manager. It will be recognized internally, by other staff, and externally by potential hires. Your organization will be known for its good practices.

- *Final thoughts.* A great employee is focused on his or her own development, whereas a great leader is focused on the development of others. Some final words of wisdom: be clear and consistent, be honest, maintain a sense of humour, and most important, never ask someone to do something that you wouldn't do yourself.

Source: Personal interview with Tom Gunter, vice-president of sales, ConAgra Foods, conducted by Lisa Violo, Brock University MBA student, November 4, 2005; personal interview with H.F. (Herb) MacKenzie, August 9, 2006.

of opportunity within the company. Other frequently cited reasons for plateauing included not being managed adequately, being bored, being burned out, and having economic needs already met. These reasons were among the highest ranked regardless of whether the sales force comprised

Exhibit 11.5

The Causes of Plateauing

Indicators	Overall	Mostly Men	Mostly Women	Salary Only	Commission Only
No clear career path	1	1	2	1	4
Not managed adequately	2	2	4	3	1
Bored	3	3	3	2	5
Burned out	4	5	1	5	2
Economic needs met	5	4	7	6	3
Discouraged with company	6	6	5	4	6
Overlooked for promotion	7	7	6	7	8
Lack of ability	8	8	9	8	7
Avoiding risk of management job	9	9	10	10	9
Reluctance to be transferred	10	10	8	9	10

Source: William Keenan, Jr., "The Nagging Problem of the Plateaued Salesperson," *Sales & Marketing Management,* March 1989, pp. 36–41. (Partial table only.) © Nielson Business Media, Inc.

mainly men or women, and regardless of whether the compensation plan was salary or commission. There were a few distinctions worthy of comment, though.

The highest ranked reason for plateauing in sales forces comprising mostly women was burnout. While the reason was not investigated, there are several possibilities. One is that women have more responsibilities at home as mothers and homemakers in addition to their normal work pressures and job demands. A second possibility is that women put more effort into their sales jobs due to a personal need to provide superior customer service after the sale, or because they have a greater motivation to succeed in their sales position.

Salespeople compensated by salary were more likely to be plateaued due to having no clear career path or by being bored than were salespeople compensated by commission. Salespeople compensated by commission were more likely to be plateaued due to burnout, or because their economic needs had been met. This indicates that salespeople on commission may have the opportunity to earn higher incomes, sufficiently high to satisfy their economic needs, and may therefore be less motivated by the opportunity to earn even higher incomes. It could also indicate that in order to earn these higher incomes, they have to work harder and are more likely to be burned out.

SUGGESTIONS TO REMOTIVATE SALESPEOPLE   There are a number of early warning signs that signal plateauing, as shown in Exhibit 11.6. The most important early warning signal is when salespeople no longer prospect hard enough. Other important early warning signs include failure to follow through, a reduction in the number of hours worked, and resisting

Exhibit 11.6

Early Warning Signals of Plateauing

Indicators	Overall	Mostly Men	Mostly Women	Sell Products	Sell Services
Doesn't prospect hard enough	1	1	1	1	1
Doesn't follow through	2	3	2	3	2
Works fewer hours	3	2	3	2	3
Resists management	4	4	4	4	4
Lives in the "good old days"	5	5	8	5	6
Doesn't keep up with new lines/products	6	6	7	6	5
Produces late/insufficient paperwork	7	7	5	7	7
Gets more customer complaints	8	8	9	9	9
Manipulates commissions/quotas	9	9	10	8	10
Sick and absent more often	10	10	6	10	8

Source: William Keenan, Jr., "The Nagging Problem of the Plateaued Salesperson," *Sales & Marketing Management*, March 1989, pp. 36–41. © Nielson Business Media, Inc.

management. These are the four most important early warning signs, regardless of salesperson gender or whether goods or services are being sold.[28]

Early warning signs may allow a sales manager to intervene before a salesperson has completely plateaued. However, given the incidence of plateauing among sales forces, it is very likely that most sales managers will have to deal at some point in their career with salespeople who have plateaued. Exhibit 11.7 provides a number of suggestions to remotivate plateaued salespeople. It is obvious that no one suggestion is likely to be successful with any particular salesperson, and a sales manager may have to use a combination of suggestions. Since salespeople plateau for different reasons, it is also likely that different suggestions will be effective with different salespeople.

Sales managers will find that, whatever suggestions they try, effectively remotivating a plateaued salesperson will unlikely be a short process. In most instances, plateauing took a long time to develop, and it will take a long time to cure. Assuming that plateaued salespeople have been successful in the past, appealing to their status and ability may help. Some may like the challenge of showing new recruits what they can do, and may even welcome the opportunity to help coach or mentor newer salespeople. Of course, care must be taken to ensure they are both qualified and motivated to do so. Another option is to increase their responsibility by giving them a special customer account or by putting them on a special project team. Again, care must be taken that the challenge that is provided is real, and that successful performance is valued and will be recognized or rewarded. Again, these opportunities should be given on the basis of good past performance and not simply because the salesperson seems demotivated. If the ability to perform is absent, any solution that does not include training will undoubtedly fail.

Exhibit 11.7

Suggestions to Remotivate Plateaued Salespeople

Talk with the salespeople and discuss the reasons they may have plateaued, along with possible solutions. These are the initial steps in coaching, and coaching—according to Brian Tracy who has trained more than 4 million people in over 1000 businesses—is the most effective thing you can do to motivate salespeople to improve. This action was favoured by approximately 70 percent of sales managers.

Hold experienced salespeople up as examples. Allow them to mentor or coach junior salespeople. This can increase the motivation of both younger and older salespeople. Of course, this will only succeed if the experienced salespeople have valuable information and skills to contribute.

Provide training on an ongoing basis. Gradually introducing training can help remotivate veteran salespeople. Many fall behind because of technology, or customer and competitor changes, and are afraid to appear weak by asking for help. Ensuring they keep their skills and knowledge current, and then rewarding small successes, can help remotivate them. Sales managers who continually train their salespeople will also reduce the likelihood of plateauing occurring in the first place.

Make all salespeople accountable. Help them set meaningful short-term goals and then monitor their performance. Know where they are going, who they are seeing, and what they are doing. Holding a weekly sales meeting lets everyone know that you want to know what is going on in their territory, and provides social pressure for everyone to have something of value to contribute.

Increase the responsibility of plateaued salespeople by giving them a special target account, responsibility for selling a major new product, or an important sales-related task, such as collecting information on a particular competitor. But don't give them too much until they prove capable. One of the least popular suggestions among sales managers was to simply give them responsibility for new products or prospects. The risk could be failure if they remain plateaued.

Source: Joe Kornik, "Motivation Makeover," *Sales & Marketing Management*, March 2007, pp. 31–33; Robin T. Peterson, "Beyond the Plateau," *Sales & Marketing Management*, July 1993, **www.managesmarter.com**; Alan Test, "Motivating Your Salespeople," *American Salesman*, May 2004, pp. 3–7; Minda Zetlin, "Is It Worth Keeping Older Salespeople?" *Sales & Marketing Management*, April 1995, **www.managesmarter.com.**

CONFLICTS OF INTEREST

It is easy for salespeople to become involved in conflict-of-interest situations. They fill boundary-spanning roles where they represent their own company, but often deal with dealers and distributors, suppliers and competitors, as well as with customers. They often have access to confidential information. Combining what they know with their networks of contacts sometimes provides opportunity for personal gain at the expense of their company. Sales managers should discuss conflicts of interest with salespeople to ensure they understand what it means, and should watch salespeople closely to see that they do not get involved in such situations. A few examples of involvement in conflict-of-interest situations follow:

1. One salesperson made sales calls four or five times too frequently to a territory that did not warrant this attention. Upon investigation, it was discovered that he was having an affair with an employee of one of the customers in that territory. By travelling there with his company car, his travel costs were paid by his company. The company also lost because he reduced his sales calls to other accounts in his territory.
2. One salesperson gave a customer prices well below what the purchase quantity suggested. The customer was eventually discovered to be a relative.
3. One salesperson, during a sales call with his sales manager, was asked by the customer about a recent purchase the customer had made. After the sales call, the sales manager wanted to know more information about the order as it covered products that the company did not sell. It was eventually revealed that the salesperson was operating as a manufacturer's agent on the side, representing other companies. His regular employer supplied a company car and paid all travel expenses to the salesperson, thinking he was a full-time employee who dedicated all of his time to them. (Termination was immediate.)

ALCOHOL ABUSE AND DRUG DEPENDENCY

There may not be reliable statistics to indicate that alcohol abuse or drug dependency is a greater problem among salespeople than people in other occupations, but there are reasons to suspect that this might be so. Salespeople are frequently faced with stressful situations, and are often required to be away from home overnight, or for extended periods of time. They are expected, and often encouraged, to entertain important prospects and customers, and in some sales positions, this can become an almost daily experience.

Alcohol abuse and drug dependency are serious problems in Canada. In 2002, an estimated 641 000 Canadians were addicted to alcohol, and 194 000 were addicted to illicit drugs.[29] The social cost of substance abuse was estimated to be $39.8 billion: tobacco, $17.0 billion (42.7 percent); alcohol, $14.6 billion (36.6 percent); and illicit drugs, $8.2 billion (20.7 percent).[30] Approximately 30 percent of Canadian companies report having problems with alcohol abuse and drug dependency in the workplace.[31]

Sales managers need to be aware of the potential for dependency problems within the sales force, and identify and help those affected. The first signs of alcohol abuse and drug dependency are usually detected by people who work closely with those at risk. Behaviours to watch for include increased absenteeism, fewer sales calls as salespeople begin their day later or quit earlier, or increased selling expenses, particularly related to entertaining or alcohol. Dealing with these dependency-related problems can be challenging for sales managers. On the one hand, occupational health and safety legislation makes employers responsible for maintaining due diligence and ensuring a safe working environment for employees. On the other hand, Canadian human rights legislation must be respected. Employees do have privacy rights, and both alcoholism and drug dependency are considered a disability under Canadian law.

Sales managers have historically played a role in counselling salespeople with alcohol abuse and drug dependency problems. While they do have an obligation to identify people at risk, and should be prepared to approach people they suspect may be at risk, they should refrain from counselling activities. These are complicated problems that often include both physical and psychological dependency, and only trained professionals should be involved. This also allows sales managers more time to focus on other tasks related to managing and leading the sales force.

HARASSMENT AND SEXUAL HARASSMENT

Harassment includes any of a broad range of behaviours that any reasonable person should know are likely to be unwelcome. It could range from physical assault or other unwelcome physical contact to threats, verbal abuse, or intimidation; to taunting, slurs, jokes, or leering; to displaying cartoons or adult pictures in the workplace. Legislation by the federal government and some provinces covers all forms of harassment; some provinces have legislation dealing only with a particular type of harassment—sexual harassment. There are two categories of sexual harassment: sexual coercion and sexual annoyance. *Sexual coercion* occurs when the sexual harassment affects a person's employment status, either providing employment benefits for allowing sexual favours, or withholding them for refusing sexual favours. *Sexual annoyance* occurs when the sexual harassment creates an intimidating, uncomfortable, offensive, or otherwise hostile or "poisoned" workplace environment. Both are serious and failure to treat them as such could result in legal action again an employer.

Regardless of legislation, responsible sales managers need to watch for harassment of all types involving members of the sales force and need to treat any instance seriously. Only four of ten Canadian women who experience sexual harassment in the workplace take any action.[32] Approximately 15 percent of sexual harassment complaints involve men.[33] While it is true that women experience sexual harassment more frequently than men, it is also possible that the difference in frequency of incidents may be smaller than suggested as men may be less likely to report it.

While it is a companywide issue, and there should be a corporate harassment policy, harassment is more likely to involve members of the sales force than other employees. One reason is because of the frequent contact salespeople have with customers. Research indicates that as the power of the customer increases, the incidence and seriousness of sexual harassment increases.[34] This places the salesperson in an uncomfortable situation when the harasser is an important customer, the loss of whom could significantly decrease sales. The sales manager has a responsibility to protect relationships with important customers, but in these situations, her first responsibility has to be to the salesperson. It would be highly inappropriate to coerce an employee to do something in this situation that would leave them still feeling victimized.

Because sexual harassment is so serious for both the victim and the company, a responsible sales manager should ensure that each new salesperson understands the issue completely. If there is a corporate harassment policy, the new employee should be completely familiarized with it. Following that, the sales manager should reinforce what should happen if an employee is victimized. They need to know what appropriate options are available to them at the time harassment occurs, and where they can go for advice. They should also be informed what actions could be taken against them if they are the perpetrator rather than the victim.

Research suggests that saleswomen will experience, on average, five incidents of some form of sexual harassment, and that they are more likely to occur early in their sales career.[35] This suggests that a sales manager should explore possible reactions to sexual harassment prior to when an actual incident occurs. When someone is harassed and it is unexpected, as it often is, the response a person makes may not be the best response that they could make if they had time to think through alternative courses of action and the consequences of each. Women who have experienced sexual harassment have responded in various ways. Some appropriate responses may include the following:

- *Leave the situation.* This may be done with or without a comment to the offending person. It is particularly appropriate if the victim is unfamiliar with the offender or feels in any way threatened with possible further physical or emotional harm.

- *Humour.* "The last person who did that to me is my ex." Another possibility: "If you do that again, I will take it as a marriage proposal and I'll have to announce our engagement." Note that this combines humour with a suggestion that a further incident would be made public.

- *Direct confrontation.* "I'm sorry, but that is completely inappropriate and unwelcome. Please do not do that again." This may be the most effective response with established customers. Following the confrontation, if the relationship is still important, the victim needs to find a reason to make quick contact with the offender to indicate that the business relationship is still important.

When harassment occurs, some people will complain but, unfortunately, some will simply decide to leave a "poisoned" work environment for employment elsewhere. This could mean leaving the company, asking for a transfer to another sales territory, or asking to be removed from a particular account. In other instances, an employee may continue in their regular work, but may be affected to the point where their performance deteriorates. An effective sales leader needs to watch for any indication of harassment involving her sales employees, and needs to deal swiftly but fairly whenever an incident has occurred.

THE UNCOOPERATIVE OR DISRUPTIVE SALESPERSON

Sales managers must frequently deal with uncooperative or disruptive salespeople. If their lack of cooperation does not interfere with the rest of the sales force and their performance is satisfactory, the best approach is probably to continue to treat them as though they were cooperative. It might be possible to find some way to motivate them to become more cooperative, or they may simply become more cooperative over time. A major factor will be why they are uncooperative. Sometimes this is because they feel they were bypassed for a promotion, maybe even believing that they should be the current sales manager. If this is the situation, then a frank discussion concerning their future possibilities is warranted. If they might have an opportunity for advancement, then some career planning and some appropriate training might help. If there is little possibility of their ever becoming a sales manager, then this should also be frankly discussed with them.

The disruptive salesperson is even more of a problem for sales managers. Left to continue his disruptive behaviour, he can eventually affect the attitudes and behaviours of the entire sales force. Be certain that everyone on the sales force will recognize his disruptive behaviour and will be watching carefully to see how the sales manager handles the salesperson. If the disruptive behaviour continues, others may see it as a sign of personal weakness, or that the sales manager is playing favourites if the disruptive salesperson is also a high-achiever. This type of salesperson has been referred to as a "lone wolf."[36] They characteristically have a high commitment to their selling job, but a low commitment to their organization. Reining them in and getting them to recognize the effect they are having on others is important. If they continue to be a problem, a threat of termination might be effective, but the threat should not be made unless the sales manager is prepared to actually terminate the disruptive salesperson if the behaviour continues. Professional sales trainer and motivational speaker Brian Tracy says, "You cannot compromise your integrity simply because that person represents a high level of sales."[37] How to terminate problem salespeople is discussed next.

TERMINATION: OPTION OF LAST RESORT

Termination should be the option of last resort, but it is sometimes a necessary option. Brian Tracy, introduced in the previous section, believes that the ability to terminate people is an essential management skill. He says, "If you don't have this skill, or if you don't develop this skill, then you are not qualified to be in management."[38] But, when should termination be necessary?

Termination should occur only if sufficient or just cause exists, and then, only after all reasonable actions to rehabilitate or salvage the employee have been taken. Acceptable reasons for termination include persistent unsatisfactory performance; behavioural misconduct, including, for example, stealing, insubordination, persistent absence or lateness, or continued harassment; and changed job requirements or the elimination of a job. However, the burden of proof of just cause rests with the employer, and Canadian courts have tended to side as often with employees as with employers. In one study, courts sided with employers in 25 percent of cases alleging incompetence, in 40 percent of cases alleging behavioural misconduct, in 54 percent of cases alleging insubordination, and in 66 percent of cases alleging conflict of interest/competing with the employer.[39] When just cause is not an issue, employers should ensure that employees receive reasonable notice as defined by provincial legislation. Even then, if the employee believes this period to be unreasonable, he can sue for wrongful dismissal. In 1997, the Supreme Court of Canada ruled in the *Wallace vs. United Grain Growers* decision that "bad faith conduct" on the part of the employer can be considered in determining a period of reasonable notice. Since then, many terminated employees have been awarded "Wallace damages" as courts have been very liberal deciding what kinds of conduct by employers are considered "bad faith." Awards have often extended periods of notice to six months, and sometimes longer.[40] As the person who is often closely involved with sales employees during the termination process, the sales manager needs to be very careful how he proceeds.

The following are some suggestions that will help protect against wrongful dismissal suits and make the termination process less stressful for the sales manager and employee:

1. *Keep a paper trail when possible.* Employees should be given written notice when they fail to meet performance expectations, or when their behaviour is deemed inappropriate. If possible, the employee should sign a copy of the documentation. Of course, there may be serious circumstances that require immediate termination.

2. *Terminate employees on Monday or Tuesday.* Some people suggest Friday so the employee can recover (although it may be to allow weaker managers to recover). Most people suggest early in the week as termination is seldom unexpected, and it gives the employee the opportunity to begin a new job search immediately. This also prevents the company rumour mill from getting into gear over the weekend.

3. *Terminate employees in private.* Even when expected, a termination can be traumatic, and employees deserve privacy. If possible, have a witness present, and preferably someone from human resources. Keep notes of the meeting.

4. *Carefully prepare what you will say.* In fact, it may be beneficial to have a written script. Be as brief as possible, but be willing to answer questions that the employee may have. Do not let the employee draw you into an argument or debate reasons for your decision.

5. *Discuss severance.* Be sure the termination meets the requirements of both federal and provincial employment legislation. If the company has assistance programs for terminated employees, make sure the employee knows about them.

6. *Be respectful and demonstrate empathy.* Regardless of the reason for termination, you should show concern for the employee. The employee will be gone following termination, so there is little value in having him leave bitter or resentful. As a manager, you need to maintain control in the situation, and you will be better able to do that if you are respectful.

There is no absolutely correct way to handle termination, but you should appreciate from the suggestions provided that the process needs to be managed carefully. Many terminated employees go on to successful careers in other positions, or with other companies. When they walk out your door, you have little control over where they will next appear, or in what employment position.

SUMMARY

1. **Understand the personal traits, personality, and needs of effective sales leaders.** There is strong research support for nine personal traits of effective leaders: dominance, high energy, self-confidence, locus of control, stability, integrity, intelligence, flexibility, and sensitivity to others. A combination of personality traits helps classify a leader's personality. These personal traits are combined into one of "The Big Five" personality dimensions: extroversion, conscientiousness, agreeableness, socially adjusted, and openness to experience. Among the needs that leaders have are the need for power (strongest), followed by the need for achievement, and then the need for affiliation.

2. **Explain how effective sales leaders use power.** Effective sales leaders have a strong need for *power,* the ability to influence others in order to get things done. There are seven bases of power they may use: legitimate, reward, coercive, expert, referent, information, and connection power. Power can only exist if there is dependence. Sales leaders who must rely on legitimate, reward, or coercive power are at a disadvantage to leaders who have expert or referent power.

3. **Understand how to effectively lead change.** Effective sales leaders must be able to manage the change process: recognize the need for change, develop a change vision, communicate change, implement change, and institutionalize change. Changes may be incremental and initiated within the sales force, or may be a crisis change mandated from senior management.

4. **Explain how to effectively lead individual salespeople.** There are two important aspects to effectively managing individual salespeople: situational leadership and coaching. *Situational leadership* recognizes that a leader's style should match the particular situation that the leader faces. The leader's style will depend on whether he is high or low task-focused and high or low relationship-focused, leading to four leadership styles: telling, persuading, partnering, and delegating. *Coaching* is defined as an interpersonal process between the sales manager and the salesperson in which the sales manager is focused on helping the salesperson improve performance on one or more specific aspects of the selling process. To be an effective sales coach, a leader must first document that a problem exists, get the salesperson's agreement that there is a problem, explore solutions, and then get a commitment from the salesperson to take action.

5. **Explain how to effectively lead the sales force.** There are two important aspects to effectively leading the sales force: building a high-performance, cohesive sales force and leading sales meetings. Building a high-performance, cohesive sales force requires building and maintaining a strong sales force culture that is results-oriented, and where each member

values his association with and involvement in the group. Sales meetings are a key venue to demonstrate leadership skills and provide a way to foster communication to and among members of the sales force. There are many types of meetings: strategy planning meetings, recognition and reward meetings, training meetings, motivational meetings, and gathering feedback meetings. To have effective meetings, a sales manager should communicate the reason for a meeting in advance, plan for the meeting process, encourage participation, manage time, be prepared but have some fun, and summarize and distribute minutes.

6. **Understand the range of personnel issues that a sales leader must face.** Dealing with personnel problems is one of the most challenging aspects of sales management. Among the many issues that sales managers must contend with are the plateaued salesperson, conflict of interest situations, alcohol abuse and drug dependency, harassment, uncooperative and disruptive salespeople, and termination. When all else fails, a sales leader must be able to engage the termination process. Termination should occur only if sufficient or just cause exists, and then, only after all reasonable actions to rehabilitate or salvage the employee have been taken.

KEY TERMS

leadership **308**

personal traits **309**

personality **310**

power **312**

situational leadership **315**

coaching **317**

sales force culture **320**

plateauing **323**

harassment **329**

REVIEW QUESTIONS

1. Explain the relationship between sales management and sales leadership. Which is most important to the sales force? Explain.

2. Describe the five dimensions of personality. Which is the most important for a sales manager to possess? Why?

3. Explain power and why it is important for sales managers to possess power.

4. Explain how you would manage change in a small sales force. Be specific.

5. Define *situational leadership*. Describe four different leadership styles that might be appropriate with different situations.

6. Coaching can be used for two different types of sales force training. Explain how it might differ depending on the purpose of the coaching.

7. Define *plateauing* and explain why it occurs. Explain what a sales manager can do about plateauing.

8. Describe how a sales manager can increase the value of a sales meeting for both the sales force and the company.

9. Explain three appropriate actions that you could take following an incident in which you were sexually harassed. Which action would you take? Explain.

10. Why should termination be the option of last resort? What guidelines would you follow if you were faced with having to terminate an employee? Explain.

APPLICATION EXERCISES

1. Psychological testing is an important tool for selecting salespeople and sales managers. A popular one is the SalesAP (Sales Achievement Predictor). Visit **www.careermotiv8.com** and view information on this test, particularly the sample report. Evaluate the information on this particular sales candidate. How might a sales leader use this information if this particular candidate were hired? Explain your answer.

2. You are concerned about Sandeep Iyengar, an experienced salesperson in your Mississauga office. "Deep," as he is called, won several annual awards when he first joined the company nearly 10 years ago, but lately, his sales have not been keeping up with price changes. That is, his sales revenue is growing slightly, but his unit sales volume is declining. The trend has been noticeable for the past three years and this year looks like it will continue. You know Deep has the skills and experience to do much better than he has been doing, and you certainly prefer not to lose him from your sales force. As an effective sales leader, determine a course of action for handling this situation. Outline what you will do and be prepared to defend your recommendations.

3. You have just announced the promotion of Veronica Hutt to a position as inside sales supervisor to oversee your staff of 15 telesales representatives and four customer service people. As you prepare to leave for lunch, Andy Cyr, your most senior telesalesperson, approaches you in your office and says, "I'm sorry, but I can't work for a woman. We all knew that Veronica's promotion was a possibility, and I think you will lose a good number of your telesalespeople unless you reconsider." Andy has been part of your telesales team for nearly five years and he has been among the top performers in your office. Explain in detail how you would handle this situation.

4. Many of you will be finishing your education soon and will be turning your attention to finding a career. One option is to simply send résumés for every job opening you might qualify for, to whatever companies you can find that have job openings. It is not necessarily a terrible option if you must pay bills and you want to gain some experience. However, there is another option. You could research companies first, and only apply to ones that might interest you. Search the annual reports of several companies (many are on the internet) and review their mission and vision statements. What can you tell about the CEO of these companies from reading the annual reports? Are any of these CEOs a leader you would like to work for? Be prepared to defend your answer.

CASE 11.1   The First Challenge

Hal Maybee had recently been transferred to the Vancouver office from Toronto. With his transfer came his promotion to sales manager and, at 35 years of age, he was very proud of being the youngest in the company. The Vancouver office was a high-performing office and had had very little turnover in recent years. In fact, sales employment with the company averaged nearly 30 years. Tony DiFranco was the most senior salesperson. He was an outstanding salesperson who had achieved membership in the President's Club more than 12 times and was among the highest sales producers in all of Canada. Tony was in his early 60s but showed no sign of slowing down. Hal was happy to have such a dedicated and experienced salesperson on the sales force, and he thought Tony would be a stabilizing factor that would help get him over the first months in his new position. Hal knew that Tony had been influential in helping the previous sales manager, who had recently taken an early retirement package.

For the first few months, everything had seemed to operate smoothly within the office. While Tony was not forthcoming with much advice, he had continued to perform extremely well in his sales role and he was pleasant to Hal each time they met. Then, without any indication that there was a problem, Tony had suddenly exploded in front of the entire sales force, and it had taken Hal completely by surprise. The issue that precipitated the event was a simple question that Hal had raised during a regular monthly sales meeting, only the third meeting that Hal had organized.

Head office in Toronto had attended a national trade show in that city and collected hundreds of sales leads from across the country. The sales leads had been distributed to the appropriate branches, and now the vice-president of sales was following up to see what action the branches had taken. Hal had noticed that almost none of the leads had been followed up by any of the sales-people. At the meeting, Hal had raised the issue. "I need a summary from each of you concerning the sales leads that came from the national office last month. They want to know if we have followed up on them and how much business we did as a result."

There was a brief silence and Hal noticed that the other salespeople all looked toward Tony to respond. When he did, it was apparent he was angered. "I trashed most of them as soon as I got them. Those are a waste of time and I won't have anyone at head office or you, for that matter, telling me what to do or how to run my territory. If those people at head office mind their own business, my sales will continue to be fine. If you mind your own business, we'll get along fine."

CRITICAL-THINKING QUESTION

If you were Hal Maybee what would you do? Explain your reasoning.

Bill Siddall's Sales Call Reports

CASE 11.2

Hal Maybee, sales manager at Power & Motion Industrial Supply, looked carefully through the sign-in book to be sure, but he was not expecting to see Bill Siddall's name there for the previous week. His expectations were confirmed. Nearly a month had passed since Bill Siddall had registered as a visitor at the pulp mill, and it was one of his most important accounts. Hal knew the answer before he asked, but he felt he had to ask anyway. "Does anyone get into this mill without registering at the gate?" The burly security guard looked directly at Hal and replied, "Mister, if a mouse doesn't have a proper I.D. and someone on the inside who wants to see him, he doesn't get in."

Hal got into his car and headed back to his office. He wasn't happy with what he had found, nor was he happy with the fact that he had had to visit the mill to check on Bill. But, now he knew for sure. Hal had been golfing over the weekend at Brae Shore Golf Club and as he frequently did, he met Rory Fisher, the mill's purchasing agent. Hal had innocently asked, "Did Bill try to sell you any pump packing last week? We just added a lot of packing to our inventory and I know Bill wants to push it because it's one of the products he knows best." Hal had been completely surprised when Rory responded, "No. Bill hasn't been in to see me for about a month." Hal had tried to hide his surprise and hoped that Rory didn't suspect anything. "Oh. I know Bill was going to concentrate on pump packing last week and I just assumed you would be one of his first calls. I guess he'll be in to see you soon. Have you broken 80 yet this season?" Hal was hoping the subject would change, and he was glad when it did.

When Hal got to work on Monday morning, he looked at Bill's call reports to be sure. There was no mistake. Bill had reported that he'd gone to the pulp mill. Further, he'd submitted a receipt on his weekly expense report and claimed for a lunch he'd had with one of the plant engineers at the mill cafeteria. When Hal went through some of Bill's previous expense reports, he noticed several more receipts from the mill cafeteria. Upon closer investigation, Hal noticed that the numbers in the corners of several receipts were almost consecutive, although the receipts had been submitted over nearly a four-month period.

Hal called Bill to his office and asked him to be seated. "Bill, I need to know where you were last Wednesday." With no hesitation, Bill replied that he had been at the pulp mill and that he had submitted his call reports on Friday as required. Hal responded, "No. I'm sorry. You were not there, Bill. Where were you?" After an awkward few moments, Bill glanced down and admitted he had not made the sales call he'd reported. "I went fishing with my son. I just needed a break, and I promised Davy that I would take him fishing. I'm sure you must have skipped off for a day sometime."

Hal knew the next response was his as he pondered what to say. He quickly decided there were a number of alternatives and he knew he had to choose one quickly.

Hal knew that he needed to demonstrate leadership in this situation and make a responsible decision that weighed the interests of many stakeholders. Then he had to act. Leadership required that.

CRITICAL-THINKING QUESTION

If you were Hal Maybee, what would you do? Explain your reasoning.

Chapter 12

Ethical and Legal Responsibilities

LEARNING OBJECTIVES

After completing this chapter, you should be able to

1. Discuss the importance of ethical behaviour for managing relationships.

2. Describe the factors that influence ethical conduct of salespeople.

3. Describe important legislation that helps manage the behaviour of salespeople.

Perhaps nothing devalues a relationship more than knowing it is built on lies, deception, or unethical behaviour. Much criticism has been directed at salespeople for unethical selling practices but, in fairness, customers often behave equally unethically, particularly when the issue relates to gifts, entertainment, or bribery. Either one party offers and the other accepts, or one party asks and the other obliges.

When a vice-president at Wal-Mart Canada requested a kickback from Montreal-based Fame Jeans in exchange for business, the manufacturer refused to pay. Fame's sales to Wal-Mart dropped from $10 million to $3 million a year. A Toronto-based supplier did pay what was reportedly a 2 percent kickback. When Wal-Mart heard of the situation, it immediately initiated an inquiry into the business dealings of its vice-president and promptly fired him. The suppliers involved in this situation would most likely not have talked to police, but Wal-Mart pressured them to do so. Wal-Mart has a reputation for strict ethical business practices that it wants to protect. The police officer who investigated the case said, "Wal-Mart was concerned and felt it was wrong—if something wasn't done about it, who's to say the accused wouldn't just go somewhere else and do the same thing again?"

Wal-Mart Canada now has a zero tolerance policy and forbids any of its 30 000 employees from accepting gifts. Wal-Mart spokesperson Kevin Groh says, "Our feeling is that gifts and gratuities to the company don't do any good for our customer." Increasingly, Canadian companies are developing and implementing codes of business ethics that help direct their relationships both internally and externally.

They are finding that good ethical behaviour provides the foundation for good business relationships.[1]

Ethics: The Foundation for Good Relationships

Ethics are the rules that direct a person's conduct and moral judgment.[2] They help people determine appropriate behaviour in all aspects of their life, and they are particularly important to salespeople for a number of reasons that will be explored throughout this chapter. Ethics vary from one community to another, and over time. However, within the current Canadian business community, there are generally recognized ethical standards. This does not mean that every company, or every salesperson, always behaves ethically. Some do, some do not, and some *really* do not—as the examples in the Sales Management Today box illustrate. There are many reasons why unethical behaviours occur, and this chapter will explore the factors that affect ethical behaviour, many of the important ethical issues that salespeople contend with regularly, legal responsibilities that must be considered when selling in Canada, and how to make better ethical decisions and develop a code of ethics for today.

Behaving ethically is important for building all types of business relationships. One particularly important type of relationship is the one that exists between employees and their employer. To one recent survey where employees were asked about the importance of various factors for creating an ideal work situation, 70 percent rated working for an ethical and trustworthy company very important. Liking their job was rated very important by only 64 percent of employees.[3]

A second type of relationship that exists is the interorganizational relationship that a company has with its customers and with its suppliers. Increasingly, companies are recognizing the value of having an ethics code and of using it in their business decision making. John Boatright, a business ethics professor at Loyola University and director of the Society for Business Ethics, says that one potential use of an ethics code is "to make customers aware of it and to transmit this through the sales force. If companies are failing to do this, they are missing a good opportunity, because it increases the credibility of the company."[4] Fortunately, many companies now recognize this and do it: 83 percent of respondents to an ethics survey reported that they train their salespeople to sell customers on their ethics and integrity, and 70 percent indicated they believed customers consider this when making a purchase decision.[5]

Ethical behaviour with respect to suppliers is no less important. As discussed in the opening vignette, when there are instances of ethical misconduct, both sellers and buyers may be involved. In fact, the behaviour can be initiated by a customer, as it was in this instance. In a broader channel perspective, a selling company to one customer is often a customer to another selling company. Treating the company that is selling to your company unethically will not engender good business relationships. While a company may make some short-term gains by treating suppliers unethically, in the longer term, the company has a lot to lose.

Colleges and universities across Canada are starting to pay more attention to business ethics. Almost every business program is now including ethics as an important topic in many of the courses, and many are including a course that is focused specifically on business ethics. AACSB (Association to Advance Collegiate Schools of Business) accreditation is becoming important globally and there are now many Canadian business schools that have received accreditation. One of the requirements for accreditation is that "the institution or the business programs of the institution must establish expectations for ethical behaviour by administrators, faculty, and students."[6] AACSB believes that the delivery of a quality business education can only occur where ethical behaviour is valued. Colleges and universities are becoming proactive in developing the character of their students. One reason to become more proactive in character development is the increasing erosion of character in business in general.

Selling Ethics: The Good, the Bad, and the Ugly

We hear a lot about ethics in selling today, but it is not all bad. There is the good. Unfortunately, there is also the "so bad," that there is the ugly. What distinguishes the good from the bad, from the ugly? Perhaps an example of each will help you decide.

■ *The good.* At Texas Instruments, all new employees get extensive ethics training. Salespeople get training in legal areas such as preparing business contracts, and non-disclosure. Sales managers get training in issues such as sexual harassment and diversity. Among the training methods used are role plays, case studies, analysis of videotaped scenarios, and even improvisational actors who act out scenes where employees must make decisions. Zoe Chapman, human resources director for sales and marketing for the Americas, says, "We tell our salespeople that if you have to do something unethical to win business, don't do it." Perhaps this is one reason why Texas Instruments was named three consecutive years to the *Business Ethics* prestigious 100 Best Corporate Citizens List. David Reid, vice-president, director of ethics compliance, says, "To be recognized at this level is validation of our basic tenet of good corporate citizenship. For TI, strong ethics are not just an afterthought, they are part of our everyday business strategy."

■ *The bad.* The Kirby Company has its difficulties with ethics—not so much the company, which has been selling vacuum cleaners door-to-door since 1935, but some of the independent salespeople that it employs. Kirby vacuum cleaners are sold in more than 60 countries around the world. Its high-priced, but quality, vacuum cleaner has a lifetime guarantee. The problem for The Kirby Company is that many of its independent distributors don't seem to follow any code of ethics. A simple review of complaints at ConsumerAffairs.com will convince most people of that. One Kirby salesperson was accused of knowingly selling vacuum cleaners to senior cit-

izens who were unable to use them because they were too large, and also falsely telling them that they had three days to cancel the sale if they were dissatisfied. To Kirby's credit, the company has a "Golden Age" policy that allows seniors to cancel a sale within one year of purchase. The court awarded each of 13 senior complainants $1000 and allowed each to keep the vacuum that was purchased. The salesperson was terminated. This is a good example of how bad people can help damage the reputation of a company and its other employees, and it demonstrates the difficulty of managing the behaviour of salespeople whose actions are largely unknown until customers complain.

■ *The ugly.* What separates the bad from the ugly? To some people, very little. To other people, it is the degree of lack of concern for the customer, the amount of financial damage caused, the premeditation behind the behaviour, or the targeting of society's most vulnerable. When all of these factors come together, you have the ugliest of the ugly. Some might say that Tyrone M. Clark deserves that honour. What did he do? He ran "Senior Financial Survivor Workshops" allegedly designed to coerce seniors to make questionable investments from companies that were founded by him. Sales associates of Clark's companies were called "Certified Elder Planning Specialists," a very fancy name for an insurance salesperson. Associates attended a two-day training school at "Annuity University." What lessons were they taught? One lesson: "Assume you are selling to a 12-year-old who is blind but smart." Another lesson: You must "probe and disturb" the elderly client. According to the complaint, "Associates learn how to alarm seminar attendees by preying on their emotions." Clark has consented to the Massachusetts Securities Division's requirement that he make a settlement, but has neither admitted nor denied the findings of fact, conclusions of law, or allegations made in the complaint issued.

Sources: Julia Chang, "Codes of Conduct," *Sales & Marketing Management,* November 2003, p. 22; Texas Instruments, "Texas Instruments Named to 100 Best Corporate Citizens List," News release, April 7, 2005, http://www.ti.com/corp/docs/press/company/2005/c05016.shtml, accessed August 7, 2006; Jennifer Gilbert, "The Right Balance," *Sales & Marketing Management,* November 2004, http://www.salesandmarketing.com, accessed August 1, 2006; ConsumerAffairs.com, http://www.consumeraffairs.com/in_home/kirby_demo.html, accessed August 7, 2006; Hoover's, "The Kirby Company," http://www.hoovers.com/kirby-company/—ID__58107—/free-co-factsheet.xhtml, accessed August 7, 2006; Secretary of the Commonwealth of Massachusetts, http://www.sec.state.ma.us/sct/sctalt/sbcn.pdf, accessed August 7, 2006.

THE EROSION OF CHARACTER

Even though businesses and business programs are showing more interest in ethics, there are indications that unethical behaviour is far too common. One survey found that nearly half of workers engaged in unethical or illegal work-related acts during the year preceding the study, and many reported that they felt pressured to do so.[7] A more recent survey conducted by *Newsweek* found that many of today's workers who responded to its study did not view lying or cheating as unacceptable.[8] Some colleges and universities in Canada are seeing increasing incidences of academic dishonesty by students, and several have hired integrity officers with responsibility to reduce it. Why are we seeing this erosion of character today?

Character is composed of your personal standards, including honesty, integrity, and personal strength. Liam Neeson, in the movie *Rob Roy,* referred to it as honour and said, "All men with honour are kings, but not all kings have honour." And when his son asked him, "What is honour?" he replied, "Honour is what no man can give you, and none can take away. Honour is a man's gift to himself." Integrity, or honour, is the basic ingredient of character. **Integrity** is exhibited when there is congruence between what you know, what you say, and what you do.[9] When salespeople lack integrity, they cannot be trusted to do what they say they will do, and they are more likely to act in their own self-interest.

Richard Sennett, author of *The Corrosion of Character,* says that the dilution of character can be traced to the world we live in today: high-stress, fast-paced, and information driven. He says that when we display loyalty, mutual commitment, and the pursuit of long-term goals, character strength builds.[10] It is difficult for employees to build character strength today through loyalty and commitment to employers, when so many are simply results-driven. Companies trade respect for employees for shareholder value, resulting in employee mistrust, low morale, and, sometimes, a willingness to take whatever they can get from their company. Some corporations have turned from being business and social institutions that serve a variety of stakeholders, to ones focused entirely on maximizing share price. Marjorie Kelly, editor of *Business Ethics,* says, "Managing a company solely for maximum share price can destroy both share price and the entire company.[11] The next section describes how management and other factors influence the ethical behaviour of salespeople.

Factors That Influence the Ethical Behaviour of Salespeople

Many factors influence the ethical behaviour of salespeople, as illustrated in Exhibit 12.1. Salespeople are especially vulnerable to moral corruption because they have both internal and external relationships to manage. Inside the firm, they may be susceptible to pressure to achieve ever-increasing sales targets and they sometimes come to accept that failure is not an option. Outside the firm, they sometimes face requests that require creative and possibly questionable tactics in order to meet customer demands. Like Willy Loman in Arthur Miller's *Death of a Salesman*— "a man way out there in the blue, riding on a smile and a shoeshine"—many salespeople travel regularly to meet with prospects and customers. Patrick Murphy, director of the Institute for Ethical Business Worldwide, says, "So, when they get hit with an ethical dilemma, often they have to deal with it on their own as opposed to in a meeting or checking with the boss down the hall."[12] Recognizing the special problems that salespeople have, it is important that effective support mechanisms exist within the company to help guide ethical behaviour. The support mechanisms must start at the very top of the organization, with the CEO.

Exhibit 12.1

Factors That Influence the Ethical Behaviour of Salespeople

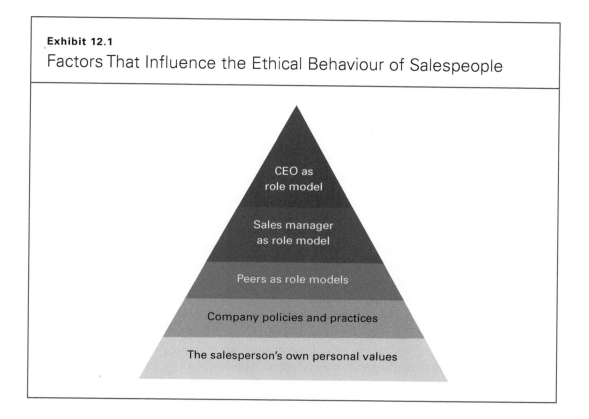

CEO as
role model

Sales manager
as role model

Peers as role models

Company policies and practices

The salesperson's own personal values

THE CEO AS ROLE MODEL

Nowhere else in an organization is ethics more important than at the very top. This is because ethics flows downhill. If it does not exist at the top, it almost assuredly does not exist at the bottom. One sales manager describes an ethical dilemma he faced when his company bid on a $30 million contract at a price that was considerably below the competition and which could not be supported over the longer term. The tactic was to get the order, then find reasons to raise the price after winning the bid. The sales manager advised the CEO that the practice was unethical, and that it would not help build the company's credibility. The CEO ignored the advice.[13] What should an ethical sales manager or salesperson do when a superior promotes or enforces unethical behaviour? There are several solutions and they are not mutually exclusive. Perhaps the easiest solution is to simply leave the organization. Unfortunately, if all employees uncomfortable in that environment left, the company would be morally bankrupt. A second solution is to stay and participate. Many people take this option because they feel they have too much at risk to do otherwise. However, many will be demoralized and demotivated, and they will pay a high personal price. A third solution is to become a whistle-blower, and people with the highest ethical standards will do this when they have no other option. Whistle-blowing is discussed in a later section.

Michael Deck, managing director of Toronto-based Ethidex Inc. and formerly a principal with KPMG Canada where he led its Ethics & Integrity Services, says, "Corporate integrity begins with senior executives visibly and actively setting an example of respect for the rules. In this way, senior management sends a clear message that unethical and illegal behaviours are not acceptable business practices."[14] The most important determinant of employee ethics is the moral tone established by people at the top of the organization. In addition, a key factor in developing employee loyalty is trust in senior leadership.[15] Salespeople will carefully monitor the importance of ethics in their organization, but, on a daily basis, their interactions with their sales manager will provide guidance concerning what the organization views as acceptable.

THE SALES MANAGER AS ROLE MODEL

The sales manager has a direct impact on the ethical behaviour of the sales force. She is the supervisor that salespeople have the closest relationship with, and they look to her for guidance and direction. Salespeople, in many instances, view the sales manager as the conduit through which company policies and values get communicated and interpreted. On an ongoing basis, the sales manager is responsible for monitoring the behaviour of each salesperson and providing feedback concerning what is acceptable. If the sales manager abrogates this responsibility, then salespeople must turn elsewhere for guidance.

Sales managers therefore have a responsibility to continually review and determine acceptable standards of behaviour and to communicate and enforce them for salespeople. Sales managers sometimes pressure salespeople to abandon personal ethical standards to achieve sales targets. One anonymous salesperson, embarrassed publicly for his behaviour, stated, "The implicit message that I got from my sales manager was that I worked for an ethical company, 'but don't lose the business.' He didn't force me to do what I did, so I accept full responsibility. However, in my mind at the time, I had little choice." Phil Rody, a former professor at the University of Western Ontario, agrees that sales managers have responsibility. He says, "A significant component of sales is dealing with the customer's reluctance to buy, anticipating objections, and coming up with ways to overcome the customer's objections. It's easy to see how that can foster an attitude of 'do whatever you have to do to get the sale.'" Rody believes that it is acceptable to train salespeople in these selling skills, but that the sales manager must ensure that the basic requirement of 'don't mislead the customer' still gets communicated.[16] The Sales Management in Action box provides a framework to help sales managers, or anyone else in an organization, make ethical decisions.

THE VALUES AND BEHAVIOURS OF PEERS

Salespeople often look to peers to help establish appropriate selling behaviour. When senior executives and sales managers abrogate their responsibility to promote honesty and integrity and to manage ethical behaviour, then salespeople view what others around them are doing and take direction from that. Bonnie Leedy, now public relations director at Go Daddy Software, describes behaviour at a sales call centre where she used to work. She says, "You could hear the top sales guy making false comments to his customers, but no disciplinary actions were ever taken. To the people who were lower in the company, it was an example of what they needed to do to be recognized."[17] Salespeople, in some organizations, over-tell, over-sell, over-promise, and over-stock customers; at the same time, they under-inform, under-deliver, under-service. Al Rosen, a former professor at York University, says that new employees quickly become a product of the company and its ethics. He says, "People are telling you to forget this and that—it becomes a birds-of-a-feather atmosphere."[18]

When there is no clear direction and enforcement of ethical standards, things can even get worse. Salespeople are not simply left to view and adopt unethical practices, they may be coached to do so. Susan Marshall, a former marketing executive with a small firm, overheard a veteran employee at her company coach a rookie on the "10 percent rule." She learned that day that it

SALES MANAGEMENT **IN ACTION**

Making Ethical Decisions

Making ethical decisions is frequently difficult. If they were easy decisions to make, then the person making an ethical decision would be able to do so with limited analysis, and little thought regarding the outcome of the decision. Some people faced with an ethical decision can decide their course of action with very little thought, either because they have already decided to behave unethically, or because they do not see that an ethical issue exists. Other people will agonize for days or months when faced with having to make an ethical decision because they recognize the costs involved for various stakeholders, including themselves, if they make a wrong decision. One thing that will help you make better ethical decisions, and be more comfortable afterward, is to follow an ethical decision-making process model. There are many that could be used, but the following six-step process will serve you well in making any ethical decision.

1. Recognize that an ethical dilemma exists.
2. Understand the important facts surrounding the ethical dilemma.
3. Identify all stakeholders that will be affected positively and negatively by your decision.
4. Identify the various ethical alternatives that you could choose.
5. Evaluate how each alternative will affect each stakeholder.
6. Choose a course of action and implement it.

Following an ethical decision-making process model will not ensure that you make sound ethical decisions, but it will help you recognize the ethics of any decision you make. Then, your personal values will decide how ethical you will be. Perhaps the most important check on any decision you make is to carefully consider how comfortable you would be if the situation became public and your involvement appeared on the front page of *The Globe and Mail* or *The National Post*.

was common practice for salespeople to add 10 percent to every expense report they filed. Susan went to her accounting department and asked that 10 percent be deducted from each salesperson's paycheque. This was more than the salespeople were over-expensing to the company, she admitted, "But, I wanted to show them what exactly they were doing to the company and demonstrate the magnitude of scale."[19] Many salespeople abuse their expense accounts because it is so easy to do: pay a $3 tip and claim $5; pay $8 for lunch and claim $12 if this is below the minimum that triggers a required receipt; claim a mileage expense for 50 kilometres more than what was actually travelled, or even submit completely false receipts for items that were never purchased. The best defence a company may have against dishonest and unethical salespeople is its internal policies and practices, assuming they are communicated and properly enforced.

COMPANY POLICIES AND PRACTICES

Company policies and practices can have a major impact on the ethical conduct of the sales force. Furthermore, research has demonstrated that companies clearly committed to ethical practices financially outperform companies less committed.[20] KPMG Canada's Ethics Survey 2000 polled 1000 CEOs: 86 percent reported written documents that stated their values and principles; 42 percent reported senior-level executives responsible for implementation, monitoring, and assurance of ethics initiatives, although most indicated that less than 10 percent of their time was spent on ethical issues.

CODES OF ETHICS   One reason why a code of ethics is important is because the process of developing it forces a company to define appropriate behaviour for its employees and how it wants to manage its business relationships. However, simply having a code of ethics is not sufficient. Marjorie Kelly, editor of *Business Ethics,* says, "You can't just slap an ethics code on a sales force like a barnacle on the side of a whale."[21] Simply developing a document that defines appropriate behaviour does not guarantee employee compliance. Enron, the now infamous energy giant that was brought down by greed and corruption, had a 65-page *Code of Ethics,* which proved to be meaningless. A copy of it now resides in the Smithsonian Institute.[22] Many people lauded Canada's Nortel Networks when it appointed a full-time ethics officer and published a 23-page code of ethics, *Living the Values—A Guide to Ethical Business Practices at Nortel Networks.* However, many people remember that Nortel had a former senior ethics advisor and a previous published code of ethics that proved equally meaningless.[23] The key to having an effective code of ethics only begins with its development. Commitment to it must be communicated internally by senior management, and it must be continually reinforced throughout the organization. Ethical conduct must be recognized and, when appropriate, rewarded. More important, unethical behaviour must be punished, and seen to be punished.

RECIPROCITY   **Reciprocity** occurs when there is a mutual exchange of benefits between organizations, as when a firm buys products from its own customers. For example, an automobile manufacturer could buy office equipment from a manufacturer whose salespeople drive automobiles that it makes. The implication is that "you scratch my back, and I'll scratch yours." This practice varies considerably by country. In the United States, the practice is watched closely by the Federal Trade Commission and the Department of Justice as it is viewed as an attempt to reduce competition. In Japan, the ties that exist between sellers and customers are often very close. In Canada, reciprocity is a widespread practice in the business-to-business marketplace. However, if it could be proven to reduce competition in Canada, the practice would be illegal.

Is this a good way to do business? Most times, yes. It becomes an ethical issue when firms feel obligated to buy from other firms simply because they are also customers. In some instances, the buyer may pay higher prices, get inferior quality products, or be taken for granted when it comes to service. Aside from the effect on competition, reciprocity can have a negative effect on the morale of purchasing people who must buy from their company's customers. It interferes with their ability to make optimal purchasing decisions for their company.

GIFTS   Giving gifts when businesspeople first meet is a common practice in China and helps build business relationships. In Canada, we also give gifts, although gifts given at first meeting are generally restricted to items of specialty advertising, such as a pen with the seller's company's name and phone number. As relationships develop, some companies continue to give gifts to customers, although the practice is beginning to decline in popularity. Anne Snowden, president of Here's Looking at You, a Toronto-based image and presentation company, notes that an increasing number of companies are instituting a zero tolerance gift policy similar to the one adopted by Wal-Mart Canada and described in the opening vignette. She offers a solution: "It sounds old-fashioned, but people are starting to go back to the hand-written thank-you card."[24] In an age of increasing electronic communication, a personalized thank-you card can be refreshing and memorable. Jim Clemmer, president of Clemmer Group in Kitchener, Ontario, has another suggestion. He suggests that instead of giving the gift to a customer's employee, consider giving the gift to the company.[25] For example, a prize could be donated to the company golf tournament.

BRIBES   When does a gift become a bribe? Some people argue that it depends on the intent of the giver: to thank the customer for a favourable purchase decision, or to entice the customer to make a purchase decision favourable to the giver. Some people argue that it depends on whether it is given before or after a purchase is made. In most instances the argument is moot. In an environment where most seller–buyer relationships are focused on the longer term, the customer that makes one purchase decision today frequently makes many future decisions that could affect the giver. Even if there were a way to determine that the intent of the giver was clearly to thank the customer, many customers would be placed in a situation where they might feel, depending on the value of what they received, an obligation to favour the giver when future purchase decisions were made. This suggests that the issue may be resolved by considering the value of what is given: 64 percent of respondents to one survey indicated that they considered personal gifts valued at more than $100 to be bribes. The bad news: 89 percent indicated that they or their colleagues offered such gifts in exchange for business.[26] Whether you view the value that differentiates a gift from a bribe as $100, or less, the problem is that any gift, even a very small one, can be dangerous. Queen's University business professor Jim Ridler has built a good part of his career around business ethics and argues that once you indulge a customer with an under-the-table gift, even a small one, you set a precedent. Colleagues who are aware of it get the message that it is acceptable practice, and customers begin to assume this is your way of doing business. What makes matters even worse is that, in business, people talk to people, and the word of your behaviour quickly spreads.[27] You may now be on a slippery slope, and you may find it difficult to get off.

ENTERTAINMENT   Entertaining customers occurs frequently in sales and, in many instances, it is simply good business practice for salespeople to do this. Some salespeople see entertaining as a way to build good relationships with buyers outside of the normal working environment. People can get to know each other better, and can discuss business over longer periods of time than might be available during a customer's busy daily routine. Other people see entertaining as another form of bribery, and some people place a value on the entertainment that they believe differentiates legitimate entertainment from bribery. Before entertaining customers, it is a good idea to find out about their personal interests and how they like to spend their leisure time. Company officials at Markham, Ontario-based Magna International, Inc. took purchasing agents for the "Big Three" automakers to strip clubs, and paid for lap dances in upstairs rooms. One account manager claimed to have entertained customers at topless bars on a weekly basis, to have taken customers to Las Vegas to play golf, to have bought one customer a tuxedo, and to have given other customers Mont Blanc pens. Many buyers did not want their names on salespersons' expense reports because their behaviour violated their company's code of ethics. To protect buyers' identities, expense reports submitted at Magna included false names.[28] Very few sales executives would argue that this is within acceptable limits for entertaining customers.

BUSINESS DEFAMATION   As part of the selling process, salespeople frequently compare their product and their company to those of their competition. Unfortunately, many comparisons are inaccurate—47 percent of managers who responded to one survey indicated that they suspect their salespeople have lied on sales calls, and nearly 78 percent said they caught a competitor lying about their company's products or services.[29] When statements are made that are inaccurate, misleading, or slander a company's business reputation, they are illegal.[30] Those that make such statements can be sued for **business defamation**. What constitutes business defamation? Steven M. Sack, coauthor of *The Salesperson's Legal Guide,* provides the following examples:

1. *Business slander.* **Business slander** occurs when an unfair and untrue statement about a competitor is made orally. It becomes legally actionable when the statement is made to a third party and can be interpreted as damaging the personal reputation of a competitor's employee or the competitor's business reputation.
2. *Business libel.* **Business libel** occurs when an unfair and untrue statement about a competitor is made in writing. It becomes legally actionable when the statement is communicated to a third party and can be interpreted as damaging the company.
3. *Product disparagement.* **Product disparagement** occurs when false or deceptive comparisons or distorted claims are made concerning a competitor's product, services, or property.[31]

While the Canadian business environment may be less litigious than in the United States, care should be exercised to prevent costly legal action because of business defamation, but also because it makes good business sense to always tell the truth. Customers are in some instances more knowledgeable about a company's competitors that its salespeople are, and if they catch a salesperson defaming a competitor, even if it is due to the salesperson's lack of knowledge, they will lose respect for the salesperson and distrust him in future.

MANAGEMENT OF CUSTOMER INFORMATION   There are two ethical issues concerning customer information: collecting it and sharing it. With the increased use of CRM applications, companies are increasingly collecting customer information, and they have a responsibility to protect that information from unlawful use. Private sector companies that misuse customer information risk legal action under the federal government's ***Personal Information Protection and Electronic Documents Act***, which has been in effect since 2001 (visit **www.privcom.gc.ca**). The Act sets out ground rules for how companies may collect, use, or disclose personal information in the course of commercial activities.

Salespeople also find themselves in situations where they are asked to or voluntarily share customer information with other customers. Salespeople often collect or are given sensitive information by customers that are seeking advice. Some things that might be divulged by the customer include production schedules, forthcoming new product or service programs, changes in marketing strategy and target customer focus, and many other things that a customer's competitors would value. Naïve salespeople believe they can gain a customer's favour by providing them with sensitive and confidential information. In most instances, this backfires as the customer getting the information loses respect for the salesperson, and will be unlikely to provide sensitive information to this salesperson concerning their own needs. They recognize that this salesperson lacks integrity and cannot be trusted.

PERFORMANCE-BASED COMPENSATION PLANS AND INCENTIVE PROGRAMS There is considerable debate about the role performance-based compensation plans and incentive programs play in encouraging unethical behaviour of salespeople. There is always the risk that paying a large percentage of a person's total income based on their sales performance will distort their judgment so that they act in their own self-interest, at odds with the interests of their customer. Andy Zoltners, a marketing professor at Northwestern University, supports this view. He says, "If salespeople have to eat what they hunt, it puts stress on them and motivates them toward bad behaviour."[32] Wesley Cragg, Gardiner professor of business at York University, agrees: "The temptation [for being dishonest] seems sharper [with commission-based sales]. This applies to real estate, insurance people, car salespeople. Compensation systems tend to push salespeople to make sales because it's in their interest."[33] But, not everyone agrees. Cameron Fellman, partner with inForm Inc., which specializes in sales force effectiveness, calls this belief simply "leftist fringe" thinking. He says, "As long as management has solid ethical terms and conditions specified in the company's compensation contract, then there is no reason that commission-based pay will encourage someone to act unethically."[34] Taken together, the two views indicate that too much performance-based compensation can lead to unethical behaviour unless management carefully defines what is appropriate and monitors the effects that commission, bonuses, and reward incentives have on the sales force.

TERRITORY ADJUSTMENTS AND HOUSE ACCOUNTS   An issue that frequently arises concerns the territory that gets to be too large, and especially if salespeople get performance-based income. From a management perspective, when a sales territory generates too many sales to be managed by a single salesperson, there needs to be an adjustment so that there is an adequate level of coverage for all customers and adequate time to prospect for and develop new accounts. The salesperson often does not share this perspective. From her perspective, the company has given her performance-based income to motivate her to grow her sales territory, and now that she has done that, she is being punished by having her territory reduced in size. A sales manager who regularly does this may find that instrumentalities among the sales force are reduced, and their performance decreases.

The same issue may arise when a sales manager decides that a particular account must become a house account, and responsibility for the account needs to be taken from the salesperson. Again, the salesperson may stand to lose a sizeable commission or bonus when this happens. Making the account a house account can be defended because large accounts need special attention, often well beyond what can be provided by a salesperson who has other responsibilities. But, this still will not satisfy the salesperson who loses commission after having worked to build the account to the size where it deserves special status and attention.

Handling either of these situations often results in misunderstanding, resentment, and dissatisfaction. Having clear guidelines and policies helps, but each situation may require special attention. Some actions that may help include providing notice as far in advance of changes as possible, protecting a salesperson's income level while the salesperson has some time to adjust to the changed conditions, or allowing the salesperson some input into how the territory will be split, or how the house account will be handled. For example, it is sometimes possible to designate only a portion of an account as a house account. Just as a manufacturer may decide to sell certain items direct to the account and other items to the same account through a distributor or manufacturer's agent, there are instances where companies will sell most items through the regular salesperson, but designate one or two items that are high value or infrequently bought to be handled by the sales manager who manages these sales as "house" sales.

WHISTLE-BLOWING   **Whistle-blowing** occurs when an employee informs on someone else in the company whose behaviour he or she believes to be unethical or illegal. In the United States, whistle-blowers are encouraged to act and are protected by law. Whistle-blowers can get rewards of 15–25 percent of any recovery, plus legal fees. They have regularly been receiving US$1 million or more, and one sales executive received US$77 million (before paying US$28 million in taxes) for exposing a scheme to bribe doctors to prescribe a particular brand of pharmaceutical product.[35] The risk to the company when a whistle-blower goes public, or when the company gets sued for retaliation, may explain why more than half of respondents to a *Sales & Marketing* survey indicated that they had a process that allowed salespeople to alert managers to unethical behaviour.[36]

In Canada, whistle-blowers do not have the same level of protection from retaliation or access to legal redress when it occurs. At least some of Canada's best-managed companies have addressed the issue. *Canadian Business* conducted an informal survey of 25 Canadian companies with top-ranked boards of directors and found that 16 of the 18 that responded had some kind of whistle-blowing policy in place.[37] These companies recognize that it is in their long-term interest to encourage and support whistle-blowing so that problems can be identified and dealt with internally. P.K. Pal, an Ottawa-based corporate governance lawyer, agrees. He says, "Generally, it seems that if you have a good system that protects whistle-blowers, this will cause the company—and therefore the country—less harm than if you didn't. Offensive acts can be nipped in the bud, so to speak, without becoming public matters."[38] Ideally, whistle-blowing should be handled internally. That is, an employee should have access to someone in an organization who will investigate questionable behaviour and, at the same time, protect the whistle-blower.

Since the risks are high, and the rewards are low, why would anyone become a whistle-blower in Canada? It obviously requires an employee with high moral values to come forward in such an environment. Russell Hayes, an employee at CMC Electronics in Montreal, wrote his CEO in 1995 alleging corrupt practices, and this precipitated his losing his job. Fortunately for Russell, the actions involved the U.S. government, and the U.S. attorney's office became involved in 2002. The resulting case against CMC Electronics was finally settled in 2004 for US$9.6 million, and Hayes got a reward of US$1.5 million.[39] However, before the case was settled, Hayes admitted that if he had to do it all again, he would have stayed with the company for selfish reasons—his paycheque. He says, "I did the right thing from a moral point of view, absolutely. But if you're morally right and broke, who gives a shit."[40]

ORDER TIMING   One issue important to some companies is when to recognize an order as a sale, and when to credit it as a sale to the salesperson. Many companies have had difficulty with this at the company level in the past, particularly technology companies such as Nortel Networks. There is always pressure to keep sales revenue growing, so increasingly some companies have reported sales revenue before the actual orders were booked. They then ran into difficulty when the recorded orders never finalized. Salespeople are sometimes prone to recording orders early as well. In one survey, 36 percent of managers reported that they had caught salespeople rushing deals through accounting before they were actually closed.[41] Sales managers need clear policies concerning when a sale can be counted as a sale. Most companies will only allow sales to be recorded after a signed purchase order has been received from the customer.

EMPLOYMENT PRACTICES: HIRING, PROMOTING, AND FIRING   Sales managers are frequently faced with ethical decisions related to hiring, promoting, and firing salespeople. Most people have a bias of some sort, and frequently their bias comes out during a hiring decision although it may never be made explicit. A sales manager could call a college or university professor, for example, and ask for the best sales candidates from a personal selling or sales management class, and then add, "But if you know they smoke, don't send them for an interview." Is this the sales manager's hiring prejudice, or does he believe there are customers who will be prejudiced against smokers when they make their purchase decisions? Even if it is only one in 20 customers, can a company afford to lose 5 percent of its sales due to smoking? Another sales manager could call and ask for the best female candidates from the class. Again, is it hiring prejudice, or could he have evidence that women perform better selling his company's product or service? Another alternative could be simply that women are underrepresented in his sales force, and he needs more women to build a stronger support group for the women he does have as his current ones are too important to risk losing. Should a sales manager consider hiring his boss's niece or nephew over a candidate who is a better qualified applicant? He would be putting the possibility of personal gain ahead of the company's best interest.

When it comes to promotion, a common consideration is whether to promote a deserving candidate from within and send a morale-boosting message to other employees that the company values its employees and wants them to succeed. An easy alternative might be to hire from outside and, that way, there would be only one position in the company where someone was learning new responsibilities. Is it ever acceptable to promote someone who is liked over someone who has better aptitude for the job? Should someone be held back from promotion because of their age?

Who should be let go when the decision has to be made? Should it be someone who has family obligations, or a single person, or does it matter? Should the oldest person be let go because they are not as aggressive as the younger salesperson, or should the younger person be let go because they have less experience? Is it acceptable to get rid of the salesperson who costs the company the most, or should it be a junior person whose compensation is a lot lower?

These are all difficult decisions and many people will be sure they know the right answer. In practice, what is done may vary considerably from one person, and one company, and one situation to another. They deserve reflection and, after they are made, the most important thing is that the decision maker can respect the decision he made and himself for making it. But, most sales managers will face these decisions many times. The decisions that are made will often result from the sales manager's personal values and his own personal code of ethics.

TOWARD A PERSONAL CODE OF ETHICS

While we hear all too frequently about unethical and dishonest salespeople, they by no means hold a monopoly on being morally corrupt. Canada has a history of political corruption—federal, provincial, and municipal—and you don't have to go back to the last century, even though that is less than a decade ago. A television newscast in Toronto recently showed what happened to a number of wallets that were left unattended on purpose in various parts of the city. Each wallet had a $20 bill inside. One wallet was picked up by what appeared to be a homeless person. He turned it in "because it was not his." Another wallet was picked up by a man in a business suit near Bay Street, Toronto's financial district. After looking around to see if anyone was watching, he took the money and discarded the wallet. While many of Canada's richest people are among the most socially responsible, the rich do not have a monopoly on integrity. Many people are hoping to see a return to higher moral values in society. Indeed, unethical and dishonest behaviour threatens the moral fabric of our whole free-enterprise system. Phil Rody, mentioned earlier in this chapter, says, "The basic principle of free enterprise is that all business transactions are voluntary transactions for mutual advantage. Deceptive sales tactics undermine that. They undermine the very system that salespeople rely on for their livelihood."[42]

There are no absolute rules for acceptable behaviour in sales, but there are certainly some guidelines that sales managers should consider that will help them and their salespeople develop a strong personal code of ethics.[43]

1. *Personal selling must be viewed as an exchange of value.* Many people would argue that the core concept of marketing is exchange. Buyers and sellers exchange with each other so that each provides value to the other. According to Ron Willingham, author of *Integrity Selling,* the role of the seller must always be to understand the buyer's needs before any attempt is made to sell.[44] Salespeople who accept this will view selling as something you do *for* people,

and not something you do *to* people. They will be as or more concerned with the process of selling—how they got there—than with the outcome of selling—how much or what they sold.

2. *Relationship comes first, task second.* Salespeople who place task first assume they know more than the customer. Sharon Drew Morgan, author of *Selling With Integrity,* tells us "the buyer has the answers; the seller has the questions.[45] The seller will only get the answers after rapport and trust have been established in the seller–buyer relationship.

3. *Be honest with yourself and with others.* The most important person in the world should be the person who looks at you in the mirror in the morning. If you can't look directly at him and say "I like you," then you will be unlikely to have a good relationship with anyone. You will like that person if he is honest with everyone he deals with. Paul Ekman, author of *Telling Lies,* says that withholding important information is a form of telling lies.[46] A compete and informative presentation should discuss the strengths and weaknesses of an offering so that customers can make a fully informed decision. Your character and integrity are revealed to others by your willingness to be candid and honest with others. Stephen Harper, prime minister of Canada, speaking about his father said, "He raised all of us with a strong sense that if you compromise your integrity to get ahead, you haven't gotten ahead."[47] As Canadians, we hope the lesson was learned well. As stakeholders in Canadian society, we hope more salespeople learn the same lesson.

Whether you are in sales or whatever your occupation, you will likely find greater comfort in your own code of ethics as you age. If you have not given your personal code of ethics much thought yet, reviewing the Canadian Professional Sales Association Sales Institute code of ethics shown in Exhibit 12.2 is a good place to start. Everyone who earns accreditation as a certified sales professional (CSP) must agree to accept and abide by this code of ethics. A personal code of ethics is one of the important things that distinguishes a sales professional from a salesperson. You will see in this code of ethics almost everything discussed in this chapter. Before leaving this chapter, a discussion of laws that affect salespeople in Canada is necessary. In the absence of a strong sense of ethical responsibility, legal responsibility should be the absolute minimum standard that directs the behaviour of salespeople.

Federal and Provincial Laws

In the field of selling there are both ethical standards and legal standards. *Ethical standards* establish appropriate behaviour for a particular community, at a particular time; that is, what is right and what is wrong; *legal standards* are enforced by statute. Sales managers should recognize that operating only within legal limits is not sufficient, and can create serious problems for the sales force; however, they should also recognize that breaking the law has serious consequences as well—for the company, for its senior executives, and for individual salespeople who may be involved. Canadian sales managers must understand both federal and provincial legislation. The following sections describe the *Competition Act*, which is the most important federal legislation, and provincial consumer protection legislation.

THE *COMPETITION ACT*

Competition legislation in Canada is more than 100 years old. Originally, the rationale for such legislation was to eliminate restrictive trade practices and to foster competition. Changes to the legislation eventually led to the **Competition Act**, passed in 1975 and revised in 1986, which is

---

Exhibit 12.2
The CPSA Sales Institute Code of Ethics

The CPSA Sales Institute Code of Ethics is the set of principles and standards that a certified sales professional will strive to adhere to with customers, organizations, competitors, communities and colleagues.

The Certified Sales Professional pledges and commits to uphold these standards in all activities.

I will:

1. Maintain honesty and integrity in all relationships with customers, prospective customers, and colleagues and continually work to earn their trust and respect.

2. Accurately represent my products or services to the best of my ability in a manner that places my customer or prospective customer and my company in a position that benefits both.

3. Respect and protect the proprietary and confidential information entrusted to me by my company and my customers and not engage in activities that may conflict with the best interests of my customers or my company.

4. Continually upgrade my knowledge of my products/services, skills and my industry.

5. Use the time and resources available to me only for legitimate business purposes. I will only participate in activities that are ethical and legal, and when in doubt, I will seek counsel.

6. Respect my competitors and their products and services by representing them in a manner which is honest, truthful and based on accurate information that has been substantiated.

7. Endeavor to engage in business and selling practices which contribute to a positive relationship with the community.

8. Assist and counsel my fellow sales professionals where possible in the performance of their duties.

9. Abide by and encourage others to adhere to this Code of Ethics.

As a certified sales professional, I understand that the reputation and professionalism of all salespeople depends on me as well as others engaged in the sales profession, and I will adhere to these standards to strengthen the reputation and integrity for which we all strive. I understand that failure to consistently act according to this Code of Ethics may result in the loss of the privilege of using my professional sales designation.

Source: **www.cpsa.com/institute.html**. Reprinted with permission.

---

the most comprehensive legislation in Canada. It is administered by Industry Canada, whose mission is to "foster a growing, competitive, knowledge-based Canadian economy," and among whose program areas is "setting rules and services that support the effective operation of the marketplace." The *Competition Act* supports a healthy Canadian marketplace by fostering competition and by protecting Canadian consumers, its two main purposes. Many of its laws and regulations can be categorized into three specific marketing areas: pricing (including price fixing, bid rigging, price discrimination, predatory pricing, and resale price maintenance); distribution (including pyramid selling, exclusive dealing, market restriction, tied selling, and refusal to deal); and promotion (including misleading advertising, referral selling, and bait-and-switch selling). Some of these are criminal offences carrying heavy fines and possibly jail sentences, and some of them are non-criminal offences subject to investigation by the Competition Tribunal, whose ruling will depend on the degree to which competition is restricted or consumers are affected. All of these activities affect salespeople, and each of them is now discussed.

1. *Price fixing.* **Price fixing** occurs when sellers collude to set prices higher than they would otherwise be in a free market. Recently, company executives have also been held personally liable when their companies have been convicted. Several companies were fined $1 million or more for price fixing graphite electrode sales in Canada. Two executives of one of the companies were given personal fines totalling $120 000 for their involvement.[48] In another case, Russell Cosburn, former vice-president of sales for Toronto-based Chinook Group Ltd., was given a nine-month sentence for his part in a conspiracy to fix prices and allocate market share for vitamin B-4.[49]

2. *Bid rigging.* **Bid rigging** occurs when sellers collude to set prices with respect to one or more specific requests for proposals. The sellers decide who will have the lowest price this time and there is an agreement that another seller will have the lowest price on a future request for proposal. However, in both instances, the price is inflated beyond what it would be in a free market. Four Toronto-based electrical contractors were convicted of bid rigging and were fined a total of $2.55 million. Winning contracts were estimated to be priced 10–15 percent higher than they should have been. Prosecutor James Sutton indicated that the bid riggers could also be sued for damages by customers who were victimized by the collusion.[50] Six Ottawa hotels were convicted of bid rigging with respect to prices charged to government employees, and were each fined up to $80 000.[51]

3. *Price discrimination.* **Price discrimination** occurs when a seller charges customers that are in competition with each other different prices for a like quantity and quality of goods. There have been very few convictions in Canada, but fines have ranged from $15 000 to $50 000.[52] Functional discounts are legal in the United States; that is, it is acceptable to offer larger discounts to wholesalers versus retailers, based on the functions they perform. In Canada, wholesalers and retailers are considered competitors, and must be treated as equals with respect to pricing and related promotional allowances. Price discrimination may be more difficult to detect and to successfully prosecute in future due to new marketing strategies used by sellers. For example, sellers now encourage repeat business and long-term relationships by offering customers discounts if they become "preferred" customers.

4. *Predatory pricing.* **Predatory pricing** occurs when companies set prices so low that they drive competitors from the market or deter competitors from entering the market. This goes beyond simply the prices charged for the goods. LePage's Inc. initiated legal action against 3M Co. for its "bundled rebates" program that it offered to retailers. LePage's, now owned by Canadian-based Conros Corp., alleged that it was dropped by Kmart after 3M offered the discount chain US$1 million in rebates if it would purchase US$15 million of 3M products in one year. LePage's argued successfully that these targets were so large that the only way retailers could meet them would be to buy everything they could from 3M and drop smaller suppliers, such as itself, that sold a much narrower product line. LePage's was awarded US$96.5 million, covering judgment, interest, and legal fees.[53]

5. *Resale price maintenance.* **Resale price maintenance** occurs when suppliers try to influence the price at which a product is to be resold by a purchaser (usually a retailer or industrial distributor). Discretionary fines or imprisonment for up to five years, or both, may be imposed. However, there are situations where a manufacturer can require a channel member to sell its branded products at an established price. Tilley Endurables, for example, now sells its products through a number of retail "partners." Tilley products are priced identically at all locations where they are sold to protect the premium image of the brand. The test for whether this is legal is whether competition is reduced or restricted as a result. Few retailers, and even few consumers, would argue that there were no acceptable alternatives to Tilley. While Tilley Endurables is an important supplier of adventure clothing in Canada, it certainly does not have sufficient market share to control the market.

6. *Pyramid selling.* **Pyramid selling** involves illegal schemes that use tiers of salespeople, sometimes referred to as members, agents, dealers, or distributors, where each succeeding tier receives credit for revenues or commissions from sales, regardless of whether they have contributed to the sales effort. The goal is to have salespeople recruit additional levels of salespeople, rather than to sell products. These schemes often exaggerate what salespeople earn, require new salespeople to purchase large quantities of inventory or expensive demonstration kits of questionable value, and fail to have a return goods policy for salespeople. The Direct Sellers Association of Canada provides a code of ethics for its members and advice on how to protect yourself from getting involved in pyramid selling. (Visit **www.dsa.ca**.) There are legitimate multi-level marketing companies, but you should be aware of questionable organizations that try to disguise themselves as multi-level marketers.

7. *Exclusive dealing.* **Exclusive dealing** requires that buyers deal only or primarily in products supplied by or designated by the seller. This practice prohibits marketing intermediaries from handling competing products. The practice is fairly widespread in Canada and seldom creates problems. Manufacturers of high quality branded items, for example, may require retailers to sell only their brand of product to ensure that they give full attention to that brand. Only if the manufacturer's or retailer's sales in the market area are sufficiently large to argue that competition is restricted is there likely to be a problem. New companies that enter a market are also able to require exclusive dealing because, being new, their market share is undoubtedly small. Once their market share becomes substantial, they will have to ensure that they do not violate the *Competition Act*.

8. *Market restriction.* **Market restriction** occurs when market intermediaries are allowed to sell only in a designated market area. There are two types of market restriction: vertical and horizontal. *Vertical market restriction* involves manufacturers and wholesalers or retailers. A manufacturer, for example, might divide the Atlantic Provinces into 10 market areas and appoint a distributor for each area, protecting each of them in their designated area by not allowing other distributors to compete with them. When manufacturers have relatively small market shares, this practice arguably increases competition. Distributors can make reasonable profit margins in their own territory and do not have to worry about other distributors who may provide lower service levels and have lower overheads undercutting prices. Distributors who do not face competition from the same brand can then concentrate on competing against brands from other manufacturers. *Horizontal market restriction* happens when wholesalers or retailers agree to avoid competition by not selling the same products in a particular market area. These agreements are more likely to restrict competition and violate the *Competition Act*.

9. *Tied selling.* **Tied selling** occurs when a buyer is required to purchase another product, or refrain from purchasing a product that is not from a specific manufacturer, as a condition of being able to buy a product from the seller. For example, a jeans manufacturer might require a retailer to carry a full range of its brands in order to sell its most popular brand. Its argument would be that it wants its resellers to have a broad representation of its products. However, if the retailer is small and has limited financial resources, this could mean that the retailer could not afford to carry other brands in its stores. That, in effect, limits competition and could trigger an investigation if the retailer complains. Tied selling is not a criminal offence but is a reviewable matter by the Competition Tribunal, which can prohibit its use after a review to determine whether competition is restricted. In what the Competition Tribunal called its most complex case, it compelled Tele-Direct, which publishes the *Yellow Pages* in many parts of Canada, to stop its practice of tied selling. The company required customers who bought advertising space to also buy its advertising services, including advice, design, and administration. By doing this, Tele-Direct restricted competition as small, independent consultants could not compete.[54]

10. *Refusal to deal.* **Refusal to deal** occurs when sellers refuse to sell to legitimate buyers. The *Competition Act* states that a seller with adequate inventory of a product that is not otherwise widely available must sell to any legitimate buyer willing to meet normal trade terms if the seller's refusal to deal would have a substantial negative effect on the buyer's business.

11. *Misleading advertising.* **Misleading advertising** includes all representations, whether in print or oral (where salespeople are more likely to be involved), that create a false or misleading impression, even if the claims are literally true. Convictions for misleading advertising have been common in Canada. Suzy Shier Ltd. was fined $1 million in 2005 and agreed to implement a corporate compliance program and publish notices in newspapers across Canada. It was fined $300 000 for a similar offence in 1995.[55] Sears Canada was fined $100 000 and also agreed to pay $387 000 for legal fees, for misrepresenting savings on its tires.[56] Health and fitness clubs have been criticized frequently by consumers for questionable marketing practices, and have had their share of convictions for misleading advertising. Good Life Fitness Clubs, which operates more than 90 locations across Canada, was fined $75 000, and Premier Health Club was fined $30 000.[57]

12. *Referral selling.* **Referral selling** is illegal and occurs when a salesperson offers a price reduction or other inducement to a customer for names of other potential customers who may subsequently buy from the seller.

13. *Bait-and-switch selling.* **Bait-and-switch selling** occurs when a seller offers a low price to attract customers and then tells them that the offered article is no longer in stock but that they can buy another, more expensive product. It is illegal; however, it is not illegal to advertise limited quantities of sale items or, as some sellers do, advertise "Compare at $200."

PROVINCIAL CONSUMER PROTECTION ACTS

Consumer protection legislation varies by province and territory across Canada. In most jurisdictions this legislation is referred to as either ***The Direct Sellers Act*** or ***The Consumer Protection Act***. The purpose is to protect the rights of buyers and sellers with respect to direct sales contracts. These sales include door-to-door sales, telephone sales, or direct mail sales, or where the buyer has been induced to a trade show, convention, or hotel, for example, for the purpose of contracting a sale for goods or services.

These laws are commonly called "cooling off laws" because one of their most important purposes is to protect the consumer's right to contract recession for a specified period after a contract is signed. The customer must be allowed to reconsider a buying decision made under a salesperson's persuasive influence. The cooling-off period ranges from two days to ten days depending on the province. Some provinces determine the period to begin when the contract is signed, while other provinces consider it to begin when the customer receives a copy of the contract. In addition, a notice informing the customer of the cooling-off period must be part of the contract in most provinces.

Other than Ontario and Quebec, all provinces provide for longer cooling-off periods under some conditions: if the salesperson was not licensed when the contract was negotiated, if the terms and conditions of the licence were not met, if the contract was not in accordance with the requirements of the appropriate legislation. For example, some consumer protection legislation specifies the minimum font size that must be used to inform consumers of the cooling-off period. Contracts may also be cancelled if the goods or services are not provided within a certain period of time. If contracts are cancelled, the seller must return the money paid by the consumer, and any trade-in that may have been part of the sale (or a sum of money equal to the value of the trade-in if its return is not possible). The Consumer Measures Committee, created under the *Agreement on Internal Trade*, is a joint federal, provincial, and territorial committee that is currently trying to harmonize consumer protection legislation across Canada. It is currently focused on direct selling, cost of credit disclosure, electronic commerce, and rules governing debt collection.[58]

CANADIAN LAW AND GLOBAL SELLING

Ethics, as defined, vary from one community to another. So, too, do laws. In the United States, the *Foreign Corrupt Practices Act* holds all employees of all companies subject to the laws of the United States, regardless of where in the world they are conducting business. Things are not so clear for Canadian companies. Joanne Paquette, senior legal counsel for Export Development Canada, says it is unclear whether Canadian businesspeople can be held accountable in Canada for paying private-sector bribes overseas. However, Canadians must appreciate that they are subject to the laws of every jurisdiction in which they violate local law, and bribes paid to foreign civil servants are certainly illegal under Canada's ***Corruption of Foreign Public Officials Act*** of 1998.[59]

SUMMARY

1. **Discuss the importance of ethical behaviour for managing relationships.** Behaving ethically is important for building all types of business relationships, both internal and external. Internally, 70 percent of employees rated working for an ethical and trustworthy company to be very important, more than the percentage who rated liking their job to be very important. With respect to seller–customer relationships, 83 percent of respondents to an ethics survey reported that they train their salespeople to sell customers on their ethics and integrity, and 70 percent indicated that they believed customers consider this when making a purchase decision. Ethics are just as important in relationships with suppliers. Because ethics are so important in business, colleges and universities are paying more attention to business ethics in their programs.

2. **Describe the factors that influence ethical conduct of salespeople.** Many factors influence the ethical behaviour of salespeople, including the CEO as a role model, the sales manager as a role model, the values and behaviours of a salesperson's peers, various

company policies and practices—codes of ethics, reciprocity, gifts, bribes, entertainment, business defamation, management of customer information, performance-based compensation plans and incentive programs, territory adjustments and house accounts, whistle-blowing, order timing, and employment practices, including hiring, promoting, and firing—and the salesperson's personal code of ethics.

3. **Describe important legislation that helps manage the behaviour of salespeople.**
    Legislation defines what is legal, not necessarily what is ethical. The most important legislation governing the behaviour of salespeople in Canada includes the federal *Competition Act,* and various provincial and territorial *Consumer Protection Acts.* The former is designed to foster healthy competition and protect Canadian consumers. It covers such things as price fixing, bid rigging, price discrimination, predatory pricing, resale price maintenance, pyramid selling, exclusive dealing, market restriction, tied selling, refusal to deal, misleading advertising, referral selling, and bait-and-switch selling, among other things. Some of these are criminal offences and some are non-criminal offences subject to investigation by the Competition Tribunal, whose ruling will depend on the degree to which competition is restricted or consumers are affected. The latter is legislation designed to protect the rights of buyers and sellers with respect to direct sales contracts. It outlines the rights of consumers and the legal obligations of direct salespeople.

KEY TERMS

ethics   **338**

character   **340**

integrity   **340**

reciprocity   **344**

business defamation   **345**

business slander   **346**

business libel   **346**

product disparagement   **346**

Personal Information Protection and Electronic Documents Act   **346**

whistle-blowing   **347**

Competition Act   **350**

price fixing   **352**

bid rigging   **352**

price discrimination   **352**

predatory pricing   **352**

resale price maintenance   **353**

pyramid selling   **353**

exclusive dealing   **353**

market restriction   **353**

tied selling   **354**

refusal to deal   **354**

misleading advertising   **354**

referral selling   **354**

bait-and-switch selling   **354**

Direct Sellers Act   **354**

Consumer Protection Act   **354**

Corruption of Foreign Public Officials Act   **355**

REVIEW QUESTIONS

1. What is the definition of *ethics?* Explain why ethics are important when building seller–buyer relationships.

2. Which is the most important role model influencing the ethical behaviour of salespeople: the CEO, the sales manager, or other members of the sales force? Be prepared to defend your answer.

3. Define *reciprocity*. Is reciprocity always an ethical issue? Be prepared to defend your answer.

4. Contrast a *gift* with a *bribe*. Is there really any difference? Be prepared to defend your answer.

5. Explain the difference between *business slander, business libel,* and *product disparagement.* Which will be more likely to create problems for you as a salesperson? Explain.

6. Define *whistle-blowing*. Should companies encourage whistle-blowing, or is it even ethical for them to do so? Be prepared to defend your answer.

7. List and describe three guidelines that will help you develop your own personal code of ethics.

8. Review the CPSA Sales Institute code of ethics in Exhibit 12.2. Select the three items that you believe will create the greatest challenge for most salespeople and explain your choices.

9. What is the *Competition Act?* Why was it passed in Canada? List 10 important selling practices that it covers.

10. What is meant by *"cooling-off" law*? How do these laws provide consumer protection?

APPLICATION EXERCISES

1. The Canadian Telecommunications Consultants Association (**www.ctca.ca**) requires all members to adhere to its code of ethics and professional conduct. Look up its code on its website. Be prepared to discuss in class why this organization has a code of ethics and professional conduct for its members.

2. You work for an industrial distributor that pays straight salary—no commissions, and no bonuses. You are the sales manager and you have just been approached by your best salesperson at the branch because she feels she deserves a raise due to her performance. Unfortunately, you know head office has a clear policy that salaries are adjusted once each year, and that would be six months in the future. When you tell her that you would be prepared to recommend a good increase for her in six months, she responds, "Thank you. I appreciate that. We both know I deserve more right now and I would like to know if you would consider another alternative since you can't adjust my income immediately. How about sending me on a trip to Montreal? I have a sister there whom I am going to visit this year, and if you sent me there on business and let me claim my expenses, that would save me about $2000, just what I would like for a raise." Do you think that her suggestion is appropriate? What would your response to her be? Be prepared to defend your response.

3. You have given a speech to the Canadian Purchasing Association on changing roles of today's salespeople. Following the meeting, a purchasing agent for a company serviced by one of your salespeople approaches you and tells you how pleased he is with a recent purchase that your salesperson recommended. You know immediately that the customer bought the wrong product, and you are also sure that the salesperson knew that when the sale was made. Explain exactly what you would do and why.

4. Visit the website of the Direct Sellers Association of Canada (DSAC) (**www.dsa.ca**). Explore the link "Consumer Protection." What guidelines does the organization offer to determine whether a company is reputable? Review its code of ethics. What is covered in its code of ethics that is not covered in the CPSA Sales Institute code of ethics in Exhibit 12.2? Why do you think there are differences? What guidelines does the DSAC provide for people to protect them from becoming involved in a pyramid scheme?

Trouble at TPG Power Source

During the 1990s and until 2001, TPG Power Source was one of the largest manufacturers of unbranded computer peripheral equipment in North America. At its peak in 2000, the company had a sales force of 270 in the United States, 33 in Canada, and 11 outside of North America. Nearly 40 percent of its sales came from its six largest accounts, all computer manufacturers. Sales to value-added resellers (VARs) that put together large systems and bought parts and components from many manufacturers accounted for 30 percent of its sales. Sales to retailers, large and small, accounted for nearly 20 percent of sales, and the remaining sales were to industrial accounts. All six computer manufacturers were located in the United States and sales were handled from there. In 2004 and again in 2005, the company downsized. In the initial downsizing, production and administrative people were most affected and even with the later cuts in 2005 only a few salespeople were let go.

The highest ranking executive in Canada was Paul Proudfoot, vice-president of sales. Paul had over 25 years with the company, having made his way through inside sales, field sales, and sales management. Under Paul, there were two sales managers, Tara Thomas and Brad Always. Tara was responsible for the salespeople in Ontario and Eastern Canada, and Brad's responsibility was for Western Canada. Both had been with the company for over 10 years and both had been hired as field salespeople.

In December 2006, Paul was having a meeting with both Tara and Brad in his Toronto office. "You know we have been lucky with the past downsizings but, unfortunately, a large one is coming and this time our sales force will take a hit. I have instructions from my boss to cut our Canadian sales force by eight people within the next month."

Tara seemed less surprised than Brad. "They sure didn't give us much time, but I was expecting it. I could see it in the sales numbers over the past year."

Paul replied, "Not much time, and not much discretion either. They want the most senior salespeople to be the ones that are let go but we have to be careful that we don't get charged with age discrimination. It really comes down to money. Some of our senior salespeople are costing us more than $250 000 per year when you include their total direct selling expenses, and most of our junior salespeople cost us less than $150 000. I was told that if I wanted to protect a senior salesperson, I would have to get rid of two junior salespeople instead. It looks like they're really trying to cut about $2 million from our selling costs."

This time, Brad was quick to respond. "There's a reason why our senior salespeople make so much money: they produce the most. Does head office realize that, with the large territories we cover in Canada, once we restructure our salespeople will have even larger territories and our costs as a percentage of sales will likely increase considerably, not to mention that customers will be put at risk due to decreased coverage?"

"I'm sure they do. They seem very serious about this cut. They don't want any hints given to anyone until we decide who is going, and then we must let them all know at the same time. We are to give them all two weeks' notice only because we will not allow them back on the company property or access to any company resources from the time they receive notice. Some good news, if it's any consolation, is that since this will be about June 1, everyone will also get reasonable vacation pay that should give them about another three or four weeks' income. You are to take their company car keys, laptops, and PDAs immediately and ensure they don't have any files outside the office that you can't recover quickly. You know the routine and the importance of confidentiality. I'm sorry we have to decide so fast, but I will give you one week to make your recommendations to me and then we will decide how we act."

Following the meeting, Brad returned to his office in Calgary, and Tara went down the hall to her office. She was located only two offices from Paul. When she sat down at her desk, Raj Nagarajan, her most senior salesperson, entered. "Tara, you look worried. Is something wrong?"

Tara smiled, "No. Just a lot to think about, but everything will be fine. I'm sure."

Raj sat beside her desk. "Tara, I need some advice."

"Sure, Raj. I'll be happy to help."

"Tara, I have been offered another job. It's basically what I do now but the pay will be about $15 000 per year more. I'm not looking for more money because you know I am very happy here. I know my accounts and my products, and I have a lot of friends in this office. Certainly, you are among my most favourite co-workers. I'm just not certain of the future here and that will be what will determine my choice. I do not want to leave, but if I stay and things don't work out here, I am putting my family at serious risk. You know my oldest daughter will be entering university this fall and my son will be there within two more years. You haven't given me poor advice in the six years we have been friends. What should I do?"

It was the kind of situation Tara feared most. She had always been proud of her ability to carefully analyze situations and select a reasoned response. However, this situation demanded an immediate answer, and she was not sure how she wanted to handle it.

CRITICAL-THINKING QUESTION

If you were Tara Thomas, what would you do? Be prepared to defend your actions.

Canadian Electrical Controller Corp.   CASE 12.2

Canadian Electrical Controller Corp. (CEC) was a large manufacturer of motor control equipment that began operations in Montreal in 1902. In 1961, it was bought by a large U.S.-based conglomerate that owned many unrelated manufacturers, none of which were industry leaders. However, they were all respectable contenders in the markets they served. The products sold by CEC ranged from small motor starting switches that sold for $10, to large motor control centres capable of operating all of the equipment in a large manufacturing plant. These motor control centres normally ranged in price from less than $40 000 to more than $300 000, and averaged about $80 000. CEC had its own sales force in Quebec and Ontario, but sold through two agents in Eastern and Western Canada. The Eastern Canadian agent was Andy Wentzell. He had been the agent for more than 20 years and had developed the territory to the point where he had approximately 30 dealers that were carrying inventory of small motor starters and popular parts items. Andy worked on a variable commission: 3 percent for motor control centres, 12 percent for direct sales to industrial customers, and 6 percent for sales that were made to any of his dealers.

One major customer that Andy handled direct was among the largest purchasers of parts and equipment. They had used CEC since the 1940s, but were now experiencing increasing trouble getting parts that were becoming obsolete; deliveries were getting longer and prices were getting much higher. Andy suggested that they consider replacing all of their old equipment with a modern motor control centre that would be worth in excess of $2 million, one of the largest units in all of Canada. After careful consideration, the customer's president decided that they would most likely go ahead with the replacement and he told Andy that he would put it in the next year's capital budget and would prepare an official call for tender within a few months. In fact, he said to Andy, "We will have to request a quotation from several sources, you know. But, you do have the inside track here. We appreciate the service you have given us and you are known and liked by all the people here. I must see that this process is handled honestly for all concerned, but be assured I will see that you get any help you want when it comes to preparing your quotation for us."

Andy was very excited, and he immediately called Peter Halfyard, the vice-president of sales for CEC, in Toronto to tell him the news. When Peter went to see Milt Zoltners, the president, Milt replied, "We need to make that a house account. We can't be giving an agent 3 percent commission on an order that large. That's more than $60 000, and he's done almost nothing for it."

Peter was surprised. "But we have always worked through Andy. He developed the territory for us from practically nothing other than about 20 large accounts that we have had for decades. Besides, we have a contract that says we must pay commissions on all sales unless either of us gives the other 30 days' notice."

"Then give Andy his 30 days' notice before it's too late. We'll continue to pay him for all of the other sales, but once a contract reaches $500 000 we will claim it as a house account in future. He doesn't need to do any work on these, but it will be in his interest to let us know about any that might develop because he'll still get the parts business and any ancillary equipment that is ordered after the initial sale."

CRITICAL-THINKING QUESTION

If you were Peter Halfyard, what would you do? Be prepared to defend your actions.

Comprehensive Cases for Part III

CASE 1	General Electric Appliances

Larry Barr had recently been promoted to the position of district sales manager (B.C.) for GE Appliances, a division of Canadian Appliance Manufacturing Co. Ltd. (CAMCO). One of his more important duties in this position was the allocation of his district's sales quota among his five salespeople. Barr received his quota for the next year in October of the current year. His immediate task was to determine an equitable allocation of that quota. This was important because the company's incentive pay plan was based on the salespeople's attainment of quota. A portion of Barr's remuneration was also based on the degree to which his sales force met their quotas.

Barr had graduated from the University of British Columbia with the degree of Bachelor of Commerce. He had immediately been hired as a product manager for a mining equipment manufacturing firm because of his summer job experience with that firm. Three years later, he had joined Canadian General Electric (CGE) in Montreal as a product manager for refrigerators. There, he had been responsible for creating and merchandising a product line, as well as developing product and marketing plans. Two years later, he had been transferred to Cobourg, Ontario, as a sales manager for industrial plastics. The next year, he had become administrative manager (Western Region), and when the position of district sales manager had become available, Barr had been promoted to it. There, his duties included development of sales strategies, supervision of salespeople, and budgeting.

Background

Canadian Appliance Manufacturing Co. Ltd. (CAMCO) had been created under the joint ownership of Canadian General Electric Ltd. and General Steel Wares Ltd. (GSW). CAMCO had then purchased the production facilities of Westinghouse Canada Ltd. Under the purchase agreement, the Westinghouse brand name had been transferred to White Consolidated Industries Ltd., where it became White-Westinghouse. Appliances manufactured by CAMCO in the former Westinghouse plant were branded Hotpoint.

The GE, GSW, and Hotpoint major appliance plants became divisions of CAMCO. These divisions operated independently and had their own separate management staff, although they were all ultimately accountable to CAMCO management. The divisions competed for sales, although not directly, because they each produced product lines for different price segments (see Exhibit 1).

COMPETITION

Competition in the appliance industry was vigorous. CAMCO was the largest firm in the industry, with approximately 45 percent market share, split between GE, GSW (Moffat and McClary brands), and Hotpoint. The following three firms each had 10–15 percent market shares: Inglis (washers and dryers only), WCI (makers of White-Westinghouse, Kelvinator, and Gibson), and Admiral. These firms also produced appliances under department store brand names such as

Source: This case was prepared by Richard W. Pollay and John D. Claxton (Professors Emeritus, University of British Columbia), and Rick Jenkner in 1984. Reproduced by permission.

Exhibit 1 Organization Chart

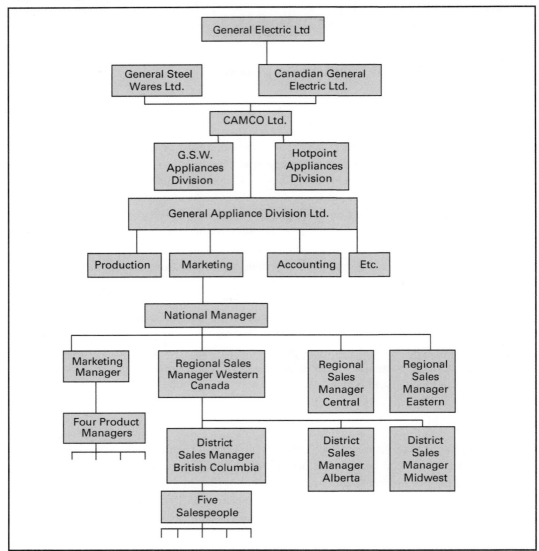

Viking, Baycrest, and Kenmore, which accounted for an additional 15 percent of the market. The remainder of the market was divided among brands such as Maytag, Roper Dishwasher, Gurney, Tappan, and Danby.

GE marketed a full major appliance product line, including refrigerators, ranges, washers, dryers, dishwashers, and television sets. GE appliances generally had many features and were priced at the upper end of the price range. Their major competition came from Maytag and Westinghouse.

THE BUDGETING PROCESS

GE Appliances was one of the most advanced firms in the consumer goods industry in terms of sales budgeting. Budgeting received careful analysis at all levels of management.

The budgetary process began in June of each year. The management of the GE Appliances division assessed the economic outlook, growth trends in the industry, competitive activity, population growth, and so forth in order to determine a reasonable sales target for the next year. The president of CAMCO received this estimate, checked and revised it as necessary, and submitted it to the president of GE Canada. Final authorization rested with GE Ltd., which had a definite minimum growth target for the GE branch of CAMCO. GE Appliances was considered an "invest and grow" division, which meant that it was expected to produce a healthy sales growth each year, regardless of the state of the economy. As Barr observed, "This is difficult, but meeting challenges is the job of management."

The approved budget was expressed as a desired percentage increase in sales. Once the figure had been decided, it was not subject to change. The quota was communicated back through GE Canada Ltd., CAMCO, and GE Appliances, where it was available to the district sales managers in October. Each district was then required to meet an overall growth figure (quota) but each sales territory was not automatically expected to achieve that same growth. Barr was required to assess the situation in each territory, determine where growth potential was highest, and allocate his quota accordingly.

THE SALES INCENTIVE PLAN

The sales incentive plan was a critical part of General Electric's sales force plan and an important consideration in Barr's allocation of quota. Each salesperson had a portion of earnings dependent upon performance with respect to quota. Also, Barr was awarded a bonus based on the sales performance of his district, making it advantageous to Barr and good for staff morale for all of his salespeople to attain their quotas.

The sales force incentive plan was relatively simple. A bonus system is fairly typical for salespeople in any field. With GE, each salesperson agreed to a basic salary figure called "planned earnings." The planned salary varied according to experience, education, past performance, and competitive salaries. A salesperson was paid 75 percent of planned earnings on a guaranteed regular basis. The remaining 25 percent of salary was at risk, dependent upon the person's sales record. There was also the possibility of earning substantially more money by selling more than quota (see Exhibit 2).

The bonus was awarded such that total salary (base plus bonus) equaled planned earnings when the quota was just met. The greatest increase in bonus came between 101 percent and 110 percent of quota. The bonus was paid quarterly on the cumulative total quota. A holdback system ensured that a salesperson was never required to pay back a previously earned bonus by reason of a poor quarter. Because of this system, it was critical that each salesperson's quota be fair in relation to those of the other salespeople. Nothing was worse for morale than one person earning large bonuses while the others struggled.

Quota attainment was not the sole basis for evaluating the salespeople. They were required to fulfill a wide range of duties, including service, franchising of new dealers, maintaining good relations with dealers, and maintaining a balance of sales among the different product lines. Because the bonus system was based on sales only, Barr had to ensure that the salespeople did not neglect their other duties.

A formal salary review was held each year for each salesperson. However, Barr preferred to give his salespeople continuous feedback on their performance. Through human relations skills, he hoped to avoid problems that could lead to the dismissal of a salesperson and the loss of sales for the company.

Exhibit 2 Sales Incentive Earnings Schedule: Major Appliances and Home Entertainment Products

Sales Quota Realization Percent	Incentive Percent of Base Salary Total	Sales Quota Realization Percent	Incentive Percent of Base Salary Total
70	0	106	37.00
71	0.75	107	39.00
72	1.50	108	41.00
73	2.25	109	43.00
74	3.00	110	45.00
75	3.75	111	46.00
76	4.50	112	47.00
77	5.25	113	48.00
78	6.00	114	49.00
79	6.75	115	50.00
80	7.50	116	51.00
81	8.25	117	52.00
82	9.00	118	53.00
83	9.75	119	54.00
84	10.50	120	55.00
85	11.25	121	56.00
86	12.00	122	57.00
87	12.75	123	58.00
88	13.50	124	59.00
89	14.25	125	60.00
90	15.00	126	61.00
91	16.00	127	62.00
92	17.00	128	63.00
93	18.00	129	64.00
94	19.00	130	65.00
95	20.00	131	66.00
96	21.00	132	67.00
97	22.00	133	68.00
98	23.00	134	69.00
99	24.00	135	70.00
100	25.00	136	71.00
101	27.00	137	72.00
102	29.00	138	73.00
103	31.00	139	74.00
104	33.00	140	75.00
105	35.00		

Barr's incentive bonus plan was more complex than the salespeople's. He was awarded a maximum of 75 annual bonus points broken down as follows: market share, 15; total sales performance, 30; sales representative balance, 30. Each point had a specific monetary value. The system ensured that Barr allocated his quota carefully. For instance, if one quota was so difficult that the salesperson sold only 80 percent of it, while the other salespeople exceeded the quota, Barr's bonus would be reduced, even if the overall sales exceeded the quota (see Exhibit 3).

Exhibit 3 Development of a Sales Commission Plan

A series of steps are required to establish the foundation upon which a sales commission plan can be built. These steps are as follows:

Determine Specific Sales Objectives of Positions to Be Included in the Plan

For a sales commission plan to succeed, it must be designed to encourage the attainment of the business objectives to the component division. Before deciding on the dimensions of a commission plan, you have to decide on which of the following objectives are important.

1. Increase sales volume
2. Do an effective, balanced selling job in a variety of product lines.
3. Improve market share
4. Reduce selling expense to sales ratio
5. Develop new accounts or territories
6. Introduce new products

Although it is probably neither desirable nor necessary to include all such objectives as specific measures of performance in the plan, they should be kept in mind, at least to the extent that the performance measures chosen for the plan are compatible with and do not work against the overall accomplishment of the component's business objectives.

Also, the relative current importance or ranking of these objectives will provide guidance in selecting the number and type of performance measures to be included in the plan.

Determine Quantitative Performance Measures to Be Used

Although, it may be possible to include a number of measures in a particular plan, there is a drawback to using so many as to overly complicate it and fragment the impact of any one measure on the participants. A plan that is difficult to understand will lose a great deal of its motivating force, as well as being costly to administer properly.

For components that currently have a variable sales compensation plan(s) for their sales, a good starting point would be to consider the measures used in those plans. Although the measurements used for sales managers need not be identical, they should at least be compatible with those used to determine commissions.

However, keep in mind that a performance measure that may not be appropriate for individual salespeople may be a good one to apply to their manager. Measurements involving attainment of a share of a defined market, balanced selling for a variety of products, and control of district or region expenses might well fall into this category.

The accompanying table lists a variety of measurements that might be used to emphasize specific sales objectives. For most components, all or most of these objectives will be desirable to some extent. The point is to select those of greatest importance where it will be possible to establish measures of standard or normal performance for individuals, or at least small groups of individuals working as a team.

If more than one performance measurement is to be used, the relative weighting of each measurement must be determined. If a measure is to be effective, it must carry enough weight to have at least some noticeable effect on the commission earnings of the individual.

As a general guide, it would be unusual for a plan to include more than two or three quantitative measures with a minimum weighting of 15-20 percent of planned commissions for any one measurement.

Establish Commission Payment Schedule for Each Performance Measure

Determine Appropriate Range of Performance for Each Measurement

The performance range for a measurement defines the percent of standard performance (R%) at which commission earnings start to the point where they reach maximum.

The minimum point of the performance range for a given measurement should be set so that a majority of the participants can earn at least some incentive pay, and the maximum set at a point that is possible

continued

Exhibit 3 continued

for some participants to obtain. These points will vary with the type of measure used and with the degree of predictability of individual budgets or other forms of measurement. In a period where overall performance is close to standard, 90 to 95 percent of the participants should fall within the performance range.

For the commission plan to be effective, most of the participants should be operating within the performance range most of the time. If a participant is either far below the minimum of this range or has reached the maximum, further improvement will not affect his commission earnings, and the plan will be largely inoperative as far as he is concerned.

Actual past experience of R% attained by participants is obviously the best indicator of what this range should be for each measure used. Lacking this, it is better to err on the side of having a wider range than one which proves to be too narrow. If some form of group measure is used, the variation and standard performance range for total District performance would probably be narrower than the range established for individual sales within a district.

Determine Appropriate Reward: Risk Ratio for Commission Earnings

This refers to the relationship of commission earned at standard performance, to maximum commission earnings available under the plan. A plan that pays 10 percent of base salary for normal or standard performance and pays 30 percent as a maximum commission would have a 2:1 ratio. In other words, participants can earn twice as much (20 percent) for above-standard performance as they stand to lose for below-standard performance (10 percent).

Reward under a sales commission plan should be related to the effort involved to produce a given result. To adequately encourage above-standard results, the reward: risk: ratio generally be at least 2:1. The proper control of incentive plan payment lies in the proper setting of performance standards, not in the setting of a low maximum payment for outstanding results that provides a minimum variation in individual earnings. Generally, a higher percentage of base salary should be paid for each 1%R up to 100%R to reflect the relative difficulty involved in producing above-standard results.

Once the performance range and reward: risk ratios have been determined, the schedule of payments for each performance measure can then be caluculated. This will show the percentage of the participants base salary earned for various performance results (R%) from the point at which commissions start to maximum performance.

Example: For measurement paying 20 percent of salary for standard performance:

Percent of Base Salary Earned	
1% of base salary for each + 1%R	0 %
	20%
1.33% of base salary for each + 1%R	60%

Percent of Sales Quota
80% or below
100% (standard performance)
130% or above

Prepare Draft of Sales Commission Plan

After completing the above steps, a draft of a sales commission plan should be prepared using the accompanying outline as a guide.

Keys to Effective Commission Plans

1. Get the understanding and acceptance of the commission plan by the managers who will be involved in carrying it out. They must be convinced of its effectiveness in order to properly explain and "sell" the plan to the salespeople.
2. In turn, be sure the plan is presented clearly to the salespeople so that they have a good understanding of how the plan will work. We find that good acceptance of a sales commission plan on the part of salespeople correlates closely with how well and understood the plan and its effect on their

continued

Exhibit 3 continued

compensation. The salespeople must be convinced that the measurements used are factors which they can control by their selling efforts.

3. Be sure the measurements used in the commission plan encourage the salespeople to achieve the marketing goals of your operation. For example, if sales volume is the only performance measure, the salespeople will concentrate on producing as much dollar volume as possible by spending most of their time on products with high volume potential. It will be difficult to get them to spend much time on introducing new products with relatively low volume, handling customer complaints, etc. Even though a good portion of their compensation may still be in salary, you can be sure they will wind up doing the things they feel will maximize their commission earnings.

4. One solution to maintaining good sales direction is to put at least a portion of the commission earnings in an "incentive pool" to be distributed by the sales manager according to his judgment. This "pool" can vary in size according to some qualitative measure of the sales group's performance, but the manager can set individual measurements for each salesperson and reward people according to how well they fulfill their goals.

5. If at all possible, you should test the plan for a period of time, perhaps in one or two sales areas or districts. To make it a real test, you should actually pay commission earnings to the participants, but the potential risk and rewards can be limited. No matter how well a plan has been conceived, not all the potential pitfalls will be apparent until you've actually operated the plan for a period of time. The test period is a relatively painless way to get some experience.

6. Finally, after the plan is in operation, take time to analyze the results. Is the plan accomplishing what you want it to do, both in terms of business results produced and in realistically compensating salespeople for their efforts?

Tailoring Commission Plan Measurements to Fit Component Objectives

Objectives	Possible Plan Measurements
1. Increase sales/order volume	Net sales billed or orders received against quota
2. Increase sales of particular lines	Sales against product line quotas with weighted sales credits on individual lines
3. Increase market share	Percent realization (%R) of shares bogey
4. Do balanced selling job	%R of product line quotas, with commissions increasing in proportion to number of lines up to quota
5. Increase profitability	Margin realized from sales
	Vary sales credits to emphasize profitable product lines
	Vary sales credit in relation to amount of price discounts
6. Increase dealer sales	Pay distributor salespeople or sales manager in relation to realization of sales quotas assigned dealers
7. Increase sales calls	%R of targeted calls per district or region
8. Introduce new product	Additional sales credits on new line for limited period
9. Control Expense	%R of expense to sales or margin ratio
	Adjust sales credit in proportion to variance from expense/budget
10. Sales Teamwork	Share of incentive based upon group results

QUOTA ALLOCATION

The total sales budget for the GE Appliance division for the following year was about $100 million, a 14 percent sales increase over the current year. Barr's share of the $33 million Western Region quota was $13.3 million, also a 14 percent increase over the previous year. Barr had two weeks to allocate the quota among his five territories. He needed to consider factors such as historical allocation, economic outlook, dealer changes, personnel changes, untapped potential, new franchises or store openings, and buying group activity (volume purchases by associations of independent dealers).

SALES FORCE

There were five sales territories within British Columbia (see Exhibit 4). Territories were determined on the basis of number of customers, sales volume of customers, geographic size, and experience of the salesperson. Territories were altered periodically in order to deal with changed circumstances.

One territory was composed entirely of contract customers. Contract sales were sales in bulk lots to builders and developers who used the appliances in housing units. Because the appliances were not resold at retail, GE took a lower profit margin on such sales.

GE Appliances recruited M.B.A. graduates for the sales force. They sought bright, educated people who were willing to relocate anywhere in Canada. The company intended that these people would ultimately be promoted to managerial positions. The company also hired experienced career salespeople in order to get a blend of experience in the sales force. However, the typical salesperson was under 30, aggressive, and upwardly mobile. GE's sales training program covered only product knowledge. It was not felt necessary to train recruits in sales techniques.

ALLOCATION PROCEDURE

At the time Barr assumed the job of district sales manager, he had a meeting with the former sales manager, Ken Philips. Philips described to Barr the method he had used in the past to allocate the quota. As Barr understood it, the procedure was as follows.

The quota was received in October in the form of a desired percentage sales increase. The first step was to project current sales to the end of the year. This gave a base to which the increase was added for an estimation of the next year's quota. From this quota, the value of contract sales was allocated. Contract sales were allocated first because the market was considered the easiest to forecast. The amount of contract sales in the sales mix was constrained by the lower profit margin on such sales.

The next step was to make a preliminary allocation by simply adding the budgeted percentage increase to the year-end estimates for each territory. Although this allocation seemed fair on the surface, it did not take into account the differing situations in the territories or the difficulty of attaining such an increase.

Exhibit 4 GE Appliances: Sales Territories

Territory Designation		Description
9961	Greater Vancouver (Alicia Rizzuto)	Hudson's Bay, Firestone, K-Mart, McDonald Supply, plus seven independent dealers
9962	Interior (Dan Seguin)	All customers from Quesnel to Nelson, including contract sales (50 customers)
9963	Coastal (Ken Block)	Eatons, Woodwards, plus Vancouver Island North of Duncan and Upper Fraser Valley (east of Clearbrook) (20 customers)
9964	Independent and Northern (Fred Speck)	All independent in lower mainland and South Vancouver Island, plus northern BC and Yukon (30 customers)
9967	Contract (Jim Wiste)	Contract sales Vancouver, Victoria. All contract sales outside 9962 (50–60 customers)

The next step was to examine the sales data compiled by GE. Weekly sales reports from all regions were fed into a central computer, which compiled them and printed out sales totals by product line for each customer, as well as other information. This information enabled the sales manager to check the reasonableness of his initial allocation through a careful analysis of the growth potential for each customer.

The analysis began with the largest accounts, such as Firestone, Hudson's Bay, and Eatons, which each bought over $1 million in appliances annually. Accounts that size were expected to achieve at least the budgeted growth. The main reason for this was that a shortfall of a few percentage points on such a large account would be difficult to make up elsewhere.

Next, the growth potential for medium-sized accounts was estimated. These accounts included McDonalds Supply, Kmart, Federated Cooperative, and buying groups such as Volume Independent Purchasers (VIP). Management expected the majority of sales growth to come from such accounts, which had annual sales of between $150 000 and $1 million. At that point, about 70 percent of the accounts had been analyzed.

The small accounts were estimated last. These had generally lower growth potential but were an important part of the company's distribution system. Once all the accounts had been analyzed, the growth estimates were summed and the total compared to the budget. Usually, the growth estimates were well below the budget.

The next step was to gather more information. The salespeople were usually consulted to ensure that no potential trouble areas or good opportunities had been overlooked. The manager continued to revise and adjust the figures until the total estimate matched the budget. These projections were then summed by territory and compared to the preliminary territorial allocation.

Frequently, there were substantial differences between the two allocations. Historical allocations were then examined, and the manager used his judgment in adjusting the figures until he was satisfied that the allocation was both equitable and attainable. Some factors that were considered at this stage included experience of the salesperson, competitive activities, potential store closures or openings, potential labour disputes in the areas, and so forth.

The completed allocation was passed on to the regional sales manager for his approval. The process had usually taken one week or longer by this stage. Once the allocation had been approved, the district sales manager then divided it into sales quota by product line. Often, the resulting average price did not match the expected mix between higher- and lower-priced units. Therefore, some additional adjusting of figures was necessary. The house account (for sales to employees of the company) was used as the adjustment factor.

Once this breakdown had been completed, the numbers were printed on a budget sheet and given to the regional sales manager. He forwarded all the sheets for his region to the central computer, which printed out sales numbers for each product line by salesperson by month. These figures were used as the salesperson's quotas for the next year.

Current Situation

Barr recognized that he faced a difficult task. He felt that he was too new to the job and the area to confidently undertake an account-by-account growth analysis. However, due to his previous experience with sales budgets, he did have some general ideas. He also had the records of past allocation and quota attainment (Exhibit 5), as well as the assistance of the regional sales manager, Anthony Foyt.

Exhibit 5 Sales Results

Territory	Previous Budget (x 1 000)	Percent of Total Budget	Previous Actual (x 1 000)	Variance from Quota (V%)
9967 (Contract)	$ 2 440	26.5	$ 2 267	(7)
9961 (Greater Vancouver)	1 790	19.4	1 824	2
9962 (Interior)	1 624	17.7	1 433	(11)
9963 (Coastal)	2 111	23.0	2 364	12
9964 (Independent Dealers)	1 131	12.3	1 176	4
House	84	1.1	235	—
Total	$9 180	100.0	$9 299	1

Exhibit 5 Sales Results (continued)

Territory	Following Year Budget (x 1 000)	Percent of Total Budget	Following Year Actual (x 1 000)	Variance from Quota (V%)
9967 (Contract)	$ 2 587	26.2	$ 2 845	10
9961 (Greater Vancouver)	2 005	20.3	2 165	8
9962 (Interior)	1 465	14.8	1 450	(1)
9963 (Coastal)	2 405	24.4	2 358	(2)
9964 (Independent Dealers)	1 334	13.5	1 494	12
House	52	.8	86	—
Total	$9 848	100.0	$10 398	5

Barr's first step was to project the current sales figures to end-of-year totals. This task was facilitated because the former manager, Ken Philips, had been making successive projections monthly since June. Barr then made a quota allocation by adding the budgeted sales increase of 14 percent to each territory's total (Exhibit 6).

Barr then began to assess circumstances that could cause him to alter that allocation. One major problem was the resignation, effective at the end of the year, of one of the company's top salespeople, Ken Block. His territory had traditionally been one of the most difficult, and Barr felt that it would be unwise to replace Block with a novice salesperson.

Barr considered shifting one of the more experienced salespeople into that area. However, that would have involved a disruption of service in an additional territory, which was undesirable because it took several months for a salesperson to build a good rapport with customers. Barr's decision would affect his quota allocation because a salesperson new to a territory could not be expected to immediately sell as well as the incumbent, and a novice salesperson would require an even longer period of adaptation.

Exhibit 6 Sales Projections and Quotas

Projected Sales Results, Current Year					
Territory	Current Year October Year to Date (x 1 000)	Current Projected Total (x 1 000)	Current Budget (x 1 000)	% of Total Budget From Quota (V%)	Projected Variance
9967	$ 2 447	$3 002	$ 2 859	25.0	5
9961	2 057	2 545	2 401	21.0	6
9962	1 318	1 623	1 727	15.1	(6)
9963	2 124	2 625	2 734	23.9	(4)
9965	1 394	1 720	1 578	13.8	(9)
House	132	162	139	1.2	—
Total	$9 474	$11 677	$11 438	100.0	2

Exhibit 6 Sales Projections and Quotas (continued)

Preliminary Allocation, Next Year			
Territory	Current Projection (x1 000)	Next Year Budget (x 1 000)	% of Total Budget
9967	$ 3 002	$3 422	25.7
9961	2 545	2 901	21.8
9962	1 623	1 854	13.9
9963	2 625	2 992	22.5
9965	1 720	1 961	14.7
House	162	185	1.4
Total	$11 677	$13 315	100.0

Barr was also concerned about territory 9961. The territory comprised two large national accounts and seven major independent dealers. The buying decisions for the national accounts were made at their head offices, where GE's regional sales staff had no control over the decisions. Recently, Barr had heard rumours that one of the national accounts was reviewing its purchase of GE appliances. If they were to delist even some product lines, it would be a major blow to the salesperson, Alicia Rizzuto, whose potential sales would be greatly reduced. Barr was unsure how to deal with this situation.

Another concern for Barr was the wide variance in buying of some accounts. Woodwards, Eaton's, and McDonald Supply had large fluctuations from year to year. Also, Eaton's, Hudson's Bay, and Woodwards had plans to open new stores in the Vancouver area sometime during the year. The sales increase to be generated by these events was hard to estimate.

The general economic outlook was poor. The Canadian dollar had fallen to 92 cents U.S., and unemployment was about 8 percent. The government's anti-inflation program, which was scheduled to end next year, had managed to keep inflation to the 8 percent level, but economists expected higher inflation and increased labour unrest during the post control period.

The economic outlook was not the same in all areas. For instance, the Okanagan Valley (territory 9962) was a very depressed area. Tourism was down, and fruit farmers were doing poorly despite good weather and record prices. Vancouver Island was still recovering from a 200 percent increase in ferry fares, while the Lower Mainland appeared to be in a relatively better position.

In the contract segment, construction had shown an increase recently. However, labour unrest was common. There had been a crippling eight-week strike recently and there was a strong possibility of another strike next year.

With all of this in mind, Barr was very concerned that he allocate the quota properly because of the bonus system implications. How should he proceed? To help him in his decision, he reviewed the development of a sales commission plan, which he had learned about while attending a seminar on sales management the previous year (Exhibit 3).

CASE 2   **Hal Maybee's Ethical Dilemmas**

The following were actual situations experienced by the case writer during more than 15 years in business-to-business sales and sales management. The names of firms and individuals have been disguised due to the nature of the material in this case.

Steelco Construction

Hal Maybee was excited when he got the unexpected phone call from Nicki Simpson, a senior buyer from Steelco Construction.

"I know it's been more than a year since we bought that reel from you for the prototype 'bear trap' that we built for the Canadian government, but we just got a contract to build 10 more bear traps and we desperately need to hold our price on these units. Could you possibly sell us 10 more reels and hold your price to what it was previously?" Nicki inquired.

"I'll see what I can do and call you back today," Hal replied.

Hal immediately retrieved the file from the previous year and saw that he had supplied the reel for $8129.00, F.O.B. the customer's warehouse. There were some notes on the file that Hal reviewed. The reel was designed as part of a "bear trap" on Canadian navy ships. These bear traps would hook onto helicopters in rough weather and haul them safely onto landing pads on the ship decks. The reel was really a model SM heavy duty steel mill reel, except some of the exposed parts were to be made of stainless steel to provide longer life in the salt water atmosphere.

There was a breakdown of the pricing on the file. Originally, the manufacturer's list price was $4000.00, but there was a 25 percent surcharge for special engineering services as the reel was a non-standard item. As a distributor, Hal got a 20 percent discount, which the manufacturer allowed on both the product and the engineering surcharge. The manufacturer had suggested at the time that Hal could easily keep the full 20 percent distributor discount as they thought there was only one other manufacturer capable of building this unit, and their price would most likely be much higher.

When Hal investigated further, he saw there was estimated currency exchange of $1064.00 and estimated duty of $1139.00. Duty was calculated as 22.5 percent of the Canadian value—distributor cost in U.S. dollars plus currency exchange—as the reel would be imported under tariff classification 44603-1, which covered a host of items manufactured from iron or steel. The estimated freight was $285.00 and the estimated brokerage fee to clear the shipment through customs was $55.00. The final estimated distributor cost was $6503.00. Hal marked the cost up by 25 percent, and quoted the customer $8129.00 for the reel.

When Hal called the manufacturer for an updated price for 10 reels, he was surprised to be quoted a price of only $3200.00 each, less 40/10 percent. When Hal asked for the price to be verified, the order desk clarified the pricing. First, there had been a 20 percent reduction in all SM series reels. That made the manufacturer's list price only $3200.00. Then, because there was a large quantity, the discount was increased from 20 percent to 40/10 percent.

As Hal estimated his cost, things got better. In the interim, the company Hal worked for got a duty remission on series SM steel mill reels as "machinery of a class or kind not manufactured in Canada," and these reels could be now imported into Canada duty-free under tariff item 42700-1, with the remitted duty supposedly passed along to the end-customer. The currency exchange rate also improved in Hal's favour, and the estimated freight and brokerage charges per unit dropped considerably because of the increased shipment size. Hal estimated the new currency exchange to be $228.00. He estimated the per unit freight to be $85.00 and the per unit brokerage fee to be $14.50.

Now that he had all the figures, Hal had to decide what price he should quote to Nikki Simpson at Steelco Construction.

Scotia Pulp and Paper

Bill Siddall had been promoted to the position of salesperson, and he was pleased when he received an order for nearly $10 000 for stainless steel fittings from the new pulp mill being built in his territory. Unfortunately, he quoted a price that was 40 percent below his cost.

"We have to honour the price quoted," Bill insisted.

"I know if you let me talk to Rory, he'll let us raise the price," replied Hal Maybee, the sales manager. "Rory used to be the purchasing agent at one of my best accounts before he came to the mill."

"No. You gave me responsibility for this account, and I want to build a good relationship with Rory myself. He gave us the order over two weeks ago. He can't change suppliers now because he needs the material next week, and I don't want to put him on the spot now because it would be unfair. Since this is our first order, I would like to supply it without any problems. We'll get back the money we lost on this order many times if we can get their future business. This material is needed for a small construction job, and they haven't even started to consider their stores inventory yet."

After much discussion, it was agreed that the order would stand, but Hal would call the fitting manufacturer's sales manager, Chuck Knowles, as the two men were good friends.

"We need some help on that last order we placed with you. Bill sold it at 40 percent below our cost," said Hal.

"How could that happen?" Chuck seemed amazed.

"Well," replied Hal, "you give us a 25 percent distributor discount and we gave 10 percent to the customer due to the size of the order. What we forgot was to double the list price because the customer wanted schedule 80 wall thickness on the fittings instead of standard schedule 40. This was Bill's first large inquiry and he made an honest mistake. He doesn't want me to get involved with the customer, and I don't want to force the issue with him, so I'm hoping you can help us on this one order. We expect to get a lot of business from this account over the next few years."

"I'll split the difference with you. What you're selling now for $0.90, you're paying $1.50 for, and if I give you an additional 20 percent discount, your cost will come down to $1.20. Can you live with that?" Chuck asked.

"It's a help. We appreciate it. We'll see you on your next trip to our territory, and I'll buy lunch."

"A deal. See you next month." The conversation ended.

When it was over, Hal was feeling reasonably satisfied with himself, but he still felt somewhat uneasy. He promised not to call Rory, and he promised not to interfere with the account, but he still thought something could be done.

On Saturday morning, Hal went to the Brae Shore Golf Club. He was confident Rory would be there. Sure enough, at 8:00 A.M., Rory was scheduled to tee off. Hal sat on the bench at the first tee and waited for Rory to appear. Promptly, Rory arrived with Bob Arnold, one of his senior buyers. The three men greeted each other pleasantly and Rory asked who Hal was waiting for.

"Just one of my neighbours. He was supposed to be here an hour ago but I guess he won't show."

"Join us. We don't mind. Besides we might need a donation this fall when we have our company golf tournament. We'll invite you of course, and we'll invite Bill if he plays golf."

"He doesn't play often, but he's pretty good. Beat me the last time we played. How is he doing at your mill? Is everything okay?" Hal asked.

"Checking up on him? Sure. He's fine. He made a mistake the other day when he went to see our millwright foreman without clearing it through my office first, but he'll learn. He'll do a lot of business with us because we want to buy locally where possible, and you have a lot of good product lines. I think he'll get along well with all of us as well. He seems a bit serious, but we'll break him in before long. We just gave him a big order for stainless fittings a few weeks ago, but we told him to visit at 10:00 next time and to bring the doughnuts."

"I know," replied Hal. "Unfortunately, we lost a lot of money on that order."

"Your price was very low. I couldn't understand it because I knew your material wasn't manufactured offshore. Did you quote the cheaper T304 grade of stainless instead of the T316 we use?"

"No. We quoted schedule 40 prices instead of schedule 80. The wall thickness for schedule 80 is twice as thick, and the price should have been double as well."

"Heck. Double the price. We'll pay it. I'll make a note on the file Monday. I know you're not trying to take us and I can appreciate an honest mistake. At double the price, you might be a bit high, but you know we want to place the order with you anyway because you're local. Eventually we'll want you to carry some inventory for us, so we might just as well make sure we're both happy with this business."

McCormick Gleason Limited

Hal Maybee telephoned Clarey Stanley, a senior buyer at McCormick Gleason Limited. "Clarey, I'm calling about that quote we made on Lufkin tapes. Can we have your order?"

"Sorry. Your price was high. I gave the order to Ken Stafford. You need a sharper pencil."

"How much sharper?" Hal asked.

"I can't tell you that. But you were close." Clarey replied. "By the way, Kenny called me from the stores department this morning and he has a large shipment of electric relays that was delivered yesterday. They weren't properly marked and he can't identify the ones with normally open contacts from the ones with normally closed contacts. Do you want them returned, or can someone see him and straighten it out here?"

"Tell him I'll see him immediately after lunch. I can tell them apart and I'll see they get properly identified."

When the conversation ended, Hal made a note to see Clarey about the tapes. There was a problem somewhere. Hal knew his cost on Lufkin tapes was the lowest available, and he quoted 12 percent on cost because he really wanted the order. The order was less than $1500, but it meant that Hal could place a multiple-case order on the manufacturer and get the lowest possible cost for all replacement inventory. That would increase the margin on sales to other customers who bought smaller quantities. There was no possibility that Stafford Industrial, a local, one-person, "out-of-the-basement" operation that bought Lufkin tapes as a jobber, not as a distributor, could match his price.

That afternoon, while waiting to see Ken MacKay, the stores manager, Hal noticed a carton from Stafford Industrial Sales being unloaded from a local delivery van. Although he knew that Stafford supplied quite a few maintenance, repair, and operating (MRO) supplies to this customer, Hal decided to play ignorant.

"What do you buy from Stafford Industrial?" he asked the young stores clerk who was handling the package.

Opening the carton, the clerk read the packing slip. "It says here we ordered 144 measuring tapes, 3/4⊄ wide by 25 ft. long."

"Are those things expensive?" Hal asked.

"Don't know. There's no price on the packing slip. Clarey Stanley in purchasing ordered them. You could talk to him." The clerk continued to unpack the shipment. As he did, Hal noticed the tapes were manufactured offshore and were poor quality compared to the Lufkin tapes that he sold, and that he had quoted to Clarey Stanley the previous day.

"Aren't those supposed to be Lufkin tapes?" Hal asked.

"Not that I know. The packing slip just says tapes. Wait and I'll haul our copy of the purchase order." The clerk went to a filing cabinet next to his desk and returned with a carbon copy of the purchase order. "No, it just says tapes. It doesn't specify any brand."

There was something wrong, and Hal was determined to get an answer.

Mercer Brothers

It was early in the afternoon and Hal Maybee had just gotten to his Halifax office. He was about to begin reviewing the previous month's sales figures when his telephone interrupted. It was Tom Bowker, the salesperson who was responsible for Newfoundland and Labrador, and Cape Breton. Tom was calling from Newfoundland where he had just spent two days at Marystown Shipyards, a large shipbuilding and repair facility on the Burin Peninsula, about three to four hours from St. John's.

"Well, Hal. I got the problem solved finally. I don't think they need a new crane although I would like very much to sell them one. The existing crane can be overhauled for about $20 000 and they can do the work in their own shop. They will fax a purchase order through to the office later today for the parts they will need."

"Tom, that's nice business. I am glad you are having a good trip. I see you just got an order for 450 furnace motors from Mercer Brothers earlier this week and I want to congratulate you on selling them their year's requirements. I think that's the first time we ever got them to commit to a blanket order for the year. Did you have to make any special arrangement with them to get the order?"

"No. I told them they could mix blower, burner, and fan motors together in each shipment as long as they took their shipments in multiples of 45 motors as that is the number required to fill a pallet, and the manufacturer only prepays freight for full pallets of motors. I didn't ask them to take shipments larger than 45 motors, but Derek Mercer said he would take 180 motors in the first shipment, and that he would take two additional shipments of 135 motors each as the season progresses. The manufacturer should be pleased as it can make only three large shipments."

"He didn't ask for any price or payment concessions?" Hal asked.

"No. I told him that there was a 16 percent discount if he ordered a full pallet of motors, and that it would increase to 24 percent if he ordered 180 motors, and 30 percent if he ordered 450 motors. Derek told me that he sells approximately 400 motors each year to small furnace repair businesses across the province so he was very comfortable giving us this order."

"Well, congratulations. That will certainly ensure you meet your sales quota for motors this year."

"Now I have a dilemma, and I need some advice." Tom paused.

"Certainly, Tom. How can I help?"

"Well, Hal, I didn't finish at Marystown Shipyards until very late yesterday so I decided to stay overnight in Marystown and drive back to St. John's today. I didn't want to risk meeting a moose on the road at dusk." Tom paused, but when Hal didn't speak, he continued. "I looked at the map and saw two small towns near Marystown, so I thought I would drive over just to see if there was any possible business for us there. One is Fortune and the other is Grand Bank. I found a furnace repair business there and when I spoke to the owner, it became apparent that he was very interested in buying motors from us. He knew the brand because he said he had been buying them for years from Mercer Brothers. In fact, he said that he and his brother-in-law would use more than 60 motors each in a typical season, and he wanted to check to see if his brother-in-law was interested in combining their needs and placing an order for 180 motors. When I left him, he said that he was certain they would agree to take four shipments of 45 motors. What should I do?"

"Well, you do have a dilemma. What do you think you should do?" Hal asked.

Part IV

Evaluating the Strategic Sales Program

CHAPTER 13 | Reviewing and Evaluating Sales Performance

Comprehensive Cases for Part IV

CASE 1 | Stavanger Safety Equipment

CASE 2 | Power & Motion Industrial Supply

Today's sales managers are responsible for reviewing and evaluating strategic sales programs. Effective sales managers must review and evaluate sales performance at two levels: the overall sales force level and the individual salesperson level. Reviewing and evaluating sales performance is discussed in Chapter 13.

Chapter 13

Reviewing and Evaluating Sales Performance

LEARNING OBJECTIVES

After completing this chapter, you should be able to

1. Perform a sales analysis at the company, SBU, or region level.

2. Discuss why conducting a sales performance evaluation is important.

3. Describe how to use input, output, and ratio measures to evaluate sales performance.

4. Discuss the use of subjective criteria for evaluating sales performance.

5. Describe how to develop and use performance matrices for sales performance evaluation.

The position of sales manager varies considerably from one organization to another. Organizations vary in terms of size, organizational structure, culture, products sold, and markets served. However, one thing sales managers have in common is that they are all involved in the evaluation of past and management of future sales performance. The goal, almost without exception, is sales growth. Jeremy Miller a partner at LeapJob, a Mississauga, Ontario-based sales force consulting firm, sees sales performance as the result of three factors: people, process, and passion.[1]

People are important. Companies today recognize that engaged and capable employees are needed throughout the organization if it wants to achieve superior performance. This is true of all organizations, but may be more so for smaller ones where there are limited resources and the loss of only a few key customers means the difference between success and bankruptcy.[2]

Process is important. Companies need a good selling process, supported by many other processes, all designed to help them meet the needs of the market they serve. Many of the most important processes are focused on the sales force: the processes for recruiting, selecting, training, motivating, and compensating salespeople.

Passion is important. Jeremy Miller sees it as the glue that holds the organization together, and the fire that drives people. People and process are both doomed to mediocrity without passion.[3] Salespeople must be passionate about delivering value to customers. Sales managers must be passionate about ensuring that the company has the right salespeople and then training, motivating, compensating and otherwise enabling them to provide value to customers. The sales manager must provide the leadership to manage the processes and the people so that the sales force achieves its goals and contributes to the organization's success. Performance evaluation is necessary to identify when there are problems with processes or people, but, in the final analysis, sales performance evaluation is also a measure of the performance of the sales manager.

The Sales Performance Evaluation Process

In her first full year as a full-time sales representative, 2007, Karen Ayanso had sales revenue of $643 262. Would you conclude that Karen was a good, average, or poor salesperson? If there were six other salespeople and Karen's sales revenue was the highest, would that make her a good salesperson? If her sales revenue was the lowest, would that make her a poor salesperson? How can you decide? That is the topic of this chapter. Sales performance evaluation is one of a sales manager's most important activities, because the outcome from sales performance evaluation should confirm that the sales force is performing at least satisfactorily, or it should point to areas of weakness and suggest changes that can be made to address them.

Evaluation, in the context of sales performance evaluation, refers to the comparison of sales results against established sales goals or objectives, as illustrated in Exhibit 13.1. When there is a variance between sales results and sales goals or objectives, the first inclination is to suggest that there

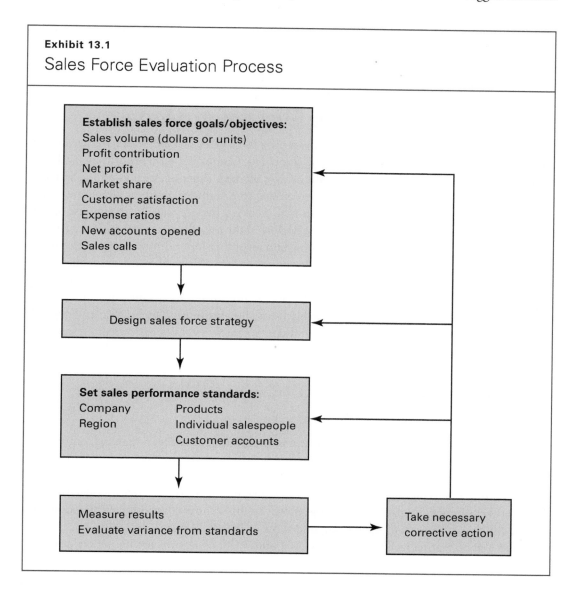

Exhibit 13.1

Sales Force Evaluation Process

Establish sales force goals/objectives:
Sales volume (dollars or units)
Profit contribution
Net profit
Market share
Customer satisfaction
Expense ratios
New accounts opened
Sales calls

Design sales force strategy

Set sales performance standards:
Company   Products
Region   Individual salespeople
                  Customer accounts

Measure results
Evaluate variance from standards

Take necessary
corrective action

is a problem with the performance of the salespeople; however, as shown in this exhibit, it is possible that the problem lies with the goals or objectives that were initially established, or with the sales force strategy that was implemented. If sales performance evaluation identifies that there is a problem with the goals or objectives, and it is caught sufficiently early, then adjustments can be made to make the goals or objectives realistically attainable, thereby maintaining motivation over the sales period. If salespeople identify early in the year that sales goals are unattainable and that they are unlikely to meet their targets, they will become demotivated, at least for the balance of that year. If sales performance evaluation identifies that there is a problem with the sales force strategy, again, changes can sometimes be made to get the sales force back on target before it is too late.

Variance from goals and objectives may also indicate that other actions need to be taken. It could indicate, for example, that training is needed. One of the outcomes of training, as identified in Chapter 8, is increased motivation. This may come simply from the act of training, or because salespeople learn the skills necessary to meet their sales goals and objectives and this becomes the motivating factor. Sometimes, sales performance evaluation may suggest changes to the compensation package to focus efforts on specific products or customers. Sales performance evaluation may also indicate that disciplinary action—even termination—is necessary. In these instances, documentation of sales performance and actions taken prior to discipline or termination may be important to protect the company from legal action.

The Sales Performance Evaluation Model

Sales performance evaluation requires that prior sales force goals or objectives have been established against which sales performance can be compared. Companies have historically used both input measures (such as number of sales calls or days worked, expenses, or non-selling activities performed) and output measures (such as sales, orders, contribution, profit, or account activity). (See Exhibit 13.2.) Research evidence suggests that there is a trend toward increasing use of output versus input measures.[4] The reason for the decline in the use of input measures is not certain, but could be related to the difficulty of tracking and recording input information as sales forces grow in size. As well, as companies focus more on sales force efficiency, many are reducing the amount of information that salespeople must provide as the time required to complete call reports and activity sheets takes away from valuable selling time. Which measures are used for sales performance evaluation varies considerably from one organization to another, and depends on the goals and objectives of the company and the level at which sales performance evaluation is being conducted: company, SBU, region, salesperson, product, or account level.

Sales Analysis at the Company, SBU, or Region Level

A first place to start sales performance evaluation is at a more aggregate level than individual salesperson, either at the company, strategic business unit (SBU), or region level. Aggregate sales figures for Canada Controllers, Inc., are provided in Exhibit 13.3. This company, disguised but still selling in Canada, sells products ranging from individual motor control starters for operating single pieces of equipment or machinery, to large motor control centres comprising numerous motor starters, which can be used to operate large sections of industrial plants, including mines, pulp mills, and manufacturing facilities. Between 2001 and 2005, company sales in one major region

B.C. Court Rules a Warning Is Not a Dismissal

Intrawest Corporation owns or is involved in more than a dozen mountain and warm-weather resorts in North America and Europe. With 24 800 employees and more than 30 years in the destination resorts and adventure travel business, it is a world leader.

When Laara Sinclaire left her position as a sales representative for the company, she quickly sued Intrawest for constructive dismissal. Laara had been selling time-share condos in Whistler, B.C. Intrawest would develop leads for its salespeople and set sales targets for them, requiring that they close 11 percent of leads or face disciplinary action.

Laara was successful for several years, but eventually she began to regularly miss her monthly sales targets. She and three other employees who failed to meet performance targets were offered a choice: (1) accept a warning letter and close 13 percent of leads in three weeks or be fired, or (2) accept a three-and-one-half month unpaid leave of absence for the fall slow season that was approaching. Laara chose to accept the leave of absence, but then quickly sued.

Initially, the court sided with Laara. However the lower court decision was overturned by the B.C. Court of Appeal. It ruled that Laara had voluntarily resigned.

In its decision, the court stated that a warning is not a constructive dismissal, but "at most, it is a threat of a future dismissal contingent on unsatisfactory future performance." It concluded that the leave of absence offer was a good-faith attempt by the employer to help salespeople who were struggling, in hopes that they would later improve their performance. For all four employees, work was still available, but with new performance conditions that the employment contract permitted. The other three salespeople chose this option.

Among the factors that saved Intrawest and that could provide guidance for other employers: draft employment contracts with a range of disciplinary actions as well as alternatives to discipline, and provide employees with a choice of how to overcome performance issues. Then, act in accordance with company policies and the employment contract.

Sources: Intrawest Corporation website, http://www.intrawest.com, accessed October 1, 2006; Howard Levitt, "Discipline Is Not the Same as Firing," *National Post*, July 6, 2005, p. FP10.

---

of Canada increased almost $6 million, from $10.3 million to $16.0 million—an increase of 56.5 percent (an annual compound growth rate of nearly 12 percent). Taken by itself, this information may be good or bad. The first indication that there may be a problem, however, is when the year-by-year sales are evaluated. A closer look reveals that sales did not increase by a constant rate each year. The sales increase from 2001 to 2002 was 15.5 percent, and the rate of increase then declined each year until it was only 9.0 percent from 2004 to 2005. This declining rate of sales growth is a cause for concern, but may be explained by industry or economic factors. An analysis of industry sales growth, however, makes it clear that Canada Controllers should be concerned. Total industry sales increased by more than $84 million during the same period—an increase of 113.0 percent (an annual compound growth rate of nearly 21 percent). If the industry growth rate is increasing faster than the company's growth rate, this indicates that the company must be losing market share, and an analysis of market share for each of the five years indicates that it has been declining each year, from 13.7 percent in 2001 to only 10.1 percent in 2005.

Exhibit 13.2

Model of Salesperson Evaluation

Salesperson behaviour:

Number of sales calls made
- Planned calls
- Unplanned calls

Number of days worked

Number of calls per day

Expenses
- Total expenses
- By type (travel, entertainment, meals, etc.)
- As a percentage of sales
- As a percentage of quota

Non-selling activities
- Letters written, telephone calls made, written proposals developed
- Number of meetings/training sessions with dealers/distributors
- Number of calls made with dealer/distributor salespeople
- Number of service calls made/complaints resolved
- Number of overdue accounts collected

Input Measures

Salesperson Evaluation

Salesperson results:

Sales
- Total revenue
- Sales by account
- Sales by product
- Unit sales volume
- Sales growth over previous period
- Sales as a percentage of quota
- Sales as a percentage of potential
- Average order size
- Average dollar value per invoice line item
- Contribution margin
- Net profit

Customers/accounts
- Number of active accounts
- Number of prospects
- Number of new accounts opened
- Number of overdue accounts
- Number of accounts lost

Output Measures

Exhibit 13.3

Sales Data: Canada Controllers*

Year	Company Sales ($)	Industry Sales ($)
2001	10 250 970	74 600 000
2002	11 844 888	92 300 000
2003	13 384 152	111 700 000
2004	14 722 155	133 500 000
2005	16 040 063	158 900 000

*All data related to Canada Controllers, and the company name, have been disguised, although the relationships among the data have been maintained.

It is clear from the analysis that Canada Controllers has a serious problem, one worthy of further investigation. However, the nature of the problem must now be explored. It is possible that the company's products have not kept pace with competitors' products. Canada Controllers could be losing sales in only one or two key market segments where one or two competitors have made specific advances. The company's prices may have had to increase more rapidly than competitors' prices, making it less competitive in the marketplace. One or more competitors may have established stronger or new distribution channels, or Canada Controllers may have become weaker in its own distribution. Finally, it may simply be a sales force issue. Maybe the company has fewer sales offices, salespeople, or distributors than needed. An effective sales manager must investigate all of these possibilities until he is sure he knows the cause for the decreasing performance. To continue his analysis, the sales manager might now look at sales by product. A first step would be to look at broad product categories, followed by even more in-depth analysis, if necessary.

SALES BY PRODUCT

As mentioned, Canada Controllers sells both single motor starters and motor control centres. Along with these two broad classes of products is a third major class of products, repair parts for its equipment. Exhibit 13.4 shows forecast and actual sales for the three classes of products, along with industry sales for each.

Exhibit 13.4

Forecast and Actual Sales Data by Product Line: Canada Controllers

Product Line	Company Forecast ($)	Company Sales ($)	Industry Sales ($)
Control centres	2 500 000	3 233 727	20 250 000
Motor starters	11 500 000	10 406 040	122 400 000
Repair parts	2 000 000	2 400 296	16 250 000
Total	16 000 000	16 040 063	158 900 000

When the company's forecast and actual total sales are compared, there does not appear to be a problem. The two figures are virtually identical. However, there are wide variations across the three product classes. Company sales for repair parts are 20.0 percent higher than forecast. Motor control centre sales are 29.3 percent better than forecast. The problem is sales for individual motor starters, which are 9.5 percent below forecast. This may not at first appear too serious. However, it could indicate that the company's long-term performance is even more at risk. Individual motor starters are the building blocks for motor control centres. Losing the motor starter business today could indicate that the company will find it increasingly difficult to sell motor control centres in the future. Another indication of future problems is that sales of repair parts were 15.0 percent of total sales for the company, but only 10.2 percent of total sales across the industry. This would be predicted by the continued decreasing market share that the company has been experiencing as its equipment, on average, will be increasingly older than competitors' equipment, and will require more repair parts.

Additional analyses can be done by looking at unit sales of motor control centres and motor starters (but not repair parts due to the large volume and variety of items, which would make them difficult to monitor). Exhibit 13.5 illustrates that the company has increased unit sales for both motor control centres and motor starters. While unit sales of motor control centres increased by 35.7 percent, sales revenue increased by 83.0 percent, indicating that the average price of a motor control centre has increased substantially. In fact, in 2004, the average price was $63 098, but in 2005, it was $85 098. While this has happened, the average price of a motor starter has dropped. Unit sales increased by 9.1 percent, but sales revenue actually decreased by 5.8 percent. In 2004, the average price of a motor starter was $658, but in 2005, it dropped to only $568. There could be several possible reasons why this has happened. The company may have been forced to reduce prices to be competitive, but may not have been able to reduce them fast enough or low enough to maintain market share. The company may still be favoured in markets that buy smaller motor starters, but may be increasingly less attractive to customers who purchase larger motor starters. Another possibility is that the company has refocused its sales efforts through its distributors, preferring to build unit market share at the expense of sales revenue market share. Clearly, the sales manager has many more things to investigate yet. Working inside the company and having knowledge of customers and competitors will no doubt provide an astute sales manager with direction for further analysis.

Exhibit 13.5

Sales Data—Unit Sales and Sales Revenue: Canada Controllers

Product Line	2004		2005	
	Sales (units)	Sales ($)	Sales (units)	Sales ($)
Control centres	28	1 766 740	38	3 233 727
Motor starters	16 775	11 041 600	18 305	10 406 040
Repair parts	*	1 913 815	*	2 400 296
Total		14 722 155		16 040 063

* Unit volume of repair parts not monitored

Expense Analysis at the Company, SBU, or Region Level

Although a sales revenue analysis is important to help a sales manager understand what is happening within his area of responsibility, this alone can provide only a partial picture. The sales manager needs also to consider an analysis of expenses to fully understand profitability. Of course, the only expenses that should concern the sales manager are those that are under his control. Frequently these include salary, travel, and entertainment expenses, although the sales manager may sometimes be responsible for controlling sales branch operating expenses as well. Commonly used evaluation measures include total expenses, selling expenses versus budgeted expenses, and selling expenses as a percentage of sales. While sales managers cannot control product costs, understanding them is important for sales managers as they are important when calculating contribution margins, and changes in contribution margins are sometimes explained by sales force activities. Product costs, or expenses, are now discussed.

COST BY PRODUCT

Sales managers should be aware of the product costs associated with the products that their salespeople sell. To continue the analysis, using Canada Controllers as an example, let us assume the following cost information provided in Exhibit 13.6. The actual cost information was not available from the company. For each of the three major product classes, the contribution margin as a percentage of sales is calculated. The relationships that exist among the three contribution margins are at least tenable. That is, the lowest gross margin is for sales of motor control centres. These have large unit selling prices, and are likely subject to the greatest competitive activity. Motor starters have much lower prices and could be expected to have higher contribution margins. However, this may be somewhat tempered by distributor sales if motor control centres are sold only through direct sales and motor starters are sold through distributors as well as through direct sales. Finally, repair parts have very high contribution margins, which may be necessary to support large inventory levels, and because repair parts are sold to a captive group of customers who have little choice but to buy parts from the manufacturer.

Looking at these figures becomes more relevant when they are compared from year to year, or from region to region. For example, a reduction in contribution margin from one year to the next could signal rising product costs without an equivalent increase in selling prices to offset the increased cost. Alternatively, it could signal an increase in price discounting by salespeople in order to close sales. The question then becomes whether this price discounting is part of the

---

Exhibit 13.6

Sales and Cost Data by Product Line: Canada Controllers

Product Line	Sales ($)	Cost of Goods ($)	Gross Margin (%)
Control centres	3 233 727	2 318 582	28.3
Motor starters	10 406 040	6 826 363	34.3
Repair parts	2 400 296	1 111 337	53.7
Total	16 040 063	10 256 337	36.1

company's strategy, was necessary due to competitive activity, or happened because salespeople are closing business to increase sales commissions or because they have simply developed poor selling habits. In any event, once a sales manager has an understanding of revenues and expenses, he is in a better position to establish future sales goals and objectives, plan sales strategy, make necessary adjustments to sales force organization, or make decisions concerning recruitment and selection, training, compensation, or motivation programs.

Evaluating Salespeople

Evaluating salespeople has the potential to be the most important duty a sales manager has, assuming it is done well. The outcome from the sales evaluation process provides an opportunity for the sales manager to communicate and interact directly with each salesperson. At a minimum, there should be a comprehensive annual sales performance review, but reviews done quarterly, or even more often, provide an opportunity to acknowledge good performance, take some action to improve poor performance, and ensure that everyone knows that performance evaluation is taken seriously. In contrast, some managers dislike the sales performance evaluation review process, rush through it, and do it poorly. The message is that it is a task that must be done, but not one that has a real benefit for either the organization or the salesperson. What are the purposes of sales performance evaluation? There are many, as illustrated in Exhibit 13.7. Sales performance evaluations:

1. Help establish the relationship between organizational sales goals and sales performance
2. Aid the sales manager in making decisions concerning sales force organization and territory alignment
3. Provide information to improve both recruitment and selection
4. Provide the bases for rewards: increased compensation, bonuses, awards, and promotions
5. Help identify when, where, and what types of training are needed
6. Motivate salespeople and help them establish career goals
7. Help the sales manager decide who should be terminated or otherwise disciplined, and document support for any action
8. Improve communication between the sales manager and salesperson, and improve salesperson performance by clearly establishing performance expectations

The measures that sales managers use to evaluate salespeople fall within two very broad categories: objective measures and subjective measures. **Objective measures** are measures that the sales manager usually collects from the company's internal information system, and do not require personal evaluations. **Subjective measures** do require personal evaluations, usually by the sales manager, but increasingly by other people with whom the salesperson interacts. Objective measures may be further divided into two categories: input measures and output measures. **Input measures** reflect the inputs to the sales process; that is, the behaviours and activities that the salesperson performs in order to generate sales. **Output measures** are the outcomes that the salesperson achieves as a result of the inputs he makes.

Objective Measures

Objective measures that are used to evaluate the sales performance of individual salespeople include input measures, output measures, and ratios of input and/or output measures. Each of these types of measures is now discussed.

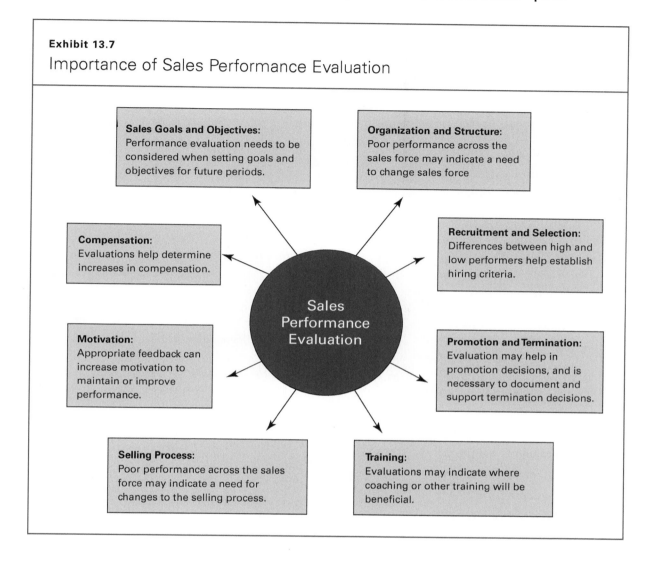

Exhibit 13.7

Importance of Sales Performance Evaluation

Sales Goals and Objectives: Performance evaluation needs to be considered when setting goals and objectives for future periods.

Organization and Structure: Poor performance across the sales force may indicate a need to change sales force

Compensation: Evaluations help determine increases in compensation.

Recruitment and Selection: Differences between high and low performers help establish hiring criteria.

Motivation: Appropriate feedback can increase motivation to maintain or improve performance.

Promotion and Termination: Evaluation may help in promotion decisions, and is necessary to document and support termination decisions.

Sales Performance Evaluation

Selling Process: Poor performance across the sales force may indicate a need for changes to the selling process.

Training: Evaluations may indicate where coaching or other training will be beneficial.

INPUT MEASURES

Salespeople perform a number of behaviours and activities for the purpose of generating sales results. These behaviours and activities are the input measures that are used to evaluate salespeople: what they did, and how often they did it. Exhibit 13.8 lists 29 input measures that companies use for evaluating salespeople, and the percentage of respondents who indicated that they use each of these measures. Most sales managers use input measures as part of a sales performance evaluation for individual salespeople because there should be a relationship between these measures and sales results. When the relationship is weaker than expected—for example, when the number of sales calls is not related strongly enough with the number of orders received—there is an indication that the salesperson is not performing appropriate behaviours, or is performing them ineffectively. Input measures are particularly relevant when the selling cycle is extended. When it takes many sales calls and many months to close a sale, or for a very large sale that may take several years of effort, input measures may be the only valid measures to use when evaluating individual salesperson performance. Understanding the important input measures that may

Exhibit 13.8

Input Bases Used for Evaluating Salespeople

Base	Percent Reporting Use	Base	Percent Reporting Use
Calls (behaviour)			
Number of customer calls	48	Number of unplanned calls	7
Number of planned calls	24	Planned to unplanned call ratio	3
Number of calls per account	23		
Time utilization (behaviour)			
Number of calls per day (per period)	42	Selling time versus non-selling time	27
Number of days worked (per period)	33	Average time spent per call	8
Selling expenses (costs)			
Selling expense versus budget	55	Average cost per sales call	12
Total expenses	53	Expenses by product category	7
Selling expenses to sales	49	Expenses by customer type	3
Selling expenses to quota	12		
Ancillary (non-selling) activities			
Number of required reports turned in	38	Number of formal proposals developed	15
Training meetings conducted	26	Advertising displays set up	13
Number of customer complaints	25	Number of demonstrations conducted	12
Number of formal presentations	22	Dollar amount of overdue accounts collected	10
Number of quotes	21	Number of letters /phone calls to prospects	9
Number of dealer meetings held	17		
Percentage of goods returned	17		
Number of service calls made	15		

Source: Adapted from Donald W. Jackson, Jr., John L. Schlacter, and William G. Wolfe, "Examining the Bases Utilized for Evaluating Salespeople's Performance," *Journal of Personal Selling & Sales Management,* Fall 1995, pp. 57–65. Copyright © PSE National Education Foundation. Used by permission of M. E. Sharpe, Inc.

lead to successfully closing the sale provides the sales manager with an opportunity to assess ongoing performance and coach the salesperson during the sales process. Input measures can be grouped into three categories: sales calls and time utilization, selling expenses, and ancillary (non-selling) activities.

SALES CALLS AND TIME UTILIZATION   Many companies provide guidelines concerning how many sales calls a salesperson is expected to make daily, or annually, on various categories of accounts, where the accounts are grouped depending on their past purchase behaviour or their future potential. In fact, this is frequently the basis for deciding the number of salespeople needed by the company, and for designing individual sales territories. The number of days a salesperson is expected to work annually multiplied by the average number of sales calls a salesperson is expected to make each day provides an estimate of the total number of sales calls available for allocation across a particular sales territory. That is, sales calls are a finite resource. The number of sales calls actually made may be determined from a salesperson's call reports.

Contact management software—such as Act! or GoldMine—has helped make the sales call reporting process more efficient. Salespeople can quickly store information concerning which accounts were called on, who at the accounts were actually visited, what products were discussed, follow-up calls needed or promises that were made, and many other aspects of the sales call. This can be routinely summarized and sent to the sales manager, or downloaded to a network server where the data can be accumulated, summarized if needed, or accessed by the salesperson or the sales manager whenever they wish. Contact management software has improved sales force efficiency, but it is questionable whether this has always been to the benefit of salespeople. A survey of 1300 salespeople asked them to evaluate 16 work-related challenges common to sales careers. Not having enough time was ranked first, followed by achieving a balance between work and family, and dealing with information overload.[5]

When there appears to be a problem with sales performance, one of the first things that a sales manager should review is the number and allocation of sales calls a salesperson makes. Most salespeople sell between 200 and 230 days per year, assuming five days per week with time for vacations, sales training, sick days, and holidays. Depending on the products sold, salespeople may be expected to make from two or three sales calls per day for some business-to-business sales positions, to six to eight sales calls per day for consumer goods salespeople who call on retailers such as grocery chains, pharmacies, or convenience stores. The number of sales calls a salesperson makes could be lower due to not working a sufficient number of days, or because fewer sales calls per day than expected were made. When a sales manager identifies that the average number of daily sales calls a salesperson makes is low, he must be careful how he chooses to get the salesperson to increase sales effort. It is quite easy for a salesperson to increase the number of daily sales calls by reducing the time and effort currently spent on making sales calls. The result could be decreased rather than increased sales. The point is that there are salespeople who achieve much higher than average sales volume or contribution margins while making a below average daily number of sales calls. The sales calls they do make are more effective as they spend more time and effort on full-line selling, up-selling, or selling product value or benefits rather than cutting price.

SELLING EXPENSES   When a sales manager evaluates a salesperson's expenses, he is evaluating the cost of the input effort that the salesperson is making. Companies routinely track total selling expenses, and expenses by expense category, such as travel, accommodation, meals, entertainment, etc. Tracking expenses as a percentage of quota or sales is also common. While it might be obvious that not tracking and controlling expenses can lead to their quickly getting excessive, it is also possible that salespeople can spend too little for travel and entertainment, and this can have a negative impact on sales.

ANCILLARY (NON-SELLING) ACTIVITIES   Many salespeople are required to perform activities that are not directly related to selling effort, and they are evaluated on these activities. Some companies that sell through channel intermediaries—retailers or wholesalers—may have salespeople who are required to monitor inventory and who, in some instances, may actually prepare purchase orders for their customers so that inventories get replenished as required. These salespeople may also stock shelves or bins, set up displays, train these resellers' salespeople, and even make sales calls with resellers' salespeople. Some companies also monitor such salesperson activities as the number of letters written, quotations prepared, telephone calls made, written proposals developed, demonstrations conducted, service calls made, or overdue accounts collected.

OUTPUT MEASURES

Output measures result from salesperson inputs (activities and behaviours). Two categories of output measures include sales- and profit-related measures—such as sales revenue, unit sales, number of orders and average order size, contribution, and margin—and customer-account activity measures—such as number of prospects, active accounts, new accounts, lost accounts, and overdue accounts. Exhibit 13.9 lists 38 output measures that companies use for evaluating salespeople, and the percentage of respondents who indicated that they use each of these measures.

SALES, ORDERS, AND PROFITABILITY Many companies track sales and order activity because, in the final analysis, these directly reflect the results the companies wish to achieve. The number of sales orders a salesperson receives is a reflection of his ability to close sales. However, the average size of the sales order is also important. A salesperson who receives many orders risks having a low average order size. The salesperson becomes focused on quantity, and not quality. Smaller accounts that buy lower volumes or fewer items from the salesperson's product line get more attention than they deserve, while large and potentially lucrative accounts never reach their full potential because the salesperson does not allocate enough of his time and effort to them. Some salespeople are so happy when they receive an order that they immediately thank the customer and rush to process the order through their sales system. A little more effort to up-sell or increase the number of items that a customer buys on each order might substantially increase the average order size that a salesperson receives.

Some companies focus attention on orders or sales volume per type of account, or per product in a product line. In some instances, it is strategically important for the long-term health of a company that it develop and support its channel intermediaries. In these instances, the sales manager may set target sales through direct sales and through channel intermediaries. Sometimes, particular products become the focus of attention. When an important product is added to a product line and that product is strategically important to the future of the company, some sales managers may set objectives for the sales of specific products, and measure sales performance related to those products.

Increasingly, companies are evaluating profitability and not simply sales revenue or orders. When companies become too focused on sales and orders, profitability may suffer for either or both of two reasons:

1. *Salespeople may reduce price in order to close sales.* When this happens, gross margins are reduced, and the sales are less profitable. There is a bias here in favour of the salesperson and against the company, and this is particularly true if the salesperson is paid on commission and gets no penalty for a reduction in gross margin. Exhibit 13.10 shows how this bias works. Assuming that a salesperson gets 10 percent commission on sales, he will get $15.00 commission on a $150.00 sale. If the company's cost of goods sold is 50 percent of list price, then the company makes $60.00 gross margin. Now, see what happens if the salesperson reduces the price by 20 percent. At a price of $120.00, the salesperson's commission is reduced to $12.00. The $3.00 reduction in commission means that the salesperson's commission is reduced by 20 percent, from $15.00 to $12.00. However, the company's gross margin is reduced from $60.00 to $33.00, a 45 percent reduction. Had the salesperson been

Exhibit 13.9

Output Bases Used for Evaluating Salespeople

Base	Percent Reporting Use	Base	Percent Reporting Use
Sales (results)			
Sales volume in dollars	79	Sales volume to market potential	27
Sales volume to previous year's sales	76	Sales volume by customer type	22
Sales volume to dollar quota	65	Sales volume to physical unit quota	9
Percentage increase in sales volume	55	Sales volume per order	7
Sales volume by product or product line	48	Sales volume per call	6
Sales volume by customer	44	Sales volume by outlet type	4
Amount of new account sales	42	Percentage of sales made by telephone or mail	1
Sales volume by units	35		
Profit (results)			
Net profit dollars	69	Gross margin in dollars	25
Gross margin as percentage of sales	34	Margin by customer type	18
Return on investment	33	Net profit per sale	14
Net profit as a percentage of sales	32	Return on sales cost	14
Margin by product category	28		
Market share			
Market share achieved	59	Market share per quota	18
Accounts			
Number of new accounts	69	Dollar amount of accounts receivable	17
Number of lost accounts	33	Number of overdue accounts	15
Number of accounts buying full line	22	Lost account ratio	6
Orders (profitability)			
Number of orders secured	47	Net orders per repeat order	10
Average size of order secured	22	Number of cancelled orders per orders booked	4
Order per call ratio (batting average)	14		
Number of orders cancelled	11		

Source: Donald W. Jackson, Jr., John L. Schlacter, and William G. Wolfe, "Examining the Bases Utilized for Evaluating Salespeople's Performance," *Journal of Personal Selling & Sales Management,* Fall 1995, pp. 57–65. Copyright © PSE National Education Foundation. Used by permission of M. E. Sharpe, Inc.

rewarded based on gross margin, then a discount would still seriously reduce the company's gross margin, but it would also have a much larger impact on the salesperson's commission, making it less likely that the salesperson would give such a large discount.

Exhibit 13.10

Effect of Price Discounting

List price	$150.00		$150.00	
Customer discount	0.00		30.00	(20%)
Selling price	$150.00		$120.00	
Less sales commission	15.00	(10%)	12.00	(10%)
	$135.00		$108.00	
Less cost of goods sold	75.00	(50%)	75.00	(50%)
Gross margin	$ 60.00		$ 33.00	

Reduction in sales commission:	20%
Reduction in gross margin:	45%

2. *Salespeople sell the wrong mix of products.* For example, companies frequently make higher gross margins on newer products that are in earlier stages of their product life cycle. These products usually do not have the same competition that drives prices down and reduces gross margins. However, left on their own, many salespeople will continue to sell products they are familiar with to customers they are familiar with, and they will not make the time or effort to establish new products or sell to new customers. If too many salespeople do this, the new product failure rate will increase, and the company's overall gross margin will continue to decline. A sales manager who astutely establishes gross margin or some other profitability target for salespeople can redirect their focus to more profitable products.

CUSTOMERS/ACCOUNTS   Many companies also track customer or account development activity. A popular measure is the number of active accounts a salesperson has in his account portfolio. What constitutes an active account may differ from one company to another. For example, some companies include any account that has made a purchase in the previous 12 months. Other companies may require at least one purchase within the previous six—or even three—months. Companies may even set a dollar value that an account must purchase in order to be classified as an active account. Sales managers can track the number of active accounts in a sales territory from one year to the next. When the number increases within a year, this indicates that the salesperson has been actively soliciting and gaining new accounts. Again, some sales managers count the number of new accounts each salesperson gains over the period. When the number of new accounts is used as the basis to evaluate performance, then the sales manager must be careful to ensure that each salesperson has the potential to open new accounts. A salesperson who has been very successful at opening accounts in her territory might find that the number of potential new accounts decreases as her success increases.

While the number of new accounts is important for many companies, many also track the number of lost accounts. These were formerly active accounts but have become inactive accounts. As this number increases, there is an indication that the salesperson is not adequately servicing her accounts, or otherwise keeping them satisfied. Finally, other customer or account measures

SALES MANAGEMENT **TODAY**

Today's Push for Profitability

Sales managers today are beginning to focus more on profitability, and less on sales volume. There is a growing recognition that not every customer is a good customer; not every product is a good product.

A company can increase its profitability if it serves only profitable customers. Jeff Multz, director of sales and marketing at FirstWave Technologies, recognized when he operated his own consulting business that he was serving far too many customers. He discovered that only approximately 20 percent of his customers contributed to his company's success. Jeff called 3000 of his less attractive customers and explained that he could no longer serve them. His sales revenue increased by 50 percent over the next year, and his profit increased by 50 percent within five months. Jeff attributes the improved performance, at least partly, to his better customer focus.

A company is at a further advantage if it can steer unprofitable customers to its competitors. This will decrease their profitability, and take their limited resources to manage unprofitable accounts, reducing their ability to focus on better opportunities. David Sutcliffe, CEO of Richmond, B.C.-based Sierra Wireless, understands the value of eliminating many smaller customers who may have limited potential but who demand special attention. He says, "I give

them a competitor's name, phone number or email address. I know they're thinking I'm out of my mind. But if your competitors are so busy choking on those small orders, you can focus on and win the more profitable opportunities."

A sales manager who performs a comprehensive sales performance evaluation is better able to determine on which customers and on what products his salespeople should focus their efforts. KMC Telecom, for example, changed the flat commission rate it paid on all products so that salespeople could earn commissions of 50–225 percent, depending on the products they sold. Thus, a management compensation decision changed salespeople's behaviours, resulting in increased profitability.

Of course, a focus on profitability must be tempered by knowledge of what is strategically important for the company. Some accounts and products that appear unprofitable in the short term may be the most profitable in the long term. Past sales to an account should not be confused with future potential. Profitable products in the decline stage of their product life cycle must be sold to generate immediate profits, but unprofitable products in the introductory stage of their product life cycle could be the future of the company.

Sources: Betsey Cummings, "You're Outta Here," *Sales & Marketing Management,* June 2001, pp. 65–66; Rhea Seymour, "Ideas That Work," *Profit,* June 2002, pp. 66–70; Betsey Cummings, "The Perfect Plan," *Sales & Marketing Management,* February 2002, p. 53.

that can be used to evaluate the sales performance of individual salespeople include the number of overdue accounts, and the number of prospects in the salesperson's prospect list. When the number of overdue accounts increases, this indicates that the salesperson has not been properly qualifying prospects. Remember that one criterion needed for a prospect to become a qualified prospect is the ability to pay. For some industries, maintaining an adequate list of prospects is also important. In insurance sales, for example, the salesperson who closes sales but who does not add prospects to her prospect list risks running out of prospects. When this happens, prospecting becomes overly important and this activity means the salesperson has little opportunity to make presentations and close sales, and her income will be reduced.

RATIOS

Many of the input and output measures discussed above can be combined into meaningful ratios that allow a sales manager to compare the performance of one salesperson to another, or to compare a salesperson's performance in one period to a previous period. Thus, ratio measures can be used for both comparative and evaluative purposes. Ratio measures can be grouped into three categories: account development ratios, salesperson activity/productivity ratios, and salesperson profitability/expense ratios. See Exhibit 13.11. Each category is now discussed.

ACCOUNT DEVELOPMENT RATIOS   One of the most commonly used ratios is the **account penetration ratio**: the number of active accounts compared to the number of potential accounts in a salesperson's territory. The ratio gets its name because it measures how effectively the salesperson is penetrating his territory. A low penetration ratio could indicate either an ineffective salesperson or a salesperson who is simply focused on a small number of accounts among the many he has. Another ratio measure that complements this one is the **sales per account ratio**: the sales dollar volume divided by the number of active accounts. This measure indicates how well the salesperson is doing, on average, per account. When the average sales volume per account is low, it could indicate that the salesperson is spending too much time and effort on small accounts and not enough time on accounts with greater potential. The **average order size ratio** (salesperson's total sales divided by number of orders), when it is low, could indicate that the salesperson is

---

Exhibit 13.11
Common Ratios Used for Salesperson Evaluation

Account Development Ratios

Account penetration ratio	=	Number of active accounts / Number of potential accounts
Sales per account ratio	=	Sales dollar volume / Number of active accounts
Average order size ratio	=	Sales dollar volume / Total number of orders
Account share ratio	=	Purchases from salesperson / Total purchases by account
New account conversion ratio	=	Number of new accounts / Total number of accounts
Lost account ratio	=	Number of lost accounts / Total number of accounts
Order cancellation ratio	=	Number of cancelled orders / Total number of orders

continued

Exhibit 13.11

continued

Salesperson Activity/Productivity Ratios

Sales per call ratio $= \dfrac{\text{Sales dollar volume}}{\text{Total number of sales calls}}$

Orders per call ratio $= \dfrac{\text{Number of sales orders}}{\text{Total number of sales calls}}$

Calls per account ratio $= \dfrac{\text{Number of sales calls}}{\text{Total number of accounts}}$

Calls per day ratio $= \dfrac{\text{Number of sales calls}}{\text{Number of days worked}}$

Dealer sales calls ratio $= \dfrac{\text{Number of calls on dealers}}{\text{Total number of sales calls}}$

Planned sales call ratio $= \dfrac{\text{Number of planned calls}}{\text{Total number of sales calls}}$

Salesperson Profitability/Expense Ratios

Gross margin $= \dfrac{\text{Total gross margin dollars}}{\text{Total sales revenue}}$

Contribution margin $= \dfrac{\text{Total contribution dollars}}{\text{Total sales revenue}}$

Profit margin $= \dfrac{\text{Total profit dollars}}{\text{Total sales revenue}}$

Sales expense ratio $= \dfrac{\text{Total direct selling expenses}}{\text{Total sales revenue}}$

Cost per call ratio $= \dfrac{\text{Total direct selling expenses}}{\text{Total number of sales calls}}$

spending too little time actually selling to each account. The salesperson completes a sale and then moves to the next account without making an attempt to sell complementary items, better quality items, or a larger volume to the customer. Other measures that the sales manager can use to further assess whether there is a problem here is the average number of items per sales order, or the average dollar value per invoice line item.

A measure that is important in some businesses, particularly for suppliers of commodities or business services such as transportation, is the **account share ratio** (percentage of an account's business given to a particular salesperson). This measures the effectiveness of the salesperson selling to a particular account. If the account can use any of 10 trucking companies to ship its finished product to market, then it would be good to assess what percentage of its shipping requirements a particular supplier satisfies. Many buyers would split their business among several trucking companies to ensure that they get competitive prices and good service. In many instances, a way for a salesperson to commence selling to an account is to convince the buyer to give him a small share of the purchase volume so he can demonstrate his ability to provide superior service. If he successfully handles the business he is given, then, over time, the salesperson can ask for a higher share of the business and penetrate the account to a greater extent. A higher percentage of volume from the account indicates how well the salesperson is building the relationship with the account. Account share is important because, as it increases, the profit from handling the account increases to an even greater extent. That is, the selling expense as a percentage of sales revenue goes down.

The **new account conversion ratio** (number of new accounts divided by total number of accounts) indicates how well the salesperson is able to prospect for and close sales to new accounts. Many companies track this because they realize that without continually adding new accounts to their active account portfolio, sales will eventually decline as customer attrition is something that cannot be avoided and is often beyond the control of the salesperson. Customers move, go bankrupt, and merge. Buyers sometimes are promoted, resign, retire, die, or simply decide to buy more from alternative suppliers. Closely related to this ratio is the **lost account ratio** (number of lost accounts divided by total number of accounts), which measures how well the salesperson is able to provide after-sale service to customers. Those that become dissatisfied will frequently stop buying from the salesperson. A final account development ratio that is important for many companies is the **order cancellation ratio** (number of cancelled orders divided by total number of orders). When this ratio increases, it may indicate that the salesperson is using high pressure to close sales and is less concerned with properly qualifying the buyer to ensure that the buyer has a need and that the right product to suit the buyer's need is selected.

ACTIVITY/PRODUCTIVITY RATIOS   Activity or productivity ratios measure the amount of effort and planning that a salesperson makes, and the results that are achieved from these activities. The **sales per sales call ratio** (sales dollar volume divided by total number of sales calls) measures the average sales revenue that the salesperson achieves per sales call. The **orders per sales call ratio** (number of orders received divided by total number of sales calls, and sometimes called the "batting average" or the "hit ratio") is a measure of how good the salesperson is at closing sales. Comparing this ratio across a number of salespeople quickly highlights those who may need training in identifying which prospects should be focused on and how to close sales once they have identified good target prospects. The *sales calls per account ratio* provides information on how well salespeople allocate their time to account coverage. Many companies categorize accounts into groups depending on account potential, and then have a target number of calls per account within each group. This helps ensure that salespeople allocate their time appropriately across a portfolio of accounts. For example, accounts may be grouped into 'A' accounts with sales potential exceeding $100 000 per year, along a continuum to 'E' accounts with sales potential of less than $1000 per year. Salespeople may be required to make six calls per year on 'A' accounts, down to one call per year on 'D' accounts, and 'E' accounts might be called only by telephone or solicited by direct mail. Other activity or productivity ratios include the *calls per day ratio*, the *dealer sales calls ratio*, and the *planned sales calls ratio*.

PROFITABILITY/EXPENSE RATIOS Two profitability ratios are contribution margin and profit margin. **Contribution margin** (total contribution dollars divided by total sales revenue) can be used to make valuable comparisons across salespeople and for the same salesperson over time. Contribution margin for a single sale is equal to total sales revenue minus total variable cost, or total cost of goods sold. The salesperson can generally only influence the total sales revenue. When the salesperson reduces price to the customer, costs remaining unchanged, the contribution dollars amount goes down, so the contribution margin goes down. A salesperson who regularly reduces price will have a lower contribution margin than the salesperson who sells based on service, quality, or value to the customer. **Profit margin** is defined as the total profit dollars divided by total sales revenue. There are companies that use profit instead of contribution; however, profit is best used only when the salesperson has control over the additional costs that are used to calculate profit.

The **sales expense ratio** compares the salesperson's total direct selling expenses to total sales revenue. Salespeople can affect the sales expense ratio by either selling more, or spending less. Management would like to see this ratio lower rather than higher, although there is often a concern when it gets too low that not enough is being spent to generate sales. Sometimes, a salesperson will have a higher sales expense ratio than other salespeople on the sales force because she has a larger geographic sales territory and must travel farther and more frequently remain overnight. For this reason, it is sometimes insightful to use categories of selling expenses, such as entertainment expenses, rather than total selling expenses. As well, expenses such as meal expenses can be compared based on the number of days away from the office; for example, average meal expenses per travel day. Some companies set maximum values for breakfast, for lunch, and for dinner; some set a per diem, or daily, maximum meal expense. A few simply manage average meal expenses over travel days so that salespeople who are regular travellers can reward themselves with an expensive meal periodically as long as their average meal expense stays within expectations.

The **cost per call ratio** (total direct selling expenses divided by total number of sales calls) estimates the average cost of a sales call for the salesperson. Total direct selling expenses are usually used, but management can use categories of selling costs as well. When salespeople are paid straight salary, for example, and salaries vary considerably for reasons that are not under the control of the salespeople, then using categories of selling expenses is sometimes more insightful. The key is for the sales manager to decide on what basis he would like to make comparisons across members of the sales force. Cost per call ratios can also be used to compare salespeople across sales forces as many trade or professional associations publish these data.

FOUR FACTOR MODEL

The previous discussion of common ratios used for salesperson sales performance evaluation suggests that there are many other ratios that could be computed that sales managers might find useful. Some sales managers may use only a few ratios, while others may use nearly all that were discussed and many more. A useful combination that can be used and that will simplify things for many sales managers is what is referred to as the *four factor model*. It considers the four things that salespeople can do to increase sales:

$$\text{Sales} = \text{Days worked} \times \frac{\text{Sales calls}}{\text{Days worked}} \times \frac{\text{Orders}}{\text{Sales calls}} \times \frac{\text{Sales}}{\text{Orders}}$$

or

$$\text{Sales} = \text{Days worked} \times \text{Call rate} \times \text{Hit rate} \times \text{Average order size}$$

This model recognizes that a salesperson can increase sales by (1) working more days, (2) increasing her average calls per day, (3) closing more sales for a particular number of sales calls, or (4) increasing her average order size. Of course, this model will not provide a complete picture for the sales manager. It ignores expenses, for example. A second problem with this four factor model is that, while any one of the factors can help explain a salesperson's performance, the four factors are not independent. For example, if the sales manager decides that the salesperson needs to improve his call rate, the salesperson may increase the number of sales calls he makes. His call rate will improve. However, if this does not result in an increase in orders closed, then the salesperson's hit rate will go down.

An important point that must be stressed, however, is that no matter which measures or how many measures are used, they are all tools to help assess performance. When numbers are calculated, they may suggest areas of weakness and where to look for additional problems, but there are often rational explanations to explain the numbers. Blind attempts to "improve" the numbers may do that, without improving overall sales performance. Objective measures of performance should aid decision-making and good judgment, but should not replace either. In the final analysis, sales managers can begin the sales performance evaluation process with standard input, output, and ratio measures, but may need some creativity to decide exactly what is best suited for their particular company and sales force.

Subjective Measures

While care must be exercised when evaluating objective measures of sales performance, even greater care is needed when evaluating salespeople with subjective measures due to the biases that can be introduced. However, subjective measures of a salesperson's performance can be useful as well. These measures focus less on the salesperson's activities and the results that they get from performing these activities, and more on how salespeople perform their role responsibilities from a behavioural or process perspective. That is, these are more "quality-related" measures rather than "quantity-related" measures. Exhibit 13.12 lists 29 subjective, or qualitative, measures that companies use for evaluating salespeople, and the percentage of respondents who indicated that they use each of these measures.

Subjective measures of salesperson performance can be used for a number of purposes. First, they may be used to identify areas of weakness where a salesperson may need development, or where corrective action may need to be taken. A salesperson with poor product knowledge is unlikely to be successful in sales for very long. A salesperson who continually reports late to the office could negatively affect the attitudes and behaviours of other members of the sales force. Many of the qualitative measures of sales performance are important to a salesperson's long-term success, either in actual sales or for their future sales careers. Review the criteria listed in Exhibit 13.12 and you will quickly see why poor performance on only a few of them would make a salesperson unsuitable for promotion to management, for example. In that sense, these criteria can be viewed as professional development criteria, and mature salespeople who perform well on these criteria will have greater career opportunities.

PROBLEMS WITH SUBJECTIVE PERFORMANCE MEASURES

There are many problems with subjective performance measures. One of the most common criticisms of salesperson performance evaluation using subjective criteria is that there is often a halo effect. A **halo effect** occurs when the rating that is assigned on one criterion affects the ratings on

Exhibit 13.12

Qualitative (Subjective) Bases Used for Evaluating Salespeople

Base	Percent Reporting Use	Base	Percent Reporting Use
Communication skills	88	Motivation	61
Product knowledge	85	Ethical/moral behaviour	59
Attitude	82	Planning ability	58
Selling skills	79	Pricing knowledge	55
Initiative and aggressiveness	76	Report preparation and submission	54
Appearance and manner	75	Creativity	54
Knowledge of competition	71	Punctuality	49
Team player	67	Resourcefulness	49
Enthusiasm	66	Knowledge of company policies	48
Time management	63	Customer goodwill generated	41
Cooperation	62	Self-improvement efforts	40
Judgment	62		

Other criteria: Care of company property (39), degree of respect from trade and competition (38), use of promotional materials (37), new product ideas (35), use of marketing/technical backup teams (33), good citizenship (22).

Source: Donald W. Jackson, Jr., John L. Schlacter, and William G. Wolfe, "Examining the Bases Utilized for Evaluating Salespeople's Performance," *Journal of Personal Selling & Sales Management,* Fall 1995, pp. 57–65. Copyright © PSE National Education Foundation. Used by permission of M. E. Sharpe, Inc.

other criteria. For example, a sales manager could rate a salesperson high on enthusiasm. As a result, the ratings given for attitude and cooperation might be higher than they would have been had the salesperson not been first rated on enthusiasm. Another issue is related to the individual rating behaviours of different sales managers. Some are prepared to rate salespeople at the extremes; that is, "very satisfactory" or "very unsatisfactory"; others tend to seldom rate at either extreme and rate everyone closer to the mean rating on a scale; that is, "somewhat satisfactory" or "somewhat unsatisfactory." This can create a real problem if performance evaluations on these criteria are used to determine salary increases or bonuses. The sales manager who tends to rate his good salespeople at the upper end of the scale will get higher rewards for his salespeople than the sales manager who tends to use more moderate measures when evaluating his sales force.

Other biases that may affect performance evaluation ratings on subjective criteria include interpersonal bias and outcome bias. **Interpersonal bias** occurs when ratings on subjective performance criteria are affected by how much the person being rated is liked or disliked by the person who is doing the performance evaluation. **Outcome bias** occurs when ratings on subjective performance criteria are affected by the sales outcomes that the salesperson has achieved.[6] When salespeople achieve higher sales results, there is a tendency to assume that they must be doing everything well; hence, there could be a tendency to rate that person higher on subjective performance criteria. The danger, of course, is that if the salesperson's colleagues believe the sales results were due to luck or other factors beyond the salesperson's control, they may be upset with what they believe to be his undeservedly high performance evaluation. It is also possible that a good salesperson—one who does everything right—gets poor results for reasons beyond his control. A sales manager who fails to recognize this, and who then rates the salesperson poorly on subjective measures, will demotivate the salesperson and increase the likelihood that a good salesperson will leave. A sales manager who does recognize this should reinforce the salesperson's behaviour.

Before ending the discussion of sales performance evaluation, there are two additional topics that should be explored: employing 360-degree feedback and using performance matrices. Both of these are now discussed.

360-Degree Feedback

One method of performance evaluation that tries to reduce the biases with subjective performance measures is **360-degree feedback**. This is an appraisal system that combines self-evaluation with evaluation from several other sources, such as customers, supervisors or managers, sales colleagues, and internal company support staff. See Exhibit 13.13. This system has been growing in popularity and is now used or planned by nearly all of the *Fortune* 1000 companies, and is increasingly becoming popular in small and medium-size companies.[7]

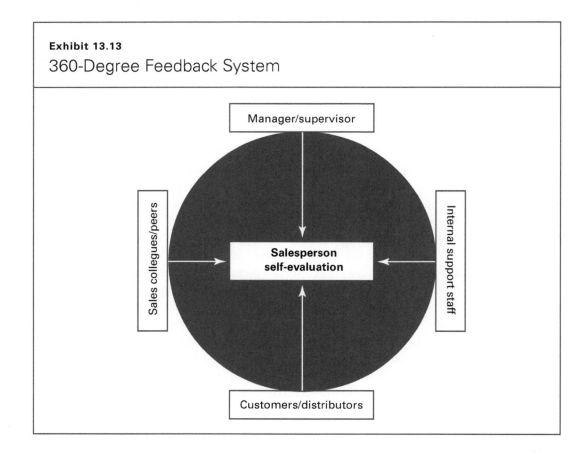

Exhibit 13.13
360-Degree Feedback System

Essentially, such a system replaces a single judge (the sales manager) with a jury (the group of evaluators), and is used to evaluate performance on such things as knowledge, skills, and behaviours. It should not be used to evaluate personality traits or styles. The strength of such an appraisal system is that it provides a view of the salesperson's performance from all angles (hence, 360-degree feedback). Further, when several customer evaluations are involved, it provides a more complete picture of how the salesperson is performing in her territory.[8]

While this type of evaluation system has tremendous intuitive appeal, and while it has benefited many companies that use it, there are still some issues with its implementation. First, when customers are involved, they must have clearly focused questions and must understand why the performance evaluation is being conducted. Evaluating another firm's employees is not within the buyer's job description, so it may raise issues of legal responsibility, or even moral responsibility, depending on the consequences of their evaluation. Second, 360-degree feedback systems are best used for developmental feedback, and not as input into the compensation and reward system. When used to determine rewards, salespeople—great game-players anyway—quickly learn to manipulate the system. When not carefully implemented, a 360-degree feedback system also risks jeopardizing relationships within the sales force, causing jealousy and retribution.[9] This risk is most likely higher when rewards or punishments are involved. Finally, the items that are used to evaluate salespeople may be more or less desirable to one group of evaluators than another. For example, a salesperson who challenges the way things are done in an organization might encourage independent thought and action among internal support staff. She may be rated higher by these support people than by the sales manager, who might give her a low rating for the same action.[10]

Whether a company decides to implement a 360-degree feedback appraisal system or not, it might still benefit by beginning the process of experimenting with such a system on a small scale. Such systems inherently foster communication between supervisors or managers and individual salespeople, who gain a greater understanding of their strengths and areas for improvement when development is the focus.

Before leaving the topic of sales performance evaluation, one of the most valuable tools that sales managers can use—performance matrices—will be discussed.

Performance Matrices

Many sales managers find that preparing performance matrices helps them better understand what is happening across their sales force, and provides them with a tool to help communicate performance to their salespeople. A **performance matrix** is a conceptual tool that helps a sales manager compare salespeople, or groups of salespeople, across several input/output measures at the same time.[11] The performance matrix illustrated in Exhibit 13.14 shows how the members of a sales force might be represented in two-dimensional space, where the dimensions are sales revenue in dollars and gross margin. In this example, the four quadrants have been given names that clearly describe the members of each group: (1) high sales–high margin, (2) high sales–low margin, (3) low sales–high margin, and (4) low sales–low margin.

Once this matrix has been prepared, it can be used to communicate the performance evaluation with each salesperson; however, there are several things that a sales manager must consider before preparing a performance matrix. First, the sales manager must decide which input or output measures to use. Two common ones are sales revenue and gross margin, as shown in Exhibit 13.14. If these are chosen, for example, then the sales manager must decide at what levels to divide high sales from low sales, and high gross margin from low gross margin. This is not a

Exhibit 13.14

Performance Matrix

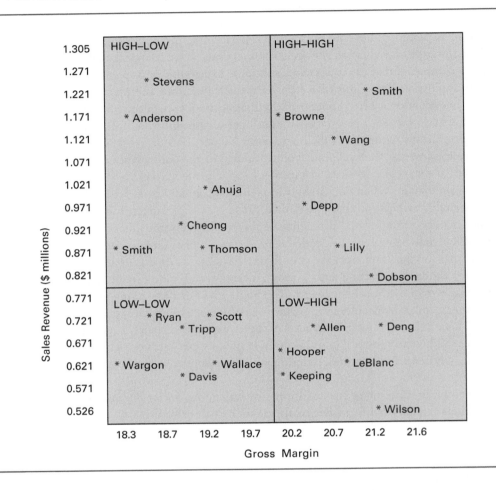

simple decision, and may require some careful thought by the sales manager. For example, a common place to begin might be to simply draw the divisions at the points of average sales and average gross margin. If the sales manager has a smaller sales force—for example, 10 to 24 salespeople—then one or two salespeople with very high sales could increase the average sales to the point where the rest of the sales force are below average. However, using average sales and average gross margin usually works quite well. If it does not, an alternative to consider would be to divide the sales force, whatever the size, so that one-half are in the high sales group and one-half are in the low sales group, and so that one half are in the high gross margin group and one-half are in the low gross margin group. This will ensure an almost equal number of salespeople in each quadrant.

Communicating with individual salespeople now becomes important and here, the sales manager needs to be careful. It might at first appear that the best quadrant to be in would be the high sales–high margin quadrant. While this might generally be true, it is also very possible that other salespeople are in other quadrants that are perfectly acceptable given the products they are selling, the particular accounts in their territory, and the competitive environment that they face. For example, Stevens (high sales–low margin) may have one or two accounts that buy high volume of a low margin product and any change in the price could put this business at risk. The sales manager also faces issues with salespeople such as Davis (low sales–low margin). To expect Davis to move from this group to the high sales–high margin group in the next year might be unrealistic. However, this matrix provides a good opportunity to discuss with Davis how he might move to either the high sales–low margin group, or the low sales–high margin group (with an expectation that there could be improvement in both sales and margin).

While the performance matrix can be a valuable tool when communicating with individual salespeople, it can also be a valuable sales force planning tool for the sales manager. Exhibit 13.15 shows the same performance matrix, but individual salespeople have been replaced with average sales, average contribution dollars per sale, and contribution margin in each quadrant. The sales manager can speculate, for example, what the impact would be of getting the six salespeople in

Exhibit 13.15

Performance Matrix

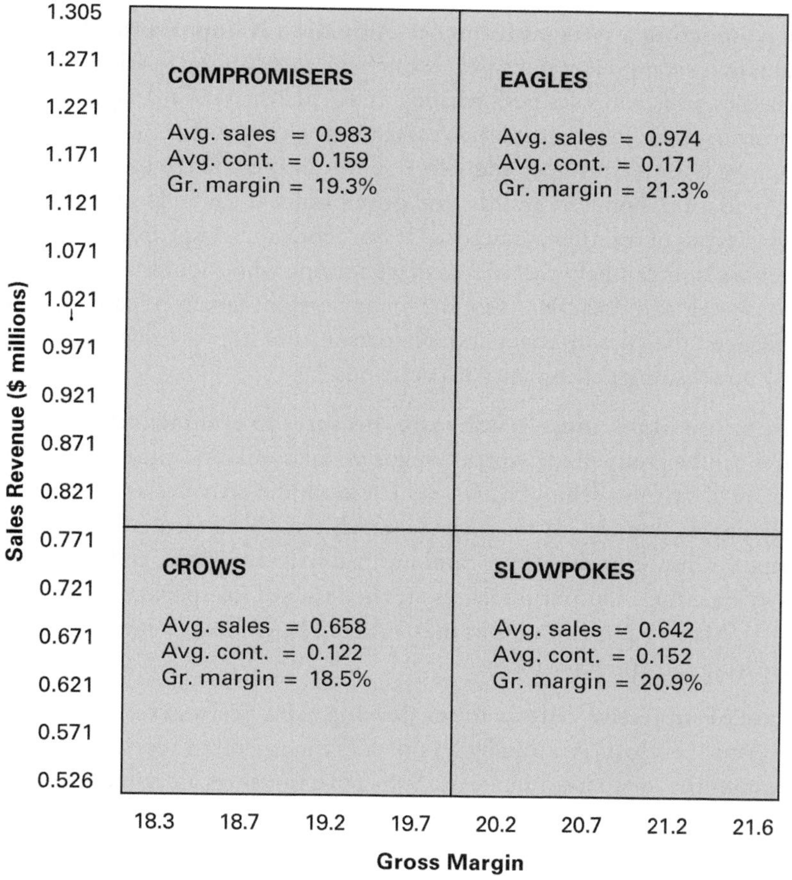

COMPROMISERS
Avg. sales = 0.983
Avg. cont. = 0.159
Gr. margin = 19.3%

EAGLES
Avg. sales = 0.974
Avg. cont. = 0.171
Gr. margin = 21.3%

CROWS
Avg. sales = 0.658
Avg. cont. = 0.122
Gr. margin = 18.5%

SLOWPOKES
Avg. sales = 0.642
Avg. cont. = 0.152
Gr. margin = 20.9%

Sales Revenue ($ millions): 1.305, 1.271, 1.221, 1.171, 1.121, 1.071, 1.021, 0.971, 0.921, 0.871, 0.821, 0.771, 0.721, 0.671, 0.621, 0.571, 0.526

Gross Margin: 18.3 18.7 19.2 19.7 20.2 20.7 21.2 21.6

the low sales–low margin quadrant to increase their gross margin to equal that of the salespeople in the low sales–high margin quadrant. The impact would be an additional $94 752 contribution for the company [($658 000 × 20.9%) – ($658 000 × 18.5%)]. Next, the sales manager could explore adding information concerning other variables in the quadrants, to explore how salespeople in each of the four quadrants might differ: number of sales calls, number of active accounts, number of lost accounts, age, years with the company, etc. If the sales manager finds that younger versus older salespeople have higher gross margins, this could suggest a plateauing issue with some of the more senior salespeople. As another example, if the sales manager finds that younger versus older salespeople have lower sales volumes, this could suggest that younger salespeople need additional sales training, possibly, but not limited to, prospecting, closing, or up-selling.

The value of performance matrices is limited only by the ingenuity of the sales manager.

SUMMARY

1. **Perform a sales analysis at the company, SBU, or region level.** A sales analysis at the sales force level is an important place to start a sales performance evaluation. It lets the sales manager assess whether the sales force is growing sales, profitability, and market share, or whether these are declining. A sales analysis at this level can help determine whether there is a problem with goals and objectives, or overall sales strategy. Sales managers should also look at sales by product or product line, and sales by customer or account type.

2. **Discuss why conducting a sales performance evaluation is important.** The sales performance evaluation serves many purposes. It can help establish the relationship between organizational sales goals and sales performance. It can aid the sales manager in making decisions concerning sales force organization and territory alignment. It can provide information to improve both recruitment and selection. It can provide the bases for rewards: increased compensation, bonuses, awards, and promotions. It can help identify when, where, and what types of training are needed. It can motivate salespeople and help them establish career goals. It can help the sales manager decide who should be terminated or otherwise disciplined, and document support for any action. Finally, it can improve communication between the sales manager and salesperson, and improve salesperson performance by clearly establishing performance expectations.

3. **Describe how to use input, output, and ratio measures to evaluate sales performance.** Input measures can be grouped into three categories: sales calls and time utilization, selling expenses, and ancillary (non-selling) activities. These are the activities and behaviours performed by salespeople (inputs) for the purpose of achieving sales results (outputs). Two categories of output measures include sales- and profit-related measures, and customer-account activity measures. Output measures are the result of salesperson inputs (activities and behaviours). Many input and output measures can be combined into meaningful ratios for evaluating sales performance.

4. **Discuss the use of subjective criteria for evaluating sales performance.** Subjective measures require personal evaluations, usually by the sales manager, but increasingly by other people with whom the salesperson interacts. Subjective measures are subject to three types of bias: halo effect, interpersonal bias, and outcome bias. One attempt to reduce these biases is the 360-degree feedback appraisal system. This system combines self-evaluation with the evaluation from several other sources.

5. **Describe how to develop and use performance matrices for sales performance evaluation.** A performance matrix is a conceptual tool that helps a sales manager compare salespeople, or groups of salespeople, across several input/output measures at the same time. Once a performance matrix has been completed, it can be used to communicate sales performance with salespeople. It can also be used as a sales force planning tool by the sales manager.

KEY TERMS

evaluation   **382**

objective measures   **388**

subjective measures   **388**

input measures   **388**

output measures   **388**

account penetration ratio   **396**

sales per account ratio   **396**

average order size ratio   **396**

account share ratio   **397**

new account conversion ratio   **398**

lost account ratio   **398**

order cancellation ratio   **398**

sales per sales call ratio   **398**

orders per sales call ratio   **398**

contribution margin   **399**

profit margin   **399**

sales expense ratio   **399**

cost per call ratio   **399**

halo effect   **400**

interpersonal bias   **401**

outcome bias   **401**

360-degree feedback   **402**

performance matrix   **403**

REVIEW QUESTIONS

1. What are the main purposes for performing sales performance evaluations? Describe how each of these purposes might affect the sales performance evaluation.

2. Distinguish between input and output measures used for sales performance evaluation. Discuss where each type of measure might best be used.

3. What is meant by ancillary (non-selling) activities? When should these be used as part of a sales performance evaluation? Explain.

4. Discuss two reasons why a salesperson's profitability (gross margin) might decline.

5. When a salesperson's gross margin declines, what action should the sales manager take? Explain.

6. Distinguish between the account penetration ratio and the account share ratio. Why is each important?

7. What is meant by the *four factor model?* Describe two limitations of this model that might reduce its usefulness for sales managers.

8. Distinguish between interpersonal and outcome bias. How can a sales manager overcome or reduce the effect of these biases?

9. Describe what is meant by a 360-degree feedback appraisal system. What are some cautions for using such a system?

10. Describe how a performance matrix can be used by a sales manager when conducting sales performance evaluations.

APPLICATION EXERCISES

1. Halogen Software Inc. is a Canadian company that provides web-based software for performing employee appraisals. One of its products, Halogen e360™, automates and simplifies feedback to employees who are evaluated using a 360-degree feedback appraisal system. Visit **www.halogensoftware.com** and take a product tour (link on the left side of the page). How might this software be of benefit to sales managers? Explain.

2. The following is a sales performance evaluation prepared by the sales manager for Geoff Curlow, one of the senior salespeople at his office. Ratings varied from 1–"far worse than average," to 4–"average," to 7–"far better than average" on each item.

Contribution margin	5
Appearance and manner	4
Sales volume	2
Sales growth	3
Product knowledge	6
Sales/quota	5
Customer goodwill	6
New accounts opened	3

   Should the sales manager give Geoff a positive or a negative review? If you were the sales manager, what would you tell Geoff?

3. Write an essay to defend either of the following positions: (1) "360-degree feedback appraisal systems are an important step forward in how sales performance evaluations should be conducted in the future"; or (2) "360-degree feedback appraisal systems are simply a 'flavour of the month' and are unlikely to be popular in another 10 years."

4. When asked about having his sales force certified through the Canadian Professional Sales Association, one sales manager remarked, "If my salespeople were compensated strictly on salary, I would want them certified because the better they are at selling, the more sales they will make for the company. However, my salespeople are compensated entirely by commission. There is no reason for me to have them certified. If I want more sales, I can simply hire more salespeople." Do you agree with this sales manager? Why or why not? Be prepared to defend your position.

CASE 13.1 Import Food Sales

Tom Bauer, vice-president of sales at Import Food Sales, was sitting in his Mississauga, Ontario, office in early February reviewing sales performance at the nine sales branches across Canada. While he was performing his analysis, he became curious about three new salespeople who had just completed their first full year of sales. From the aggregate data he had, Tom noticed that, on average, the company's 56 salespeople made 7.9 sales calls per day. Salespeople normally worked 230 days per year. Tom did not personally know any of the salespeople, although he had met Preet Chaterjee on several occasions as the two worked from the same office. All three salespeople reported directly to branch sales managers, who then reported to Tom.

Tom thought it would be good to look at the sales performance of the three salespeople and then discuss each of them with their sales manager. The following is the data that Tom had available for his review.

	Vivian Zhang	Preet Chatterjee	Jessica MacIsaac
Territory	Vancouver	Toronto	Halifax
Days worked	230	230	230
Calls per day	10.1	8.3	6.5
Direct selling expenses	$72 300	$74 600	$83 500
Hit rate (batting average)	22.4%	26.1%	29.2%
Average sales per call	$3666	$4123	$3255
Contribution margin	21.1%	22.6%	23.3%
Average time per sales call	25 minutes	31 minutes	43 minutes

CRITICAL-THINKING QUESTION

If you were Tom Bauer, how would you evaluate these salespeople, and what questions would you ask their respective sales managers?

Upper Canada Clothing   CASE 13.2

Upper Canada Clothing Company has been selling its industrial clothing across Canada for over 20 years. It has a four-member sales force, of whom three are in Ontario and one is in Quebec. Total sales by this sales force in 2006 were $3.9 million. Total industry sales for competing products in Ontario and Quebec were $15.8 million. The company also has nine manufacturer's agents, who are paid an 8 percent commission on sales. Their 2006 performance follows.

Territory	Number of Agents	Sales ($)	Market Share (%)
British Columbia	2	886 458	17.5
Alberta	2	742 458	13.4
Saskatchewan and Manitoba	2	1 244 553	19.5
Atlantic Provinces	3	937 887	26.3
Total		3 811 356	

The agents that sell for Upper Canada Clothing also sell between three and eight other noncompeting product lines. One of the agents in British Columbia has recently complained about the commission she is being paid, and has informed Upper Canada Clothing that a major competitor is paying its agents a 10 percent commission. The sales manager at Upper Canada Clothing thinks that it is time to evaluate his entire sales force, including those who work directly for the company and those who are manufacturer's agents. Specifically, he is wondering whether he should continue with the current sales strategy, or replace all of the manufacturer's agents with company salespeople. The direct selling costs (salaries and selling-related expenses) for each new salesperson hired would be $90 000. One salesperson would be needed for each of the four territories.

CRITICAL-THINKING QUESTION

If you were the sales manager for Upper Canada Clothing, what would you recommend?

Comprehensive Cases for Part IV

CASE 1	**Stavanger Safety Equipment**

Hui Zhou, known to his English-speaking friends and business associates as Henry, was pleased with his recent appointment as Ontario sales manager for Stavanger Safety Equipment. Henry had come to Canada from China in 1992 and had completed his last year of secondary school in Toronto, where he had quickly become fluent in English. He had then completed a four-year degree at an Ontario university and been fortunate to get a job with a consumer goods company. Within six months, Henry had been promoted to a sales position, one he had kept for almost four years before deciding to return to university for an M.B.A. Throughout his program, he had remained dedicated to getting another sales job. This was one aspect of business he really enjoyed, and one for which he had considerable aptitude.

Just before graduation, Henry had met a fellow student who had worked for Stavanger Safety Equipment and who had left to pursue a career in finance. He had mentioned to Henry that the company was looking for an Ontario sales manager, and that he would give Henry a great recommendation. Henry had not been sure that he was ready for a sales management position, but he had been impressed with the company and the owners had been impressed with Henry during his initial job interview. Henry had been hired and he'd been told that his first task would be to "stir the pot" a bit. The owners were concerned that sales were not as good as they should be in Ontario, but they were unsure if or where there might be problems.

Company Background

Stavanger Safety Equipment Corp. (SSE) was a Canadian manufacturer of a broad range of safety clothing and equipment that it sold to general industrial accounts as well as to municipalities for use by police and fire departments. The company manufactured about 40 percent of the products that were in its product line, and supplemented these products with many that were manufactured overseas with the SSE brand name. The pricing policy of the company was to set the suggested list price of all products so that if any were sold at list price, the gross margin would be 35 percent; however, as will be explained shortly, the company gave discounts to all customers that it sold to, and only the company's distributors sold the products at full list price. In fact, in some regions, small distributors even charged a premium over the list price when they sold small quantities to individual consumers.

The company had regional sales offices across Canada and employed its own sales force, many of whom lived within their respective territories but who reported to a regional sales office. The largest regional office in Canada was located in Toronto. Nine salespeople reported directly to the Ontario region sales manager. Two salespeople served the Toronto area. One salesperson lived in each of London, Cambridge, Hamilton, Kingston, Ottawa, Windsor, and Thunder Bay.

Source: This case was prepared as the basis for classroom discussion only, and is not intended to demonstrate either effective or ineffective handling of a management situation. © 2007 by H.F. (Herb) MacKenzie, Brock University, Faculty of Business Administration, St. Catharines, ON, L2S 3A1. Reprinted with permission.

Salespeople sold directly to municipalities and to selected large industrial accounts, referred to as "target user accounts." Otherwise, the company sold through a number of "distributors," which could range from small retail stores to wholesalers who sold to smaller industrial accounts. There was often some conflict between Stavanger Safety Equipment and its distributors, as they were often competing for the same user accounts. Not all distributors were satisfied selling only to smaller accounts.

Management recognized the conflict and was prepared to let it continue as long as the company's overall goals were met. In particular, with the exception of the two Toronto area salespeople, management wanted each salesperson to sell 60 percent of his or her sales through distributors and 40 percent to user accounts. In the larger metropolitan area, the target split was established at 70 percent to 30 percent in favour of distributors because it was thought that since many of these distributors sold to customers throughout Ontario, they would have larger sales than might otherwise be expected. The company owners wanted to sell mainly through distributors because many sales would only be made if the products were immediately available for sale at the point where the customer wanted to make a purchase. On the other hand, the company wanted to maintain sales to important user accounts to reduce dependence on distributors. As well, the owners recognized that sales made to user accounts improved the company's gross margin.

Distributors received a 15 percent resale discount from list prices. They got an additional 2 percent discount when individual orders were between $5000 and $9999. For orders over $10 000, they received a 5 percent additional discount. Target user accounts got a 10 percent discount from the list price, but salespeople could negotiate discounts as high as 15 percent when necessary. However, they were discouraged as, when they gave larger discounts, they also received reduced commission on their sales. The discount structure was quite effective at keeping distributors from selling to target user accounts. Occasionally, however, a distributor would take a large order at a very low margin, and would then add additional items to the order to get a better price on those items for its own inventory.

The Stavanger Safety Equipment Ontario Sales Force

The first thing that Henry looked at was the total Ontario sales over the previous three years. There was nothing that immediately raised a concern. Sales increased each year; however, part of the increase could be attributed to annual price increases of 5 percent on January 1, 2005, and January 1, 2006. In all three years, the region achieved its target gross margins, and sales quotas were surpassed by anywhere from 5 percent to 8 percent. In fact, during 2006, total sales reached $11.2 million, while the target sales quota was only $10.5 million (see Exhibit 1). It was apparent that if there were problems, they would be with individual salespeople.

When Henry looked at the sales data for individual salespeople, there were three salespeople with whom he had concerns: Antony Jones (Ottawa), Tom D'Video (London), and Bud Carson (Toronto). He wasn't sure there were problems, but he certainly had questions he wanted to ask. Henry decided to meet with each of them. The following summarizes what happened during each of the meetings.

ANTONY JONES

Henry took an immediate liking to Antony when the two first met. Similar to himself, Antony had not been born in Canada but had moved to Ottawa from Nigeria when he was very young. Antony had gotten his entire education in Canada, however. He was tall and very thin, with a friendly smile and an infectious laugh. Antony had been with the company for four years.

Henry's questions about Antony's territory mainly concerned the increasing percentage of sales that were coming from distributors. Antony offered a defence: "I am very good at managing distributor accounts. You can ask any of them and they will tell you that they don't get better service from any other company that they represent. I like them, and I know how to manage them. I am not comfortable calling on user accounts. They just want to argue about price and they never appreciate what you do for them. Don't worry about me. Maybe my end-user sales are down, but I always deliver my total quota. If I wasn't making my quota, I could understand your wanting to get involved in my territory but since I am, I trust you will let me manage things myself."

Henry knew that there would be some concern if the owners of the company became aware of what was happening in this territory, but overall, the Ontario branch was nearly meeting its total target for user accounts. Henry decided to think about the situation before taking any further action.

TOM D'VIDEO

Henry had a concern with Tom because he had been with the company for less than two years and his sales seemed to be steadily decreasing. He had not achieved his target sales during his first six months with the company in 2005, and he had fallen further behind in 2006. Early indications were that sales would continue to decline in 2007. Henry had just heard that one of Tom's most important user accounts had recently decided it did not want to see Tom again. When Henry contacted the company for a reason, the purchasing manager advised that he had told Tom on a previous occasion that he did not want Tom in the office smelling of tobacco. The purchasing manager stated that on Tom's next visit, the warning had been repeated. Tom's clothing reeked of stale tobacco smoke and he had obviously just been smoking in his car. The purchasing manager commented, "There are far too many salespeople for me to buy from. I don't need to do business with someone who doesn't respect my office." Henry agreed that the purchasing agent was certainly within his rights, and he apologized for Tom's behaviour.

When Henry finally had a chance to speak with Tom, he decided to mention the decreasing sales performance first. Tom responded, "I know. I was waiting for Ken (the previous sales manager) to call me on this. I knew it would only be a matter of time before you did. I do take full responsibility for my behaviour. I have been making fewer calls than I should and, in fact, some days I simply stop selling early. I was committed to this job when I first took it. I was having some marital problems and I thought that if I took this job and moved back to London where my wife's family live, things would get better. Unfortunately, things got worse and we separated just over a year ago. I still haven't gotten over it. I have been drinking a bit too much and I spend a lot of time just too depressed to really do much. I am just starting to appreciate what this job means to me. I do like selling and I do like this company. If you will give me a chance to prove myself, I will certainly try. I want to succeed, and I know if I can simply get over my separation, I *will* succeed."

At this point, Henry did not want to mention the lost account. He wanted some time to think about what should be done. He made no promises to Tom other than to say that it was necessary to have some time to think about this and that the two of them would talk again in approximately two weeks.

BUD CARSON

Henry was totally unprepared for what happened when he met with Bud Carson. Henry knew he would have to treat Bud with considerable respect as he was the oldest and most senior salesperson with the company. As well, he had the largest quota of all of the Ontario salespeople. Although he had not made his sales quota in 2006, he'd come very close and this was the only

Exhibit 1 Summary Information on Ontario Sales Performance 2004–2006

Antony Jones (Ottawa)	2006		2005		2004	
	Actual	Target	Actual	Target	Actual	Target
Sales (distributor)	842 428	600 000	727 765	540 000	701 901	510 000
Sales (end user)	269 557	400 000	255 609	360 000	256 675	340 000
Sales (total)	1 111 985	1 000 000	983 374	900 000	958 576	850 000
Gross margin (dist.)	21.6%	22.0%	22.0%	22.0%	22.2%	22.0%
Gross margin (user)	26.9%	26.0%	27.0%	26.0%	27.3%	26.0%
Gross margin (total)	22.9%	23.6%	23.3%	23.6%	23.6%	23.6%
Total accounts (dist.)	67		70		72	
Total accounts (user)	56		49		46	
Active accounts (dist.)	62		67		67	
Active accounts (user)	52		43		40	
Sales calls (dist.)	292		284		268	
Sales calls (user)	222		216		210	
Tom D'Video (London)*						
Sales (distributor)	513 244	600 000	241 540	270 000		
Sales (end user)	363 388	400 000	172 387	180 000		
Sales (total)	876 632	1 000 000	413 927	450 000		
Gross margin (dist.)	21.7%	22.0%	21.8%	22.0%		
Gross margin (user)	26.8%	27.0%	27.0%	27.0%		
Gross margin (total)	23.8%	24.0%	24.0%	24.0%		
Total accounts (dist.)	60		62			
Total accounts (user)	44		48			
Active accounts (dist.)	54		58			
Active accounts (user)	39		44			
Sales calls (dist.)	277		135			
Sales calls (user)	208		100			
Bud Carson (Toronto)						
Sales (distributor)	933 222	980 000	905 900	945 000	962 853	910 000
Sales (end user)	422 905	420 000	451 564	405 000	435 098	390 000
Sales (total)	1 356 127	1 400 000	1 357 464	1 350 000	1 397 951	1 300 000
Gross margin (dist.)	21.6%	20.0%	21.2%	20.0%	21.0%	20.0%
Gross margin (user)	24.8%	26.0%	25.0%	26.0%	25.5%	26.0%
Gross margin (total)	22.6%	21.8%	22.5%	21.8%	22.4%	21.8%
Total accounts (dist.)	58		53		52	
Total accounts (user)	69		66		64	
Active accounts (dist.)	56		50		50	
Active accounts (user)	68		64		64	
Sales calls (dist.)	282		270		279	
Sales calls (user)	240		232		248	
Ontario (Sales)	**11 233 334**	**10 500 000**	**10 402 111**	**10 000 000**	**9 906 867**	**9 500 000**
Ontario (Gross Margin)	**23.8%**	**23.8%**	**24.1%**	**24.0%**	**24.2%**	**24.0%**

* Tom joined SSE on July 1, 2005.

time during the previous three years when he had not. What concerned Henry most was that Bud's quota was growing at a slower rate than the annual price increases, so even if he met his sales quota, sales in his territory would not necessarily be improving. When he asked Bud why this might be happening, Bud became very loud and aggressive: "Until you can get someone who can handle the volume of sales that I can, you need to focus more on the other salespeople. However, since you raised the issue, I want to tell you that I am not happy with the way this company pays its commissions. We get 3 percent commission on all sales except when we give discounts to user accounts. Then, we are penalized as our commission percentage gets reduced as the discount we allow increases. If you look at my sales last year, you will see that I was just short of my total sales quota. Although I only got 24.8 percent gross margin on my sales to user accounts, I beat my total target gross margin by almost a whole percentage point. If you took the time to multiply my actual sales by my actual gross margin, you would see that I actually contributed more gross margin sales dollars than my quota. You should be thankful you have guys like me on the sales force, so leave me alone."

Henry wasn't sure what to do. There was certainly more he wanted to say, but he realized that now might not be the appropriate time. After several seconds of uncomfortable silence, he replied, "We will continue our discussion at a later time, after you have had some time to think about things."

CASE 2 | Power & Motion Industrial Supply

It was 7:00 P.M. on Sunday evening when Hal Maybee returned to his office. He had spent the afternoon golfing with one of his customers, and he now had to decide what he was going to tell head office on Monday morning with regard to new salaries for the sales staff at his branch.

Hal had just been appointed sales manager for one of Canada's largest industrial distributors. Power & Motion Industrial Supply had sales agreements with over 400 manufacturers, but about 100 of them accounted for 80 percent of the branch's sales.

Hal's promotion had followed the sudden death of Fergie McDonald who, at 48 years old, had been in charge of the company's most profitable branch. It was a complete surprise to Hal when he was promoted, and he knew there were people at the branch who expected they deserved it more. Exhibit 1 shows the performance evaluations that Fergie had completed on the six salespeople just before he died. Head office had intended to send only five forms to Hal, but one of the secretaries mistakenly included Fergie's evaluation of Hal as well.

Nearly three weeks previously, Fergie and Hal had been making joint calls on some pulp mills in Northern New Brunswick, the territory that Fergie kept for himself, even though head office wanted him to stop selling and spend more time on sales administration. During the trip, Fergie had told Hal that he was given 6 percent of the total sales staff salary to be divided among them for the coming year. This was the customary way of giving salary increases at the branches as it gave head office the discretion to decide the total increase in the salary expense, but it gave the district managers responsibility for allocating salary increases. Fergie was told that nationally,

Source: © 2007 H.F. (Herb) MacKenzie, Brock University, Faculty of Business, St. Catharines, ON, L2S 3A1. All names in this case are disguised. Reprinted with permission.

sales increases would average about 3 percent, but his branch was among the lowest paid in the company and had been the best performing branch for several years.

Hal did not want to express his opinions as he knew that he and Fergie would disagree. However, he did allow Fergie to express his own thoughts on the staff. There were two salespeople that Fergie had a real problem with. He viewed Jim Stanley as his biggest problem. Jim actually had seniority at the branch. He had been hired as shipper, order desk salesperson, and secretary when the branch was only large enough to support one person other than Bob Laird, the first salesperson the company had in Atlantic Canada. Bob and Jim operated the branch for almost two years when Bob decided to hire Fergie as a salesperson to help develop the territory. When Bob retired, Jim thought he would get the position of sales manager as he had seniority, and he had experience with all aspects of the business including managing the office and warehouse, which had grown to include seven people. He was very disappointed when head office gave the position to Fergie as he had no experience other than sales.

Within a year, Jim decided he wanted to get into sales. He was finally resigned to the fact that office management was a dead-end job, and the only possibility for advancement was through sales. Now, after five years, Jim was not performing as well as he should. In fact, he hated selling and spent an increasing amount of time drinking while away from home. He hinted that he wanted to get back into the office. However, when these rumours started to spread, the staff let it be known that they did not want to work under Jim again if there were any alternatives.

Fergie was thinking about giving Jim a good salary increase. First, it might make him appreciate his job more and maybe he would put more effort into selling. Second, it would make the position more attractive than a possible return to the office as he would not want to take a tremendous salary cut.

The other problem was Arne Olsen, the other senior salesperson. As the territory developed quickly, the branch hired a secretary just after Fergie was hired. A month later, a warehouseman was hired and Jim was promoted to office manager. Jim immediately hired Hal Maybee as an order desk salesperson. Within a year, another salesperson, Arne, was hired, along with a second secretary. The branch growth slowed, but was steady from that point on. Arne was always an average salesperson. He never really had much motivation to perform, but he always did whatever he had to do so that he was never in any serious trouble as far as his job was concerned. Lately, he was starting to slip a bit, and rumour had it that he was having at least one affair. He also had recently bought a Mazda Miata that he drove on weekends as he was not allowed to drive anything but the company car during the week.

Dave Edison had been with the company for just under one year. If he'd had a few more years with the company, Hal knew he would have probably been the new sales manager. He came to the company from the life insurance industry, and rumour had it that he was slated for a national sales manager position within the next year as the company was rumoured to be taking on a new line of capital equipment from Europe that would be sold nationally, but would have one person at head office responsible for national sales.

Tanya Burt had also been in sales for only a year. She had been hired as a secretary, but it soon became apparent that she had exceptional telephone skills. She had been promoted to order desk salesperson within a year, and three years later, she requested and was given an outside sales territory. There was some concern with her product knowledge, but no concern with her attitude or sales ability. Tanya was the first and only woman to have been promoted to one of the company's 80 outside sales positions.

Buck Thompson had a very solid, established territory. He needed little direction as he was doing most things very well. Fergie had been a bit concerned that he was not making enough sales calls, but he certainly was performing well.

As Hal reviewed the performance evaluations, he agreed that Fergie had been very thorough and accurate in his assessment of each of the individuals. Hal wondered about the amount of salary increase he should give to each person. While he had to make this decision quickly, Hal realized there were other important decisions he would have to make soon. He recognized some of the problems Fergie had had in trying to decide salary increases, and these were more important for Hal as he had to get the support of the sales staff before he could hope to overcome some of these problems. He also had to start thinking about hiring another salesperson to cover Newfoundland and Northern New Brunswick, as head office was determined that he give up responsibility for all accounts in the region. He would, however, be allowed and encouraged to call on customers with the sales staff.

Exhibit 1   Evaluation of Salespeople*

	Dave Edison	Arne Olsen	Hal Maybee	Tanya Burt	Jim Stanley	Buck Thompson
Attitude	5	3	5	4	3	4
Appearance and manner	6	3	4	4	3	4
Selling skill	6	3	4	5	3	5
Product knowledge	4	4	5	3	4	6
Time management	4	3	6	5	2	4
Customer goodwill	4	3	6	5	3	4
Expenses to budget	4	5	4	4	3	3
New accounts opened	4	3	2	5	2	2
Avg. daily sales calls	4	6	4	5	4	3
Sales to quota	5	3	5	5	5	4
Sales volume	4	4	2	4	4	4
Sales growth	5	3	3	5	5	4
Contribution margin	6	3	2	5	5	4
Total score	**61**	**46**	**52**	**59**	**46**	**51**

* Salespeople are rated on a 7-point scale, where 1 = "far below average," 4 = "average," and 7 = "far above average."

Additional notes from salespeople's performance evaluation forms are as follows:

- *Dave Edison:* Current salary $52 000. Territory is about three hours' drive from the sales branch. Needs more product knowledge, but has learned a lot since hired. A bit aggressive, but he has developed some excellent new accounts through attention to detail and follow-up support.

- *Arne Olsen:* Current salary $44 500. Territory is about three hours' drive from the sales branch. Although he has increased the number of sales calls as agreed at our last review, sales have not gone up accordingly. Some concern with product knowledge. Arne knows all of our major product lines very well, but has not shown much effort to learn about many of the new lines we have added that may become our best product lines in the future. Some concern with his contribution margin. This is the fourth year in a row that it has dropped although it is almost the same as last year.

- *Hal Maybee:* Current salary $38 500. Although still the office manager, Hal has taken over the most distant territory from the sales branch, about five hours away. He travels to it about one week per month. Hal has expert product knowledge on electric and pneumatic products, and is particularly knowledgeable concerning the mining and pulp and paper industries. Hal is very focused and successful with the big sales, but needs to develop knowledge of and interest in some of the lower sales volume, less-technical products as they are generally higher-margin items. Hal has a lot of respect in the office and our efficiency has improved greatly, as has the general work atmosphere within the office.

- *Tanya Burt:* Current salary $36 000. Very impressed with her performance. Has good knowledge of product pricing and sourcing, but needs to learn more about product applications. Tanya sells many less-expensive expendable supplies, but she has a number of accounts that buy large annual volumes. Her territory surrounds the sales branch. Tanya is dedicated and dependable. She has opened many new accounts for us, and I predict good success for her as she continues to develop her knowledge and selling skills.

- *Jim Stanley:* Current salary $42 000. Jim seems to be performing quite well, but there is concern with his behaviour. I hope that a salary increase and some direction from me will improve his performance next year. He has been making some suggestions that he might like to move back to office management because everyone thinks I will be promoting Hal to full-time sales and letting him take over my territory. I really do not want Jim back in the office, and I think he should be a good salesperson. His sales and contribution margin are good, but part of his sales increase this year came from a new customer that has a manufacturing plant in his region, but actually buys from an office located in Tanya's territory. Tanya and Jim have agreed to split the credit for the sales as Tanya must do the selling, but Jim has to service the account.

- *Buck Thompson:* Current salary $49 000. Sells in a very concentrated, established territory with a customer base that represents a great variety of industries. Territory is about one-hour drive from the sales branch. Buck knows all of his customers very well as he has lived in the area all of his life. He has very good selling skills and product knowledge, and has been the main reason we have done so well in his territory.

Glossary

Account analysis   Estimating sales potential for each prospect and customer in a sales territory.

Account penetration ratio   Number of active accounts compared to the number of potential accounts in a territory.

Account relationship strategy   Carefully conceived plan to acquire, maintain, and develop customer accounts.

Account share ratio   Percentage of an account's business given to a particular salesperson.

Activity-based quota   Quota based on sales-related activities to ensure salespeople do the right things.

Advocate   Or champion, helps a salesperson by providing valuable information related to a particular purchase decision, and may actively support the salesperson within the buying organization.

Alternative evaluation   Stage of the buying-decision process in which the customer uses information from the search to evaluate alternatives that have been previously identified.

Average order size ratio   Salesperson's total sales divided by number of orders.

Bait-and-switch selling   Occurs when a seller offers a low price to attract customers and then tells them that the offered article is no longer in stock but that they can buy another, more expensive product.

Bid rigging   Occurs when sellers collude to set prices with respect to one or more specific requests for proposals.

Bonus   Cash or some form of cash equivalent paid to salespeople who achieve a specific sales objective.

Breakdown sales approach   Approach to determining appropriate sales force size by starting with a company's total sales forecast and dividing it by the average expected sales per salesperson.

Break-even sales volume per sales call   The volume of sales that is need to exactly cover the cost a making a single sales call.

Business defamation   Occurs when statements are made that are inaccurate, misleading, or slander a company's business reputation.

Business libel   Occurs when an unfair and untrue statement about a competitor is made in writing.

Business slander   Occurs when an unfair and untrue statement about a competitor is made orally.

Buyer remorse   Doubt in the buyer's mind concerning whether in fact she made the correct purchase decision.

Buying centre   Comprises all of the people involved in a particular buying decision.

Buying conditions   One or more qualifications that must be fulfilled or available before the buyer will agree to make a purchase.

Buying-decision process   Process a customer uses that ultimately results in a particular buying decision.

Buying power index   Method of forecasting sales for a particular sales territory as a percentage of total forecast sales.

Career stage   One of four stages people go through during their career: exploration, establishment, maintenance, and disengagement.

Carryover effects   Sales that continue in a territory after sales resources have been reduced in the territory.

Character   Your character is composed of your personal standards, including honesty, integrity, and personal strength.

Closed question   Question that requires a simple Yes or No response.

Coaching   An interpersonal process between the sales manager and the salesperson in which the sales manager provides constructive feedback and encouragement to the salesperson with the goal of improving sales performance.

Co-branding   The practice of using two established brands on the same product.

Cognitive dissonance   Doubt in the buyer's mind whether the correct purchase decision was made. See *buyer remorse*.

Cold calling   Contacting, by phone or in person, each prospective customer among a group of identified prospects.

Combination compensation plan   Compensation plan that includes any combination of salary, commission, and bonus.

Commitment stage   Highest stage of relationship evolution where the buyer and seller are committed to long-term working relationships.

Compensation plan   Plan that determines the direct and indirect monetary payments given to a salesperson for the job she performs.

Competencies   Knowledge, skills, aptitudes, and other personal characteristics needed to achieve superior performance.

Competition Act   Comprehensive federal legislation designed to foster healthy competition and protect Canadian consumers.

Concentrated targeting   Targeting a single market segment.

Confirmation question   Question designed to verify the accuracy and assure a mutual understanding of information shared between the buyer and salesperson.

Confirmation step   Confirmation by the salesperson that reassures the customer that he has made the right decision.

Consultative relationship   Relationship based on two-way communication, bilateral problem solving, and considerable negotiation so that at the end of the process, both parties will gain from the relationship.

Consultative selling approach   Foundation for modern selling where the salesperson assess customer needs in consultation with the customer.

Consumer Protection Act   Provincial and territorial legislation designed to protect the rights of buyers and sellers with respect to direct sales contracts.

Contribution margin   Total contribution dollars divided by total sales revenue.

Corruption of Foreign Public Officials Act   Federal legislation that makes it illegal for Canadian businesspeople to pay bribes to foreign civil servants.

Cost per call ratio   Total direct selling expenses divided by total number of sales calls.

Cross-selling   Selling items that are unrelated to the items that a customer is currently buying from the salesperson.

Culture See *sales force culture.*

Customer benefit approach Approach where the salesperson immediately focuses on the superior benefit his company can offer to its customers.

Customer relationship management Business strategy to acquire and retain the most valuable customer relationships.

Customer strategy Carefully conceived plan that will result in maximum customer responsiveness.

Decomposition method Sales forecasting method used when a seasonal pattern is evident in the sales data.

Delphi method Qualitative sales forecasting method similar to jury of executive opinion method but less subject to group influence.

Differentiated targeting Targeting two or more market segments with a specific marketing program for each segment.

Direct Sellers Act See *Consumer Protection Act.*

Direct selling expenses Any expenses that are attributable to a particular salesperson and that would not be incurred if the salesperson were not employed.

Diversity Variance within a group with respect to gender, ethnicity, culture, race, age, disability, sexual orientation, and religious affiliation.

Economic buyer Person with the ultimate decision-making authority as he has financial control.

Emotional link Connector between what the salesperson says and the prospect's emotions.

Employee benefits An indirect form of compensation intended to improve the quality of the work lives and personal lives of employees.

Ethics The rules that direct a person's conduct and moral judgment.

Evaluation Comparison of sales results against established goals or objectives.

Evaluative criteria Objective and subjective criteria that are important to the customer and are used to make comparisons among alternatives.

Exclusive dealing Requires that buyers deal only or primarily in products supplied by or designated by the seller.

Expansion selling Any of three techniques to expand business from an existing customer: full-line selling, cross-selling, and up-selling.

Expansion stage A stage that follows the exploration stage and in which customers may place additional business with a supplier based on the supplier's satisfactory past performance.

Expectancy Belief that effort will lead to performance.

Expense account padding Claiming inappropriate expenses, or expenses that were not actually made.

Exploration stage Early stage in relationship evolution where the customer explores the capability of a supplier to meet its needs, often involving a trial purchase.

Exponential smoothing method Sales forecast method similar to moving averages method but where the most recent sales data play a more important role and older data get systematically discounted.

First-line manager Manage nonmanagerial sales staff and have a short-term perspective; report to more senior management and are generally focused on implementing company sales policies and procedures.

Framing Way of describing a particular alternative that will have an impact on a customer's evaluation of an alternative.

Full-line selling Attempt to sell products that are related to other products that a customer is already buying.

Functional specialization A way to organize the sales force whereby salespeople are responsible to perform specific selling-related activities or functions.

Gatekeeper Person who controls the flow of information to members of the buying centre.

General survey question Question that helps a salesperson discover facts.

Geographic specialization A way to organize the sales force whereby salespeople are usually responsible for a specific geographic area and call on all accounts and potential accounts within that area, attempting to sell the company's complete product line.

Goals Specific performance targets that a firm wishes to achieve.

Halo effect Occurs when the rating that is assigned to one criterion affects the ratings on other criteria.

Harassment Any of a broad range of behaviours that any reasonable person should know are likely to be unwelcome.

Incremental approach Approach to determining appropriate sales force size by adding additional salespeople until the cost of adding one more salesperson will not be covered by the estimated additional contribution dollars the salesperson will generate.

Independent sales agent Also called a manufacturer's agent, sells for several non-competing manufacturers and receives a commission from each based on the sales made for each manufacturer.

Information search Occurs when customers use either internal or external search to acquire information on possible alternative products or sources to solve their buying problem.

Informative presentation One where the primary purpose is to inform the buyer concerning factual information about the product, its superior benefits, and its technical or operating specifications.

Input measures Measures of the behaviours and activities that a salesperson performs in order to generate sales.

Instrumentality Belief that performance will lead to reward.

Integrated marketing communications Providing a consistent, persuasive message to customers through all forms of marketing communications: personal selling, advertising, sales promotion, publicity, and public relations.

Integrity You exhibit integrity when there is congruence between what you know, what you say, and what you do.

Interpersonal bias Occurs when ratings on subjective performance criteria are affected by how much the person being rated is liked or disliked by the person who is doing the performance evaluation.

Job analysis Systematic approach to define specific roles or activities that will be required to be performed in a particular job (job description), and to determine the personal characteristics that a successful applicant should possess (job qualifications).

Job description Formal written document that describes the requirements and responsibilities for a particular job.

Job qualifications Required knowledge, skills, and abilities, or KSAs.

Jury of executive opinion method
Qualitative sales forecasting method that employs the opinions of a group of people who might all add insight into likely future sales.

Leadership　Manager's ability to influence the actions of salespeople to achieve the goals of the organization.

Leading indicator　Measurable indicator that is closely related to sales, but that changes before sales occur.

Lost account ratio　Number of lost accounts divided by total number of accounts.

MAPE　Mean absolute percentage error, a method of assessing forecast accuracy.

Market forecast　Industry-level forecast of the most likely sales that will be achieved, recognizing that ideal conditions do not exist.

Marketing mix　Consists of four elements: product, price, distribution, and promotion.

Marketing program　Set of integrated decisions that relate to the elements of the marketing mix.

Marketing strategy　Set of integrated decisions that begin with market segmentation, target marketing, and positioning, and then include the marketing program.

Market orientation　Focus on aligning all business activities and processes toward maximizing performance in the competitive marketplace.

Market potential　Industry-level forecast of the best possible sales that can be achieved across an entire industry, under ideal conditions.

Market restriction　Occurs when market intermediaries are allowed to sell only in a designated market area.

Market segmentation　Either aggregating customers into groups, or dividing the total market into smaller, relatively homogeneous groups.

Market segments　Groups that result from market segmentation and comprise people or businesses that share one or more common characteristics, or have similar needs and purchase behaviours.

Market specialization　A way to organize the sales force whereby salespeople are responsible to sell to a limited number of industries or vertical markets, thereby becoming experts on the needs of specific types of customers.

Micromarketing　Targeting customers by postal code, by occupation, or even as individuals.

Middle manager　Have management positions above and below them; have a mid-term perspective and communicate policies and procedures from top management to lower management levels.

Misleading advertising　Includes all representations, whether in print or oral, that create a false or misleading impression, even if the claims are literally true.

Mission statement　Statement that defines a firm's goals and objectives, which, if achieved, will enable the firm to become what it wishes to be.

Modified rebuy　Buying situation that generally involves limited problem-solving as the customer is considering product modifications or a new supplier.

Motivation　An internal drive to initiate and expend sufficient effort over time to perform appropriate selling activities to accomplish specific sales objectives.

Moving averages method　Sales forecast method based on observations from two or more previous periods where, when each newer period is added, the older period is dropped from the estimation.

Multiple regression method　Sales forecasting regression model where the dependent variable is sales and there are two or more independent or predictor variables.

Multiple-sourcing　Occurs when a customer buys from several suppliers to ensure supply and lowest price.

Naïve forecast method　Sales forecast method that assumes sales in the next period will be equal to sales in the last period.

Need discovery　Asking questions and carefully noting the responses to clearly establish the prospect's needs.

Need recognition　First stage of the buying-decision process, where the customer recognizes a difference between a current situation and their desired state.

Need-satisfaction question　Question designed to move the buyer to commitment and action.

Negligent hiring　Occurs when an employer hires an employee and fails to do an adequate background check, and that employee later harms another employee.

Negligent retention　Occurs when an employer retains an employee when the employer is aware that the employee is unfit for employment, and the employee later causes harm to another employee.

Negotiating　Process of working to reach a win–win agreement between the buyer and seller.

Networking　People meeting people and benefiting from the personal connections.

New account conversion ratio
Number of new accounts divided by total number of accounts.

New task buy　Most complicated buying situation, often requiring extensive problem-solving, as the customer has no prior experience making this purchase.

Objective measures　Measures usually collected from the company's internal information system, and do not require personal evaluations.

Objectives　Goals expressed in more specific, measurable terms.

Open question　Question that requires the buyer to provide more thoughtful and insightful answers.

Order cancellation ratio　Number of cancelled orders divided by total number of orders.

Orders per sales call ratio　Number of orders received divided by total number of sales calls, also called "hit ratio" or "batting average."

Outcome bias　Occurs when ratings on subjective performance criteria are affected by the sales outcomes that the salesperson has achieved.

Output measures　Outcomes that the salesperson achieves as a result of the inputs he makes.

Partnering relationship　Highest-level buyer–seller relationships requiring close cooperation and the investment of considerable resources by both parties.

Percentage of sales approach
Approach to determining appropriate sales force size by starting with the company's total sales forecast, estimating the sales force budget, and then dividing the budgeted amount by the direct cost per salesperson.

Performance matrix　Conceptual tool that helps a sales manager compare salespeople, or groups of salespeople, across several input/output measures at the same time.

Personal Information Protection and Electronic Documents Act Federal legislation that sets out ground rules for how companies may collect, use, or disclose personal information in the course of commercial activities.

Personal selling Involves person-to-person communication with a prospect or customer with the intention of discovering their needs, matching product solutions to their needs, and building satisfying relationships with them by satisfying their needs.

Personal selling philosophy Salesperson's commitment to value personal selling, adopt the marketing concept, and see themselves as consultants and problem solvers for their customers.

Personal traits A person's distinguishing characteristics.

Personality Combination of personal traits that classifies a person's behaviour.

Persuasive presentation One where the primary purpose is to influence the buyer's beliefs and attitudes, and ultimately to move the buyer to take action and make a buying decision.

Plateauing Occurs when salespeople reach the disengagement career stage too early in their career, when they stop growing professionally and are satisfied with maintaining performance standards, often well below their capability.

Portfolio model Model used for account classification where accounts are classified based on multiple factors, most commonly using four cells.

Positioning Creating and maintaining a firm's intended image with respect to its product, brand, or itself in the minds of target customers, relative to competition.

Post-purchase evaluation Evaluation of a purchase decision after the decision has been made, and that may affect future purchase decisions.

Power The ability to influence others in order to get things done.

Predatory pricing Occurs when companies set prices so low that they drive competitors from the market or deter competitors from entering the market.

Predictors Measurable or visible indicators of a selection criterion.

Presentation strategy Well-developed plan that includes preparing the sales presentation objectives, preparing a presentation plan to meet these objectives, and renewing commitment to provide outstanding customer service.

Price discrimination Occurs when a seller charges customers that are in competition with each other different prices for a like quantity and quality of goods.

Price fixing Occurs when sellers collude to set prices higher than they would otherwise be in a free market.

Probing question Question designed to help the salesperson uncover and clarify the buyer's problem, or what has sometimes been referred to as "pain."

Product approach Approach where the salesperson focuses immediately on the product that he sells, and may include a product display, a demonstration, or even simply a picture or brochure.

Product disparagement Occurs when false or deceptive comparisons or distorted claims are made concerning a competitor's product, services, or property.

Product specialization A way to organize the sales force whereby salespeople are responsible to sell a limited number of products or product lines, thereby becoming experts on the products they do sell.

Product strategy Plan that helps salespeople make correct decisions concerning the selection and positioning of products to meet identified customer needs.

Profit-based quota Quota based on profit rather than just sales revenue.

Profit margin Total profit dollars divided by total sales revenue.

Prospecting Systematic process of identifying potential customers.

Pull strategy Promotion directed to end-users instead of channel intermediaries.

Purchase decision Stage of the buying-decision process in which the terms of sale are negotiated.

Push strategy Promotion directed to channel intermediaries instead of end-users.

Pyramid selling Illegal schemes that use tiers of salespeople, sometimes referred to as members, agents, "dealers," or distributors, where each succeeding tier receives credit for revenues or commissions from sales, regardless of whether they have contributed to the sales effort.

Qualifying the prospect Evaluating prospect opportunities by assessing need, authority to buy, financial resources, and willingness to buy.

Quota Quantitative goal assigned to an individual salesperson.

Reciprocity Occurs when there is a mutual exchange of benefits between organizations, as when a firm buys products from its own customers.

Recognition programs Formalized programs designed to recognize salespeople for superior sales performance.

Referral Prospect who has been recommended by a current customer or by someone familiar with the product or salesperson.

Referral approach Approach where the salesperson uses a third-party referral to gain the prospect's attention and interest.

Referral selling Occurs when a salesperson offers a price reduction or other inducement to a customer for names of other potential customers who may subsequently buy from the seller.

Refusal to deal Occurs when sellers refuse to sell to legitimate buyers.

Relationship selling approach Increasingly popular selling approach used when both salespeople and customers recognize the value of closer, longer-term buyer–seller relationships.

Relationship strategy Well thought out plan for establishing, building, and maintaining quality relationships.

Reminder presentation One where the primary purpose is to remind or reinforce to the buyer what is already known.

Resale price maintenance Occurs when suppliers try to influence the price at which a product is to be resold by a purchaser (usually a retailer or industrial distributor).

Reverse marketing Customer-initiated, long-term relationships in which the customer actively attempts to create the supplier it wants through formalized evaluations and supplier communications.

Sales budget Document that itemizes planned expenses and provides a basis for the sales manager to monitor and control sales activities.

Sales call response function A function that relates sales volume to the number of sales calls that a salesperson makes.

Sales contests Contests focused usually on achievement of specific short-term sales objectives.

Sales expense ratio Total direct selling expenses divided by total sales revenue.

Sales force automation A variety of information and communication technologies that address sales force efficiency.

Sales force composite method Sales forecasting method that uses sales estimates from individual salespeople.

Sales force culture Total of values, attitudes, and behaviours that are shared by members of the sales force and that are expected of and reinforced to new members.

Sales forecast Company-level forecast of the most likely sales that will be achieved by a particular company, recognizing its limitations to develop and implement a perfect marketing plan.

Sales management Management of the company's personal selling function.

Sales per account ratio Salesperson's total sales divided by number of active accounts.

Sales per sales call ratio Sales dollar volume divided by total number of sales calls.

Sales potential Company-level forecast of the best possible sales that can be achieved by a particular company, under ideal conditions.

Sales process model Model used for account classification where accounts are classified based on where they are in the sales process.

Sales territory Group of customers and prospective customers assigned to a single salesperson.

Sales volume quota Quota based on dollar sales, unit sales, or on a point system.

Satisfactions Positive benefits from a purchase.

Selection criteria Characteristics that are necessary for a person to be successful at a specific job.

Selling expenses All of the expenses that salespeople incur as a result of selling-related activities that they perform for their company.

Selling team Groups of people, often from different functional areas within a sales organization, who are responsible for managing strategic accounts when the buying process or

product solutions are complex and customized.

Servicing the sale Providing post-sale service, including all of the activities that are performed to facilitate or enhance the purchase and use of the product.

Sexual harassment See *harassment.*

Single-factor model Model used for account classification where accounts are classified based on a single factor, most commonly sales.

Single regression method Sales forecasting regression model where the dependent variable is sales and there is a single independent or predictor variable.

Situational leadership An approach to leadership based on the theory that the most effective leadership style is one that matches the particular situation that the leader faces.

Sole-sourcing Occurs when a customer buys all of a particular product from a single supplier.

Specific survey question Question designed to give buyers a chance to describe in greater detail their current buying problem, issue, or dissatisfaction that they are experiencing.

Straight commission plan Compensation plan where income is tied directly to performance.

Straight rebuy Simplest buying situation where the customer simply buys what she bought previously, from a familiar supplier.

Straight salary plan Fixed monetary income that is paid at regular intervals for the performance of specific duties or responsibilities.

Strategic account programs Also called key, major, national, or global account programs, provide increased attention and customized solutions for important accounts that require this level of support.

Strategic business unit Business unit within a larger, more diversified organization that has its own management, resources, objectives, and competitors, making it important that it manages its business strategy planning separately.

Strategies Means to achieve goals and objectives.

Subjective measures Measures that require personal evaluations, either from the sales manager or from other people with whom the salesperson interacts.

Summary confirmation question Question that brings several buying conditions temporally close for the customer and ensures that the customer understands and remembers what his buying conditions were.

Survey of buyer intentions method Sales forecasting method that uses estimates obtained from customers or potential customers concerning their expected purchases for a future period.

Survey question Designed to gain knowledge concerning the buyer's current situation, also called an *information-gathering question.*

Target marketing Occurs when the decision is made to allocate resources to gain a sales response from one or more of the identified market segments.

Technical buyer Person who influences and sometimes determines product specifications.

Telemarketing Practice of using telephone contact to prospect for, qualify, sell to, and service customers.

Test market method Sales forecasting method useful for predicting sales for new products as they are tested in the real marketplace under, hopefully, real market conditions.

360-degree feedback An appraisal system that combines self-evaluation with evaluation from several other sources, such as customers, supervisors or managers, sales colleagues, and internal company support staff.

Tied selling Occurs when a buyer is required to purchase another product, or refrain from purchasing a product that is not from a specific manufacturer, as a condition of being able to buy a product from the seller.

Time-series regression Sales forecasting regression model where the dependent variable is sales and the independent or predictor variable is time periods.

Total target compensation Total monetary compensation that a salesperson can earn assuming that she meets expected target results.

Training needs assessment Assessment of what salespeople should know, what should be their attitude, and how they should sell.

Transactional relationship Low-level relationships based on being able to meet the customer's short-term needs for price and convenience.

Transactional selling
Traditional approach to s[...]
"pushes" product on custome[...]

Trend projection method   Number o[...]
simple time-series forecasting methods that all assume that past sales
and rates of change in past sales can
be used to predict future sales.

Trial close   Sometimes called *minor
point close*—is a comment or question at any point in a sales presentation designed to help the salesperson
discover how close the prospect actually is to making a purchase decision.

Turnover rate   Percentage of salespeople who leave the sales force

U[...]
the e[...]
keting progr[...]
mass marketing[...]

User buyer   Person focuse[...]
with operating characteristics a[...]
when the purchase will affect their jo[...]
performance or operating budget.

Up-selling   Attempt to sell better
quality items to a customer.

Valence   Personal value for a specific
reward.

[...]
territo[...]
amount by [...]
sales calls a sales[...]

3. Ro...
   Selling...
   the New...
   *Journal of Per...
   Sales Managemer.*
   pp. 17–32.

4. Thomas A. Stewart, "Aft..
   You've Done for Your
   Customers, Why Are They Still
   Not Happy?" *Forbes,* May 23,
   1995, pp. 178–182.

5. Foreign Affairs and International
   Trade Canada, "Sixth Annual
   Report on Canada's State of
   Trade: Trade Update, April 2005.
   http://www.international.gc.ca/
   eet/trade/sot_2005/sot_2005-en.
   asp, downloaded January 17,
   2007.

6. Robert G. Cooper, "Winning
   With New Products," *Ivey
   Business Journal,* 64, 6,
   July–August 2000, pp. 54–60.

7. "Angiotech Introduces COSTA-
   SIS^R (VITAGEL^TM) to
   Orthopedic & Spinal Surgery
   Market Through Distribution
   Agreement With Orthovita,"
   press release, June 24, 2004.
   http://www.angiotech.com,
   downloaded July 30, 2004.

May
...and Marian
...vigating
...gh Waters: The
...e of Trust in
...ng Sales Representatives
...mes of Change," *Industrial
Marketing Management,* 28, 1,
1999, pp. 37–49.

13. Gregory A. Rich, "The Sales
    Manager as a Role Model:
    Effects on Trust, Job Satisfaction,
    and Performance of
    Salespeople," *Journal of the
    Academy of Marketing Science,*
    25, 4, 1997, pp. 319–328.

14. Laura Pratt, "Get In the
    Trenches With Your Sales
    Troops," *Financial Post,*
    March 1, 2004, pp. FE1-2.

15. Bob Thompson, "What Is
    CRM?" in *Customer Think Guide
    to CRM.* CRMguru.com,
    January 2003, p. 1.

16. Thomas N. Ingram, Raymond
    W. LaForge, and Thomas W.
    Leigh, "Selling in the New
    Millennium: A Joint Agenda,"
    *Industrial Marketing
    Management,* 31, 2002,
    pp. 559–567.

17. David Greenall, "The National
    Corporate Social Responsibility

...Risks,
...ortunities," The
...oard of Canada,

p. 24.

...n Hobel, "If It Works In
Poker . . . ," *Canadian HR
Reporter,* April 19, 2004, p. 22.

20. "Marmon/Keystone Canada
    Announces Promotions,"
    Canada News Wire, May 17,
    2004. ProQuest document
    637895611, downloaded
    July 15, 2004.

21. Gerald L. Manning, Barry L.
    Reece, and H.F. (Herb)
    MacKenzie, *Selling Today:
    Building Quality partnerships,*
    Canadian edition (Toronto:
    Prentice Hall, 1998), p. 33.

22. Ibid.; "Anne Mulcahy Named
    Xerox Chief Executive Officer,"
    http://www.xerox.com/go/xrx/
    template/inv_rel_newsroom.
    jsp?ed_name=Anne+Mulcahy+
    Named+Xerox+CEO_11990460
    &app=InvestorRelations&view=
    newsrelease&format=article&
    Xcntry=USA&Xlang=en_US,
    downloaded July 25, 2004.

23. Gabrielle Birkner, "Who Says
    Titles Don't Matter," *Sales &
    Marketing Management,* July
    2001, p. 14.

24. Montrose Sommers and James
    G. Barnes, *Marketing,* Tenth
    Edition (Toronto, ON: McGraw-
    Hill Ryerson, 2004), p. 341.

CHAPTER 2

1. Google website, http://www.
   google.com/corporate/facts.html,
   accessed December 28, 2006;
   Adam Lashinsky, "No. 1 Search
   and Enjoy," *Fortune,* January 22,
   2007, pp. 70–82; Google 2005

Annual Report; Julia Chang, "The World According to Google," *Sales & Marketing Management,* April 2006, pp. 24–28; Julia Chang, "More Content from the April Feature, 'The World According to Google,'" http://www.managesmarter.com/msg/search/article_display.jsp?vnu_content_id=100287616, accessed December 29, 2006.

2. Daniel G. Simpson, "Why Most Strategic Planning Is a Waste of Time and What You Can Do About It," *Long Range Planning,* 31, 3, 1998, pp. 476–480.

3. Bob Urichuck, *Up Your Bottom Line* (Carp, ON: Creative Bound, 2001), p. 57.

4. Peter Yannopoulos, *Marketing Strategy* (Scarborough, ON: Thomson Nelson, 2007), p. 78.

5. Louis E. Boone, David L. Kurtz, H.F. (Herb) MacKenzie, and Kim Snow, *Contemporary Marketing,* First Canadian Edition (Scarborough, ON: Thomson Nelson, 2007) p. 317.

6. David Menzies, "Meeting the Challenge," *Profit,* June 1998, pp. 148–150.

7. Xerox Corporation news release, "Printers Worldwide Choose Xerox iGen3 Presses to Expand Their Businesses, Grow Profits, Meet Customer Demand," May 16, 2005. http://www.xerox.com/go/xrx/template/inv_rel_newsroom.jsp?ed_name=NR_2005May16_iGen3CustomerSuccesses&app=Newsroom&view=newsrelease&format=article&Xcntry=USA&Xlang=en_US, accessed January 2, 2007.

8. Montrose S. Sommers and James G. Barnes, *Fundamentals of Marketing,* 10th Canadian ed. (Toronto, ON: McGraw-Hill Ryerson, 2004), p. 287.

9. "Selling Power 500: The Major Sales Forces in America," *Selling Power,* October 2006, pp. 57–60.

10. Ibid.

11. Ibid.

CHAPTER 3

1. Mark Riehl, "Xerox's product rollout success dependent on channels, says IDC," *eChannelLine Daily News,* May 1, 2003, accessed February 19, 2004, www.integratedmar.com/ECLprinter.cfm?item=DLY050103-02; "Xerox changes strategy, prices and products," www.globeandmail.com, posted April 30, 2001, accessed February 19, 2004; Hewitt Associates, "Best Employers in Canada," http://was7.hewitt.com/bestemployers/canada/the_list_2007.htm, accessed January 24, 2007.

2. Gerald L. Manning, Barry L. Reece, and H.F. (Herb) MacKenzie, *Selling Today: Creating Customer Value* (Toronto: Pearson Prentice Hall, 2004), p. 38.

3. Gerald L. Manning, et al. *Selling Today: Creating Customer Value,* p. 210.

4. Mark Evans, "Phone sellers to face new rules: Telemarketers have to prepare for U.S. do-not-call lists," *National Post* (Index-only), November 21, 2003, p. FP04.

5. David Myron, "Outsourcing HOT spots," *Customer Relationship Management* 8, 2, February 2004, pp. 26–30.

6. Gerald L. Manning, et al. *Selling Today: Creating Customer Value,* p. 42.

7. www.minacs.com/en/company/about, downloaded March 1, 2004.

8. Email correspondence from Jim Domanski, February 21, 2004.

9. Email correspondence from Jim Domanski, February 16, 2004.

10. www.jftaylor.ca downloaded February 17, 2004.

11. Telephone interview with Paul Flack, Elkay Canada, February 17, 2004.

12. Henry Canaday, "Independent Rep's Comp," *Selling Power* (January–February 2001): p. 79.

13. Christian Homburg, John P. Workman, Jr., and Ove Jensen, "Fundamental Changes in Marketing Organization: The Movement Toward a Customer-Focused Organizational Structure," *Journal of the Academy of Marketing Science* 28, 4, 2000, pp. 459–478.

14. Ibid.

15. Gerald L. Manning, et al. *Selling Today: Creating Customer Value,* p. 16.

16. Erika Rasmusson, "3M's Big Strategy for Big Accounts," *Sales & Marketing Management,* September 2000, pp. 92–98.

17. Bob Macdonald, president and CEO, Maritz Canada. Presentation to Brock University MBA Association, St. Catharines, Ontario, February 24, 2004.

18. Phil Wallace, "The Sales Role in Transition," *Canadian Printer,* September 2003, p. 32.

CHAPTER 4

1. Wendy Zellner, "Wal-Mart," *Business Week,* November 24, 2003, p. 104.

2. "RFID Update," *The RFID Industry Daily,* http://www.rfidupdate.com/articles/index.php?id=1178, accessed December 9, 2006.

3. ABI Research Press Release, "RFID Software and Services

2007 Revenue Forecasts Down 15%: What This Says About the Industry," http://www.abiresearch.com/abiprdisplay.jsp?pressid=700, accessed December 9, 2006.

4. Douglas D. Donnait, honorary chairman of the board, OCR Ltd. http://www.ocr.ca/company/letter.asp, accessed December 9, 2006.

5. Rolph Anderson, Rajiv Mehta, and James Strong, "An Empirical Investigation of Sales Management and Training Programs for Sales Managers," *Journal of Personal Selling & Sales Management,* Summer 1997, pp. 53–66.

6. Robert D. Klassen and Benito E. Flores, "Forecasting Practices of Canadian Firms: Survey Results and Comparisons," *International Journal of Production Economics,* 2001, pp. 163–174.

7. "Boston Market in Canadian Test," *Marketing,* November 5, 1002, p. 1.

8. Jim McElgunn, "The Ultimate Test Market," *Marketing,* February 10, 2003, http://www.marketingmag.ca/magazine/current/editorial/article.jsp?content=20030210_24163, accessed December 3, 2007.

9. Chris Powell, "Sink or Swim?" *Marketing,* October 30, 2000, http://www.marketingmag.ca/magazine/current/feature/article.jsp?content=20001030_15362, accessed December 3, 2007.

10. Robert D. Klassen and Benito E. Flores, "Forecasting Practices of Canadian Firms: Survey Results and Comparisons."

11. Ernie Stokes and Robin Somerville, "Statistics Newfoundland and Labrador: Towards an Assessment of the Benefits of the Canadian Economic Union," April 2003, p. 23; http://www.gov.nl.ca/publicat/royalcomm/research/stokes-n-someville.pdf#xml=-http://search.gov.nl.ca/texis/search/pdfhi.txt?query=NAICS&pr=provincial&prox=page&rorder=500&rprox=750&rdfreq=250&rwfreq=500&rlead=500&sufs=2&order=r&cq=2&id=431f77657, accessed December 7, 2006.

12. Robert D. Klassen and Benito E. Flores, "Forecasting Practices of Canadian Firms: Survey Results and Comparisons."

13. Teresa M. McCarthy, Donna F. Davis, Susan L. Golicic, and John T. Mentzer, "The Evolution of Sales Forecasting Measurement: A 20-Year Longitudinal Study of Forecasting Practices," *Journal of Forecasting,* 2006, pp. 303–324.

14. Ibid.

15. Chaman L. Jain, "Business Forecasting Practices in 2003," *The Journal of Business Forecasting Methods & Systems,* Fall 2004, pp. 2–6.

16. Ibid.

17. Teresa M. McCarthy, et al., "The Evolution of Sales Forecasting Measurement: A 20-Year Longitudinal Study of Forecasting Practices."

18. Ibid.

19. Ibid.

20. Douglas C. West, "Number of Sales Forecast Methods and Marketing Management," *Journal of Forecasting,* August 1994, pp. 395–407.

21. Robert D. Klassen and Benito E. Flores, "Forecasting Practices of Canadian Firms: Survey Results and Comparisons."

22. Ibid.

23. Chaman L. Jain, "Business Forecasting Practices in 2003."

24. Teresa M. McCarthy, et al., "The Evolution of Sales Forecasting Measurement: A 20-Year Longitudinal Study of Forecasting Practices."

25. Ibid.

26. Robert D. Klassen and Benito E. Flores, "Forecasting Practices of Canadian Firms: Survey Results and Comparisons."

27. Teresa M. McCarthy, et al., "The Evolution of Sales Forecasting Measurement: A 20-Year Longitudinal Study of Forecasting Practices."

28. Robert D. Klassen and Benito E. Flores, "Forecasting Practices of Canadian Firms: Survey Results and Comparisons."

29. Ibid.

CHAPTER 5

1. Personal interview with Patrick Morrissey, May 27, 2004; L. Brody, W. Cukier, K. Grant, M. Holland, C. Middleton, and D. Shortt, "True Control is Being Needed," in *Innovation Nation* (Etobicoke: John Wiley & Sons, 2002), pp. 92–97; www.creo.com, downloaded May 17, 2004.

2. Nicole Coviello, Roderick Brodie, Peter Danaher, and Wesley Johnston, "How Firms Relate to Their Markets: An Empirical Examination of Contemporary Marketing Practices," *Journal of Marketing,* 66 (July 2002), pp. 33–46.

3. Ibid.

4. Leslie Angello–Dean, "Converting Salespeople to Consultant/Advisors," *Sales & Marketing Training,* March–April 1990, p. 18.

5. David Wilson, "Deep Relationships: The Case of the Vanishing Salesperson," *Journal of Personal Selling & Sales Management,* 20 (Winter 2000), p. 53.

6. *Modern Purchasing,* "Commodity Partnerships:

Saving Time and Money on MRO Materials at Nortel Semiconductors," November 1996. Download ProQuest, May 3, 2004.

7. Robert D. McWilliams, Earl Naumann, and Stan Scott, "Determining Buying Centre Size," *Industrial Marketing Management,* 21, 1992, pp. 43–49.

8. George S. Day, "Creating a Superior Customer-Relating Capability," Marketing Science Institute working paper. Report No. 03-001, 2003.

9. John F. Tanner, Jr., "Users' Role in the Purchase: Their Influence, Satisfaction, and Desire to Participate in the Next Purchase," *Journal of Business and Industrial Marketing,* 13 6, 1998, pp. 479–491.

10. Frederick F. Reichheld and W. Earl Sasser, Jr. "Zero Defections: Quality Comes to Services," *Harvard Business Review,* September–October 1990, pp. 105–111.

11. William Weeks and Lynn Kahle, "Salespeople's Time Use and Performance," *Journal of Personal Selling & Sales Management,* 10 (Winter 1990), pp. 29–37.

12. Gerald L. Manning, Barry L. Reece, and H.F. (Herb) MacKenzie, *Selling Today: Creating Customer Value,* 3rd Canadian edition (Toronto: Pearson Prentice Hall, 2004), p. 54.

13. "Joe Girard: The World's Greatest Salesman." www.usdreams.com/Girard. html, downloaded May 10, 2004.

14. Alan Test, "Cold Calls Are Hot," *Agency Sales Magazine,* September 1995, p. 28.

15. Alan Lucas, "Leading Edge," *Sales & Marketing Management,* June 1995, pp. 13–14.

16. Ben Chapman, "The Trade Show Must Go On," *Sales & Marketing Management,* June 2001, p. 22.

17. Barry Siskind, "Questions, Questions, Questions," *Sales Exchange,* May 3–9, 2004. e-newsletter published by The Canadian Professional Sales Association.

18. Sheldon Gordon, "Punch Up Your Profits," *Profit,* May 1999, pp. 17–22.

19. Mark Stevenson, "The Lean, Mean Marketing Machine," *Canadian Business,* January 1994, pp. 32–36.

20. Rhea Seymour, "Ideas That Work," *Profit,* June 2002, pp. 66–70.

21. Tony Parinello, "Keeping Track of Prospects," http://www.entrepreneur.com/article/0,4621,306013,00.html, January 13, 2003, downloaded May 21, 2004.

CHAPTER 6

1. Personal interviews, Brenda Fisher, beginning February 24, 1997.

2. Personal interviews, Susan Green, beginning July 18, 1999.

3. www.jimpattison.com, accessed June 20, 2002; Diane Francis, "What Makes Jim Pattison Run—and Whistle?" *Financial Post,* March 5–7, 1994, p. S3.

4. Personal interviews, Joe Murphy, beginning June 9, 1999.

5. Gerald L. Manning, Barry L. Reece, and H.F. (Herb) MacKenzie, *Selling Today: Creating Customer Value,* 4th Canadian edition. (Toronto, ON: Pearson Prentice Hall, 2007), p. 19.

6. Susan Bixler, *The Professional Image* (New York, NY: Putnam Publishing Group, 1984), p. 216.

7. Gerald L. Manning, et al., p. 91.

8. Gerald L. Manning, et al., p. 19.

9. Michael Hammer and James Champy, *Reengineering the Corporation: A Manifesto for Business Revolution* (New York, NY: Harper Business, 1993), p. 18.

10. Gerald L. Manning, et al., p. 22.

11. Regina Eisman, "Justifying Your Incentive Program," *Sales & Marketing Management,* April 1993, p. 52.

12. Gerald L. Manning, et al., p. 214.

13. Gerald L. Manning, et al., p. 236.

14. Susan Bixler and Nancy Nix-Rice, *The New Professional Image* (Holbrook, MA: Adams Media Corporation, 1997), p. 3.

15. Gerald L. Manning, et al., p. 240.

16. Stephanie G. Sherman and V. Clayton Sherman, *Make Yourself Memorable* (New York, NY: AMACOM, 1996), pp. 58–59.

17. Gerald L. Manning, et al., pp. 311–312.

18. Rick Kang, "Management by Defiance," *Profit,* June 1999, pp. 63–64.

19. Kristine Ellis, "Deal Maker or Breaker?" *Training,* April 2002, p. 37.

20. "Why Customers Leave," *Sales & Marketing Management,* May 1998, p. 86.

21. Geoffrey Brewer, "The Customer Stops Here," *Sales & Marketing Management,* March 1998, pp. 31–32.

22. Max Morden, "Service With a Smile," *In Touch* (Richard Ivey School of Business, Fall 1999), p. 37.

23. Melinda Ligos, "The Joys of Cross-Selling," *Sales & Marketing Management,* August 1998, p. 75.

24. Jo Ann Brezette, "Smart Answers to Clients' Questions," *Window Fashions Design & Education Magazine*, September 2001, p. 120.

25. William F. Kendy, "Skills Workshop," *Selling Power*, June 2000, pp. 33–34.

26. Michael Abrams and Matthew Paese, "Winning and Dining the Whiners," *Sales & Marketing Management*, February 1993, p. 73.

CHAPTER 7

1. Personal experience as the manager involved. Only the name of Jim MacDonald is disguised.

2. Jennifer Gilbert, "Smart Hiring," *Sales & Marketing Management*, October 2004; Christine Galea, "Smart Hiring," *Sales & Marketing Management*, March 2005.

3. "Pharma Reps Flee," *Sales & Marketing Management*, Online exclusive November 28, 2004, http://www.salesandmarketing. com/smm/search/article_display. jsp?vnu_content_id=100072665, downloaded April 12, 2006.

4. Brett Ruffell, "The 2006 Salary Report," *Contact*, December 2006, pp. 18–24.

5. Andy Holloway, "Finding the Right Fit," *Canadian Business*, November 25, 2002, pp. 119–122.

6. Earl Naumann, Scott M. Widmier, and Donald W. Jackson, Jr., "Examining the Relationship Between Work Attitudes and Propensity to Leave Among Expatriate Salespeople," *Journal of Personal Selling & Sales Management*, Fall 2000, pp. 227–241; Thomas R. Wotruba and Pradeep K. Tyagi, "Met Expectations and Turnover in Direct Selling," *Journal of Marketing*, July 1991, pp. 24–35.

7. Robert L. Mathis, John H. Jackson, and Deborah M. Zinni, *Human Resource Management* (Toronto, ON: Nelson Canada, 2008), p. 207.

8. Andrew J. Vinchur, Jeffrey S. Schippmann, Fred S. Switzer III, and Philip L. Roth, "A Meta-Analytic Review of Predictors of Job Performance for Salespeople," *Journal of Applied Psychology*, August 1998, pp. 586–597; Murray R. Barrick, Greg L. Stewart, and Mike Piotrowski, "Personality and Job Performance: Test of the Mediating Effects of Motivation Among Sales Representatives," *Journal of Applied Psychology*, February 2002, pp. 43–51.

9. Michele Marchetti, Chad Kaydo, Andy Cohen, Tricia Campbell, and Sarah Lorge, "Give Us 2 Weeks and We'll Give You a New Sales Force," *Sales & Marketing Management*, December 1998, pp. 31–32.

10. Carole Ann King, "Frustration Mounts as Recruiting Gets Harder," *National Underwriter*, March 19, 2001, pp. 6–7.

11. Rene Darmon, "Where Do the Best Sales Force Profit Producers Come From?" *Journal of Personal Selling & Sales Management*, 1993 (3), pp. 17–29.

12. Thomas Wotruba and Stephen Castleberry, "Job Analysis and Hiring Practices for National Account Hiring Positions," *Journal of Personal Selling & Sales Management*, 1993 (3), pp. 49–65.

13. Andy Holloway, "Finding the Right Fit," ibid.

14. Virginia Galt, "Hiring Firms Employ the Buddy System," *Globe and Mail*, www.globeandmail.com, accessed April 30, 2006.

15. Peopleclick website, http://www. peopleclick.com/knowledge/ ind_lefkow.asp, viewed April 20, 2006.

16. General Mills website, http:// www.generalmills.com/ corporate/careers/ lifestyle_canada.aspx, viewed April 20, 2006.

17. Procter & Gamble Canada website, http://www.pg.com/en_CA/ careers/internships.jhtml, viewed April 19, 2006.

18. The Directory of Canadian Recruiters website, http://www. directoryofrecruiters.com/faqs. html, viewed April 20, 2006.

19. William Keenan, "Time Is Everything," *Sales & Marketing Management*, August 1993, p. 60.

20. The Directory of Canadian Recruiters website, ibid.

21. Rene Darmon, "Where Do the Best Sales Force Profit Producers Come From?" ibid.

22. William Keenan, "Time Is Everything," ibid.

23. HR Chally Group, http://www. chally.com/assess/samples/ interview-guides.html, accessed August 17, 2006.

24. Glynne Jenkins, "Attracting Good Sales People," *Canadian Printer*, April–May 2003, p. 30.

25. Personal interviews with and correspondence from Alex Pettes, November 2004 through March 2006.

26. Wonderlic, Inc. website, www.wonderlic.com, viewed April 26, 2006; Canada Revenue Agency, *Handbook for Candidates*, http://www.cra-arc.gc.ca/careers/ working/wonderlic-e.html, accessed August 16, 2006.

27. The HR Chally Group, "How to Select a Sales Force that Sells,"

revised 6th edition, p. 15. Downloaded from www.chally. com, April 26, 2006.

28. Julia Chang, "Born to Sell?" *Sales & Marketing Management,* July 2003, pp. 34–38.

29. Robert P. Tett, Douglas N. Jackson, and Mitchell Rothstein, "Personality Measures as Predictors of Job Performance: A Meta-Analytic Review," *Personnel Psychology,* 1991, pp. 703–742.

30. Les Rosen, "Effective Pre-Employment Background Screening," *Protective Operations,* Spring 2002, pp. 1–5.

31. Laura Cassiani, "Upfront Checking Means Fewer Fraud Investigations After the Fact," *Canadian HR Reporter,* November 20, 2000.

32. Office of the Privacy Commissioner of Canada, Fact Sheet, "Complying With the *Personal Information Protection and Electronic Documents Act,*" http://www.privcom.gc.ca/fs-fi/ 02_05_d_16_e.asp, accessed August 17, 2006.

33. Kevin Wilson, "The Hiring Game," *Contact,* October 2005, pp. 32–38.

34. Robert L. Mathis, et al., p. 235.

35. Equifax, Inc., 2005 Annual Report. http://www.equifax. com/corp/investorcenter/ annualReport2005/ greatsolutions.html, accessed August 17, 2006.

36. Robert L. Mathis, et al., p. 236.

37. Ibid., p. 237.

CHAPTER 8

1. Personal interview, Ed Holloway, vice-president, rentals and leasing, Maxim Transportation Services, May 30, 2006;

"Leveraging Certification," *Contact,* August 2005, p. 11.

2. "Industry Report 1998," *Training,* October 1998, p. 55.

3. Robert Klien, "Nabisco Sales Soar After Sales Training," *Marketing News,* January 6, 1997, p. 23.

4. Christine Galea and Carl Wiens, "2002 Sales Training Survey," *Sales & Marketing Management,* July 2002, pp. 34–37.

5. Frederick A. Russ, Kevin M. McNeilly, James M. Comer, and Theodore B. Light, "Exploring the Impact of Critical Sales Events," *Journal of Personal Selling & Sales Management,* Spring 1998, pp. 19–34.

6. Charles M. Futrell and A. Parasuraman, "The Relationship of Satisfaction and Performance to Salesforce Turnover," *Journal of Marketing,* Fall 1984, pp. 33–40; George H. Lucas, Jr., A. Parasuraman, Robert A. Davis, and Ben M. Enis, "An Empirical Study of Salesforce Turnover," *Journal of Marketing,* July 1987, pp. 34–59.

7. William Moncrief, Ronald Hoverstad, and George Lucas, Jr., "Survival Analysis: A New Approach to Analyzing Sales Force Retention," *Journal of Personal Selling & Sales Management,* Summer 1989, pp. 19–30.

8. Brian Jeffrey, "Commanding Performance," *Contact,* April 1998, www.cpsa.com, accessed July 12, 2006.

9. Carolyn Green, "In Pursuit of a Top-Notch Sales Team," *Contact,* April 2004, pp. 20–22.

10. Ibid.

11. Marc Hequet, "Product Knowledge: Knowing What They're Selling May Be the Key

to How Well They Sell It," *Training,* February 1988, p. 18.

12. Steve Atlas, "Warm and Fuzzy Tips From Buyers for Closing More Sales," *Selling Power,* October 2001, pp. 74–78.

13. "Ontario Global Traders Awards," *Profit,* September 2001, Advertising Supplement.

14. Ian Gelenter, "Build Satisfaction With a Service Contract," *Selling,* May 1998, p. 7.

15. Laura Pratt, "Training the Team? Start at the Top," *National Post,* April 12, 2004, p. FP7.

16. Chris Chase, "Toyota's Truck Division Changes Its Marketing," *The Province* (Vancouver), September 2, 2005, p. C13.

17. "Pfizer Canada Consistently Chosen Among the Best Companies to Work for in Canada," Canada News Wire, Ottawa, December 31, 2004, p.1.

18. Jennifer Myers, "Letters From Canada's Fastest Growing Companies," *Profit,* June–August 2001, pp. 22–32.

19. Michael R. Williams and Jill S. Attaway, "Exploring Salespersons' Customer Orientation as a Mediator of Organizational Culture's Influence on Buyer–Seller Relationships," *Journal of Personal Selling & Sales Management,* Fall 1996, pp. 33–52.

20. Interview with Mike Urquhart, May 20, 1997.

21. Colette A. Frayne and J. Michael Geringer, "Self-Management Training for Improving Job Performance," *Journal of Applied Psychology,* June 2000, pp. 361–372.

22. "Data Trends," *Selling,* June 1999, p. 1.

23. Cy Charney, *The Salesperson's Handbook* (Toronto, ON: Stoddart Publishing, 2002), p. 277.

24. Laura Pratt, "Twenty-five Hours a Day," *Profit*, November 2001, p. 41.

25. Erika Rasmusson, "Wanted: Profitable Customers," *Sales & Marketing Management*, May 1999, pp. 28–34.

26. Rhea Seymour, "Fighting the Pressure," *Profit*, November 2001, p. 43.

27. Brenda Bouw, "In Praise of an Ethical Education," *Globe and Mail*, March 18, 2002, p. C1.

28. Suzanne Wintrob, "The Right Connections Can Pay Off," *National Post*, April 14, 2003, p. BE7.

29. "Turning Managers Into Trainers," *Selling Power*, www.sellingpower.com, accessed July 12, 2006.

30. Erika Rasmusson, "Getting Schooled in Outsourcing," *Sales & Marketing Management*, January 1999, p. 49; Christine Galea and Carl Wiens, "2002 Sales Training Survey," *Sales & Marketing Management*, July 2002, p. 37.

31. Brandon Hall, "Sales Training Makeovers," *Training*, May 2005, pp. 15–22.

32. Christine Galea and Carl Wiens, "2002 Sales Training Survey," p. 37.

33. Ibid.

34. Ibid., p. 35.

35. Brandon Hall, "Sales Training Makeovers."

36. Ibid.

37. Steve Alexander, "Reducing the Learning Burden," *Training*, September 2002, pp. 32–34.

38. Christen P. Heide, *Dartnell's 30th Sales Force Compensation Survey: 1998–1999* (Chicago, IL: Dartnell Corporation, 1999), p. 141.

39. Christine Galea and Carl Wiens, "2002 Sales Training Survey," p. 38.

40. Donald L. Kirkpatrick, "Techniques for Evaluating Training Programs," *Journal of the American Society for Training and Development*, 1959, pp. 3–9; Donald L. Kirkpatrick, "Great Ideas Revisited," *Training and Development*, January 1996, pp. 55–57.

41. Mark P. Leach and Annie H. Liu, "Investigating Interrelationships Among Sales Training Evaluation Methods," *Journal of Personal Selling & Sales Management*, Fall 2003, pp. 327–339.

42. Ibid.

43. Ibid.

44. SellingPower.com, "Training for Managers," *Sales Management Newsletter*, July 19, 2004. Featured articles by Lain Ehmann, www.sellingpower.com, accessed April 29, 2006.

45. Rolph Anderson, Rajiv Mehta, and James Strong, "An Empirical Investigation of Sales Management Training Programs for Sales Managers," *Journal of Personal Selling and Sales Management*, Summer 1997, pp. 53–66.

CHAPTER 9

1. Maritz Inc., http://www.maritz.com and http://www.maritzcanada.com, accessed August 19, 2006.

2. Barry L. Reece and Rhonda Brandt, *Effective Human Relations in Organizations*, Sixth Edition (Boston, MA: Houghton Mifflin, 1996), p. 153.

3. Bernadette Johnson, "Visionary Heights," *Contact*, October 2004, p. 19.

4. Katharine Kaplan, "Better With Age," *Sales & Marketing Management*, July 2001, pp. 58—62.

5. Ibid.

6. "2006 Compensation Study," *Sales & Marketing Management*, p. 29 www.salesandmarketing.com, accessed July 13, 2006.

7. Thomas R. Wotruba and Michael L. Thurlow, "Sales Force Participation in Quota Setting and Sales Forecasting," *Journal of Marketing*, April 1976, pp. 11—16.

8. "2006 Compensation Study," p. 11.

9. *CPSA's Guide to Non-Financial Rewards and Recognition*, Ed., Anna Fredericks. (Toronto, ON: Canadian Professional Sales Association, 2003), p. 30.

10. Ibid., p. 23.

11. Ibid., p. 7.

12. Anna Fredericks, "Are You Rewarding Your Sales Team With the Right Stuff? CPSA Survey Says . . . ," *Contact*, June 2005, pp. 34–35.

13. Melanie Chambers, "What's Driving Sales?" *Contact*, April 2006, p. 26.

14. "2006 Compensation Study," p. 23.

15. "2006 Compensation Study," p. 24.

CHAPTER 10

1. Andy Cohen, "Extreme Makeovers, Case Study #1: A Push for Product Diversity," *Sales & Marketing Management*, May 2004, pp. 36–40.

2. *Canadian Sales Management Manual* (Toronto, ON: Canadian Professional Sales Association, 2005), pp. 3–13.

3. Fay Hansen, "A New Way to Pay," *Workforce Management*, October 24, 2005, pp. 33–37.

4. Andris Zoltners, Prabhakant Sinha, and George Zoltners, *The Complete Guide to Accelerating Sales Force Performance* (New York, NY: AMACOM, 2001), p. 50.

5. Andris Zoltners, Prabhakant Sinha, and Sally E. Lorimer, *The Complete Guide to Sales Force Incentive Compensation* (New York, NY: AMACOM, 2006), p. 2.

6. George John and Barton Weitz, "Salesforce Compensation: An Empirical Investigation of Factors Related to Use of Salary Versus Incentive Compensation," *Journal of Marketing Research,* February 1989, p. 9.

7. Andris Zoltners, Prabhakant Sinha, and Sally E. Lorimer, *The Complete Guide to Sales Force Incentive Compensation,* p. 2.

8. Ibid.

9. Brett Ruffell, "The 2006 Salary Report," *Contact,* December 2006, pp. 18–24.

10. T&E Report, *Sales & Marketing Management,* July 2003, p. 62.

11. Monica Belcourt, Arthur Sherman, George Bohlander, and Scott Snell, *Managing Human Resources,* Second Canadian Edition. (Toronto, ON: ITP Nelson, 1999), p. 428.

12. John F. Tanner, Jr., and George Dudley, "International Differences—Examining Two Assumptions About Selling," reported in *Baylor Business Review,* Fall 2003, pp. 44–45.

13. Andris Zoltners, Prabhakant Sinha, and Sally E. Lorimer, *The Complete Guide to Sales Force Incentive Compensation,* p. 158.

14. Ibid.

15. Bill Gates, *Business @ The Speed of Thought,* (New York, NY: Warner Books, 1999) p. 67.

16. James G. Barnes, *Secrets of Customer Relationship Management: It's All About How You Make Them Feel,* (Toronto, ON: McGraw-Hill, 2001).

17. Eilene Zimmerman, "Quota Busters," *Sales & Marketing Management,* January 2001, pp. 58–63.

18. Andris Zoltners, Prabhakant Sinha, and Sally E. Lorimer, *The Complete Guide to Sales Force Incentive Compensation,* p. 205.

19. Aaron Bernstein, "Women's Pay: Why the Gap Remains a Chasm," *Business Week,* July 14, 2004, pp. 58–59.

20. Ibid.

21. Rhea Seymour, "Ms. Versus Mr." *Profit,* October 2000, p. 53.

22. Sridhar N. Ramaswami and Jagdip Singh, "Antecedents and Consequences of Merit Pay Fairness for Industrial Salespeople," *Journal of Marketing,* October 2003, pp. 46–66.

23. Hari Das, *Recruitment, Selection, and Deployment of Human Resources: A Canadian Perspective.* Andrew Templar, series editor. (Toronto, ON: Pearson Education Canada, 2007), p. 326.

24. Michele Marchetti, "Paring Expatriate Pay," *Sales & Marketing Management,* www.salesandmarketing.com, accessed July 1, 2006.

CHAPTER 11

1. Kim Wright Wiley, "How a Leader Masters Change," *Selling Power,* June 2006, pp. 50–55.

2. Adam Lashinsky, "The Hurd Way," *Fortune,* April 17, 2006, pp. 92–102.

3. "Recipe for a Turnaround," *Contact,* October 2005, p. 29.

4. All searches were made July 6, 2007.

5. Robert N. Lussier and Christopher F. Achua, *Leadership: Theory, Application, Skill Development,* Second Edition. (Toronto, ON: Thomson Southwestern, 2004), p. 33.

6. S.S.K. Lam and J. Schaubroeck, "The Role of Locus of Control in Reactions to Being Promoted and to Being Passed Over: A Quasi Experiment," *Academy of Management Journal,* 43 (2000), pp. 66–78.

7. N.M. Ashkanasy and C.S. Daus, "Emotion in the Workplace: The New Challenge for Managers," *Academy of Management Executive,* 16 (2002), pp. 76–86.

8. Nataniel Branden, *Self-Esteem at Work* (San Francisco, CA: Jossey-Bass, 1998), p. 35.

9. L.R. Goldberg, "An Alternative 'Description of Personality': The Big-Five Factor Structure," *Journal of Personality and Social Psychology,* 59 (1990), pp. 1216–1229.

10. Robert N. Lussier and Christopher F. Achua, p. 30.

11. Steve Bates, "Personality Counts: Psychological Test Can Help Peg the Job Applicants Best Suited for Certain Jobs," *HR Magazine,* February 2002, pp. 28–34.

12. Robert N. Lussier and Christopher F. Achua, p. 40.

13. D.C. McClelland, *Human Motivation* (Glenview, IL: Scott Foresman, 1985).

14. Robert N. Lussier and Christopher F. Achua, p. 42.

15. John French, Jr. and Bertram Raven, "The Bases of Social Power," in *Studies in Social Power,* D. Cartwright (ed.) (Ann Arbor, MI: The University of Michigan Press, 1959).

16. Robert N. Lussier and Christopher F. Achua, p. 103.

17. Paul Busch, "The Sales Manager's Bases of Social Power

and Influence Upon the Sales Force," *Journal of Marketing,* Summer 1980, p. 98.

18. Price Pritchett, "Overcome Resistance," *Executive Excellence,* February 1997, pp. 13–14.

19. Robert N. Lussier and Christopher F. Achua, p. 396.

20. Rhea Seymour, "The Mentor's Reward," *Profit,* November 2001, p. 35.

21. Kenneth R. Phillips, "The Achilles' Heel of Coaching," *Training & Development,* March 1998, p. 41.

22. Susan M. Drake, Michelle J. Gulman, and Sara M. Roberts, *Light Their Fire* (Chicago, IL: Dearborn Trade Publishing, 2005), p. 3.

23. Ibid., p. 16.

24. Ibid., p. 45.

25. David Kirkpatrick, "Star Power: Kevin Johnson, Microsoft," *Fortune,* February 6, 2006, p. 58.

26. Robin T. Peterson, "Beyond the Plateau," *Sales & Marketing Management,* July 1993, pp. 78–82.

27. William Keenan, Jr., "The Nagging Problem of the Plateaued Salesperson," *Sales & Marketing Management,* May 1989, pp. 36–41.

28. Ibid.

29. Michael Tjepkema, "Alcohol and Illicit Drug Dependence," Statistics Canada, Catalogue 82-003, Supplement to Health Reports, Volume 15, 2004, accessed http://www.statcan.ca/english/freepub/82-003-SIE/2004000/pdf/82-003-SIE20040007447.pdf, accessed July 26, 2006.

30. Canadian Centre for Substance Abuse, "The Costs of Substance Abuse in Canada 2002,"

accessed http://www.ccsa.ca/NR/rdonlyres/18F3415E-2CAC-4D21-86E2-CEE549EC47A9/0/ccsa0113322006.pdf, accessed July 26, 2006.

31. M. Johne, "Clean and Sober: Dealing With Drugs and Alcohol in the Workplace," *HR Professional,* October–November 1999, pp. 18–22.

32. "Sexual Harassment," *CACSW Fact Sheet,* Canadian Advisory Council on the Status of Women, March 1993.

33. William L. Cron and Thomas E. DeCarlo, *Dalrymple's Sales Management,* Ninth Edition (Hoboken, NJ: John Wiley & Sons, 2006), p. 276.

34. Leslie M. Fine, C. David Shepherd, and Susan L. Josephs, "Insights Into Sexual Harassments of Salespeople by Customers: The Role of Gender and Customer Power," *Journal of Personal Selling & Sales Management,* Spring 1999, pp. 19–34.

35. Ibid.

36. Thomas N. Ingram, Keun S. Lee, and George H. Lucas, Jr., "Commitment and Involvement: Assessing a Salesforce Typology," *Journal of the Academy of Marketing Science,* Summer 1991, pp. 187–197.

37. Mary Klonizakis, "Dealing With Difficult People," *Contact,* May 2001, p. 18.

38. Ibid.

39. T. Wagar, "Wrongful Dismissal: Perception vs. Reality," *Human Resources Professional,* June 1996, p. 10.

40. J. Miller, "Lower Courts Raise Employers' Costs With Higher Extended-Notice Damages," *Canadian HR Reporter,* May 31, 1999, p. 5.

CHAPTER 12

1. Sources: Zena Olijnyk, "Former VP of Wal-Mart Canada Charged With Taking Kickbacks," *National Post,* February 1, 2000, http://www.flipside.org/vol3/feb00/00fe02b.htm, accessed April 9, 2002; Marina Strauss, "Wal-Mart Supplier Was Asked for Kickbacks," *Globe and Mail,* February 2, 2000, pp. B1, B7; Marina Strauss, "Wal-Mart Initiated Police Investigation," *Globe and Mail,* February 3, 2000, p. B3; Matthew Sylvain, "Creative Gift-Giving," *Contact,* October 2005, pp. 21–25.

2. Vivian Arnold, B. June Schmidt, and Randall L. Wells, "Ethics Instruction in the Classrooms of Business Educators," *Delta Pi Epsilon Journal,* Fall 1996, p. 185.

3. S&MM Impulse, *Sales & Marketing Management,* June 2006, p. 18.

4. Jennifer Gilbert, "A Matter of Trust," *Sales & Marketing Management,* March 2003, accessed www.salesandmarketing.com, August 1, 2006.

5. Ibid.

6. AACSB, "Eligibility Procedures and Standards for Business Accreditation," Adopted April 2003. Revised January 2006. http://www.aacsb.edu/accreditation/standards.asp, accessed August 1, 2006.

7. "Nearly Half of Workers Take Unethical Actions—Survey," *Des Moines Register,* April 7, 1997, p. 18B.

8. Sharon Begley, "A World of Their Own," *Newsweek,* May 8, 2000, pp. 53–56.

9. Nathaniel Branden, *Self-Esteem at Work* (San Francisco, CA: Jossey-Bass, 1998), p. 35.

10. Patrick Smith, "You Have a Job, But How About a Life?" *Business Week,* November 16, 1998, p. 30.

11. Marjorie Kelly, "Waving Goodbye to the Invisible Hand," *Business Ethics,* March–April, 2002, p. 4.

12. Theodore B. Kinni, "An Ethical Dilemma," *Selling Power,* http://www.sellingpower.com/article/display.asp?aid=SP2036997, accessed August 5, 2006.

13. Betsey Cummings, "Ethical Breach," *Sales & Marketing Management,* July 2004, www.sales&marketing.com, accessed August 1, 2006.

14. Michael Deck, "Good Intentions Aren't Enough," *Globe and Mail,* October 23, 1997, p. B2.

15. "Survey Reveals What Motivates Loyalty," *Selling,* September 2000, p. 2.

16. Brenda Hampton, "Ethics in Sales: Walking the Fine Line Between What's Right and Wrong," *Contact,* February 2006, pp. 20–21.

17. Erin Strout, "To Tell the Truth," *Sales & Marketing Management,* July 2002, pp. 40–47.

18. Brenda Bouw, "In Praise of an Ethical Education," *Globe and Mail,* March 18, 2002, p. C1.

19. Erin Strout, "Are Your Salespeople Ripping You Off?" *Sales & Marketing Management,* February 2001, pp. 56–61.

20. Corinne McLaughlin, "Workplace Spirituality Transforming Organizations From the Inside Out," *The Inner Edge,* August–September 1988, p. 26.

21. Theodore B. Kinni, "An Ethical Dilemma."

22. Ibid.

23. Steve Maich, "Selling Ethics at Nortel," http://www.macleans.ca/switchboard/columnists/article.jsp?content=20050124_98842_98842, accessed August 6, 2006.

24. Matthew Sylvain, "Creative Gift-Giving."

25. Ibid.

26. Melinda Ligos, "Gimme! Gimme!" *Sales & Marketing Management,* March 2002, pp. 33–40.

27. Deborah Aarts, "Why Bribery Should Worry You," *Canadian Business Online,* November 17, 2005, www.canadianbusiness.com, accessed August 1, 2006.

28. Janet McFarland and Greg Keenan, "Harassment Suit Puts Heat on Big 3," *Globe and Mail,* September 10, 1997, p. A1.

29. Erin Strout, "To Tell the Truth," *Sales & Marketing Management,* July 2002, www.salesandmarketing.com, accessed August 1, 2006.

30. Steven Sack, "Watch the Words," *Sales & Marketing Management,* July 1, 1985, p. 56.

31. Steven Sack, "Watch the Words."

32. Erin Strout, "To Tell the Truth."

33. David Menzies, "Deciding Which Route to Take," *Contact,* May 2001, pp. 12–13.

34. David Menzies, "Deciding Which Route to Take."

35. Charles Haddad and Amy Barrett, "A Whistle-Blower Rocks an Industry," *Business Week,* June 24, 2002, pp. 126–130.

36. Erin Strout, "To Tell the Truth," *Sales & Marketing Management,* July 2002,

www.salesandmarketing.com, accessed August 1, 2006.

37. Matthew McClearn, "A Snitch in Time," *Canadian Business,* December 29, 2003–January 14, 2004, p. 61.

38. Matthew McClearn, "A Snitch in Time."

39. Matthew McClearn, "Court Sides With Snitch," *Canadian Business,* December 2003, April 12–April 25, 2004, p. 14.

40. Matthew McClearn, "A Snitch in Time."

41. Erin Strout, "Are Your Salespeople Ripping You Off?"

42. Brenda Hampton, "Ethics in Sales: Walking the Fine Line Between What's Right and Wrong," *Contact,* February 2006, pp. 20–21.

43. See Gerald L. Manning, Barry L. Reece, and H.F. (Herb) MacKenzie, *Selling Today: Creating Customer Value* (Toronto, ON: Pearson Prentice Hall, 2006), p. 118.

44. Ron Willingham, *Integrity Selling* (New York, NY: Doubleday, 1987) p. xv.

45. Sharon Drew Morgan, *Selling With Integrity* (San Francisco, CA: Berrett-Koehler Publishers, 1997) pp. 25–27.

46. Gerhard Gschwandtner, "Lies and Deception in Selling," *Personal Selling Power,* Fifteenth Anniversary Issue, 1995, p. 62.

47. "Stephen Harper Talks to Linda Frum," *Maclean's,* March 6, 2006, p. 14.

48. Competition Bureau Canada, "Former UCAR Executive Pleads Guilty to Price Fixing," news release, May 16, 2005, http://www.competitionbureau.gc.ca/internet/index.cfm?itemID=193&lg=e, accessed August 5, 2006.

49. Leonard Zehr, "Five Vitamin Giants Hit With Record Fines for Price Fixing in Canada," *The Globe and Mail,* September 23, 1999, pp. B1, B4.

50. Thomas Claridge, "Four Convicted of Rigging Bids," *Globe and Mail,* December 20, 1997, p. B5.

51. "Hotels Fined for Price Fixing," *Calgary Herald,* April 28, 1987, p. D1.

52. *Competition Law* (North York, ON: CCH Canadian Limited, 1995), p. 4202.

53. Christina Campbell, "Tale of the Tape," *Canadian Business,* April 24–May 7, 2006, pp. 39–40.

54. Canadian Press News Wire, "Competition Tribunal Offers Mixed Ruling in Phone Directory Case," Toronto, February 27, 1997.

55. Industry Canada, "Competition Bureau Investigation Leads to $1-Million Settlement with Suzy Shier Inc," news release, January 29, 2004, http://www.ic.gc.ca/, accessed May 26, 2005.

56. "Sears to Pay $487K in Fines and Costs for Misleading Tire Ads," *National Post,* April 2, 2005, p. FP4.

57. Industry Canada, "Premier Health Club Found Guilty of Misleading Advertising Under the *Competition Act,* news release, April 19, 2005, http://www.ic.gc.ca/, accessed May 27, 2005; Mitch Moxley, "Good Life to Pay $75 000 for Misleading Advertising," *National Post,* February 10, 2005, p. FP5.

58. Industry Canada, "About the CMC," http://www.cmcweb.ca/epic/internet/incmc-cmc.nsf/en/h_fe00013e.html, accessed August 5, 2006.

59. Deborah Aarts, "Why Bribery Should Worry You."

CHAPTER 13

1. Jeremy Miller, "The 3 P's of Sales Performance," http://www.leapjob.com/art-3psofsalesperformance.htm, accessed October 9, 2006.

2. Hari Das and Andrew Templer, eds. *Performance Management* (Toronto, ON: Prentice Hall, 2003), p. 12.

3. Jeremy Miller, "The 3 P's of Sales Performance."

4. Donald W. Jackson, Jr., John L. Schlacter, and William G. Wolfe, "Examining the Bases Utilized for Evaluating Salespeople's Performance," *Journal of Personal Selling & Sales Management,* Fall 1995, pp. 57–65.

5. "Data Trends," *Selling,* June 1999, p. 1.

6. Mark W. Johnston and Greg W. Marshall, *Churchill/Ford/Walker's Sales Force Management,* Seventh Edition (Toronto, ON: McGraw-Hill Irwin, 2003), p. 493.

7. Team Builders Plus, http://www.360-degreefeedback.com/FAQ, accessed October 8, 2006.

8. John F. Milliman, Robert F. Zawacki, Carol Norman, Lynda Powell, and Jay Kirksey, "Companies Evaluate Employees From All Perspectives," *Personnel Journal,* November 1994, pp. 99–103.

9. Kenneth Bettenhausen and Donald Fedor, "Peer and Upward Appraisals," *Group and Organization Management,* June 1997, pp. 236–263.

10. Sabrina Salam, Jonathan Cox, and Henry Sims, Jr., "In the Eye of the Beholder: How Leadership Relates to 360-Degree Performance Ratings," *Group and Organization Management,* June 1997, pp. 185–209.

11. Douglas J. Dalrymple and William M. Strahle, "Career Path Charting: Frameworks for Sales Force Evaluation," *Journal of Personal Selling & Sales Management,* Summer 1990, pp. 59–68.

Company/Name Index

A

AACSB (Association to Advance Collegiate Business Schools), 338
ABI Research, 93
Abramson, Susan, 165
Acadia University, 126, 194, 195
Accenture, 244
AccountPro, 284
Acklands-Grainer, 319
Act!, 391
Adey, Trevor, 11
Aetna Life & Casualty, 217
Aflak Inc., 281
A.L. Van Houtte, 234
Albanese, Frank, 70
Alliance of Manufacturers, 107
Amazon.com, 308
American Express, 92
Anderson, Dave, 13, 242
Angiotech Pharmaceuticals, 10
Anthony, Mitch, 212, 220
Aon Consulting, 87
AstraZeneca, 75
Avanade Inc., 244
Avon Canada, 31
Avon for North America, 16

B

Babej, Anne, 236
Baldassarre, Mod, 132
Barnes, Jim, 300
The Bay, 241
The Beer Store, 308
Bell Mobility, 84
Bixler, Susan, 152
Black & Decker, 217
Blakeway, Doug, 30
Blanchard, Ken, 211
Blanchard Training and Development, 211
The Blue Book of Canadian Business, 134
Boatright, John, 338
Book, Howard E., 214
Bourke, Michael, 242
Brandt Group of Companies, 259
Branson, Richard, 320
The Brick, 241
Brock Placement Group Inc., 206
BT Group PLC, 242
Burdett, Kevin, 104
Burke, Ron, 301
Business Ethics, 339, 344
Business Objects, 204

C

Cadbury Trebor Allan, 84
Caliper Corp., 197
callcenterjob.ca, 206

Canada Business, 31
Canada Cement LaFarge, 72
Canada Controllers Inc., 382, 383, 385, 386, 387
Canada IT, 134
canada411.ca, 134
Canadian Centre for Stress and Well-Being, 239
Canadian Computers, 134
Canadian Directory of Industrial Distributors, 134
Canadian Grocer, 134
Canadian House & Home, 165
The Canadian Key Business Directory, 134
Canadian Plastics Magazine, 134
Canadian Professional Sales Association, 18, 197, 207, 234, 236, 244, 259, 272, 350, 351
Canadian Trade Index, 134
Canadian Underwriter, 134
Carlson Marketing Group, 273
Carnegie, Dale, 158
Carruthers, Court, 319
Carson, Bill, 81
Cascioli, Teresa, 308, 311
Center for Exhibition Industry Research, 135
Century 21, 244
Channel Partners, 32
Chapman, Zoe, 339
Chapters.indigo.ca, 308
Charney, Cy, 238
Charney & Associates, 238
Charon Systems Inc., 135
Chinook Group Ltd., 352
Cisco, 281
Clark, Al, 264
Clark, Tyrone M., 339
Clemmer, Jim, 344
Clemmer Group, 344
CMC Electronics, 348
Coca-Cola, 92
Colgate-Palmolive Company, 107, 108
Competition Tribunal, 352, 354
Computing Canada, 126
ConAgra Foods, 299, 323, 324
Conference Board of Canada, 16
Conros Corp., 352
Consilient Technologies, 11
Consumer Measures Committee, 355
ConsumerAffairs.com, 339
Cooper, Donald, 318
Cooper, Robert G., 10
Cormier, Jean, 72

Corporate Express Canada Inc., 27
Cosburn, Russell, 352
Cowan, Rory, 5
Cozyn, Martin, 257
Creo Inc., 119–120

D

DDI International, 196
Deck, Michael, 341
Dell Computer Corporation, 31, 171, 199, 207
Department of Justice, 344
Direct Sellers Association of Canada, 353
dnb.ca, 134
Document Sciences, 76
Domanski, Jim, 78, 80
Dow Chemical, 217

E

Eaton Cutler-Hammer, 299
Eddie Bauer, 10
Edward Jones, 202
Ekman, Paul, 350
Elizabeth Arden, 84
Elkay Canada, 81
Elwood, Mark, 238
Enron, 344
Equifax Canada, 216
Equifax Inc., 216
Equisure Financial Network Inc., 169
Ethidex Inc., 341
European Commission, 217
Export Development Canada, 355
Exporters Canada, 107

F

Fame Jeans, 337
Federal Express, 242, 280
Federal Trade Commission, 344
FirstWave Technologies, 395
Fisher, Brenda, 149
Food Network, 165
Forbes, 253
Ford, 10
Ford Motor Company of Canada, 87
Fortune, 24, 228, 280, 402
Franklin, Barbara Hackman, 217
Franklin Templeton Investments, 242
Fraser's Canadian Trade Directory, 134
Frito-Lay Canada, 324
Fulton, Mark, 319
Fung, David, 135
Future Shop, 241

G

Gallant, Paul, 273
The Gallup Organization, 202
Gates, Bill, 299
General Foods, 75
General Mills Canada, 204, 207
Girard, Joe, 133
GlaxoSmithKline, 37
The Globe and Mail, 273
The Globe and Mail's Report on Business, 70
Go Daddy Software, 342
Gold, Christina, 16
Goldmine, 391
Good Life Fitness Clubs, 354
Goodwin, Bill, 170
Google Inc., 24, 25, 134, 308
Grand & Toy, 8
Grantham, Kevin, 16
Green, Susan, 149, 150
Greenberg, Herbert, 197
Groh, Kevin, 337
Gschwandtner, Lisa, 6
Gunter, Tom, 323, 324

H

Hammer and Champy, 155
Hanson, Linda, 14
Harper, Stephen, 350
Harry Rosen Inc., 171
Hayes, Russell, 348
Here's Looking at You, 344
Herrman, Gerlinde, 215
Hewlett-Packard, 75, 87, 307
HGTV, 165
Holloway, Ed, 225
Home To Go, 165
HR Chally Group, 208, 212
Human Resources Professionals Association of Ontario, 215
Hurd, Mark, 307
Husky Injection Molding Systems Ltd., 238
Hutchinson, George, 169

I

IBM Software Group, 75, 76, 87, 135, 207
IBM Storage, 85
IDC Canada, 70
Industry Canada, 351
Institute for Ethical Business Worldwide, 340
Intrawest Corporation, 383
Intrinsyc Software Inc., 237

J

Janssen-Ortho Inc., 149
J.D. Power & Associates, 8
Jeffery, Brian, 232

Jeffery, Scott, 274, 275
Jenkins, Glynne, 209
Jennings, Mark, 280
jobWings, 206
Johnson, Kevin, 320
Johnson & Johnson, 217

K

Kahle, Dave, 154, 247
Keane, Patrick, 25
Kelly, Majorie, 340, 344
Kirby Company, 339
Kitchen Equipped, 165
Kmart, 352
KMC Telecom, 395
Kofax, 76
Kohn, Archie, 257
Kowlaczyn, Tara, 96
KPMG Canada, 341, 343
Kraft Canada, 103

L

Laird, Michael, 93
Lakeport Beverage Corporation, 308
LeapJob, 380
Leedy, Bonnie, 342
Leo, Elisa, 15
Leon's, 241
LePage's Inc., 352
Lionbridge Technologies, 4–5
LLH Enterprises, 14
Loyola University, 338

M

Magna International Inc., 345
Manning, Ted, 19
Maritz Canada, 86–87, 253
Maritz Inc., 253, 257
Marketing Magazine, 253
Marmon/Keystones Canada Inc., 16
Marshall, Susan, 342–343
Marsulex, 234
Massachusetts Securities Division, 339
MasterCard, 92
Maxim Transportation Services, 225, 226
Mayer, Marissa, 24
Mazzotta, Sam, 240
McCain Foods Canada, 84, 104
McCarthy, John, 85
McDermott, Bill, 307
McDonald's, 103–104
McGarry, Diane, 16
McGarry, Rachel, 165
MCI Canada, 240
McInnis, Patricia, 126
McMaster University, 10
Memorial University of Newfoundland, 149
Merck Frosst Canada, 319
Michael Stern Associates, 204
Microsoft, 87, 135, 207, 244, 321
Miller, Arthur, 340

Miller, Jeremy, 380
Minacs Worldwide, 79, 80
Molson Canada, 324
Morgan, Sharon Drew, 350
Morrissey, Patrick, 119
Mulcahy, Anne M., 16
Multz, Jeff, 395
Murphy, Joe, 149, 150
Murphy, Patrick, 340

N

Nabisco, 227
The National Post, 273
Natural Resources Canada, 236
NCR, 307
Neeson, Liam, 340
Newsweek, 340
Niagara Windpower Inc., 19
Nortel, 87
Nortel Networks, 257, 344, 348
Nortel Semiconductors, 122–123
Novartis AG, 37

O

Ocean Spray Cranberries, 94, 96
OCR Ltd., 92, 93
Ogilvie, David, 126
Orthovita, 10

P

Pampered Chef, 31
Paquette, Joanne, 355
Patel, Roopesh, 37
Pattison, Jim, 149, 150
PepsiCo, 84
Peszat, Lucille, 239
Pettes, Alex, 211
Pfizer, 36, 37, 207
Pfizer Canada, 237
Polaroid Canada, 135
Polk City Directory, 134
Porter, Michael, 28
Proctor & Gamble, 30, 84, 92, 103, 207
Proctor & Gamble Canada, 204
Propp, Jeff, 204
Pulp & Paper Canada, 134
Pulvermedia, 32
PureEdge Solutions, 76

Q

Queen's University, 345
Quick & Reilly, 172

R

Ralston Purina, 217
Red Carpet Vending & Refreshment Services, 77, 234
Reese, Sean, 96
Reid, David, 339
retailjob.ca, 206
Richardson, 319
Richardson, Linda, 319

Ridler, Jim, 345
R.J. Reynolds, 217
Rody, Phil, 342, 349
Rogers Cable 10, 165
Rosen, Al, 239, 342
Rosen, Larry, 171
Royal Bank of Canada, 238

S

Saab, 244
Sales & Marketing Management, 106, 205, 207, 245, 290
SalesForce Training & Consulting, 232
salesrep.ca, 206
Sandberg, Sheryl, 24, 25
SAP America, 307
Sauvageau, Christian, 319
Schwartz, Steven J., 133
Scotiabank, 87
Scott Paper, 324
Scott's Directories, 134
Sears, 241
Sears Canada, 354
Selling Power, 6, 70
Sellutions Inc., 206
Semple, Gavin, 259
Seneca College, 165
Sennett, Richard, 340
Shannon, Paula, 4, 5
Siebel Systems, 300
Sierra Wireless, 136, 395
Sinclaire, Laara, 383
Siskand, Barry, 134, 135
SJS Productions, 133
Skin Health, 3M Medical, 319
Smithsonian Institute, 344
Snowden, Anne, 344
Sobczak, Art, 235
Sobeys, 105–106
Society for Business Ethics, 338
St. Francis Xavier University, 194, 195
State Farm, 264
Statistics Canada, 106
Stein, Steven J., 214
Stern, Michael, 204
Stevens, Jeff, 81
The Stevens Company Limited, 81
Stewart, Rob, 71
Stotz, Rodger, 257
Strategic Technologies Inc., 30
Sutcliffe, David, 136, 395
Suzy Shier Ltd., 354
Swarm Enterprises, 31

T

TalkSwitch, 31, 32
Target Training International, 232
Taylor, Mark, 242
Tele-Direct, 354
Teleconcepts Consulting, 78, 80
Tenaquip Industrial Equipment and Supplies, 31, 131, 132
Texas Instruments, 339

TFI Food Equipment Sales, 211
3M, 170, 352
3M Storage Systems Business, 85
Tilley Endurables, 353
Tomikawa, Kenji, 237
Toyota, 103
Toyota Canada, 237
Tracy, Brian, 330, 331
Training, 226
TT&T Marketing, 19
Tupperware Canada, 31
2 Great Gals, 165

U

University of Waterloo, 257, 274
University of Western Ontario, 342
Upson, Mark, 76
Urichuck, Bob, 28
Urquhart, Mike, 238

V

VARBusiness, 32
Vasella, Daniel, 37
Virgin, 320

W

W Network, 165
Wabi Iron and Steel Corp., 235
Wal-Mart, 84, 92
Wal-Mart Canada, 337, 344
Wallace, Phil, 87
Weber, Mike, 172
Welch, Tim, 32
West, Marlene, 204
Westinghouse Electric, 217
Whirlpool Corporation, 240, 241
White Radio, 32
Willingham, Ron, 349
Windsor Factory Supply (WFS), 291, 295
Women's Wear Daily, 134
World Incentives Inc., 274
WorldCom Canada, 240

X

Xerox, 135, 150, 207, 240
Xerox Canada, 30, 31, 70, 149, 240
Xerox Corporation, 9, 16, 70, 71
Xerox Office Group, 71

Y

Yellow Pages, 134, 354
York University, 239, 301, 342
Young Electric Sign Company, 172

Z

ZedIT Solutions, 85
Zunin, Leonard, 160

Subject Index

Note: Key terms and their page references appear in boldface. The letter *f* denotes an exhibit.

A

A-B-C account classification method, 138–139
account analysis, 138
account classification, 138–139, 138*f*
account development activity, 394–395
account development ratios, 396–398
account maintenance selling, 281
account penetration ratio, 396
account relationship strategy, 120–121
  consultative relationships, 122
  enterprise relationships, 122–123
  partnering relationships, 122–123
  transactional relationships, 121–122
  types of, 120–123, 121*f*
account relationships
  buyer-seller relationship evolution, 129–133, 130*f*
  buying centre, 124–125
  buying decision, 124–125
  buying-decision process, 125–129
  customer's buying task, 123–124
  emphasis on, 166
  helping customers buy, 123–129
  management of, 120, 120*f*
  management of portfolio of accounts, 136–142
  prospecting for new accounts, 133–135
  qualifying the prospect, 135
  technology purchases, 126
  trust, 131–133
  types of strategies. *See* account relationship strategy
  value creation, 133
account share ratio, 398
achievement need, 311
activity-based quotas, 269
activity/productivity ratios, 398
advertisement
  building awareness, 31
  misleading, 354
  recruitment, 205
advocate, 125
affiliation need, 311
agreeableness, 310
Agreement on Internal Trade, 355

alcohol abuse, 328
alternative evaluation, 128
ancillary (non-selling) activities, 391
appeals, 167
applicant interview form, 210*f*
application forms, 208–209
the approach, 160–161
aptitude tests, 212–213
attitude, 228
audiotapes, 244
autonomy, 259
avatar, 242
average order size ratio, 396
awards, 272–273

B

background checks
  credit checks, 216
  drug testing, 216–218
  educational background embellishment, 215
  negligent hiring, 216
  negligent retention, 216
  physical examinations, 216–218
  reasons for, 215
  references, 215–216
bait-and-switch selling, 354
bid rigging, 352
blind ad, 205
bonuses, 286
  advantages, 287
  described, 286–287
  limitations, 287
  short-term objectives, 287
  where used, 287
break-even sales volume per sales call, 136
breakdown sales approach, 33–34
bribes, 345
business defamation, 345–346
business ethics. *See* ethics
business libel, 346
business slander, 346
business strategies
  distribution strategy, 30–31
  marketing strategy, 28–31
  Porter's generic business strategies, 29*f*
  price strategy, 30
  product strategy, 30, 155

  promotion strategy, 31
  pull strategy, 31
  push strategy, 31
  sales force budgeting, 39–40
  sales force investment, 33–35
business strategy planning
  market planning process, 26*f*
  mission statement, 25–28
  strategic business unit, 25–27
buyer remorse, 170
buyer-seller relationship evolution
  commitment stage, 131
  expansion stage, 130–131
  exploration stage, 130
  stages in, 130*f*
buying centre, 124
  advocate, 125
  economic buyer, 125
  gatekeeper, 125
  technical buyer, 124
  user buyer, 124
buying conditions, 162
buying-decision process, 125
  alternative evaluation, 128
  cognitive dissonance, 129
  general model, 127*f*
  information search, 127–128
  need recognition, 126–127
  post-purchase evaluation, 129
  purchase decision, 128–129
buying power index, 106
buying task
  modified rebuy, 123–124
  new task buy, 123
  straight rebuy, 124

C

California Psychological Inventory, 213
career paths in sales management, 16–18
career stage, 261–262
  described, 261–262, 262*f*
  disengagement, 265
  establishment, 264
  exploration, 262
  implications for sales managers, 263*f*
  maintenance, 264–265
carryover effects, 38

cases
  Aries Corporate Coffee Services, 305–306
  B.C. Business Equipment Sales, 251–252
  Bill Siddall's Sales Call Reports, 335–336
  Bridgehead Cutting Tools, 176
  Canadian Electrical Controller Corp., 359–360
  Centre for the Arts, 117–118
  Eastern Canada Pulp & Paper, 146–147
  Electronics and More, 44–45
  The First Challenge, 334–335
  General Electric Appliances, 361–372
  Haines & Associates, 176–177
  Hal Maybee's Ethical Dilemmas, 372–376
  Hi-T Mill Supply Inc., 183–191
  Import Food Sales, 408–409
  Leisure Lady Lingerie, 147–148
  Maritime Bank, 46–55
  Performance Auto Sales, 278
  Power & Motion Industrial Supply, 414–417
  Prairie Ag Products, 306
  Robert Mendes, 278–279
  Royal Corporation, 56–66
  Scotia Electric Sales and Service, 22
  Shoes for Moos, 43–44
  Stavanger Safety Equipment, 410–413
  Tandy Safety Clothing, 91
  TFI Food Equipment Solutions, 178–180
  Tortran Digital, 23
  Trecourt Valve and Fittings, 90–91
  Trends, 117
  Trouble at TPG Power Source, 358–359
  Upper Canada Clothing, 409
CDs, 244
centralized training, 240
CEO as role model, 341
change management, 313–315
change vision, 314–315
changing environment of sales management
  changes in selling and sales management, 10–12
  competitors, 10
  customers, 8–9
  important changes, 9f
character, **340**
classroom instruction, 243
closed question, **162**
closing, 170–171
cluster of satisfactions, 164, 164f
co-branding, **10**

co-op students, 204
coaching, **15**, **317–320**
codes of ethics, 344
coercive power, 312
cognitive ability tests, 212
cognitive dissonance, **129**, 170
cognitive intelligence, 310
cold calling, **133**
collaborative demand planning, 108
colleges, 206
combination compensation plans, **287**
  advantages, 288
  described, 287
  limitations, 288
  where used, 288
commitment stage, **131**
company ethics policies and practices
  bribes, 345
  business defamation, 345–346
  codes of ethics, 344
  employment practices, 348–349
  entertainment, 345
  gifts, 344
  hiring, 348–349
  house accounts, 347
  management of customer information, 346
  order timing, 348
  performance-based compensation and incentive plans, 346–347
  promoting, 348–349
  reciprocity, 344
  termination, 348–349
  territory adjustments, 347
  whistle-blowing, 347–348
company knowledge, 237–238
company records, 229–231
company training specialists, 241
company websites, 207
compensation issues
  customer satisfaction, 299–300
  global considerations, 302
  pay equity, 300–301
  team incentive compensation, 301
compensation plans, **281**
  advantages, 282–283
  appropriate mix, 296–297
  bonuses, 286–287
  changes, 297–298
  combination compensation plans, 287–288
  comparison of various methods, 289f
  compensation/performance model, 294f
  design of, 281
  employee benefits, 291, 292f, 293f
  evaluation, 297–298
  high compensation, 294–296
  importance of, 281

  limitations, 283
  limited repayment plans, 290
  low compensation, 293–294
  per diem payment plans, 291
  performance-based compensation, increasing, 298f
  performance-based compensation and ethics, 346–347
  putting the plan together, 293–297
  redirecting behaviour, 299
  selling expense reimbursement plans, 290–291
  straight commission plan, 284–286
  straight salary plan, 282–283
  summary, 288
  total target compensation (TTC), 281
  unlimited reimbursement plans, 290
  when used, 283
competencies, **12**
  effective sales managers, 12f
  leading and coaching competency, 13–15
  managing diversity competency, 16
  strategic planning and implementation, 12–13
  technology competency, 15–16
Competition Act, **350**
  bait-and-switch selling, 354
  bid rigging, 352
  described, 351–352
  exclusive dealing, 353
  market restriction, 353
  misleading advertising, 354
  predatory pricing, 352
  price discrimination, 352
  price fixing, 352
  pyramid selling, 353
  referral selling, 354
  refusal to deal, 354
  resale price maintenance, 352–353
  tied selling, 354
competitive knowledge, 236–237
competitor alliances, 10
competitors
  changes, 10
  competitor alliances, 10
  globalization of competition, 10
  product and service life cycles, 10
  as source of recruitment, 207
comprehensive cases. *See* cases
concentrated targeting, **28**
concerns, 167–169
confirmation question, **162**
confirmation step, **170**
conflicts of interest, 327–328
connection power, 313
conscientiousness, 310
consultative relationships, **122**
consultative selling approach, **150**

The Consumer Protection Act, 354
contact management software, 391
contribution (loss) projection, 40*f*
contribution margin, 399
cooling off laws, 355
corporate goals and objectives. *See* goals; objectives
Corruption of Foreign Public Officials Act, 355
cost per call ratio, 399
costs, 82*f*
CPSA Sales Institute Code of Ethics, 351*f*
credit checks, 216
cross-functional selling teams, 85, 86*f*
cross-selling, 171–172
customer benefit approach, 161
customer knowledge, 237
customer relationship management (CRM), 15
customer strategy, 155
customers
    buying centre, 124–125
    buying decision, 124–125
    buying-decision process, 125–129
    buying task, 123–124
    customer power, 9
    decreasing supplier bases, 8
    dissatisfied customers, 172–173
    focus on value, 9
    gaining customer knowledge, 158
    helping customers buy, 123–129
    improved relationships, and sales training, 227
    management of customer information, 346
    as output measure, 394–395
    rising customer expectations, 8
    satisfaction, and sales force compensation, 299–300
    selling approaches, 150–151
    shifts in customer marketplace, 8–9
    as source of recruitment, 207

D

decentralized training, 240
decision models, 140–141
decomposition method, 101–102, 101*f*
delegating style, 317
delivery, 236
Delphi method, 103
demonstrations, 167
differentiated targeting, 28
The Direct Sellers Act, 354
direct selling expenses, 136
direction, 254
directories, 134
disengagement stage, 265
disruptive salesperson, 330

dissatisfied customers, 172–173
distribution strategy, 30–31
diversification selling, 281
diversity, 16
dominance, 309
downsizing the sales force, 36–38
downsizing trend, 18
drug dependency, 328
drug testing, 216–218
dual distribution, 32

E

economic buyer, 125
educational seminars, 134–135
Edwards Personal Preference Schedule (EPPS), 213
effective sales presentations. *See* sales presentations
efficient consumer response (ECR), 15
effort, 255–256
electronic data interchange (EDI), 15
emotional intelligence, 214, 310
emotional link, 167
employee benefits, 291, 292*f*, 293*f*
employee referral programs, 204
employment practices, 348–349
enterprise relationships, 122–123
entertainment, 345
entry-level jobs, 209*f*
erosion of character, 340
establishment stage, 264
estimate of potential. *See* potential
ethical standards, 350
ethics, 338
    bribes, 345
    business defamation, 345–346
    and business relationships, 338
    CEO as role model, 341
    codes of ethics, 344
    company policies and practices, 343–349
    employment practices, 348–349
    entertainment, 345
    erosion of character, 340
    gifts, 344
    hiring, 348–349
    house accounts, 347
    importance of ethical behaviour, 338
    influencing factors, 340–350, 341*f*
    making ethical decisions, 343
    management of customer information, 346
    order timing, 348
    performance-based compensation and incentive plans, 346–347
    personal code of ethics, 349–350
    promoting, 348–349

reciprocity, 344
    sales manager as role model, 342
    in selling, 339
    termination, 348–349
    territory adjustments, 347
    values and behaviours of peers, 342–343
    whistle-blowing, 347–348
evaluation, 382
    changes in evaluation, 11–12
    expense analysis, 387–388
    importance of evaluation, 389*f*
    input measures, 388, 389–392
    objective measures, 388, 400
    output measures, 388, 392–395
    performance matrix, 403–406, 404*f*
    ratios, 396–399
    sales analysis, 382–386
    of salespeople, 388–403
    subjective measures, 388, 400–402
    360-degree feedback, 402–403
evaluative criteria, 128
exclusive dealing, 353
executive opinions methods, 102–103
expansion selling, 171–172
expansion stage, 130–131
expatriate salespeople, 302
expectancy, 254, 255–256
expense account padding, 290
expense analysis, 387–388
expert power, 312
exploration, 262
exploration stage, 130
exponential smoothing method, 98, 99*f*
external search, 127
external sources of recruitment
    colleges, 206
    company websites, 207
    competitors, 207
    customers, 207
    described, 205
    online sources, 207
    print advertisements, 205
    private employment agencies, 205–206
    professional associations, 206–207
    suppliers, 207
    trade associations, 206–207
    universities, 206
external trainers, 241–243
extroversion, 310

F

face-to-face interaction phase
    the approach, 160–161
    closing, 170–171
    described, 159–160
    effective sales presentations, 161–167

negotiating buyer concerns, 167–169

family decision-making unit (DMU), 124

federal and provincial laws
Competition Act, 350–354
cooling off laws, 355
global selling, 355
legal standards, 350
provincial *Consumer Protection Acts*, 354–355

feedback, 259–260, 322
field sales managers, 242
figurative language, 167
firing. *See* termination
first-line managers, 17
flexibility, 310
focusing behaviour, 299
forecast methods
buying power index, 106
choice of appropriate method, 111
comparison of methods, 112*f*
decomposition method, 101–102, 101*f*
Delphi method, 103
executive opinions methods, 102–103
exponential smoothing method, 98, 99*f*
familiarity with methods, 108–110, 109*f*
jury of executive opinion method, 102
leading indicators, 102
moving averages method, 97–98
multiple regression model, 100
naïve forecast method, 97
sales force composite method, 104
single regression model, 100
survey of buyer intentions method, 103
test market method, 103–104
time-series regression, 100, 100*f*
trend projection method, 99
use of methods, 108–110, 110*f*

forecasting sales. *See* sales forecasts
four factor model, 399–400
framing, **128**
full-line selling, **171**
functional specialization, **76**–77, 77*f*
future sales performance
executive opinions methods, 102–103
leading indicators, 102
sales force composite method, 104
survey of buyer intentions method, 103
test market method, 103–104

G

gatekeeper, **125**
gathering feedback meetings, 322
general model of sales motivation, 254–258, 255*f*
general survey question, **162**
geographic specialization, **72**, 73*f*
gifts, 344
global selling
and Canadian law, 355
global account programs. *See* strategic account programs
global compensation considerations, 302
globalization of competition, 10
goals, **27**
and business strategies, 28
and mission statement, 27–28
of recruitment, 203
good quota plans, 266–267
group interviews, 211

H

halo effect, **400**
harassment, **329**–330
high compensation, 294–296
high energy, 309
high-performance, cohesive sales force, 320–321
horizontal market restriction, 353
house accounts, 347

I

implementation, 12–13
incremental approach, **35**
incremental selection decision model, 219*f*
independent sales agents, **80**
advantages of, 81
choosing, 83
costs of, 82*f*
management of, 83
when to use independent sales agents, 81–82

individual-related motivation factors, 260–265
industry knowledge, 237
inflation of job titles, 18
informal interviews, 211
information-gathering question, 162
information power, 312–313
information search, **127**–128
informative ad, 205
informative presentation, **166**
input measures, **388**
ancillary (non-selling) activities, 391
described, 389–390
input bases, 390*f*
sales calls, 390–391
selling expenses, 391

time utilization, 390–391
instrumentality, **254**, 256–257
integrated marketing communications, **31**
integrity, 310, **340**
intelligence tests, 212, 310
intensity, 254
internal search, 127
internal sources of recruitment
co-op students or interns, 204
employee referral programs, 204
promotion from within, 203–204
internal trainers, 241–243
internalizers, 310
interns, 204
interpersonal bias, **401**

J

job analysis, **198**
described, 198
job description, 198–199, 200*f*
job qualifications, 199–202
valid predictors, 202–203
job description, **198**–199, 200*f*
job qualifications, **199**–202
job-related motivation factors
autonomy, 259
feedback, 259–260
job value, 258
opportunity, 259
skill variety, 259
job value, 258
jury of executive opinion method, **102**
justifiability, 274

K

key account programs. *See* strategic account programs

L

the law. *See* federal and provincial laws
leadership, **308**
advice for, 324
change, 313–315
coaching, 317–320
delegating style, 317
high-performance, cohesive sales force, 320–321
of individual salespeople, 315–320
leading the sales force, 320–323
vs. management, 308
needs, 311–312

partnering style, 317
personal traits, 309–310
personality, 310–311
personnel issues, 323–332
persuading style, 317, 318
and power, 311, 312–313
relationship-focused, 316
sales force culture, 320
sales meetings, 321–323
situational leadership, 315–317, 316*f*
task-focused, 316
telling style, 316
leading and coaching competency, 13–15
leading indicators, 102
legislation. *See* federal and provincial laws
legitimate power, 312
leverage selling, 281
limited repayment plans, 290
locus of control, 310
lost account ratio, 398
low compensation, 293–294

M

maintenance contracts, 236
maintenance stage, 264–265
major account programs. *See* strategic account programs
management
    see also sales management
    account relationships, 120, 120*f*
    CEO as role model, 341
    change management, 313–315
    customer information, 346
    independent sales agents, 83
    vs. leadership, 308
    portfolio of accounts, 136–142
    of quota plans, 269–270
    self-management, 227
    strategic account programs, 84–85
    strategic sales program, 8
    telemarketing, 78–80
    territory management, 238
    training needs assessment, objectives of, 228–229
manufacturer's agent. *See* independent sales agents
MAPE (mean absolute percentage error), 113–114
market forecast, 94
market orientation, 25
market potential, 94
market restriction, 353
market segmentation, 28
market segments, 28
market specialization, 74–75, 75*f*
marketing
    relationship with sales, 11

reverse marketing, 129
marketing mix, 28
marketing program, 28
marketing program development
    distribution strategy, 30–31
    price strategy, 30
    product strategy, 30
    promotion strategy, 31
marketing strategy, 28
    distribution strategy, 30–31
    market segmentation, 28–29
    marketing program development, 29–31
    micromarketing, 28
    positioning, 29
    price strategy, 30
    product strategy, 30
    promotion strategy, 31
    target marketing, 28–29
mass marketing, 28
McClelland's Theory of Learned Needs, 311
mean validities for entry-level jobs, 209*f*
metaphors, 167
micromarketing, 28
middle managers, 17–18
minor point close, 170
misleading advertising, 354
mission statement, 25
    Corporate Express Canada, Inc., sample, 27*f*
    and corporate goals and objectives, 27–28
    importance of, 27
modified rebuy, 123–124
morale, 228
motivation, 254
    autonomy, 259
    "B" team, 257
    career stage, 261–265
    common needs of salespeople, 261*f*
    expectancy, 254, 255–256
    feedback, 259–260
    general model of sales motivation, 254–258, 255*f*
    individual motives, 260–261
    individual-related factors, 260–265
    instrumentality, 254, 256–257
    job-related factors, 258–260
    job value, 258
    motivation theories, 260*f*
    opportunity, 259
    quotas, 265–270
    recognition programs, 270–273
    remotivation suggestions, 325–326, 327*f*
    sales contests, 270–273
    skill variety, 259
    valence, 254, 257–258
motivation theories, 260*f*

motivational meetings, 321
moving averages method, 97–98
multiple regression model, 100
multiple-sourcing, 128
Myers-Briggs Type Indicator (MBTI), 213

N

naïve forecast method, 97
national account programs. *See* strategic account programs
need discovery, 161–164
need discovery worksheet, 163–164, 163*f*
need recognition, 127
need-related concerns, 168
need-satisfaction presentation, 165–166
need-satisfaction question, 162
negligent hiring, 216
negligent retention, 216
negotiating, 167–169
networking, 135
neuroticism, 310
new account conversion ratio, 398
new markets, 38
new product launches, 38
new task buy, 123
non-selling activities, 391

O

objections, 167
objective measures, 388
    account development ratios, 396–398
    activity/productivity ratios, 398
    ancillary (non-selling) activities, 391
    customers/accounts, 394–395
    four factor model, 399–400
    input measures, 389–392
    output measures, 392–395
    profitability/expense ratios, 399
    ratios, 396–399
    sales, orders, and profitability, 392–394
    sales calls, 390–391
    selling expenses, 391
    time utilization, 390–391
objectives, 28
    and business strategies, 28
    and mission statement, 27–28
    sales call objectives, 158–159
    sales training objectives, 232–234
    training needs assessment, 228–229
Occupational Personality Questionnaire, 213
on-the-job training, 245
online sources, 207
online training, 244
open question, 162
openness to experience, 310

opportunity, 259
order activity, 392–394
order cancellation ratio, 398
order timing, 348
orders per sales call ratio, 398
organizational hierarchies, 17*f*, 18
organizing the selling function. *See* sales force organization
outcome bias, 401
output measures, 388
  customers/accounts, 394–395
  described, 392
  output bases, 393*f*
  sales, orders, and profitability, 392–394

P

paper trail, 331
partnering relationships, 122–123
partnering style, 317
past sales performance
  decomposition method, 101–102, 101*f*
  exponential smoothing method, 98, 99*f*
  moving averages method, 97–98
  naïve forecast method, 97
  time-series regression, 100, 100*f*
  trend projection method, 99
pay equity, 300–301
peer values and behaviours, 342–343
penetration selling, 281
per diem payment plans, 291
percentage of sales approach, 34
performance
  see also sales performance
  coaching for performance improvement, 318
  compensation/performance model, 294*f*
  compensation plans, and ethics, 346–347
  and effort, 255–256
  expectancy, 255–256
  formula for, 254
  instrumentality, 256–257
  and reward, 256–257
performance data and specifications, 236
performance matrix, 403–406, 404*f*
performance testing, 231–232
perquisites, 292*f*, 293*f*
persistence, 254
personal code of ethics, 349–350
Personal Information Protection and Electronic Documents Act, 346
personal interviews, 209–211
personal selling, 5

changes in, 10–12
customer strategy, 155
organization of selling function. *See* sales force organization
prerequisites to success, 152–157
presentation strategy, 155–157
product strategy, 155
relationship strategy, 152–154
relationship with marketing, 11
selling process model. *See* selling process model
strategic-consultative selling model, 152–157, 153*f*
personal selling philosophy, 152, 154
personal traits, 309–310
personality, 310–311
personality profiles, 310–311
personality tests, 213
personalized power, 311
personnel issues
  alcohol abuse, 328
  conflicts of interest, 327–328
  drug dependency, 328
  harassment, 329–330
  plateauing, 323–326
  sexual harassment, 329–330
  termination, 331–332
  uncooperative or disruptive salesperson, 330
personnel needs, 196–197
persuading style, 317, 318
persuasive presentation, 166–167
pharmaceutical industry, 37
physical examinations, 216–218
planning for recruitment and selection, 196–203
planning the interaction, 158–159
plateauing, 323
  causes of, 323–325, 325*f*
  early warning signals, 326*f*
  remotivation suggestions, 325–326, 327*f*
portfolio models, 139, 140*f*
portfolio of accounts
  account analysis, 138
  account classification, 138*f*
  decision models, 140–141
  management of, 136–142
  portfolio models, 139, 140*f*
  sale process models, 141–142
  single-factor model, 138–139
  when account is too small, 136–138
positioning, 29, 30
post-purchase evaluation, 129
post-sale phase
  described, 171
  dissatisfied customers, 172–173
  expansion selling, 171–172
  servicing the sale, 171

potential
  see also sales forecasts
  importance of estimating, 93–95
  market potential, 94
  relationships among forecasts and estimate of potential, 95*f*
  sales potential, 94, 269
power, 312
  coercive power, 312
  connection power, 313
  expert power, 312
  information power, 312–313
  and leadership, 311, 312–313
  legitimate power, 312
  need for, 311
  personalized power, 311
  referent power, 312
  reward power, 312
  socialized power, 311
pre-contact phase
  described, 157–158
  gaining prospect or customer knowledge, 158
  planning the interaction, 158–159
  sales call objectives, 158–159
predatory pricing, 352
predictors, 202–203
presentation strategy, 155–157
price, 236
price discounting, 394*f*
price discrimination, 352
price fixing, 352
price-related concerns, 168–169
price strategy, 30
primary effect, 167
print advertisements, 205
private employment agencies, 205–206
prizes, 272–273
probing question, 162
product approach, 161
product development process, 235
product disparagement, 346
product knowledge, 235–236
product life cycles, 10
product-related concerns, 168
product selection, 164–165
product specialization, 73–74, 74*f*
product strategy, 30, 155
productivity, 39
professional associations, 206–207
profit-based quotas, 268–269
profit margin, 399
profitability, 392–394, 395
profitability/expense ratios, 399
promotion strategy, 31
promotions
  from within, 203–204
  and ethics, 348–349
prospecting, 133

cold calling, 133
directories, 134
educational seminars, 134–135
finding prospects, 133–135
gaining prospect knowledge, 158
good prospecting, 133
networking, 135
qualifying the prospect, 135
referrals, 134
trade publications, 134
trade shows, 134–135
websites, 134
provincial *Consumer Protection Acts*, 354–355
provincial laws. *See* federal and provincial laws
pull strategy, **31**
purchase decision, **128**–129
push strategy, **31**
pyramid selling, **353**

Q

qualifying the prospect, **135**
quality improvement process, 235
quasi-concerns, 169
quotas, **265**
activity-based quotas, 269
establishment of quota plans, 269–270
good quotas, 266–267
management of quota plans, 269–270
profit-based quotas, 268–269
reasons to use, 266
sales volume quotas, 267–268
types of quotas, 267–269

R

ratios
account development ratios, 396–398
account penetration ratio, 396
account share ratio, 398
activity/productivity ratios, 398
average order size ratio, 396
common ratios for evaluation, 396*f*
contribution margin, 399
cost per call ratio, 399
described, 396
lost account ratio, 398
new account conversion ratio, 398
order cancellation ratio, 398
orders per sales call ratio, 398
profit margin, 399
profitability/expense ratios, 399
sales expense ratio, 399
sales per account ratio, 396
sales per sales call ratio, 398

recency effect, 167
reciprocity, **344**
recognition and reward meetings, 321
recognition programs, **270**
duration of, 272*f*
evaluation, 275
planning, 271
prizes and awards, 272–273
promoting, 271–272
tangible incentives, 274–275
records management, 238
recruitment
co-op students or interns, 204
colleges, 206
company websites, 207
competitors, 207
customers, 207
employee referral programs, 204
and ethics, 348–349
external sources, 205–207
goal of, 203
internal sources, 203–205
online sources, 207
personnel needs, 196–197
print advertisements, 205
private employment agencies, 205–206
professional associations, 206–207
promotion from within, 203–204
suppliers, 207
trade associations, 206–207
universities, 206
recruitment and selection process
described, 195*f*
importance of, 195
incremental selection decision model, 219*f*
job analysis, 198–203
planning for recruitment and selection, 196–203
recruitment stage. *See* recruitment
role of sales manager, 196
sales force culture, 197–198
sales force turnover, 196–197
selection stage. *See* selection
validation of selection process, 218–220
reduced turnover, 227–228
references, 215–216
referent power, 312
referral approach, **161**
referral selling, **354**
referrals, **134**
refusal to deal, **354**
relationship-focused leadership, 316
relationship selling approach, **151**

relationship strategy, **152**
reminder presentation, **166**
remotivation suggestions, 325–326, 327*f*
resale price maintenance, **353**
restructuring trend, 18
résumés, 208–209
reverse marketing, **129**
reward, 256–257, 258
reward power, 312
RFID (radio frequency identification), 92–93
right-sizing the sales force
breakdown sales approach, 33–34
considerations, 33
incremental approach, 35
percentage of sales approach, 34
typical sales response and cost functions, 36*f*
workload approach, 34–35
role-playing, 243–244

S

sale process models, **141**–142
sales analysis, 382–386
sales budget, **39**
administering the sales budget, 40
contribution (loss) projection, 40*f*
planning the sales budget, 39
sales call objectives, 158–159
sales call response function, **140**, 141
sales calls, 390–391
sales contests, **270**
evaluation, 275
planning, 270–271
popular objectives, 271*f*
prizes and awards, 272–273
promoting, 271–272
tangible incentives, 274–275
sales crows, 294
sales cycle, 141
sales eagles, 294–295
sales expense ratio, **399**
sales force
see also salespeople
budgeting, 39–40
changes in structure, 11
compensation. *See* compensation issues; compensation plans
costs of, 82*f*
culture, 197–198
high-performance, cohesive sales force, 320–321
leadership of, 320–323
and market orientation, 25
observation of, 231–232
productivity, 39
recruitment. *See* recruitment
sales crows, 294

sales eagles, 294–295
sales liabilities, 295
selection. *See* selection
size decisions. *See* sales force
    investment
telemarketing, integration of, 78
turnover, 196–197
sales force automation (SFA), 15
sales force composite method, 104
sales force culture, 320
sales force investment
    additional factors, 35–39
    breakdown sales approach, 33–34
    downsizing the sales force, 36–38
    incremental approach, 35
    key decision, 33
    new markets, 38
    new product launches, 38
    percentage of sales approach, 34
    productivity, 39
    right-sizing the sales force, 33–35
    workload approach, 34–35
sales force organization
    complexity of, 85–87
    described, 71–72
    functional specialization, 76–77,
        77f
    geographic specialization, 72–73, 73f
    importance of sales force organization,
        71f
    independent sales agents, 80–83
    market specialization, 74–75, 75f
    product specialization, 73–74, 74f
    strategic account programs, 83–85
    telemarketing programs, 77–81
sales forecasts, 94
    additional topics, 104–114
    as basis of decisions, 94
    choice of appropriate method, 111
    collaborative demand planning, 108
    decomposition method, 101–102,
        101f
    early adjustment of forecasts,
        111–113
    executive opinions methods,
        102–103
    exponential smoothing method, 98,
        99f
    familiarity with methods, 108–110,
        109f
    future sales performance, 102–104
    importance of, 93–95
    information for forecasting purposes,
        107
    involvement in forecasting, 107
    leading indicators, 102
    MAPE (mean absolute percentage
        error), 113–114
    market forecast, 94
    moving averages method, 97–98
    naïve forecast method, 97

past sales performance, 97–102
preparation of, 96–104
relationships among forecasts and
    estimate of potential, 95f
review and evaluation, 113–114
sales force composite method, 104
survey of buyer intentions method,
    103
territory forecasts, 105–107
test market method, 103–104
time-series regression, 100, 100f
trend projection method, 99
trends, 111
types of, 93f
use of methods, 108–110, 110f
sales funnel, 142f
sales liabilities, 295
sales management, 5
    see also management
    activities, changes in, 11
    career paths, 16–18
    changes in, 10–12
    changing environment, 8–12
    and distribution strategy, 30–31
    leadership. *See* leadership
    management decisions, 14
    and price strategy, 30
    and product strategy, 30
    promotion strategy, 31
    reasons for considering, 18–20
sales management process, 6–8, 7f
sales managers
    competencies, 12–16
    described, 18
    field sales managers, 242
    first-line managers, 17
    influence of, 5
    middle managers, 17–18
    recruitment and selection, role in,
        196
    as role models, 342
    role of, 14
    training, 246–248
sales meetings, 321–323
sales organizational hierarchy, 17f
sales per account ratio, 396
sales per sales call ratio, 398
sales performance
    account development ratios,
        396–398
    activity/productivity ratios, 398
    changes in evaluation, 11–12
    evaluation of, 8
    four factor model, 399–400
    future sales performance, 102–104
    importance of evaluation, 389f
    improved, and sales training, 227
    input measures, 388, 389–392
    objective measures, 388, 400
    output measures, 388, 392–395
    past sales performance, 97–102

people, process, and passion, 380
performance matrix, 403–406, 404f
profitability/expense ratios, 399
ratios, 396–399
review of, 8
salespeople, evaluation of, 388–403
subjective measures, 388, 400–402
360-degree feedback, 402–403
sales performance evaluation model,
    382–388
sales performance evaluation process,
    381–382, 381f
sales potential, 94, 269
sales presentations
    confirmation question, 162
    effective sales presentations,
        161–167
    information-gathering question,
        162
    informative presentation, 165–166
    need discovery, 161–164
    need-satisfaction presentation,
        165–166
    need-satisfaction question, 162
    persuasive presentation, 166, 167
    probing question, 162
    product selection, 164–165
    reminder presentation, 166
    survey questions, 162
sales process knowledge, 236
sales strategy model, 282f
sales territory, 238
sales training
    behavioural changes, 246
    customer relationships, 227
    importance of, 225–228
    meetings, 321
    morale, 228
    organizational objectives, 246
    outcomes, 226f
    participant learning, 246
    participant reactions, 246
    reduced turnover, 227–228
    for the sales manager, 246–248
    sales performance, 227
    self-management, 227
    selling skills, 227
sales training budget, 234
sales training process
    evaluation of sales training,
        245–246
    framework, 229f
    Kirkpatricks' four-stage model of
        evaluation, 246
    objectives, 232–234
    sales training budget, 234
    sales training program development,
        234–245
    steps in, 228
    training needs assessment, 228–232
sales training program

CDs and audiotapes, 244
centralized training, 240
classroom instruction, 243
common training topics, 235f
company knowledge, 237–238
company training specialists, 241
competitive knowledge, 236–237
customer knowledge, 237
decentralized training, 240
development of, 234–245
external trainers, 241–243
field sales managers, 242
how to train, 243–245
industry knowledge, 237
internal trainers, 241–243
on-the-job training, 245
online training, 244
other topics, 239
product knowledge, 235–236
role-playing, 243–244
sales process knowledge, 236
self-management, 238–239
webcasting, 244
what to train, 235–239
when to train, 239–240
where to train, 240–243
whom to train, 234–235
sales volume, 392–394
sales volume quotas, 268
salespeople
see also sales force
building trust, 131–133
character, 131
common needs of salespeople, 261f
competence, 131
customer orientation, 131
dependability, 131
disruptive salesperson, 330
expatriate salespeople, 302
likeability, 132
personnel issues. *See* personnel issues
training. *See* sales training
uncooperative salesperson, 330
satisfactions, 164
screening interviews, 209
selection
application forms, 208–209
background checks, 215–218
described, 208
and ethics, 348–349
incremental selection decision model, 219f
personal interviews, 209–211
résumés, 208–209
screening interviews, 209
subsequent interviews, 211
tests, 211–215

validation of selection process, 218–220
selection criteria, 202, 218–219
self-confidence, 309
self-management, 227, 238–239
selling. *See* personal selling
selling approaches
consultative selling approach, 150
relationship selling approach, 151
transactional selling approach, 150
selling expenses, 290
expense account padding, 290
limited repayment plans, 290
per diem payment plans, 291
and sales performance evaluation, 391
unlimited reimbursement plans, 290
selling process
changes in, 11
selling process model
described, 157f
face-to-face interaction phase, 159–171
phases of, 157
post-sale phase, 171–173
pre-contact phase, 157–159
selling seminars, 134–135
selling skills, 227
selling teams, 85
sensitivity to others, 310
service contracts, 236
service life cycles, 10
servicing the sale, 171
sexual harassment, 329–330
single-factor model, 138–139
single regression model, 100
situational leadership, 315–317, 316f
16 Personality Factors, 213
skill variety, 259
smoking, 217
social adjustment, 310
social reinforcement, 274
socialized power, 311
sole-sourcing, 128
source-related concerns, 168
specific survey question, 162
stability, 310
stall technique, 169
straight commission plan, 284
advantages, 284
described, 284
limitations, 284–285
vs. straight salary plan, 285f

when used, 286
straight rebuy, 124
straight salary plan, 282
advantages, 282–283
described, 282
limitations, 283
vs. straight commission plan, 285f
where used, 283
strategic account programs, 83
creation of separate sales force, 85
cross-functional selling teams, 85, 86f
existing sales force, use of, 84–85
management of, 84–85
selection of accounts, 84
use of, 84
strategic business unit, 25–27
strategic-consultative selling model
customer strategy, 155
five strategic steps in, 156f
personal selling philosophy, 152, 154
presentation strategy, 155–157
product strategy, 155
relationship strategy, 152–154
strategic planning and implementation, 12–13
strategic sales program
development, 7
implementation, 8
management of, 8
strategies, 28
account relationships strategies, 120–123
business strategies. *See* business strategies
customer strategy, 155
personal selling strategies, 152–157, 153f
presentation strategy, 155–157
relationship strategy, 152–154
sales strategy model, 282f
strategy planning meetings, 321
stress management, 239
Strong Interest Inventory, 212
subjective measures, 388, 400–402
subsequent interviews, 211
summary confirmation question, 162
suppliers
decreasing supplier bases, 8
as source of recruitment, 207
survey of buyer intentions method, 103
survey question, 162

T
tangible incentives, 274–275
target marketing, 28
concentrated targeting, 28

differentiated targeting, 28
undifferentiated targeting, 28
task-focused leadership, 316
team incentive compensation, 301
technical buyers, **124**
technology competency, 15–16
technology purchase decisions, 126
telemarketing, **77**
current telemarketing activities, 79*f*
future of telemarketing, 80
integration with sales force, 78
management of, 78–80
motivation challenges, 79–80
staffing challenges, 79
Telephone Consumer Protection Act,
77–78
training challenges, 80
when to use telemarketing, 78
Telephone Consumer Protection Act,
77–78
telling style, 316
termination, 331–332, 348–349
territory adjustments, 347
territory forecasts, 105–107
territory management, 238
test market method, **103**–104
testimonials, 167
tests
aptitude tests, 212–213
cognitive ability tests, 212

concerns about use of, 213–215
intelligence tests, 212
personality tests, 213
as selection tool, 211
Theory of Learned Needs, 311
360-degree feedback, **402**–403
tied selling, **354**
time management, 238
time-related concerns, 169
time-series regression, **100**, 100*f*
time utilization, 390–391
total target compensation (TTC),
281
trade associations, 206–207
trade publications, 134
trade shows, 134–135
training. *See* sales training
training needs assessment, **228**
company records, 229–231
management objectives, 228–229
performance testing, 231–232
quick assessment tool, 233*f*
sales force observation, 231–232
transactional relationships, **121**–**122**
transactional selling approach, **150**
trend projection method, **99**
trial close, **170**
trust, 131–133
turnover, 227–228
turnover rate, **197**

U
uncooperative salesperson, 330
undifferentiated targeting, **28**
universities, 206
unlimited reimbursement plans, 290
up-selling, **172**
user buyers, **124**

V
valence, **254**, 257–258
valid predictors, 202–203
validation of selection process,
218–220
value analysis, **128**
value creation, 133
vendor analysis, **128**
vertical market restriction, 353

W
Wallace vs. United Grain Growers,
331
webcasting, 244
websites, 134, 207
whistle-blowing, **347**–348
Wonderlic Personnel Test, 212
workload approach, **34**–35